THE ART OF MASTERS OF THE UNIVERSE REVOLUTION

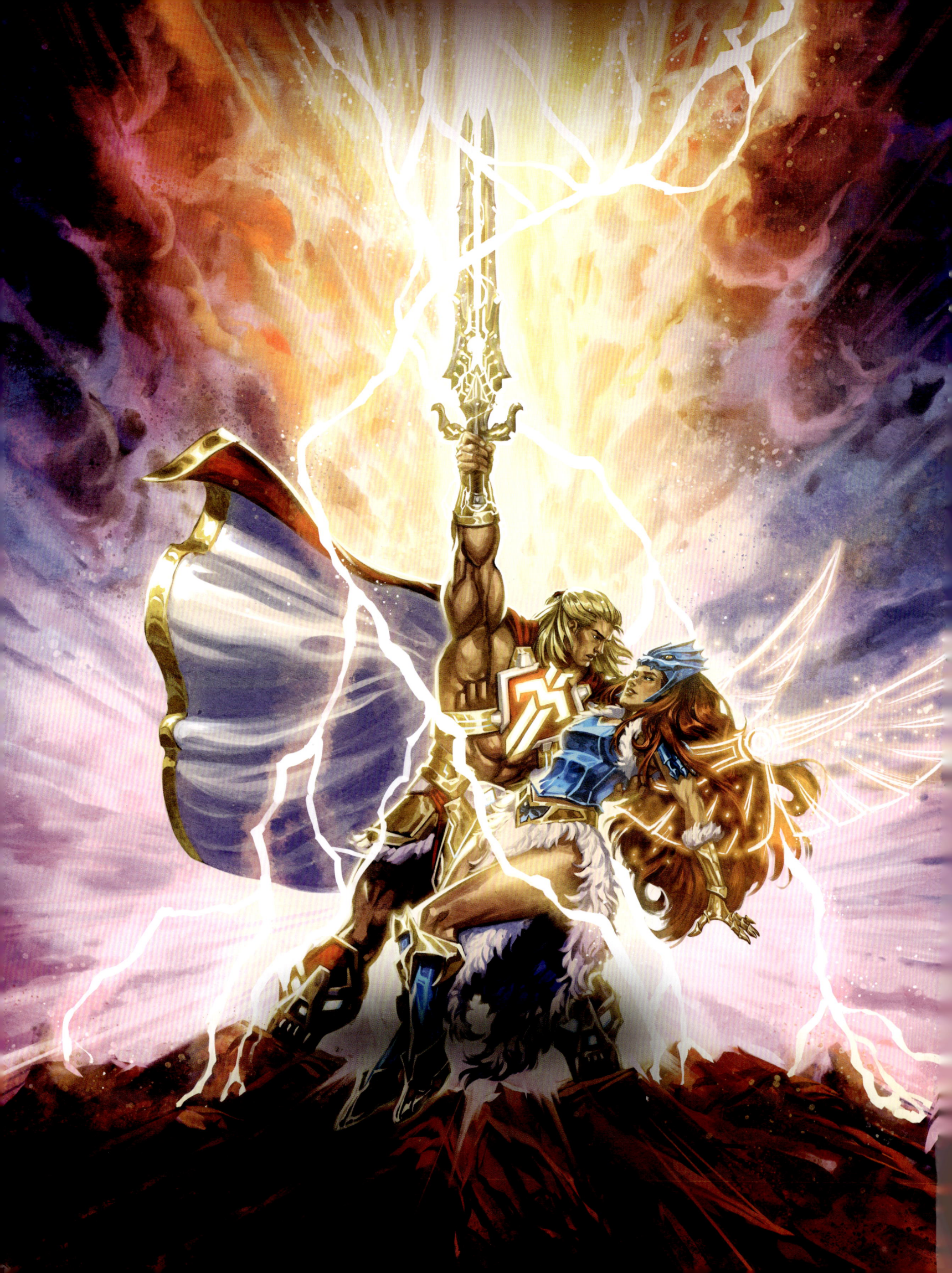

THE ART OF MASTERS OF THE UNIVERSE
REVOLUTION

CAPTIONS BY
Adam Conarroe
Jessica McNeme
Stage McNulty
Patrick Stannard

COVER ART AND FACING PAGE BY
Nate Baertsch

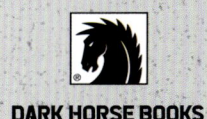

DARK HORSE BOOKS

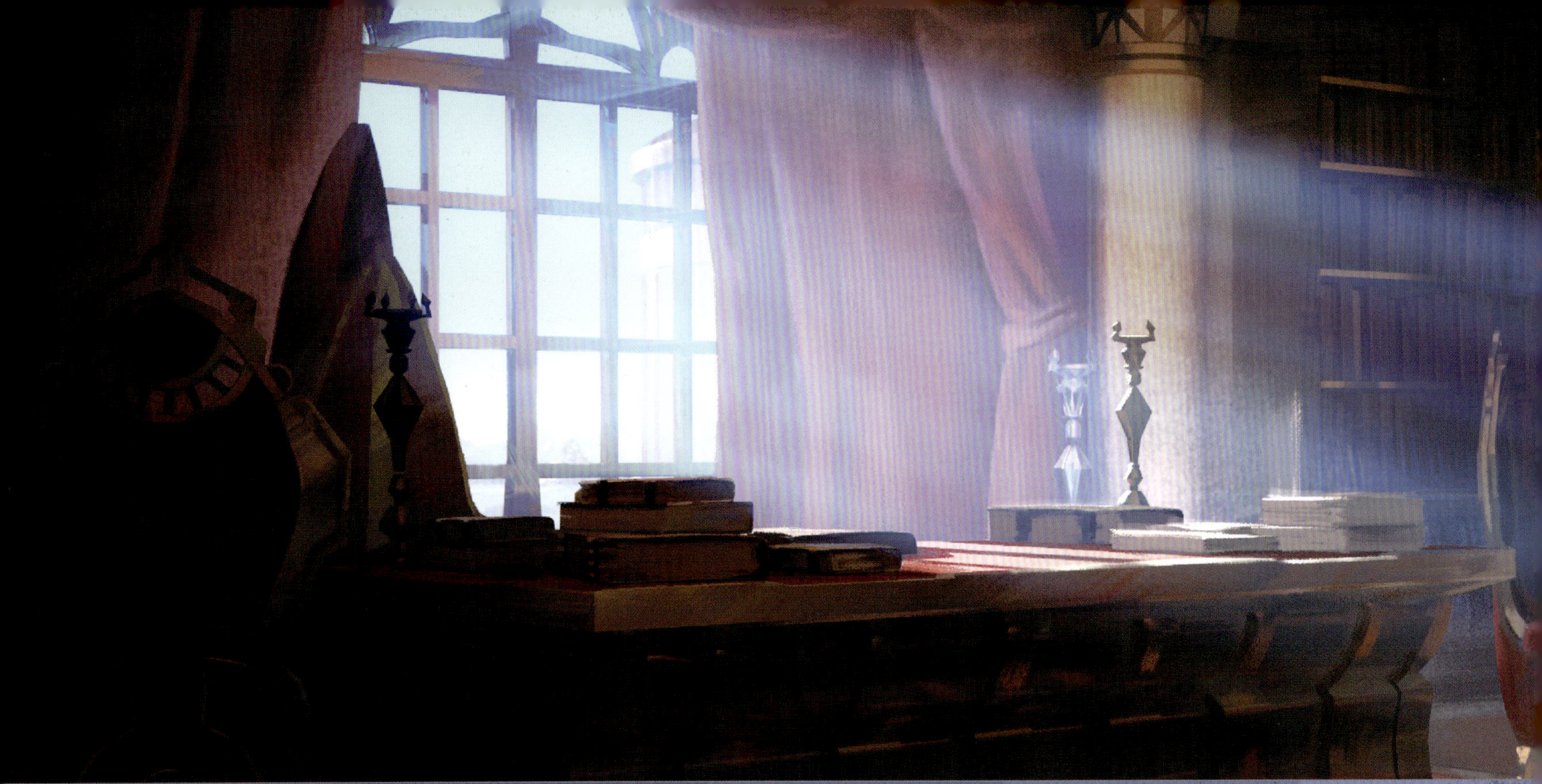

PRESIDENT & PUBLISHER **MIKE RICHARDSON**

EDITOR **BRETT ISRAEL**

ASSISTANT EDITOR **TARA MCCARRON**

DESIGNER **LIN HUANG**

CONCEPT DESIGNER **SARAH TERRY**

DIGITAL ART TECHNICIAN **TYLER LI**

Special thanks to: Rob David, Melanie Shannon, Rowenna Otazu, Alix Rosenberg, and Ryan Ferguson at Mattel. Shane Minshew, Brad Graeber, and Lexi Lassiter at Powerhouse Animation.

THE ART OF MASTERS OF THE UNIVERSE: REVOLUTION

The Art of Masters of the Universe: Revolution © 2024 Mattel. Dark Horse Books® and the Dark Horse logo are registered trademarks of Dark Horse Comics LLC, registered in various categories and countries. All rights reserved. Dark Horse is part of Embracer Group. No portion of this publication may be reproduced or transmitted, in any form or by any means, without the express written permission of Dark Horse Comics LLC. Names, characters, places, and incidents featured in this publication either are the product of the author's imagination or are used fictitiously. Any resemblance to actual persons (living or dead), events, institutions, or locales, without satiric intent, is coincidental.

Published by Dark Horse Books
A division of Dark Horse Comics LLC
10956 SE Main Street, Milwaukie, OR 97222

DarkHorse.com
Facebook.com/DarkHorseComics
X.com/DarkHorseComics

To find a comics shop in your area, visit ComicShopLocator.com.

First edition: December 2024
Ebook ISBN 978-1-50674-505-3
Hardcover ISBN 978-1-50674-481-0

10 9 8 7 6 5 4 3 2 1
Printed in China

Library of Congress Cataloging-in-Publication Data

Names: Mattel, Inc. | Powerhouse Animation.
Title: The art of Masters of the universe revolution.
Description: First edition. | Milwaukie, OR : Dark Horse Books, 2024.
Identifiers: LCCN 2024017928 (print) | LCCN 2024017929 (ebook) | ISBN 9781506744810 (hardcover) | ISBN 9781506745053 (ebook)
Subjects: LCSH: Masters of the universe: revelation (Television program) | Animated television programs–Pictorial works.
Classification: LCC PN1992.77.M296 A79 2024 (print) | LCC PN1992.77.M296 (ebook) | DDC 791.45/72–dc23/eng/20240502
LC record available at https://lccn.loc.gov/2024017928
LC ebook record available at https://lccn.loc.gov/2024017929

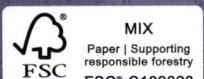

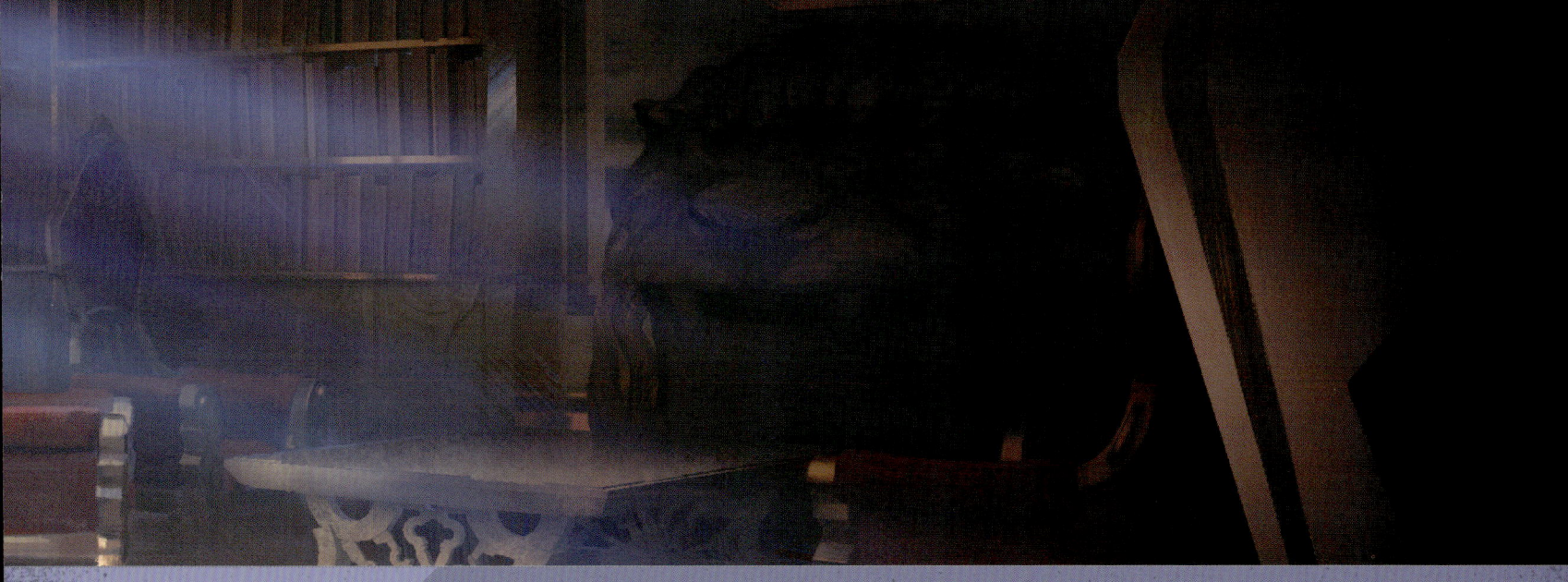

TABLE OF CONTENTS

HEROES 007

VILLAINS 045

VEHICLES AND ARTIFACTS 071

LOCATIONS 097

STORYBOARDS AND ANIMATION . . 157

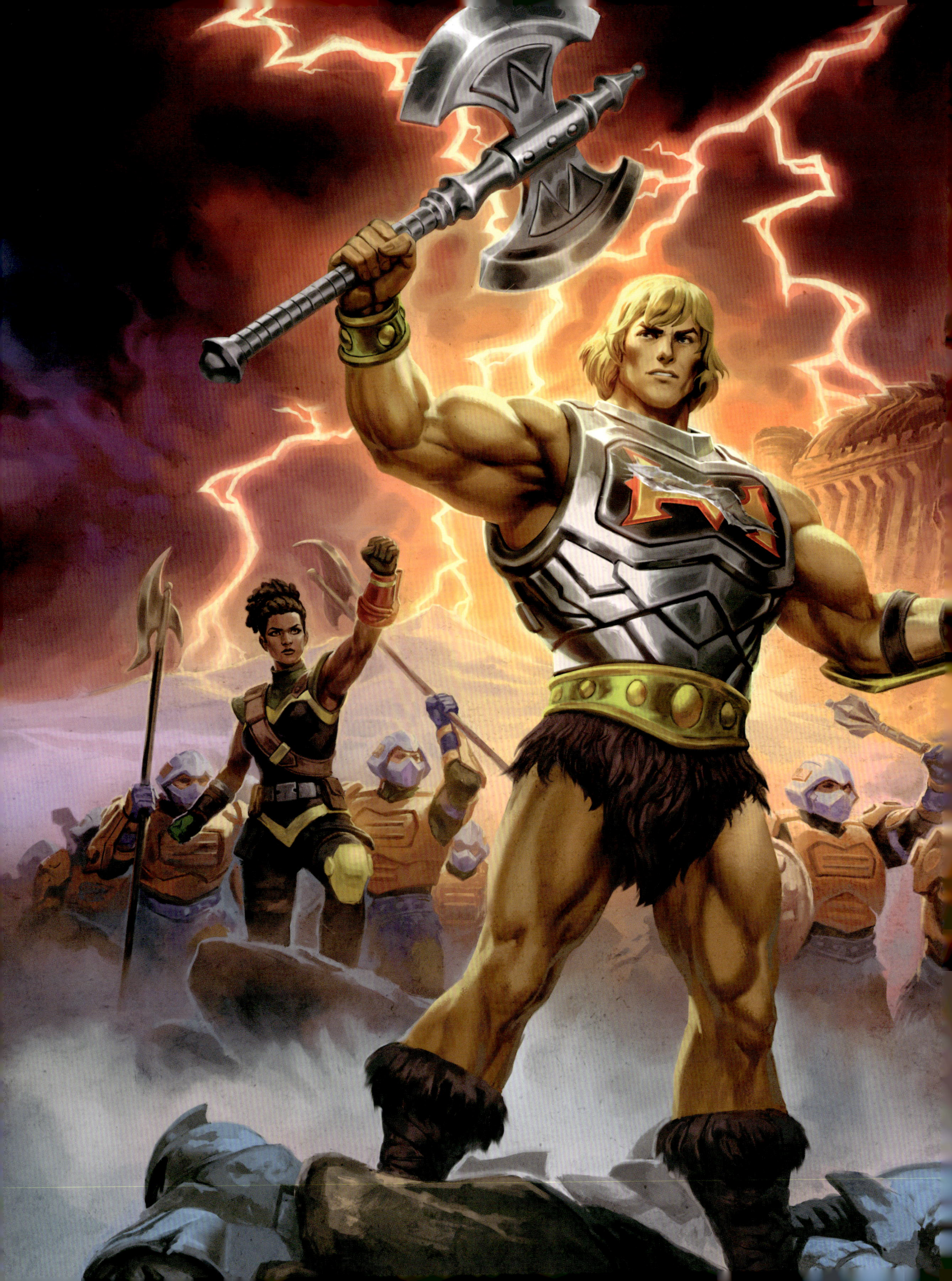

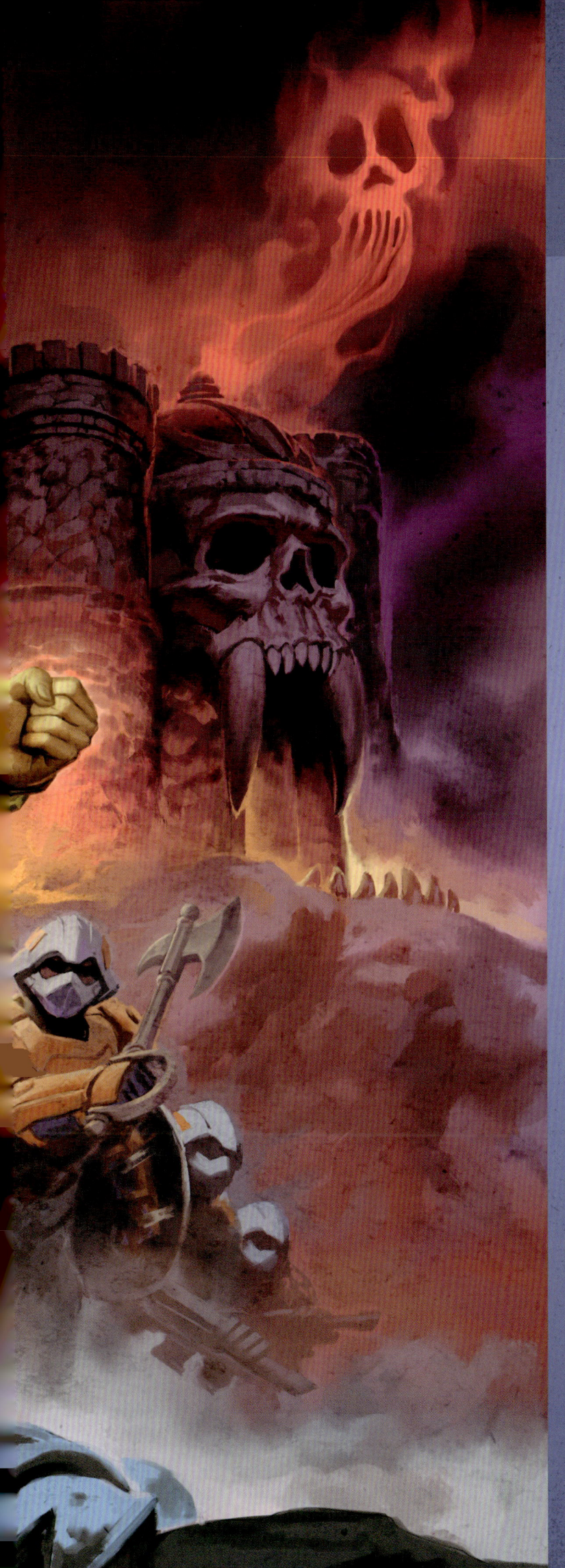

CHAPTER 1
HEROES

THIS SEASON, WE WERE ABLE TO EXPAND *Revelation*'s already-substantial roster with even more heroes pulled from Masters of the Universe lore. While it was a joy to "unbox" these characters for the screen, the greater challenge came from the returning heroes.

The events of this season push the heroes to overcome greater obstacles than ever before. They're thrust into new roles, they must acquire new abilities, and naturally their designs had to evolve beyond their familiar and iconic appearances in a way that reflects their growth while still feeling familiar and paying homage to what makes the characters so beloved.

It was a tall order made tenable by a team of talented designers. And since this is a Mattel show, we were always conscious of the possibility that new toys might be based on our models, so we sought to find designs that would look just as good on the shelf as they do on the screen.

HE-MAN

This is He-Man leveled up! We strove to intertwine magic and technology into an elegant new look without replacing or distracting from the iconic elements that make He-Man so timeless. The flashy red cape was included as a nod to the 1987 film.

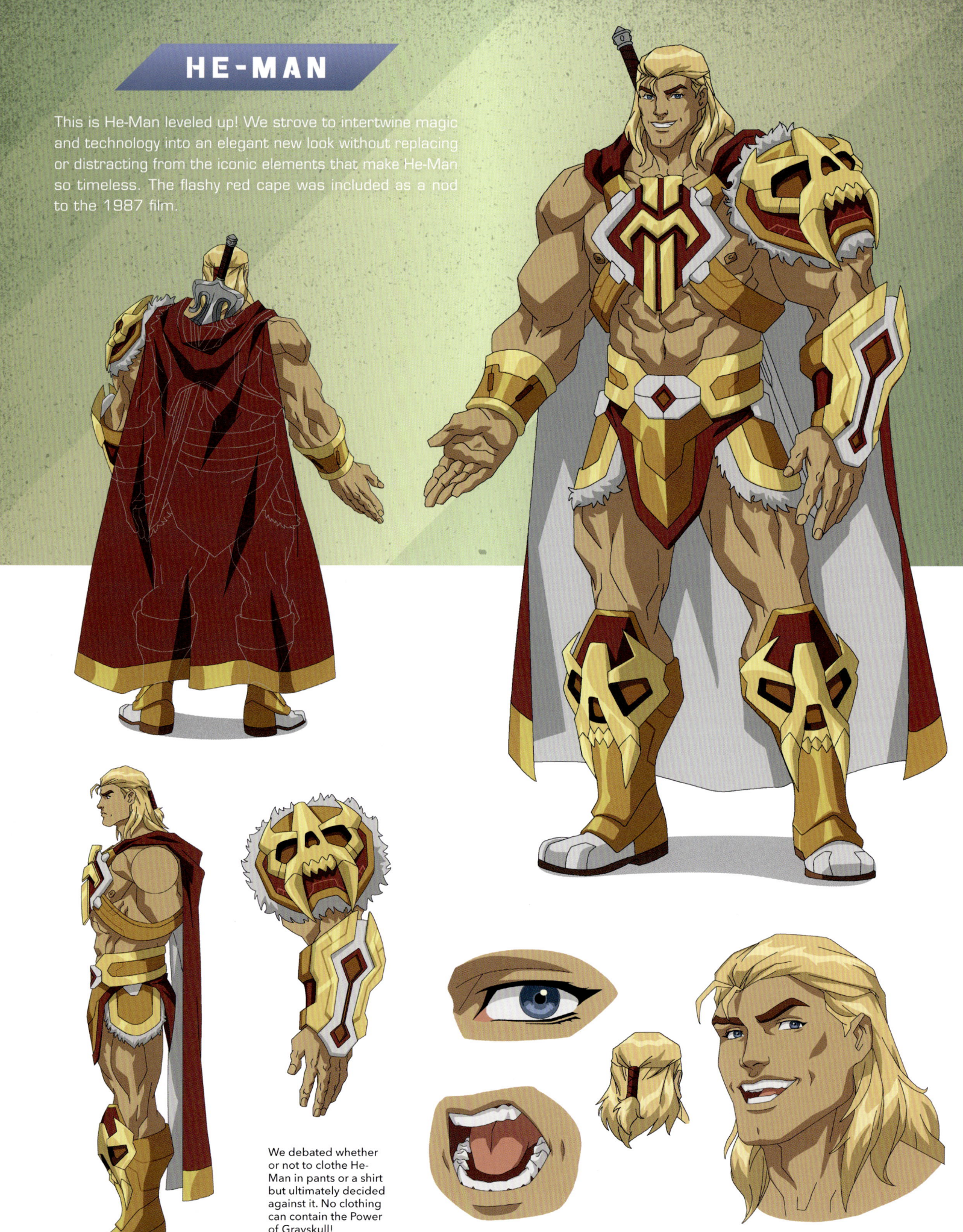

We debated whether or not to clothe He-Man in pants or a shirt but ultimately decided against it. No clothing can contain the Power of Grayskull!

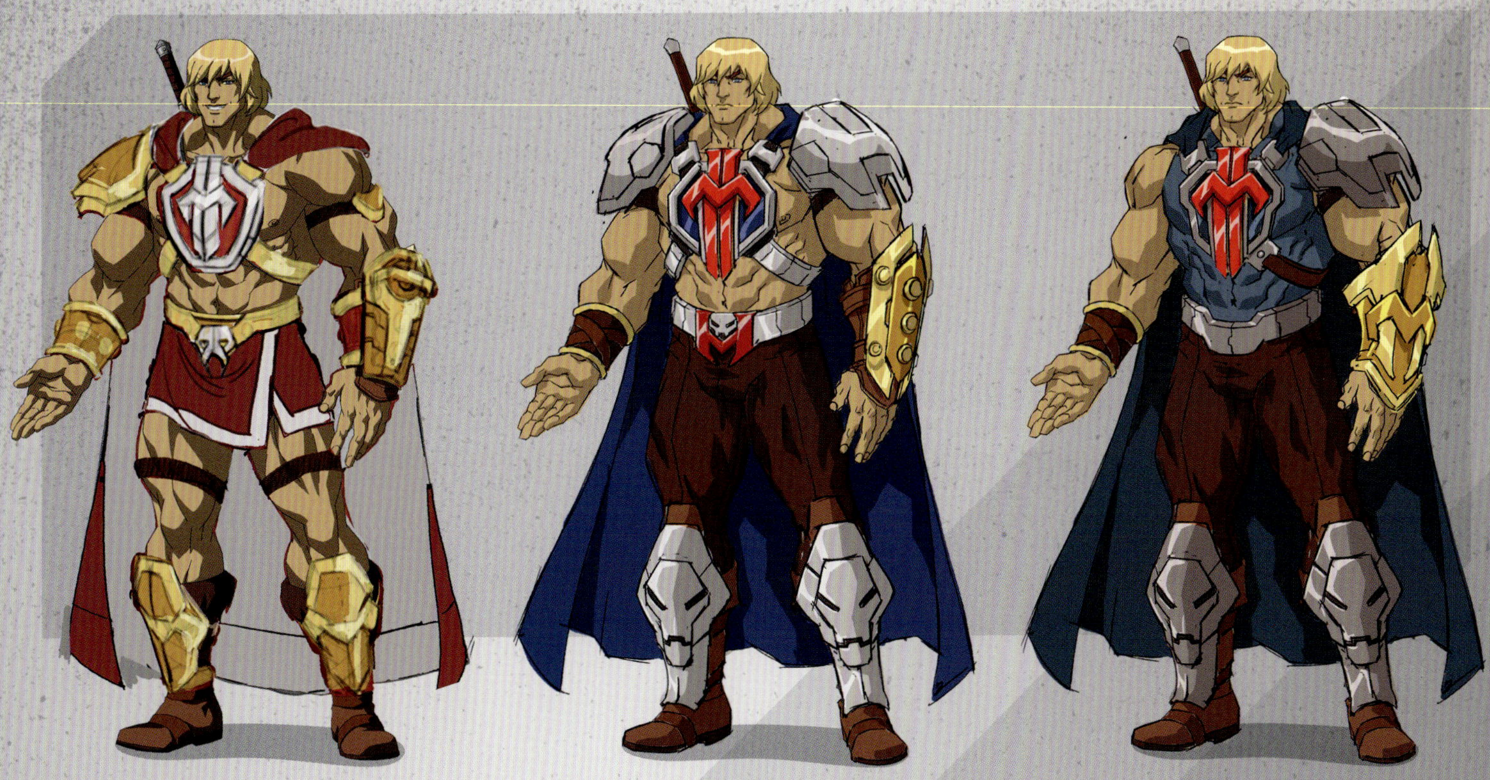

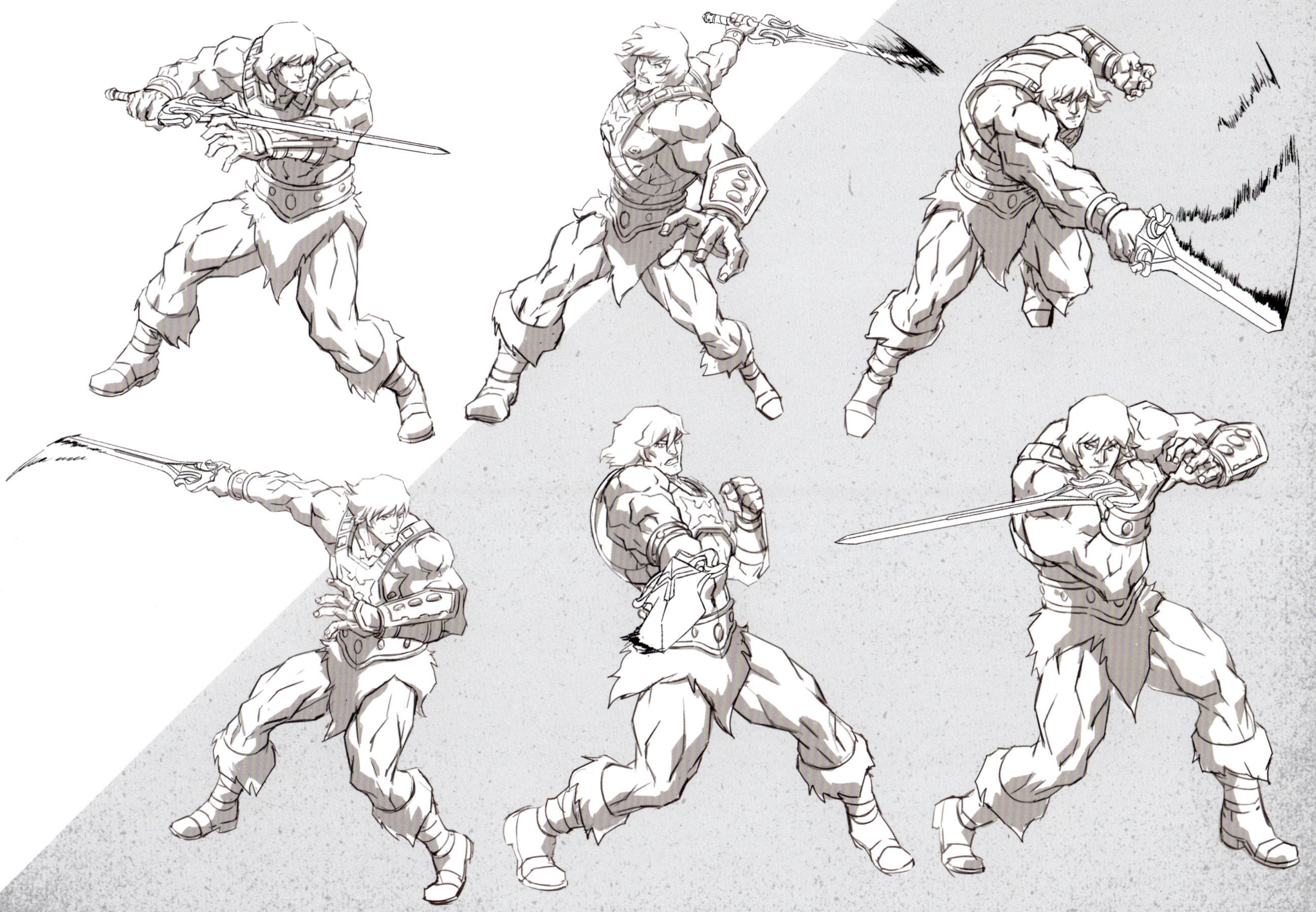

HEROES \\ 9

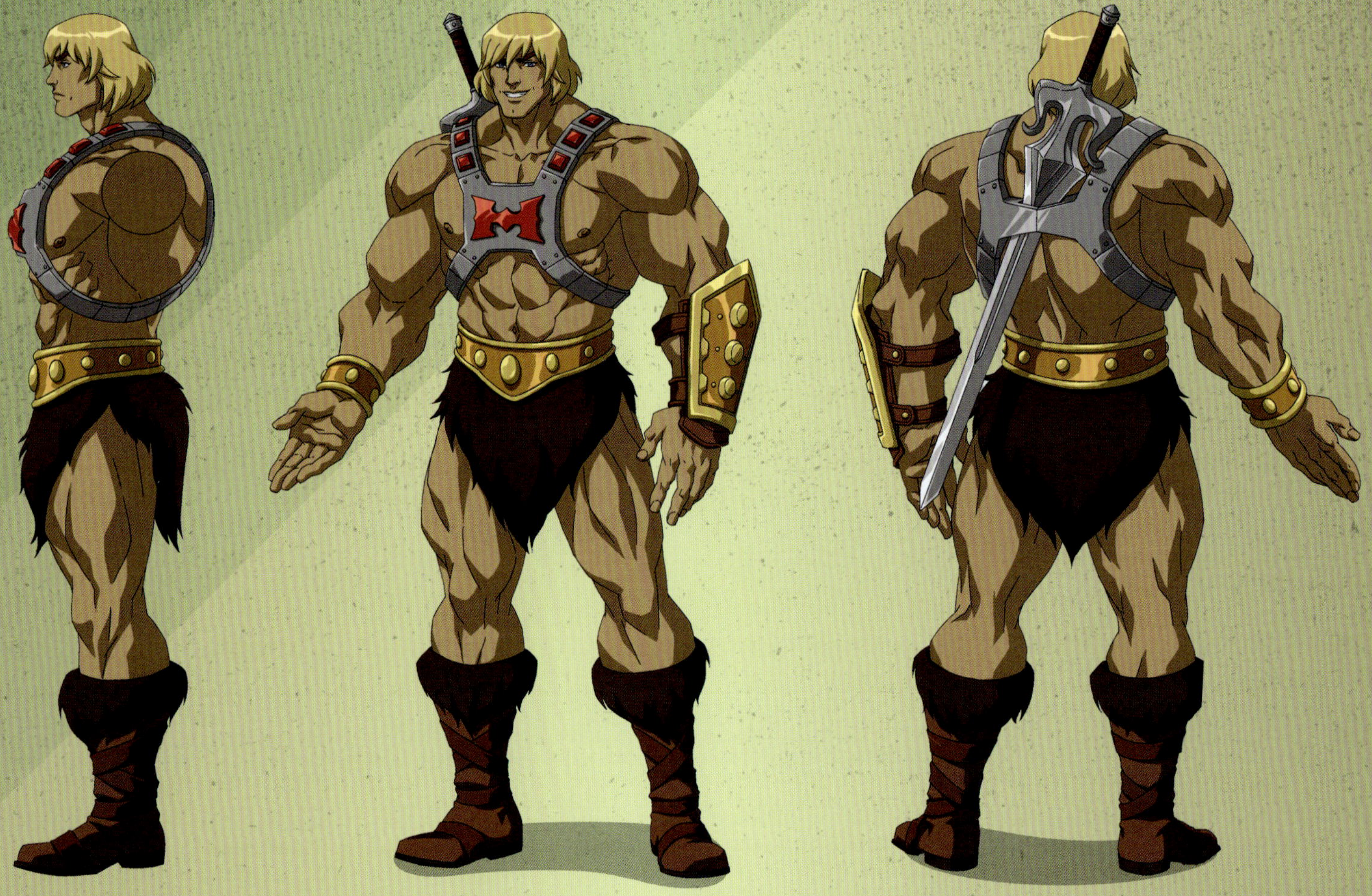

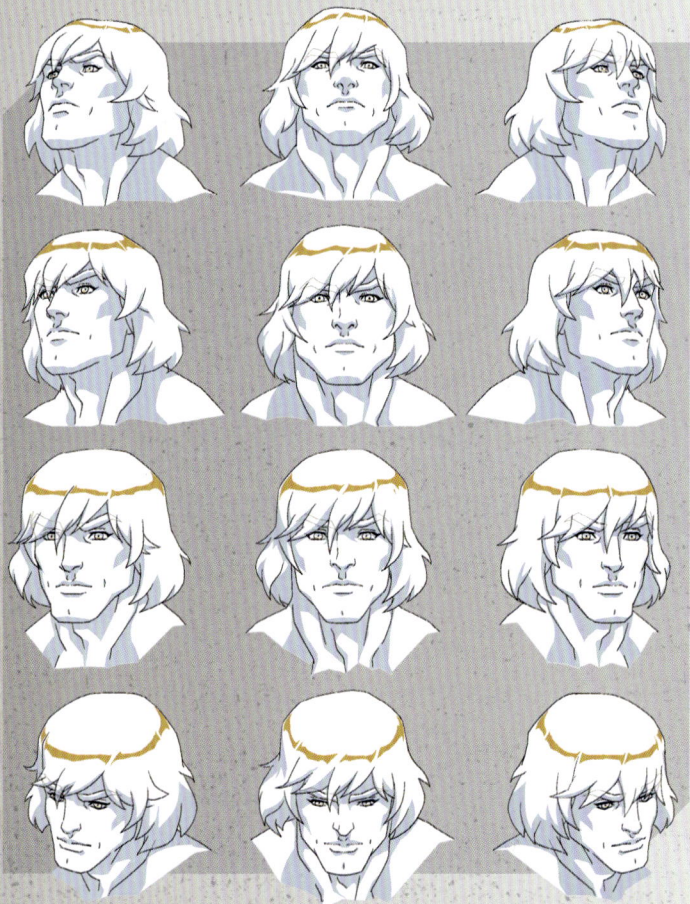
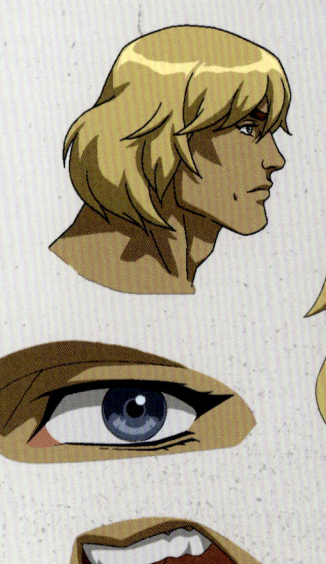
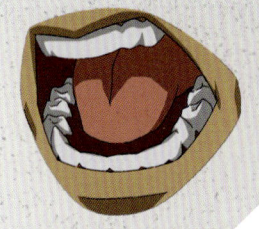
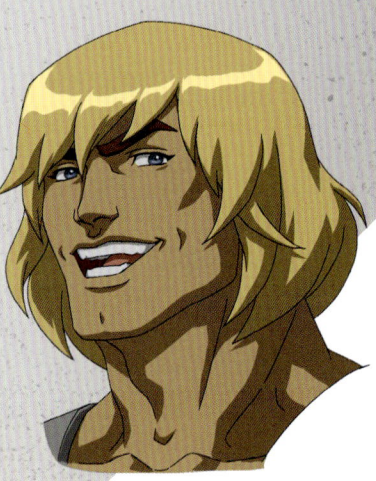

He-Man's flashy new upgrade includes a fresh new hairstyle to match. We experimented with several different looks but ultimately settled on a shoulder-length cut which emphasizes He-Man's growth.

10 // THE ART OF MASTERS OF THE UNIVERSE: REVOLUTION

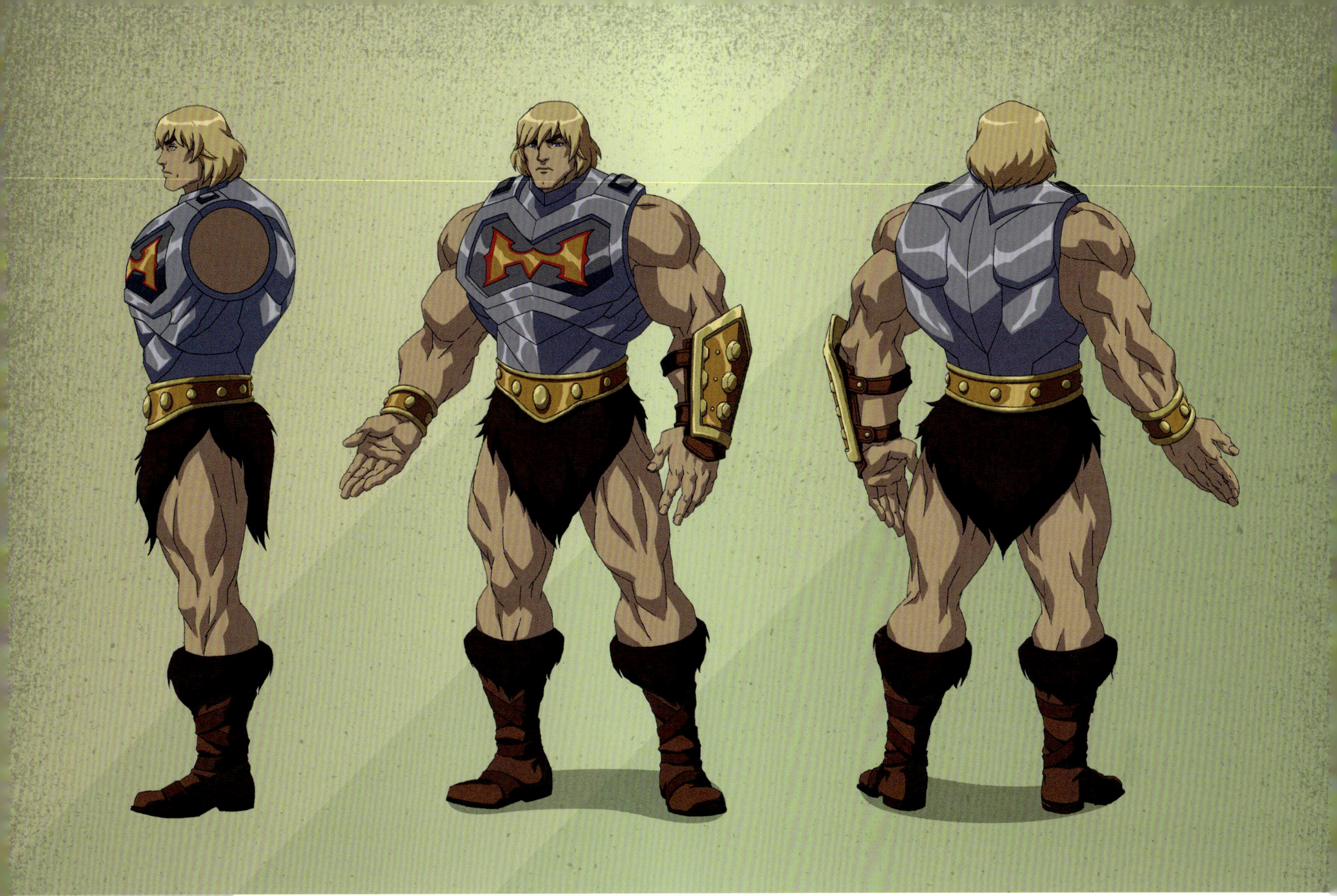

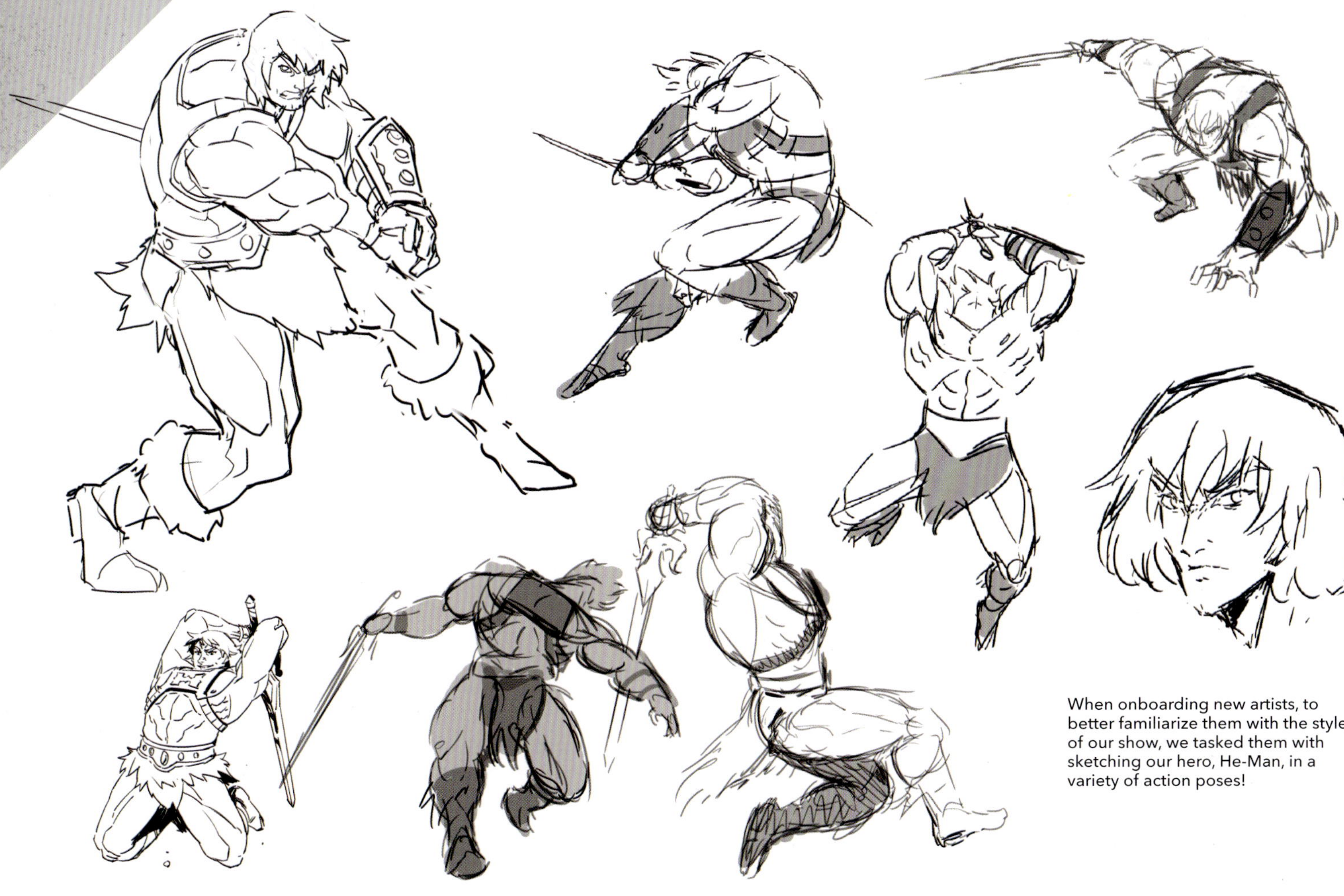

When onboarding new artists, to better familiarize them with the style of our show, we tasked them with sketching our hero, He-Man, in a variety of action poses!

HEROES \\ 11

PRINCE ADAM

Adam spends much of the season in somber funeral attire. Since he transforms into He-Man while wearing this outfit, we see it again when Motherboard disconnects him from the power. The costume serves as a visual reminder of Randor's death and the potential end of Adam's time as champion.

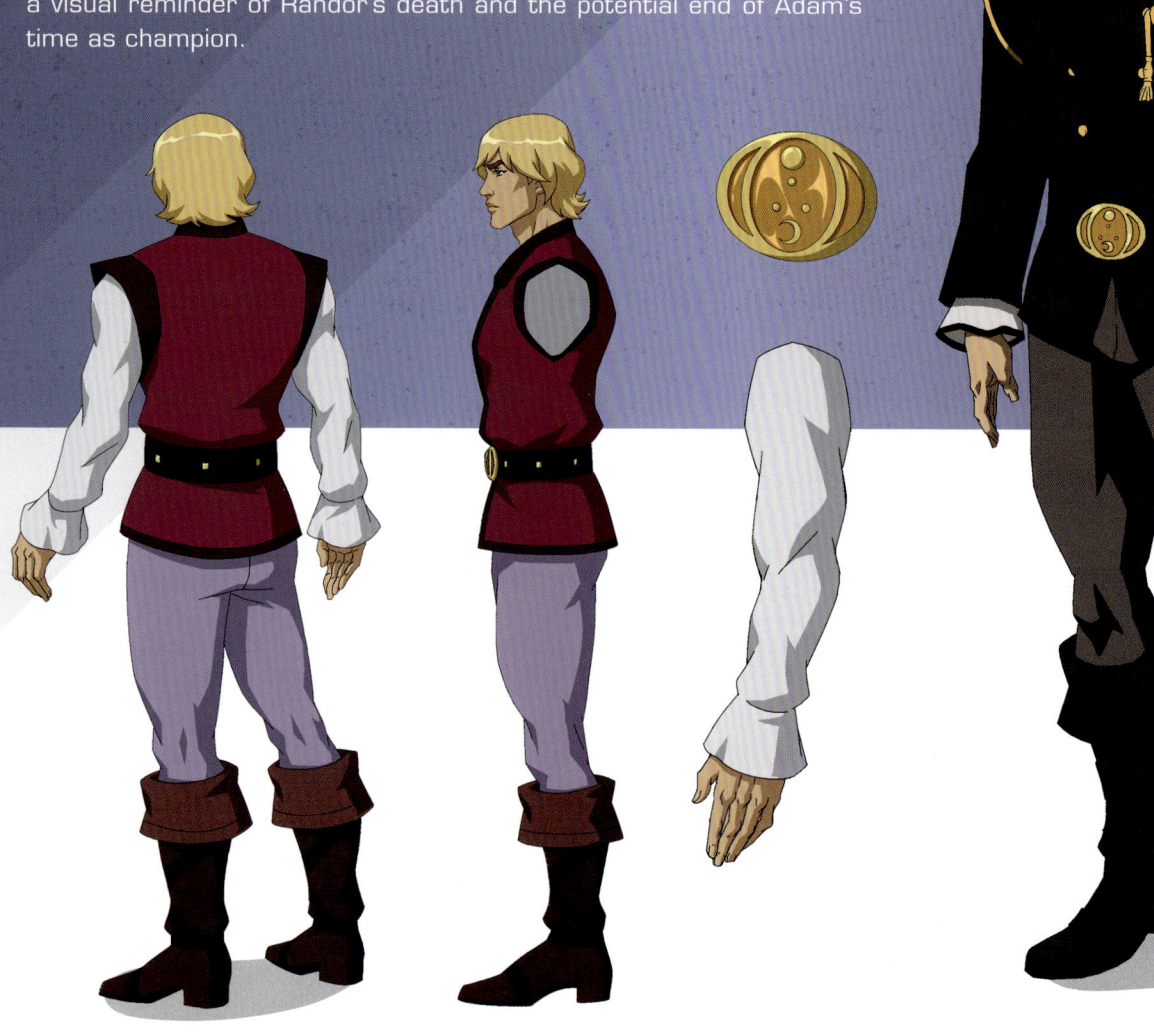

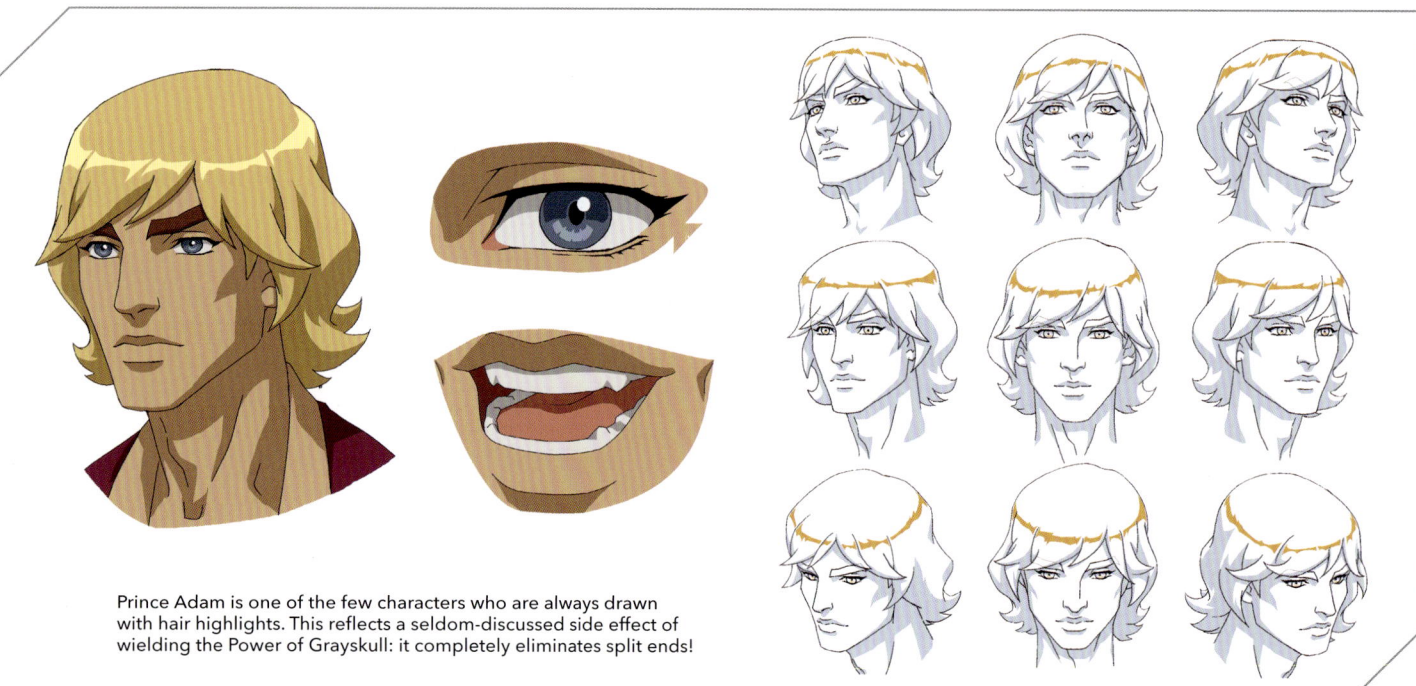

Prince Adam is one of the few characters who are always drawn with hair highlights. This reflects a seldom-discussed side effect of wielding the Power of Grayskull: it completely eliminates split ends!

THE ART OF MASTERS OF THE UNIVERSE: REVOLUTION

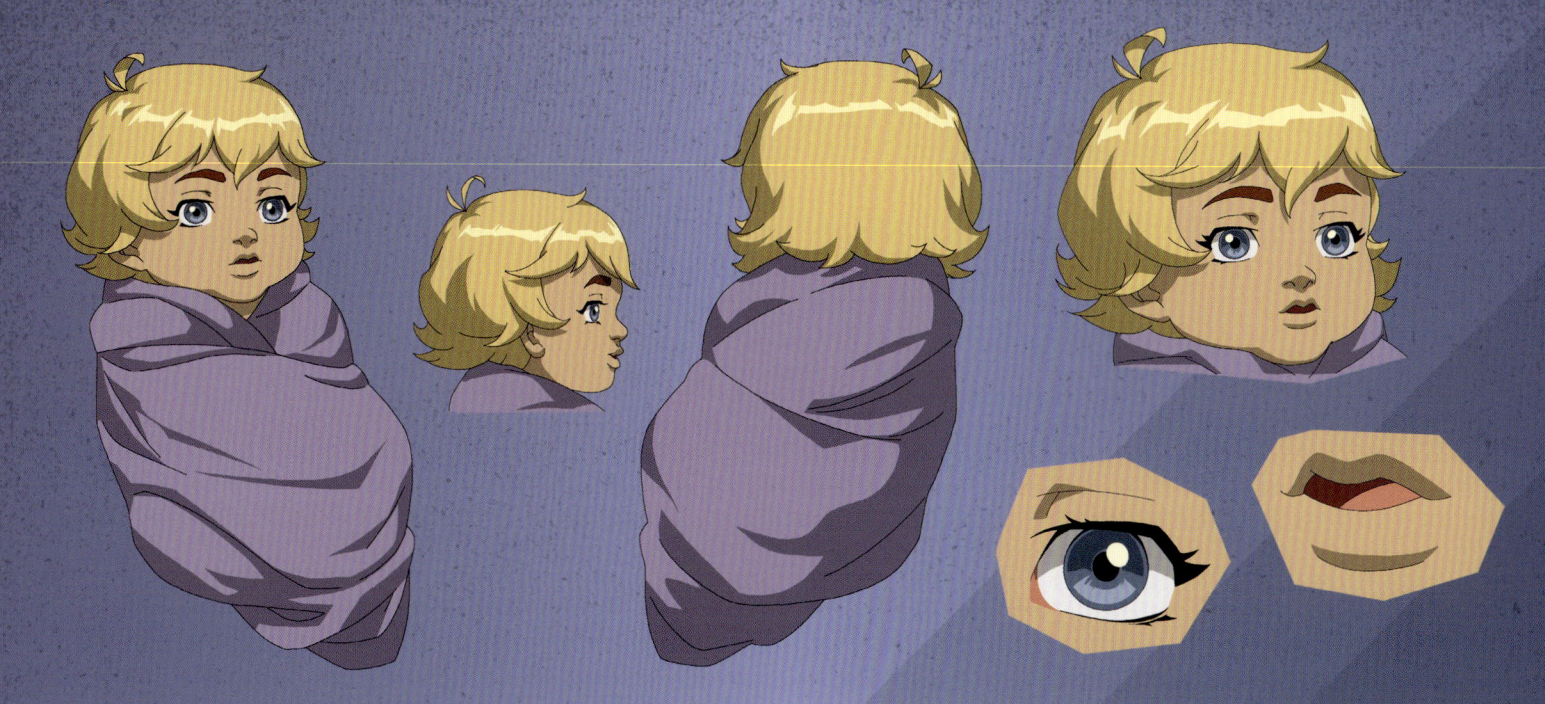

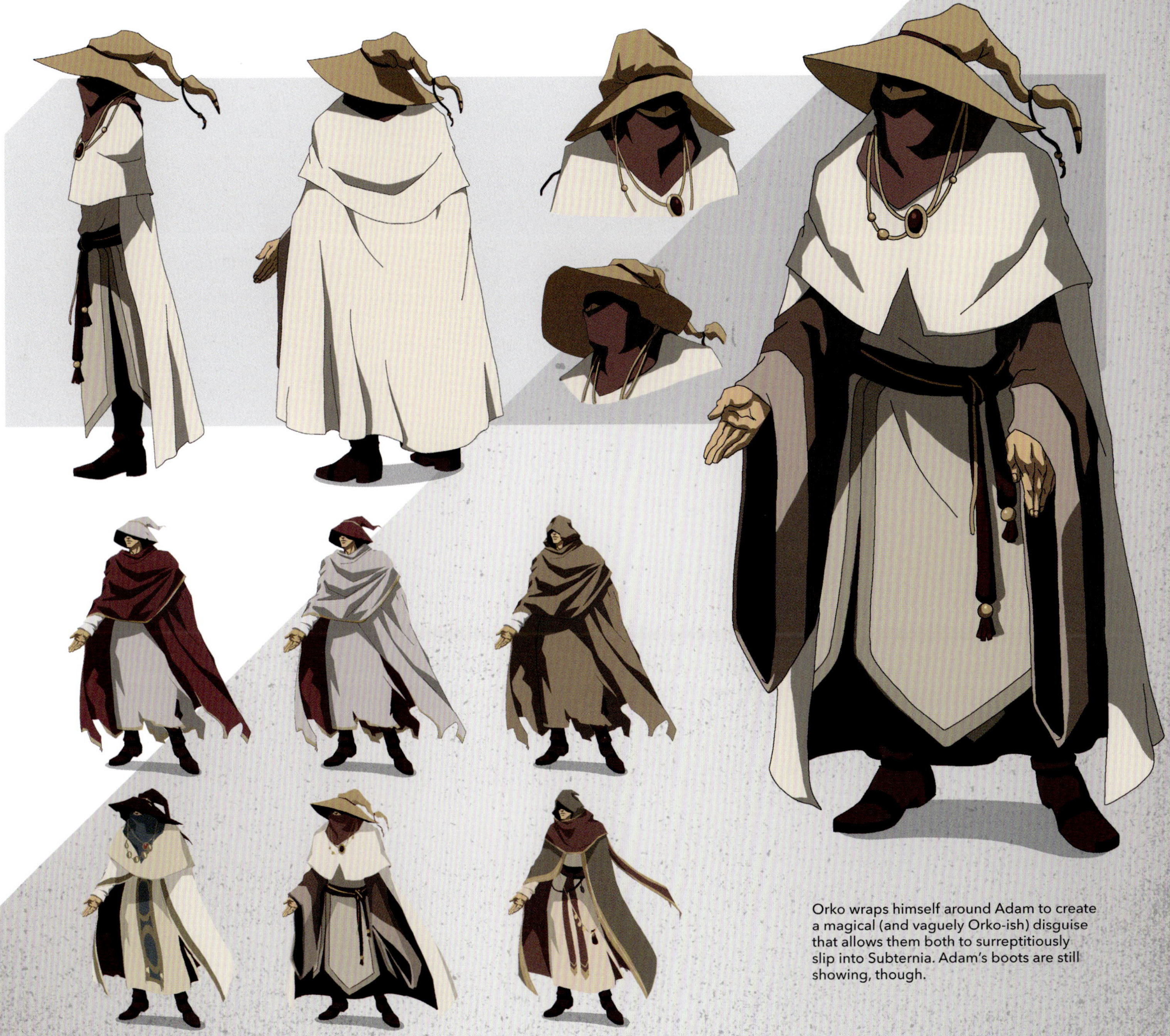

Orko wraps himself around Adam to create a magical (and vaguely Orko-ish) disguise that allows them both to surreptitiously slip into Subternia. Adam's boots are still showing, though.

HEROES // 13

TEELA

This season no other character goes through quite so many wardrobe changes as Teela—she's practically her own fashion show! Most of these reskins were necessary for the story, but occasionally, as with her winterized Sorceress outfit below, we'll throw them in just for fun.

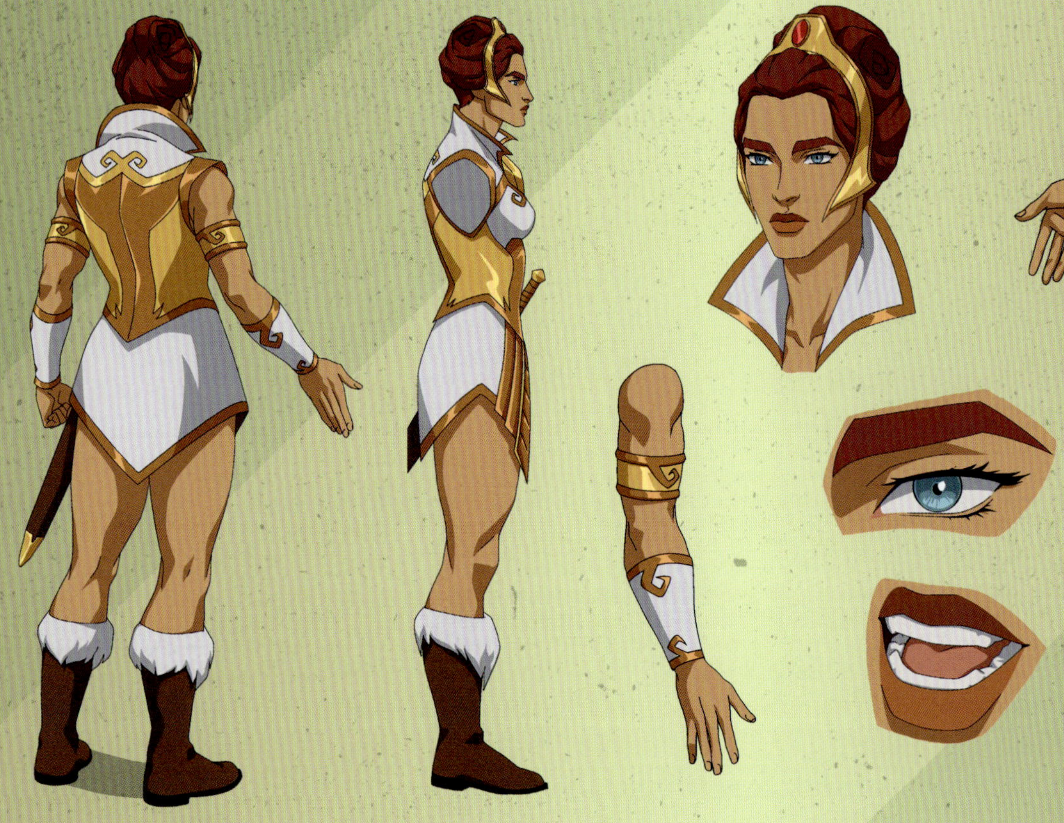

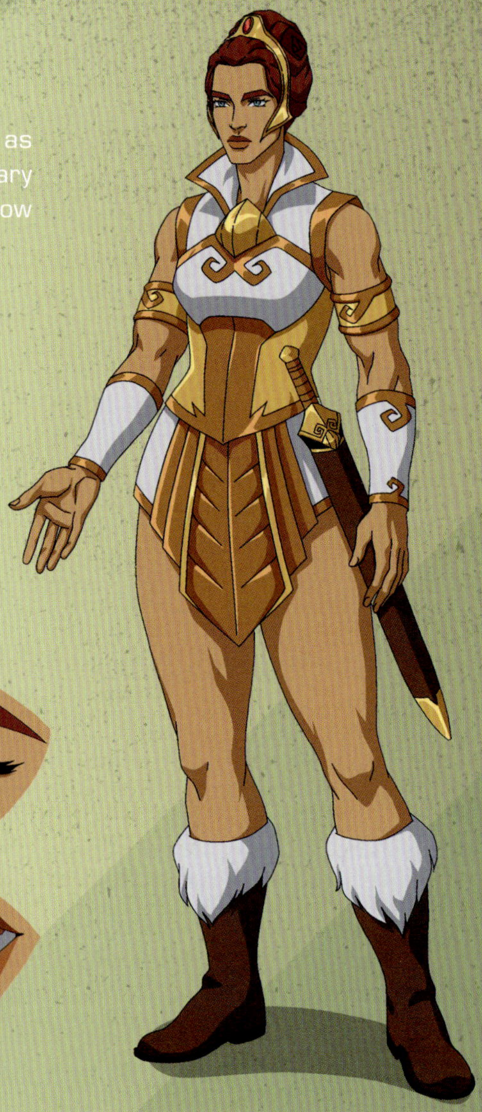

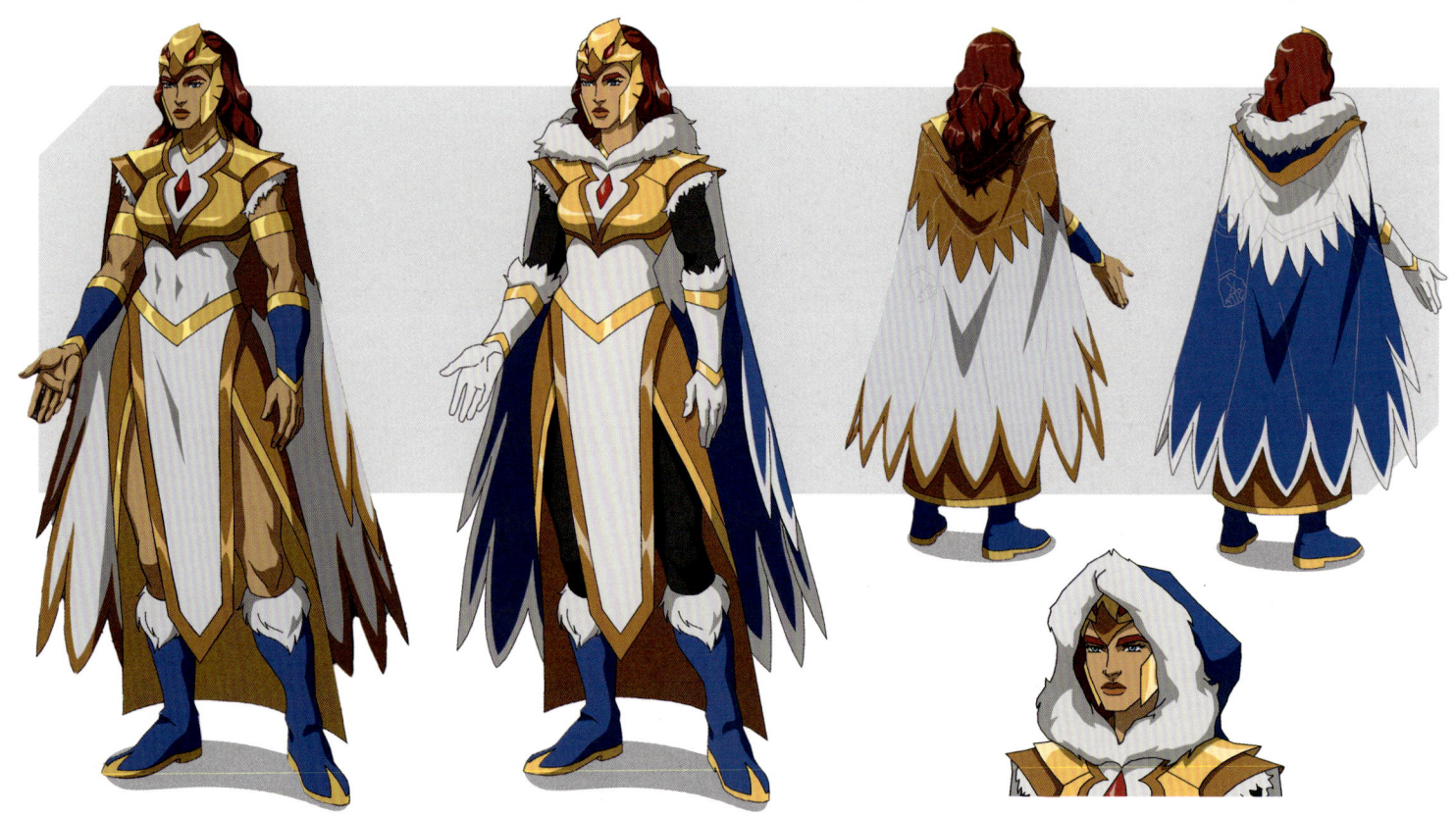

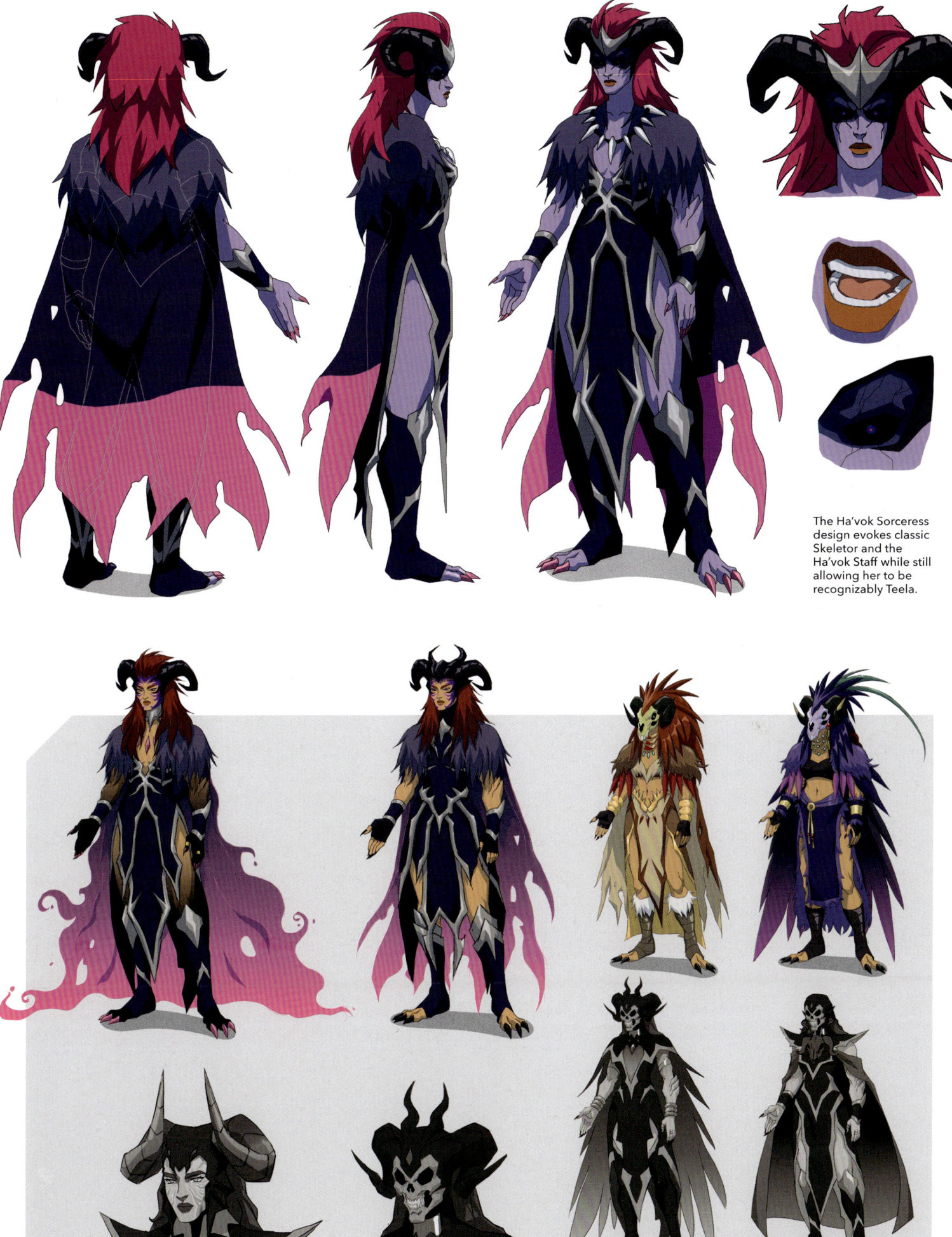

The Ha'vok Sorceress design evokes classic Skeletor and the Ha'vok Staff while still allowing her to be recognizably Teela.

HEROES \\ 15

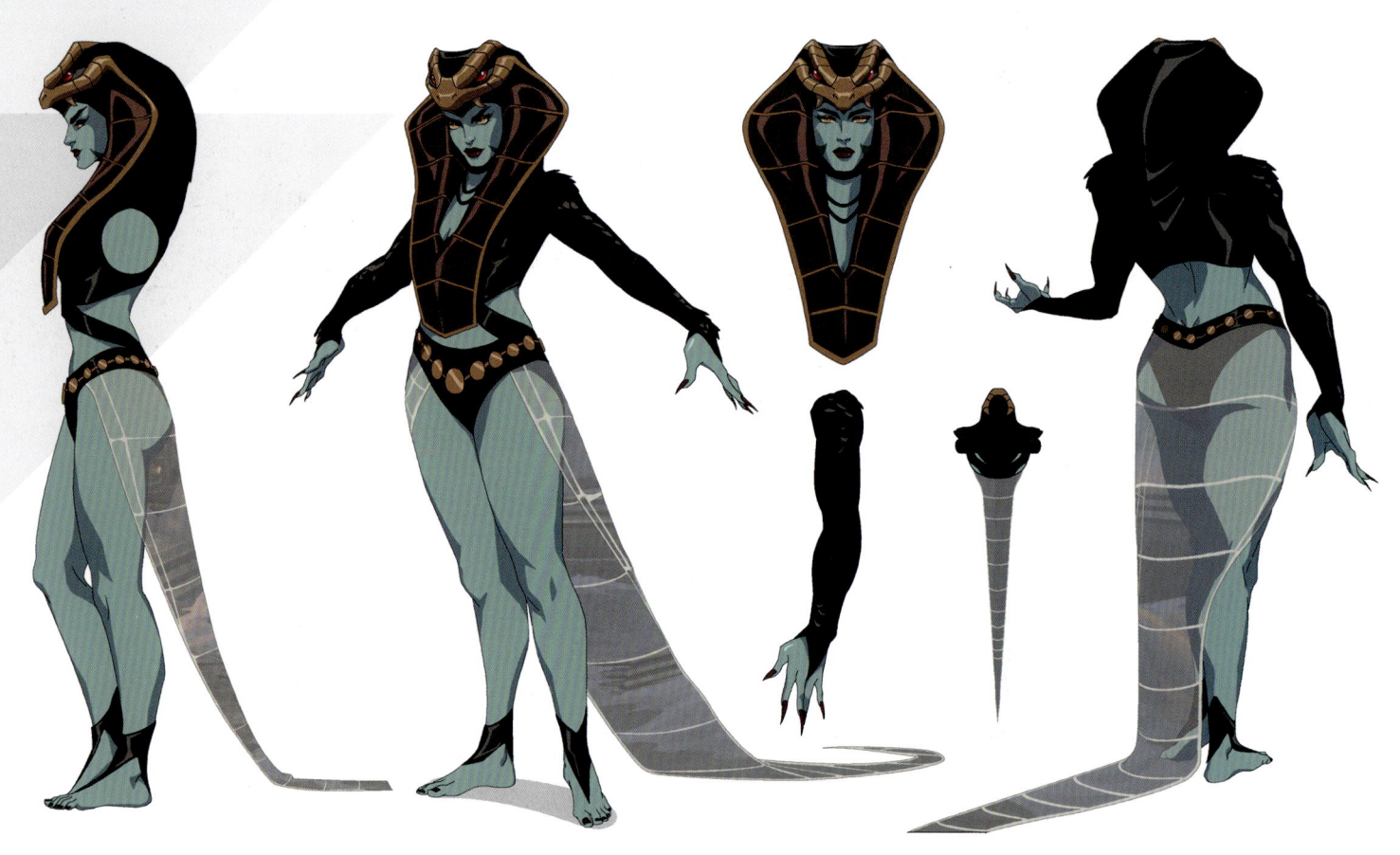

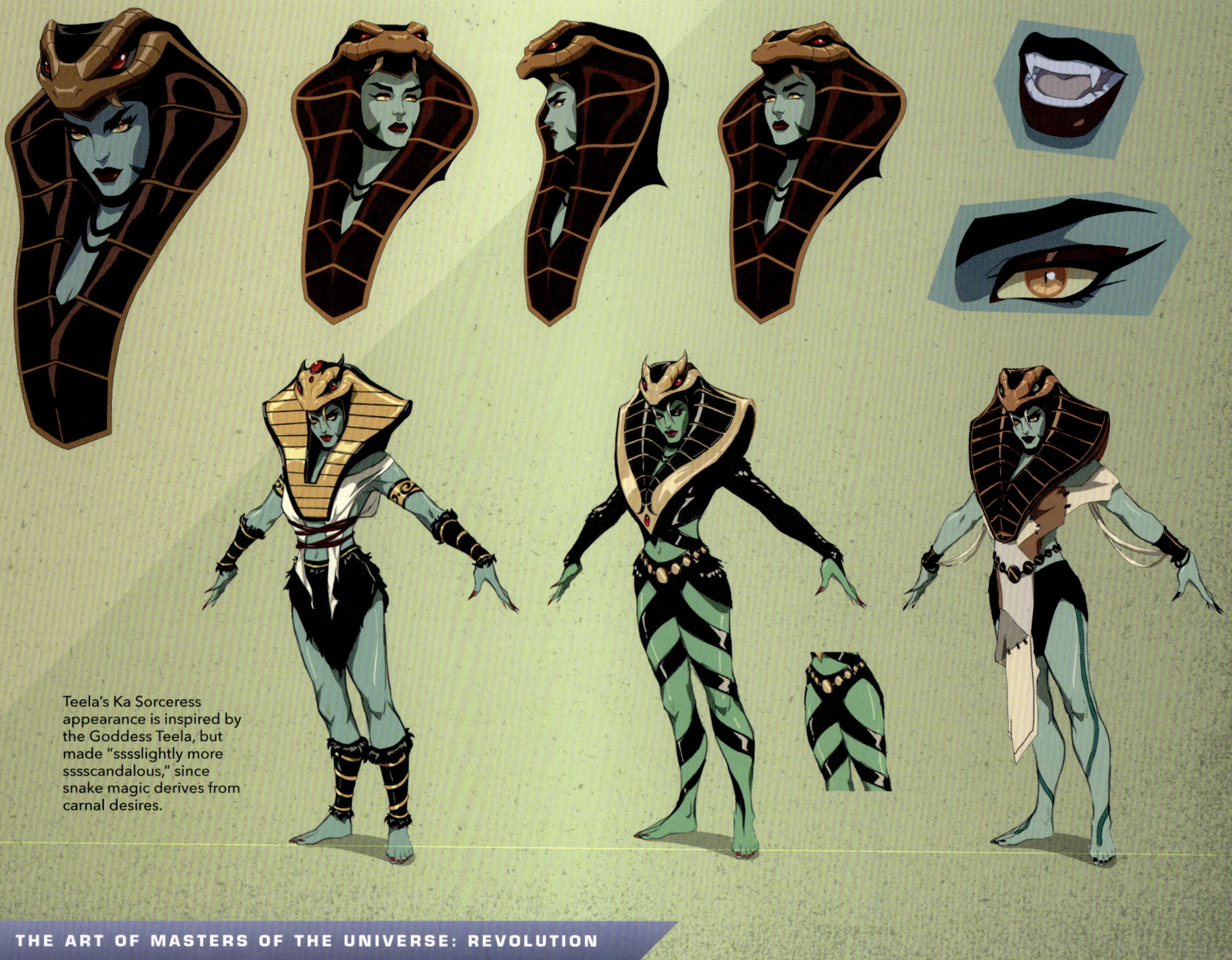

Teela's Ka Sorceress appearance is inspired by the Goddess Teela, but made "sssslightly more sssscandalous," since snake magic derives from carnal desires.

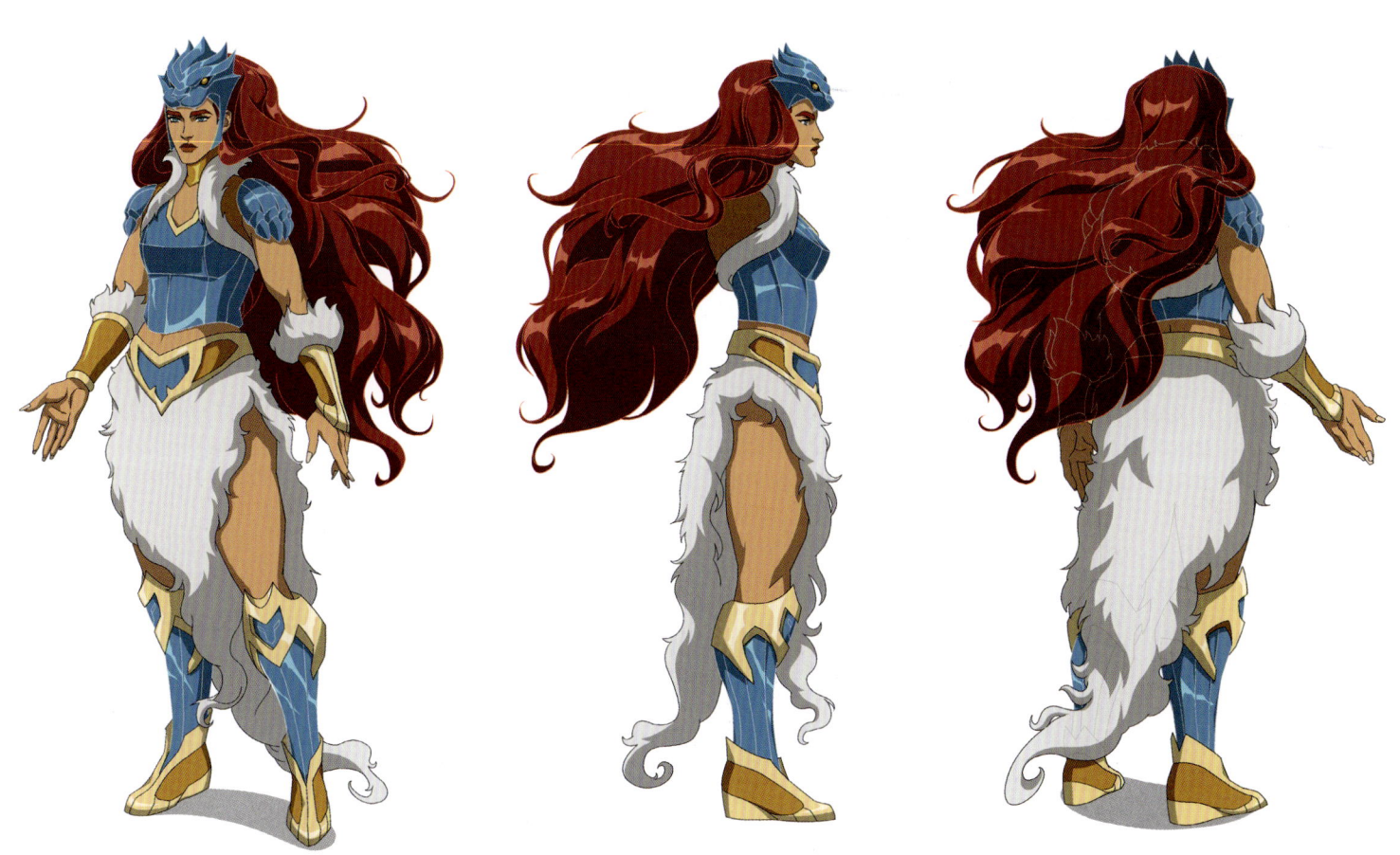

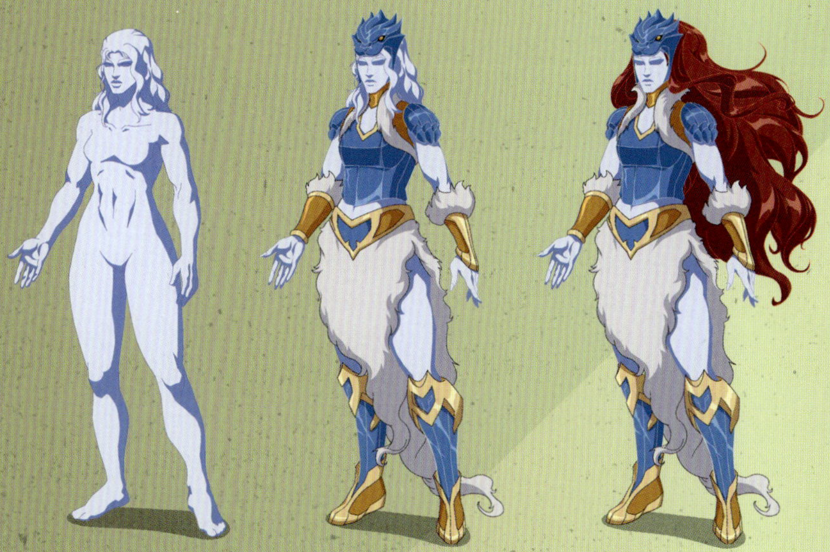

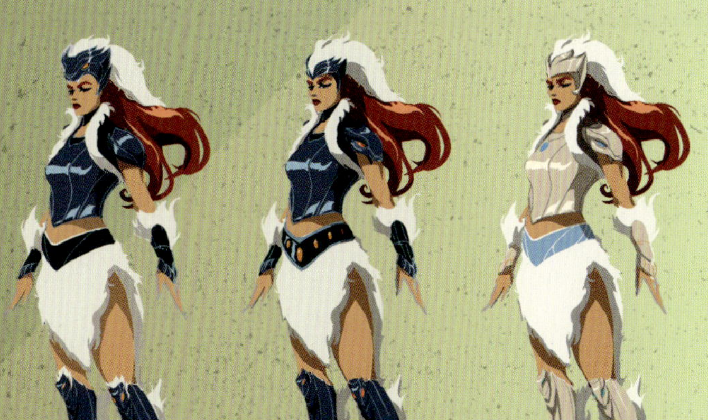

Representing the balance of all three magics in harmony, Teela's Tri-Sorceress appearance is based on Preternia's Central Tower. The fabulous hair is just a bonus.

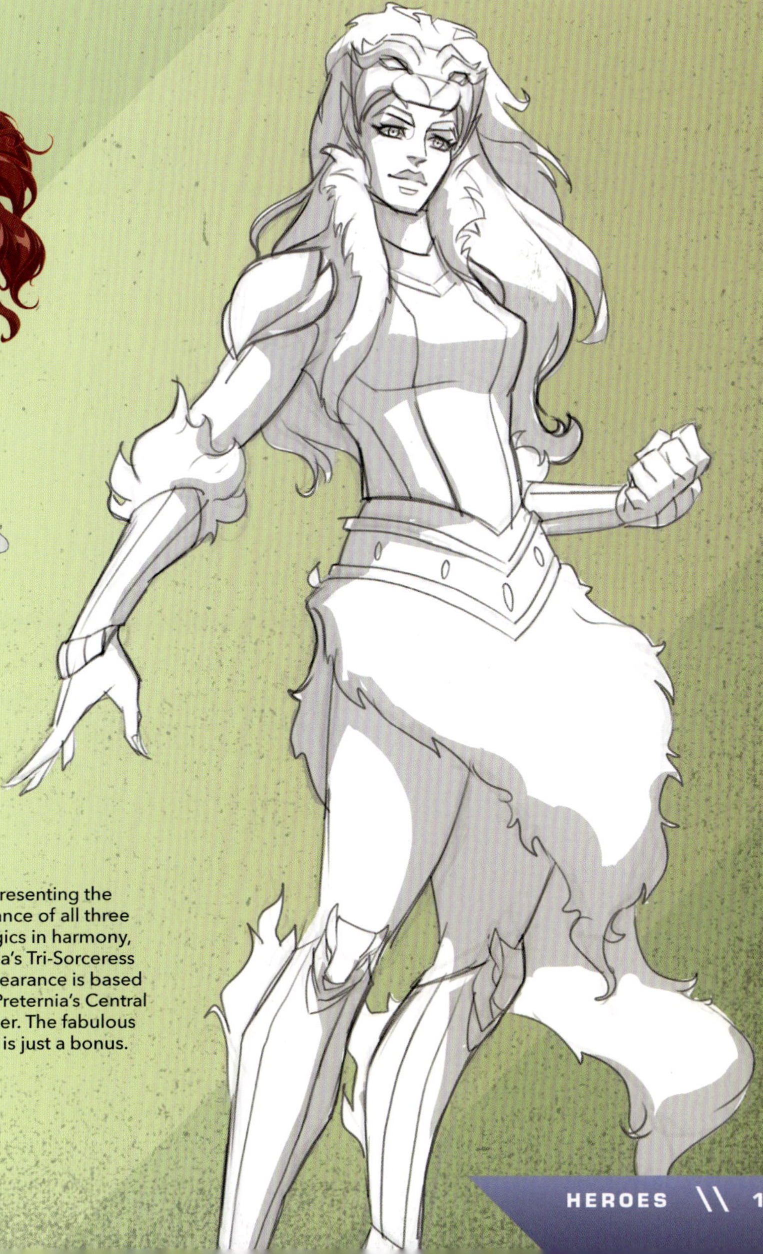

HEROES \\ 17

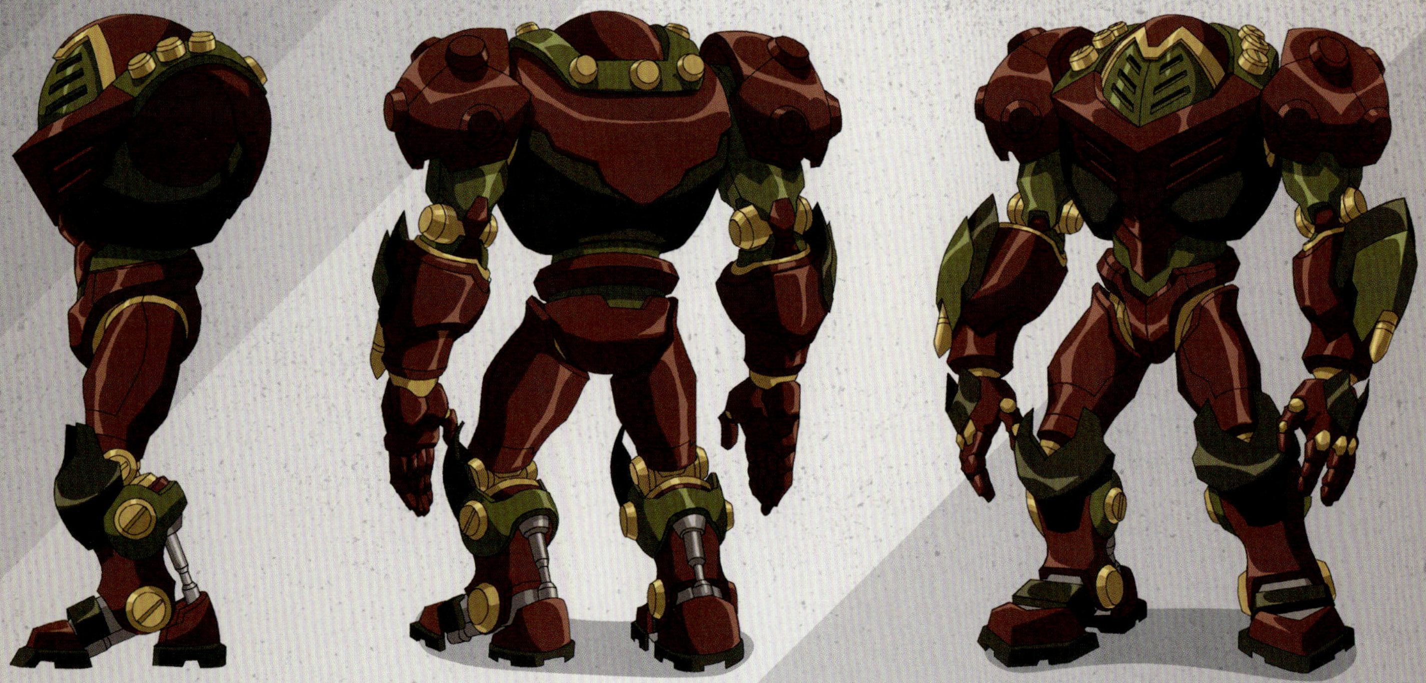

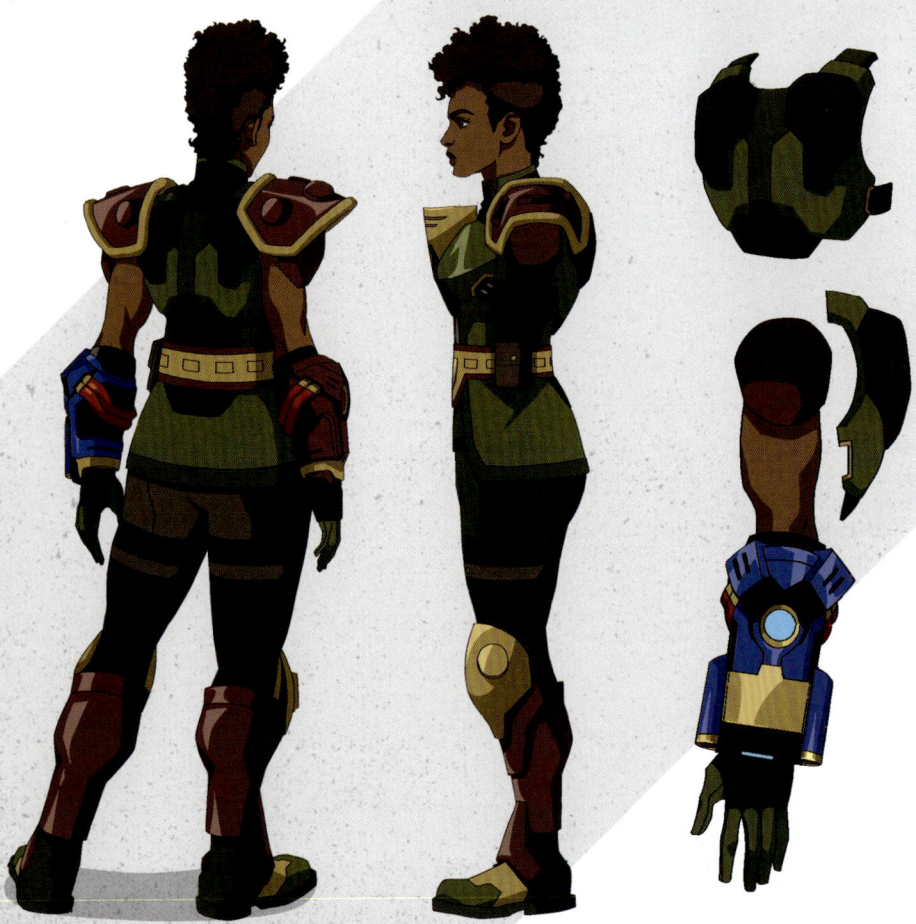

ANDRA

Eternia's technological mastermind returns this season with a brand-new feat of engineering: the He-Mech. As Man-At-Arms, Andra retains her original color palette but adopts Duncan's armor's classic shape language. She also gains a gauntlet upgrade from Keldor, providing a distinctive blue pop.

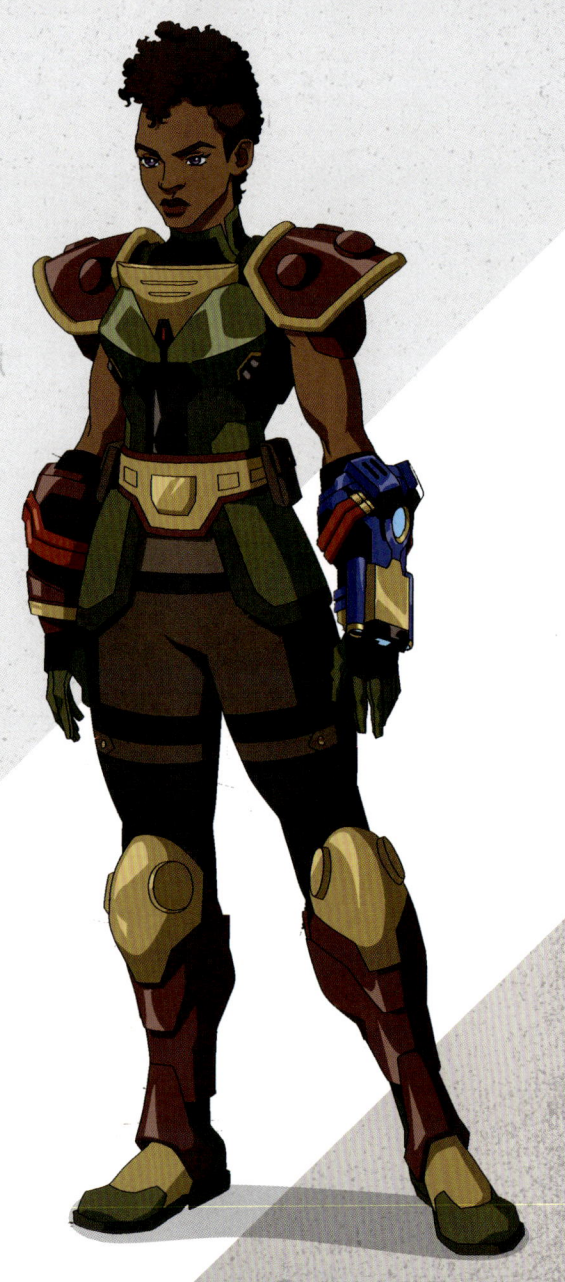

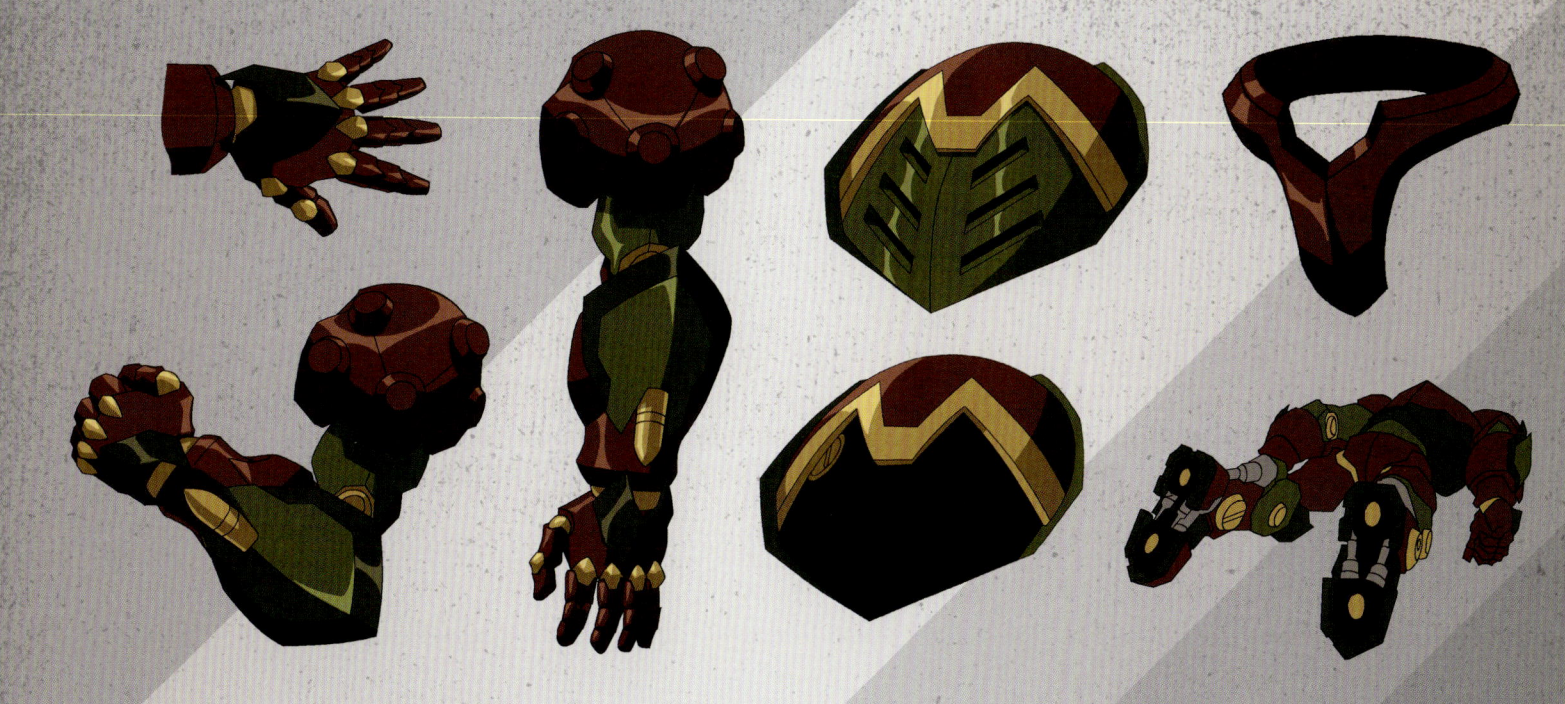

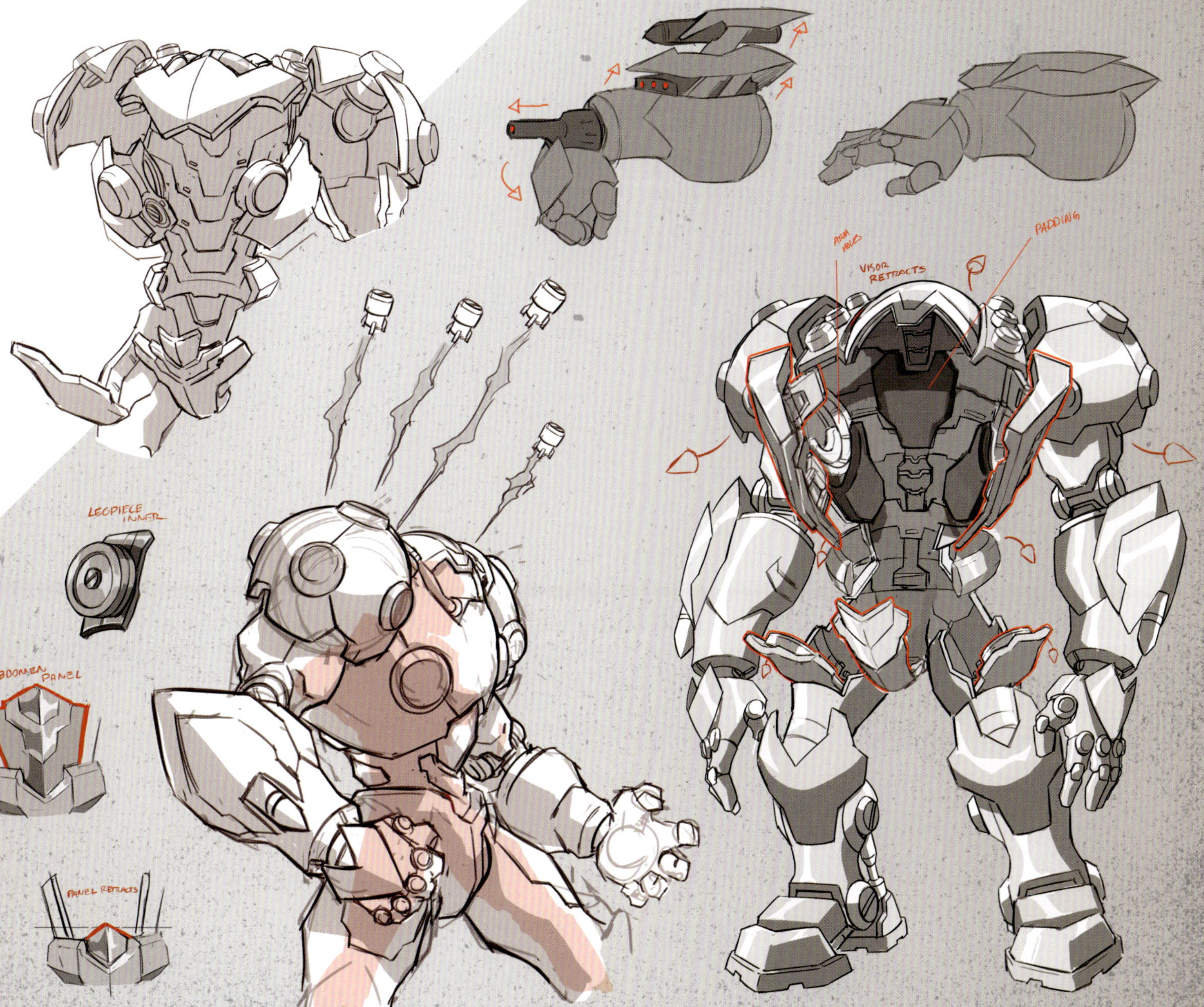

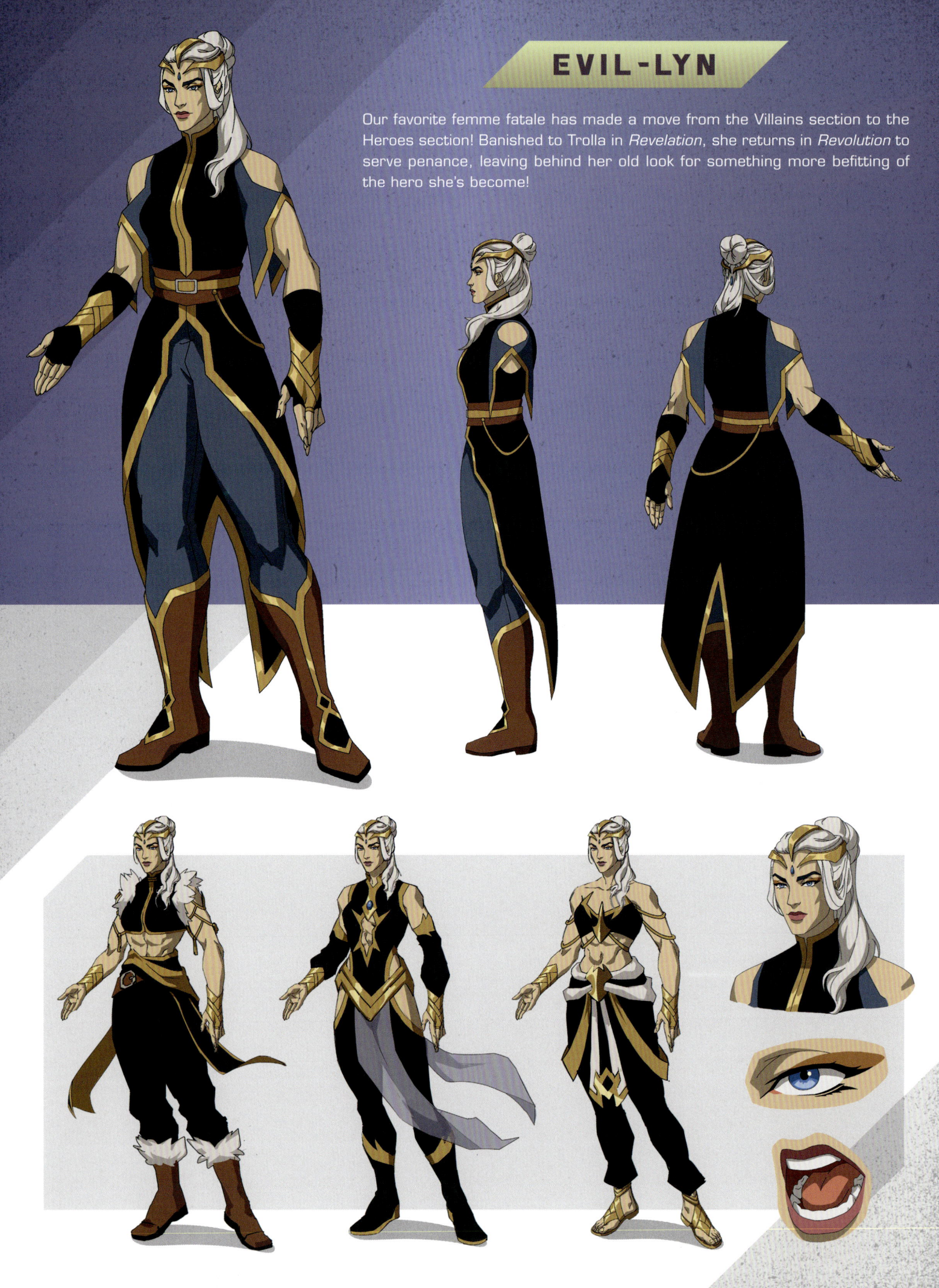

EVIL-LYN

Our favorite femme fatale has made a move from the Villains section to the Heroes section! Banished to Trolla in *Revelation*, she returns in *Revolution* to serve penance, leaving behind her old look for something more befitting of the hero she's become!

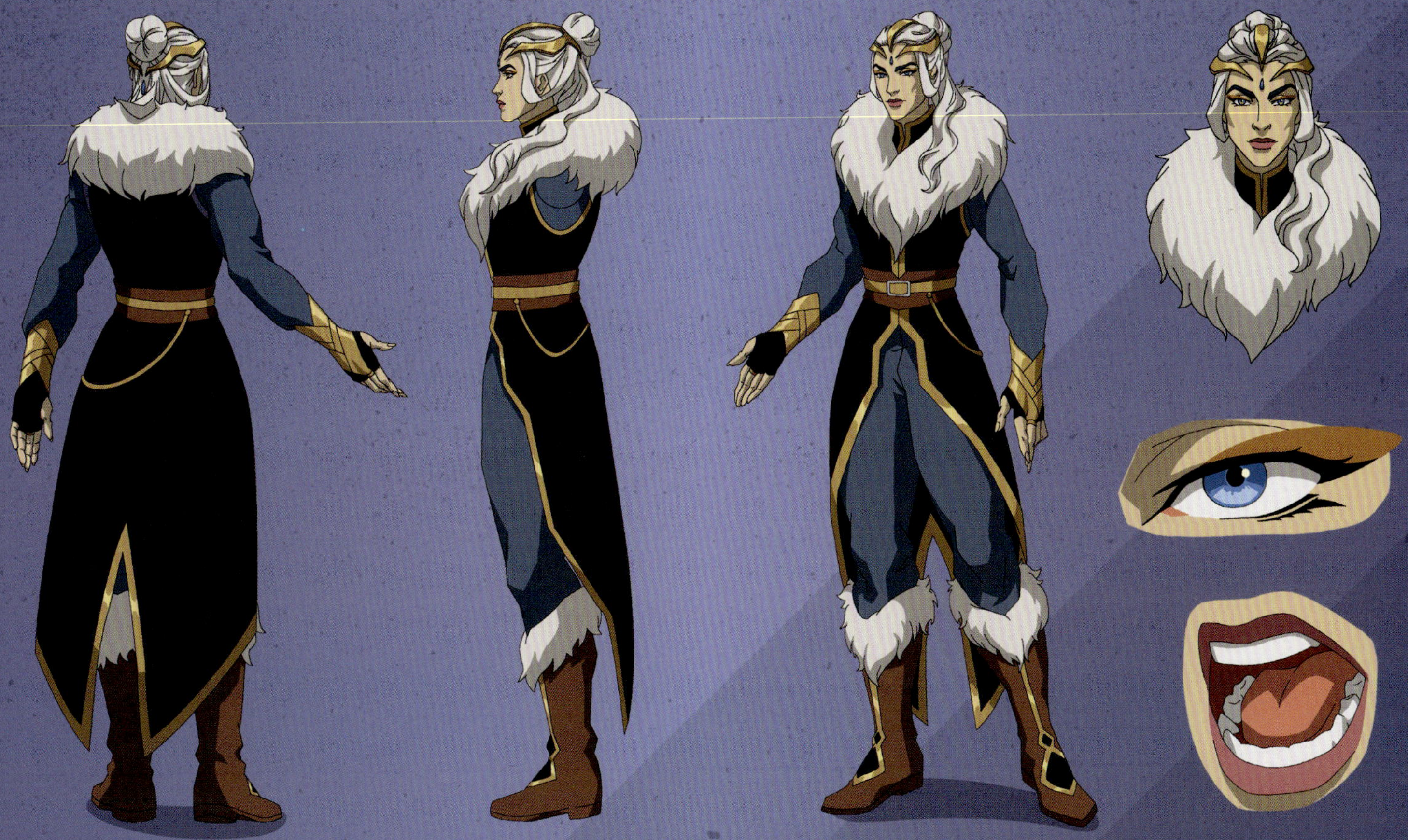

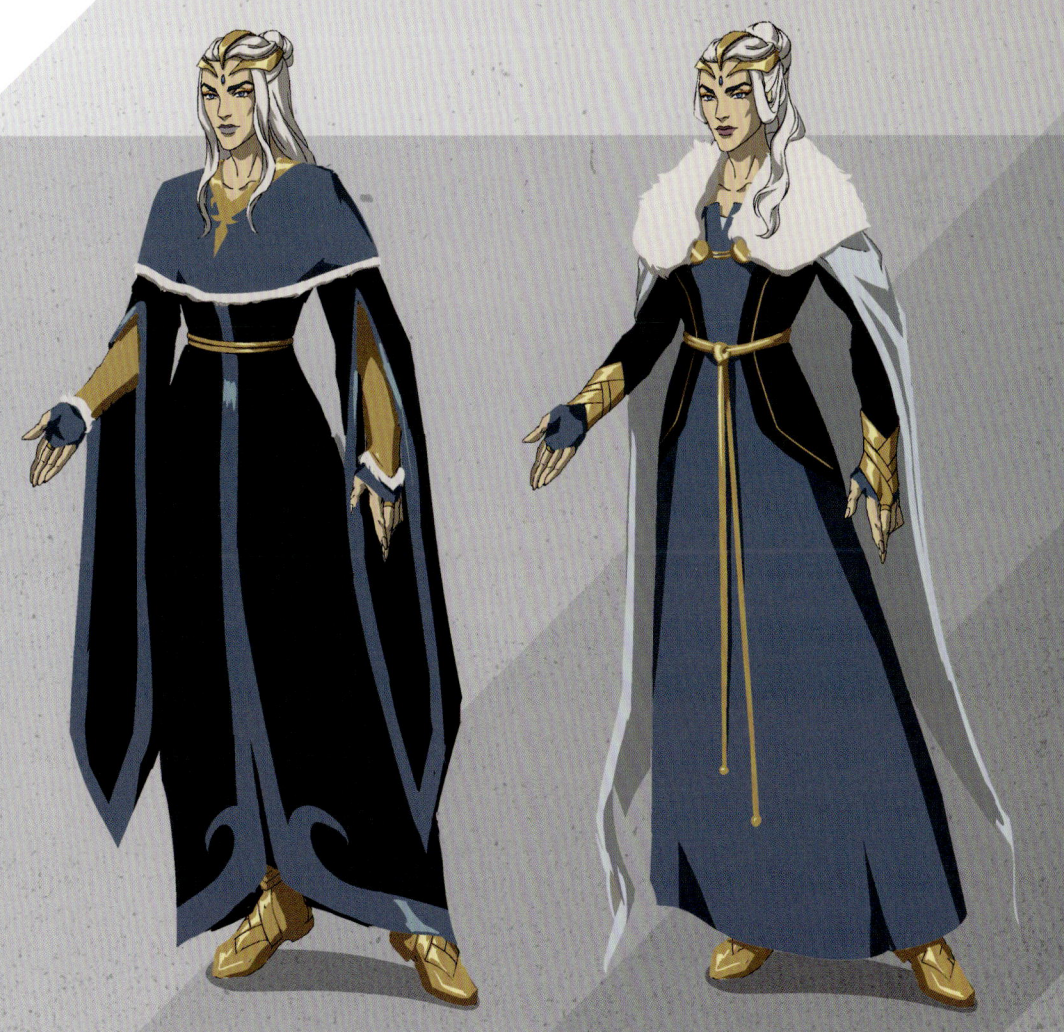

This season, Evil-Lyn's cozy ensemble derives from the "liberated" look she adopted during her exile to Trolla, but updated to be more suitable for the frigid drafts of Darksmoke. Her new look, affectionately dubbed "Winter-Lyn," is complete with gold trim, fur-lined boots, and an opulent collar showing that even in exile, Lyn has acquired a taste for the refined.

HEROES

MAN-OF-WAR

Since Andra has taken over Duncan's role as Man-At-Arms, the most dangerous man in Eternia has moved into an advisory role. But that doesn't mean that he's not still tinkering on the side, as seen when his newest invention single-handedly destroys Hordak's mother ship.

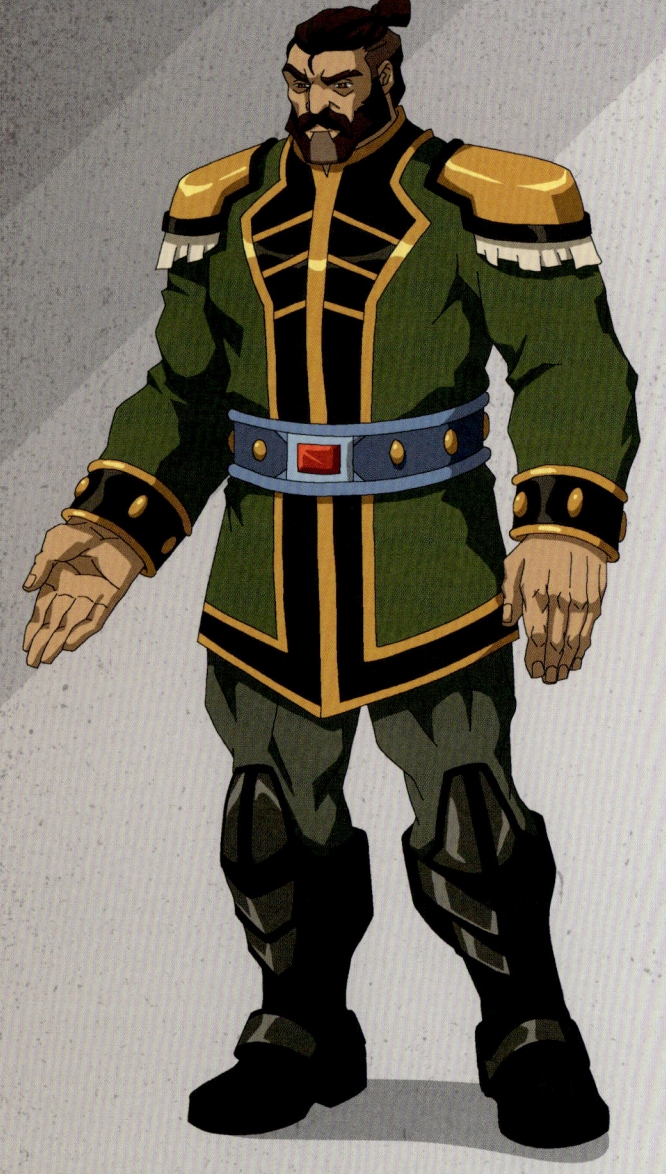

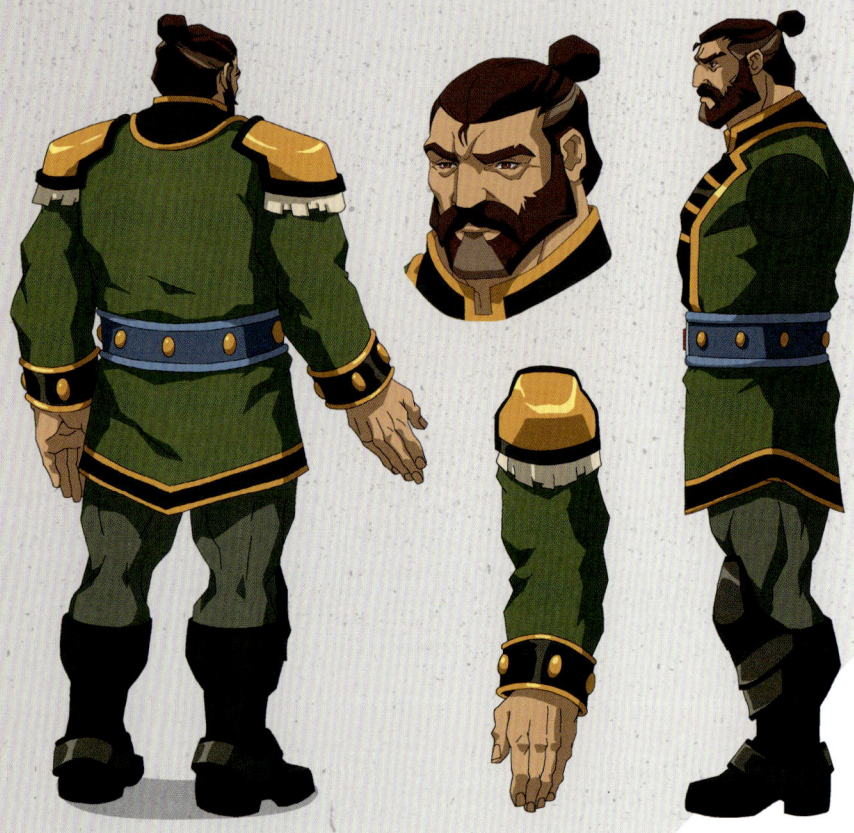

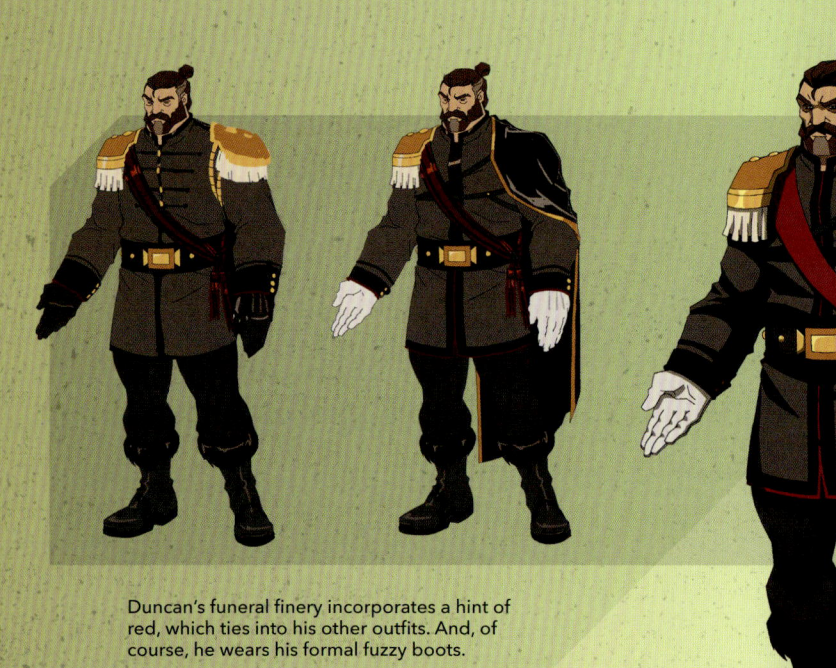

Duncan's funeral finery incorporates a hint of red, which ties into his other outfits. And, of course, he wears his formal fuzzy boots.

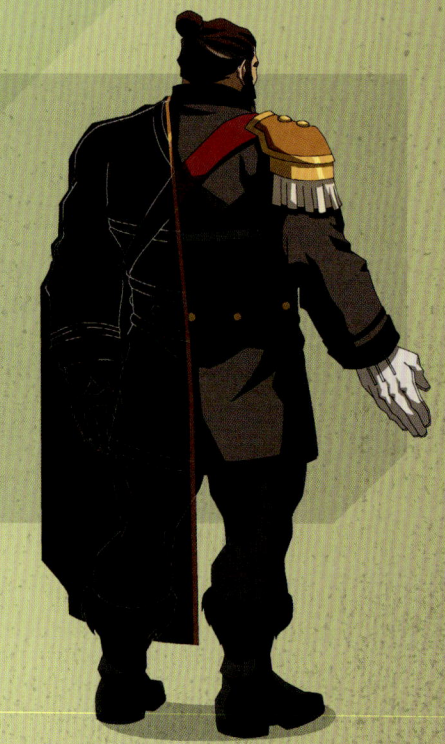

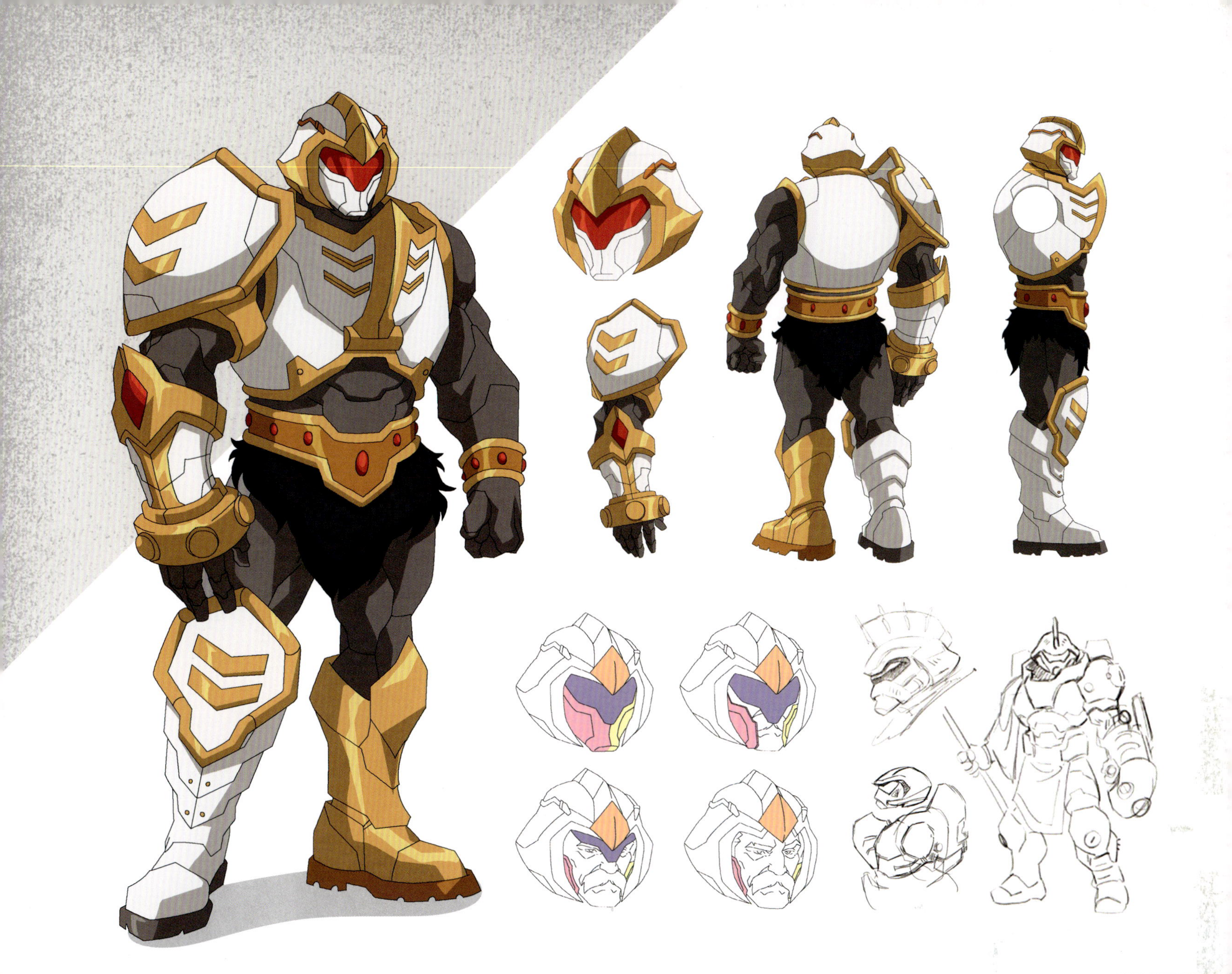

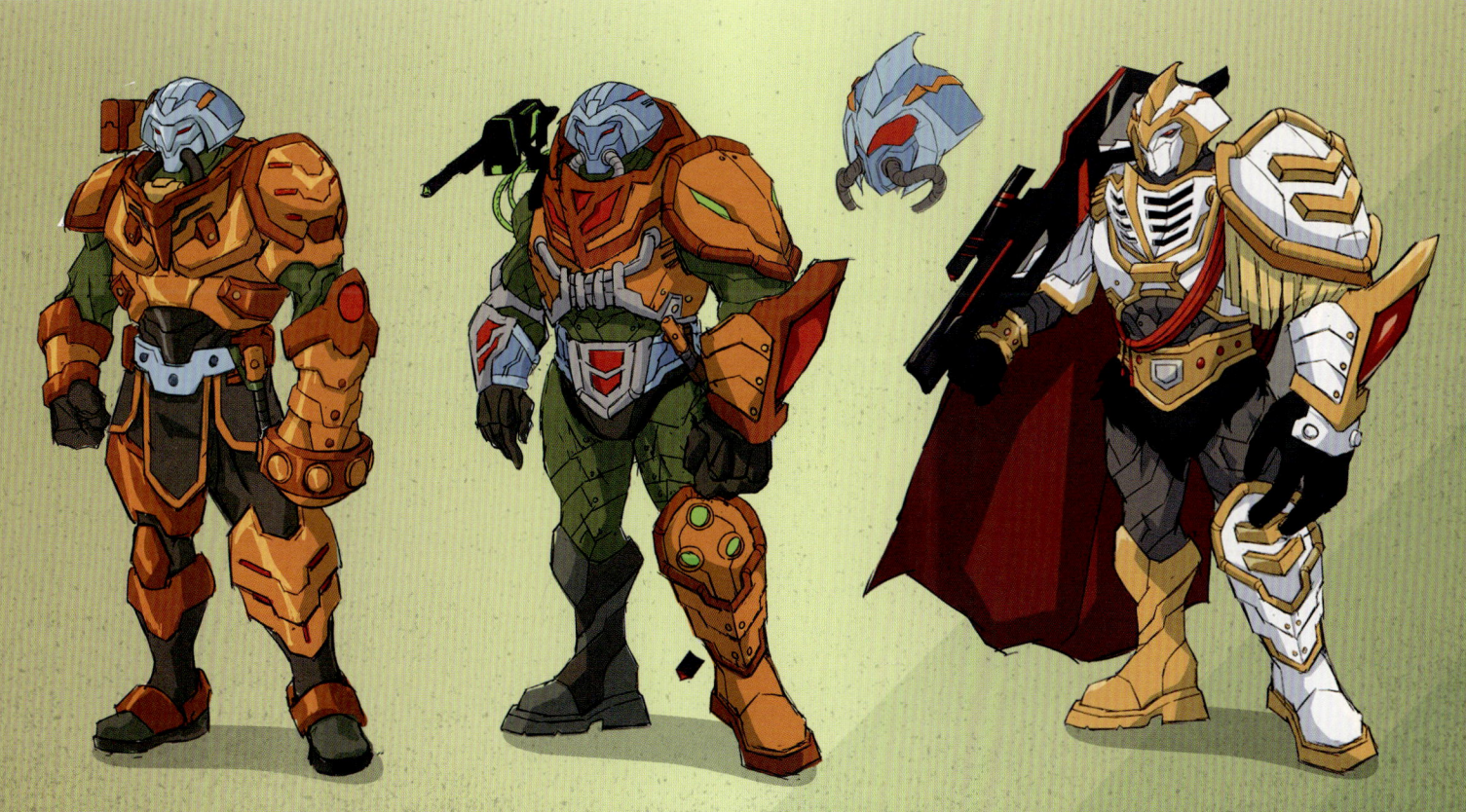

HEROES \\ 23

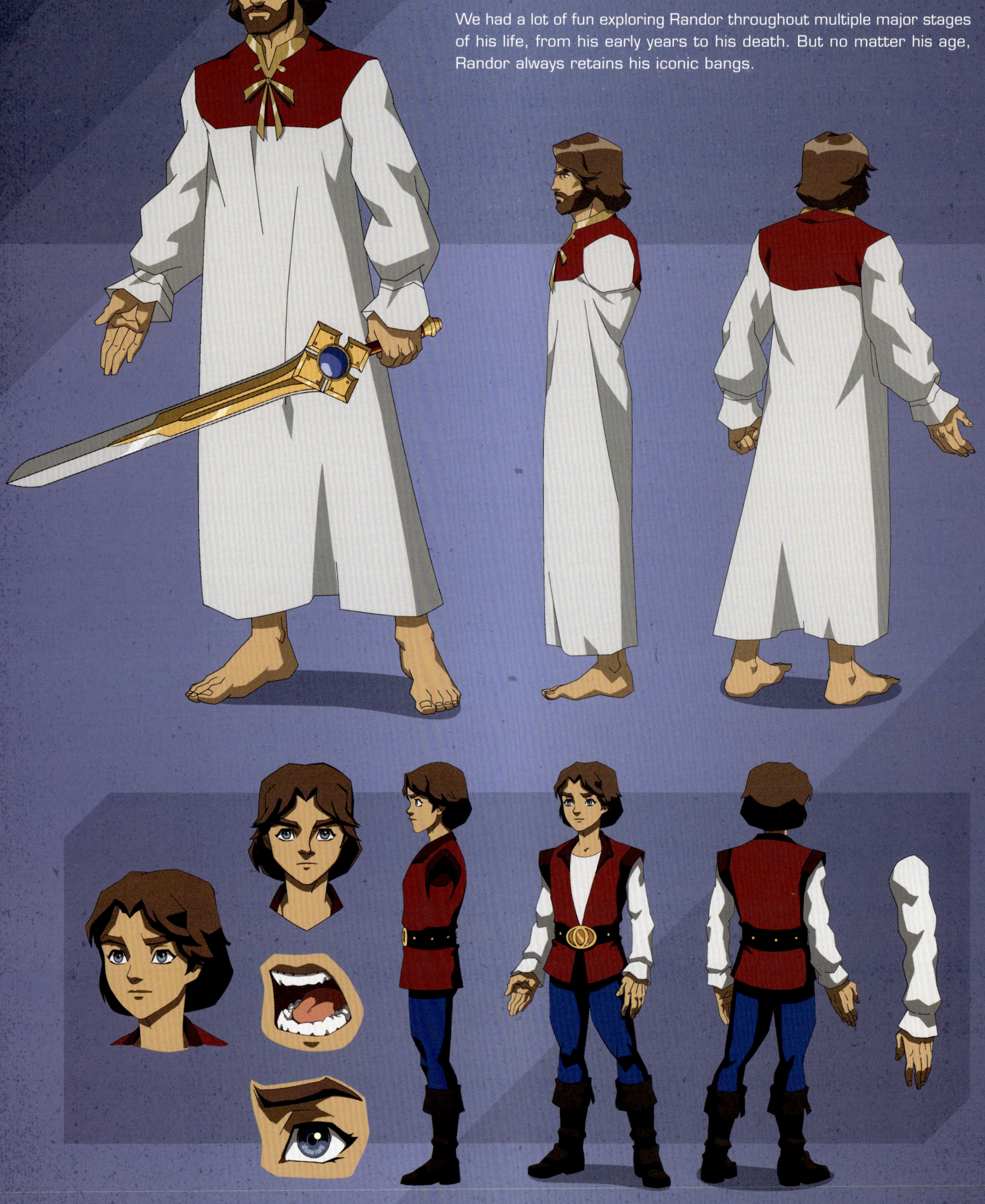

KING RANDOR

We had a lot of fun exploring Randor throughout multiple major stages of his life, from his early years to his death. But no matter his age, Randor always retains his iconic bangs.

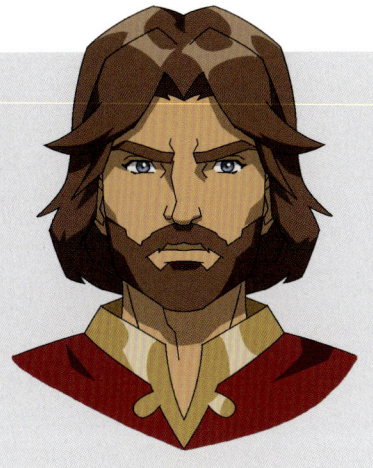 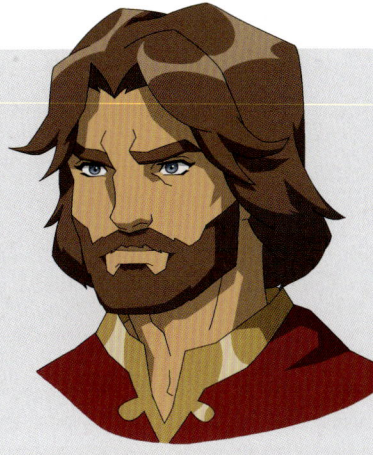 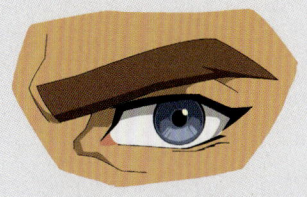 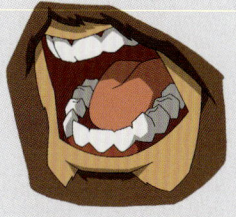

In season 1, Randor and Adam's shared eye color links them together—even when fighting. This season, it emphasizes their improved relationship and Randor's overall legacy.

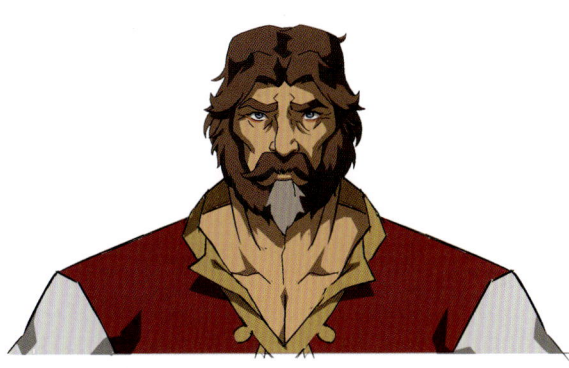 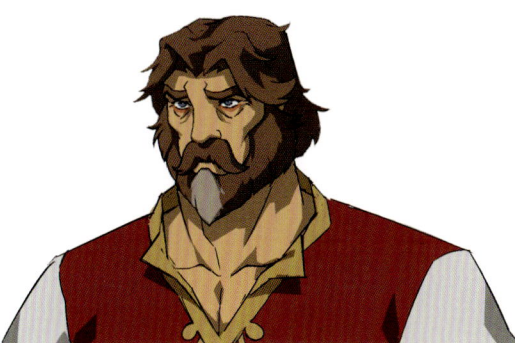 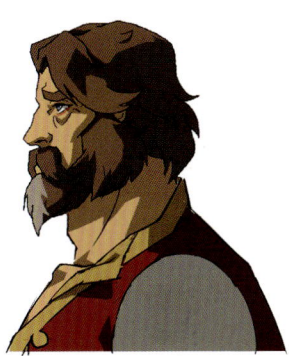

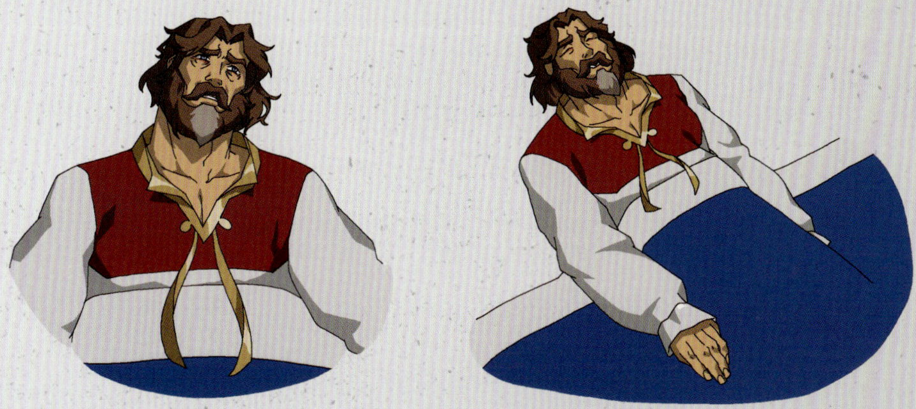

Since Randor's illness was an internal one, the only external signs we needed to show were swollen, heavy eye bags and unkempt hair. We utilized the same nightgown design for both Randor's modern-day and flashback looks. Even the king of Eternia can wear an outfit twice!

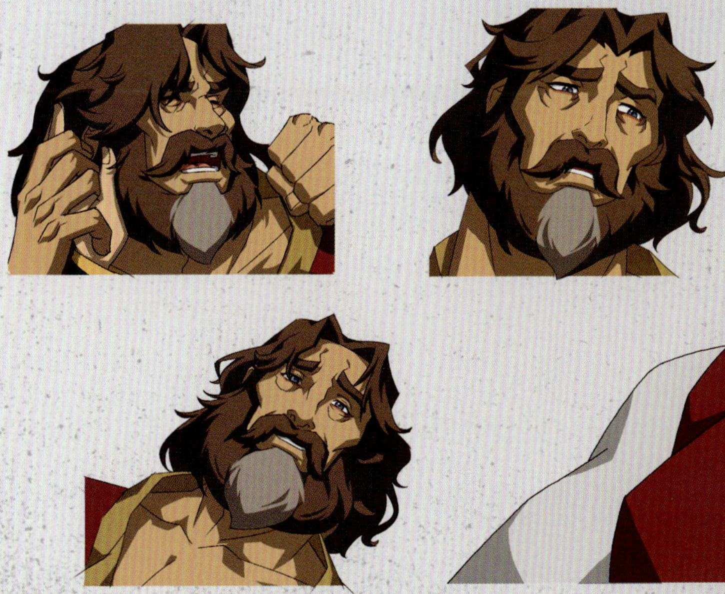

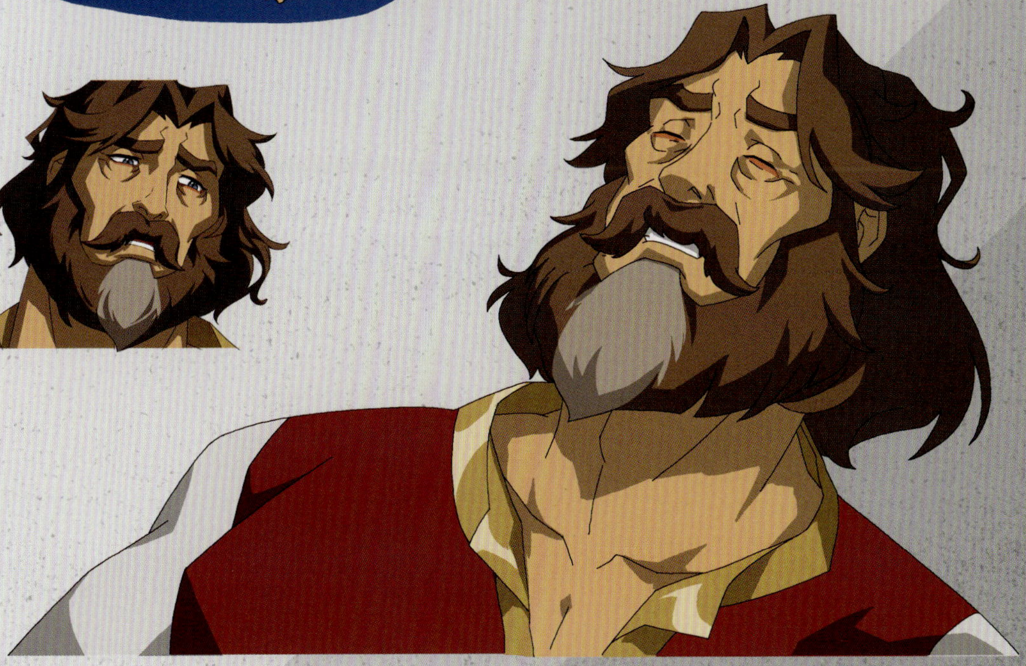

HEROES \\ 25

QUEEN MARLENA

Queen Marlena goes through a lot this season, between the loss of her husband, the invasion of her kingdom, and her eventual capture. Yet throughout it all, she remains poised. We also got the opportunity to design her younger self for a flashback.

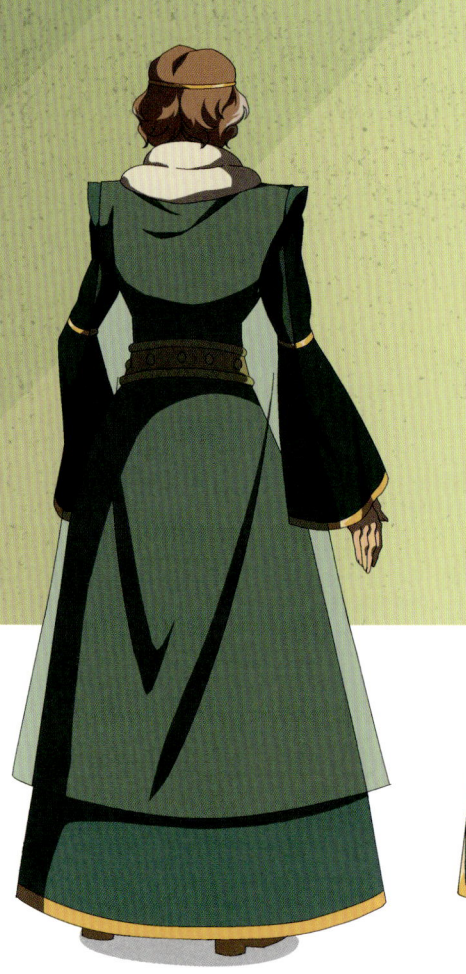
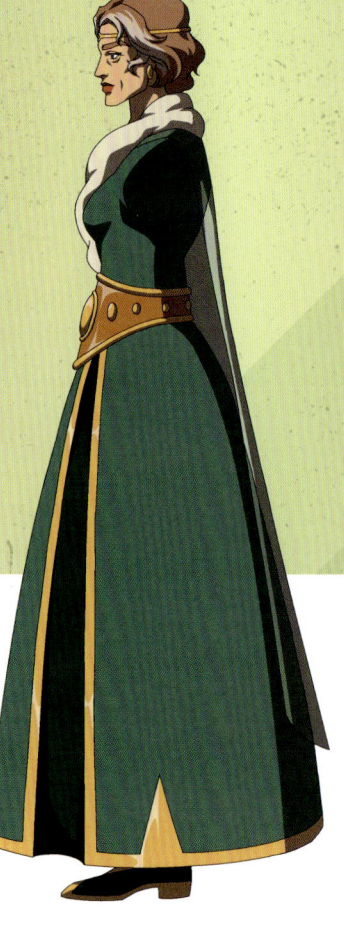
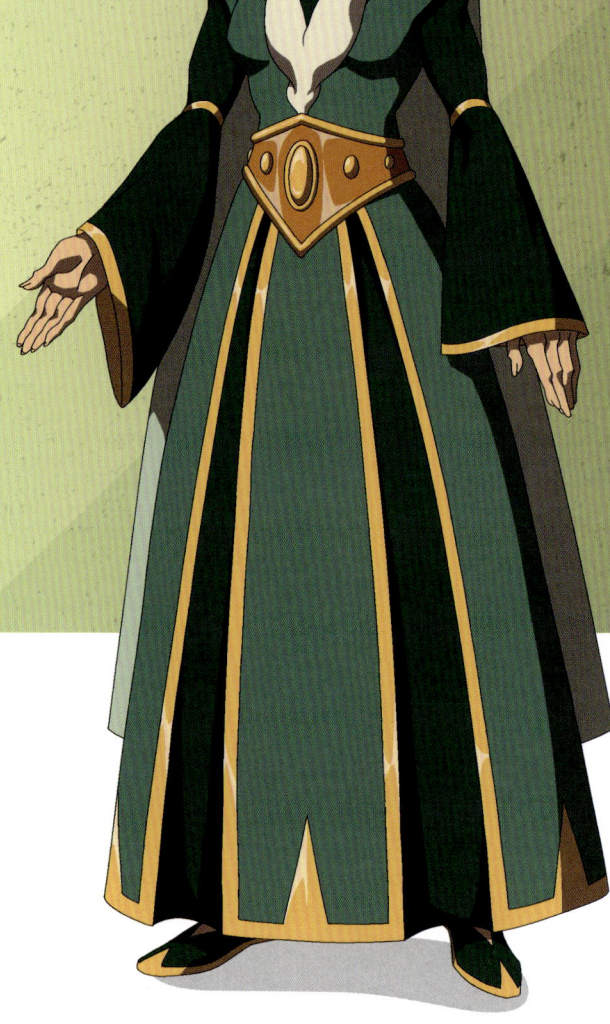

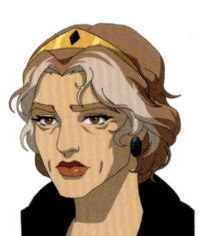
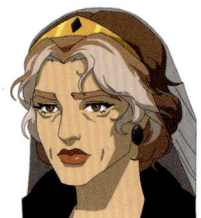
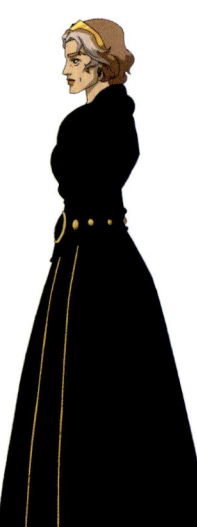
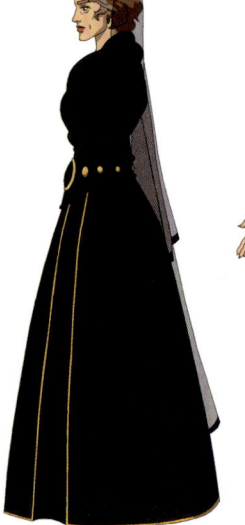
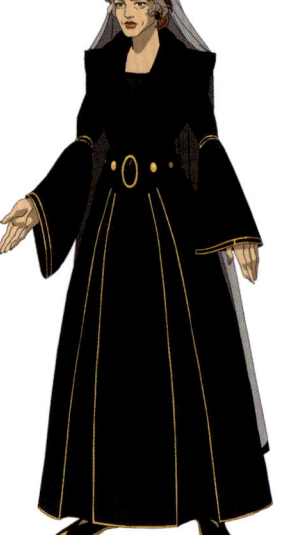
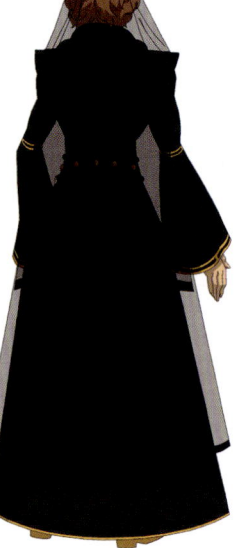

Marlena's mourning gown is elegant and understated.

26 // THE ART OF MASTERS OF THE UNIVERSE: REVOLUTION

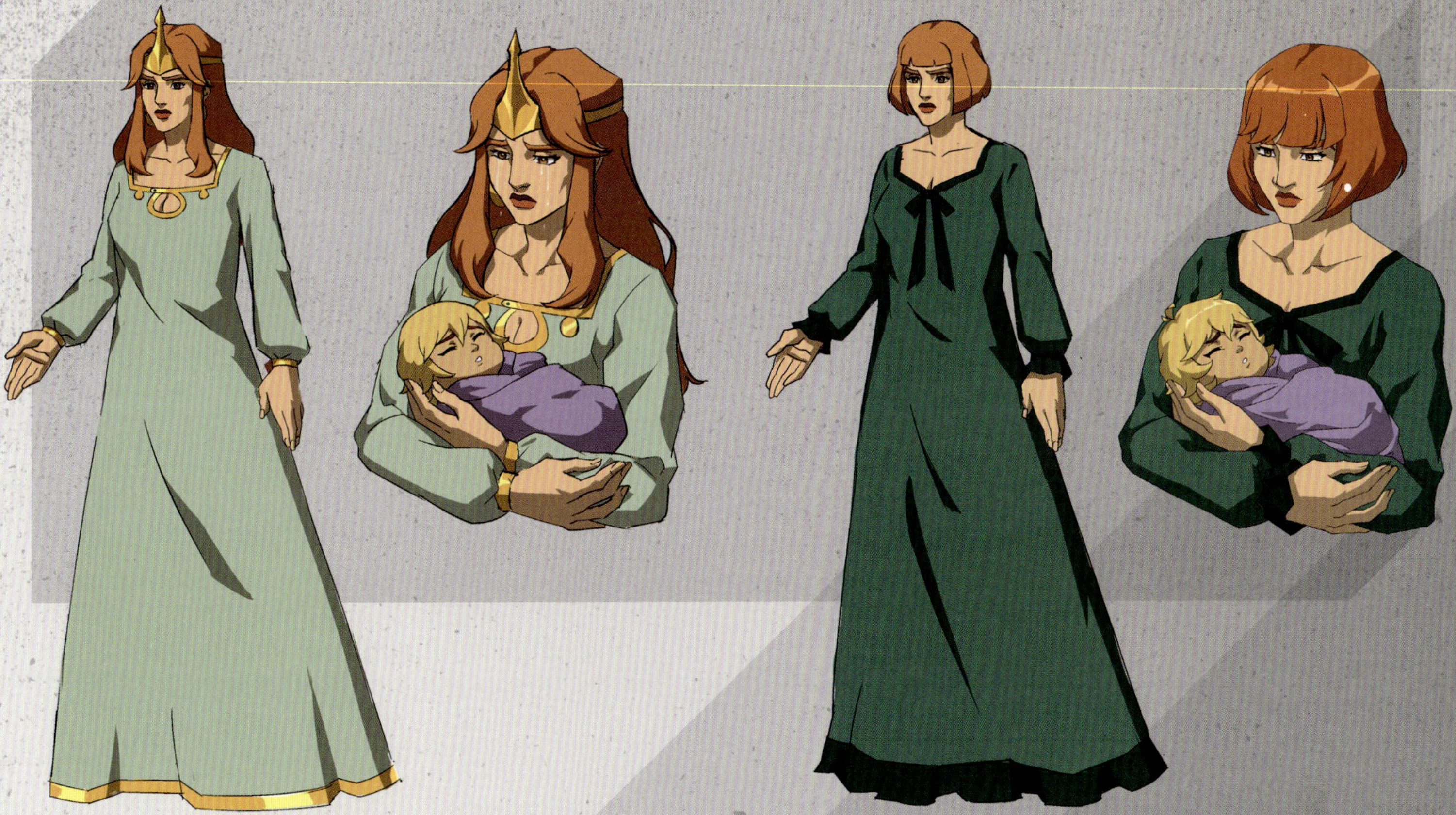

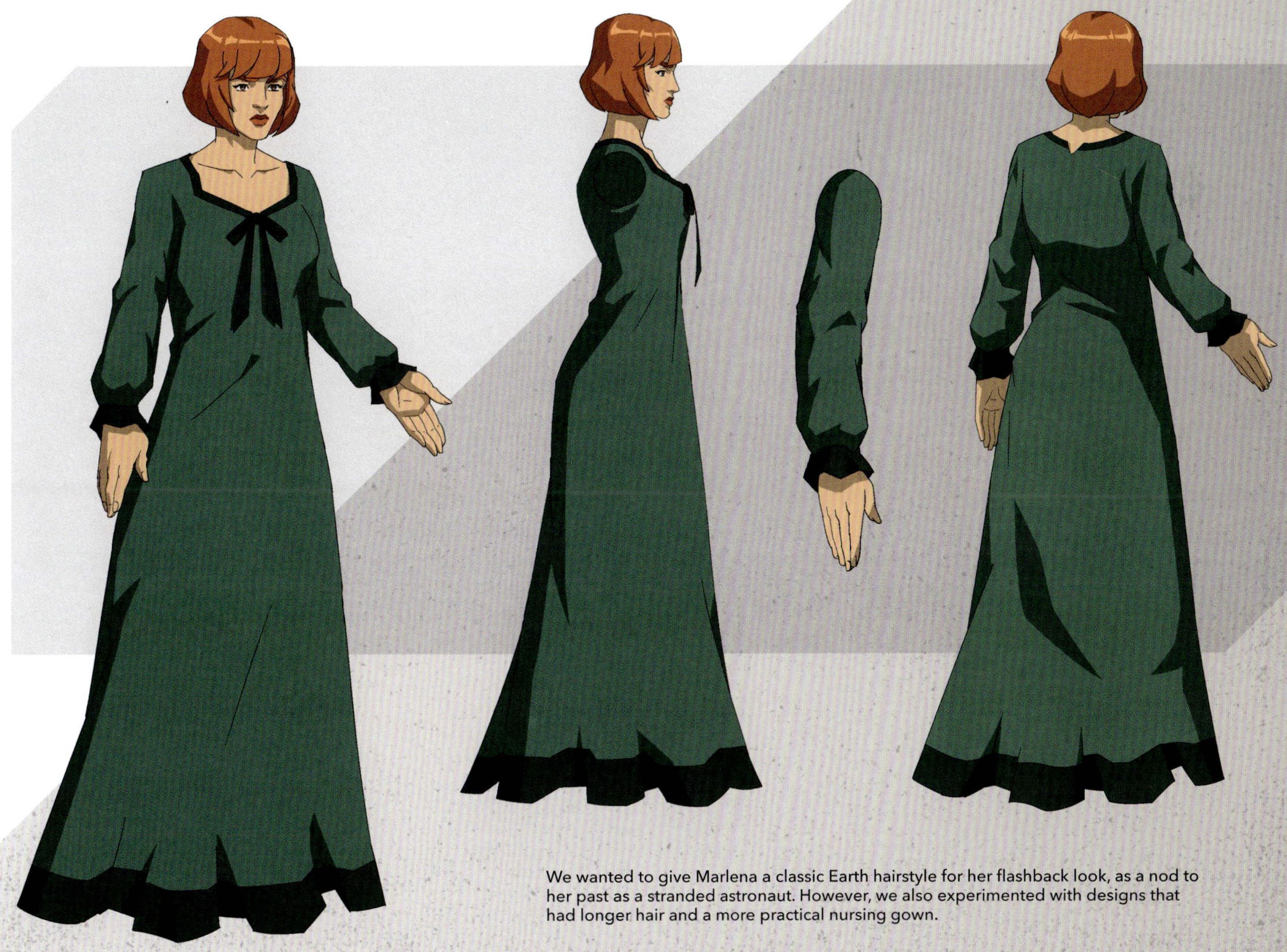

We wanted to give Marlena a classic Earth hairstyle for her flashback look, as a nod to her past as a stranded astronaut. However, we also experimented with designs that had longer hair and a more practical nursing gown.

HEROES \\ 27

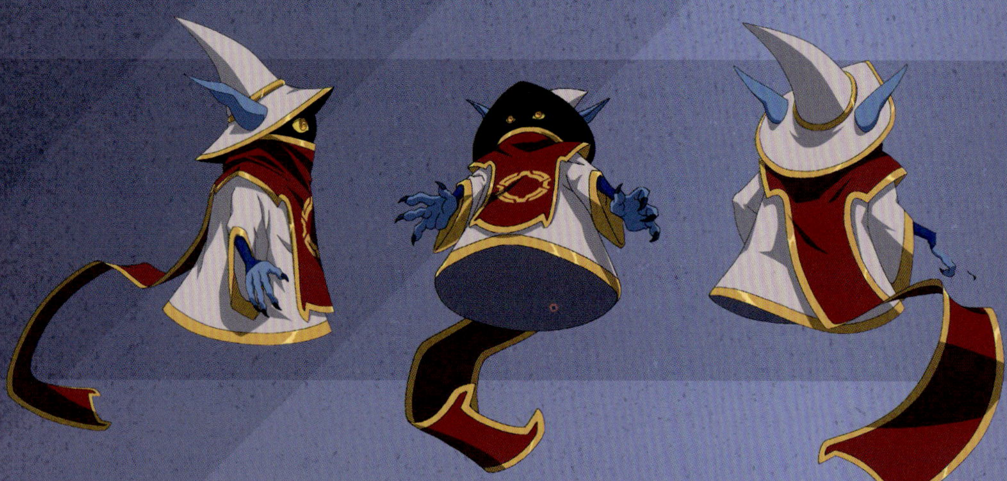

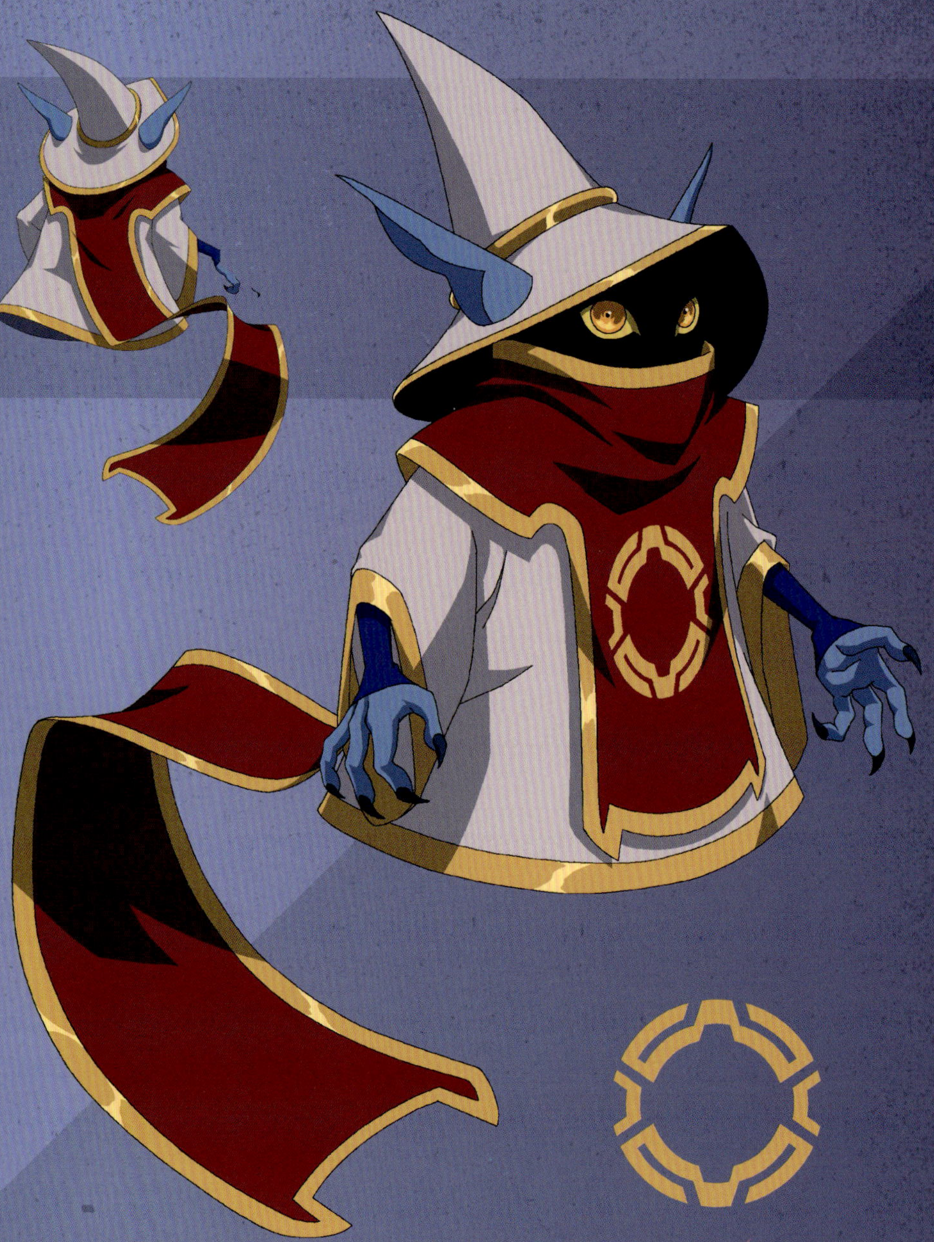

ORKO

This little mage is back this season, more powerful than ever! After a rough journey to Subternia, he's ready to showcase a variety of new spells alongside our favorite heroes. Behold the Oracle!

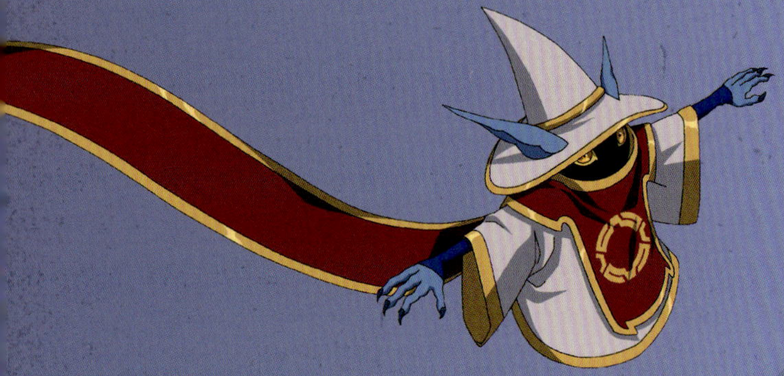

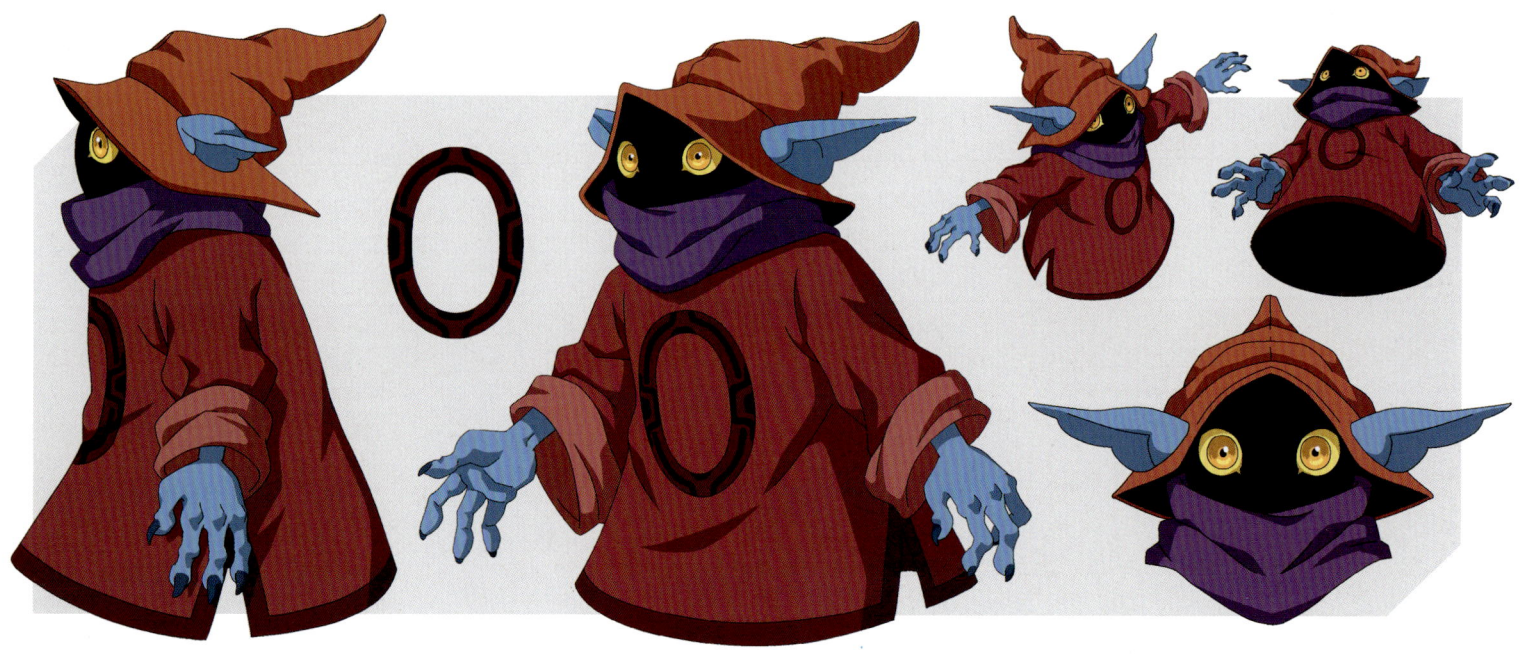

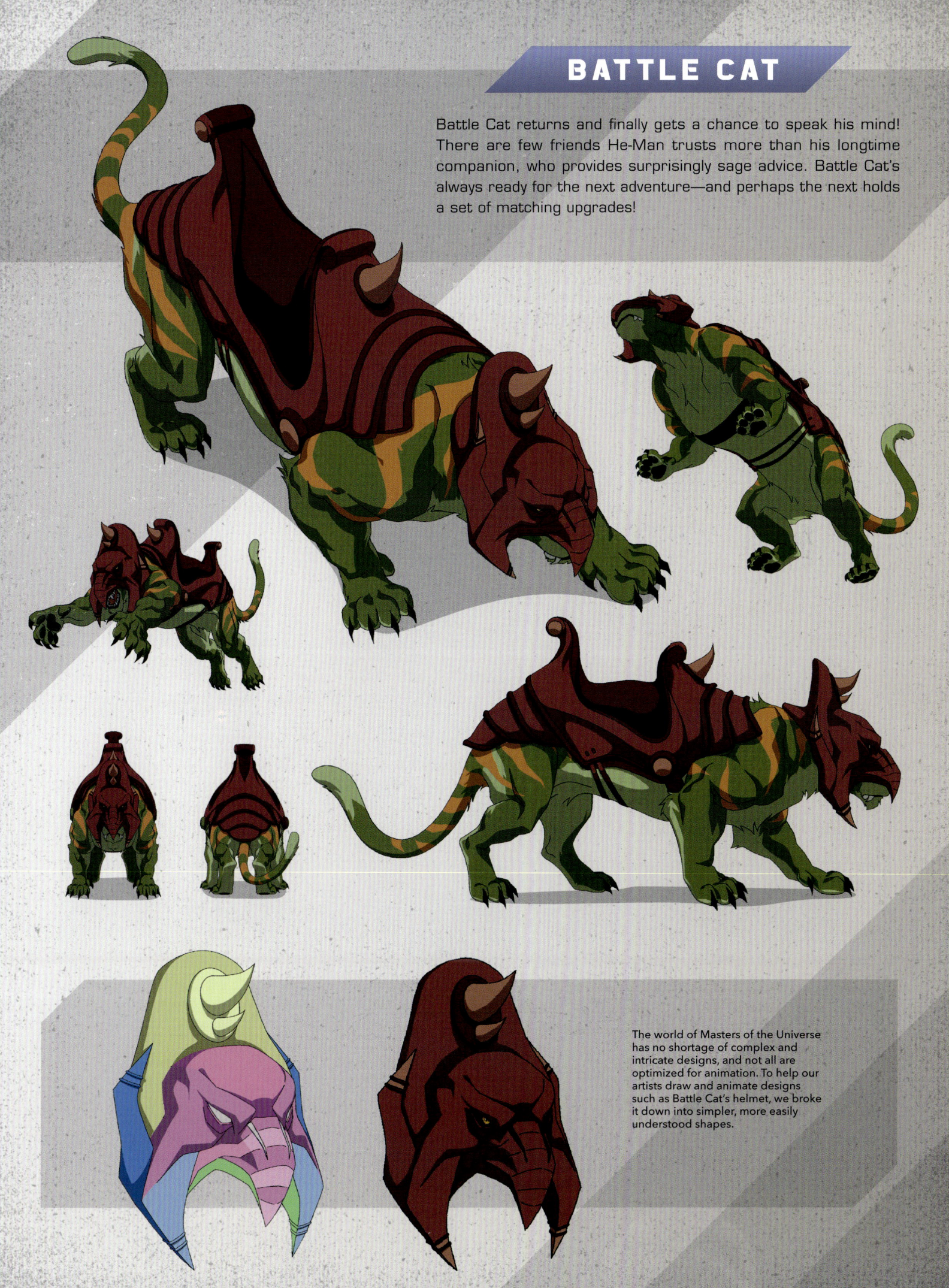

BATTLE CAT

Battle Cat returns and finally gets a chance to speak his mind! There are few friends He-Man trusts more than his longtime companion, who provides surprisingly sage advice. Battle Cat's always ready for the next adventure—and perhaps the next holds a set of matching upgrades!

The world of Masters of the Universe has no shortage of complex and intricate designs, and not all are optimized for animation. To help our artists draw and animate designs such as Battle Cat's helmet, we broke it down into simpler, more easily understood shapes.

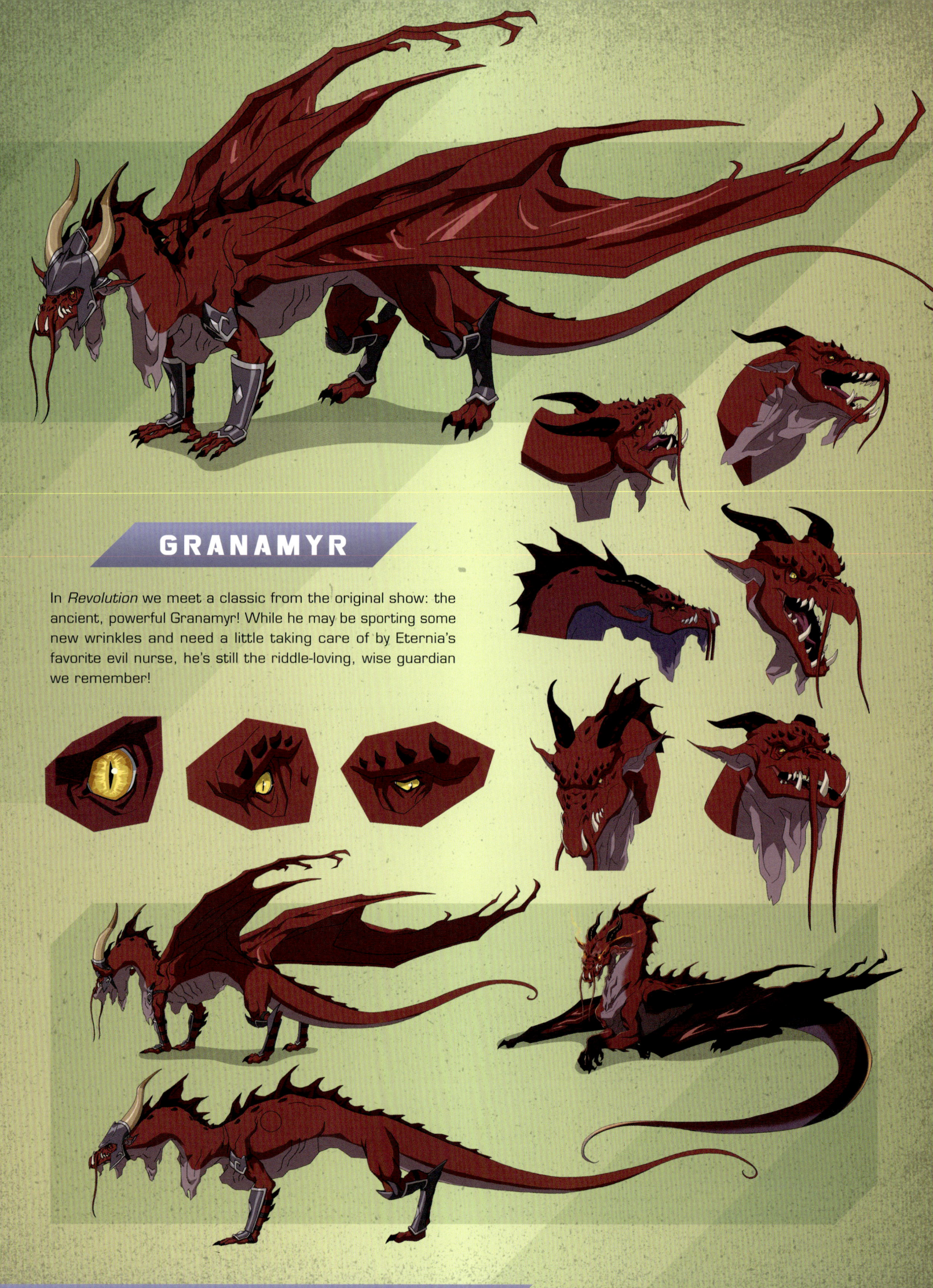

GRANAMYR

In *Revolution* we meet a classic from the original show: the ancient, powerful Granamyr! While he may be sporting some new wrinkles and need a little taking care of by Eternia's favorite evil nurse, he's still the riddle-loving, wise guardian we remember!

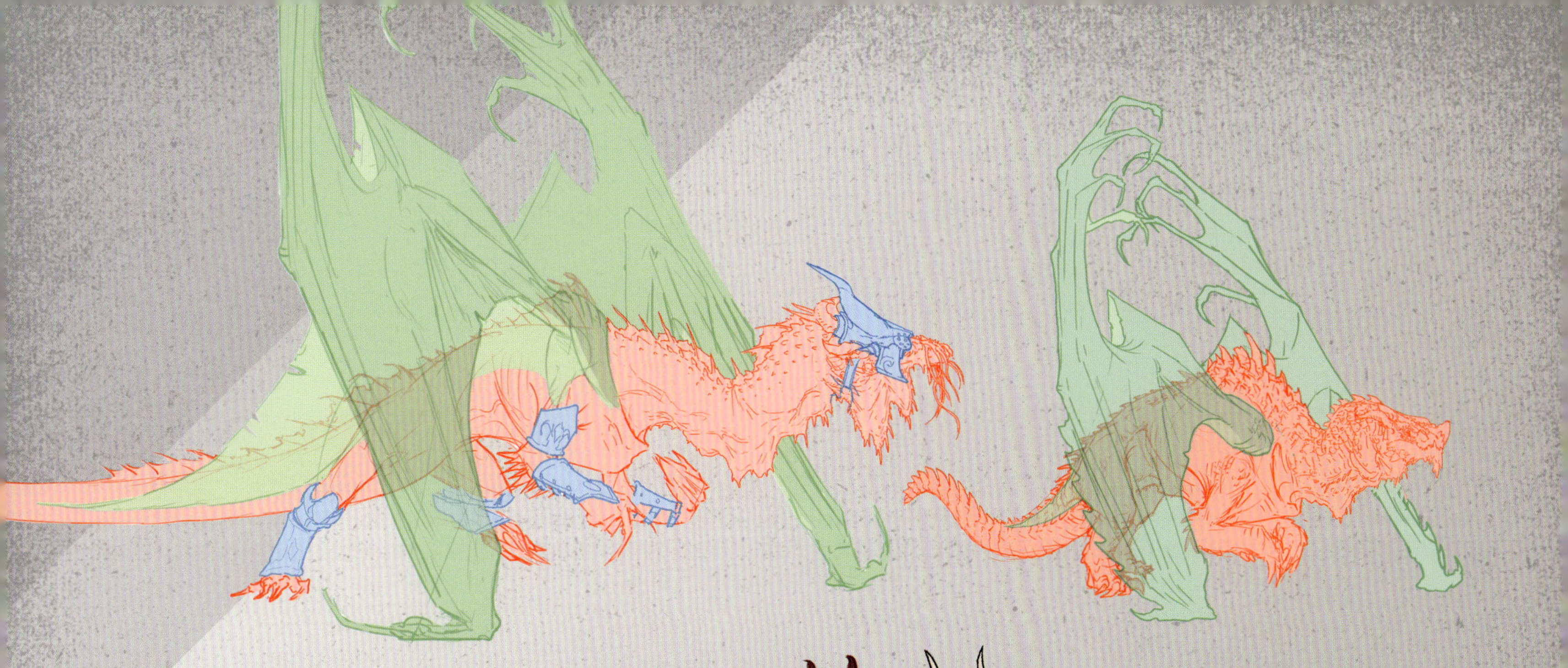

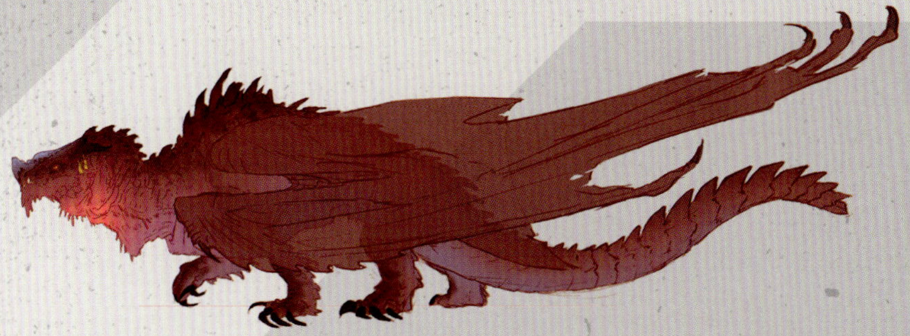

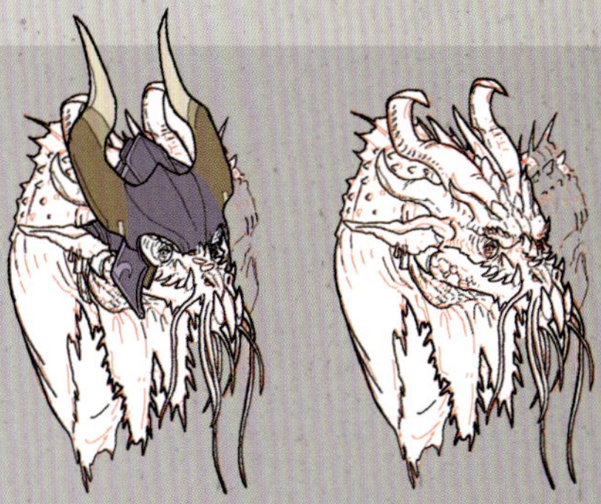

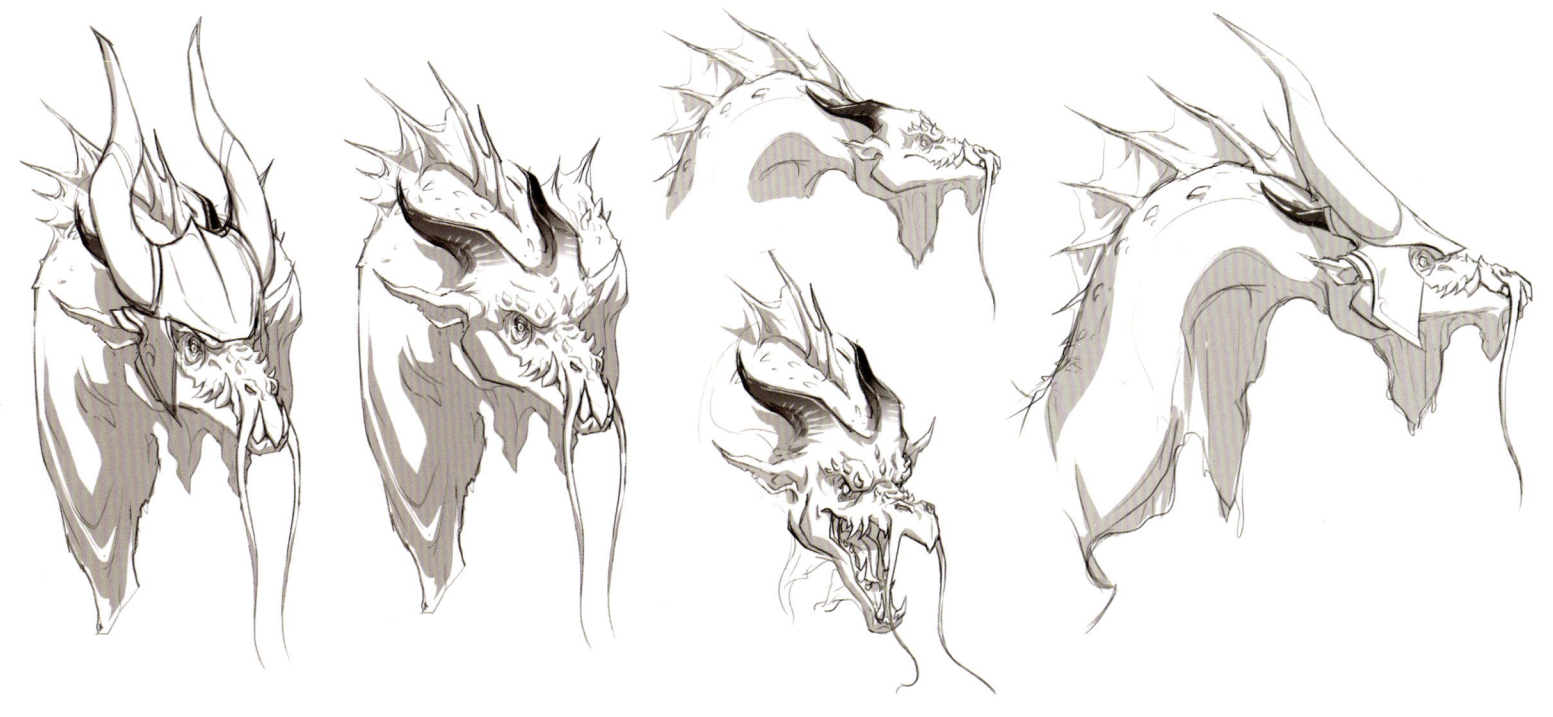

The design team was sure to include Granamyr's classic helmet, even while playing with new palettes and styles.

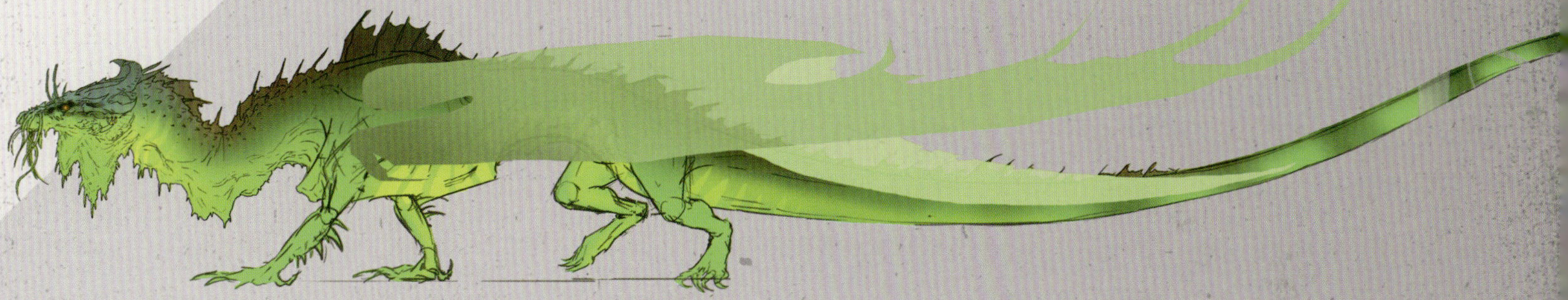

GWILDOR

We couldn't wait to bring Gwildor from the silver screen into the world of *Revolution*, especially considering it would canonize the live-action film. Our designers translated his eccentric movie appearance into something suitable for animation but still carried over his quirks and charm.

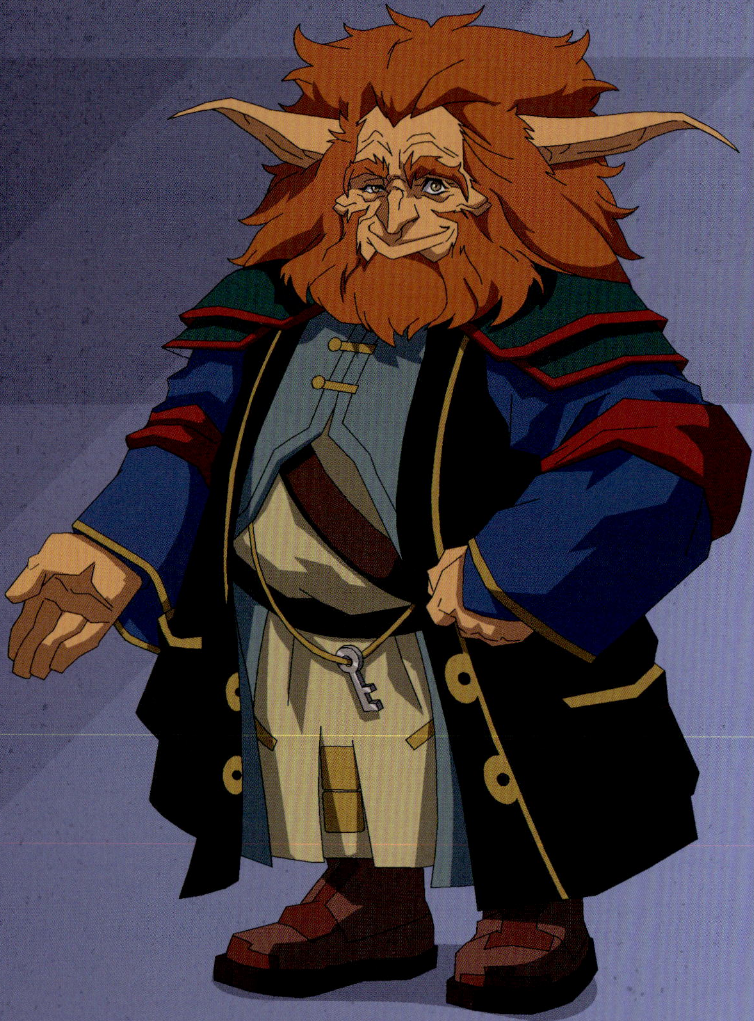

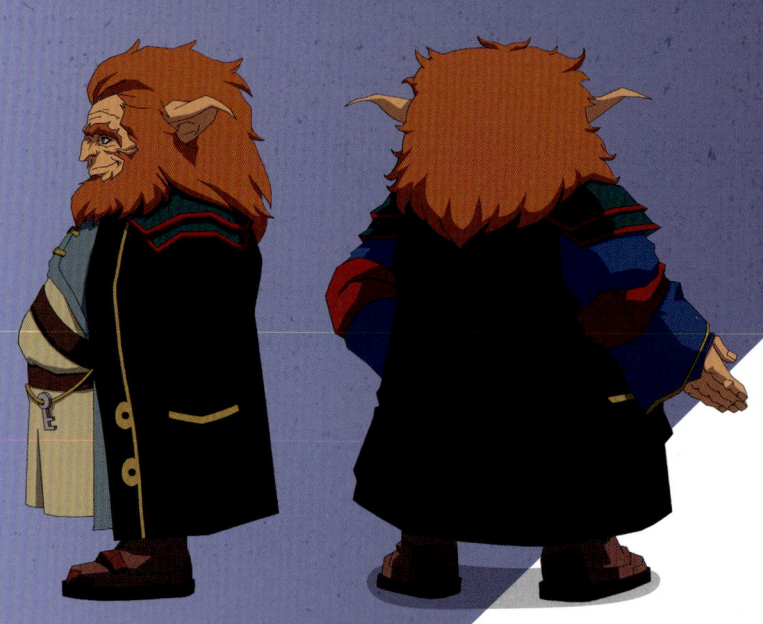

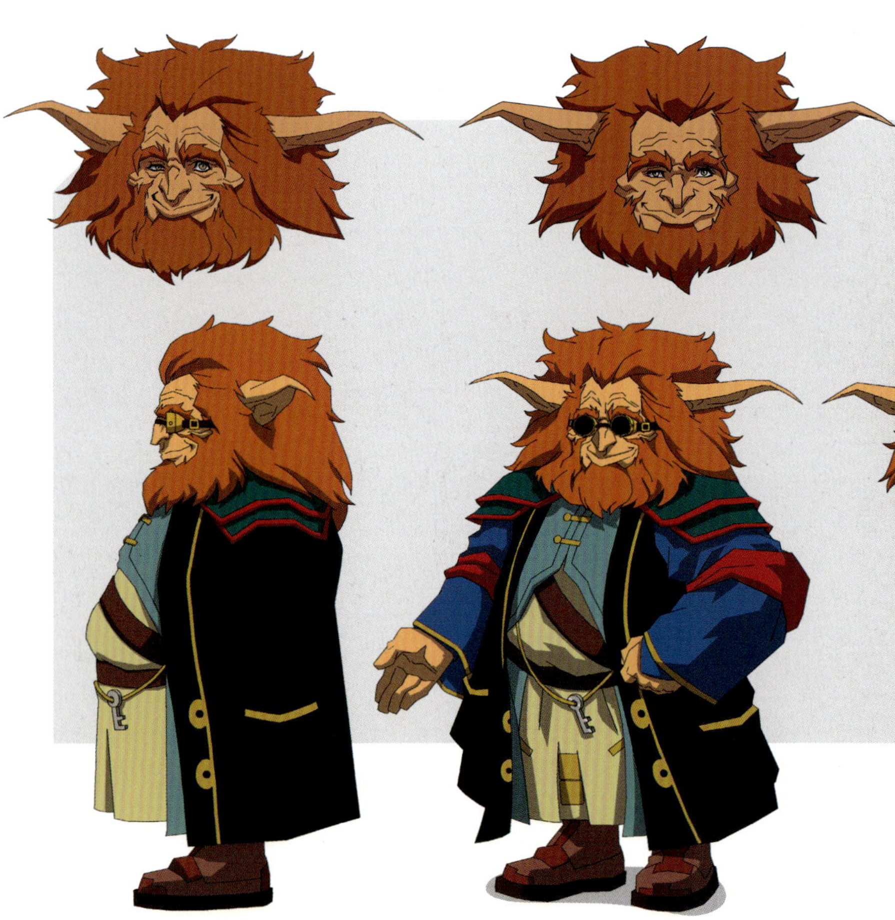

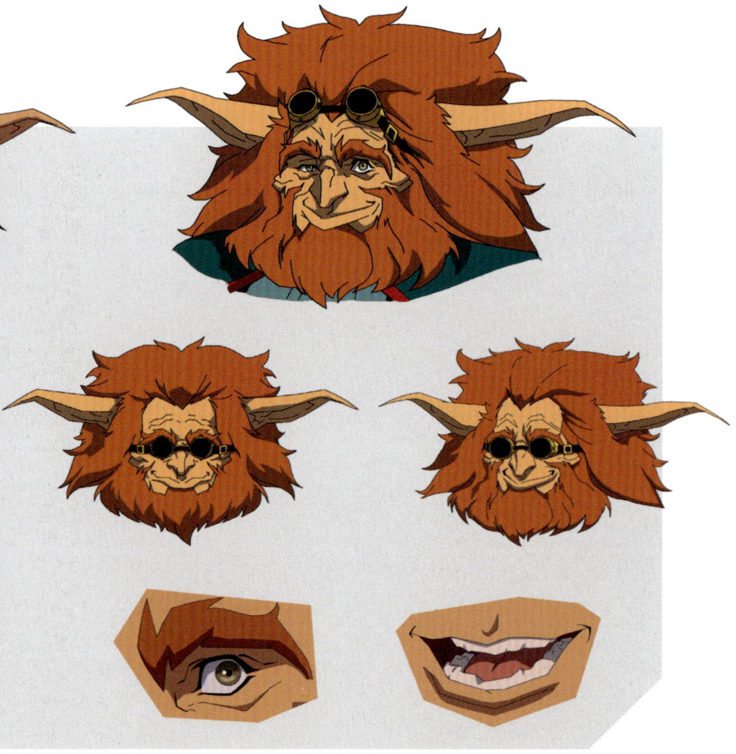

As he would be working with lots of powerful blacksmithing tools, we made sure Gwildor could follow all the necessary safety protocols with a stylish pair of goggles.

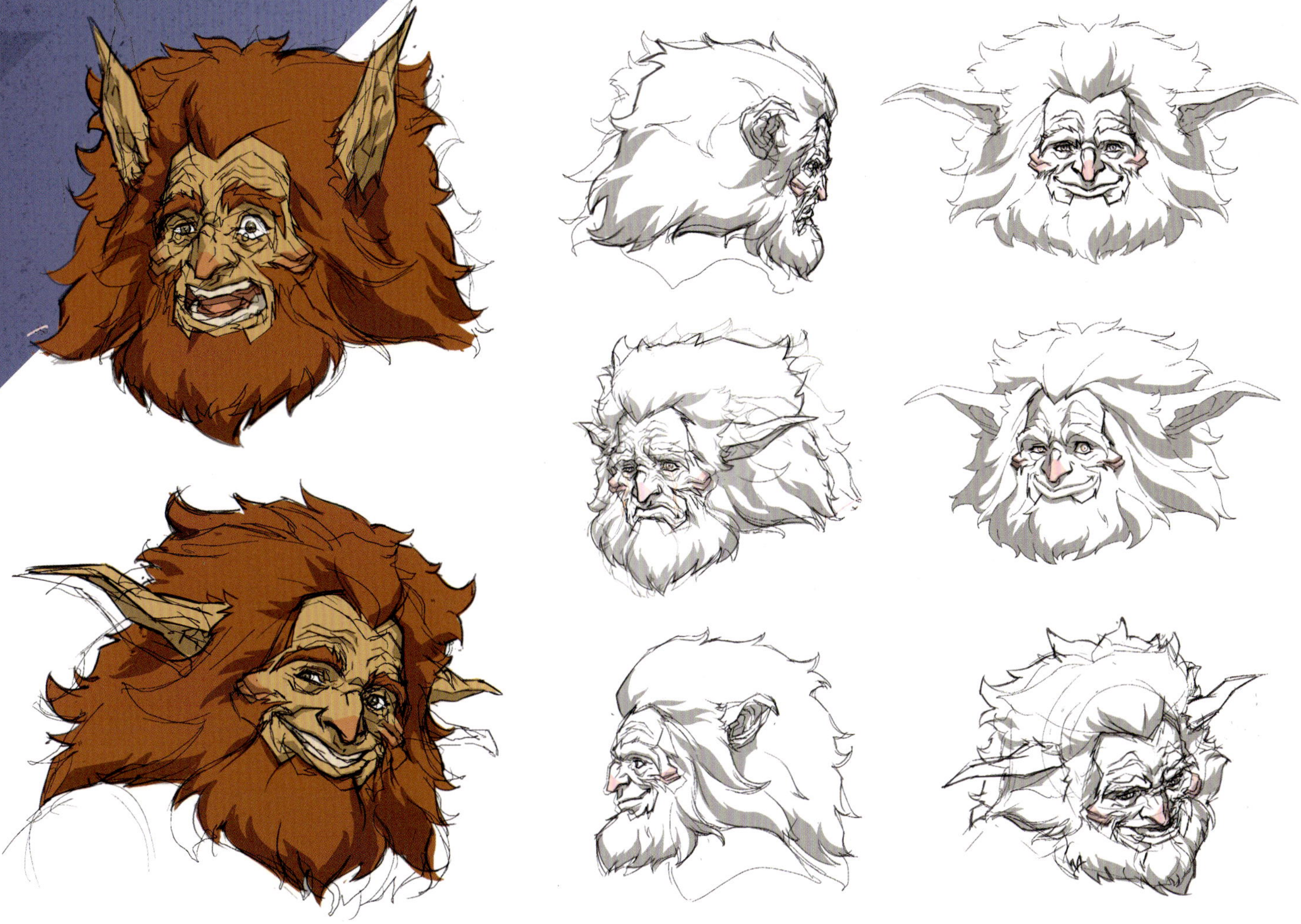

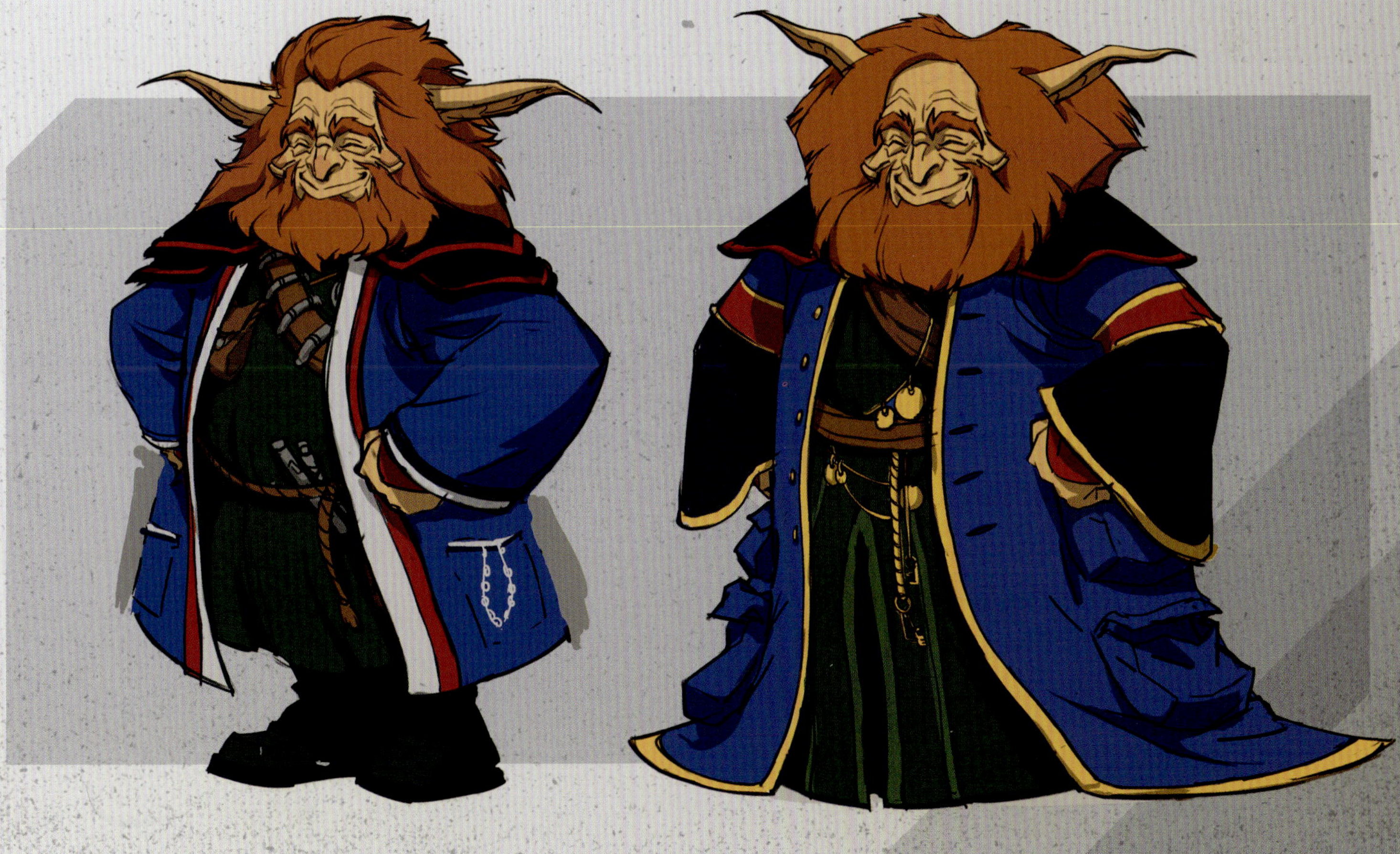

HEROES \\ 33

KING MIRO

The conflicted former king of Eternos. When he sent his son Keldor away, he unknowingly caused a chain reaction that would lead to the creation of the infamous Lord of Destruction—Skeletor! Miro's not exactly winning any Father of the Year awards.

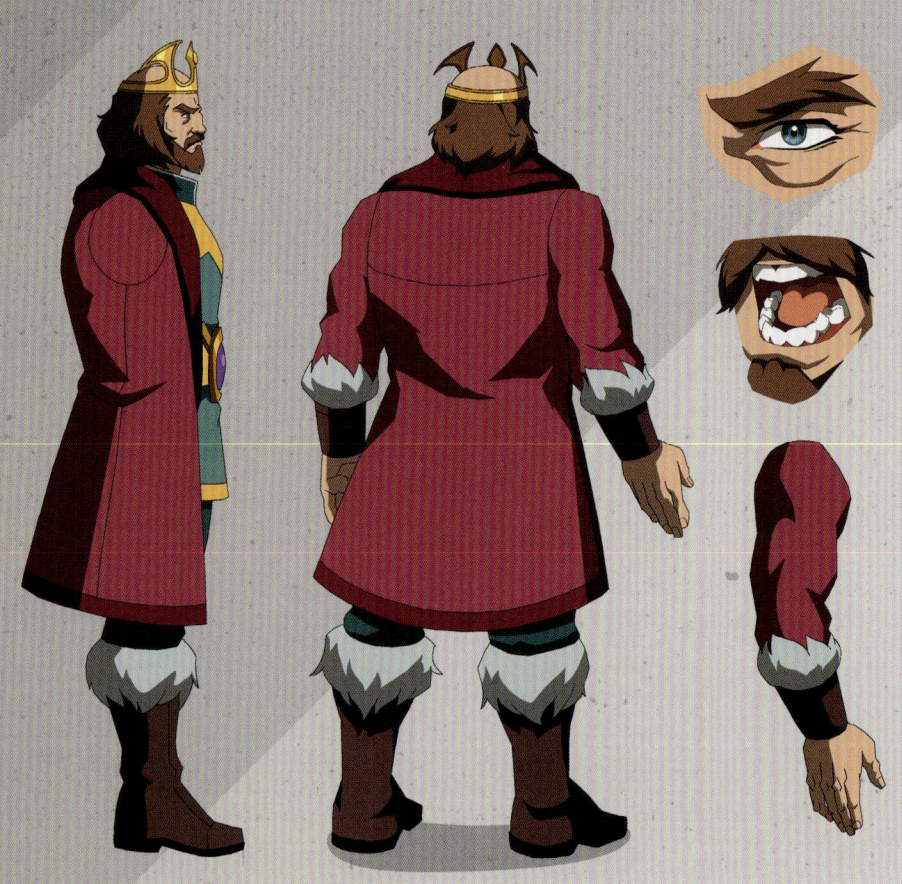
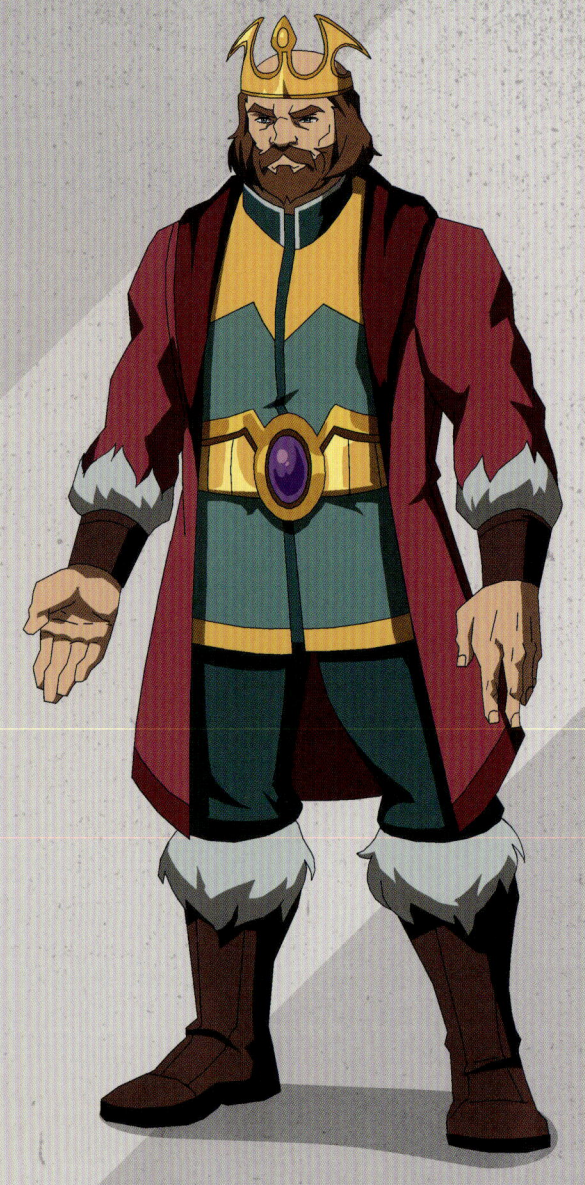
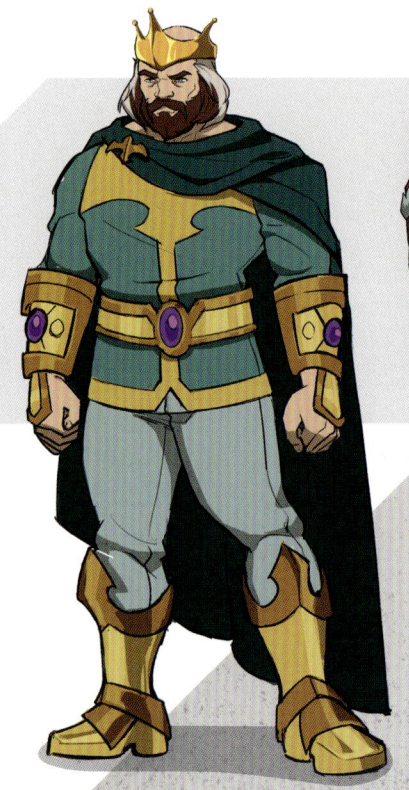
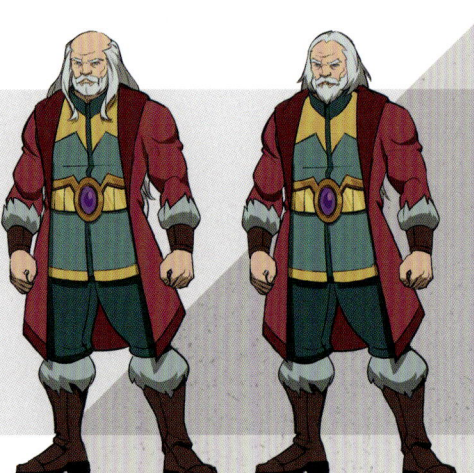
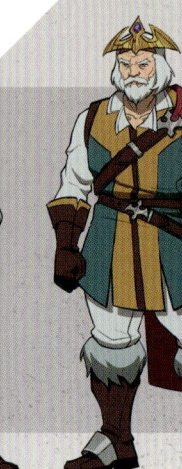
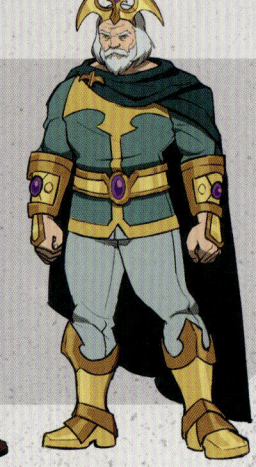
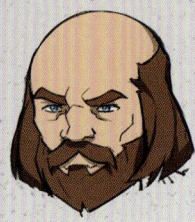
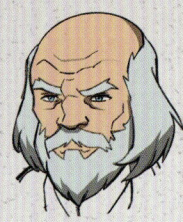
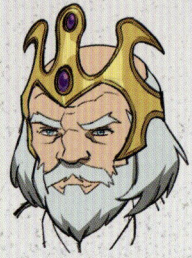

While many of the previous depictions of Miro had white hair, we wanted to emphasize his family resemblance to young Prince Randor.

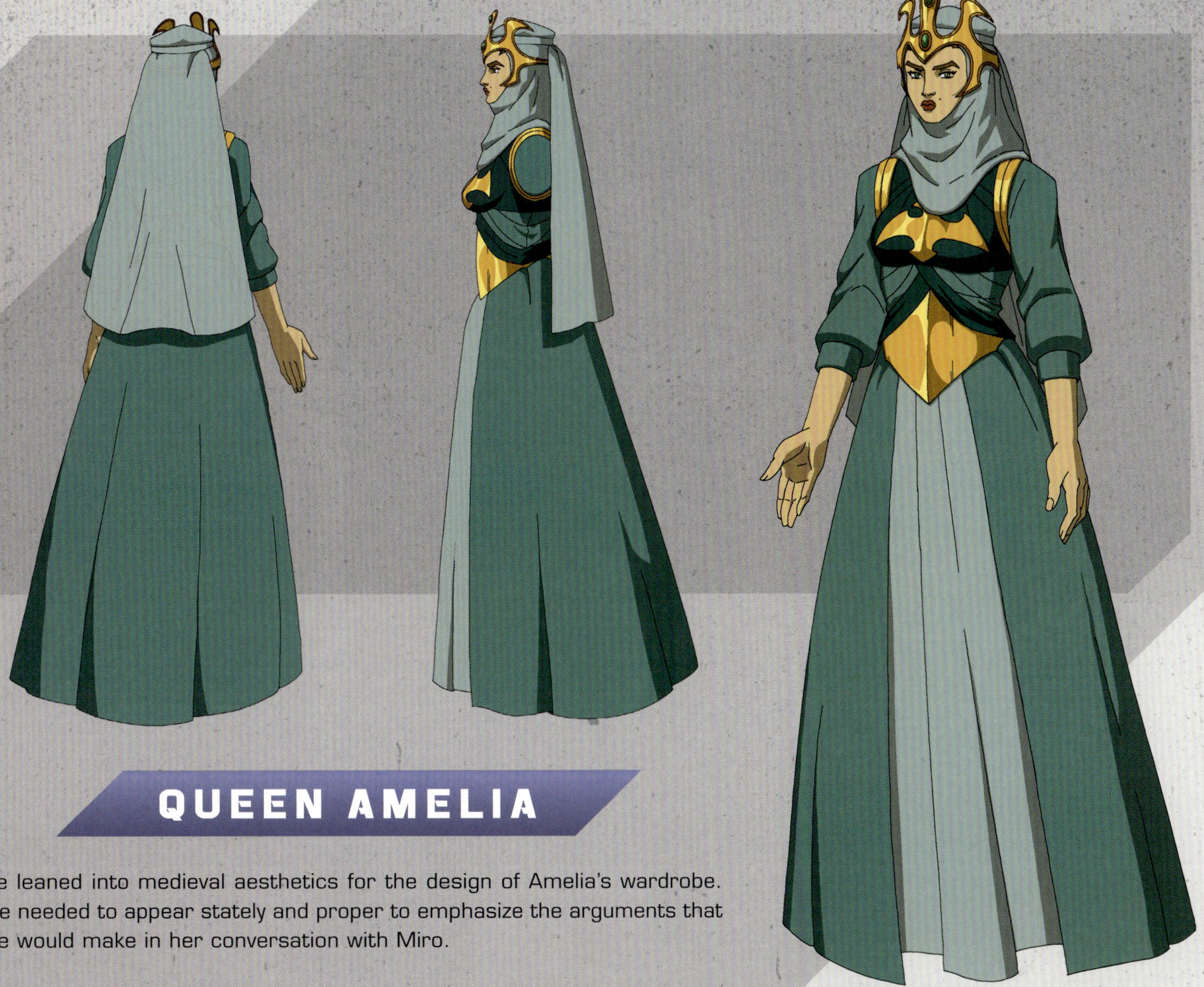

QUEEN AMELIA

We leaned into medieval aesthetics for the design of Amelia's wardrobe. She needed to appear stately and proper to emphasize the arguments that she would make in her conversation with Miro.

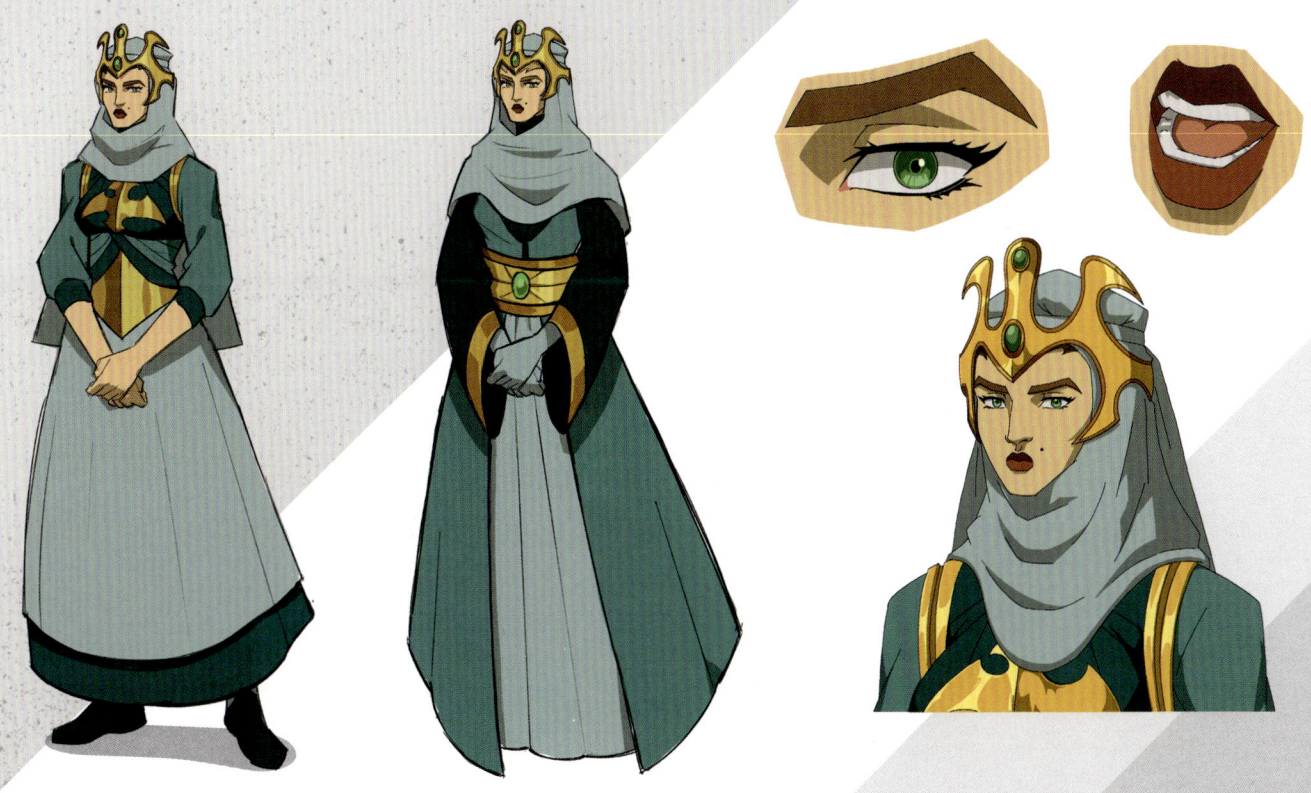

HEROES \\ 35

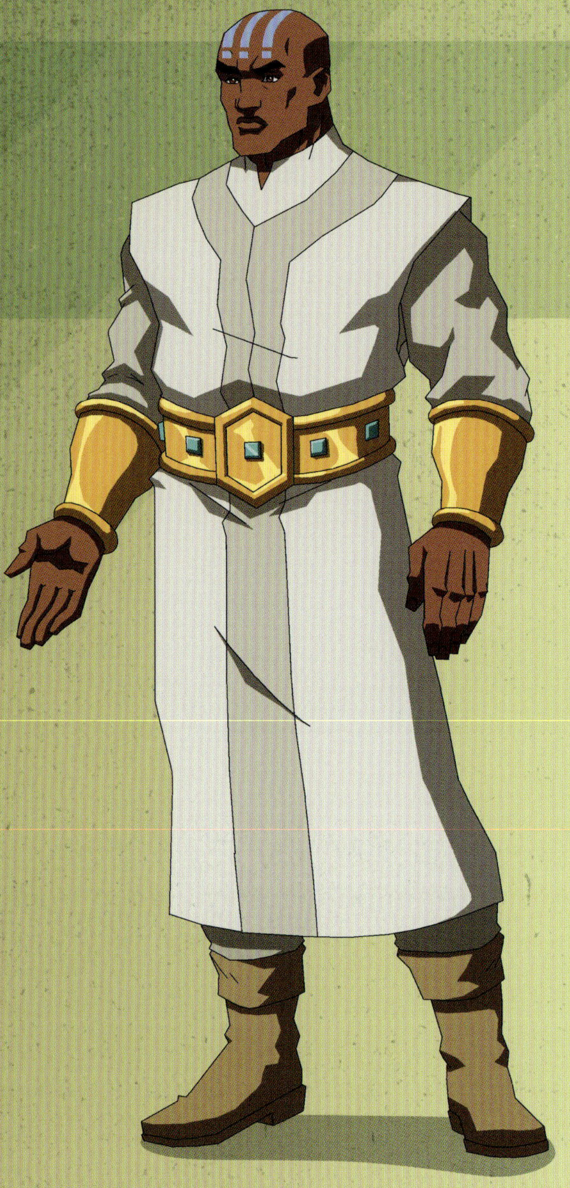

MENDOR

As Royal Physician, Mendor needed clean robes to work in. We didn't want to use plain scrubs, so his final look combines fashion and practicality—plus that classic Eternian bling!

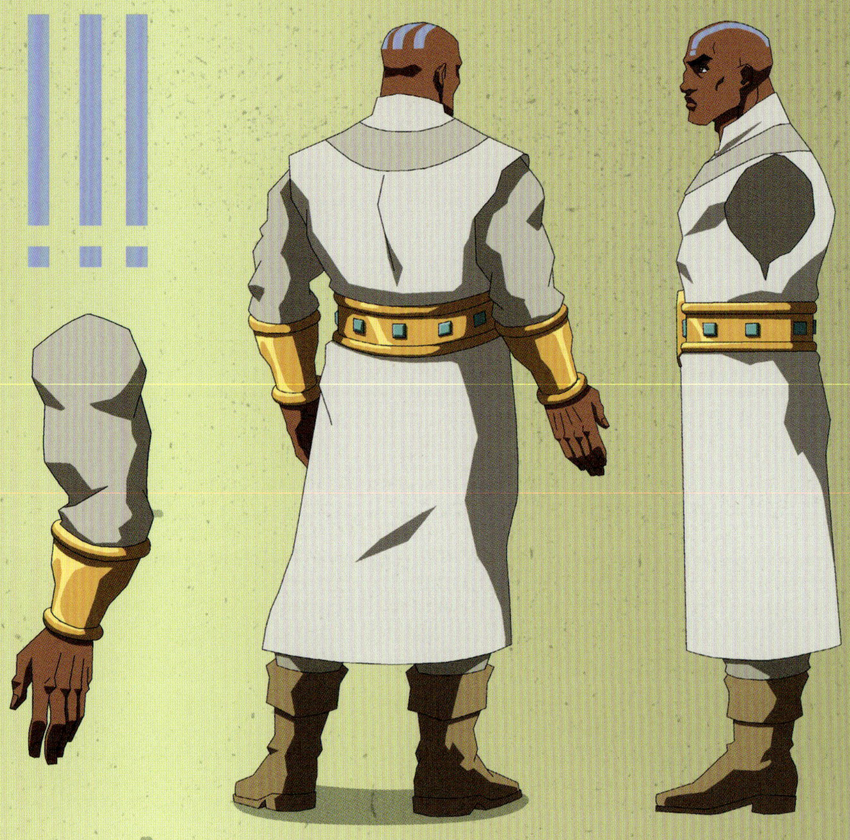

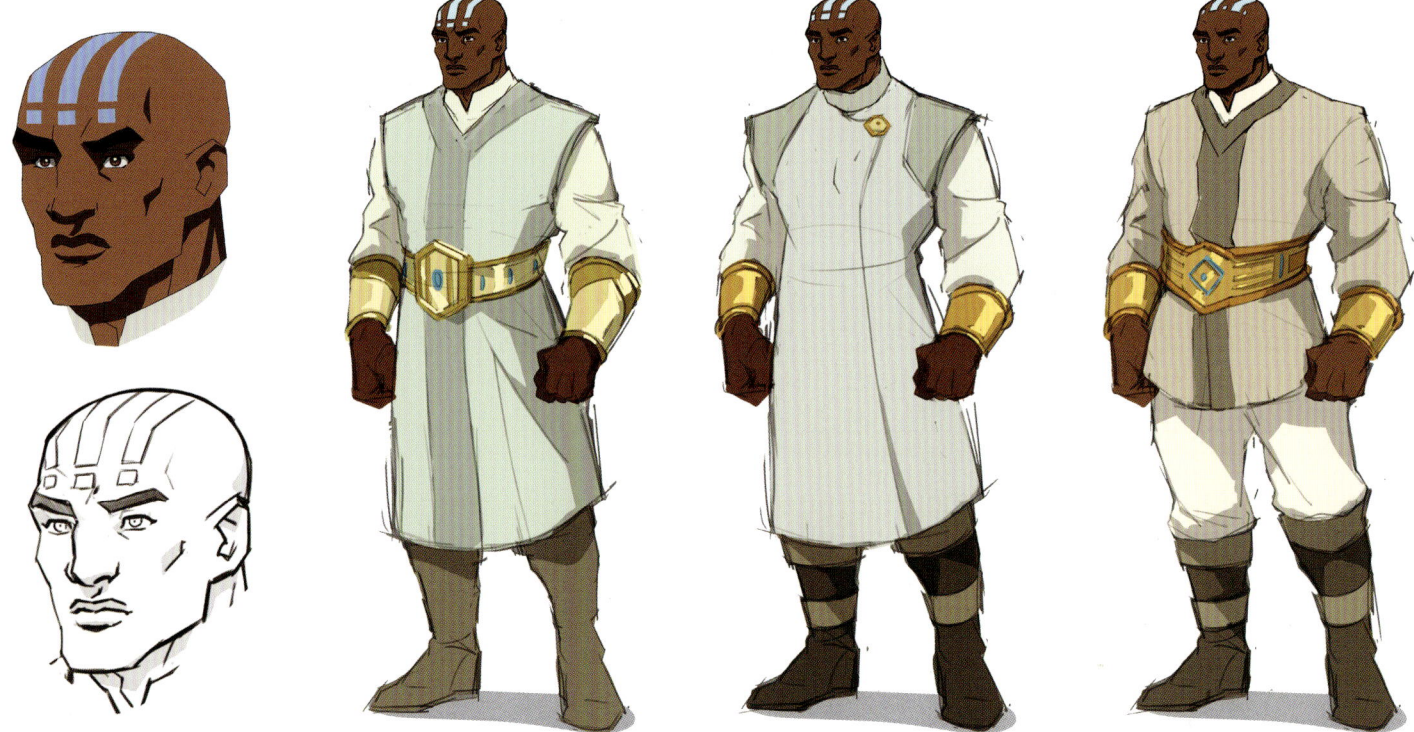

SNAKE FAMILIAR

Along with Teela's newfound control over the magic of Ka came plenty of new and powerful perks, including this sneaky little guy, acting as her eyes and ears from a distance during the Horde's siege of Eternos.

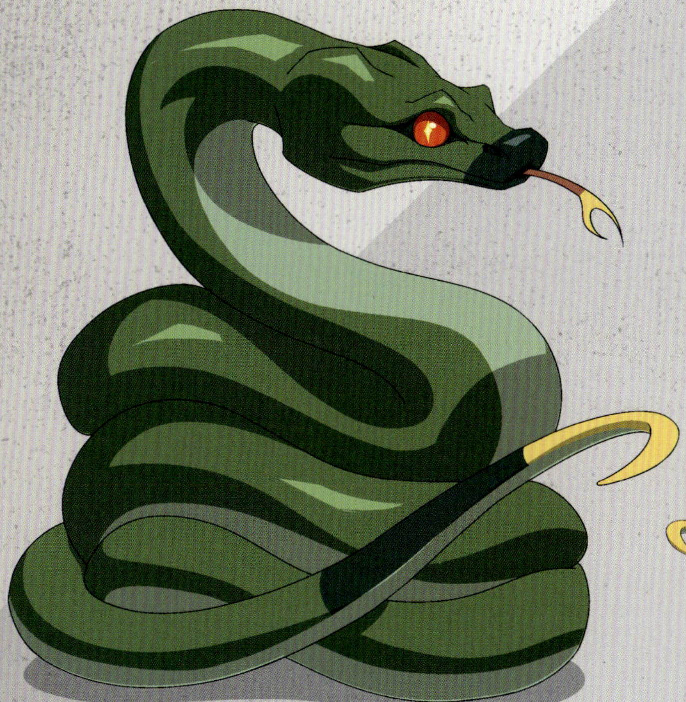

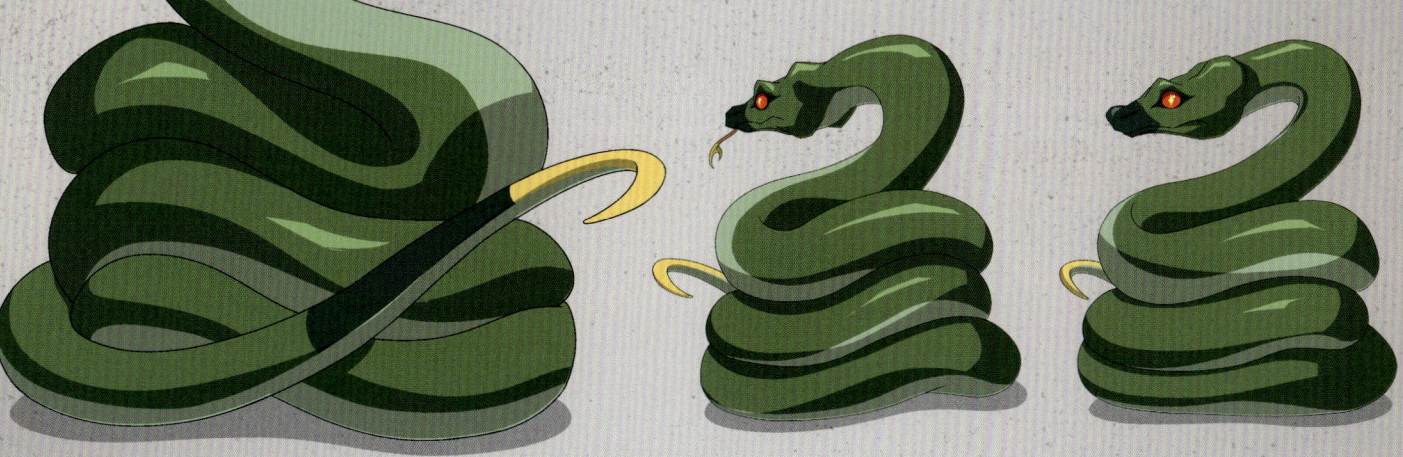

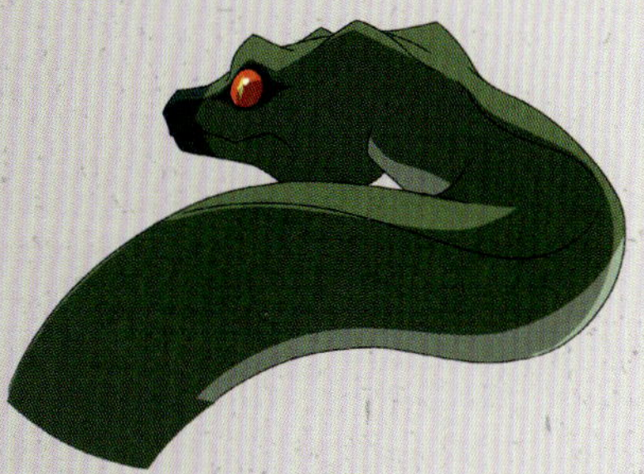

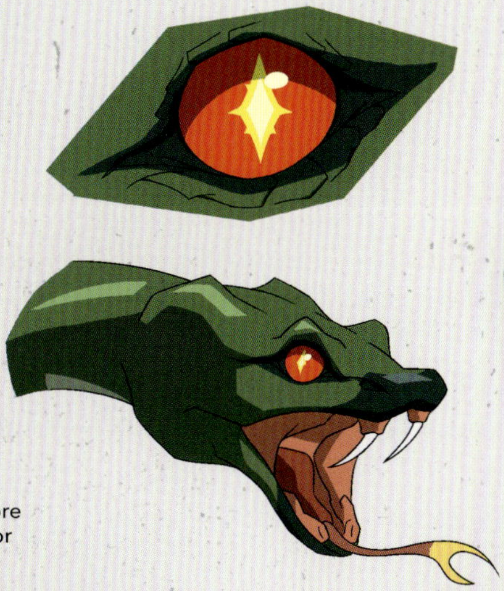

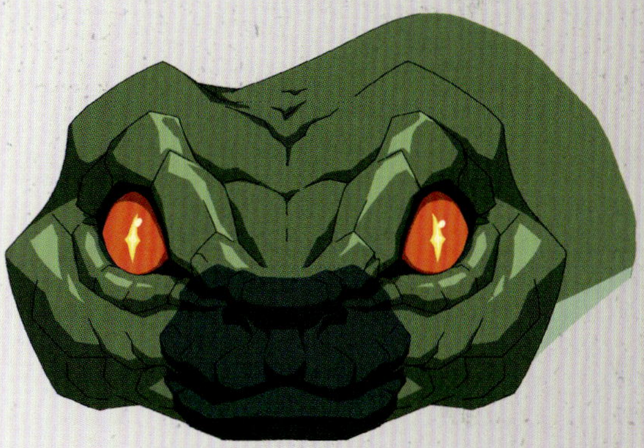

The artists on the team tried several different magical looks for the spell before settling on a simple snake look—better for going unnoticed by the Horde.

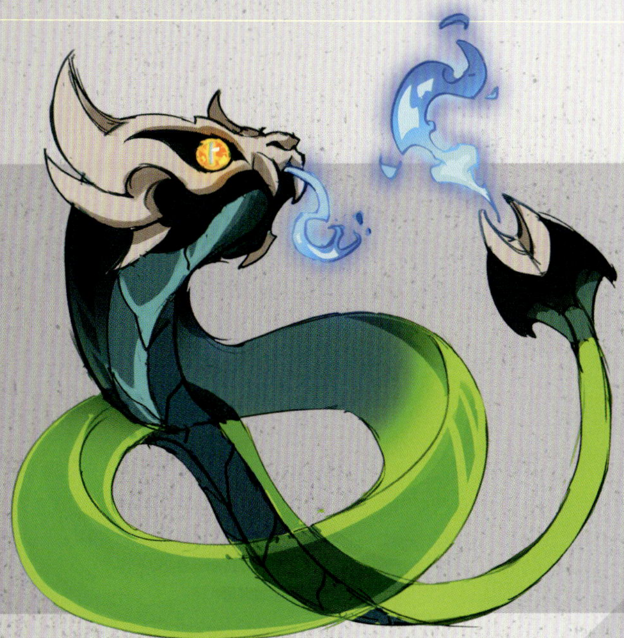

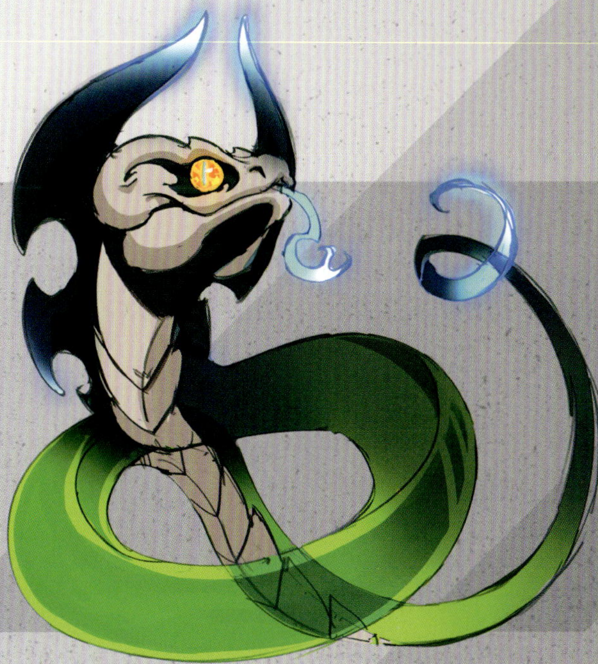

RIO BLAST

It was important to us to be faithful to the toys both in design and in the fun they inspired through play. Ensuring that Rio Blast maintained his arsenal of hidden blasters, including his knee lasers and massive chest compartment, was crucial.

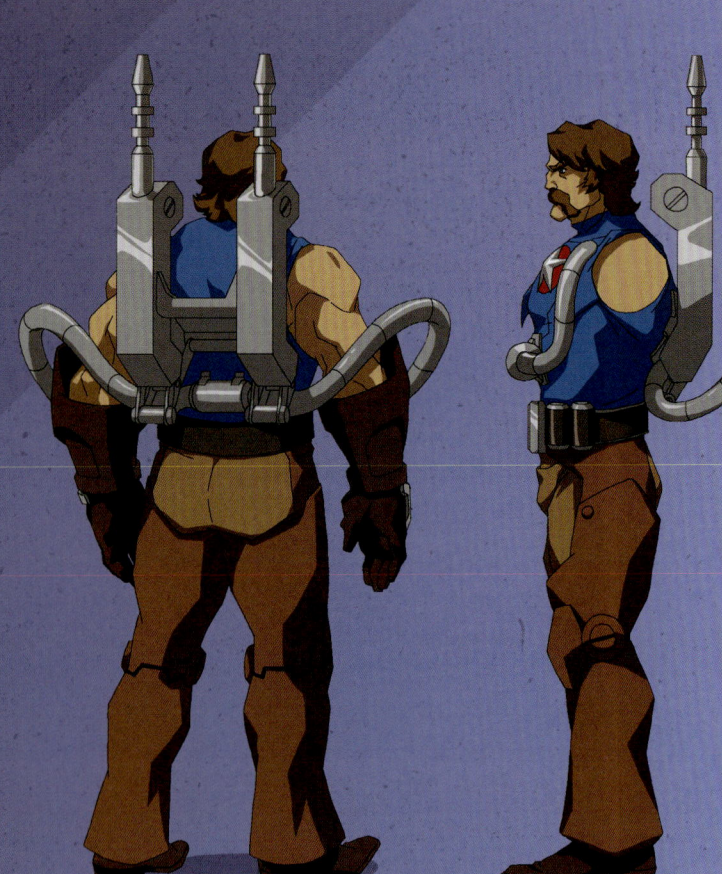
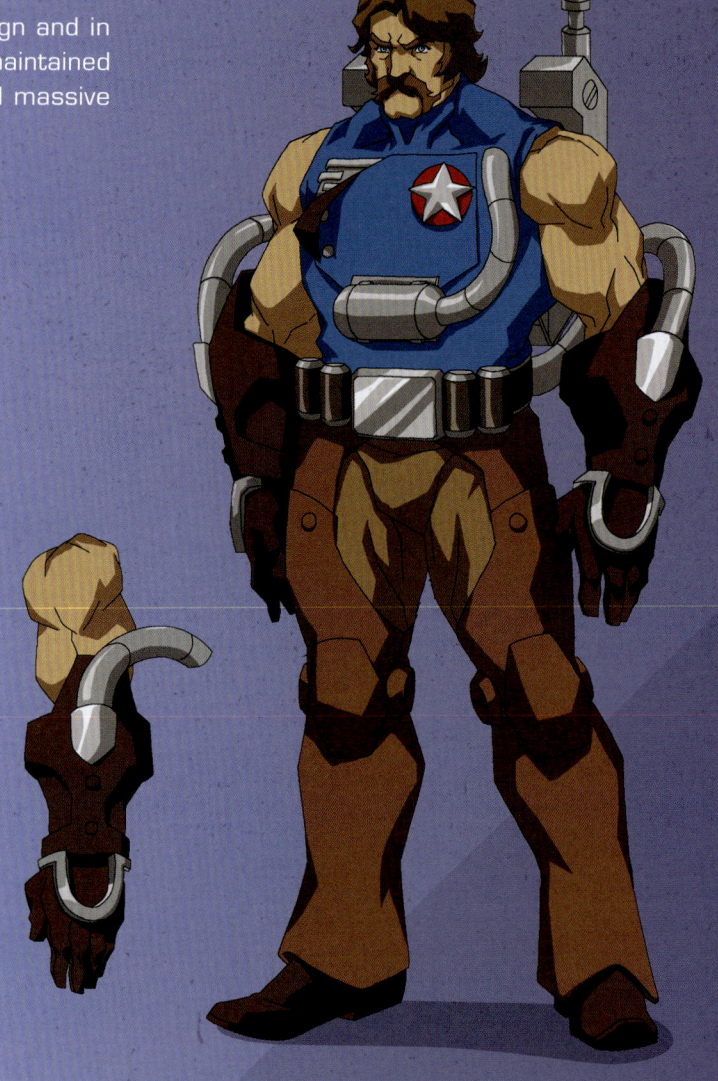
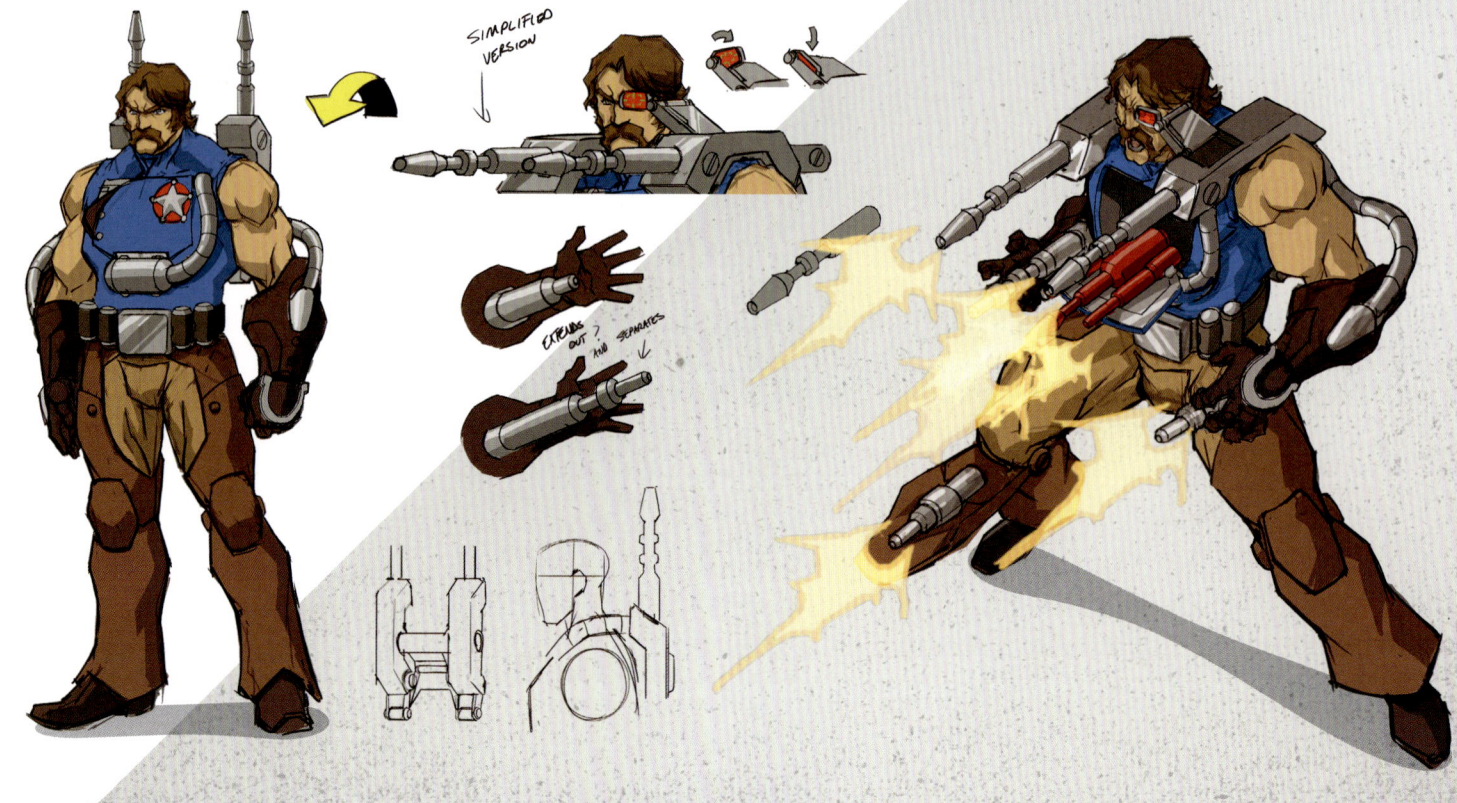

SNOUT SPOUT

We had a blast, no pun intended, creating all of the little details for Snout Spout's design. With two sleek water tanks on his back, a sharpened axe, and heavy elephant-style boots, we ensured he'd be ready for anything while on a mission.

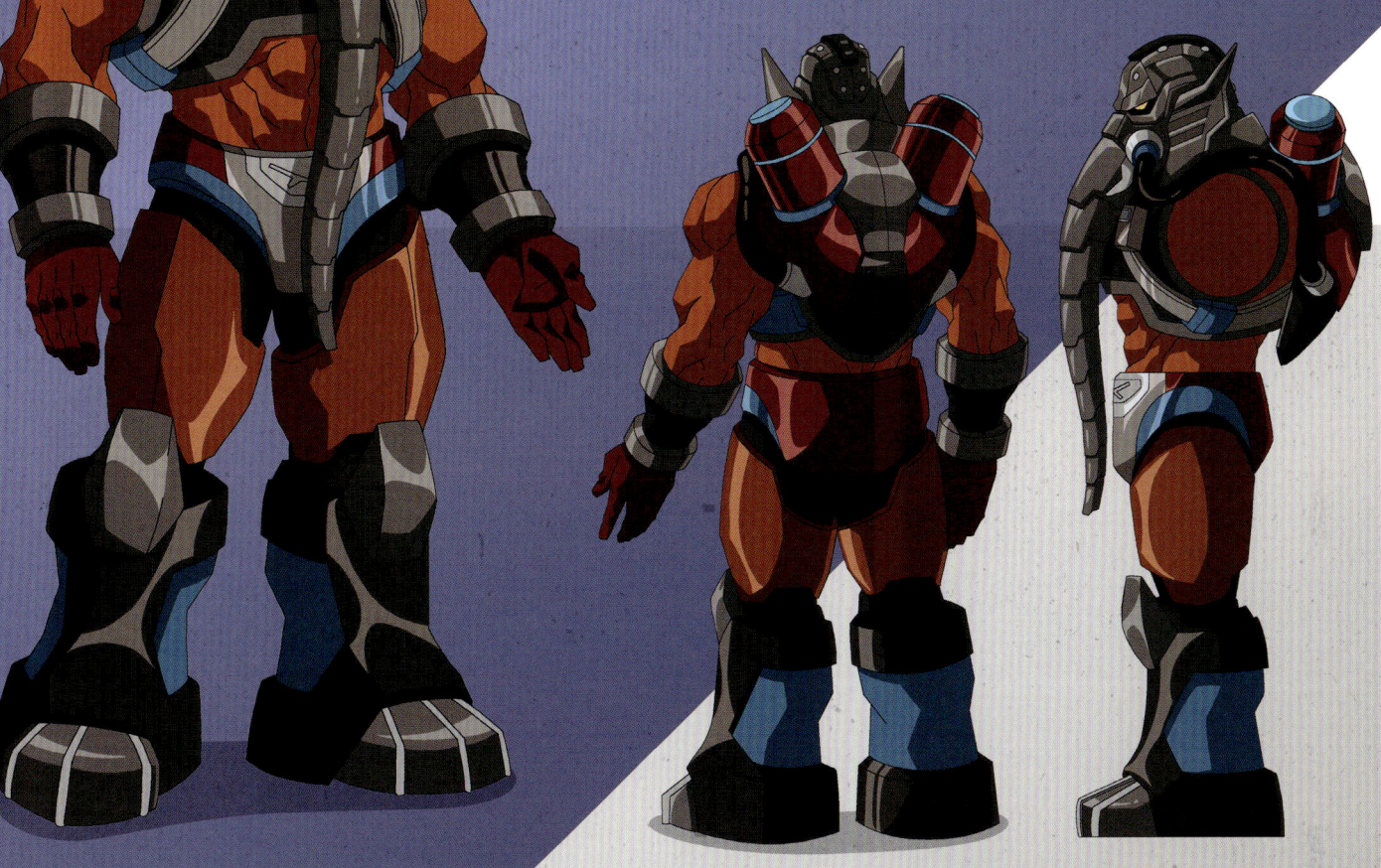

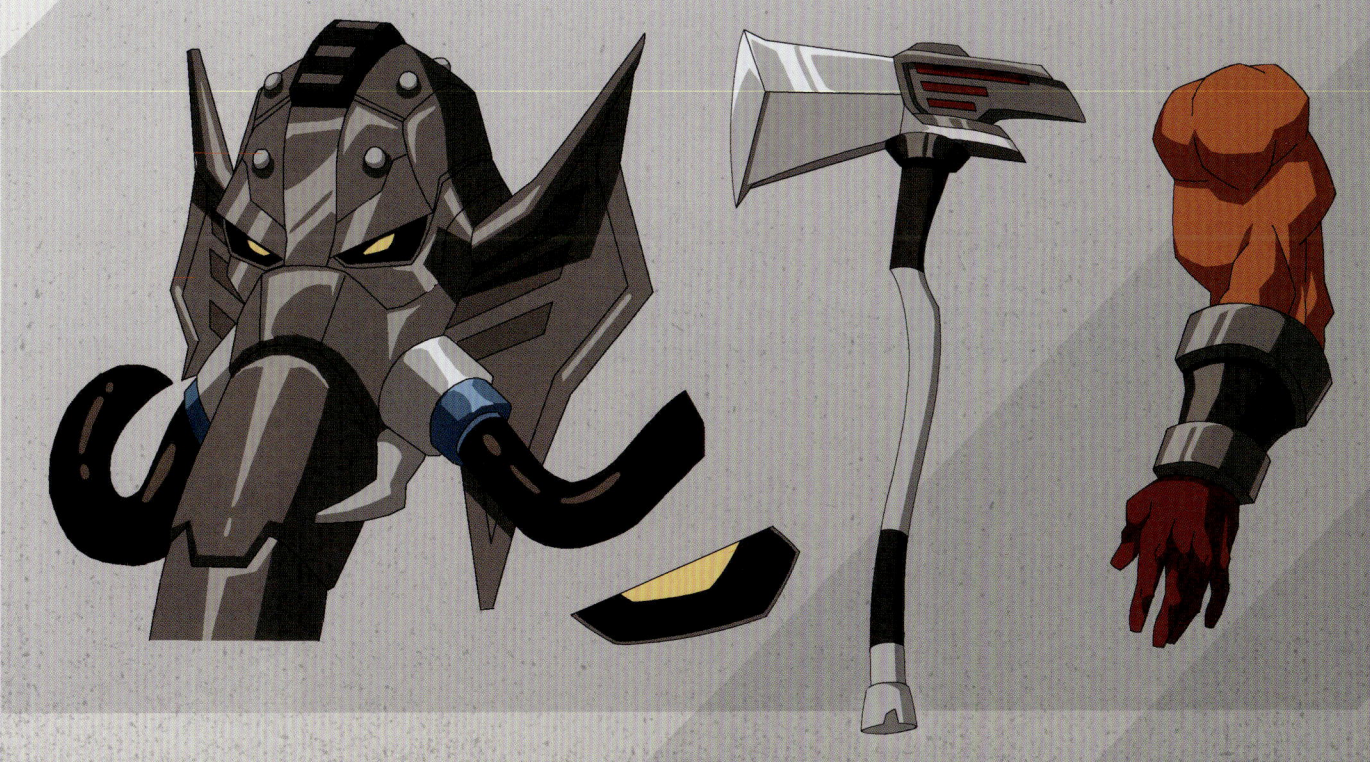

STONEDAR

Stonedar acts as defender to his planet in the same way that He-Man is champion of Eternia. When Grizzlor, Mantenna, and Leech claw, blast, and then bleed him dry as a riverbed, it shows exactly how Hordak means to deal with He-Man.

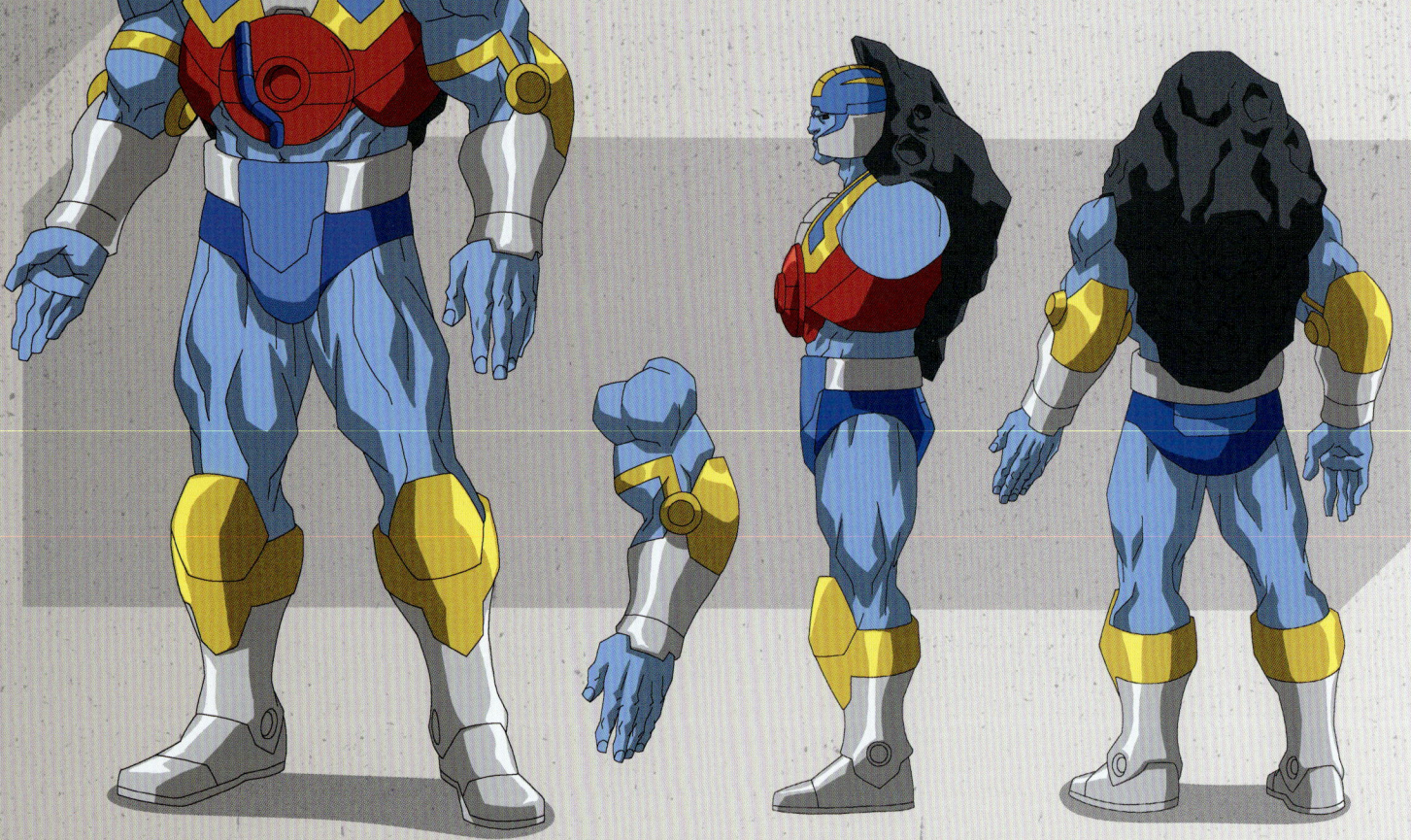

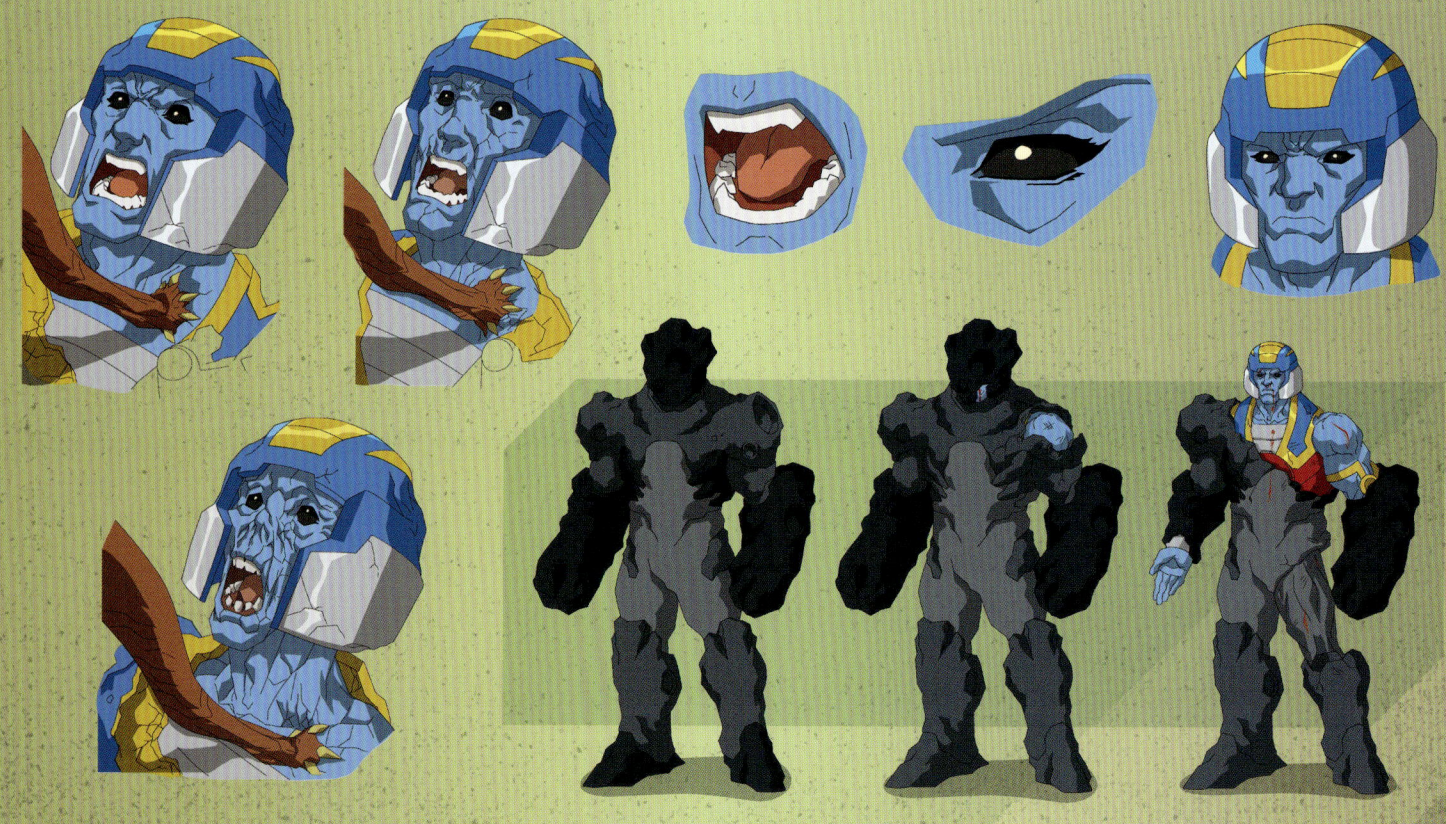

STROBO

We kept Strobo's final look true to his classic design, though in earlier concepts we tested out different appearances for his reflector. All the Cosmic Enforcers ended up sharing the same helmet design to keep them looking like a cohesive and organized team.

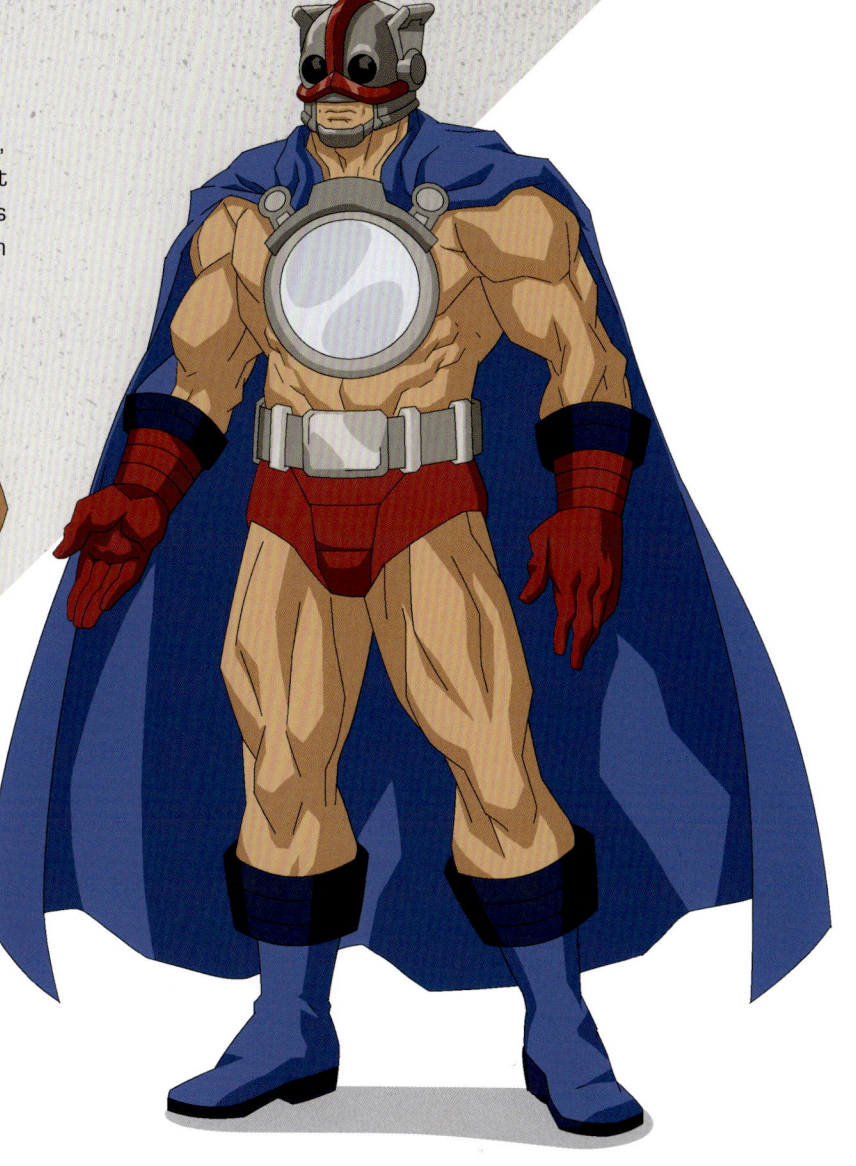

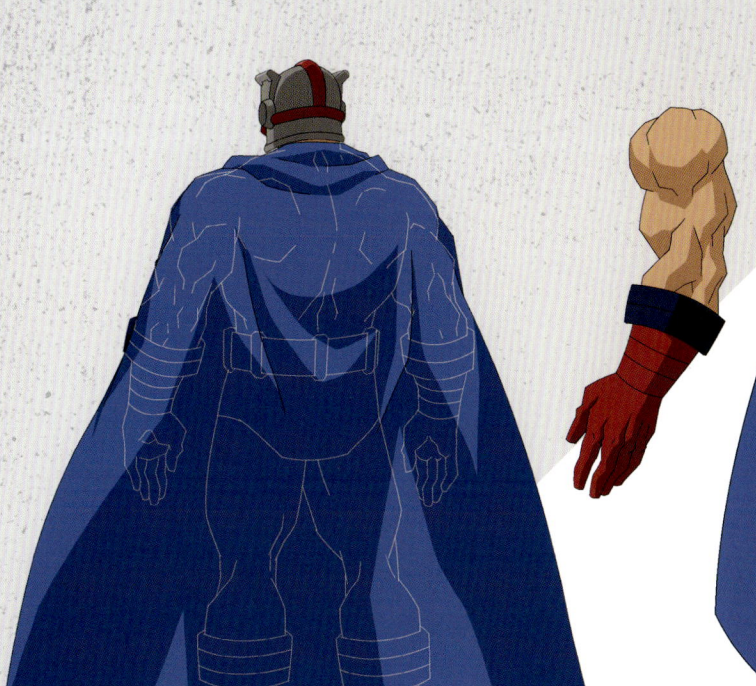

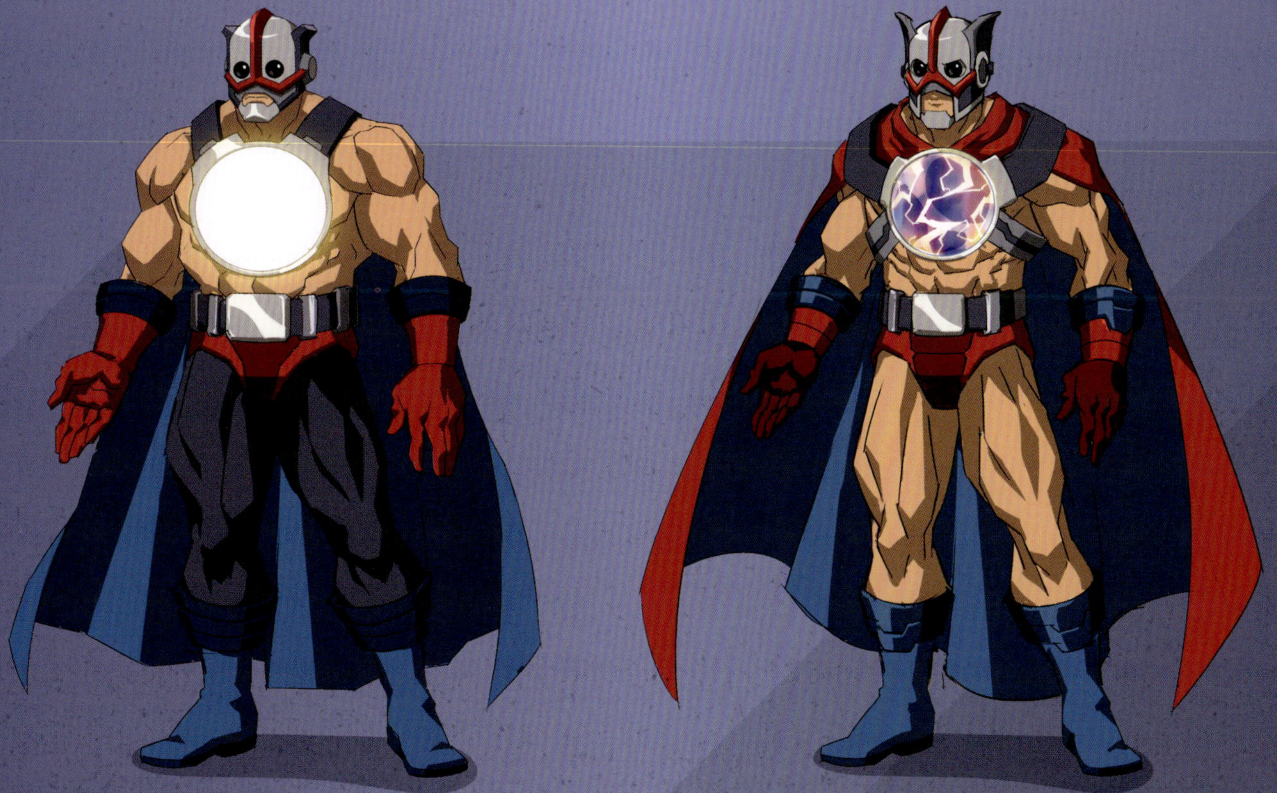

ZANTHOR

Among the various Cosmic Enforcers in the council's chambers, you can spy Zanthor's iconic facial hair peeking through just below his helmet. His outfit is similar to those of the other Enforcers but has some of its own flair to indicate his more elevated position.

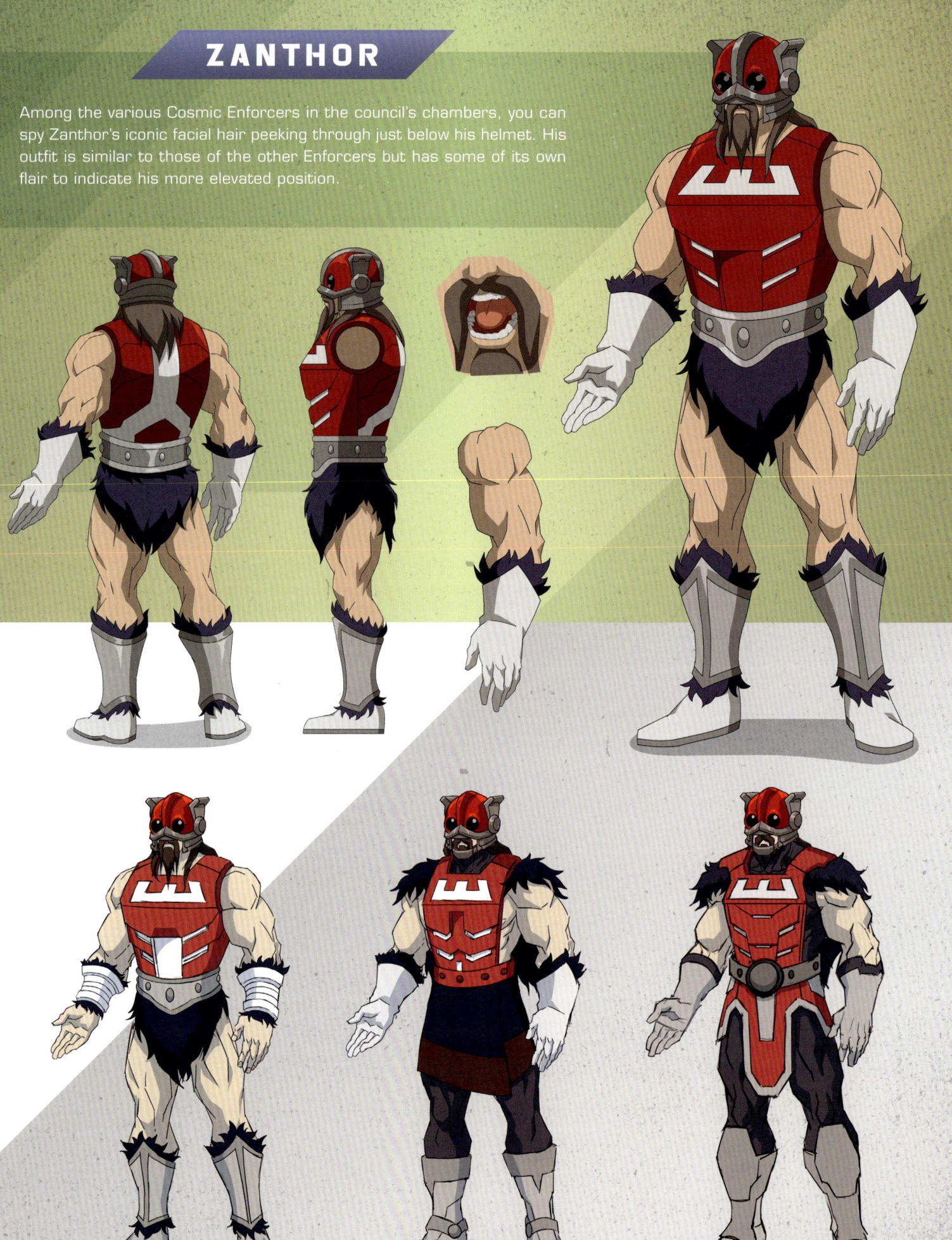

SPIRITS

In Eternia, death doesn't mean you're out of the fight. Some of our favorite heroes return to us from Preternia to protect their home and friends. Fisto, Clamp Champ, Moss Man, King Grayskull, and King Randor join He-Man on the battlefield one last time.

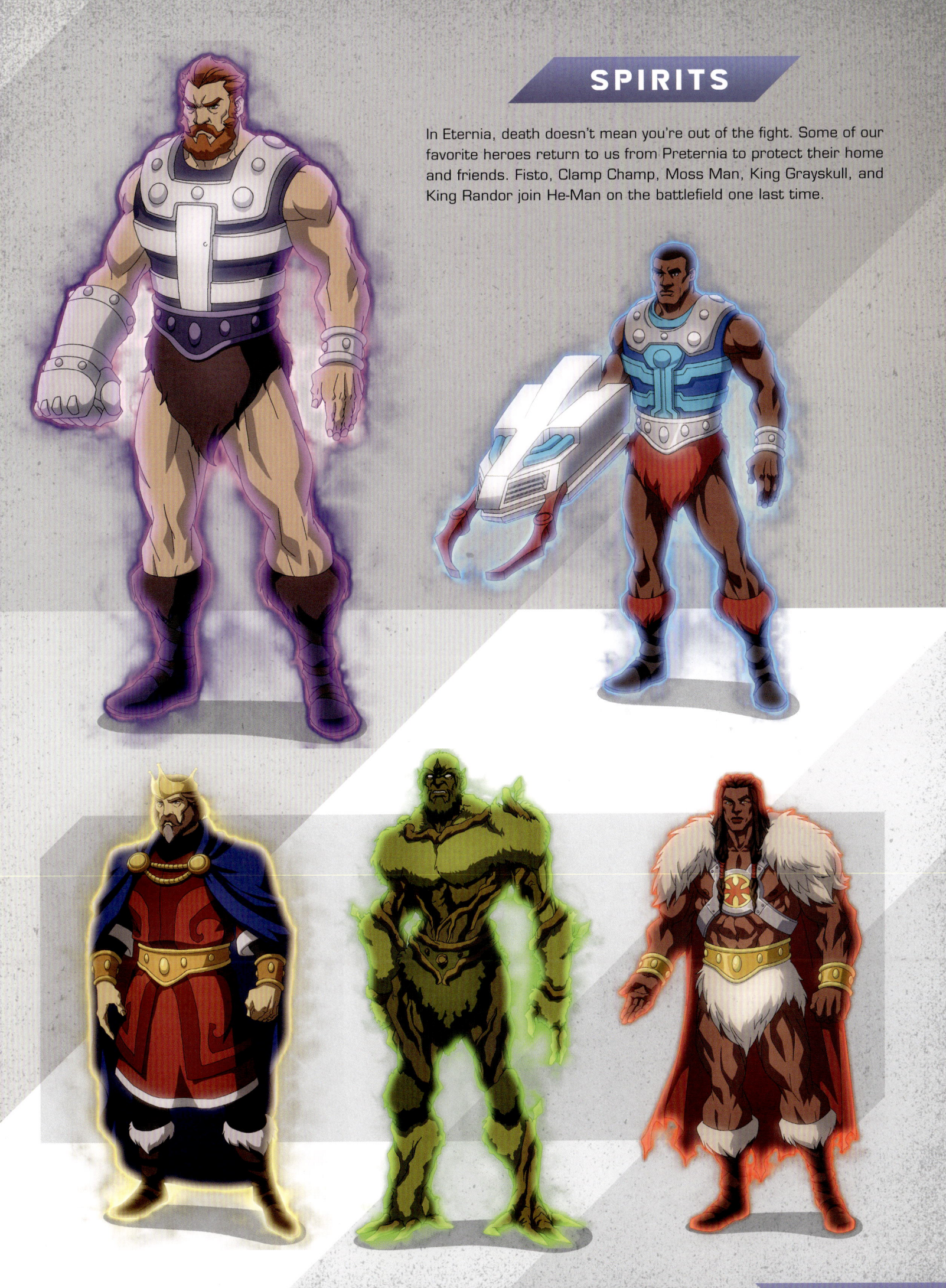

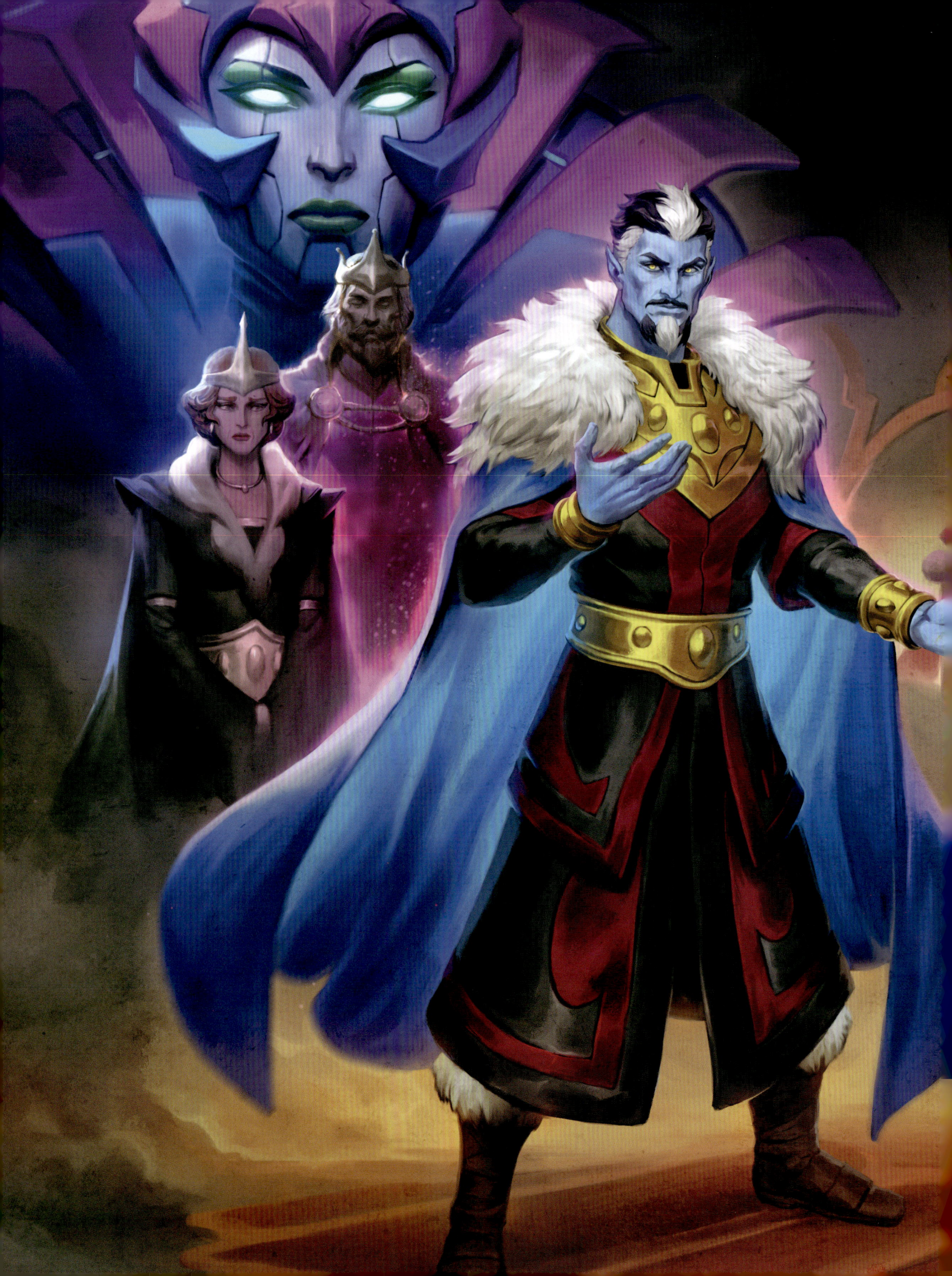

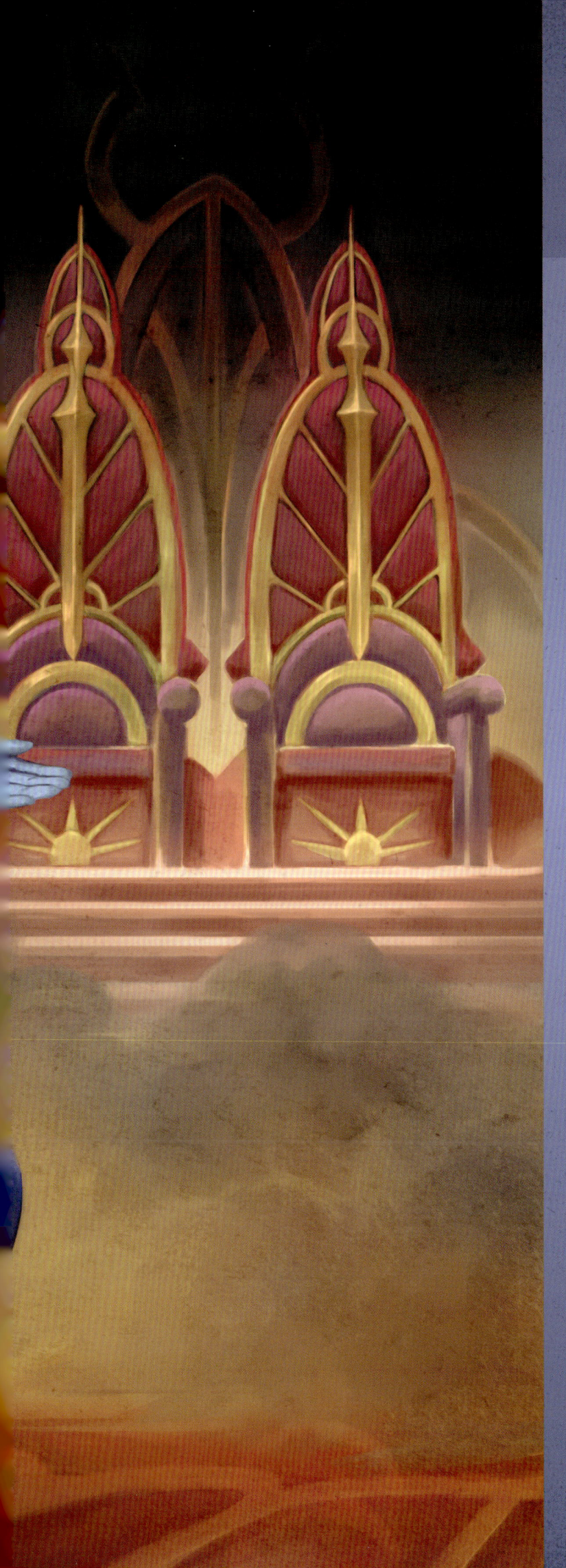

CHAPTER 2
VILLAINS

A NEW SEASON OF *MASTERS OF THE UNIVERSE* means a new cast of villains. The designers not only imagined new looks for Skeletor and his crew, but also brought in many more evildoers from all over the universe. And we do mean that quite literally. From the hallowed halls of Snake Mountain to the interstellar conquering armies of the Horde, this season is chock full of villains, new and old.

In *Revolution*, it is the power of magic versus the might of technology! With the takeover of Motherboard's technological cult, practically everyone is getting a new outfit and new upgrades. The hot new look for Eternia's baddest powerhouses is wires, circuits, and lots of neon! And these design enhancements are more than just a thematic aesthetic; with each detail and technological advancement there comes powerful abilities to make things interesting for our favorite heroes.

SKELETOR

The tech-modified "Skeletek" we saw at the start of *Revelation* is now dethroned and subjugated. The half hood covering his face, asymmetrical silhouette, and almost blasphemous replacement of his arm with the Ha'vok Staff portray Motherboard's technology as an invasive injury inflicted upon the once-mighty Skeletor.

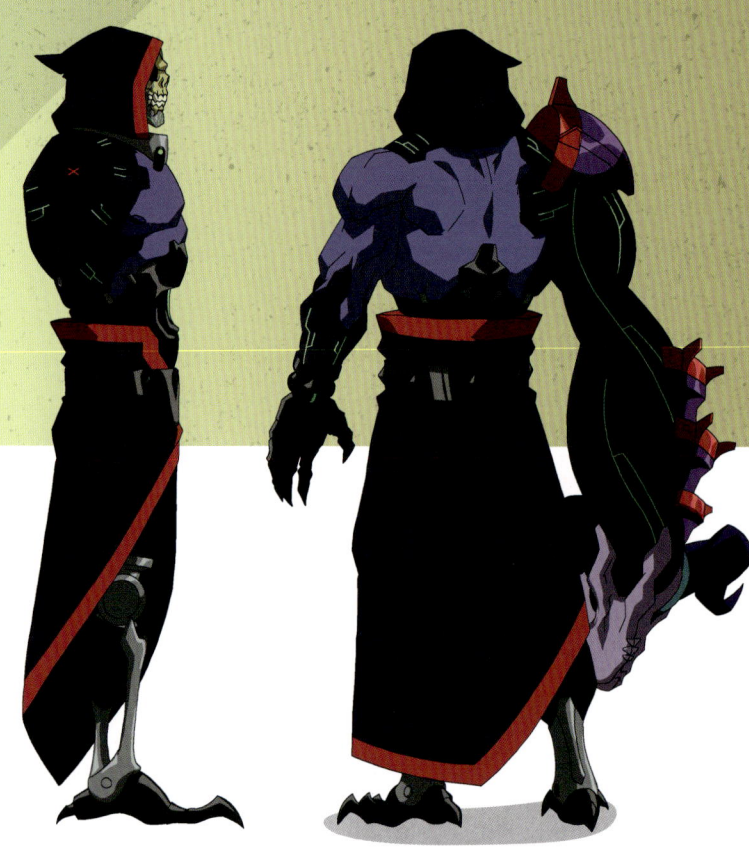

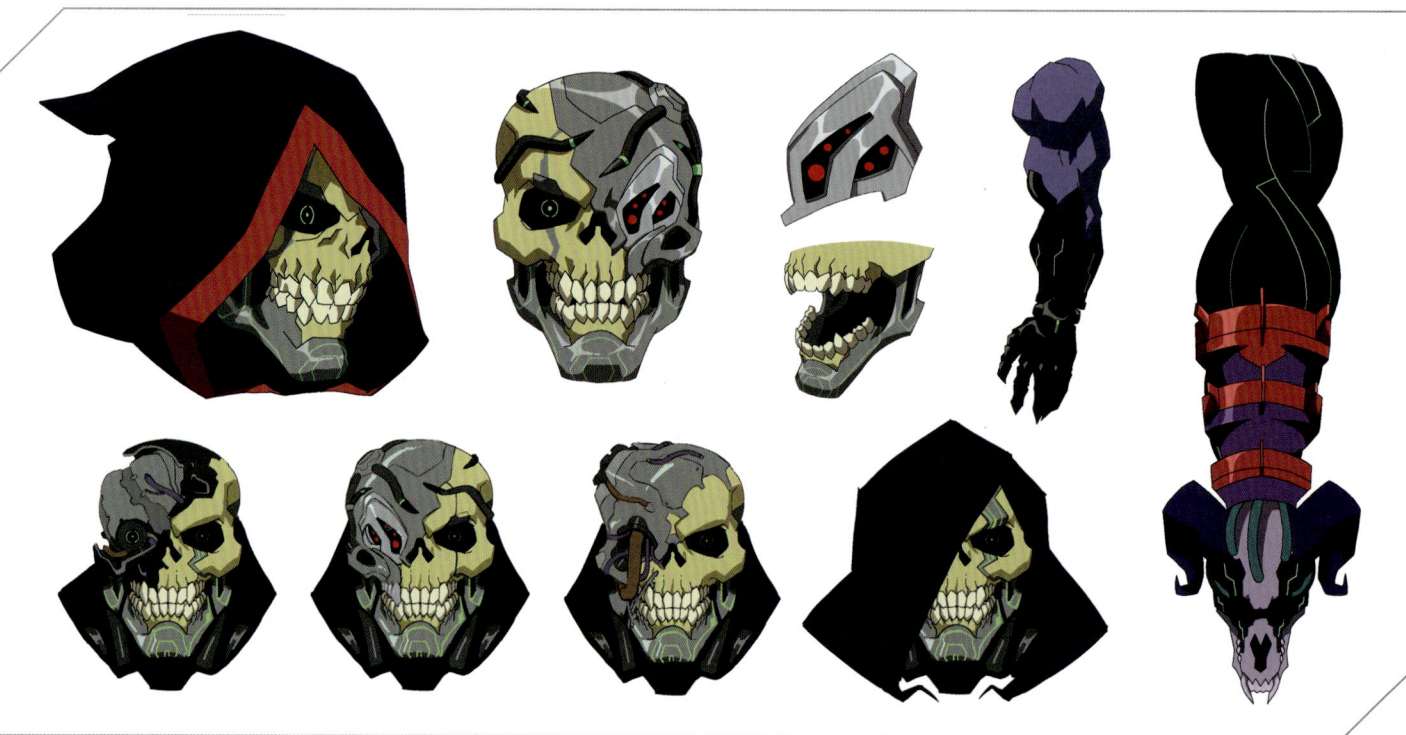

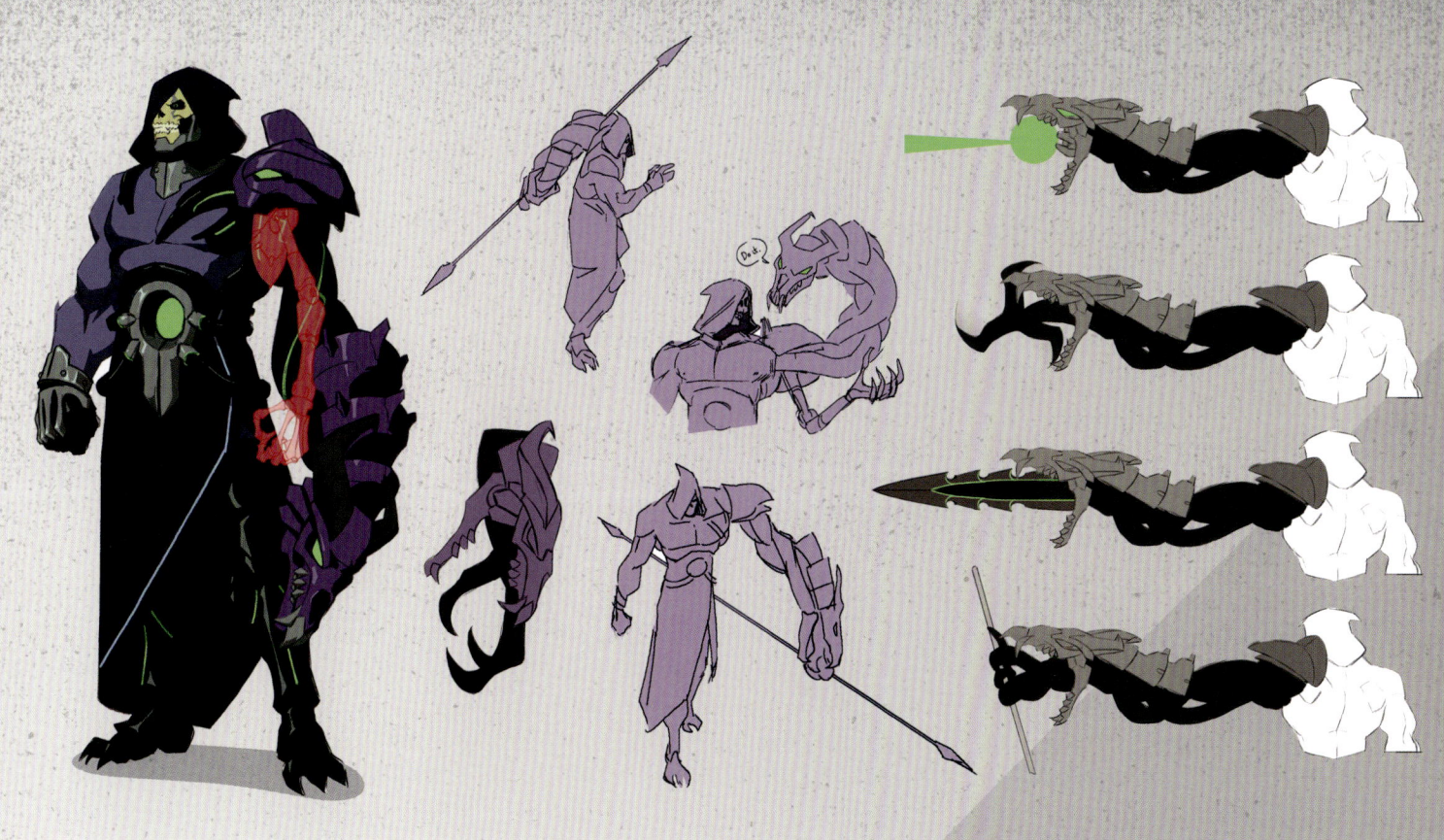

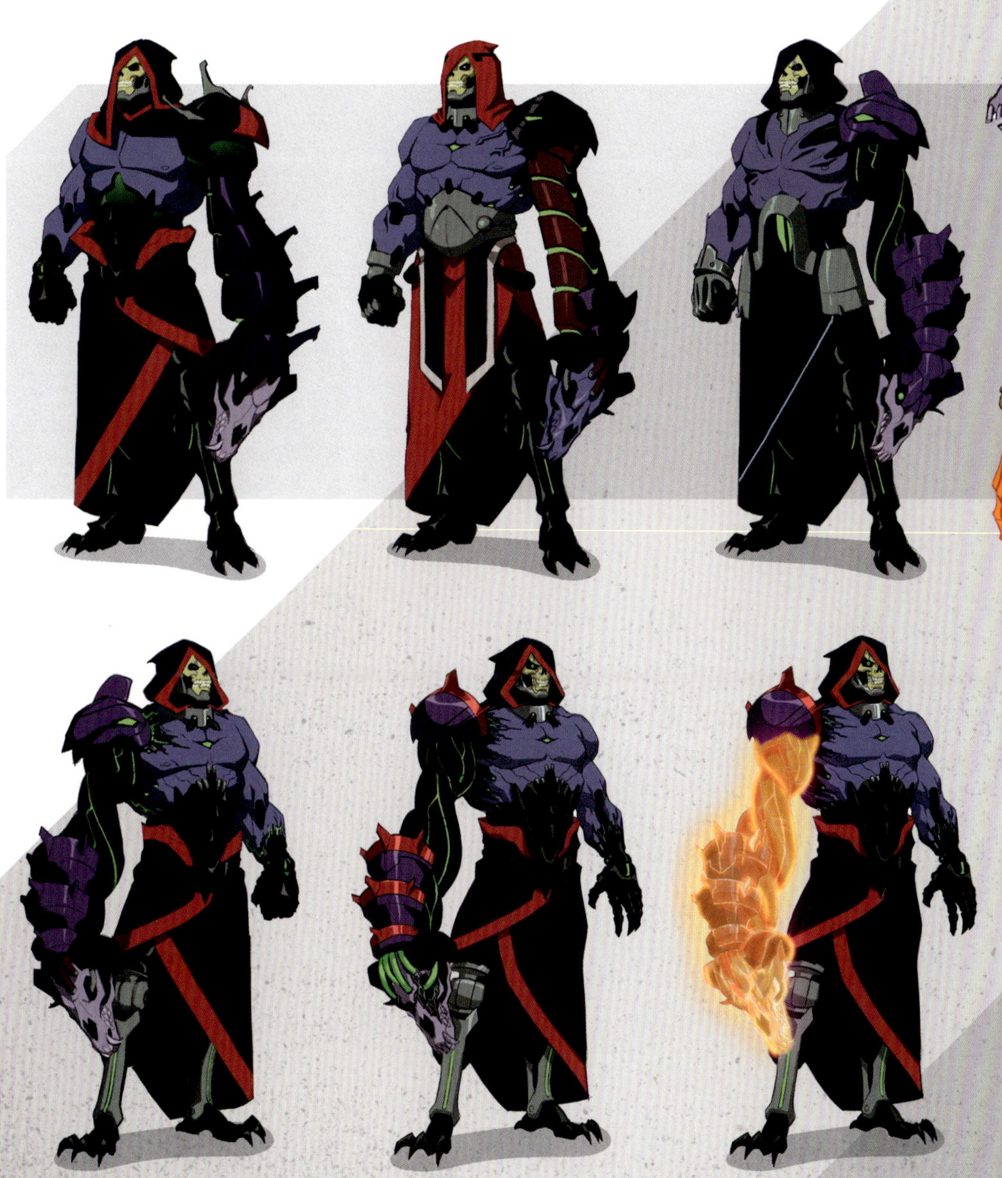

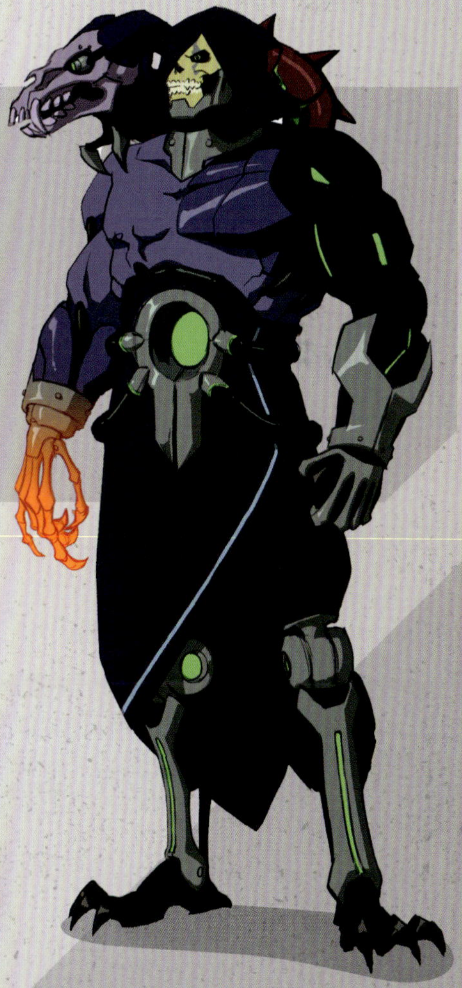

We explored a wide variety of mechanics and designs for Skeletor's new Ha'vok Arm, including references to Laser-Light Skeletor, Dragon Blaster, and even a separate sentient Ha'vok companion that could operate independently.

VILLAINS \\ 47

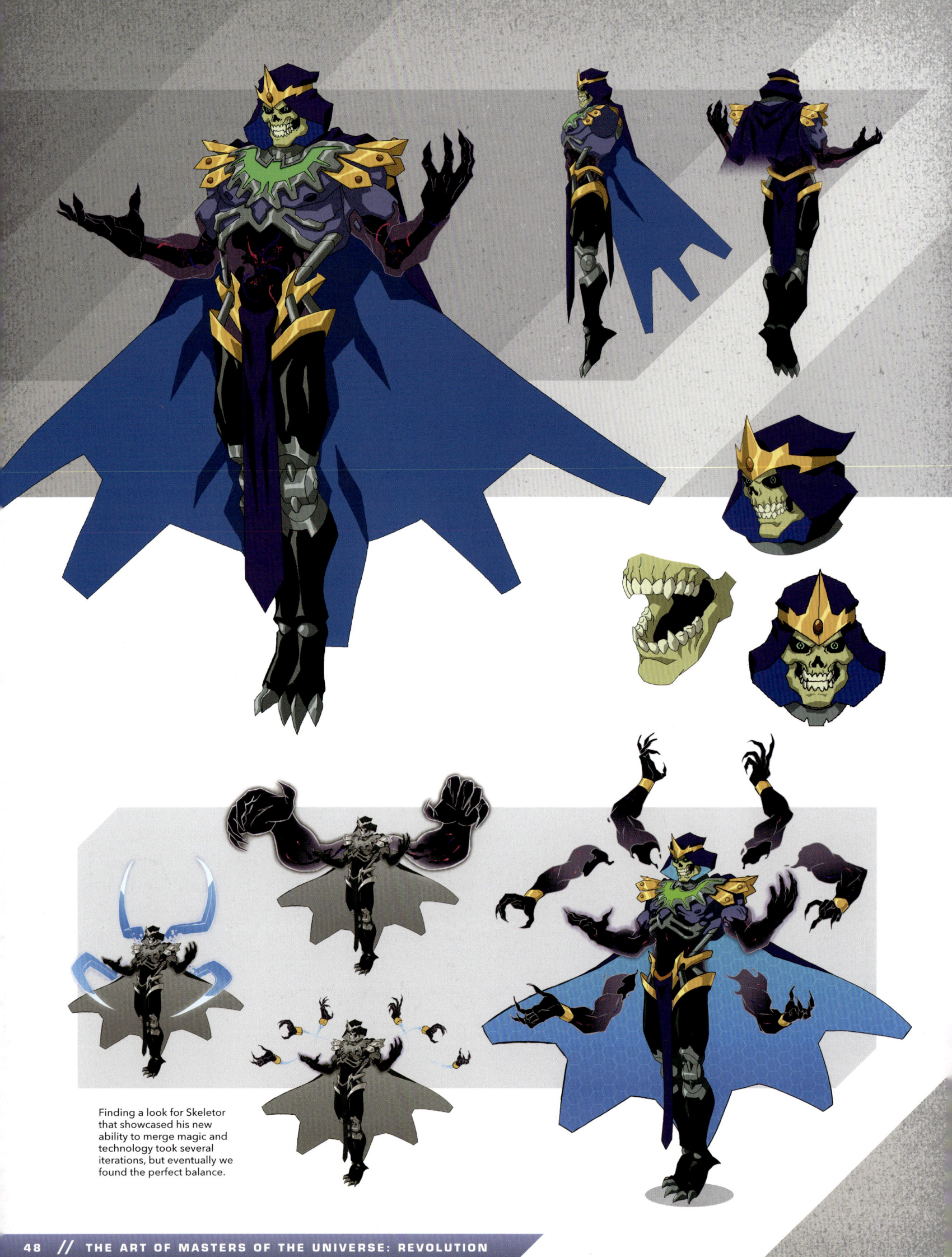

Finding a look for Skeletor that showcased his new ability to merge magic and technology took several iterations, but eventually we found the perfect balance.

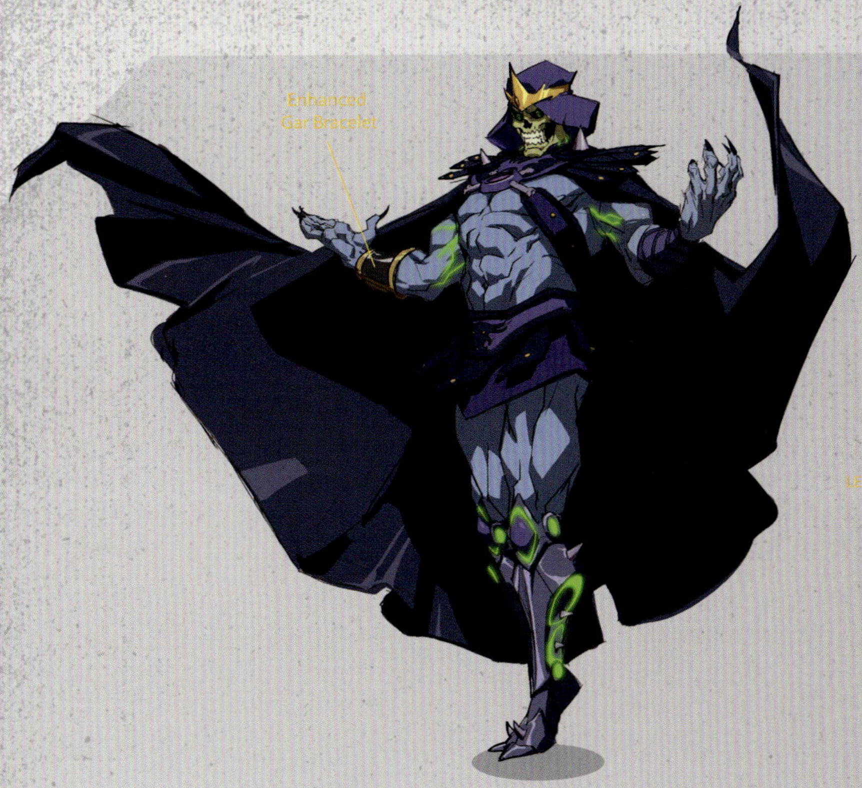

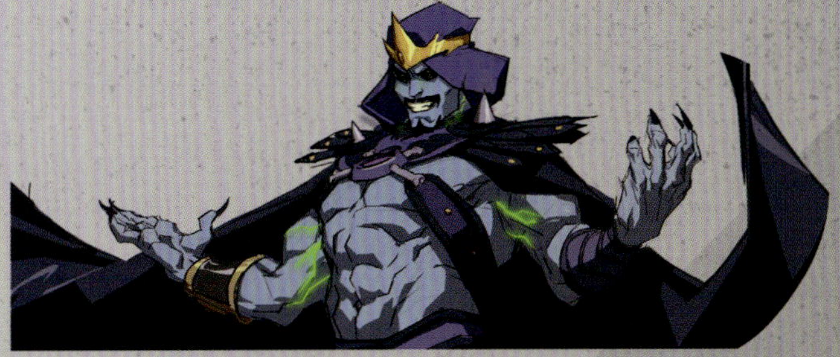

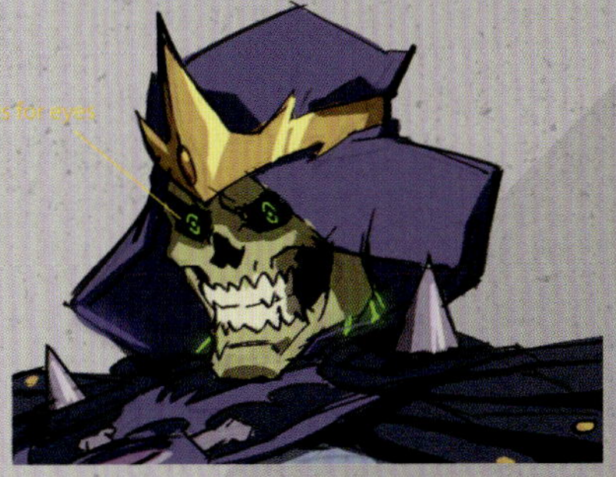

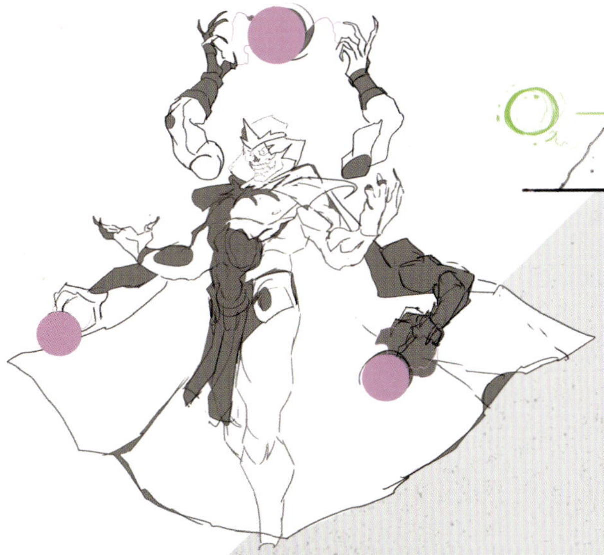

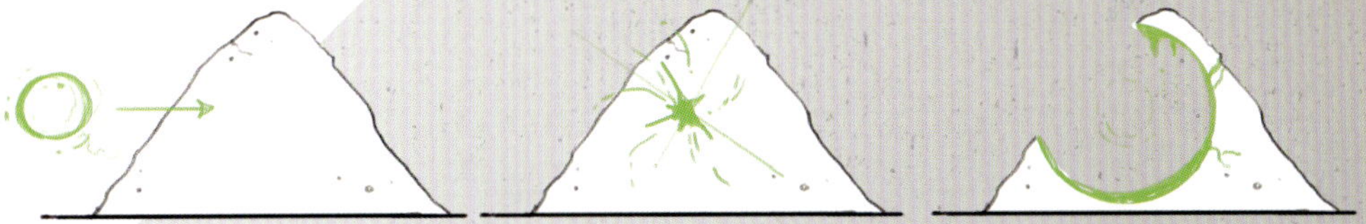

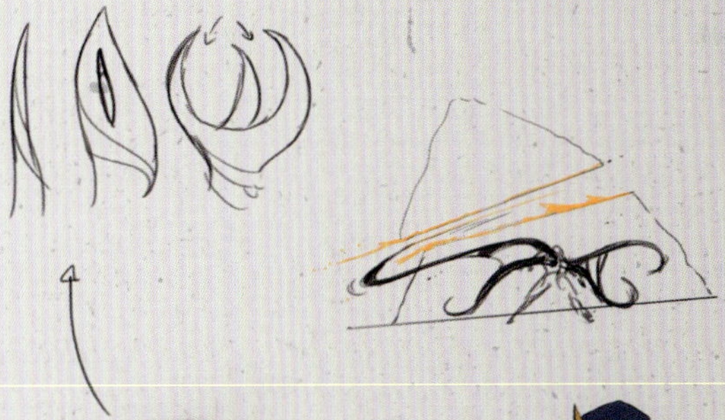

Enhanced Gar'bnazehh

As well as the costume, the team designed the look of a new kind of magic, lovingly called "skele-magic" by the artists and directors at Powerhouse.

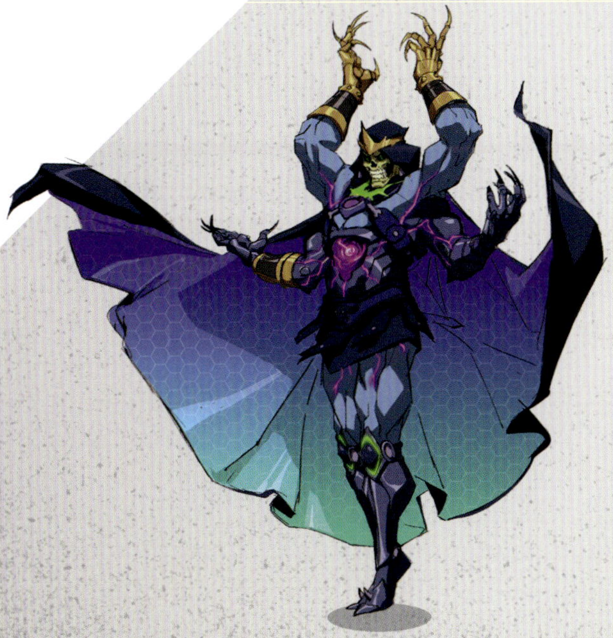

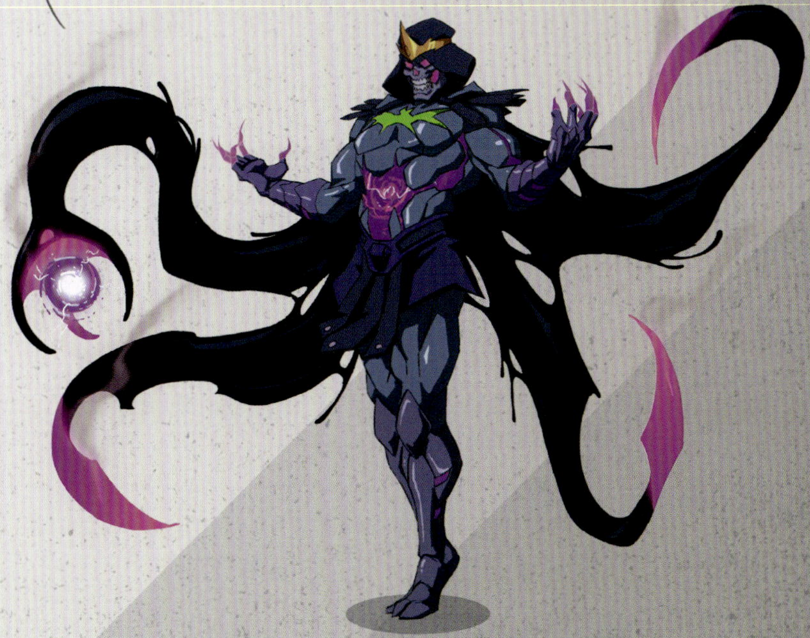

VILLAINS \\ 49

KELDOR

Aged up compared to his appearance in the 2002 series, Keldor has a beard that features the same gray accents as Randor's. After all, it's been over twenty years; who wouldn't be more gray? Skeletek achieves this convincing illusion through a combination of hard-light holograms and nanobots.

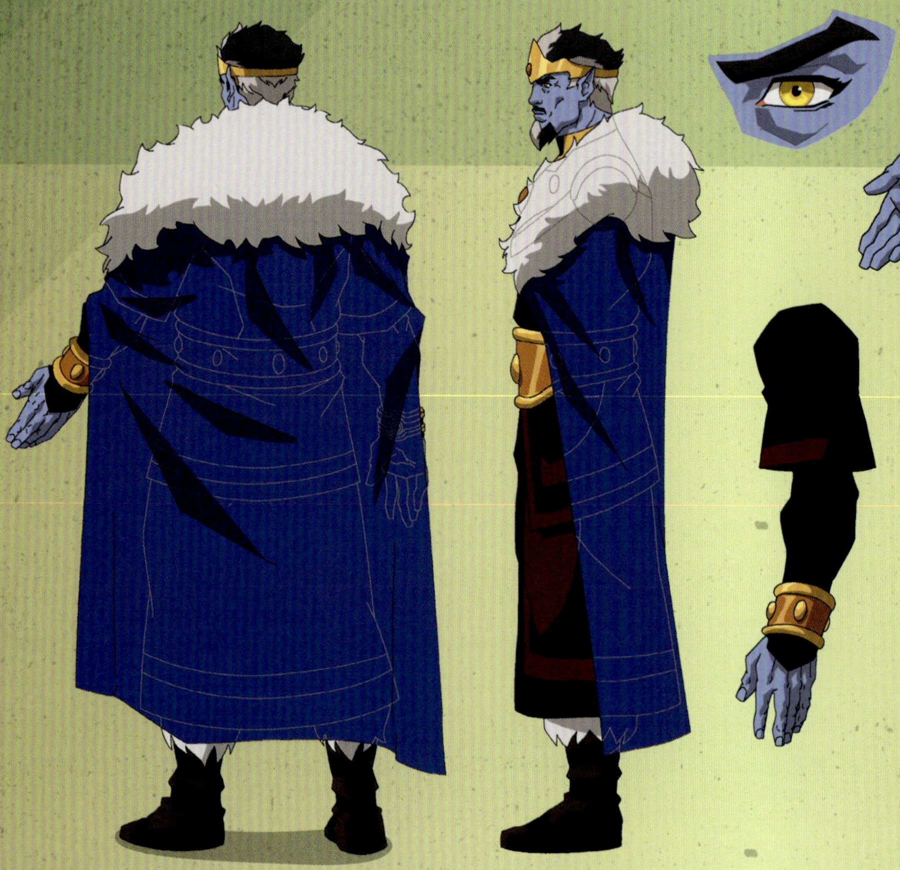

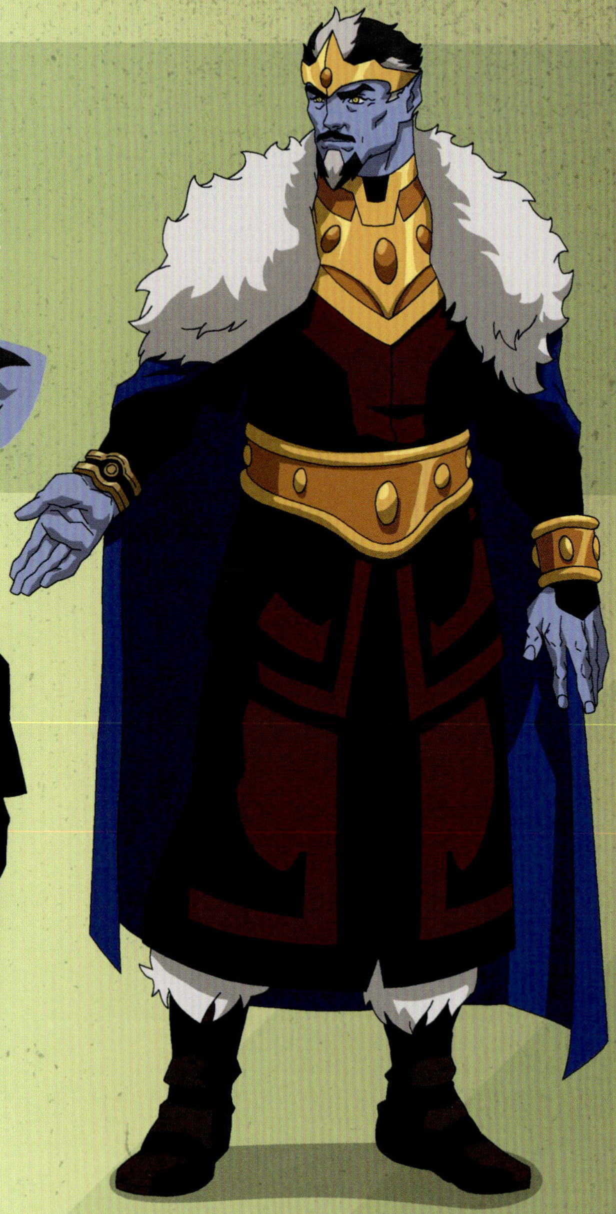

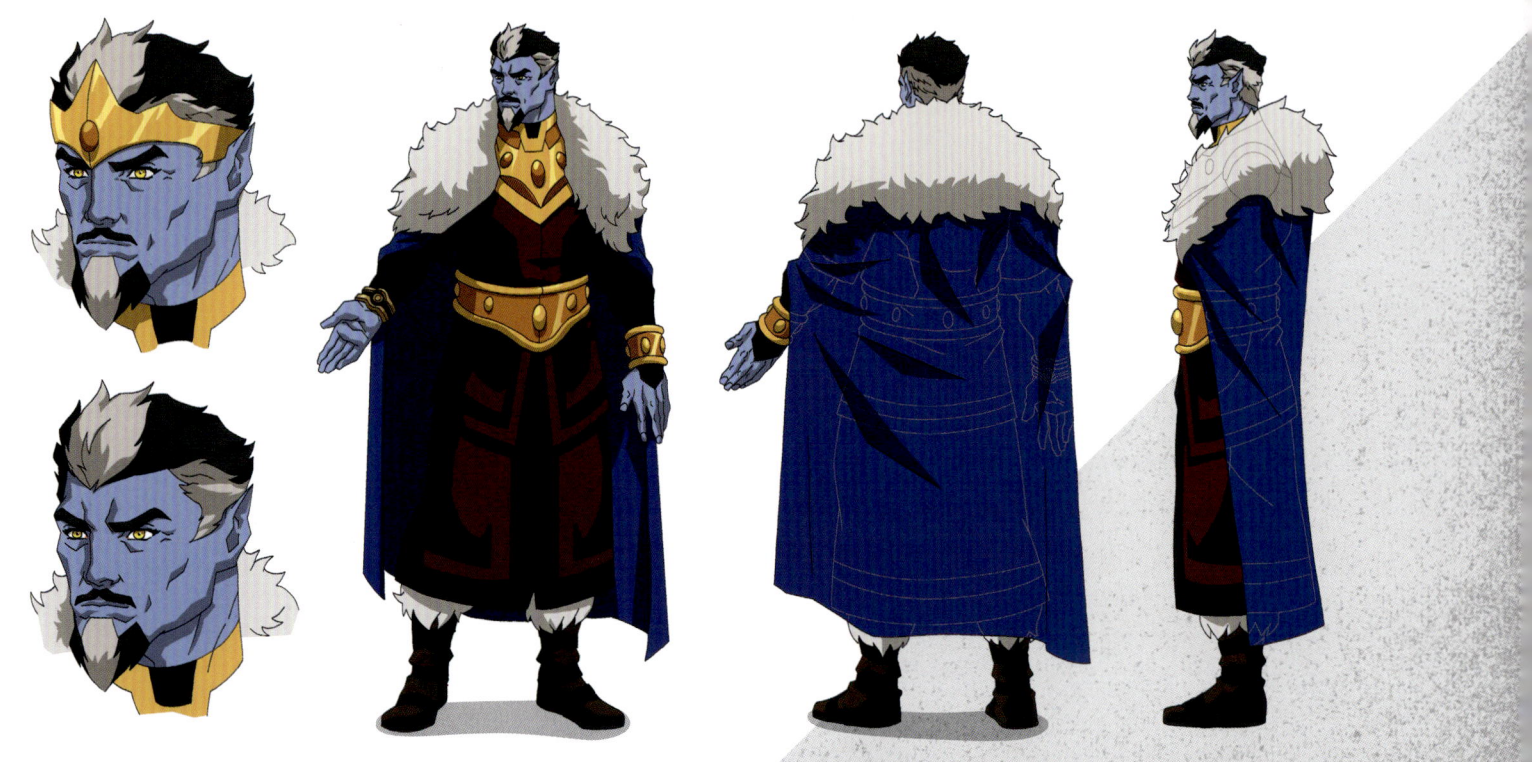

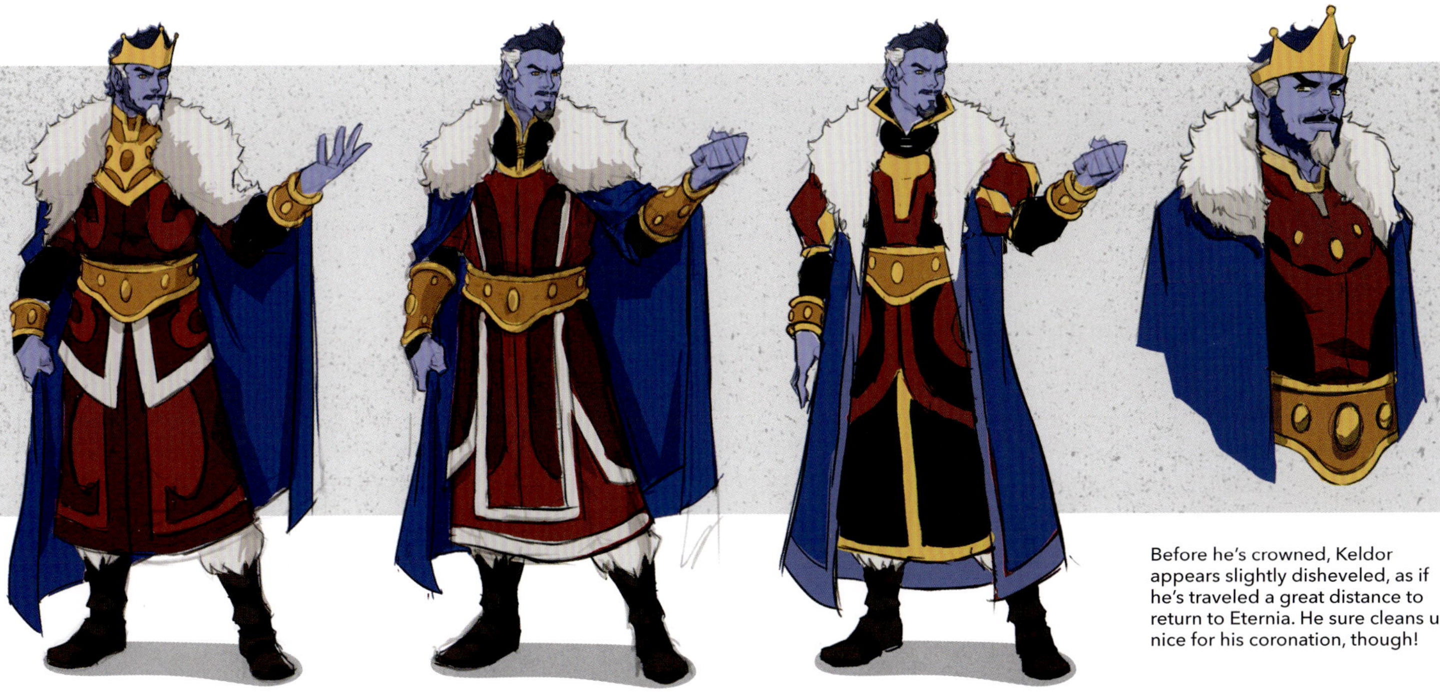

Before he's crowned, Keldor appears slightly disheveled, as if he's traveled a great distance to return to Eternia. He sure cleans up nice for his coronation, though!

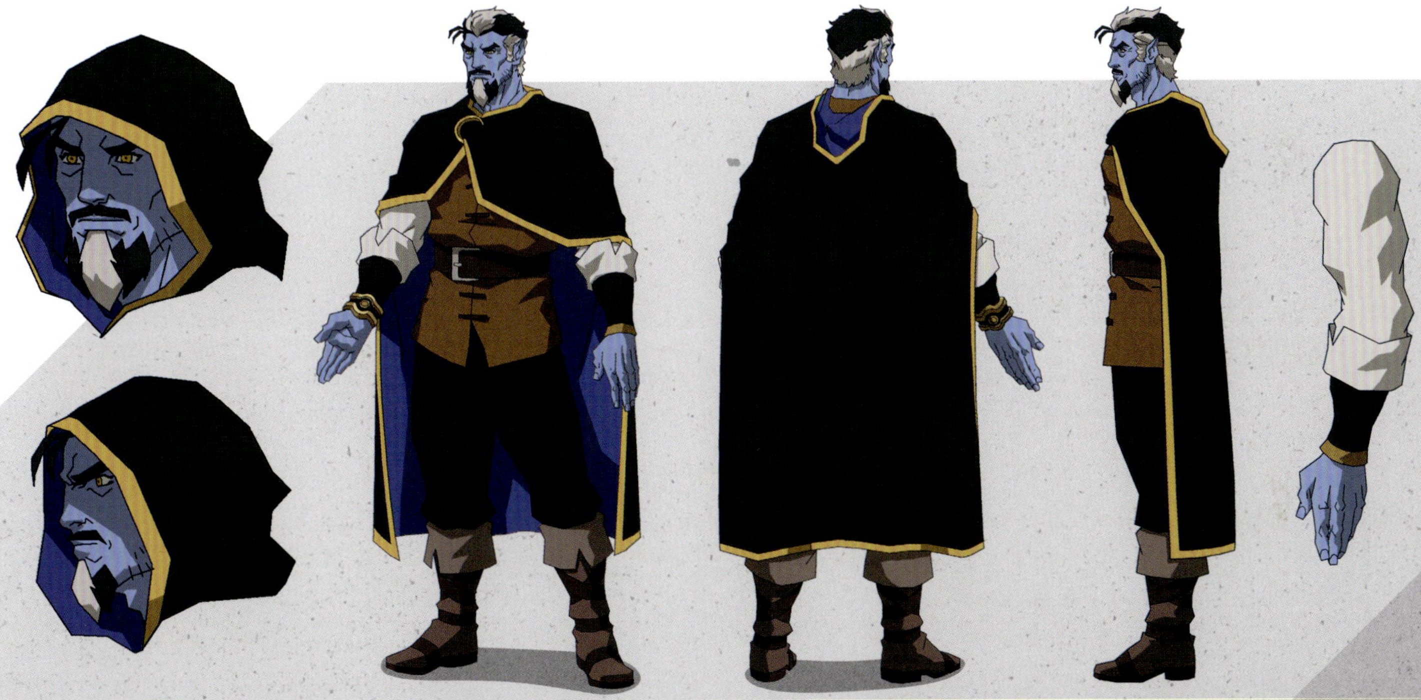

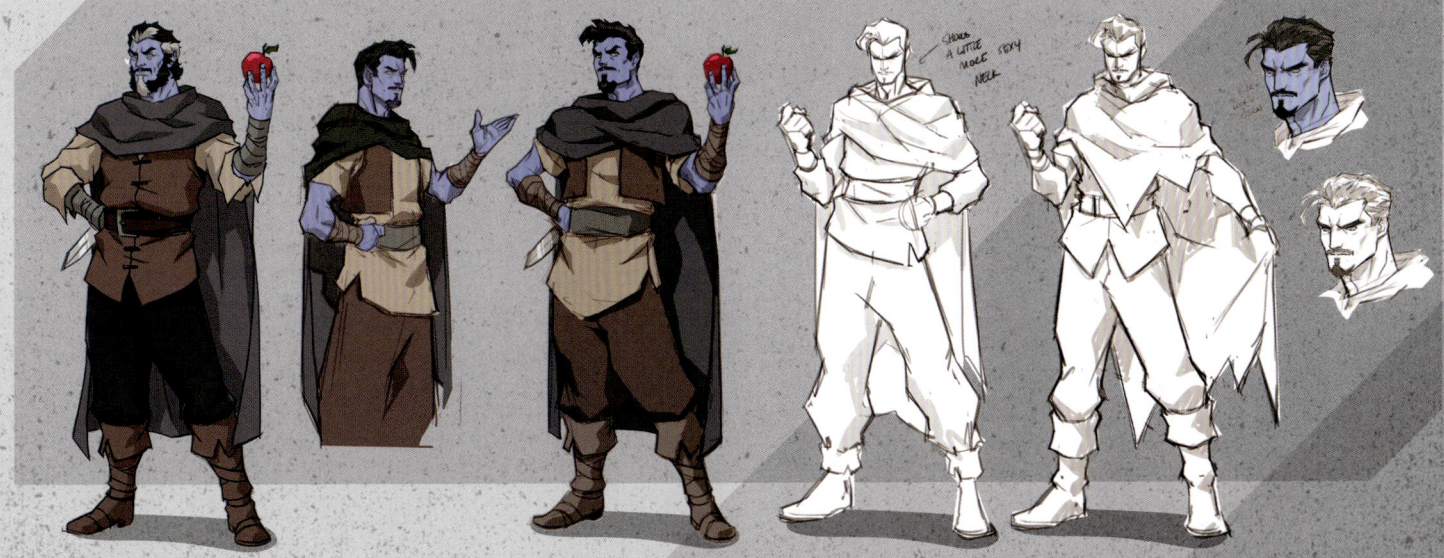

VILLAINS \\ 51

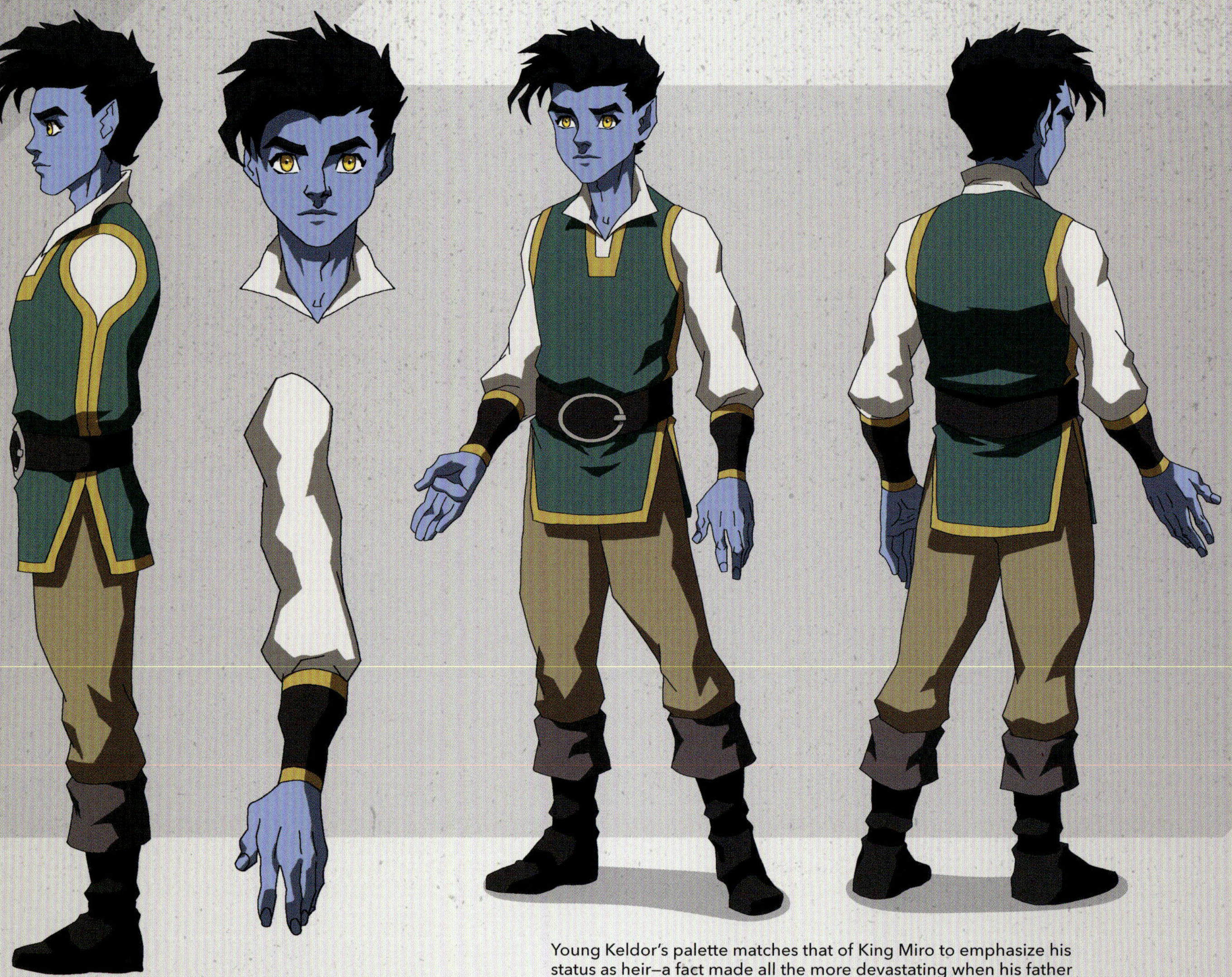

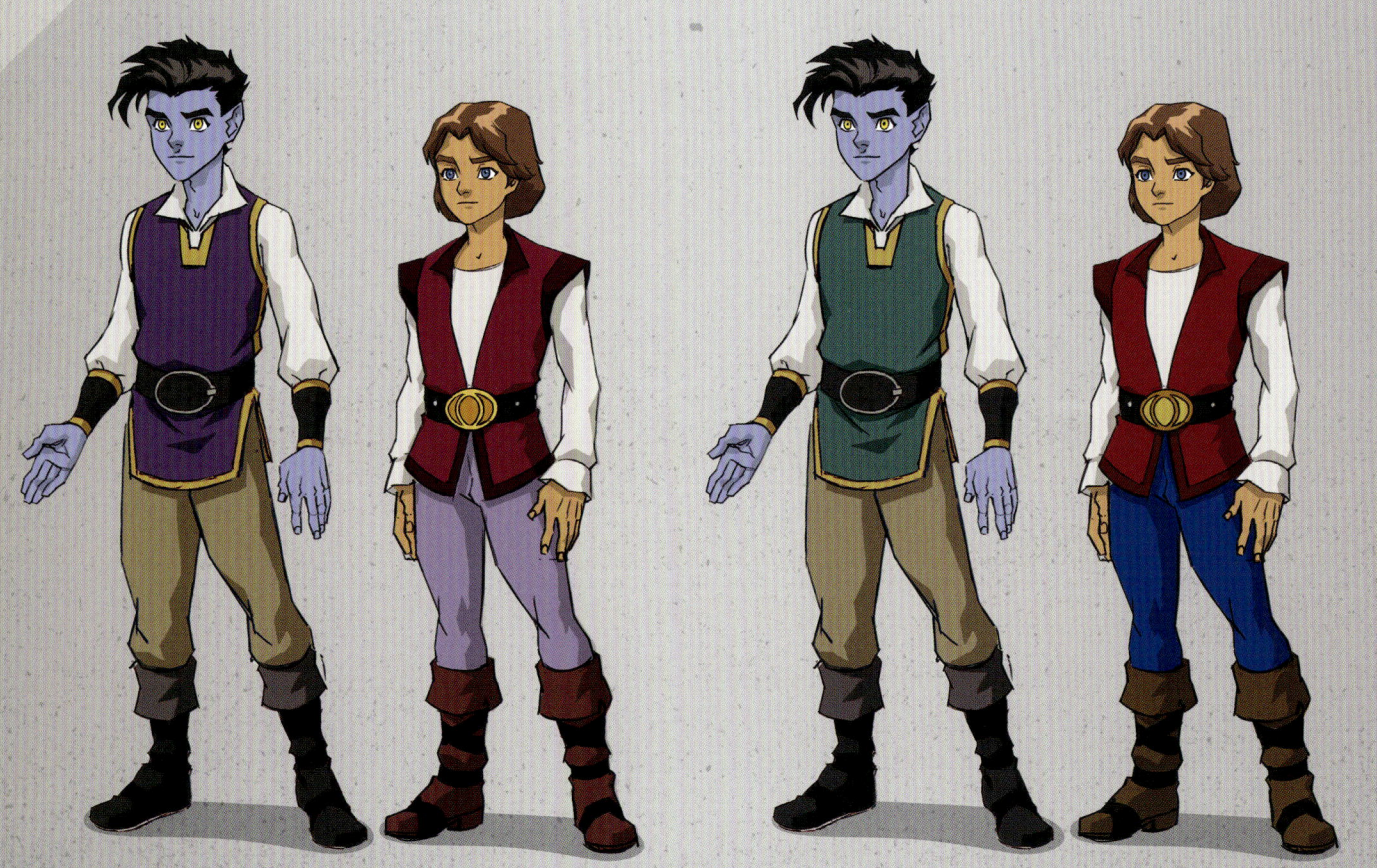

Young Keldor's palette matches that of King Miro to emphasize his status as heir—a fact made all the more devastating when his father banishes him to Anwat Gar.

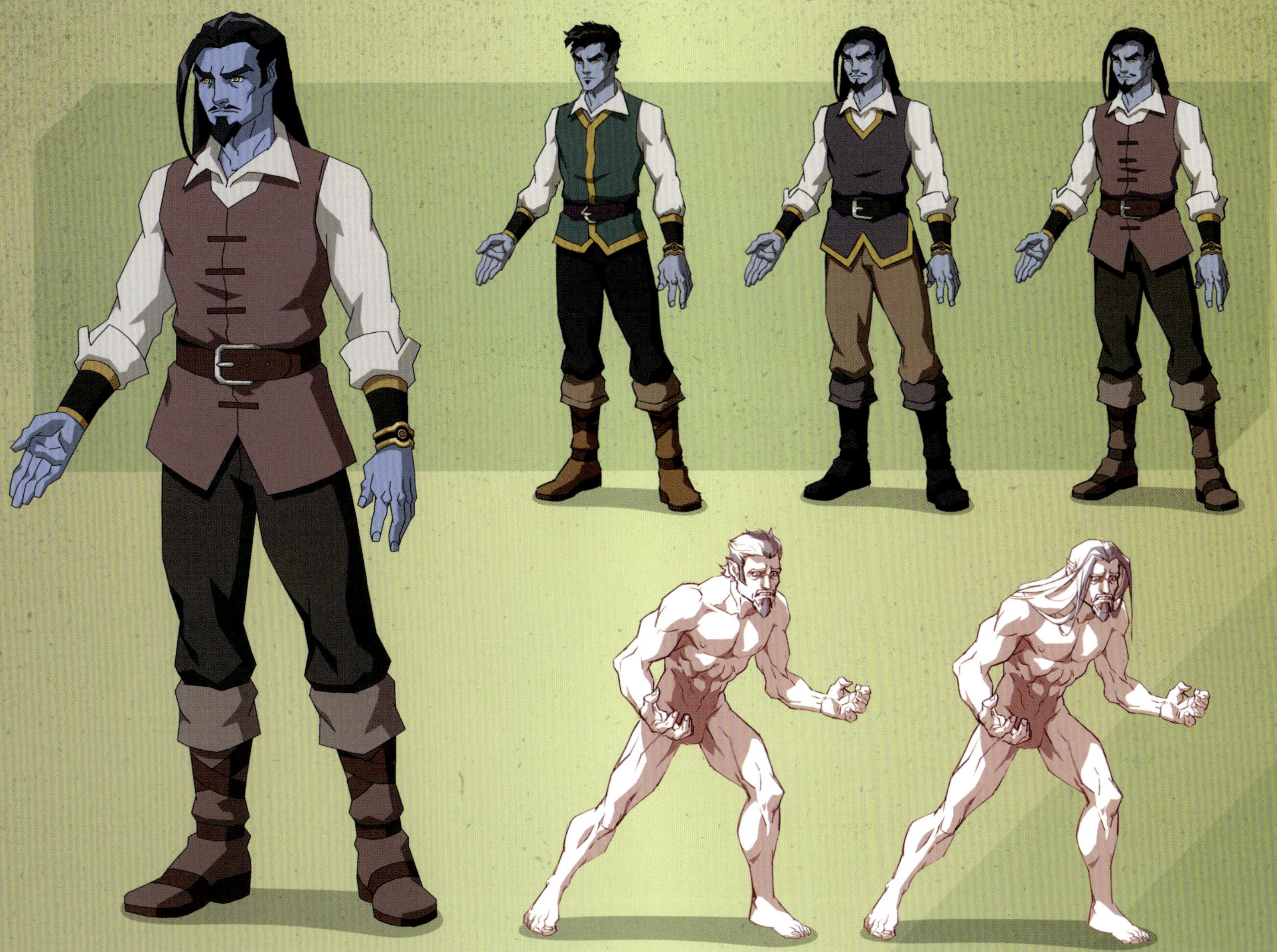

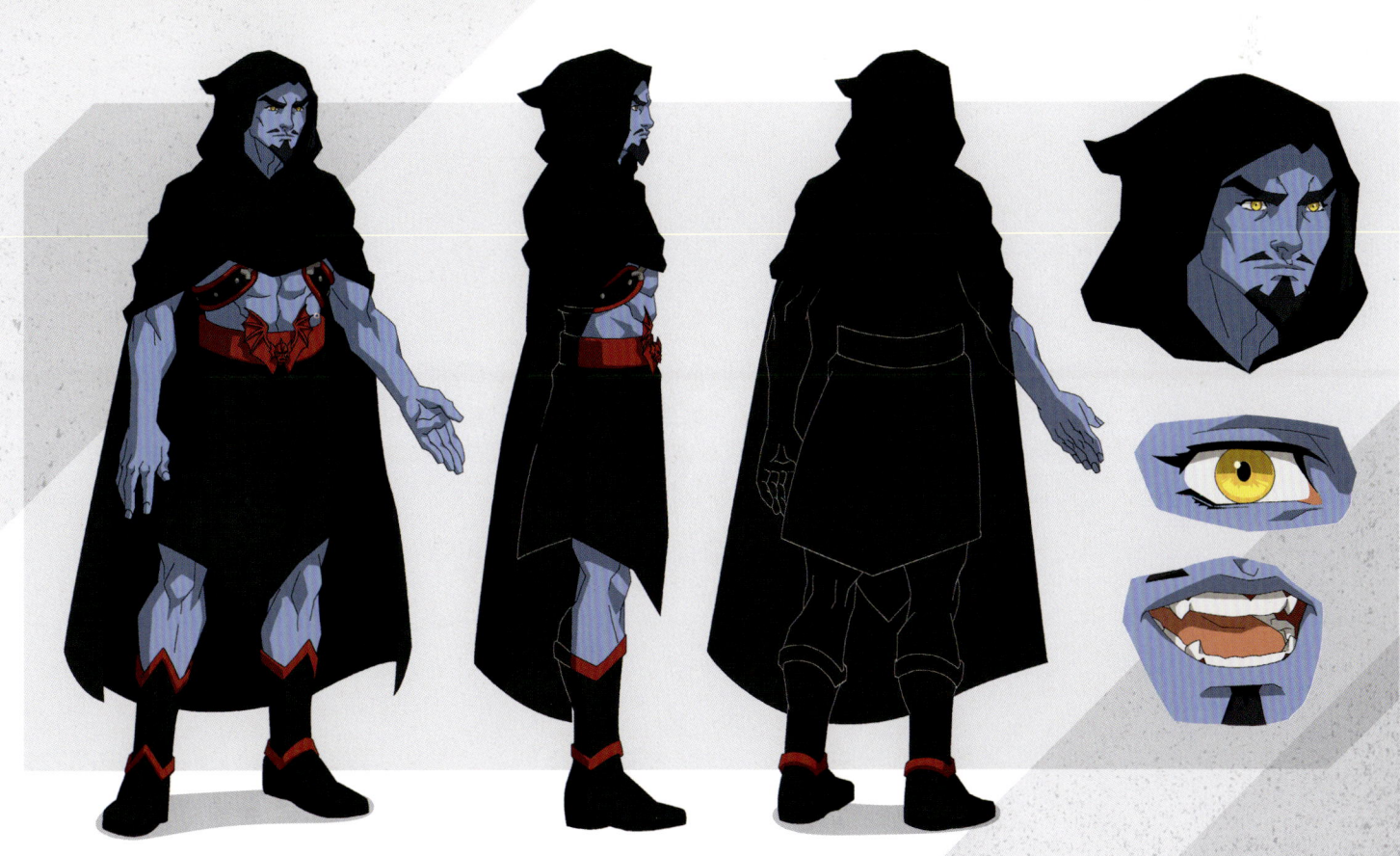

VILLAINS \\ 53

HORDAK

We wanted Hordak's initial appearance to be more "emperor" than "warrior"—someone who no longer needs to fight his own battles. This way, we could insert a big moment when he transforms into his battle form to show that he means business.

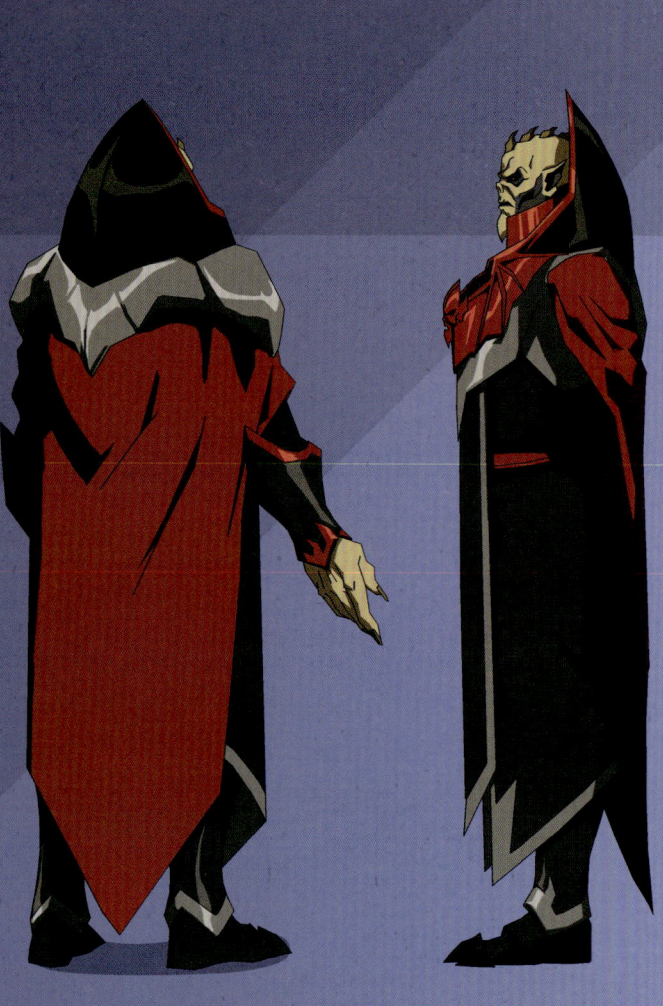
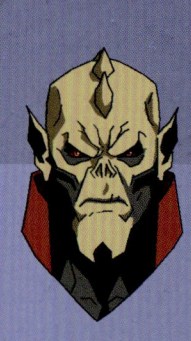
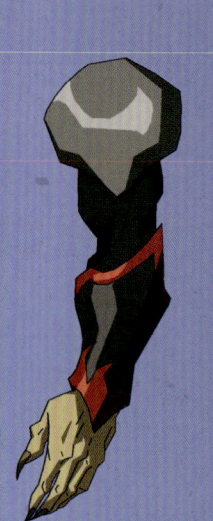
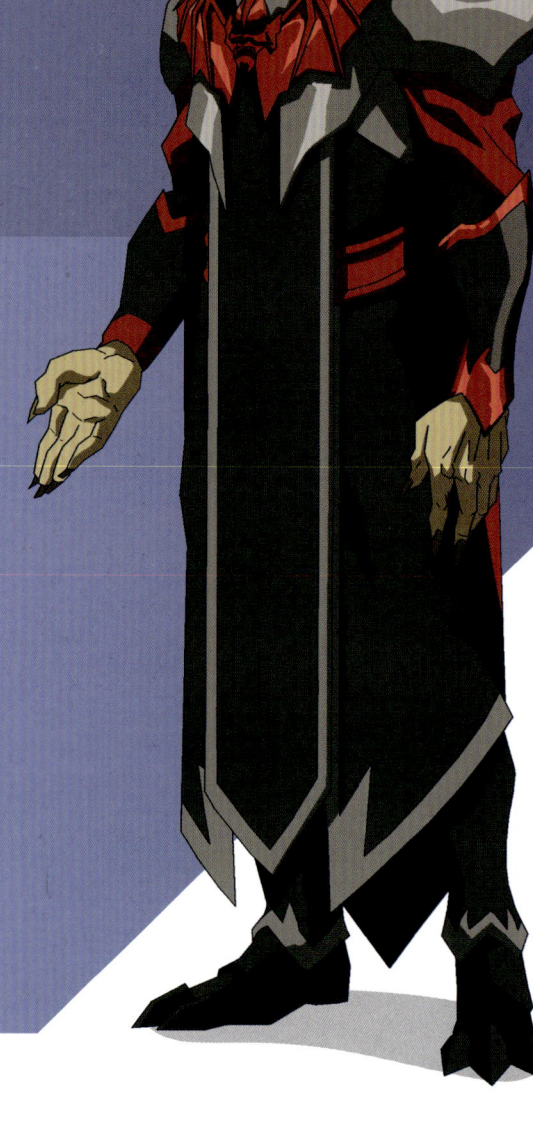
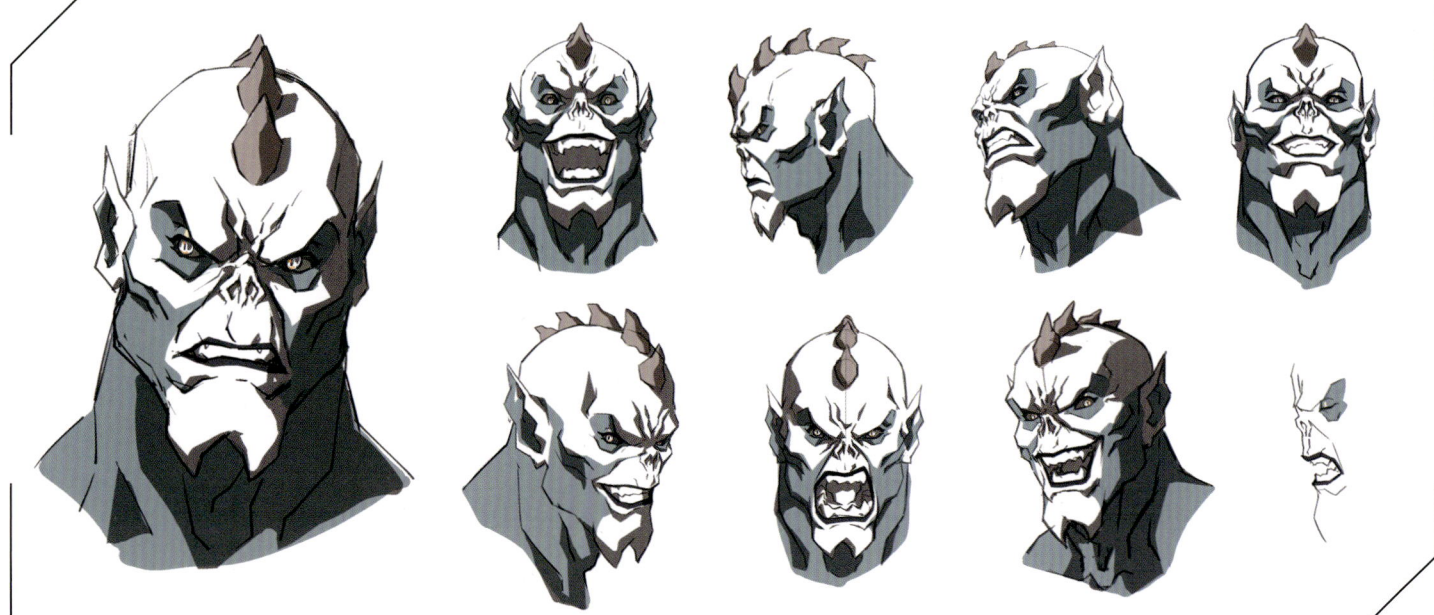

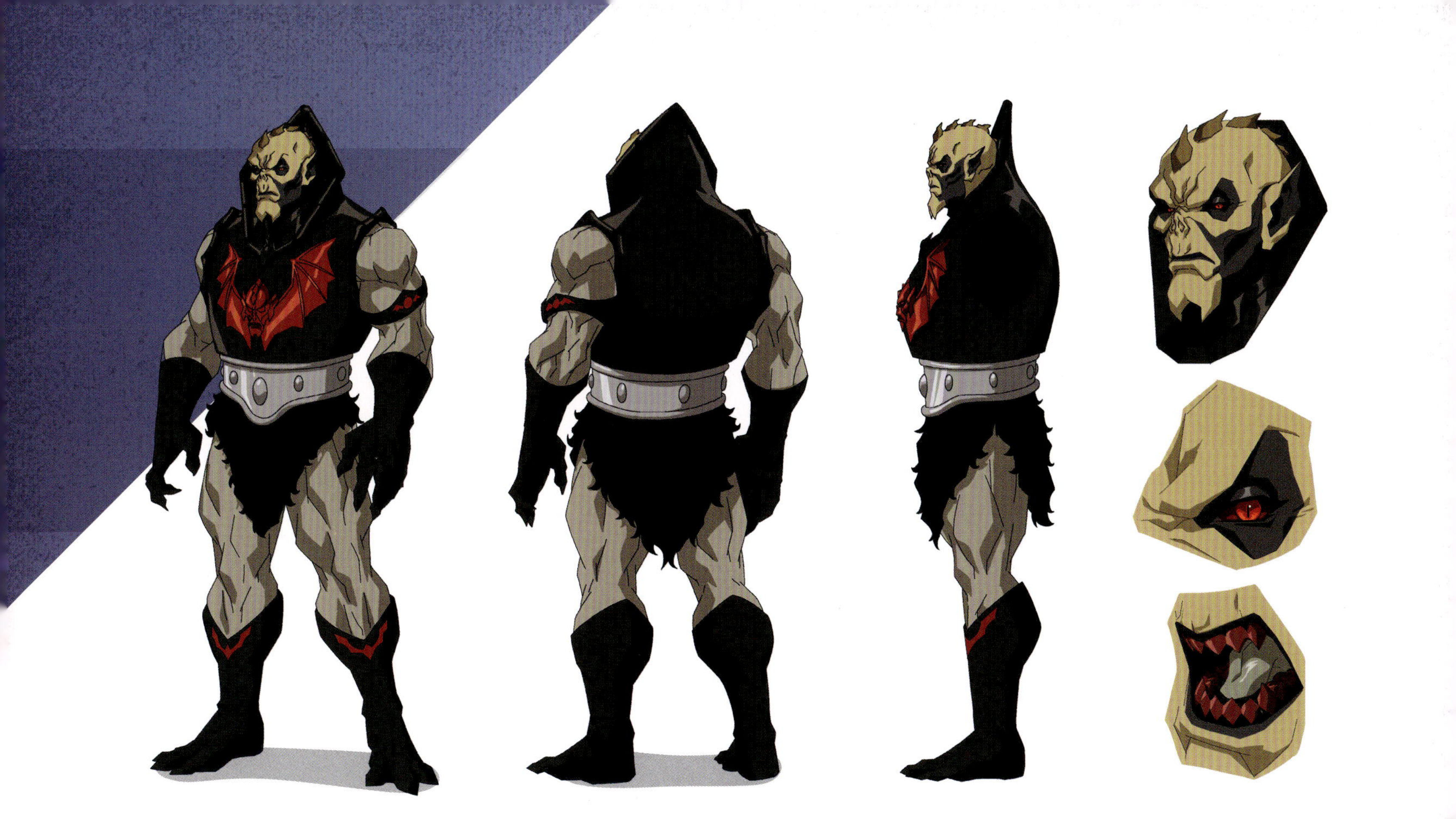

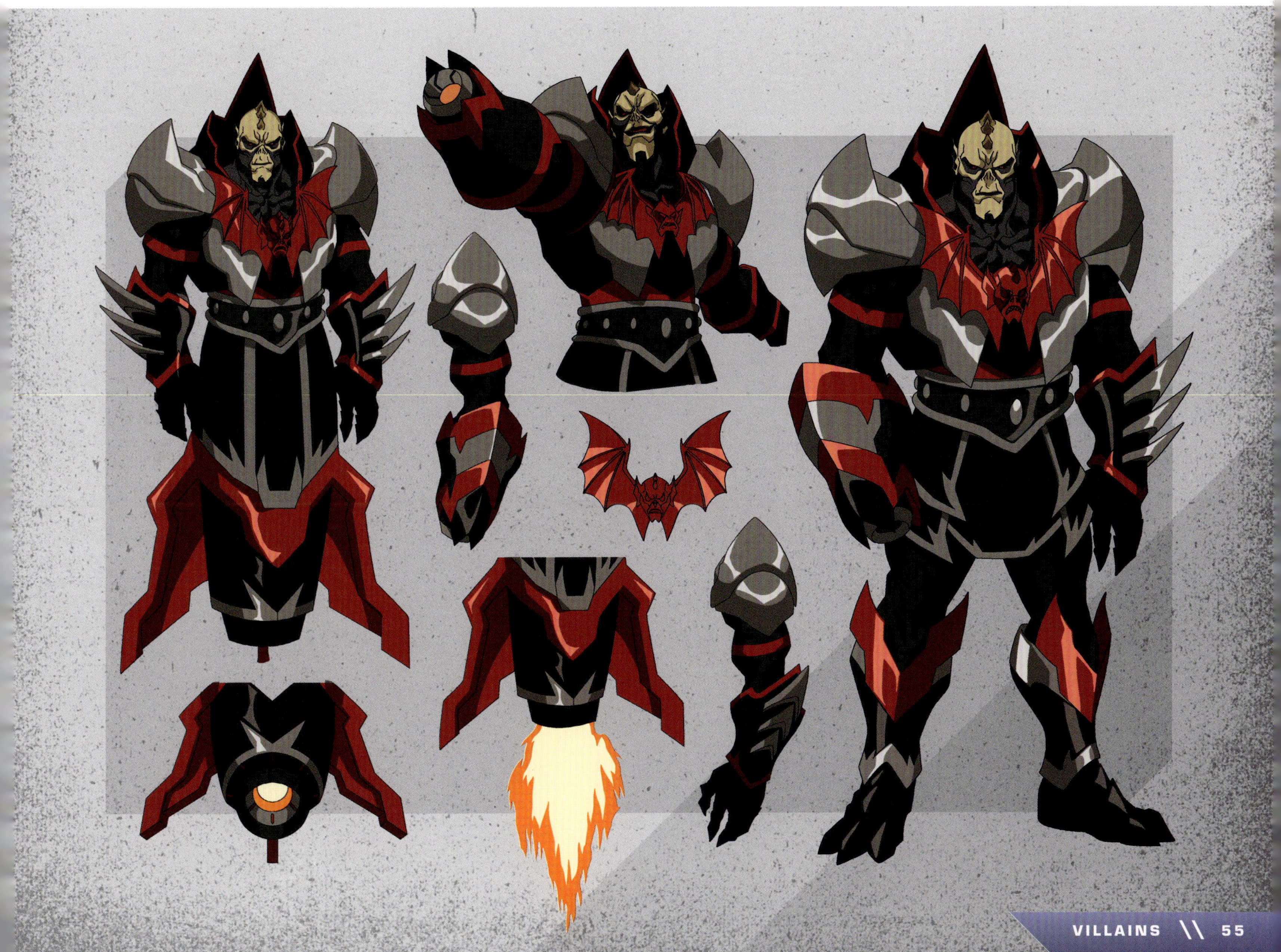

VILLAINS

LEECH

Among the ranks of Hordak's biggest and baddest is the life-draining slug man known as Leech! He's got mouths everywhere: hands, feet, and even *a mouth in his mouth*. It's easy to see why this absolute monster is proof that Hordak hires well.

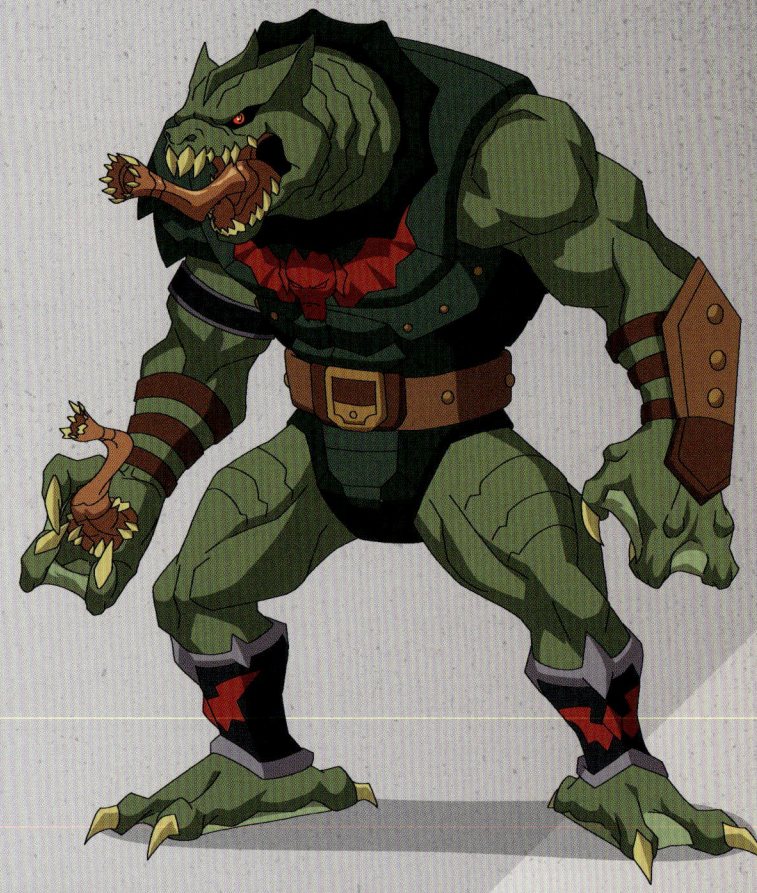

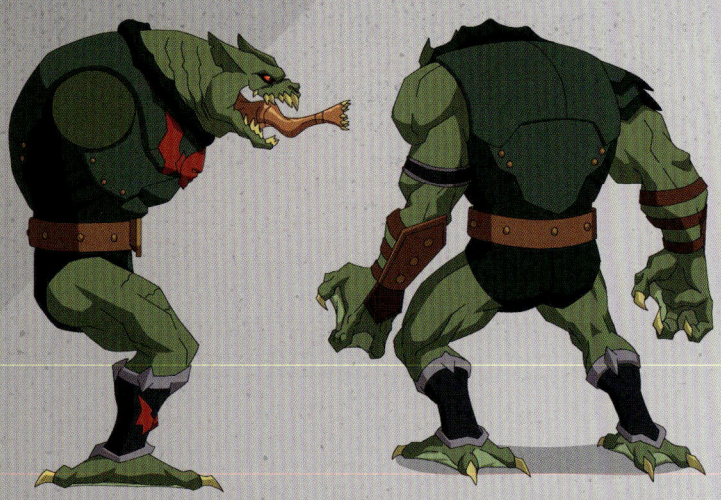

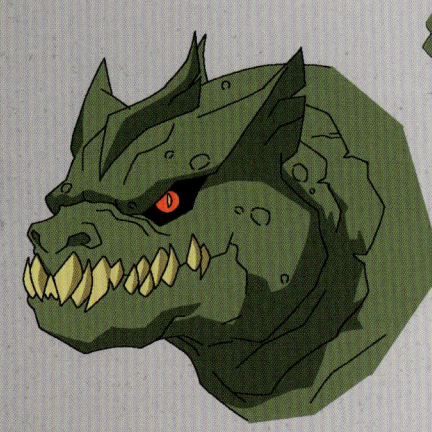

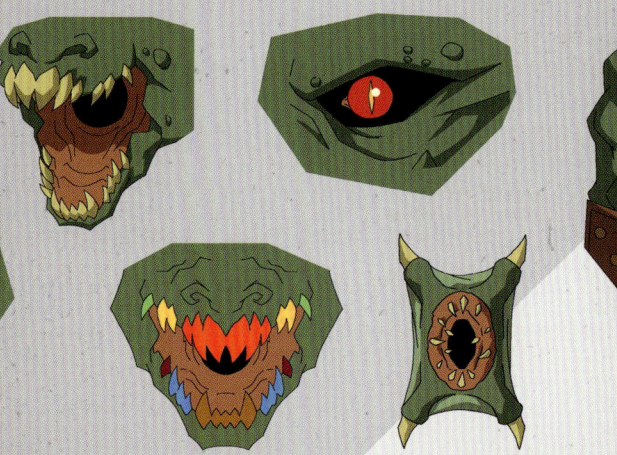

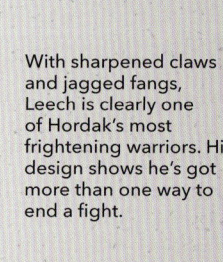

With sharpened claws and jagged fangs, Leech is clearly one of Hordak's most frightening warriors. His design shows he's got more than one way to end a fight.

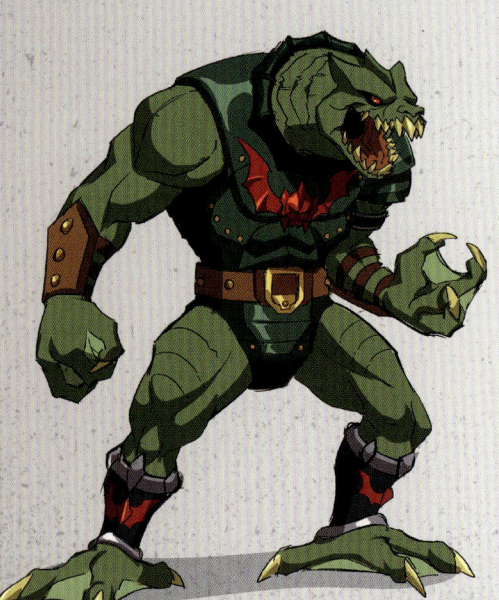

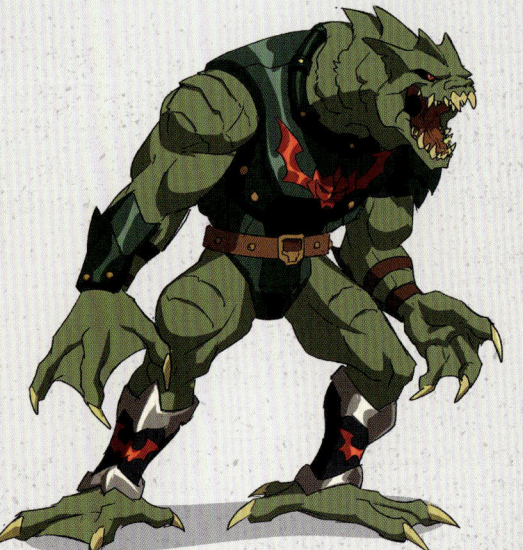

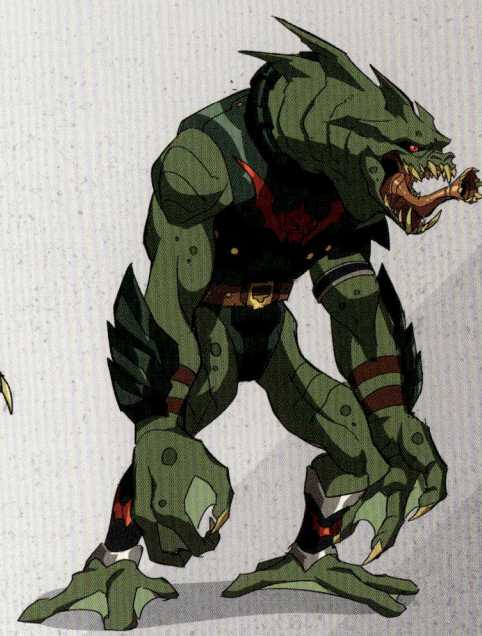

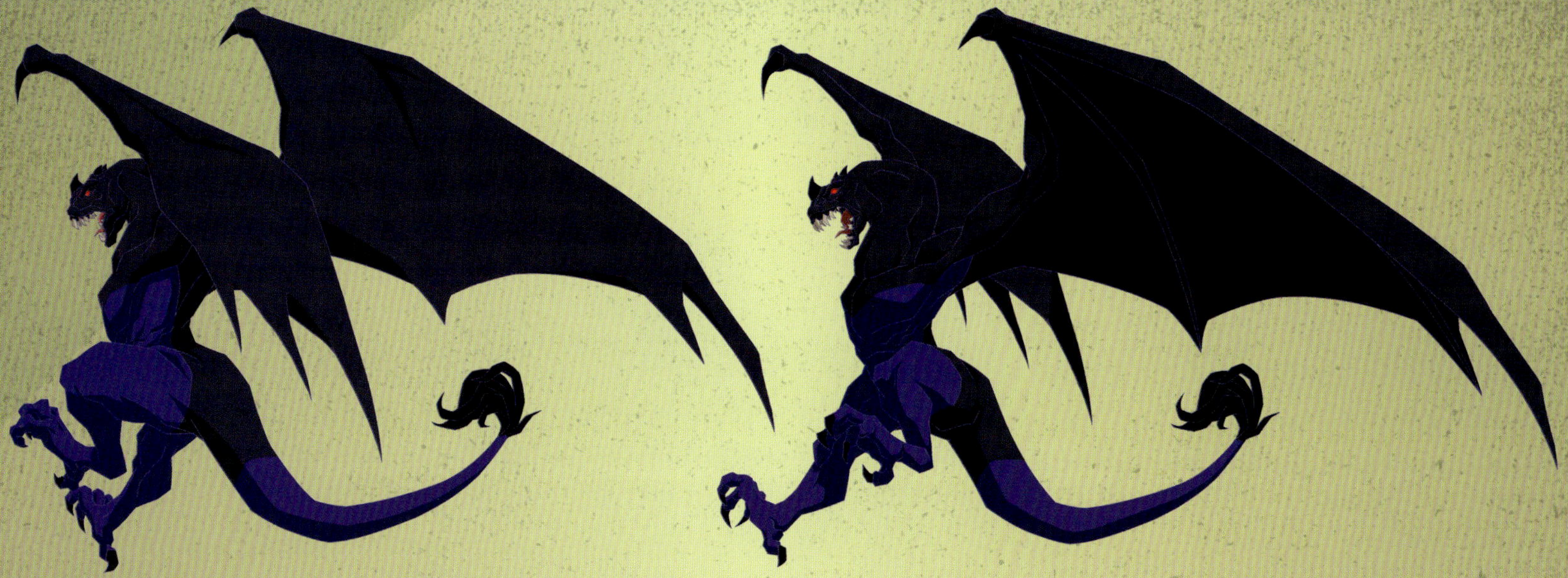

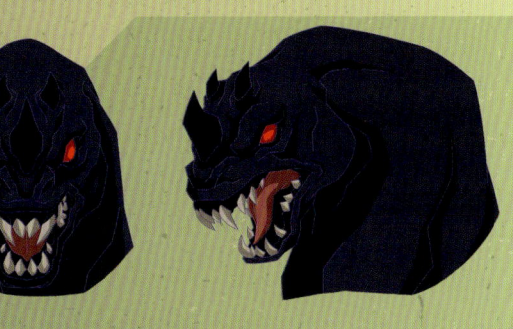

SHADOW WYVERN

It was important that we designed a unique flying creature to challenge our heroes while not "overshadowing" the previous and more dragon-like creature in *Revelation*. To this end, their snout was shortened to further distinguish them from the Shadow Dragon.

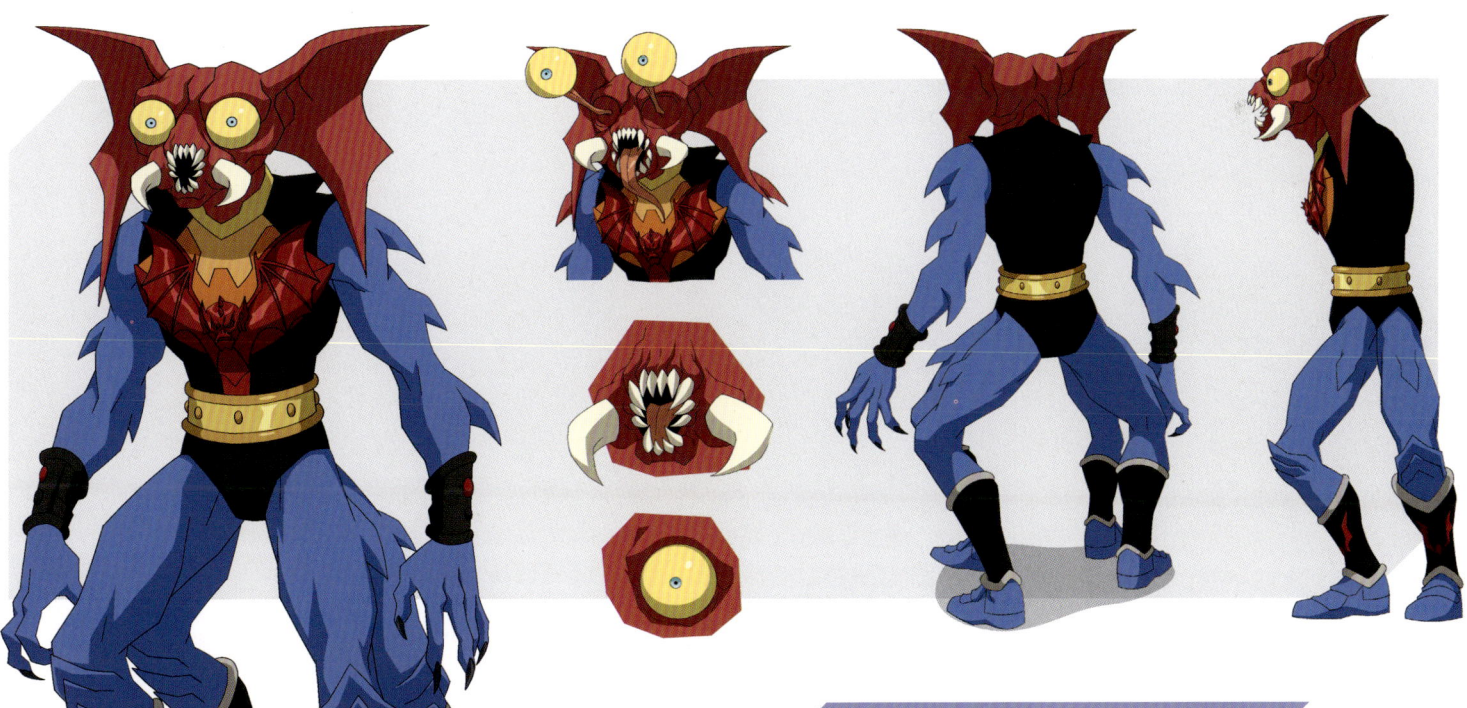

MANTENNA

Another one of Hordak's strongest warriors: the terrifying insectoid Mantenna! Definitely a fun character to both design and animate, with four legs, extendable eyestalks, and gnashing pincers. And if that wasn't enough to send our heroes running the other way, check the eyes again—*they shoot lasers*.

VILLAINS \\ 57

GRIZZLOR

And finally, leading Hordak's special forces, the creature that still haunts Eternian legends: Grizzlor! This savage beast hails from the planet of Jungulia. With awesome strength and unstoppable ferocity, he is reason number one that Hordak rarely needs to fight his own battles.

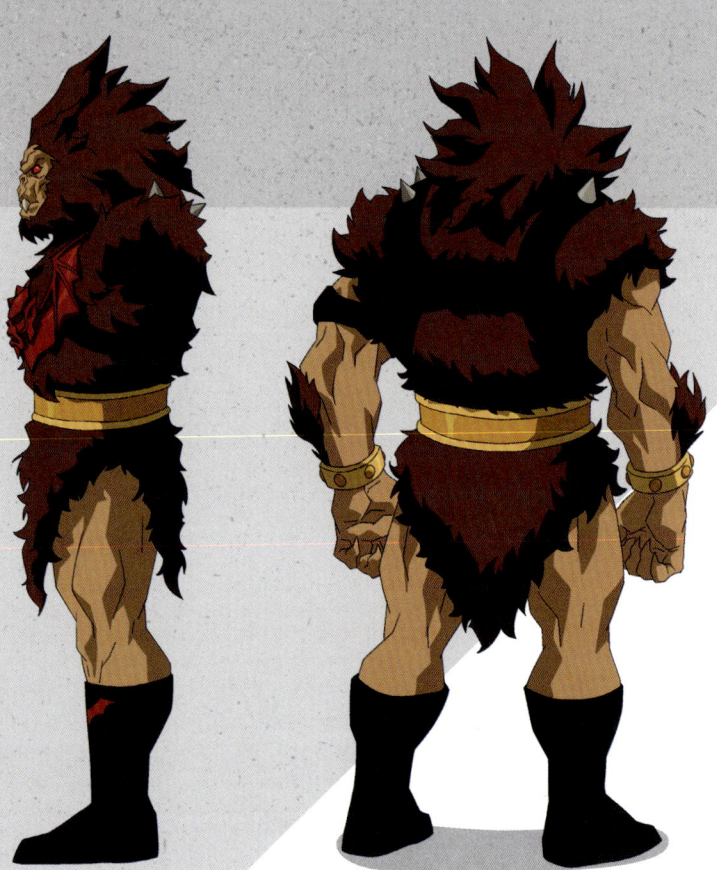
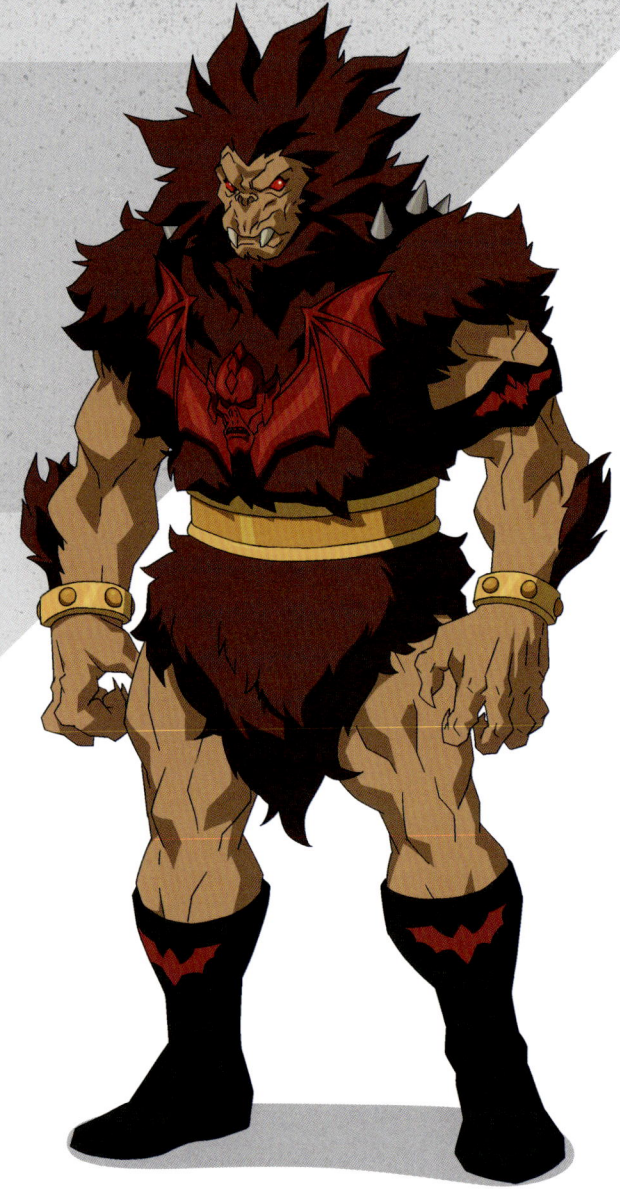
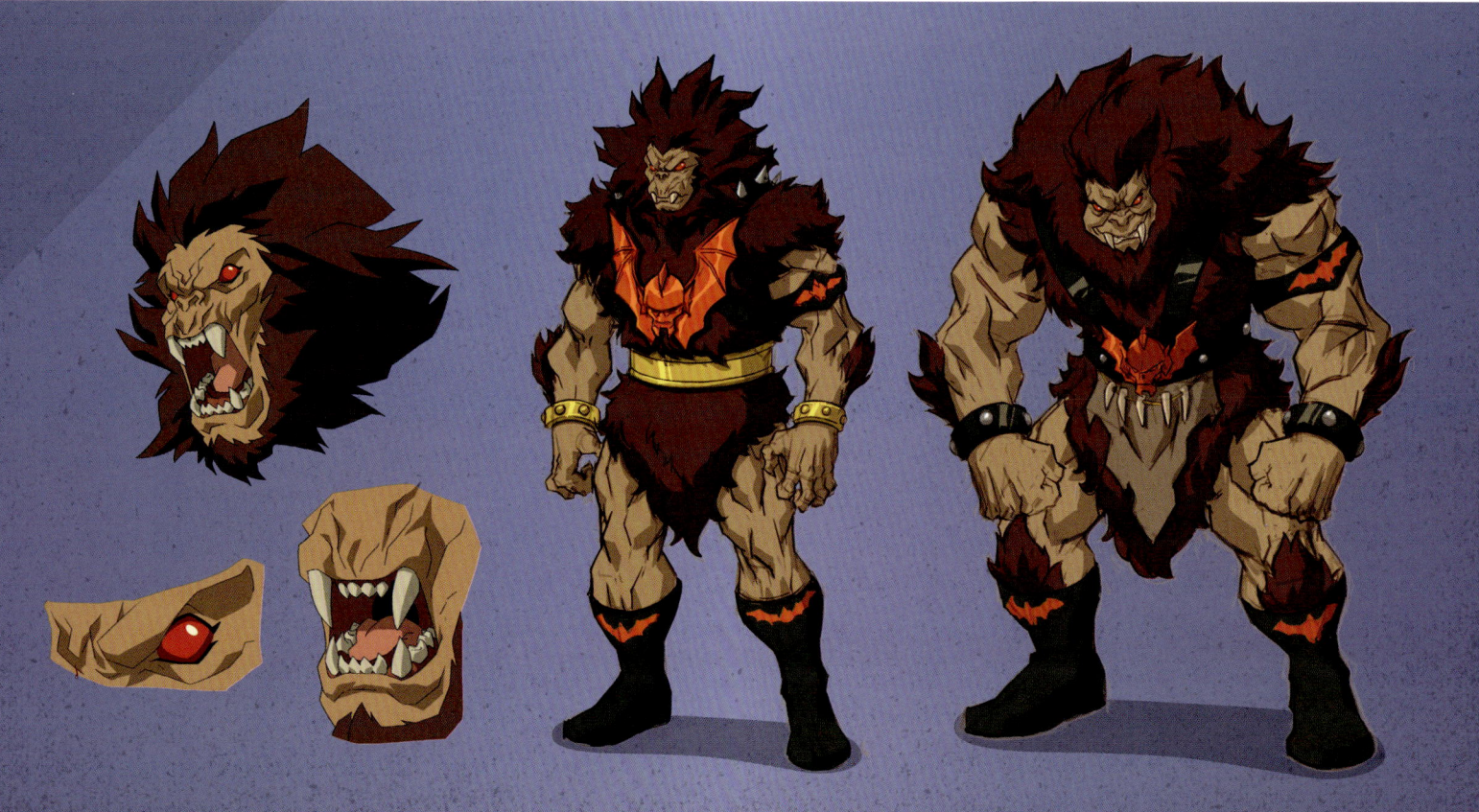

// THE ART OF MASTERS OF THE UNIVERSE: REVOLUTION

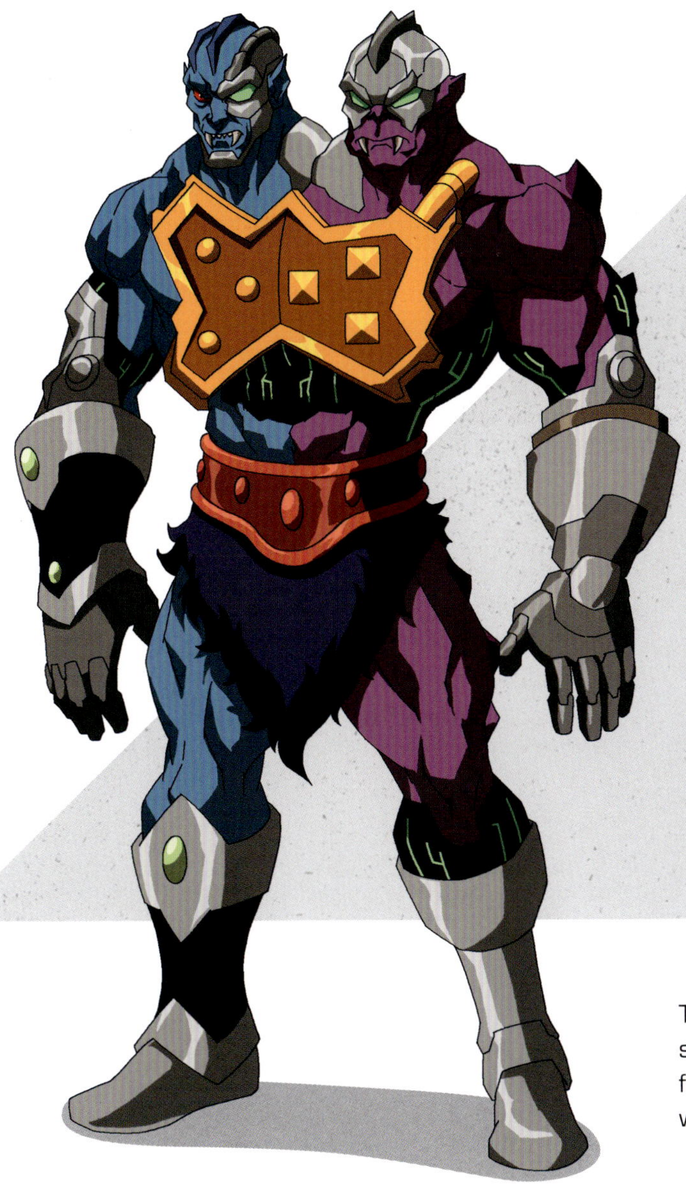

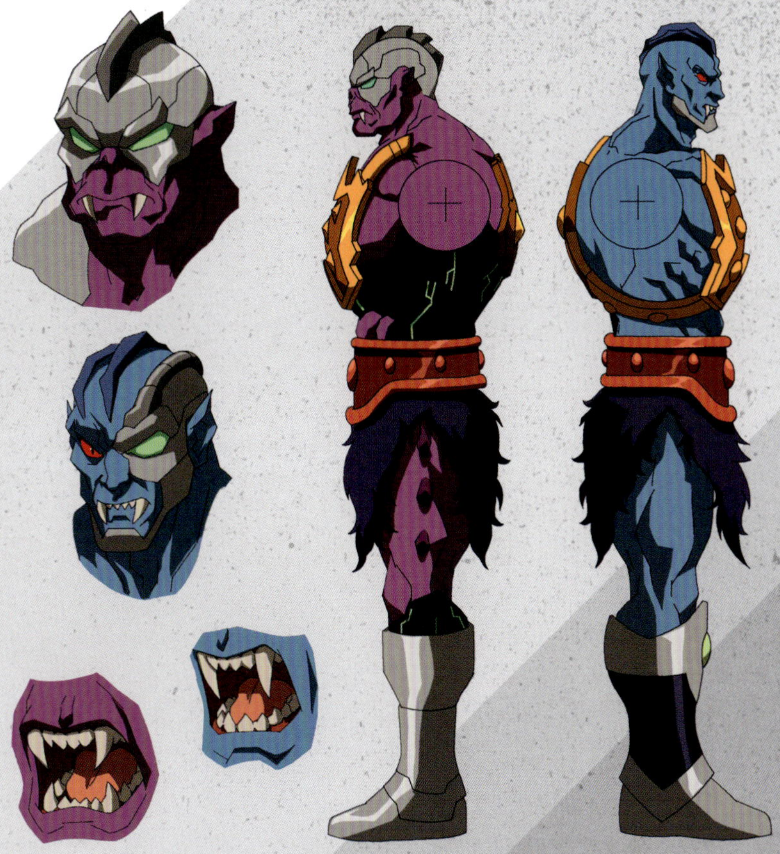

TWO BAD

The latest addition to Skeletor's forces, Two Bad starts out this season admittedly not having the best time. With a little extra juice from Motherboard and her acolytes, the two heads find themselves with some new upgrades, all to help with the revolution.

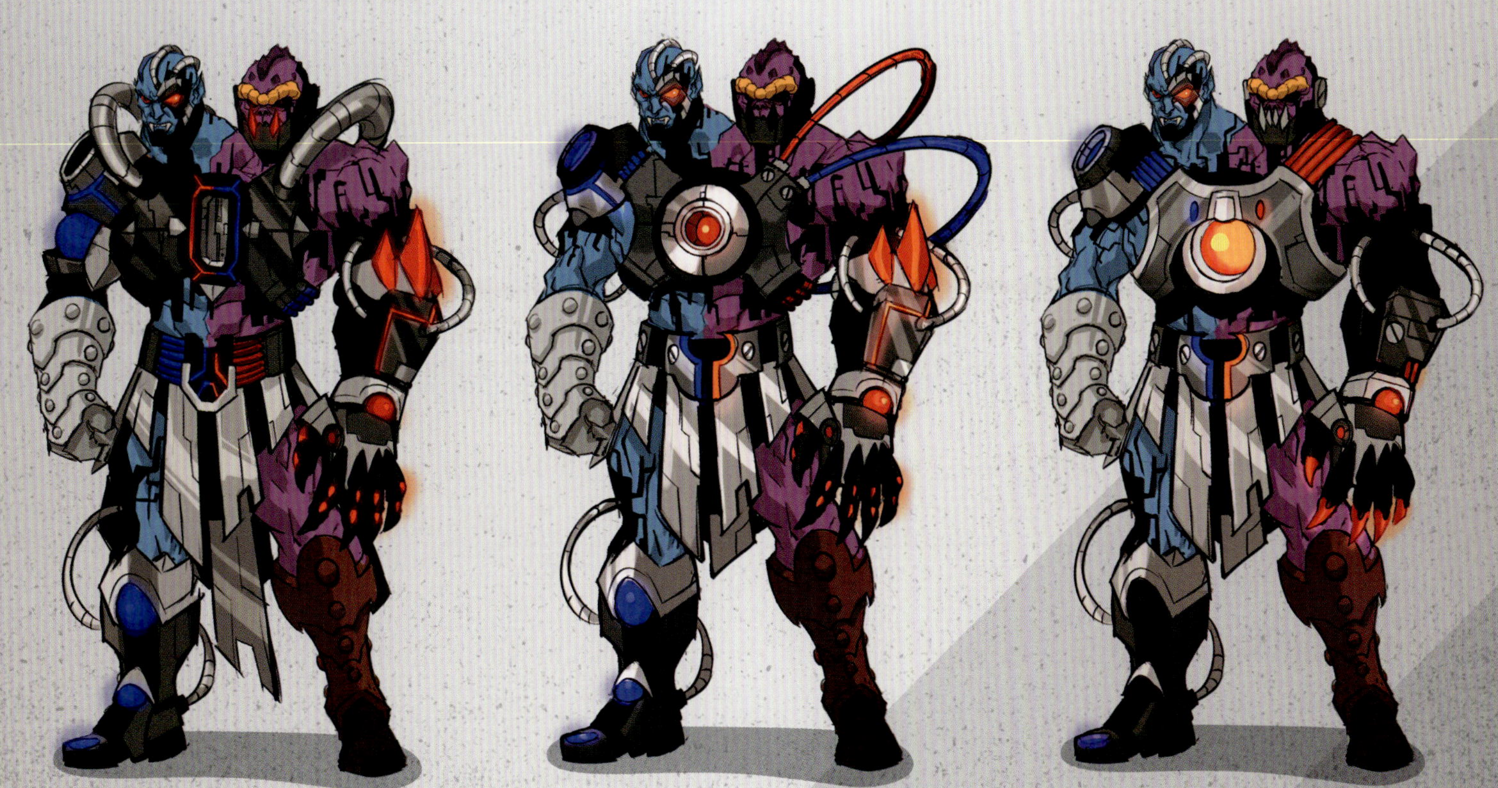

VILLAINS \\ 59

SCARE GLOW

The opportunity for Scare Glow to utilize the spirits of both Clamp Champ and Fisto as weapons was too good to pass up! We designed his mechanics like a toy. The fist was designed to shoot out and retract as if it were spring loaded.

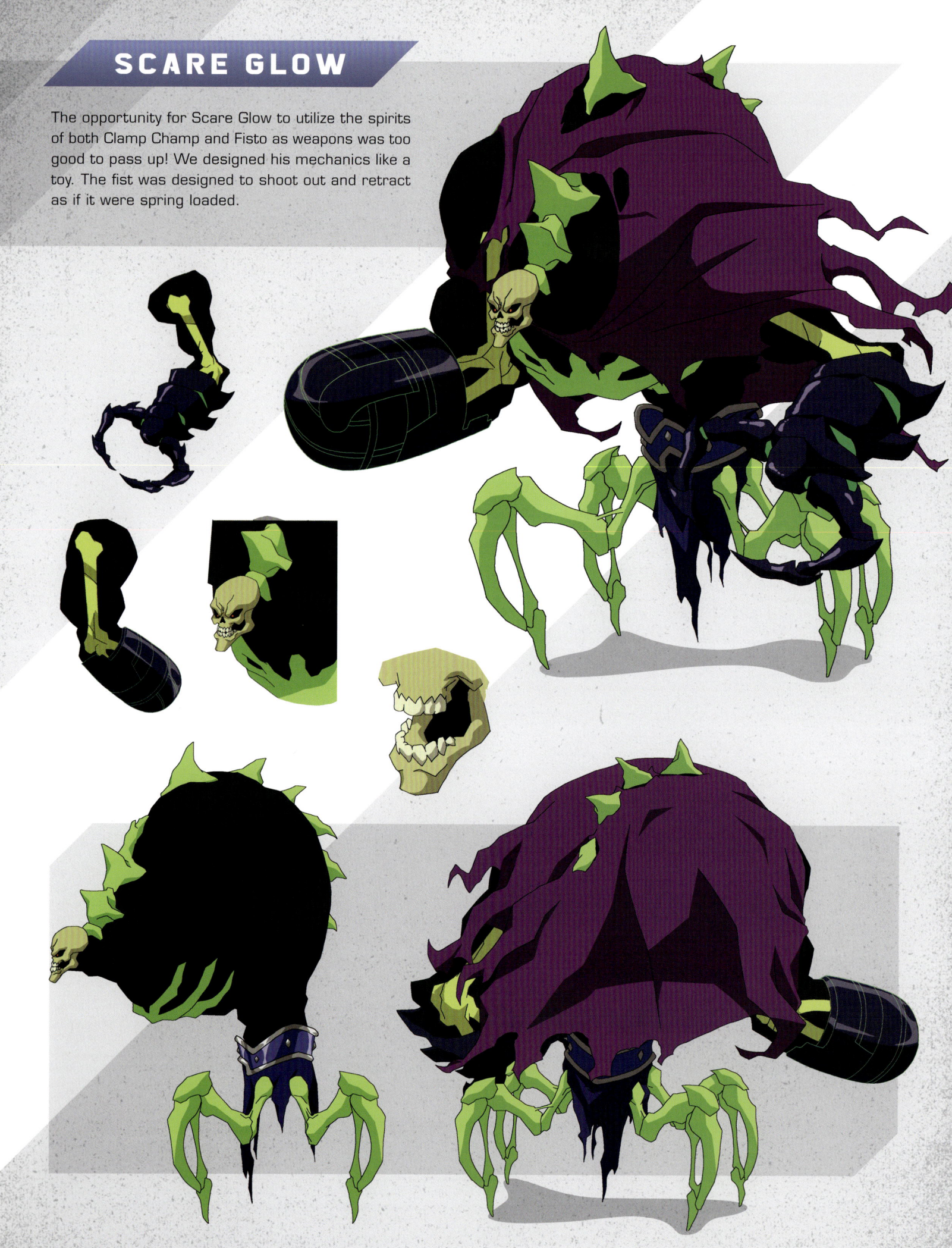

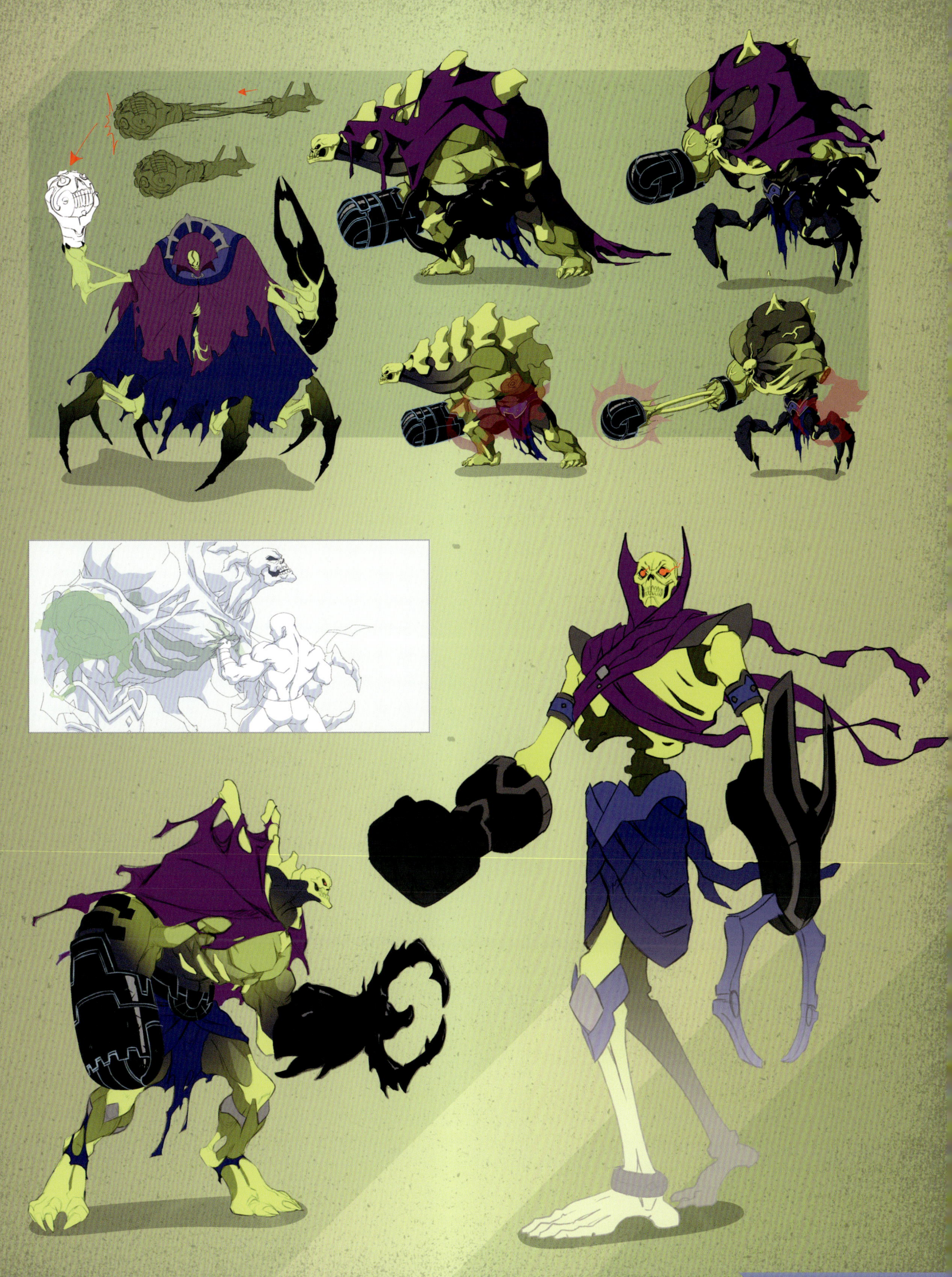

VILLAINS \\ 61

MOTHERBOARD

This maleficent matron is worshiped by the technocult inhabiting Snake Mountain. Though first unveiled at the tail end of *Revelation*, she was only seen from the front. Naturally, this season most of our exploration focused on how she looks from the back.

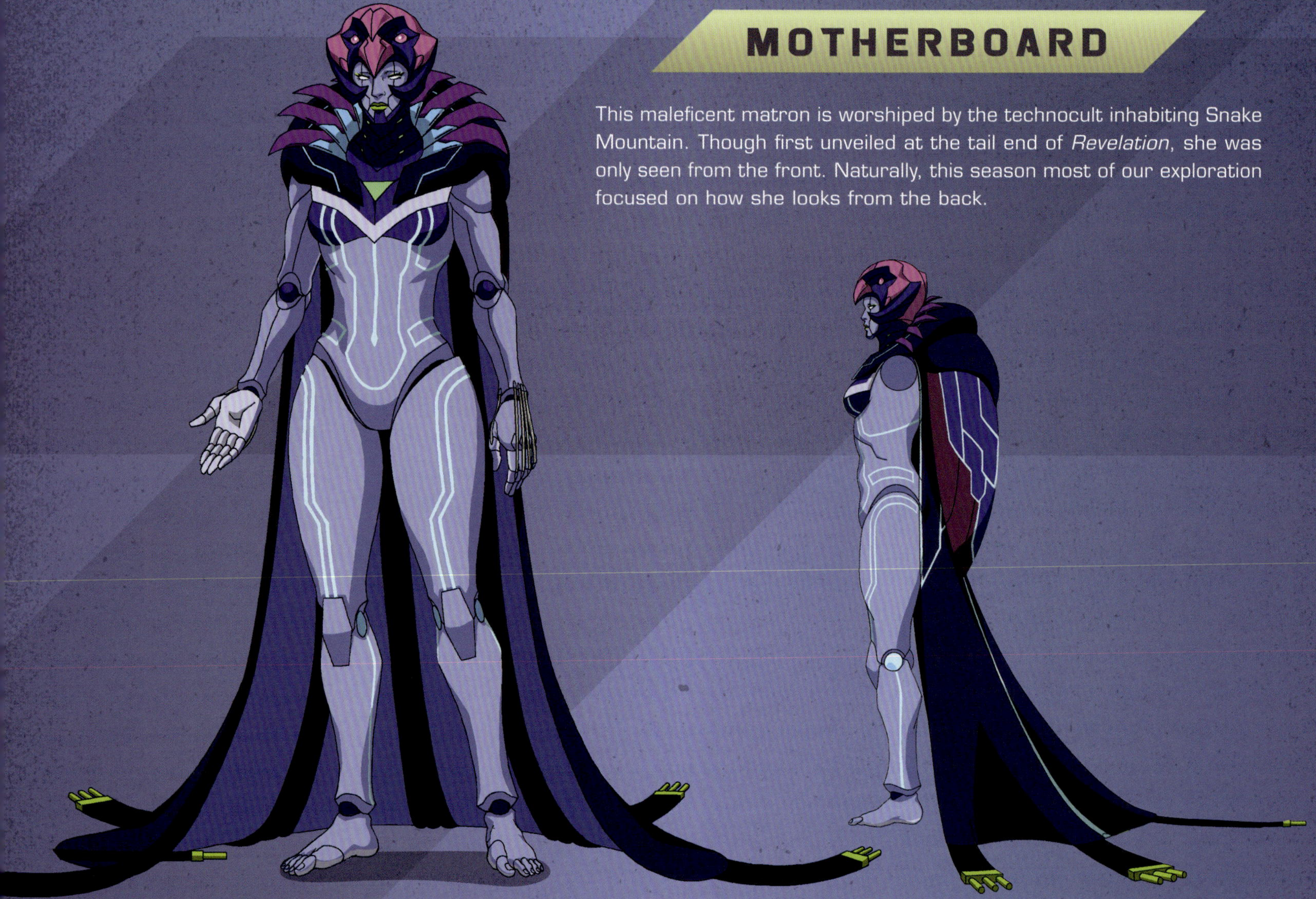

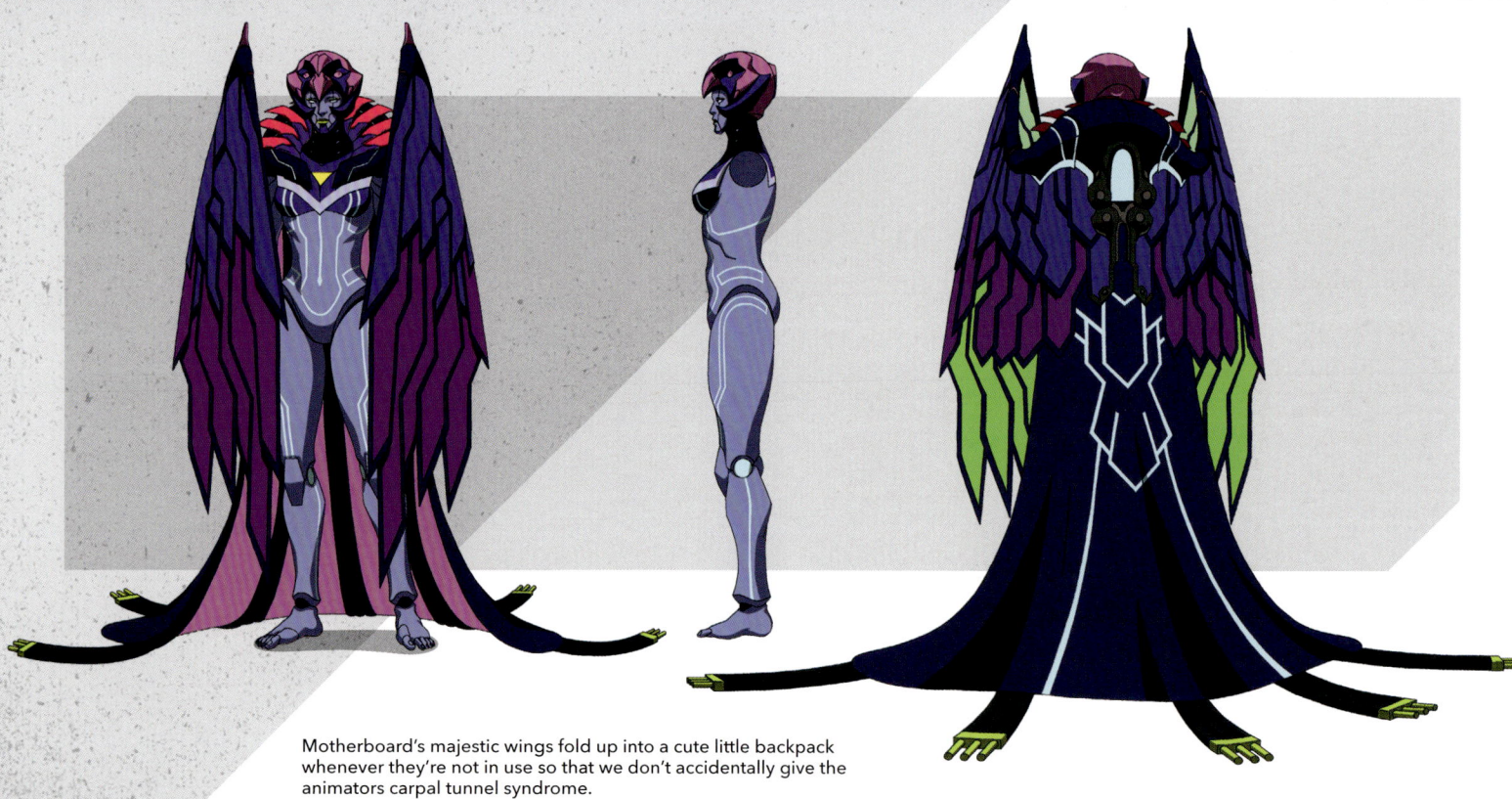

Motherboard's majestic wings fold up into a cute little backpack whenever they're not in use so that we don't accidentally give the animators carpal tunnel syndrome.

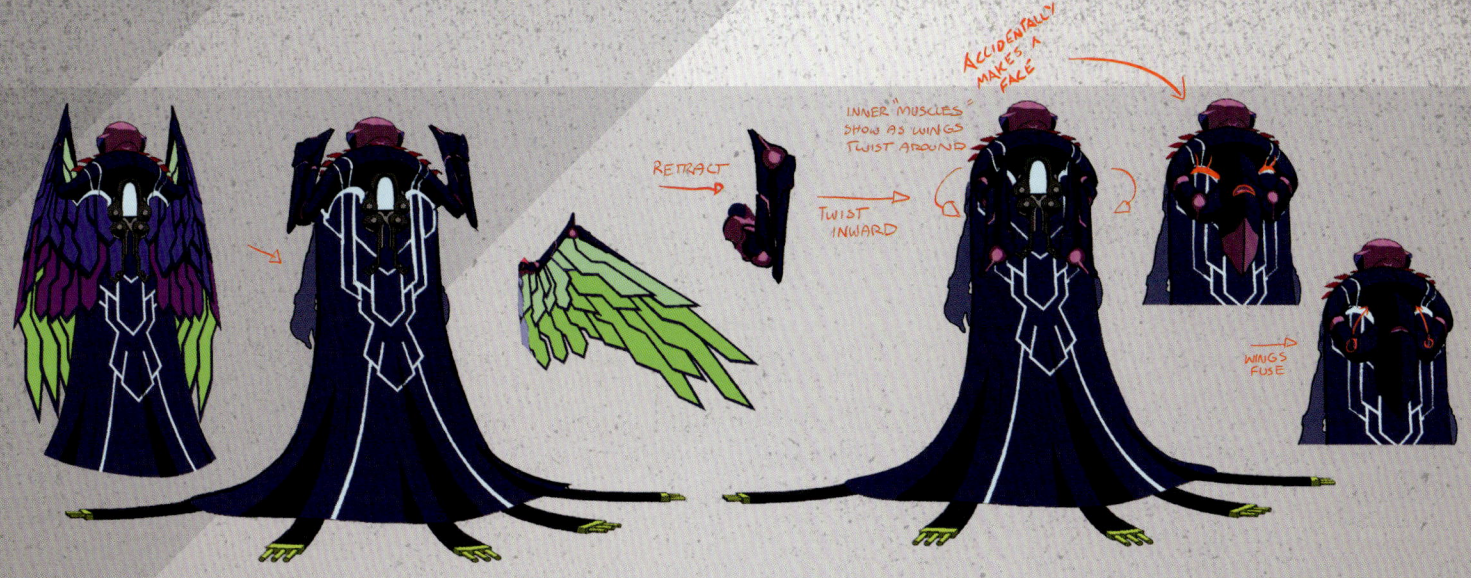

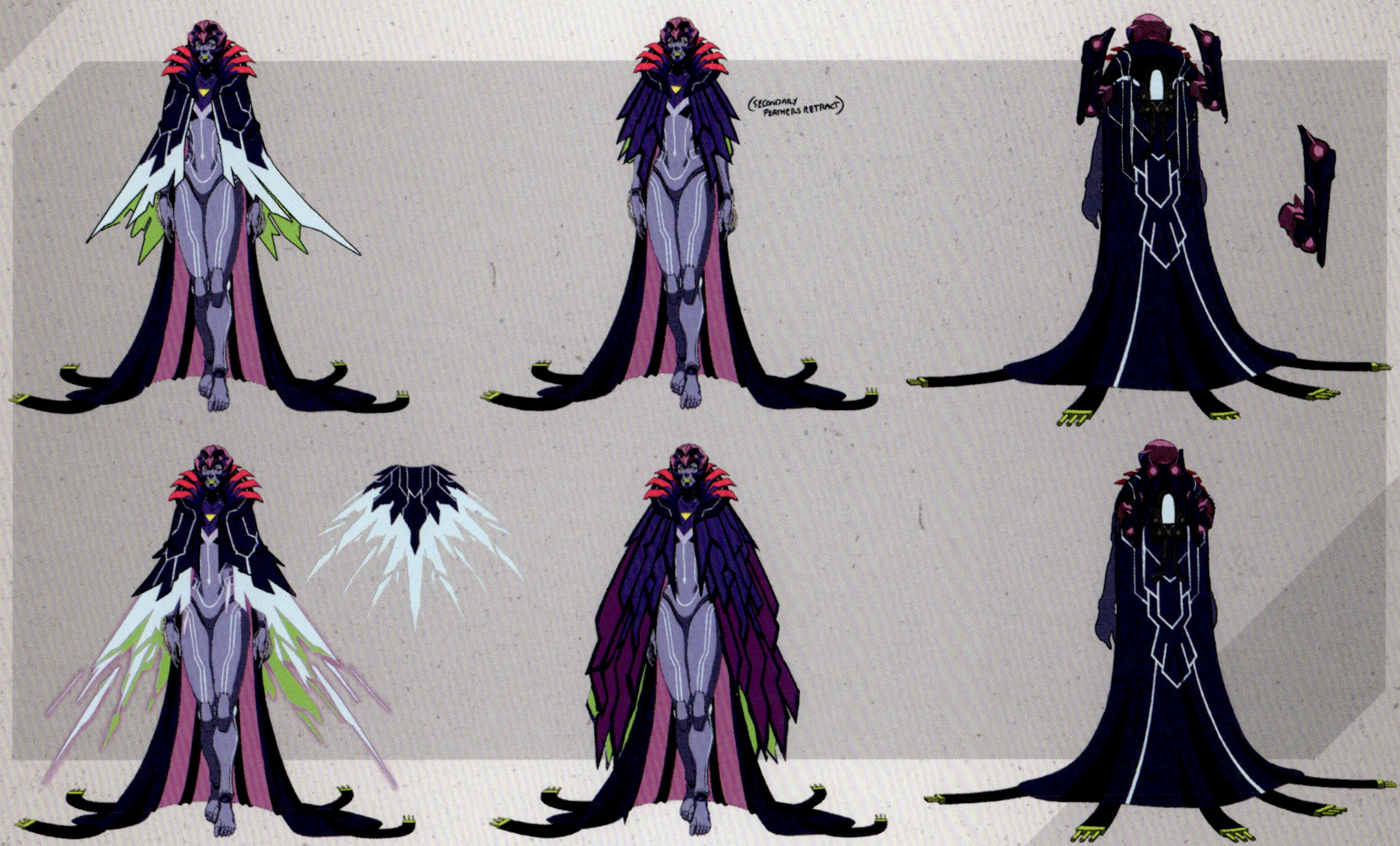

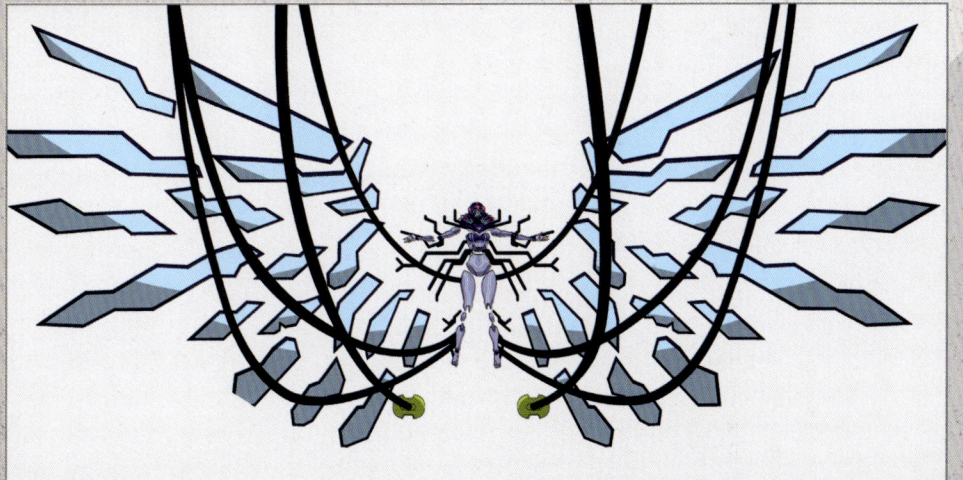

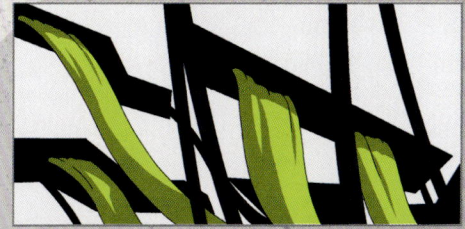

Motherboard integrates herself into Castle Grayskull, allowing her to download its safeguarded secrets. Ultimately, this proves to be her undoing, as the process leaves her completely defenseless and gives Skeletek a chance to "download" her head.

VILLAINS \\ 63

TECHNO-TITAN

The twisted and alien forms of the Techno-Titans are relics from a bygone age left slumbering under the mantle of Eternia. Each one is unique yet equally ancient. We referenced obelisks, effigies, and ruins, combined with metal limbs that resembled bone and carapace, so that they could be equally grotesque and cosmic.

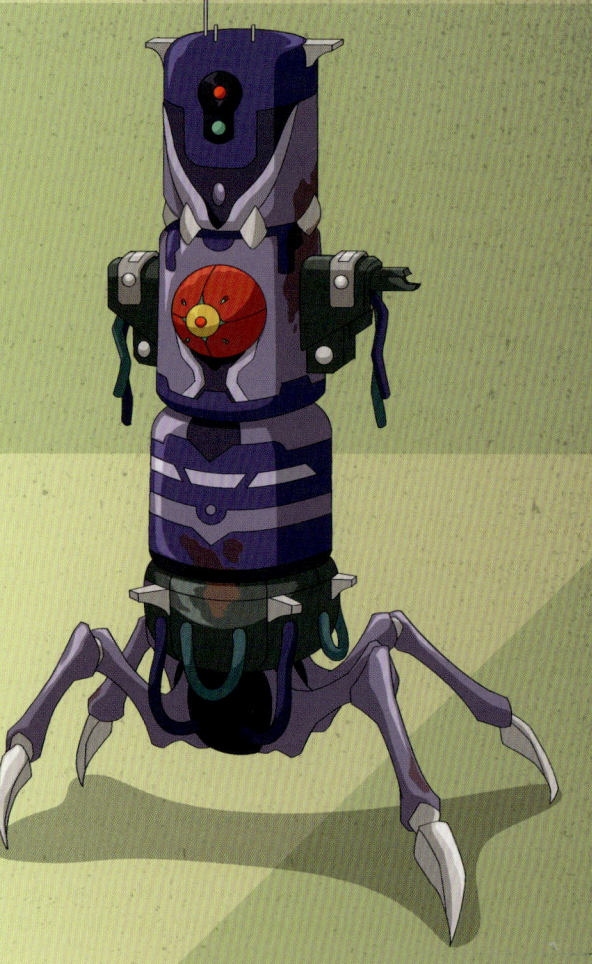

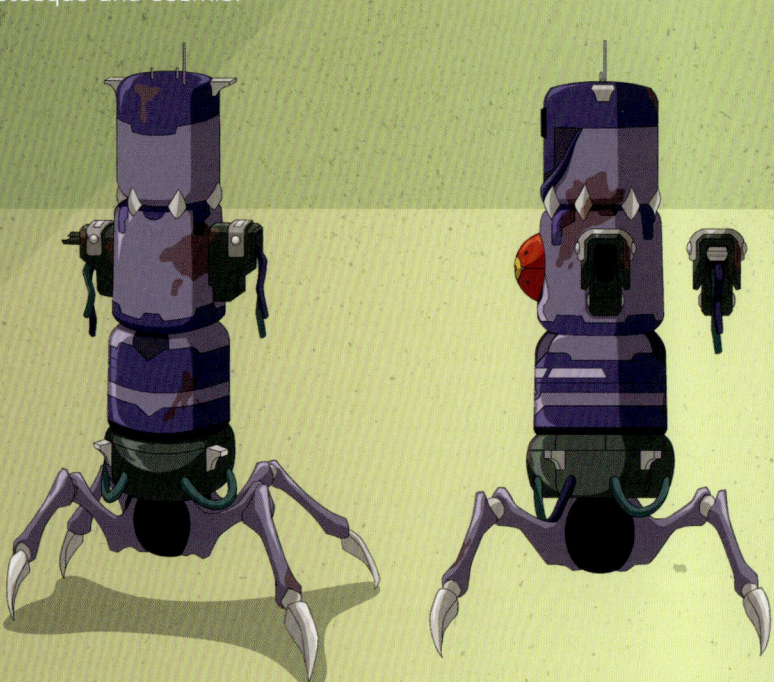

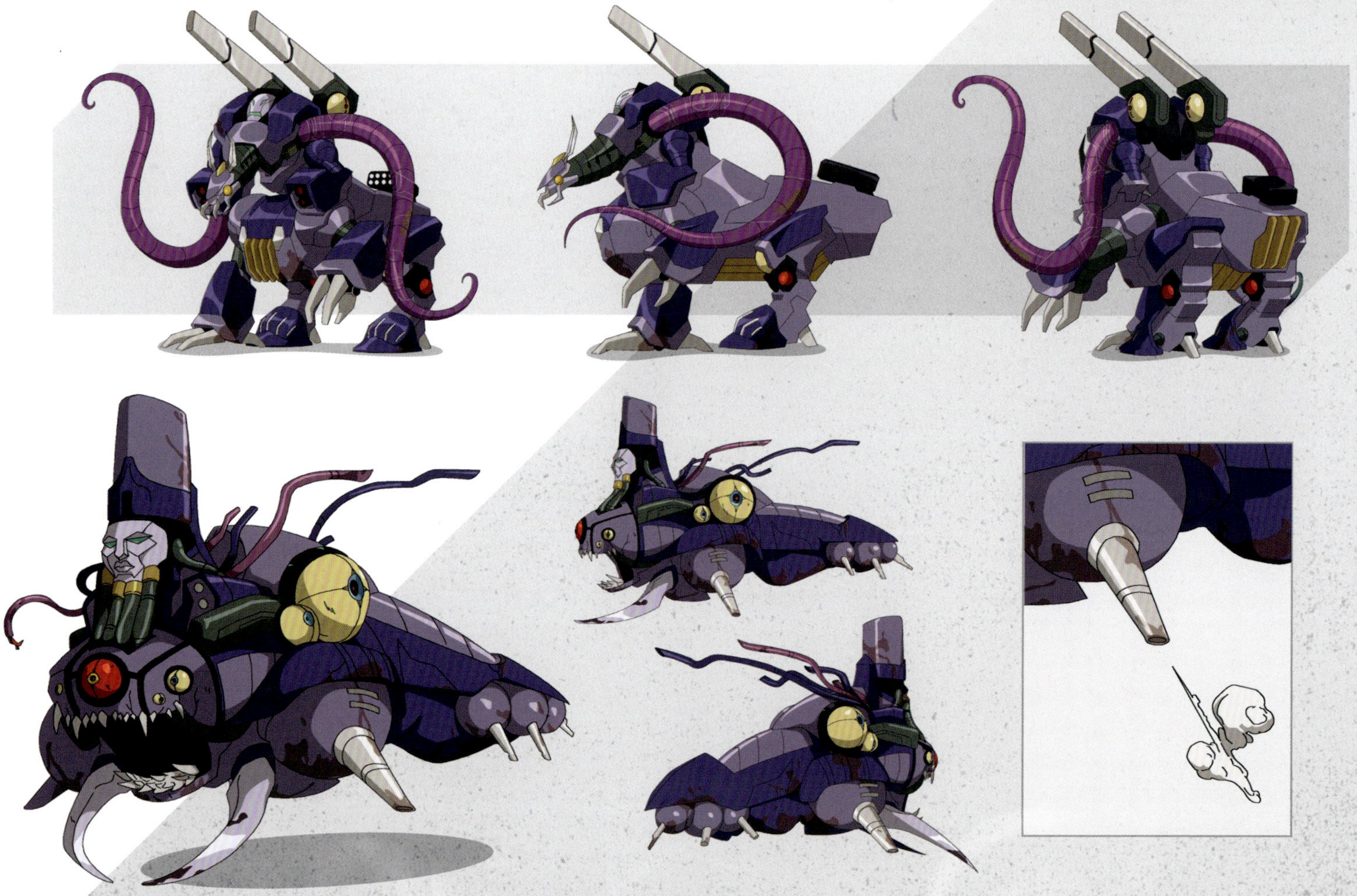

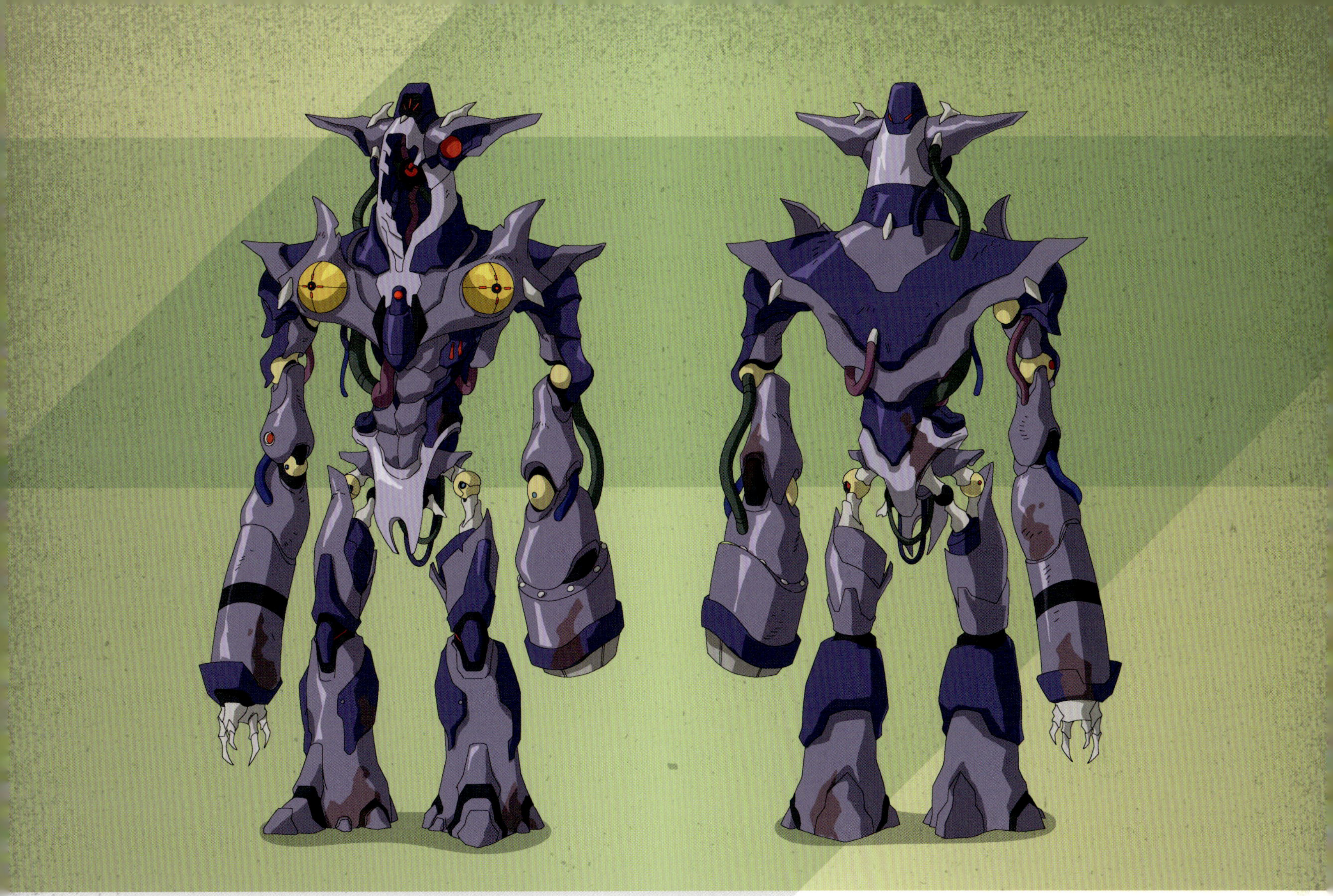

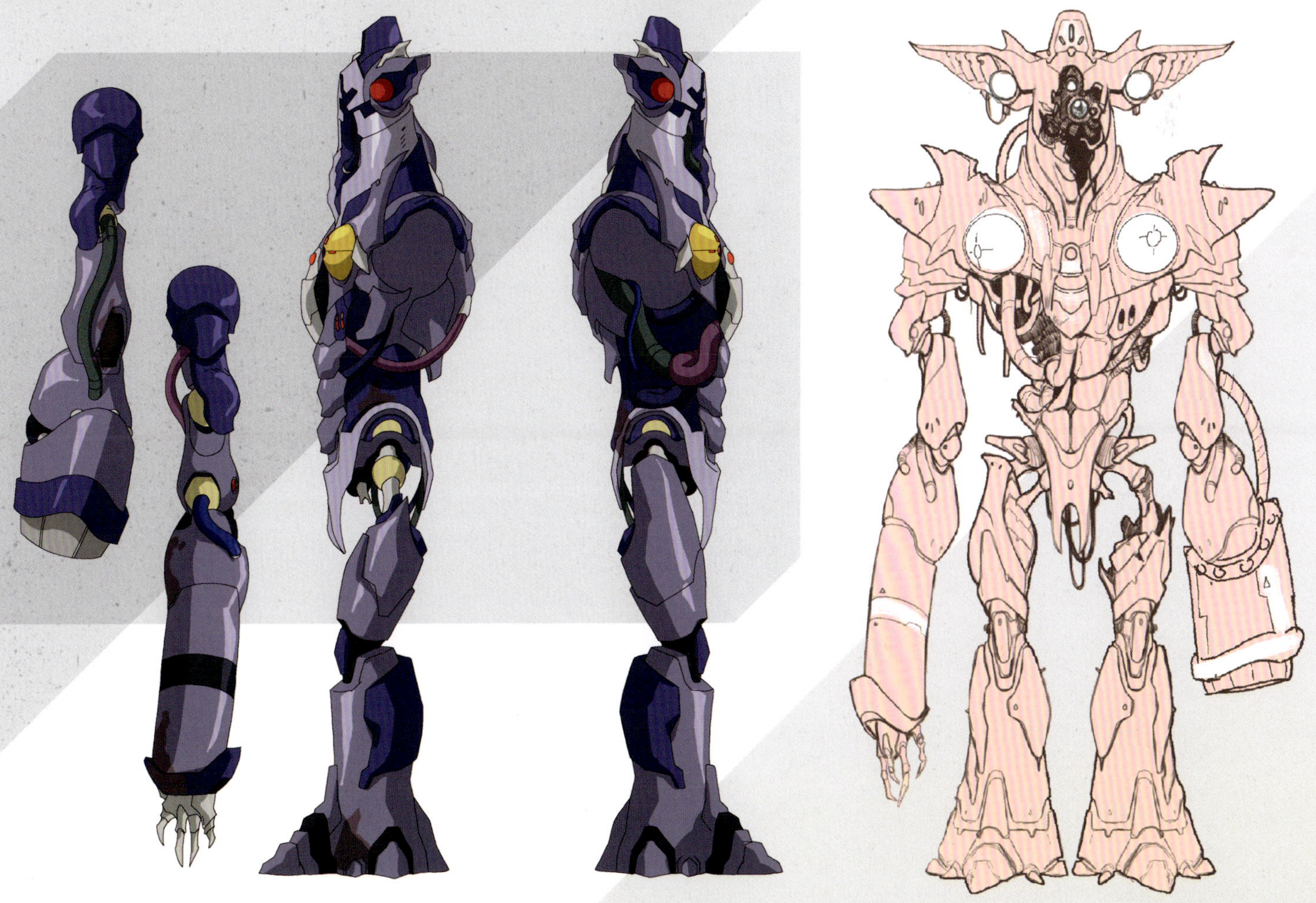

VILLAINS \\ 65

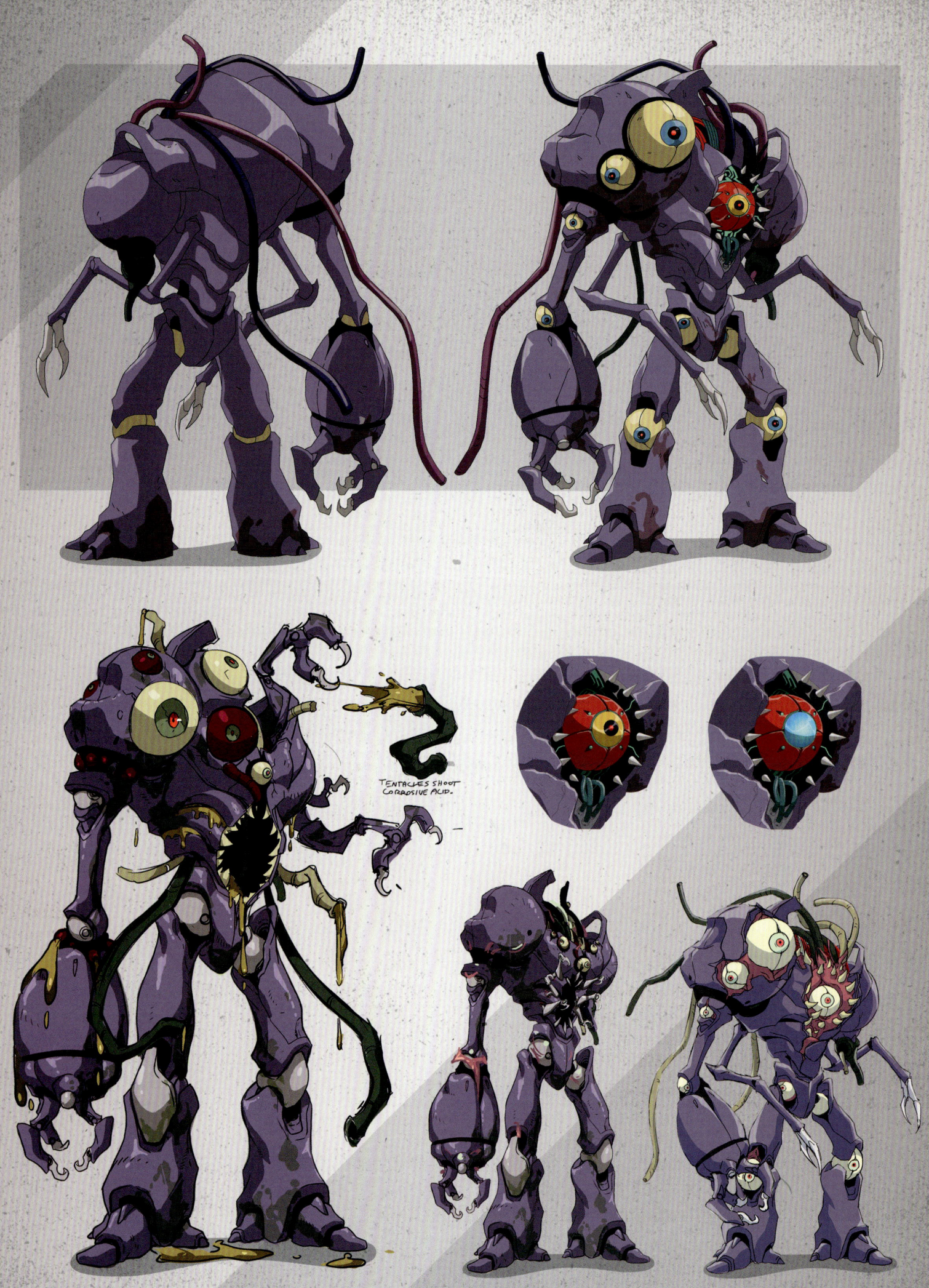

WEBSTOR

Webstor returns this season with a few new technological upgrades to match the other members of Motherboard's cult! He gains a set of controllable metallic spider arms to match his already-arachnoid appearance and now rocks a couple of pairs of entirely digitized eyes.

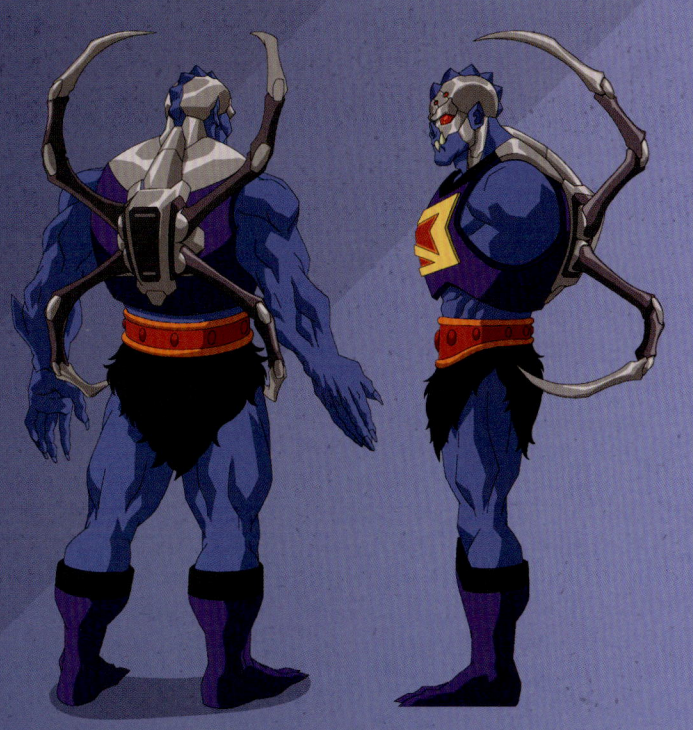
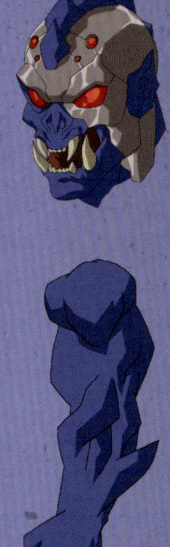
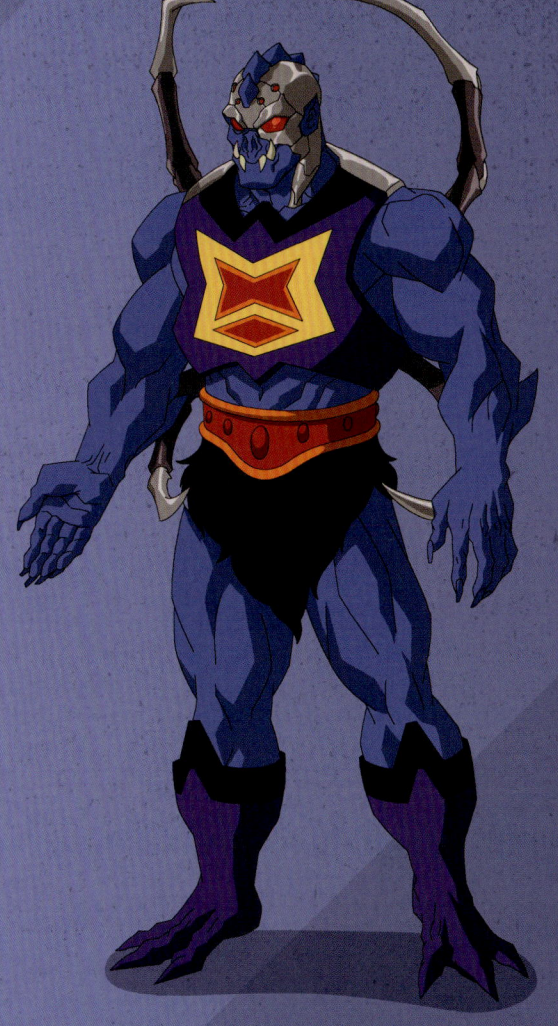

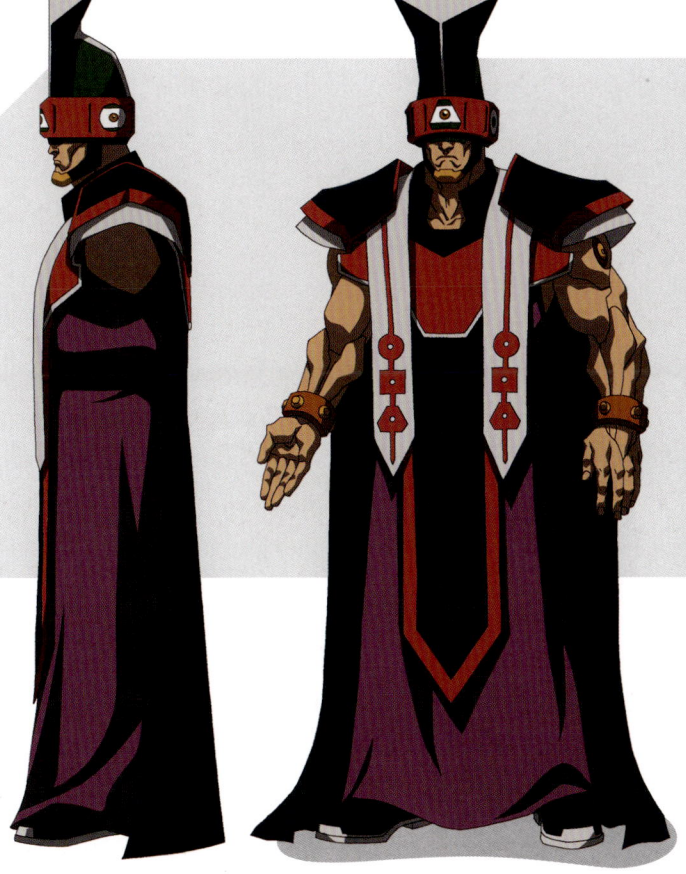
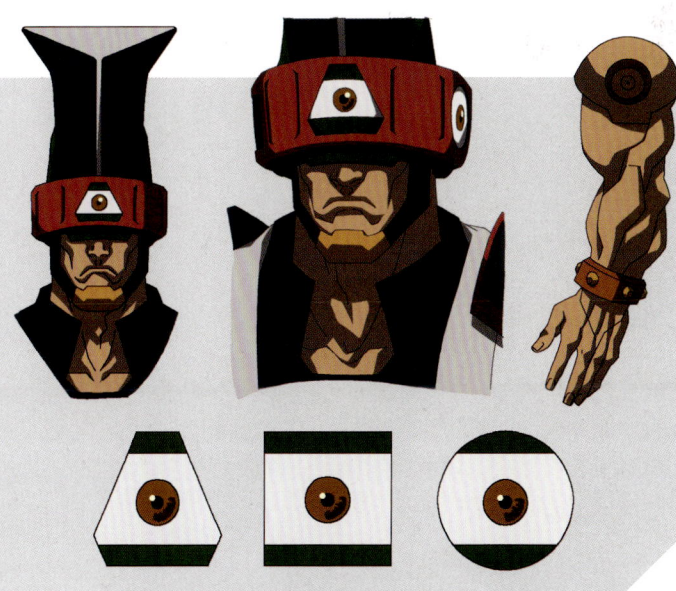

TRI-KLOPS

Tri-Klops resumes his reign as high priest of Motherboard's technocult, but his role is minimized this season while under her direct supervision. Either way, he continues to rock his modified miter.

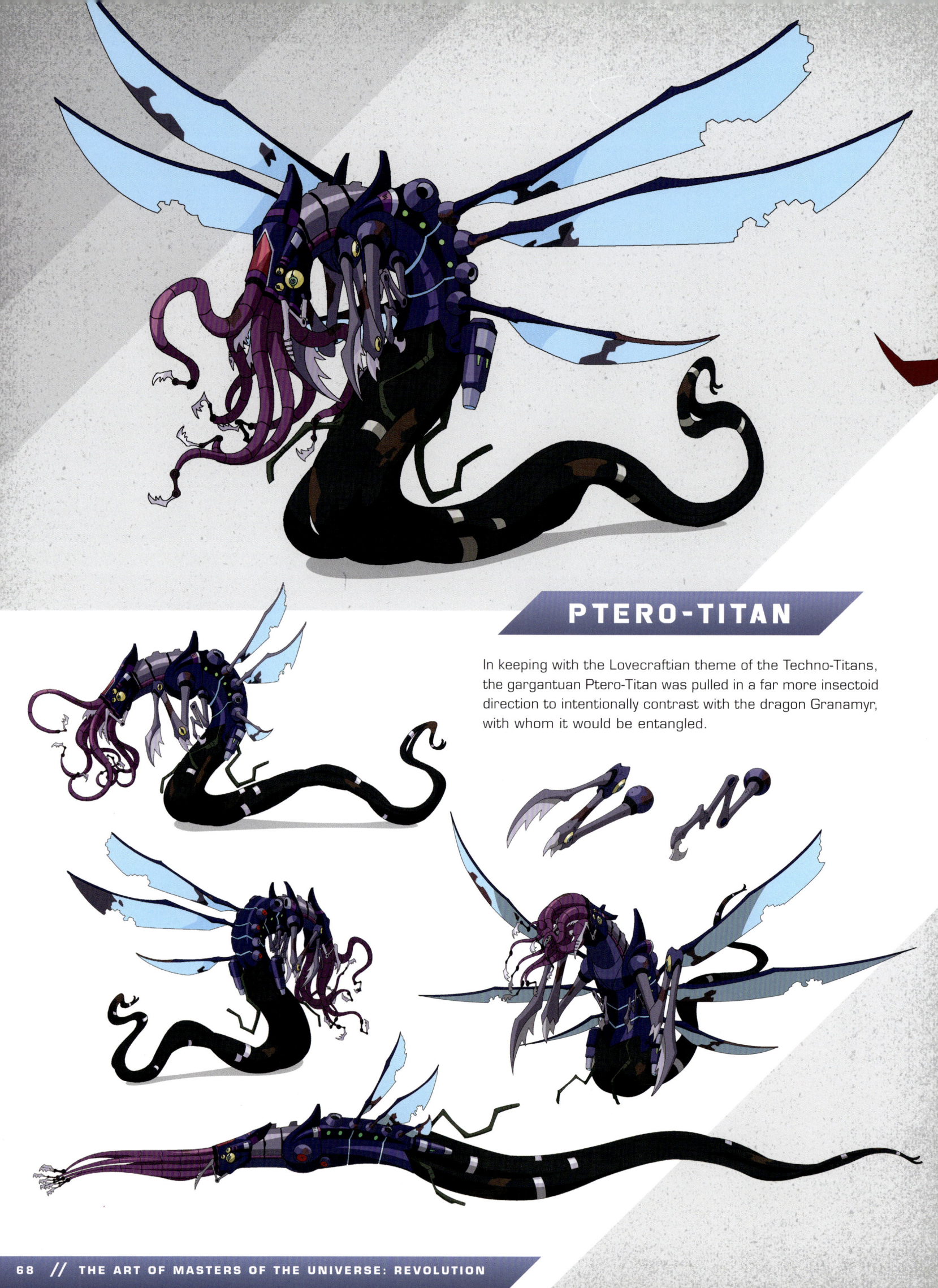

PTERO-TITAN

In keeping with the Lovecraftian theme of the Techno-Titans, the gargantuan Ptero-Titan was pulled in a far more insectoid direction to intentionally contrast with the dragon Granamyr, with whom it would be entangled.

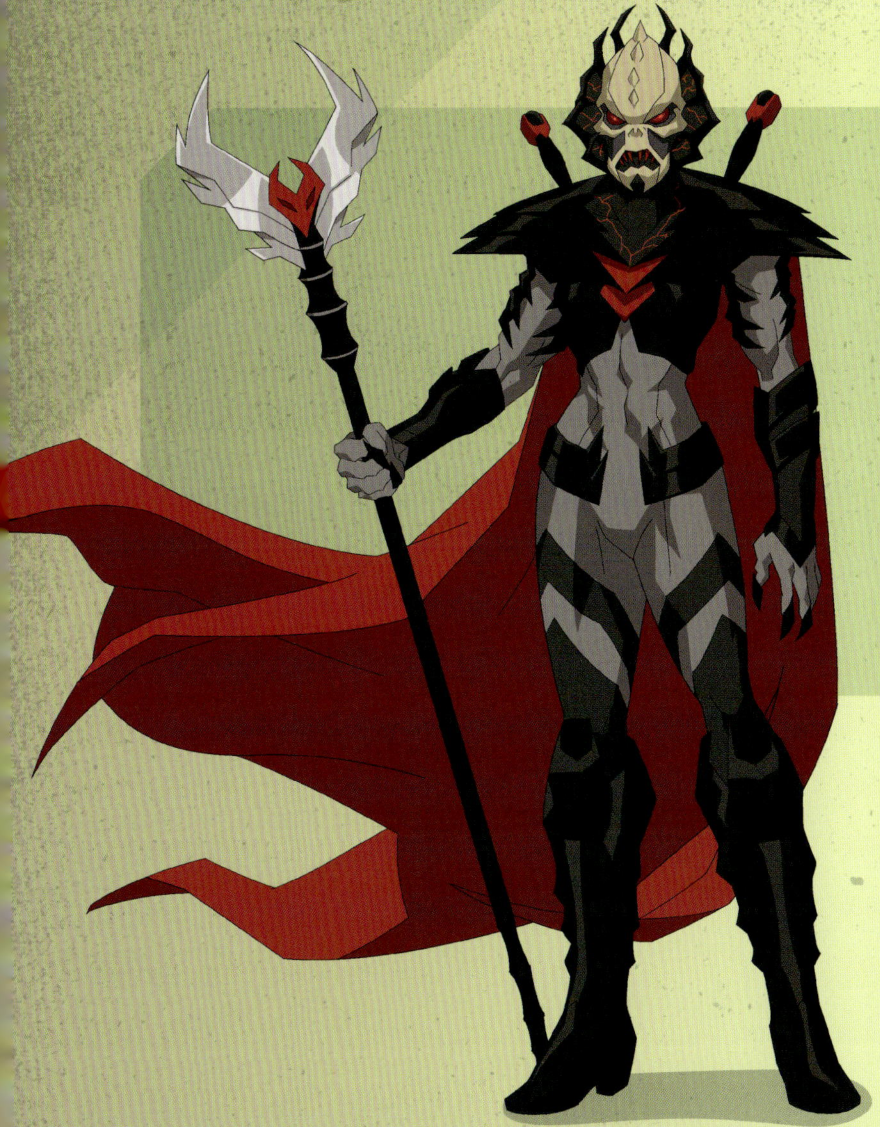

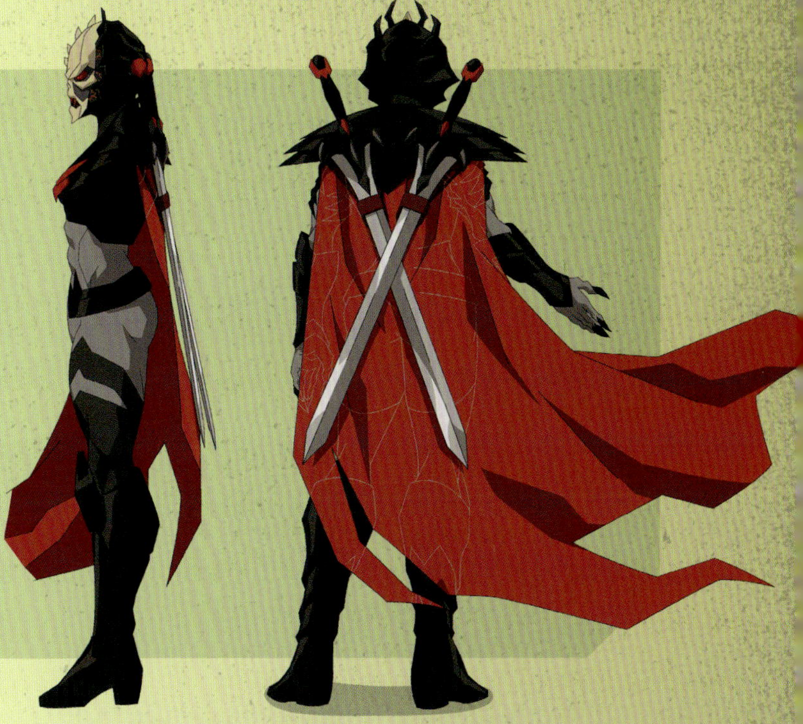

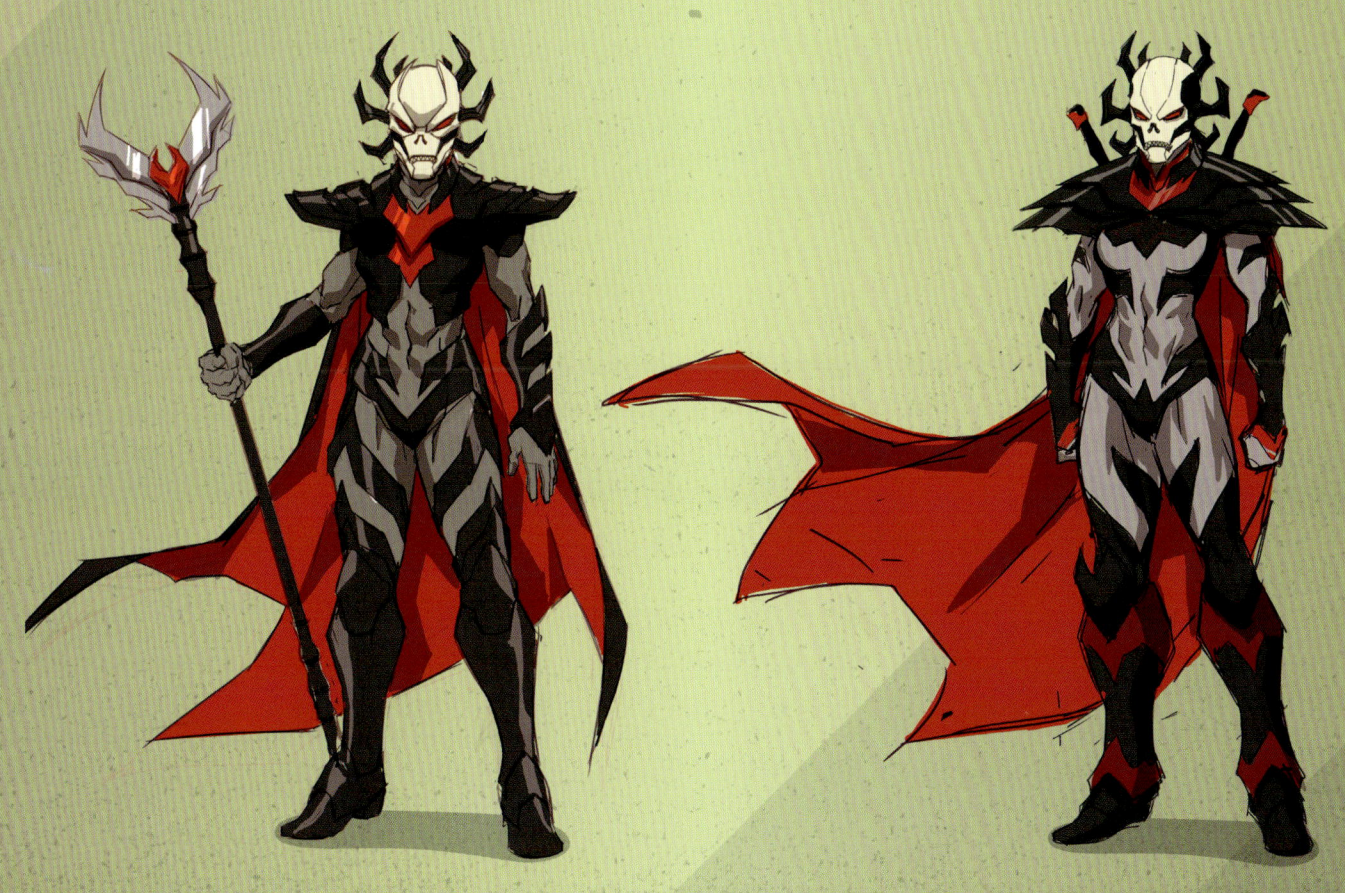

DESPARA

Though Despara's design is directly drawn from her counterpart in the comics, even we don't know who's behind the menacing mask. Whoever it is, they're completely devoted to Hordak and eager to inflict their vengeance upon those who dare oppose the Horde.

VILLAINS \\ 69

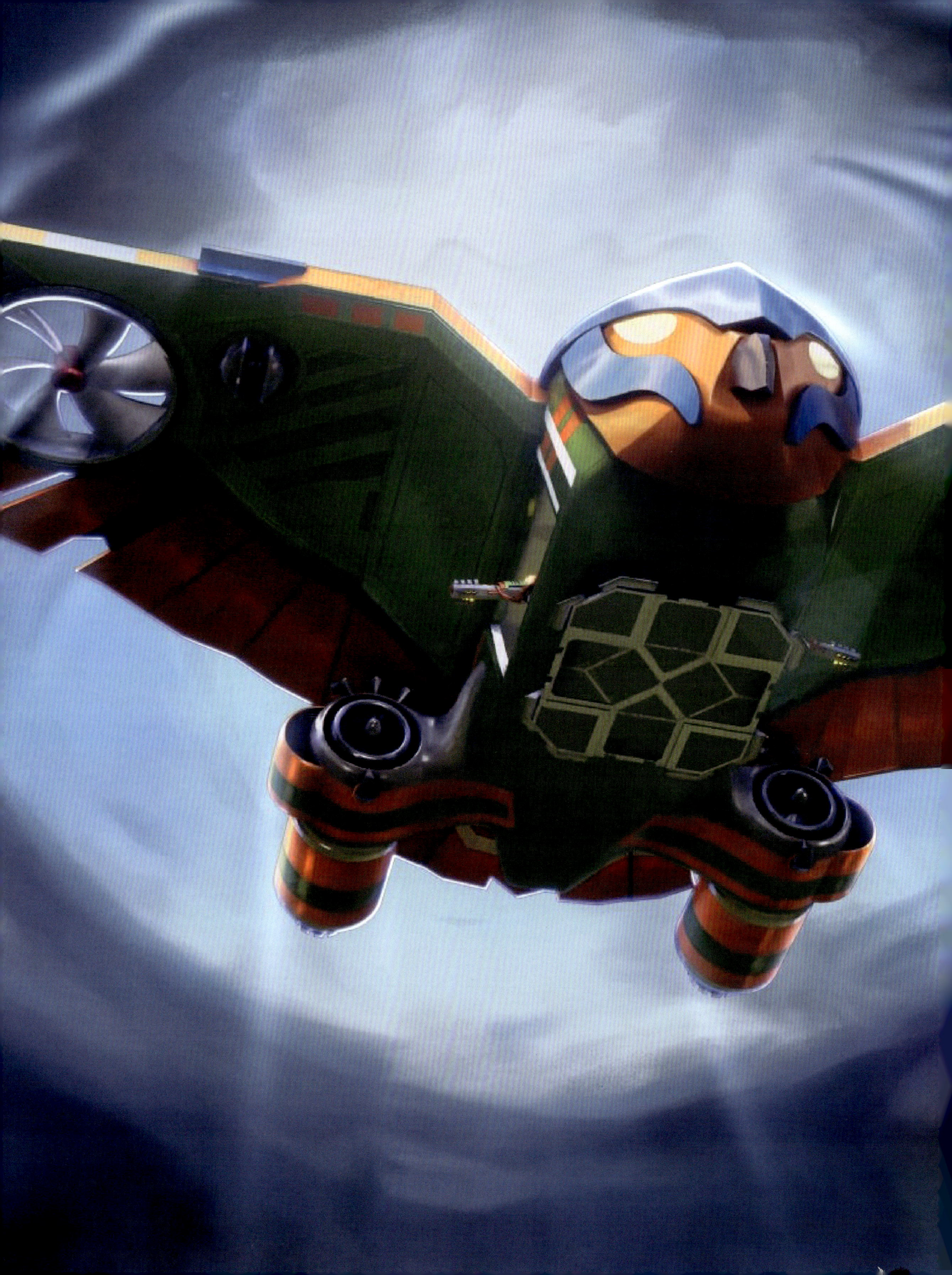

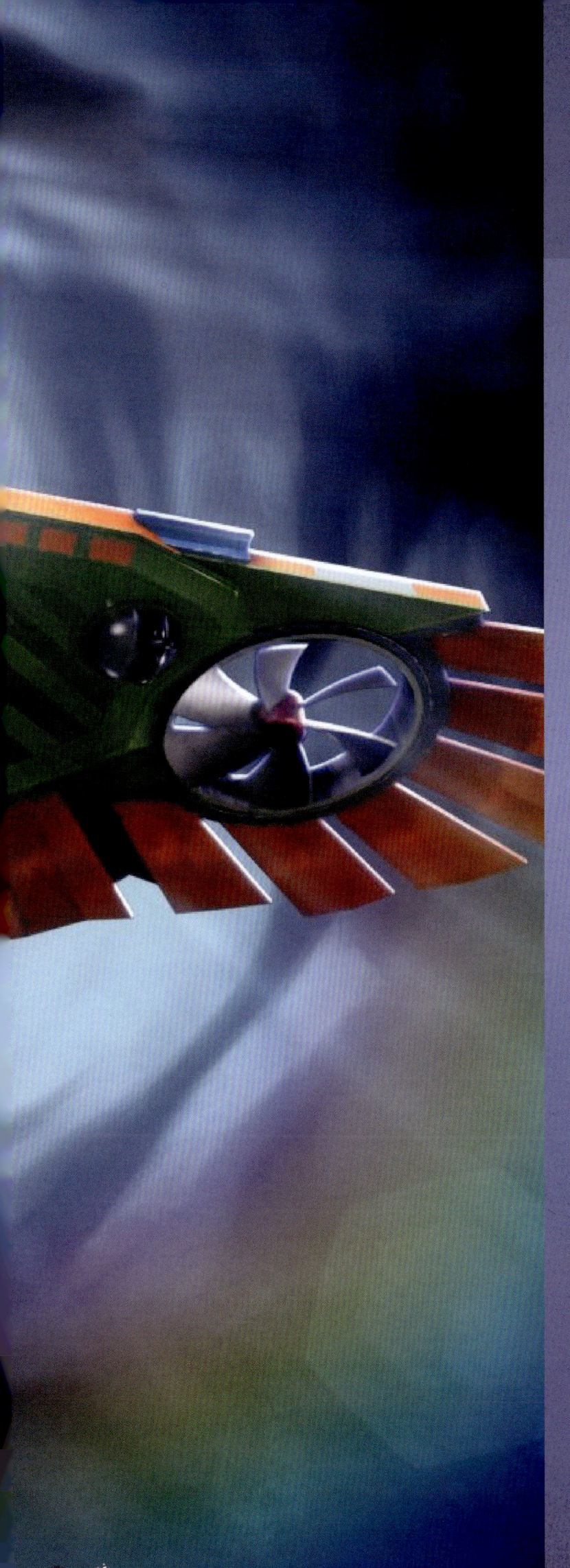

CHAPTER 3
VEHICLES AND ARTIFACTS

NO GOOD ACTION FIGURE IS COMPLETE without a set of matching accessories! As *Revolution* gave our favorite heroes and villains massive upgrades, we knew each aspect of their arsenal would need a few power-ups to match. Magical weapons shape-shift and transform, new classes of aircraft soar effortlessly through the sky, and technological tools provide enhancements beyond even normal Masters of the Universe standards!

This season, the battle between magic and technology extends over centuries and between planets! Each side has its own unique aesthetic identity—the sleek but decaying Gar technology, the mysterious magical artifacts of the Tri-Sorceress, the futuristic might of the Horde, and of course, the classic animal motifs of Eternia. It was vital that we kept a sense of childhood whimsy and wish fulfillment in each design—every artifact should look just as much at home in a toy box as it does on a television screen.

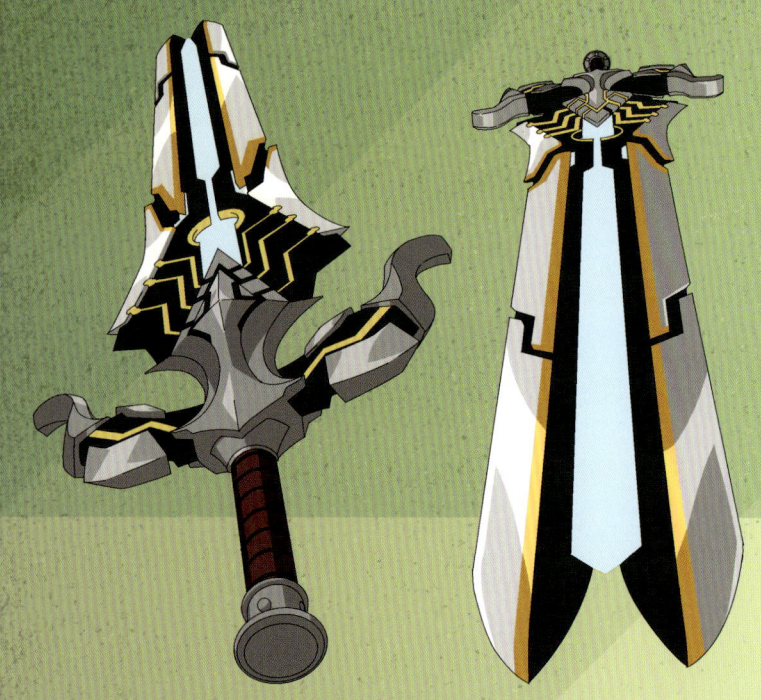

POWER SWORD

We didn't want to veer too far away from the Power Sword's familiar silhouette, so we decided that the sword should transform. In its powered-up state, the weapon grows to the size of a great sword, and the blade splits down the middle, revealing a white-hot beam that shows magic and technology in perfect balance.

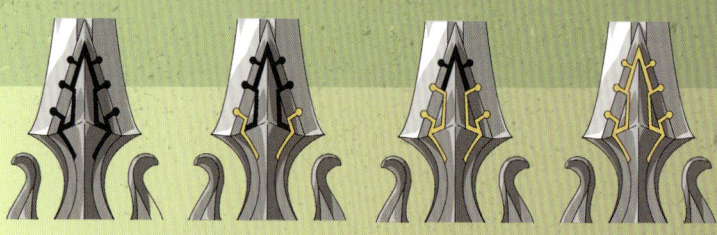

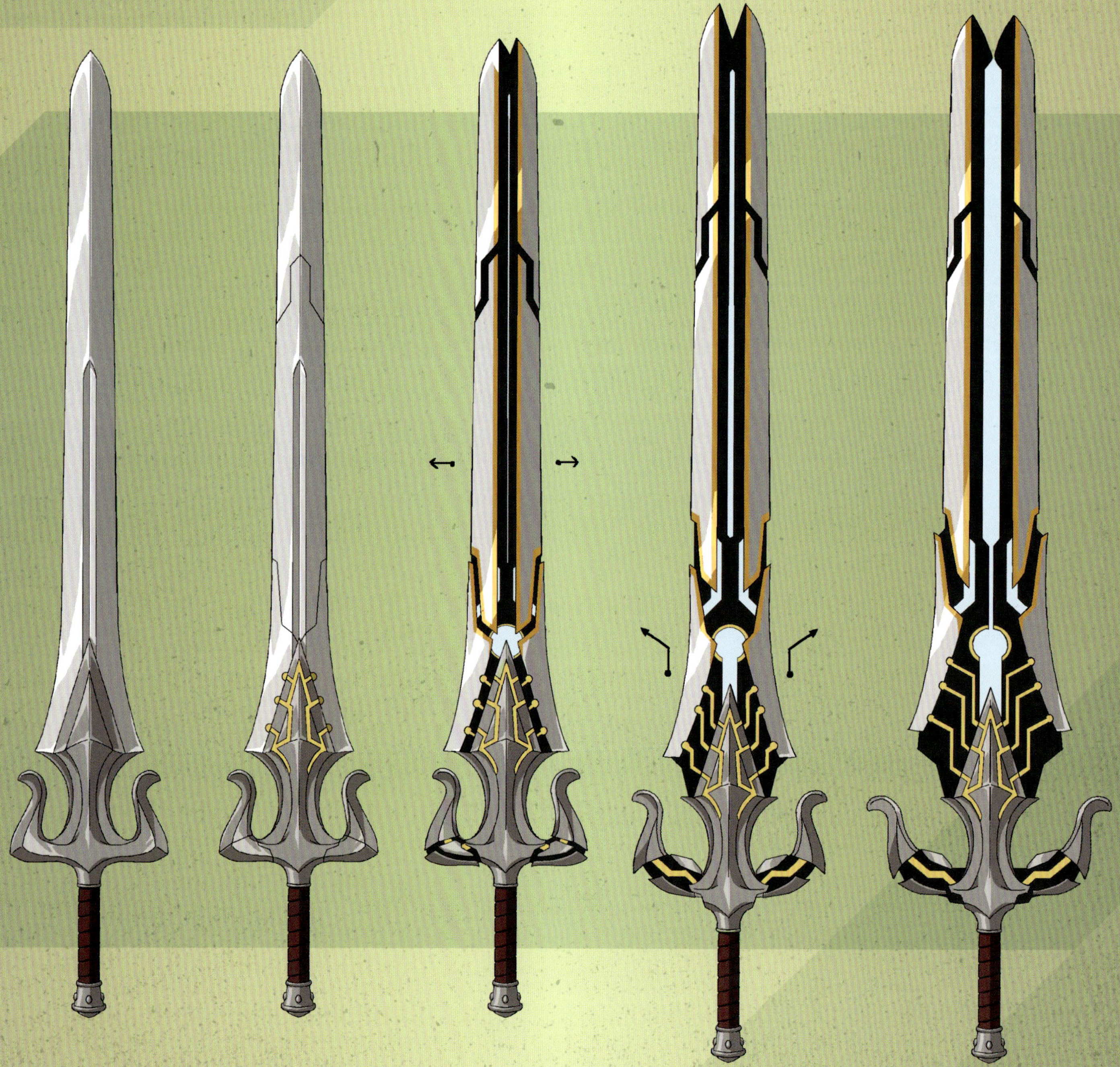

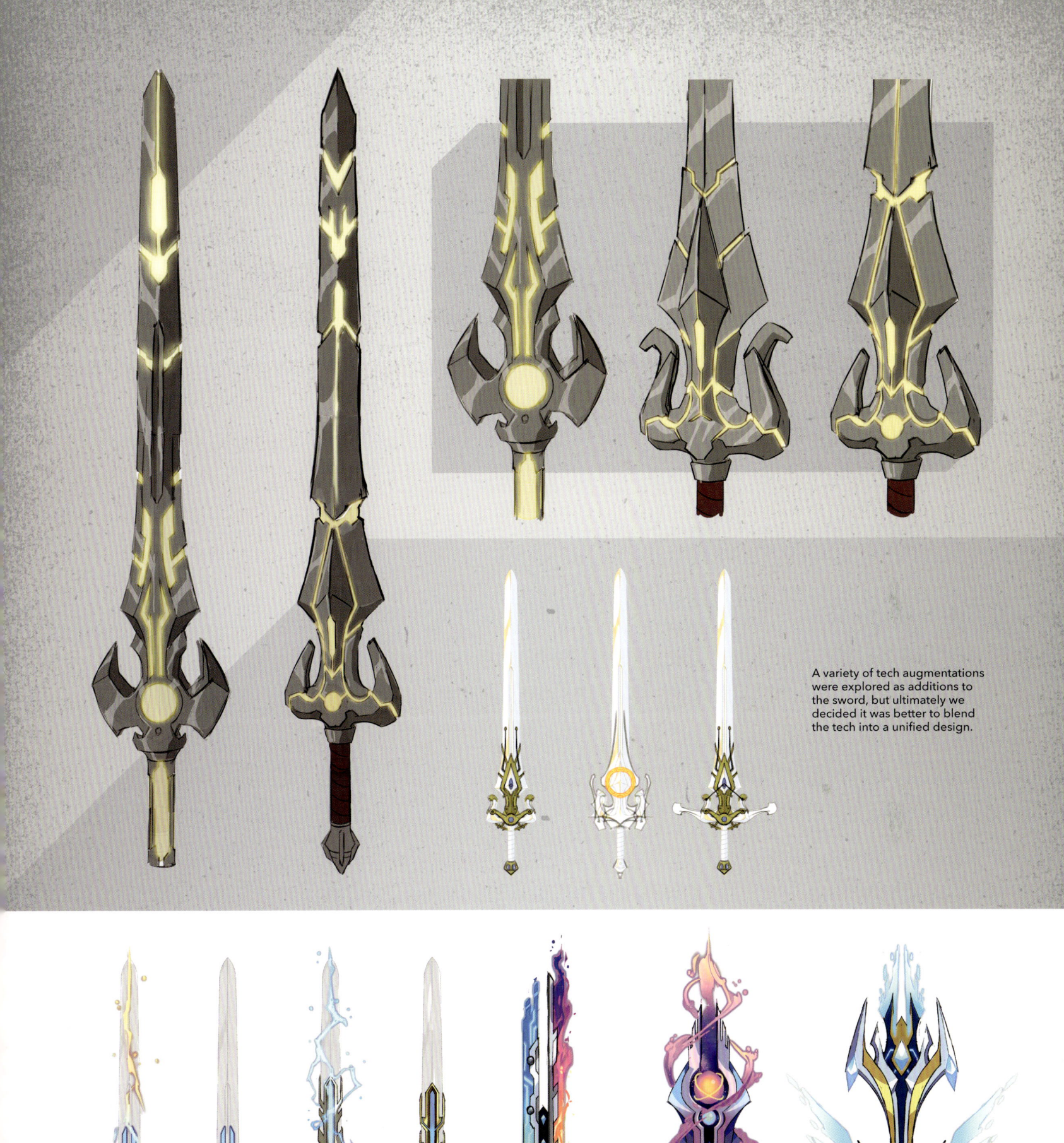

A variety of tech augmentations were explored as additions to the sword, but ultimately we decided it was better to blend the tech into a unified design.

VEHICLES AND ARTIFACTS

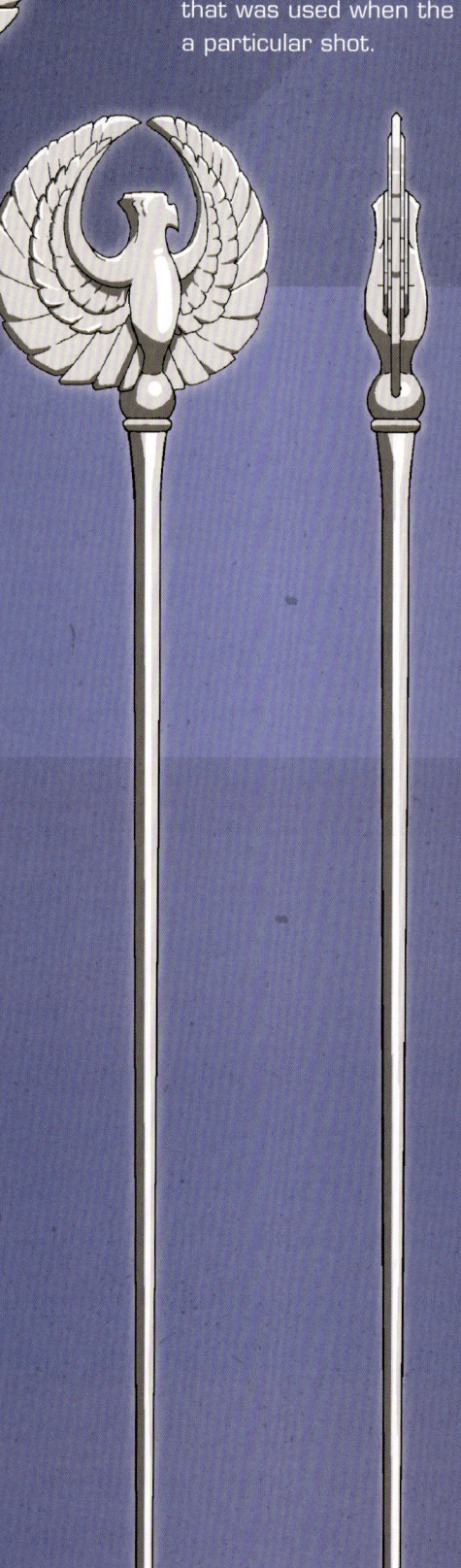

POWER STAFF

Teela finally wields the iconic Power Staff this season—passed down to her from her mother, the Sorceress. We didn't need to meddle much with its classic design—though we created a simplified variant that was used when the staff appeared further away or smaller in a particular shot.

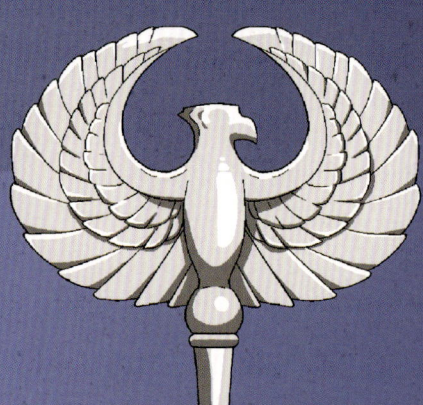

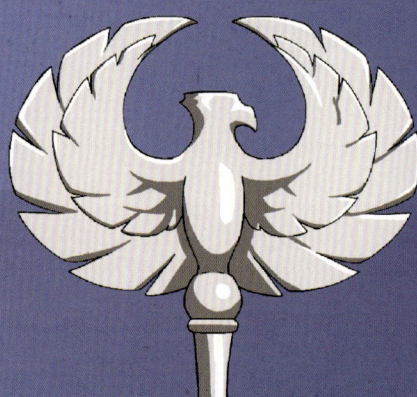

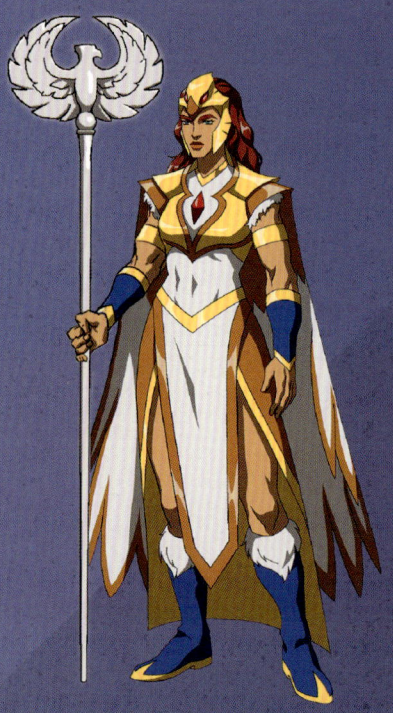

74 // THE ART OF MASTERS OF THE UNIVERSE: REVOLUTION

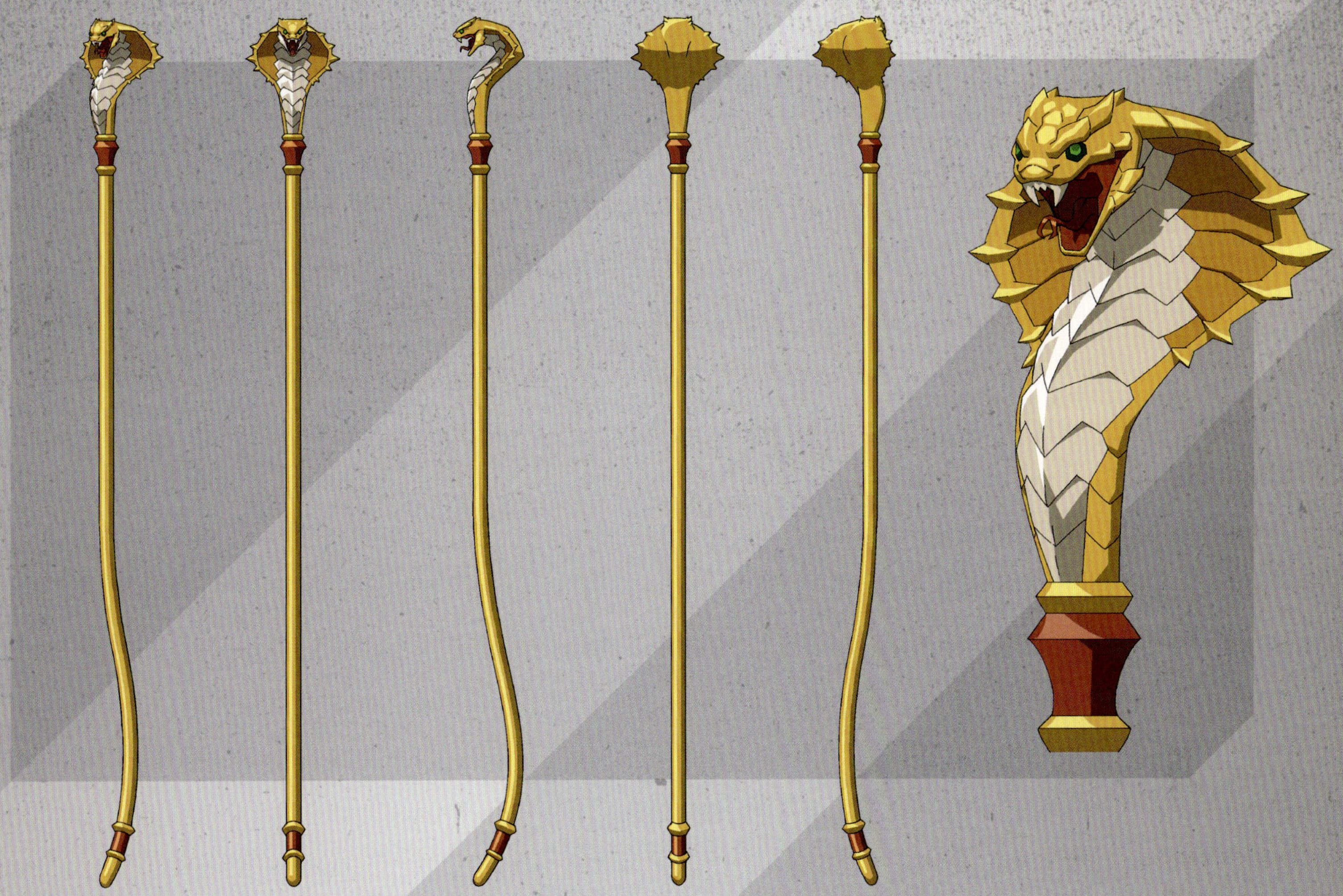

STAFF OF KA

The Staff of Ka represents Teela's new ability to wield snake magic, the energy representing passion, gifted by Granamyr. This staff draws inspiration from one of Teela's older toy designs, when the characters of Teela and the Goddess were combined into one figure. In those designs she is seen carrying the snake-like staff, as well as being decked out in cobra-themed armor, rather than her more current Captain of the Guard regalia.

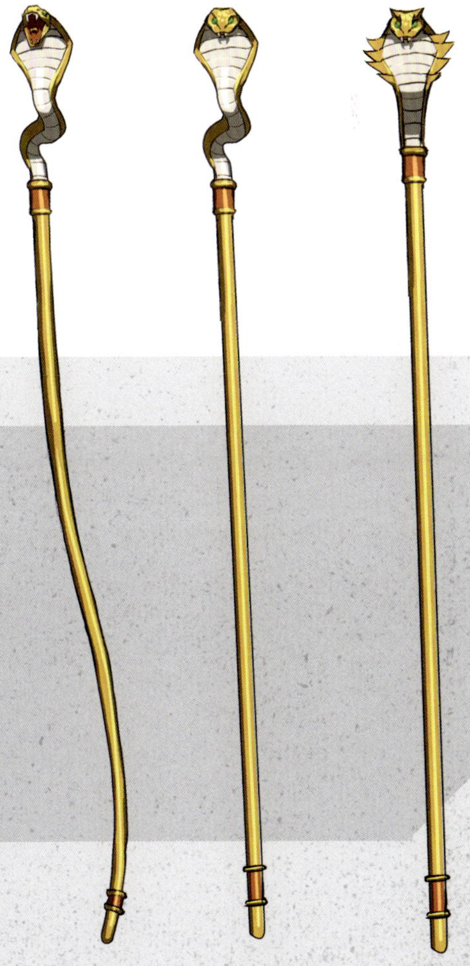

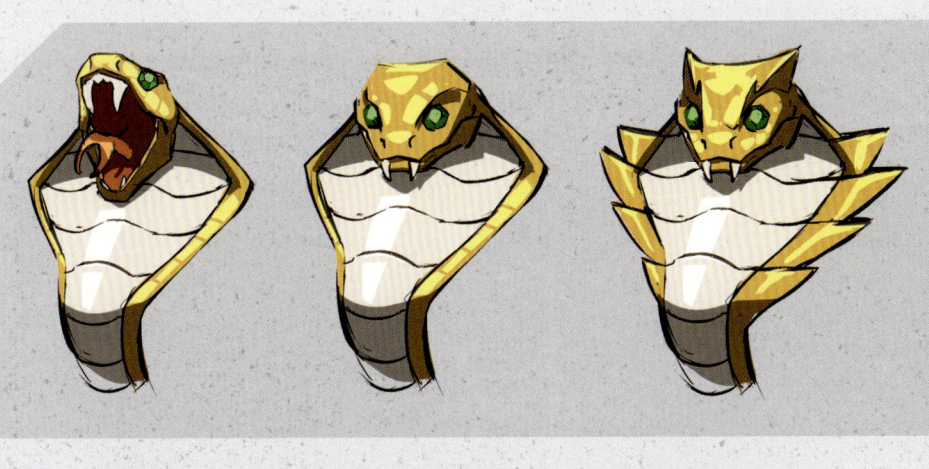

While the general shape and palette for the staff were chosen early, the design team went through several iterations to nail down the snake's pose and defining details.

VEHICLES AND ARTIFACTS \\ 75

TRI-SORCERESS STAFF

It was difficult to settle on a design for the Tri-Sorceress Staff that presented all three of the old gods without becoming overcomplicated. We explored having the lion's head from the central Preternian tower in the center but ultimately decided to represent Baelon through the use of blue and white metal accents.

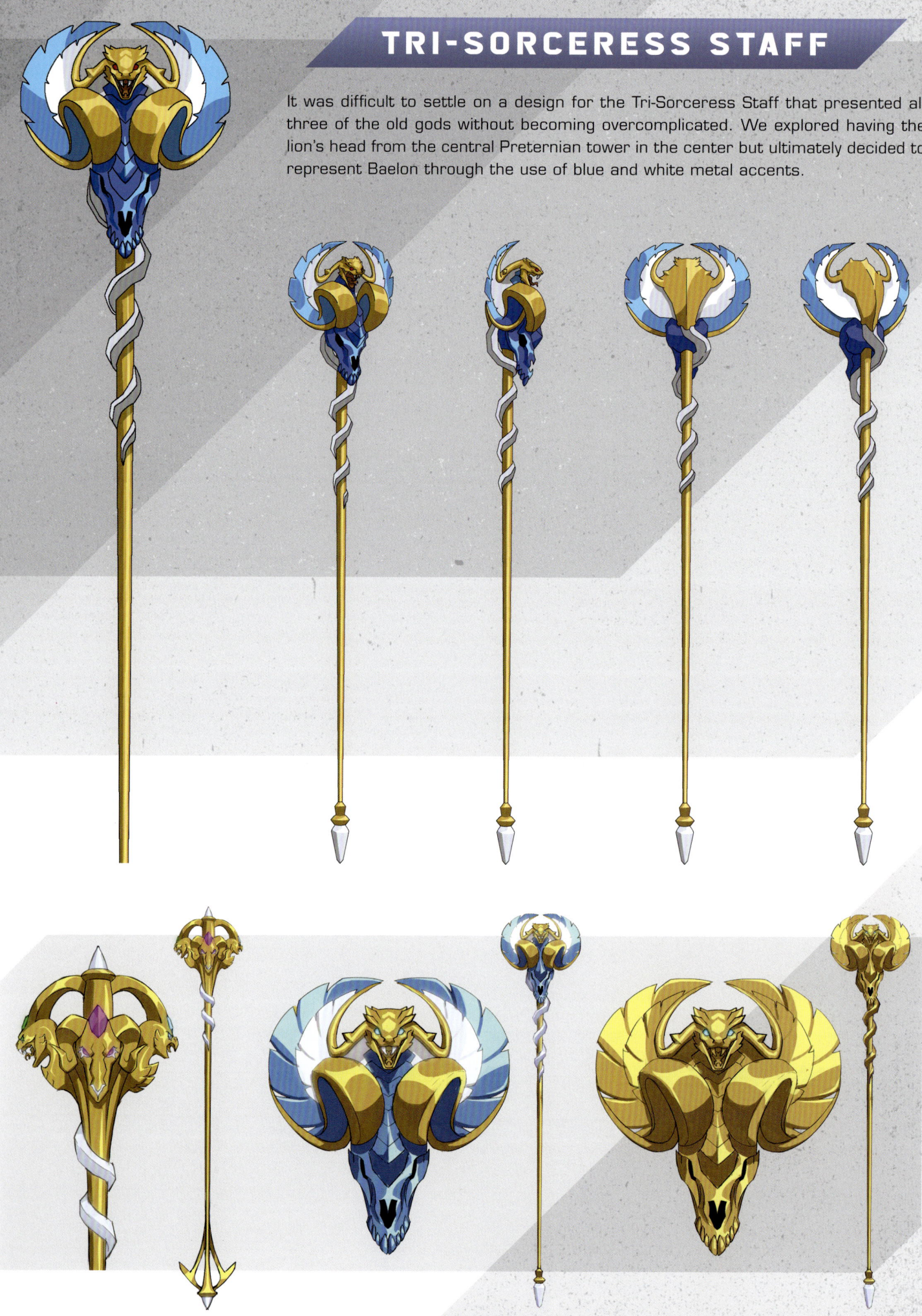

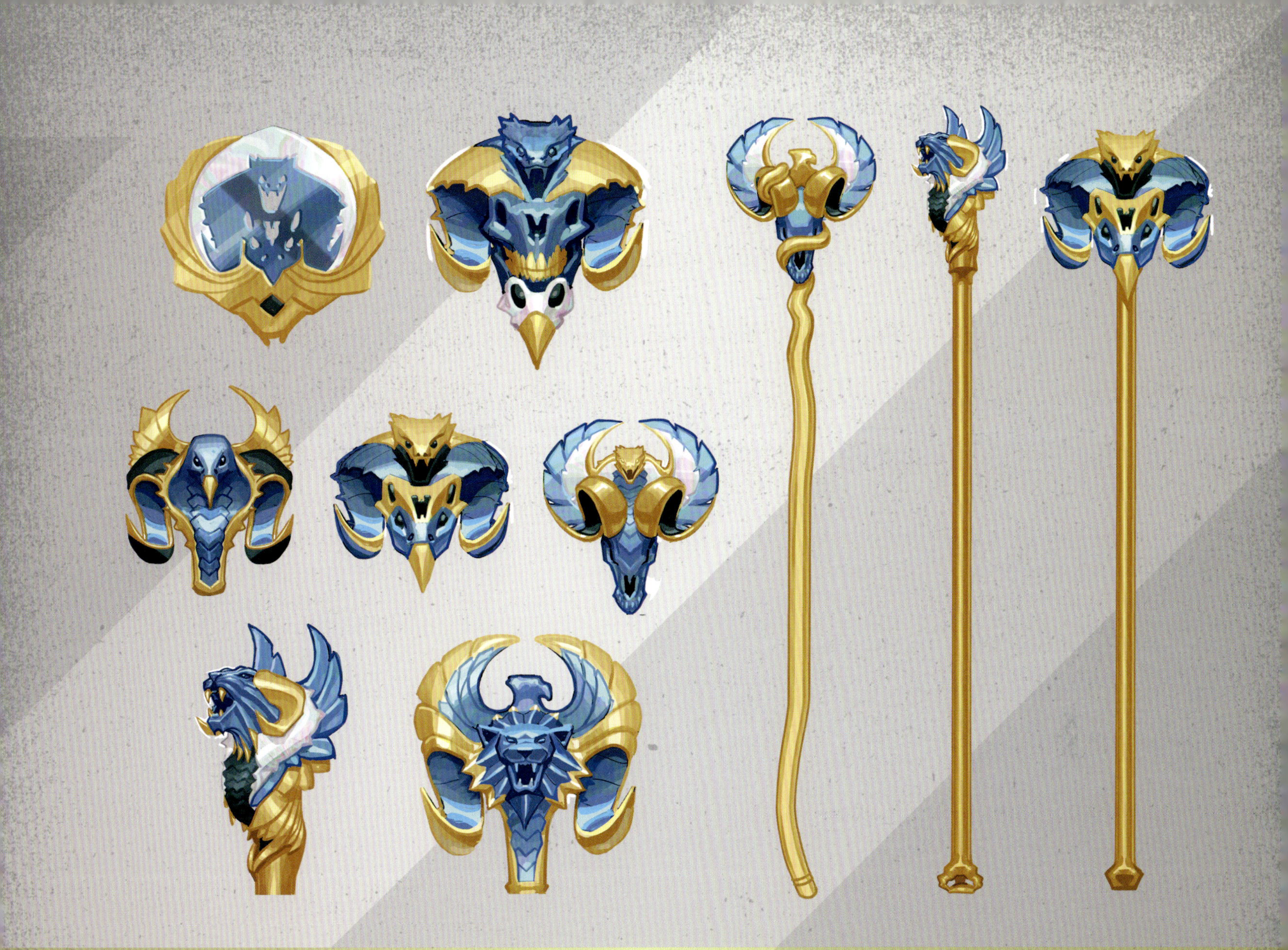

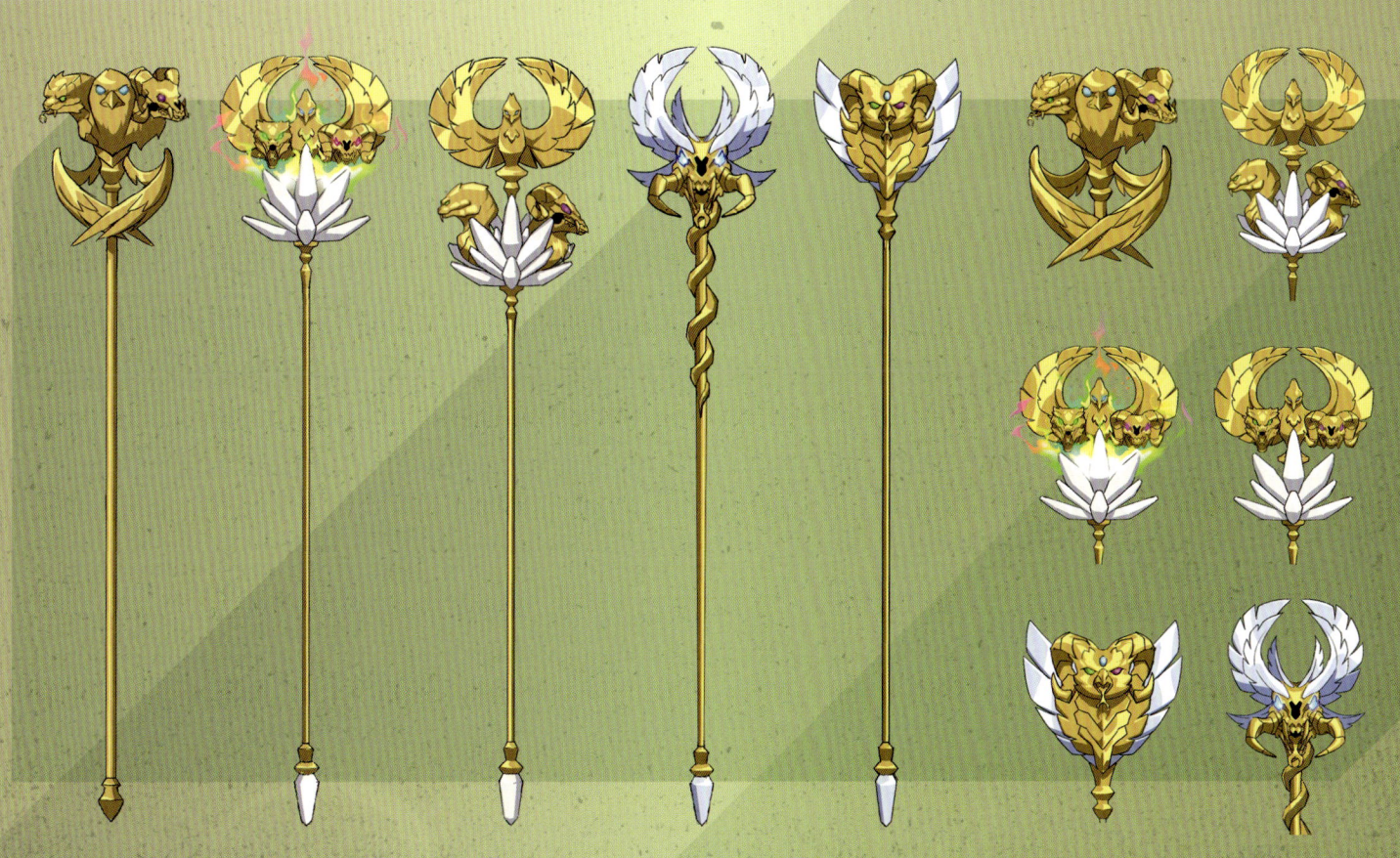

VEHICLES AND ARTIFACTS

SOUL FIST

When thinking of how to visualize Clamp Champ's and Fisto's souls, we didn't need to look any further than their iconic gear. Covered in ghostly flames, these weapons seem even more imposing in death than they were in life. And as Scare Glow demonstrated, they can still pack a real punch!

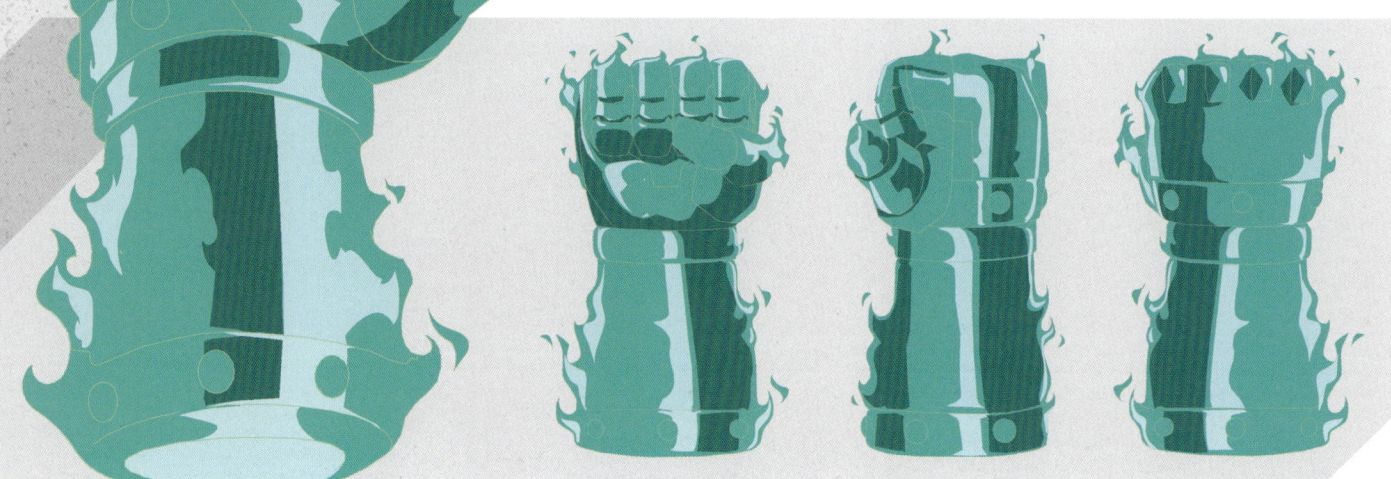

SOUL CLAMP

Scare Glow is able to wield both Clamp Champ's and Fisto's souls as weapons, transforming himself into a towering monster. However, once He-Man frees them from Scare Glow's grasp, they shift back into their base forms, unharmed. Initially, their souls were going to be involved further in the quest for Preternia's return.

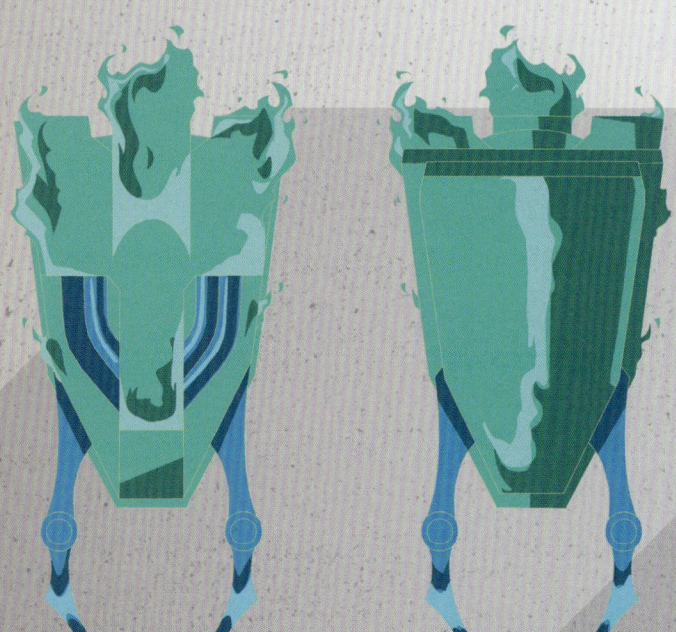

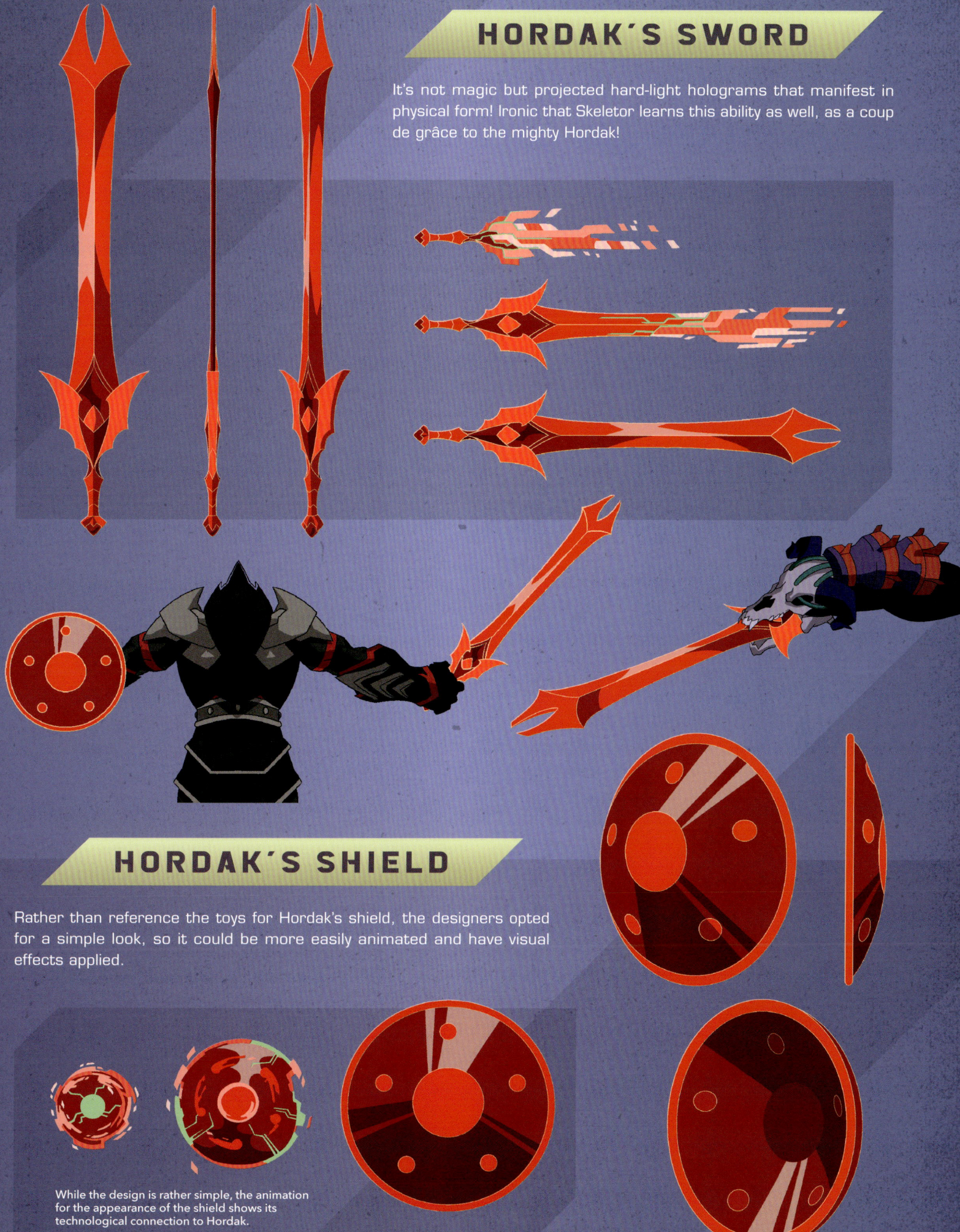

HORDAK'S SWORD

It's not magic but projected hard-light holograms that manifest in physical form! Ironic that Skeletor learns this ability as well, as a coup de grâce to the mighty Hordak!

HORDAK'S SHIELD

Rather than reference the toys for Hordak's shield, the designers opted for a simple look, so it could be more easily animated and have visual effects applied.

While the design is rather simple, the animation for the appearance of the shield shows its technological connection to Hordak.

VEHICLES AND ARTIFACTS \\ 79

HORDAK'S STAFF

Hordak doesn't bring out his staff lightly, and its appearance signifies that he's getting serious. The nanobots swarming within the device seep into his body, providing additional mass that facilitates his transformation into his battle form. This also strengthens Hordak's technomorph abilities. Though called the Magik Staff by some, our version is pure technology.

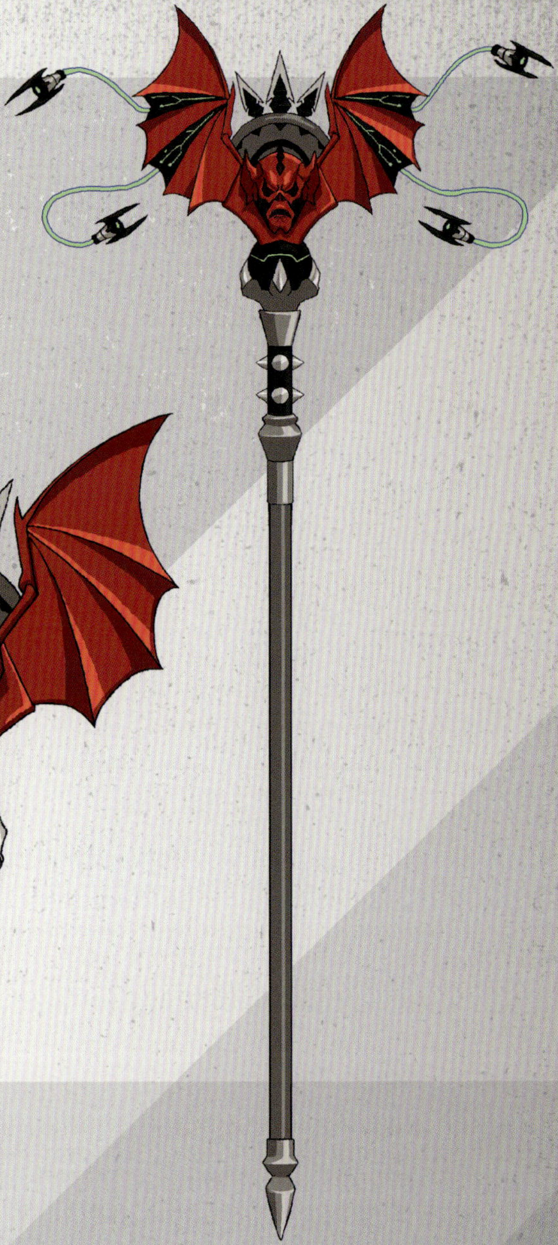

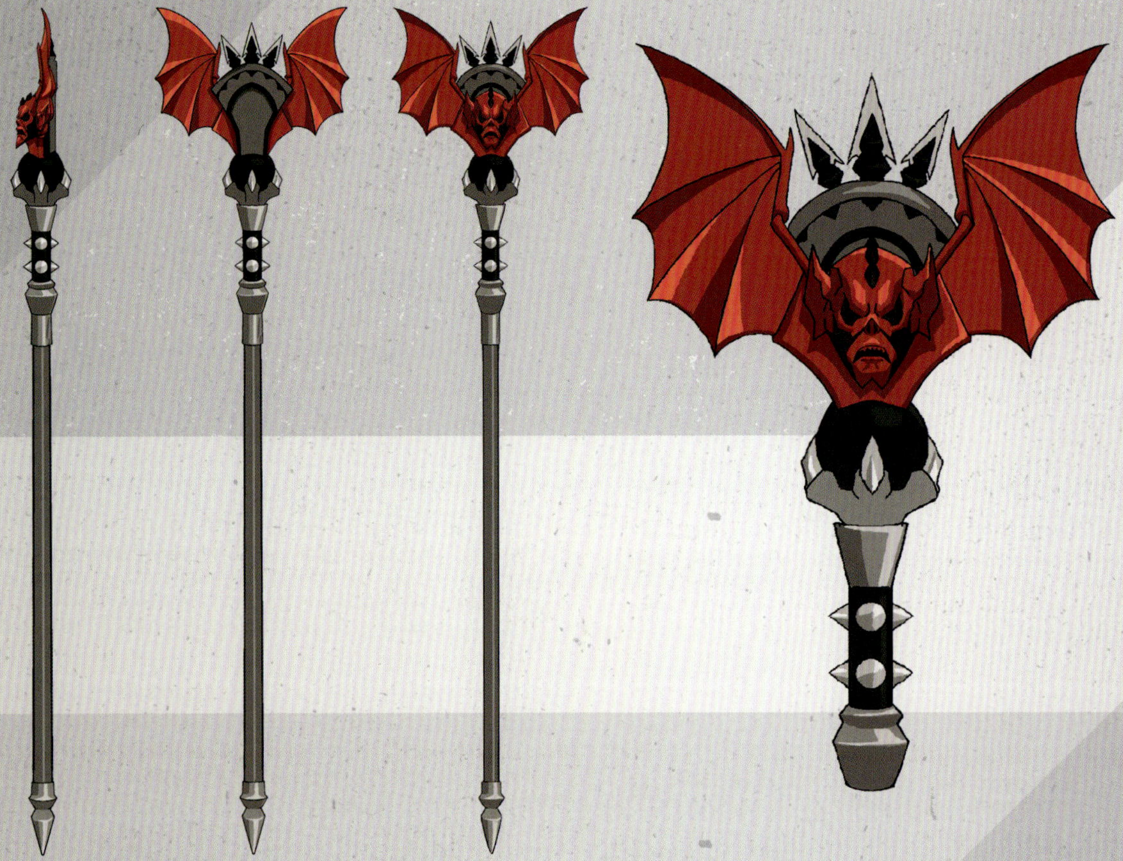

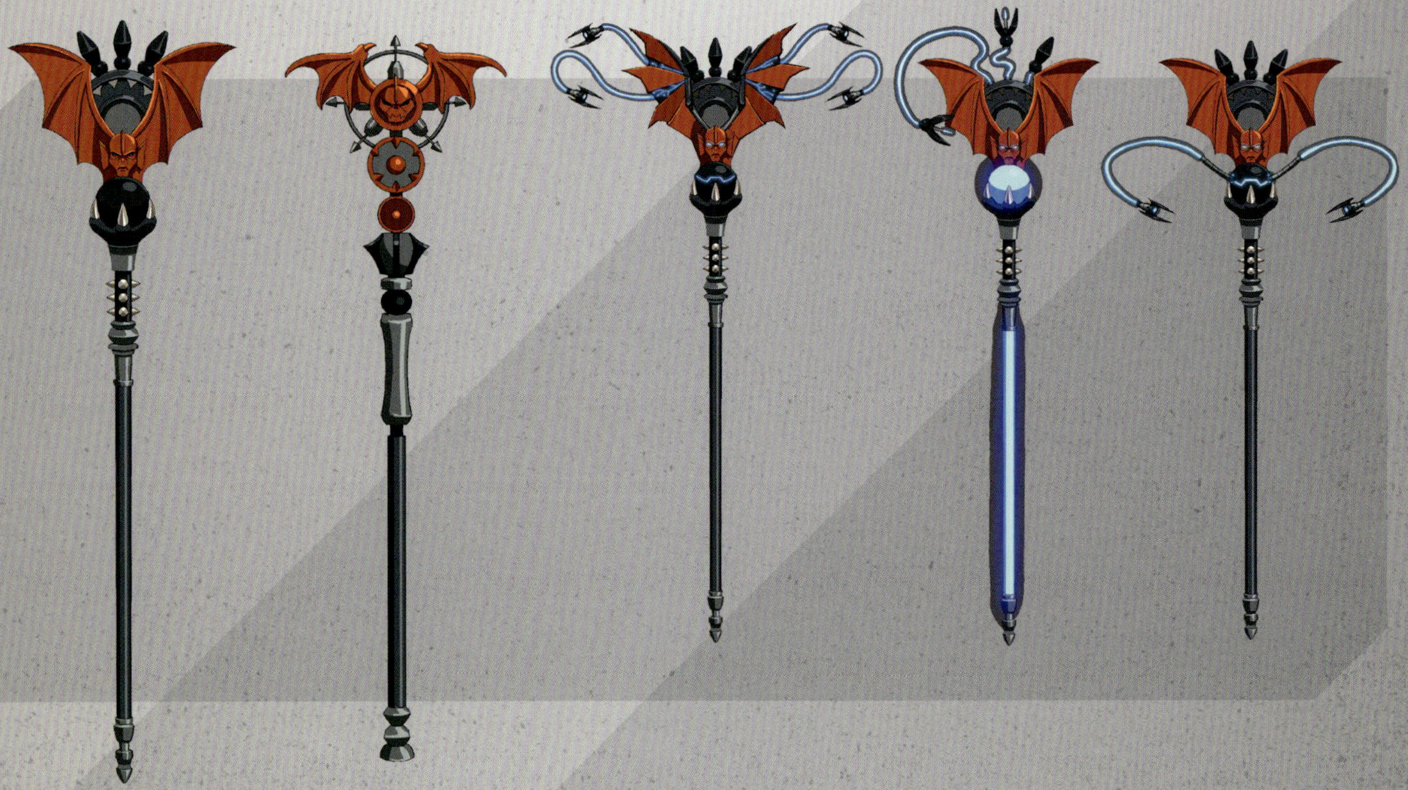

MAN-OF-WAR WEAPON

When Duncan rises to his new position as Man-Of-War, we thought his arsenal would naturally need to be elevated as well and decided to turn his armor into a Swiss Army knife of destructive power! Among his many gadgets are wrist-mounted lasers, rocket boots, and even his trusty collapsible tech claymore.

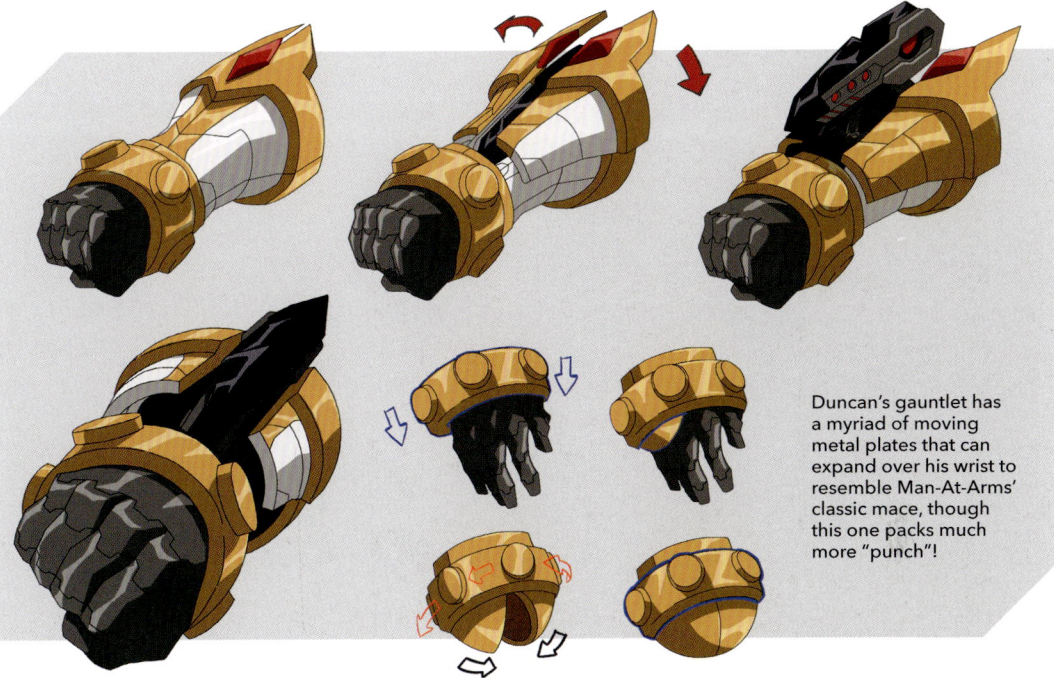

Duncan's gauntlet has a myriad of moving metal plates that can expand over his wrist to resemble Man-At-Arms' classic mace, though this one packs much more "punch"!

MAN-OF-WAR GRENADE

These compact remote detonators may look small, but they're exceptionally powerful! Carried in clusters on Man-Of-War's utility belt, they can be flung in handfuls at villainous vehicles or structures. They possess the ability to stick to almost any surface, and a short time after making contact, they will detonate to devastating results!

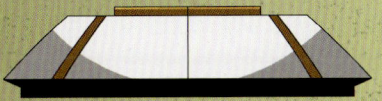 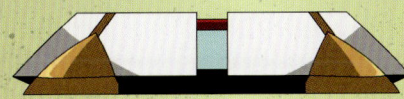

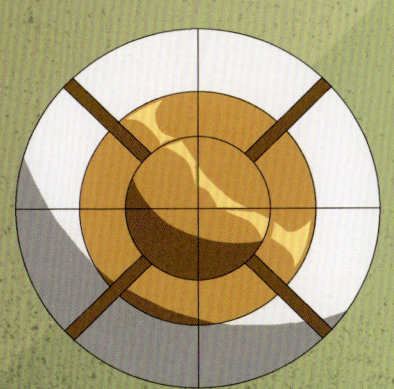 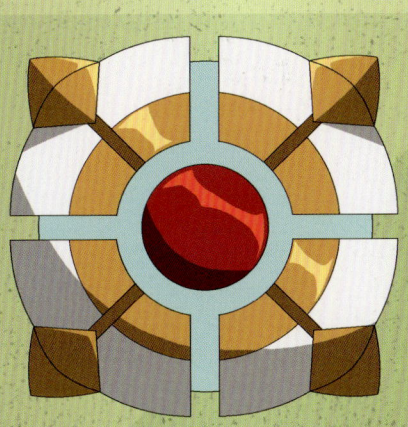 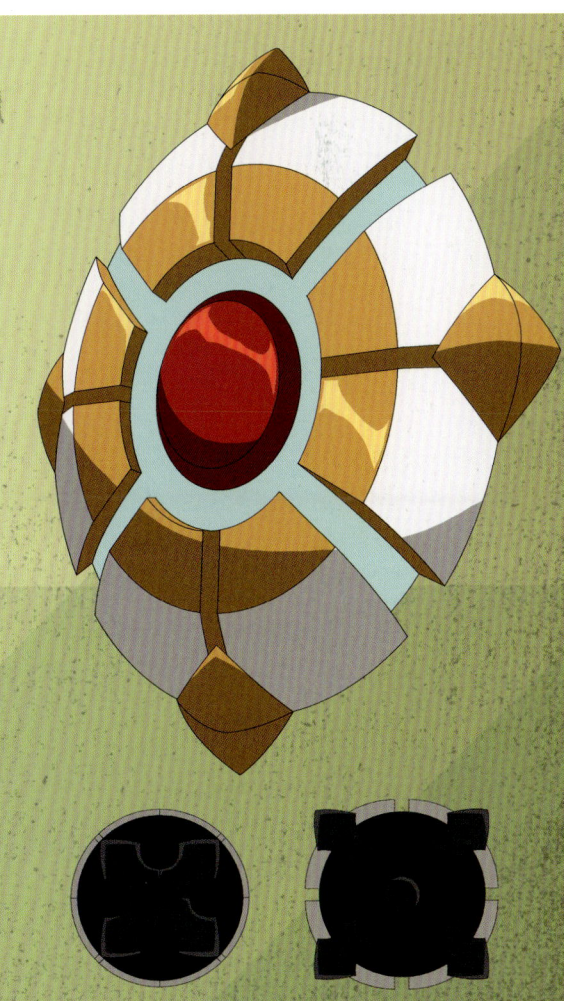

VEHICLES AND ARTIFACTS \\ 81

TECHNOVIRUS GRENADES

The grenades were designed to reference Motherboard's palette. Activated by the button on top, they detonate with a large explosion, polluting the air around them and affecting any poor soul in the blast radius with her technovirus, taking hold of their mind and forcibly bringing them into the fold of her technocult.

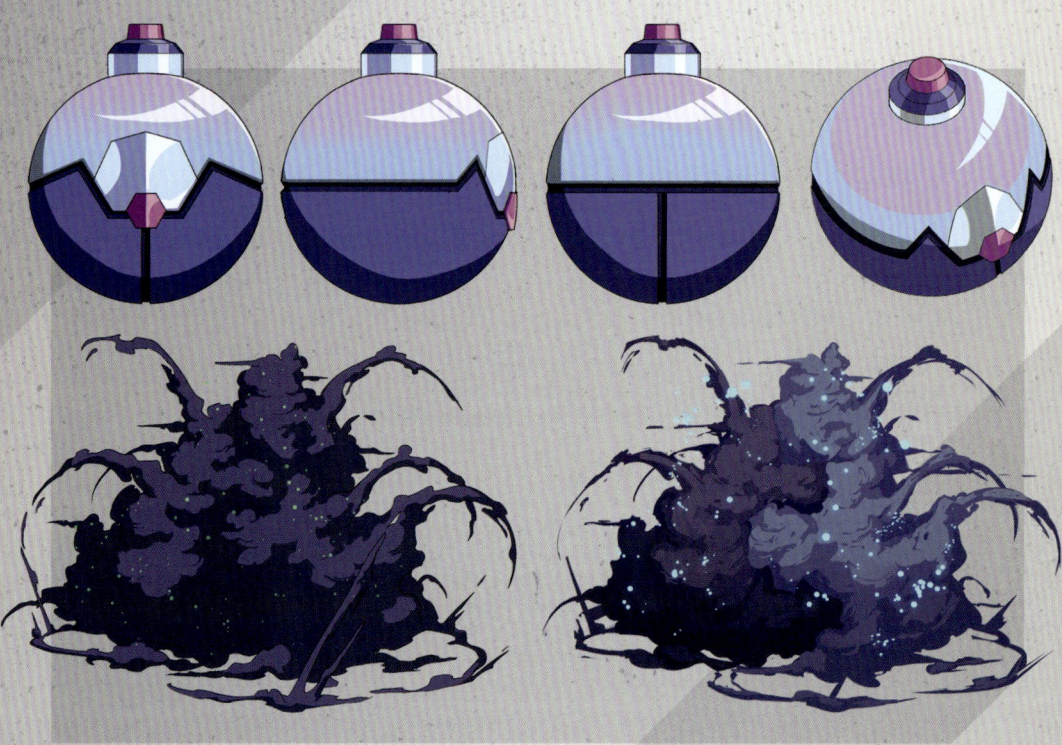

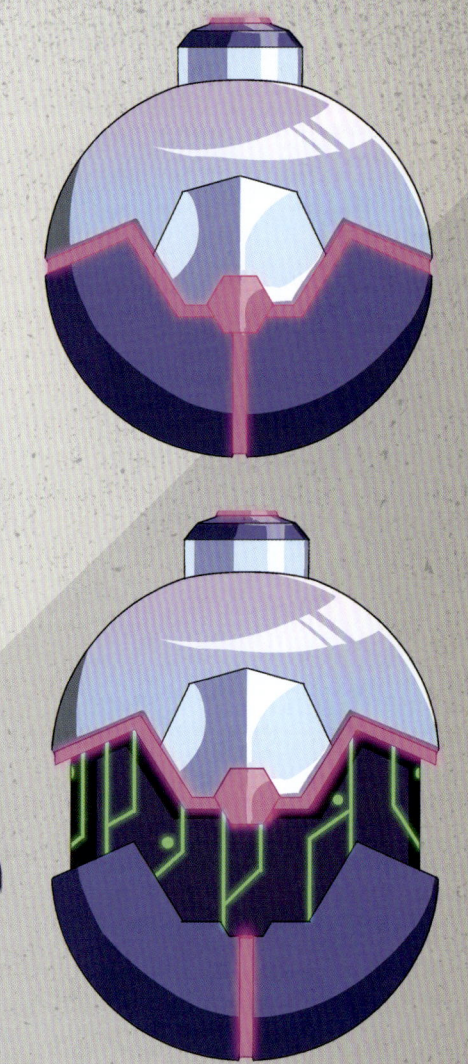

TECH WAFERS

The Tech Wafers are another way the Horde forcibly recruit Eternians. The blue-and-gold color palette signifies their connection to Keldor, while the circuitry in the design indicates the connection to Motherboard. Designed to evoke the imagery of Communion, one Tech Wafer, when consumed, is enough to put the victim under the Horde's control.

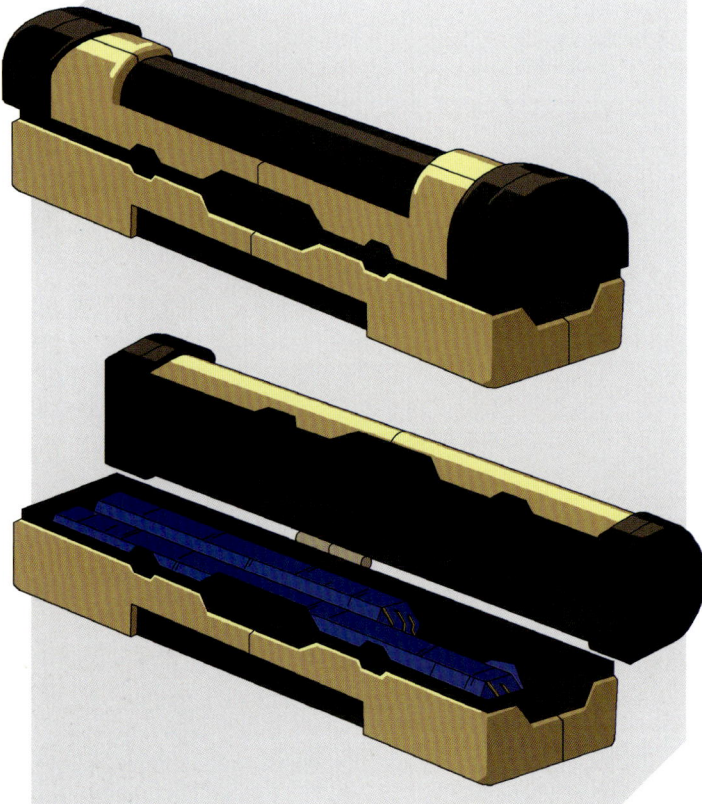

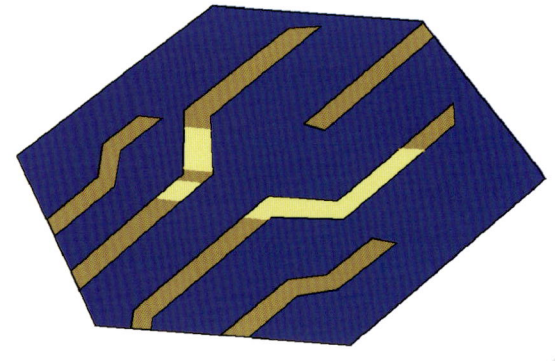

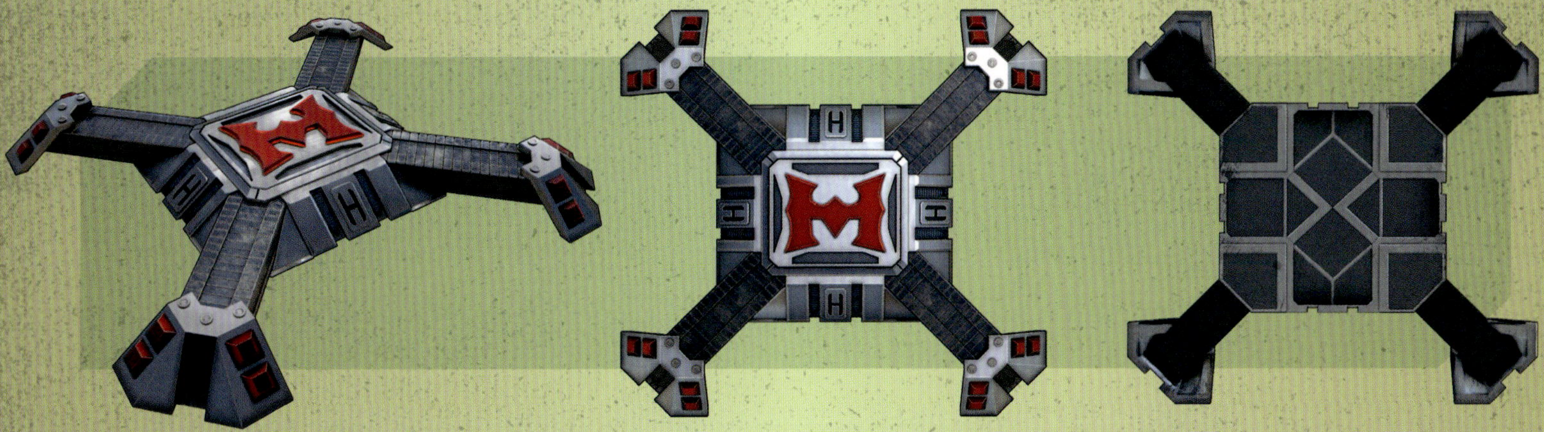

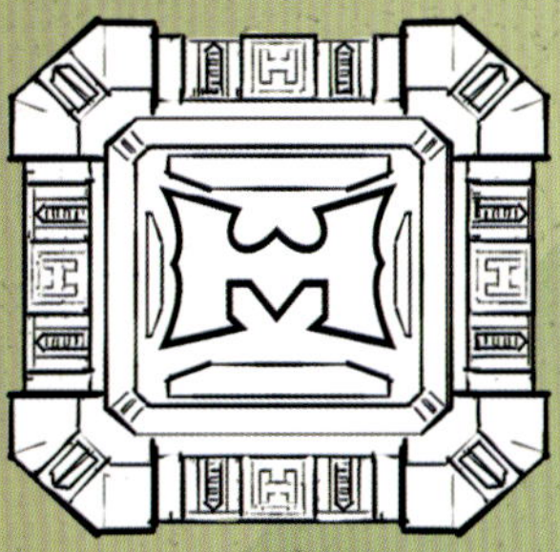

POWERSEAL

The Powerseal provides an early example of just how powerful magic and technology can be when combined. Even after being dropped from the bay of the Cloud Crusher, it still functions perfectly. With Andra's engineering skill and Teela's magical prowess, the Powerseal can keep even the door to Subternia sealed shut!

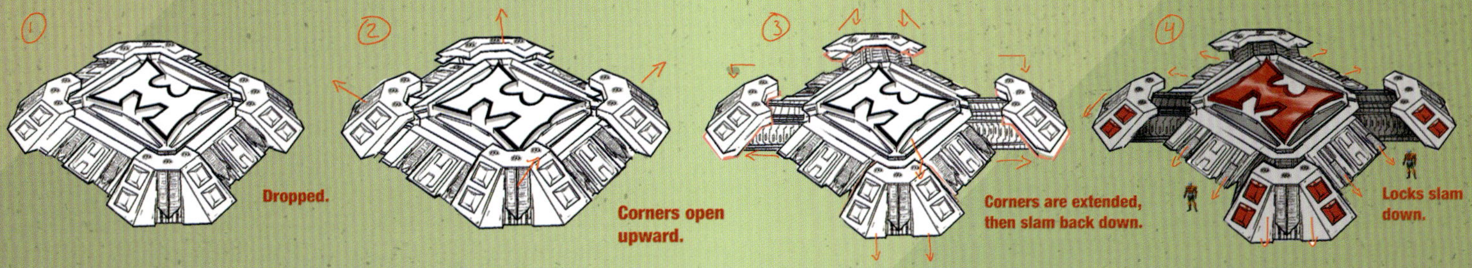

① Dropped.
② Corners open upward.
③ Corners are extended, then slam back down.
④ Locks slam down.

BATTLE ARMOR POD

By having the Battle Armor start out as an attachable pod, we were able to create a badass sequence showing the armor building itself around He-Man while he's in combat. The pod's sleek design perfectly attaches and conforms to He-Man's existing harness to keep things low profile when not in battle.

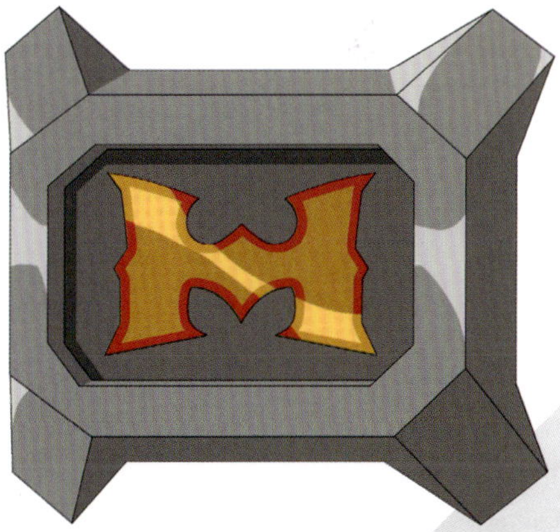

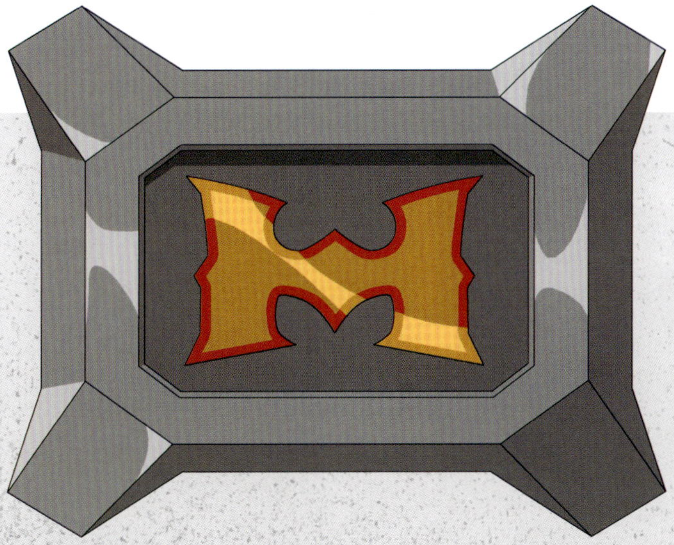

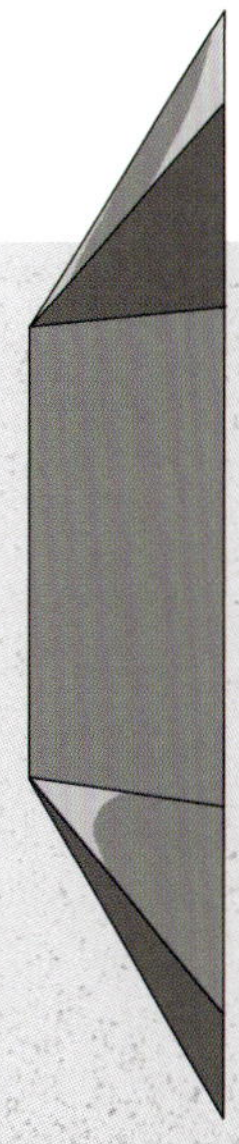

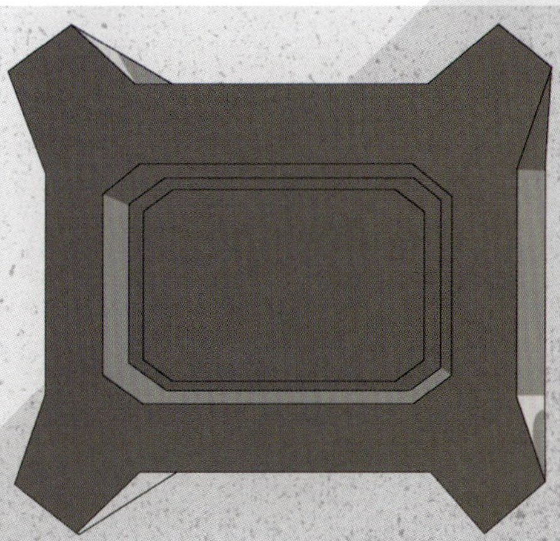

VEHICLES AND ARTIFACTS \\ 83

RIO BLAST'S GUNS

The fastest draw in the universe *has so many guns*. A lot of work went into figuring out how the myriad of lasers opened, fired, and even just fit on that one body. The design and animation teams worked together to create this truly impressive design while still keeping it possible to animate.

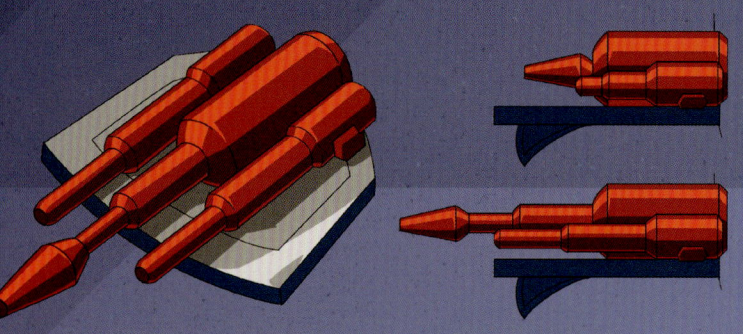

On top of the chest cavity of guns, Rio Blast has several lasers on his shoulders and hidden in his forearms. His shoulders also come equipped with a scope.

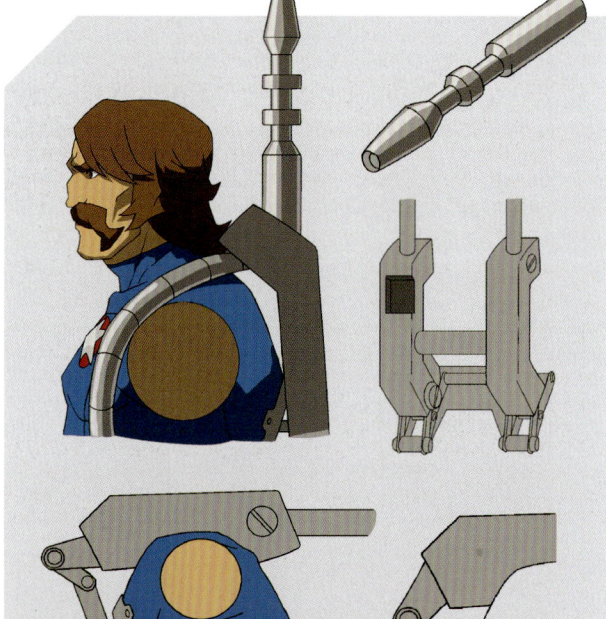
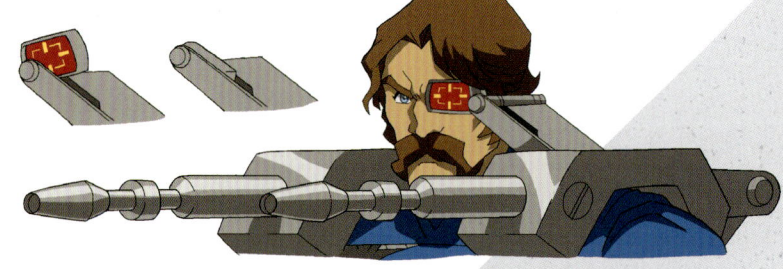
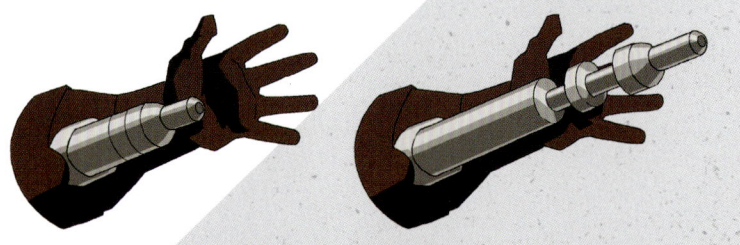

NANOBOTS

The nanobots, while tiny, are pretty much the source of every terrible thing happening to our friends in Eternia. Infecting citizens and taking over Grayskull—none of it's possible without these little guys.

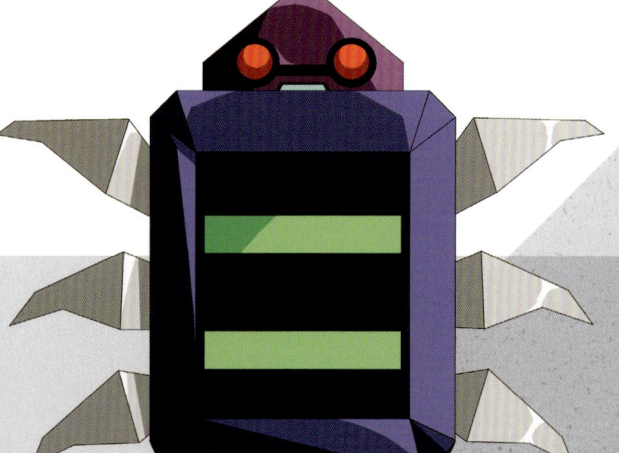
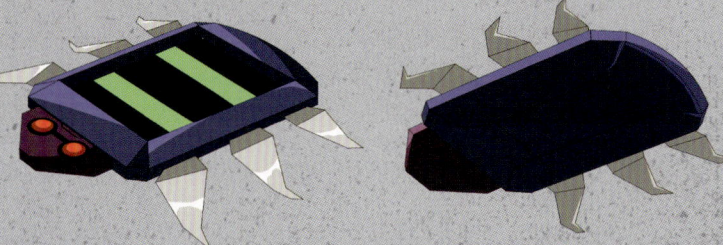

84 // THE ART OF MASTERS OF THE UNIVERSE: REVOLUTION

MANTENNA'S CROSSBOW

You thought Mantenna had enough bells and whistles? Think again! In addition to his crazy eyes, terrifying teeth, and numerous legs, he comes equipped with this wonderfully designed, Horde-approved crossbow. Of course, one of the Horde's most terrifying soldiers can't be walking around shooting simple arrows . . . so it shoots more lasers!

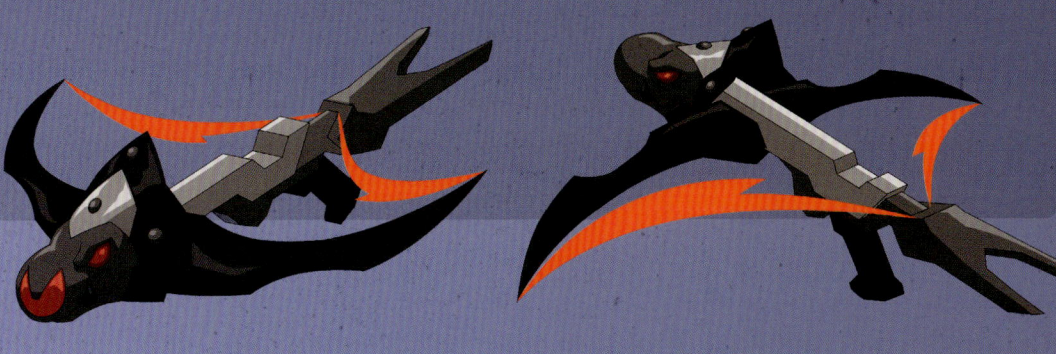
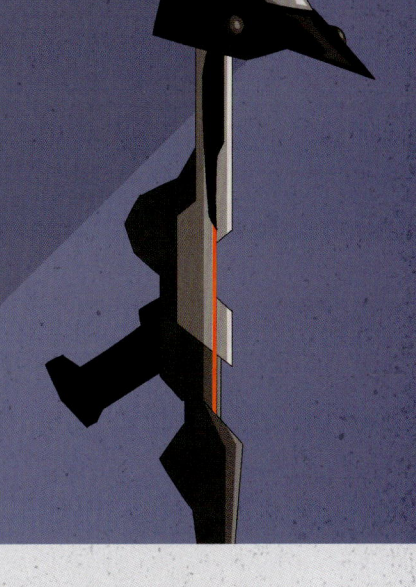

GAUNTLET CABLE

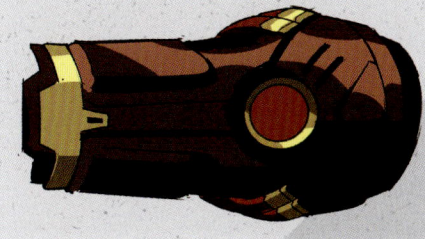

In the first battle against the Techno-Titan, Keldor bestows Andra with an upgraded Gar blaster that allows her to fire a "data beam." And let's be honest, uploads and downloads would be a lot more entertaining if there were lasers involved. In reality, Skeletek uses Motherboard's nanobots to achieve this transformation.

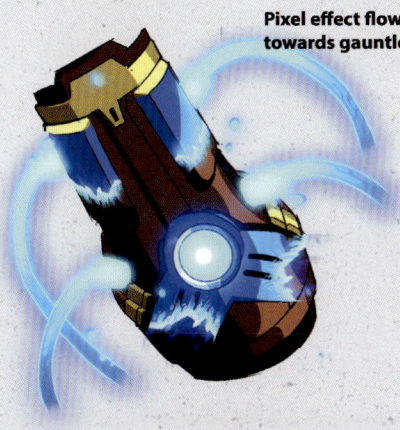

Pixel effect flows towards gauntlet.

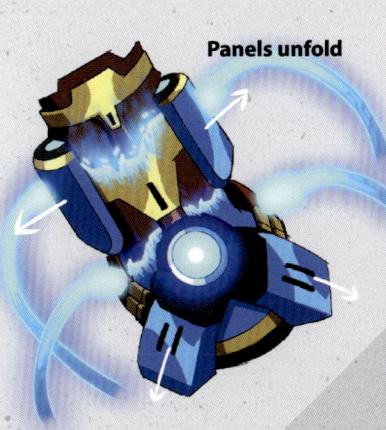

Panels unfold

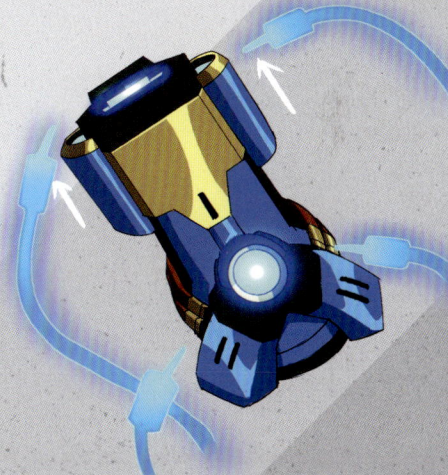

DUNCAN'S WHIP

On top of an upgraded look this season, Duncan also got a few new weapons to go with that fancy armor, including this whip. Designed with his new palette, this whip gives Man-Of-War several updated fighting styles to choose from and can be used at range and in a melee to control the battlefield.

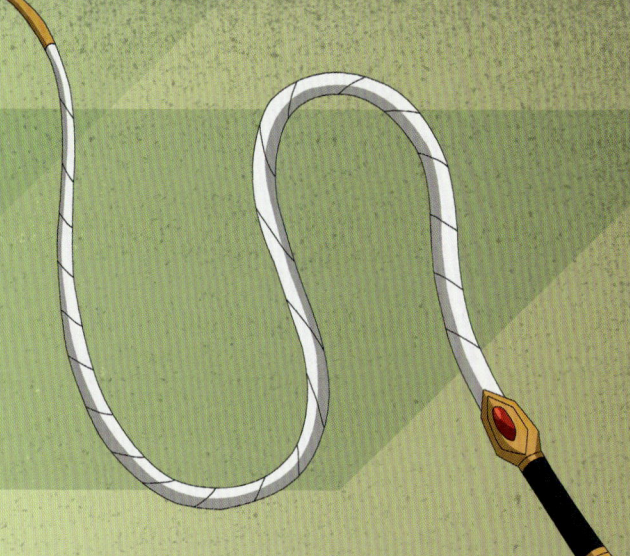

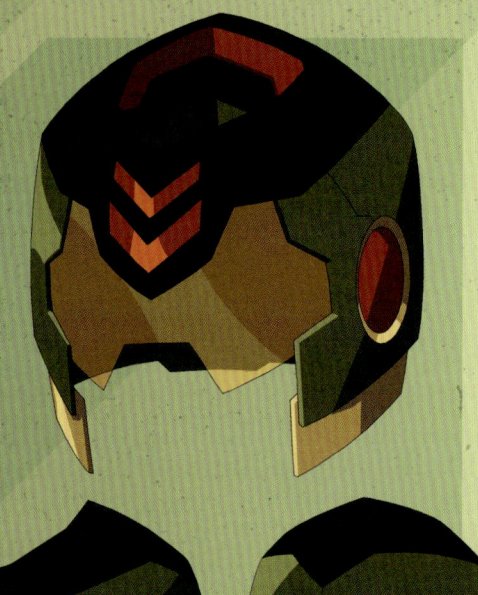

ANDRA'S HELMET

Andra is never seen actually wearing this helmet in the show, but we wanted to make sure it would still fit her look—and appear incredibly stylish! And the design is durable too: even after being thrown to the ground, it doesn't have a dent or scratch on it!

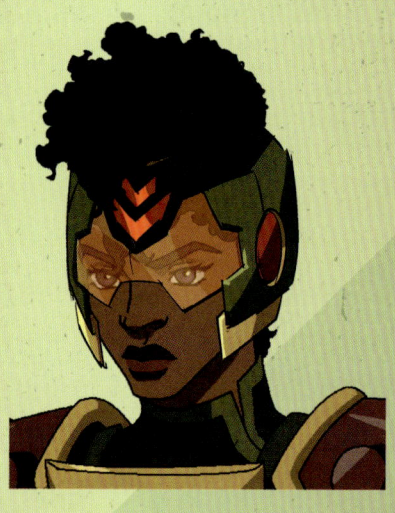
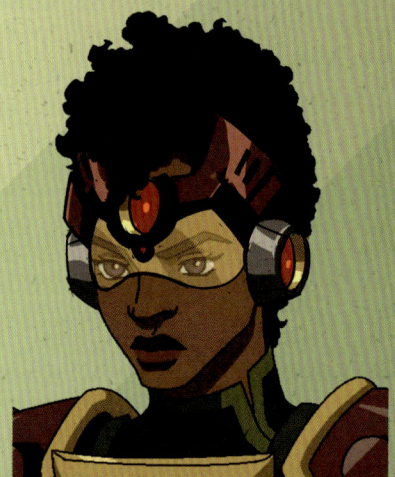

PRONGED CABLE

Yet another part of Gwildor's endless toolbox—this odd apparatus helps Gwildor perform his initial calibration on the Power Sword. Synthesizing magic and technology is no small task, and after Duncan provides a convincing argument, Gwildor eventually rises to the challenge of making the Power Sword even . . . "eleganter."

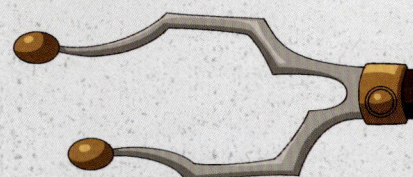

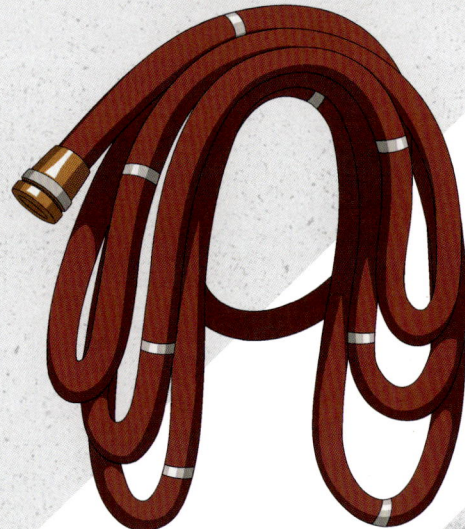

RIVET GUN

The original idea for how to seal the door to Subternia was more technology than magic. The Eternian rivet gun was designed as a construction tool with the ability to hold even the most powerful of doors shut. This was later made obsolete by Teela's powerful magic.

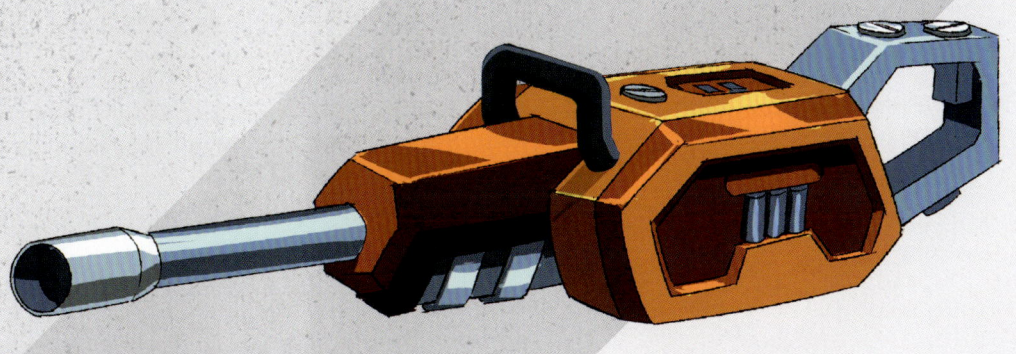
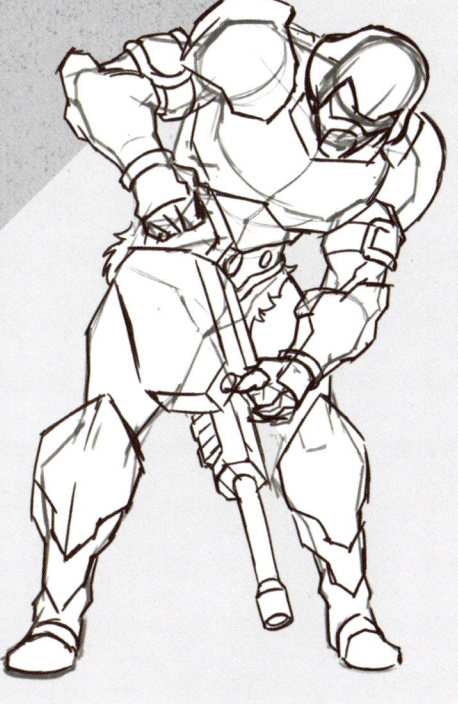

TINKERING TOOLS

Gwildor makes use of multiple odd contraptions while working on the Power Sword. Not all these tools are recognizable to us earthlings; Thenur truly has some unusual machinery! These durable instruments are able to augment even the mythically strong Power Sword—we'd love to grab a set at the hardware store!

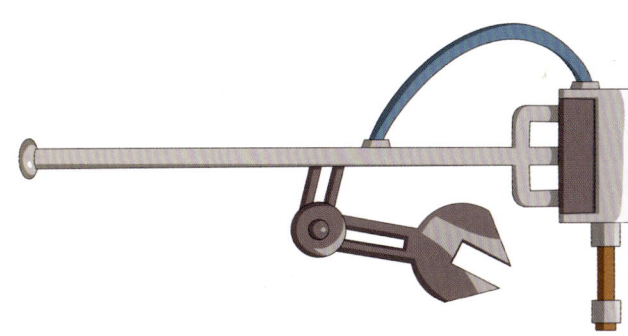

WHALE QUARK CANNON

Even the converts of almighty Motherboard must adhere to the unwritten rule of cool in Eternia: if you have a large vehicle or structure, you must apply an animal motif to it! Plus, dorsal fins make anything look stylish.

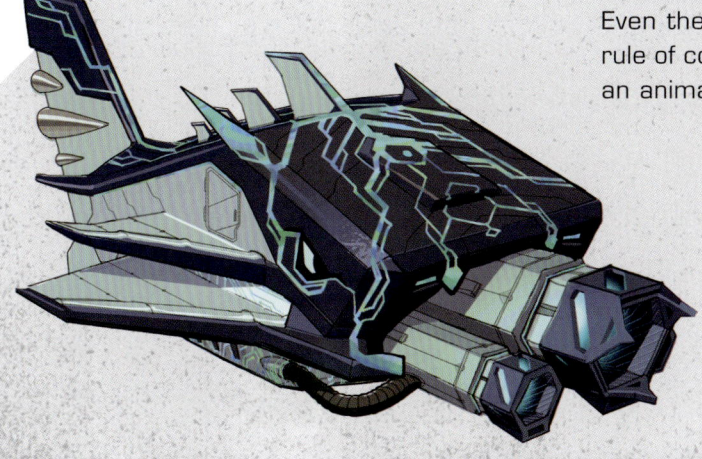
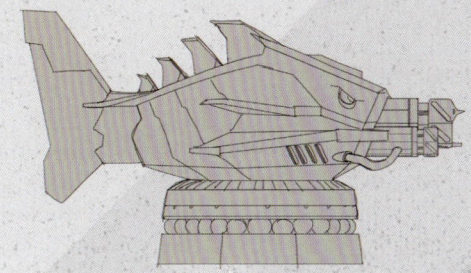
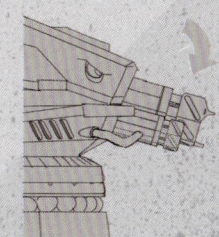

VEHICLES AND ARTIFACTS \\ 87

KELDOR'S BRACELET

Keldor's bracelet is an amazing piece of technology. Not only able to display schematics and assist with upgrading any device at will, it also controls Skeletor's disguise and the Eternians he's infected. Truly, what can't this bracelet do?

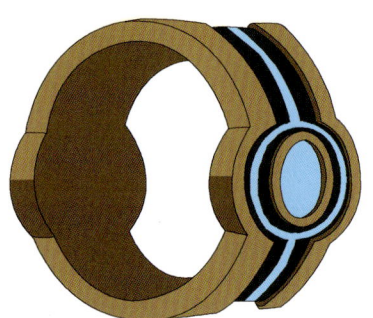
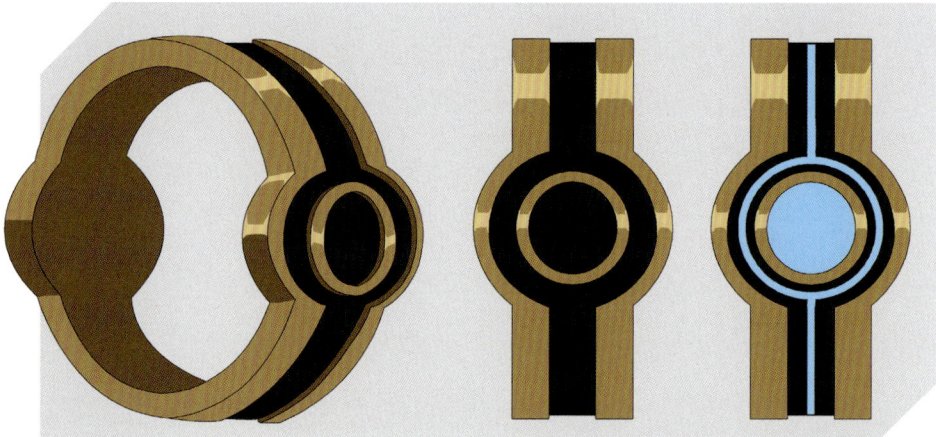

ROYAL FLASK

The royal flask, seen in episode 2, belongs to King Miro. It went through several iterations before the team landed on the final design, opting for a Sorceress-inspired wing pattern with red jewels. The placement of the jewels is meant to allude to the two moons featured on the Eternian flag.

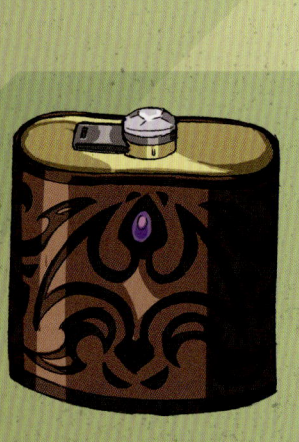
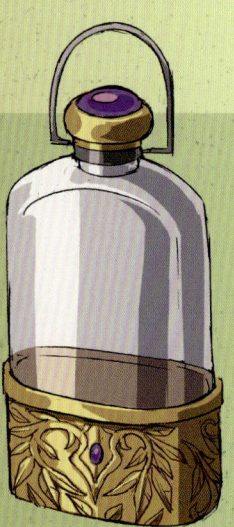
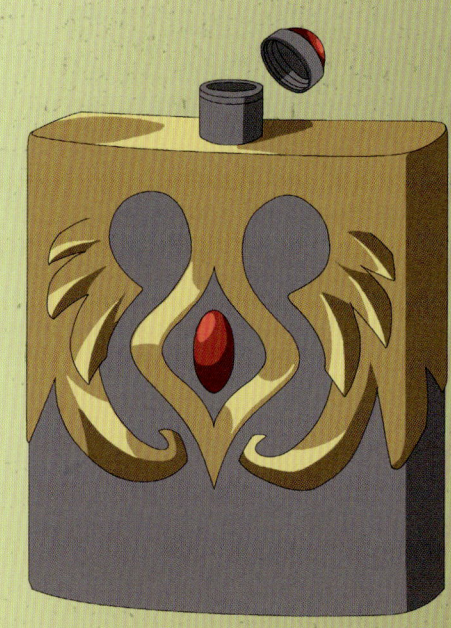
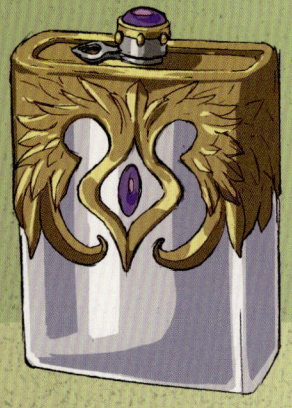
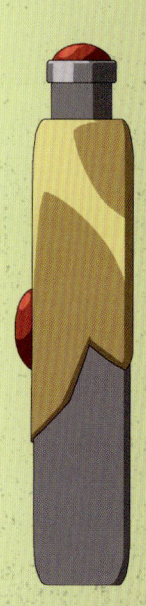
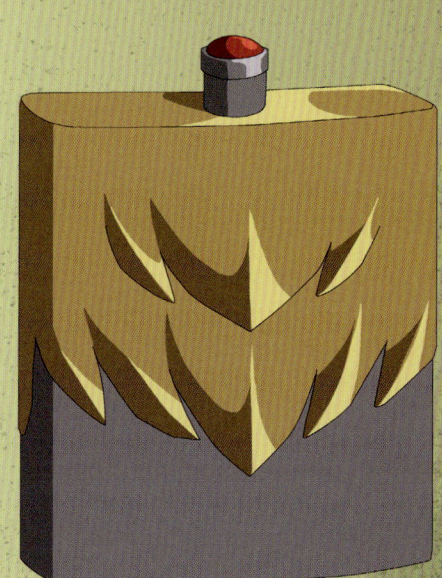

In the other options for the design, artists played with different materials and colors, even considering referencing the shape of Miro's crown rather than the standard Eternian iconography.

KING'S STUDY BOOK

The book featured in the king's study only appears for a short time onscreen, but if you look closely you will see the beautifully designed image of Granamyr hidden in its pages.

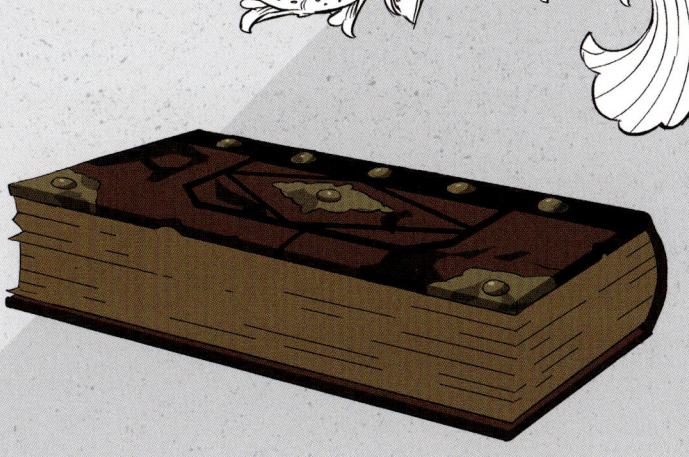

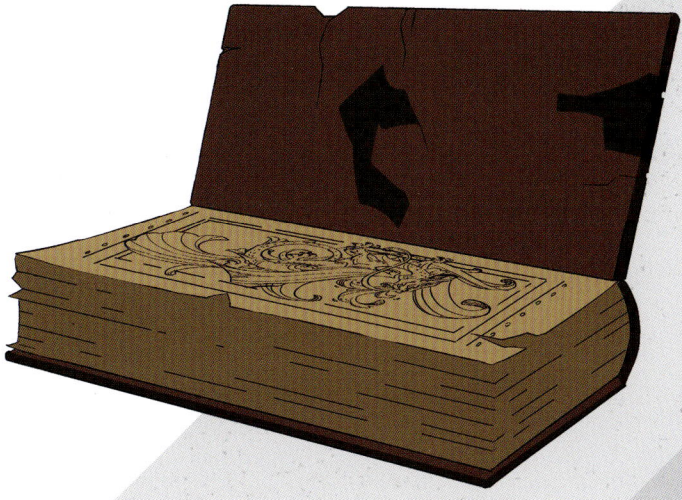

KELDOR'S CROWN

We made the decision that Randor should be buried with his crown. This ties in with Randor's final message to Adam that each king should forge his own destiny. As an added bonus, we were able to give Keldor/Skeletor's crown a sharper and more angular design that hints at his sinister motives.

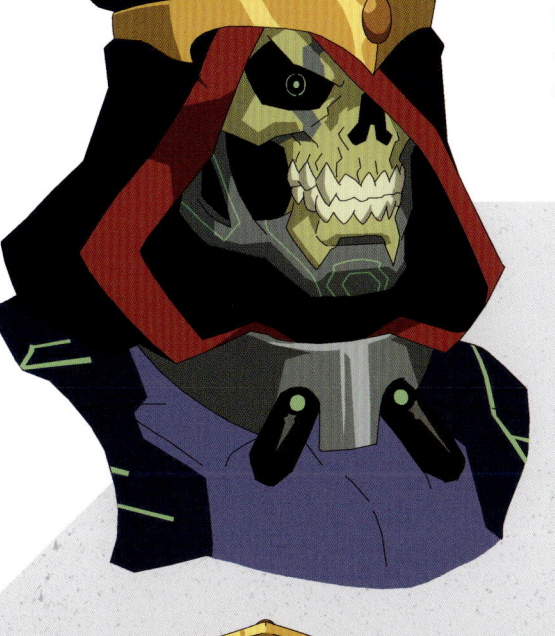

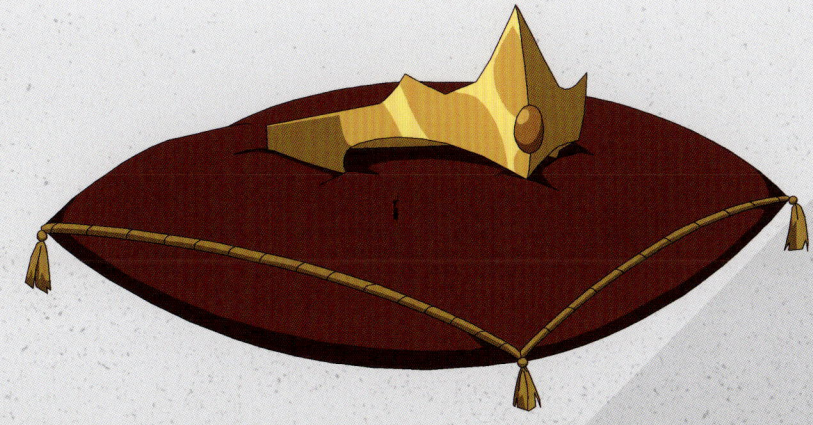

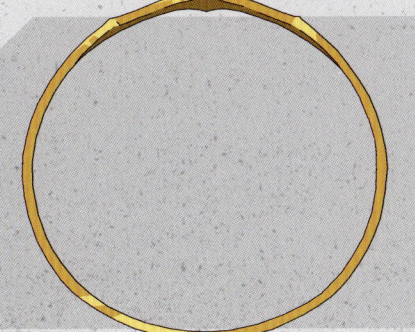
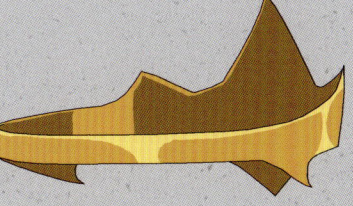
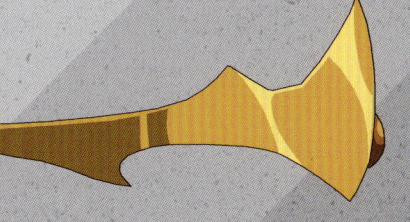

VEHICLES AND ARTIFACTS \\ 89

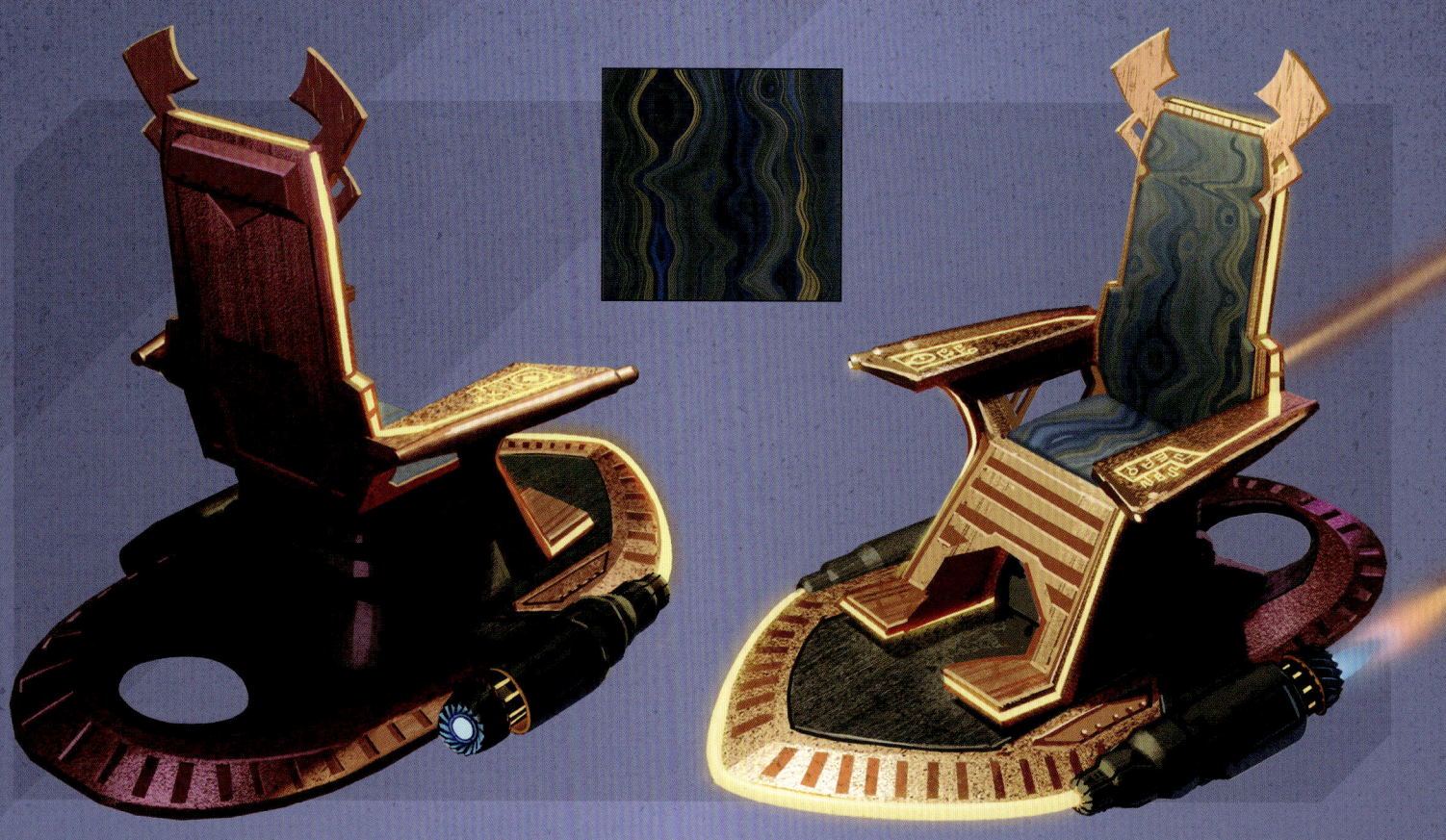

ZODAC'S CHAIR

Zodac sits atop this hovering throne, overseeing the balance of the universe. The design is based on the original vehicle shown in Zodac's classic toy, though with a few added details, such as metal armrests with digital displays and detailed upholstery fabric with patterns that reference gas giant planets. Only the best of the best for the leader of the Cosmic Enforcers!

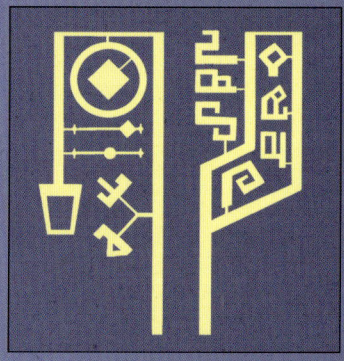

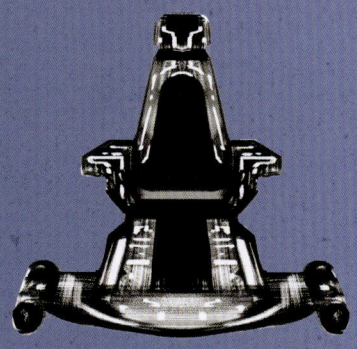 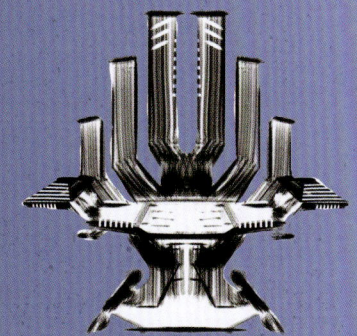 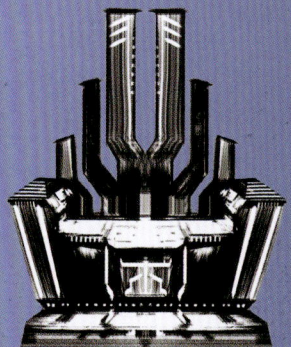 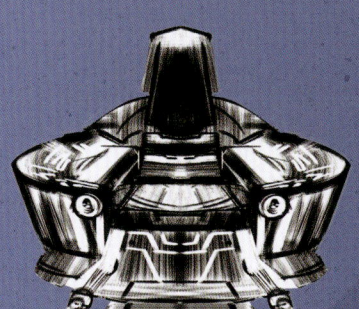

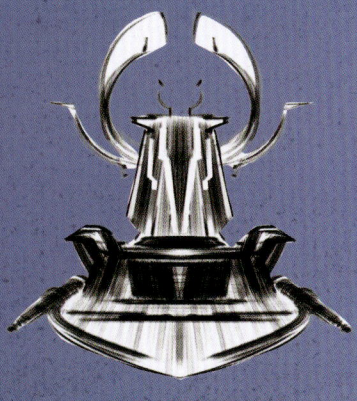 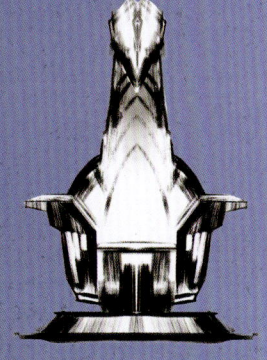 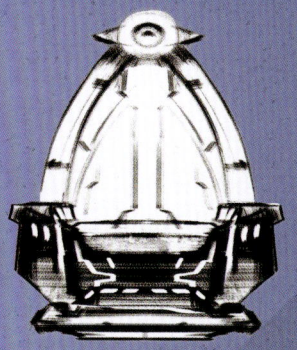 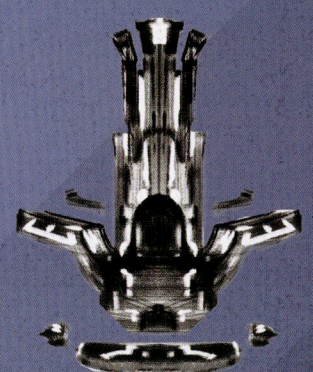

GIFT BOX

Though it turns out not to be the gift that Hordak was hoping for, you have to appreciate the extra effort that Skeletor went through to gift-wrap it. Skeletor even chose a ribbon with circuitry, since he knows how much Hordak loves technology.

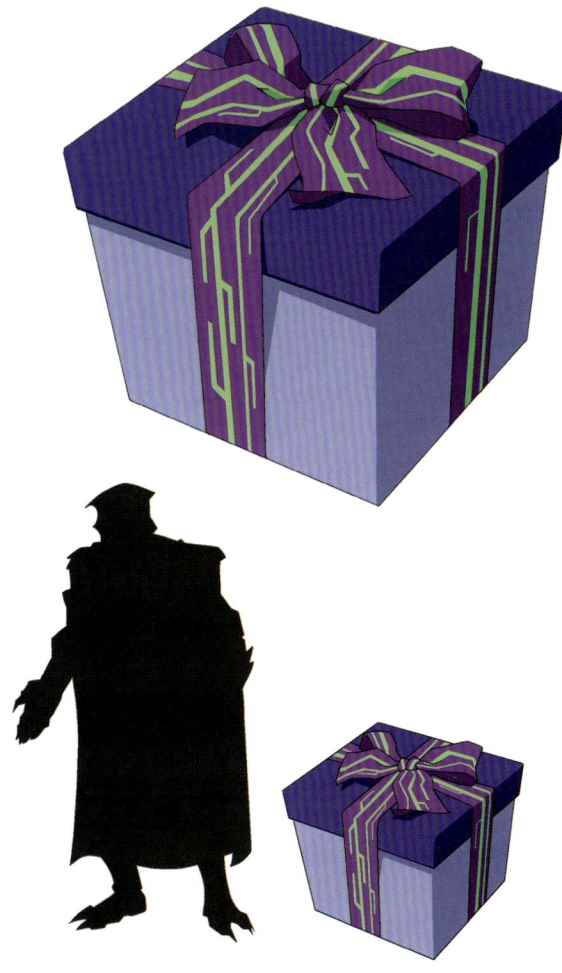

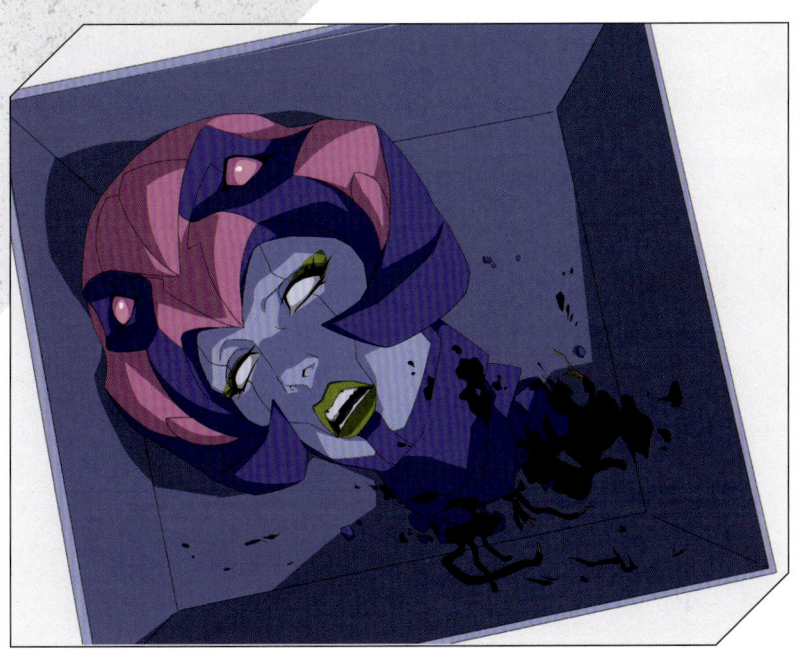

HA'VOK STAFF

Despite Motherboard's makeover, the Ha'vok Staff reverted completely to its original form once severed from Skeletor's arm. Here we see it still covered in nanobots but ready to make its way to Teela. No matter what shape it takes, the Ha'vok Staff is sure to exert its ominous influence on its wielder.

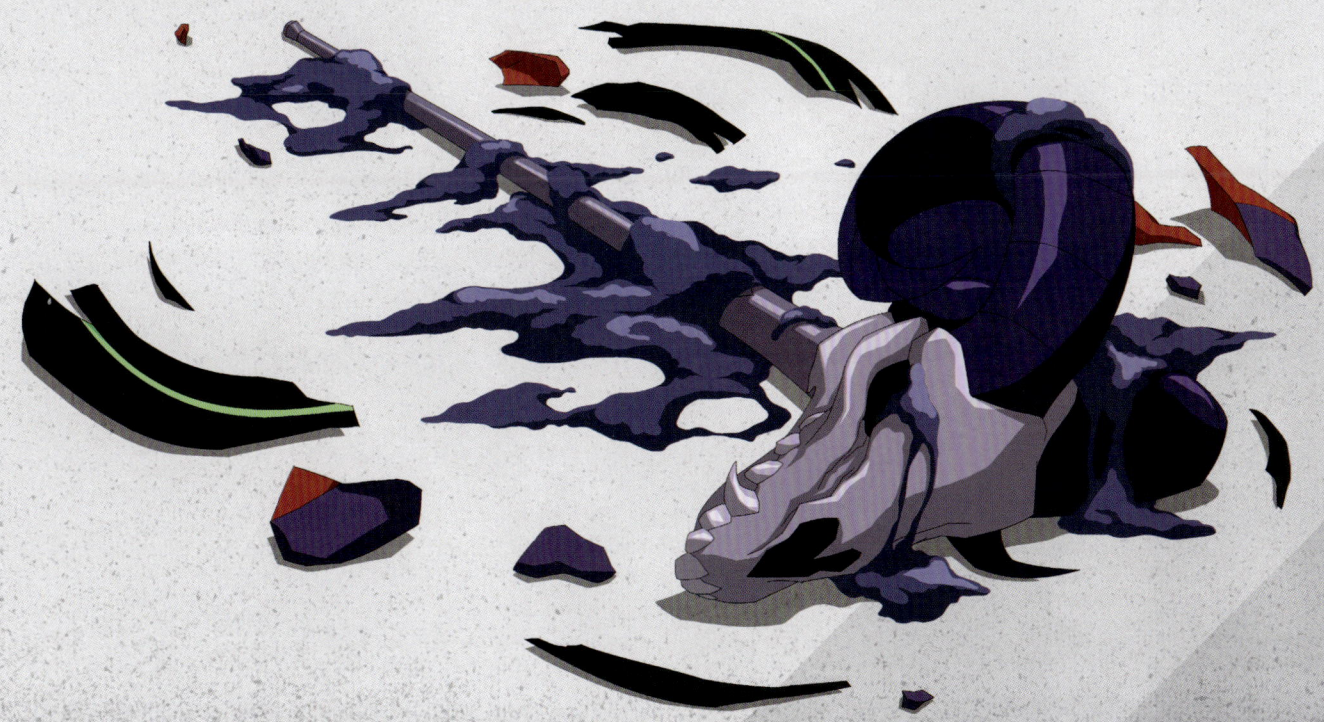

VEHICLES AND ARTIFACTS \\ 91

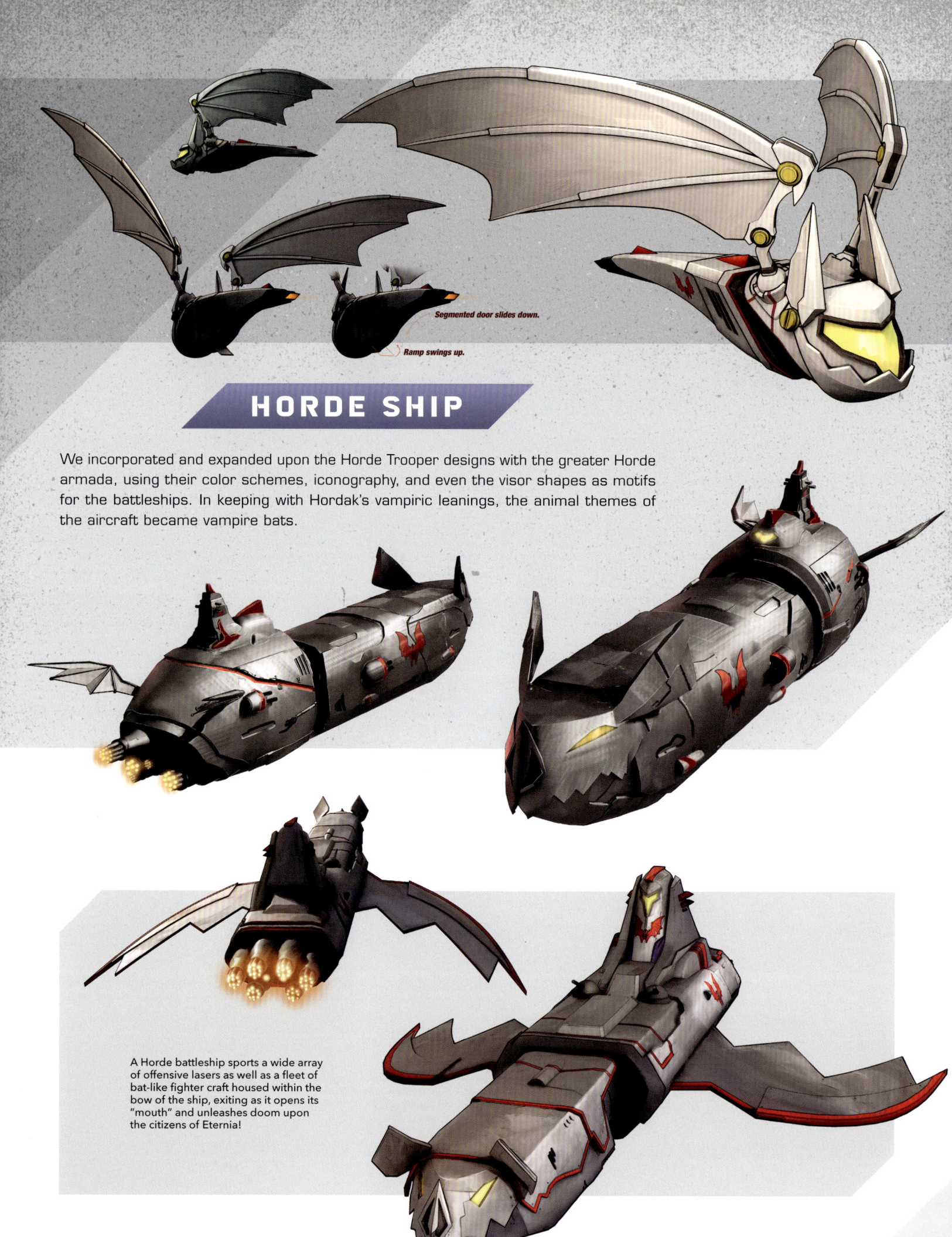

Segmented door slides down.
Ramp swings up.

HORDE SHIP

We incorporated and expanded upon the Horde Trooper designs with the greater Horde armada, using their color schemes, iconography, and even the visor shapes as motifs for the battleships. In keeping with Hordak's vampiric leanings, the animal themes of the aircraft became vampire bats.

A Horde battleship sports a wide array of offensive lasers as well as a fleet of bat-like fighter craft housed within the bow of the ship, exiting as it opens its "mouth" and unleashes doom upon the citizens of Eternia!

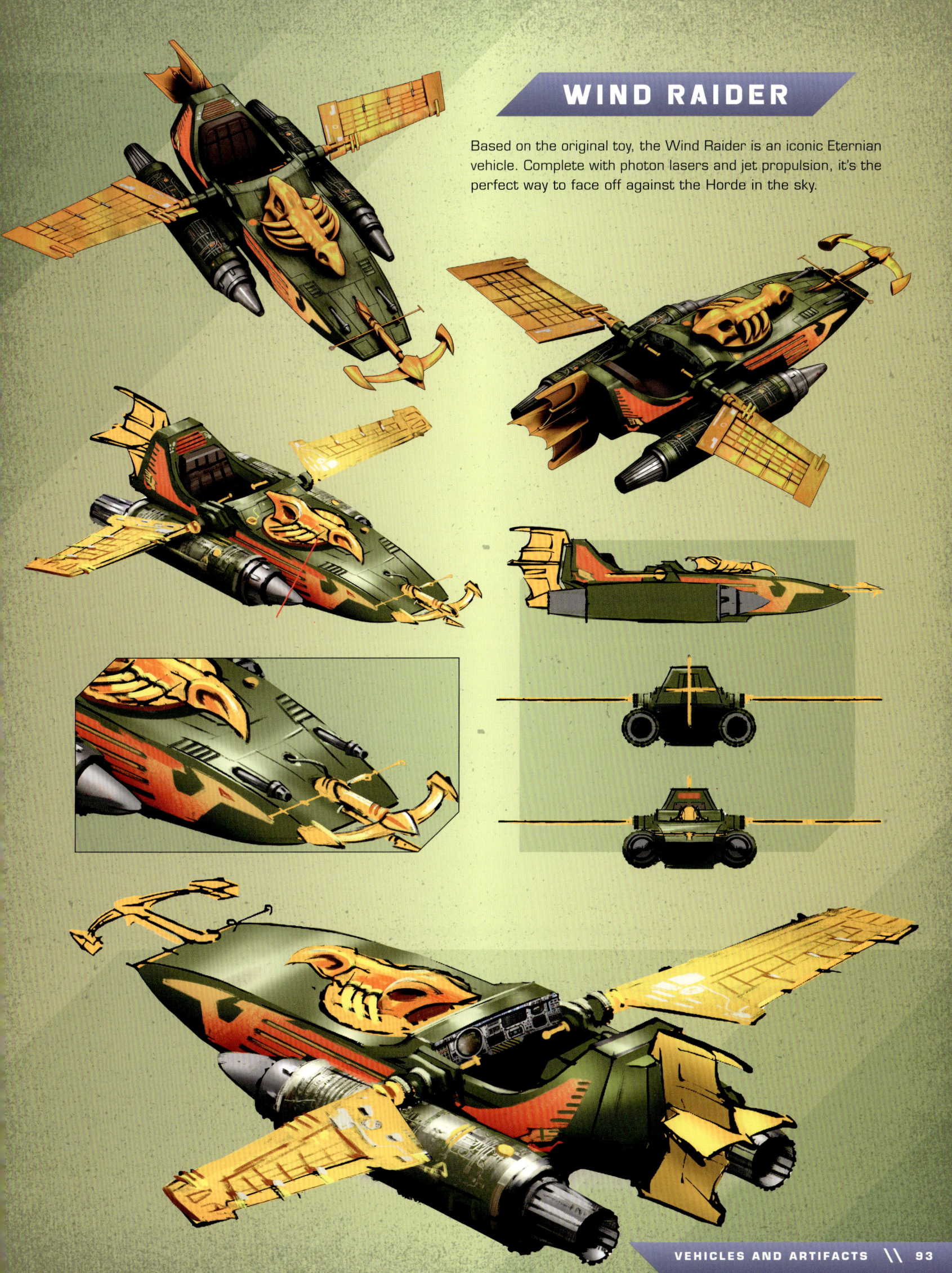

WIND RAIDER

Based on the original toy, the Wind Raider is an iconic Eternian vehicle. Complete with photon lasers and jet propulsion, it's the perfect way to face off against the Horde in the sky.

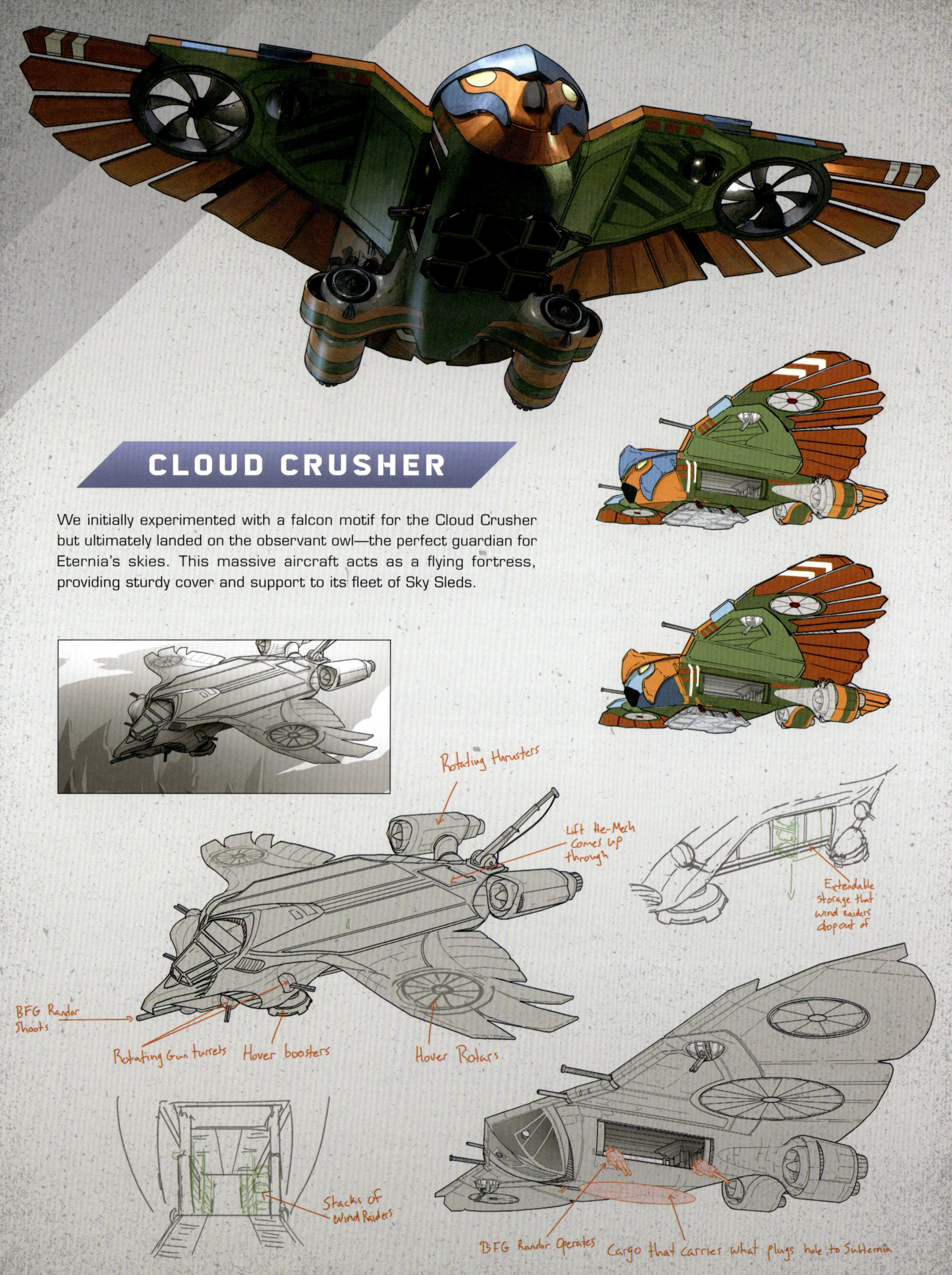

CLOUD CRUSHER

We initially experimented with a falcon motif for the Cloud Crusher but ultimately landed on the observant owl—the perfect guardian for Eternia's skies. This massive aircraft acts as a flying fortress, providing sturdy cover and support to its fleet of Sky Sleds.

BLASTER HAWK

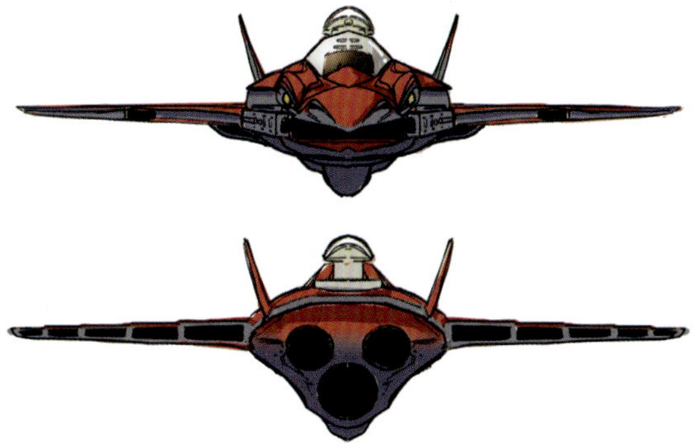

Marlena shows off her flashy piloting skills once again this season, using the Blaster Hawk's iconic laser disks to cut effortlessly through the shambling army of Techno-Titans. The ship's streamlined design gives it incredible maneuverability in the air.

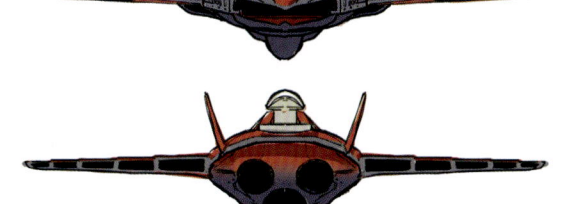

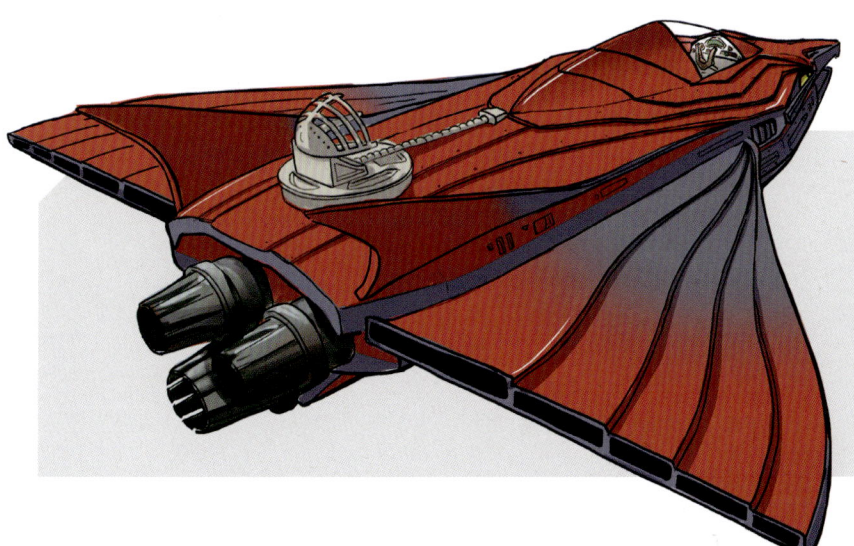

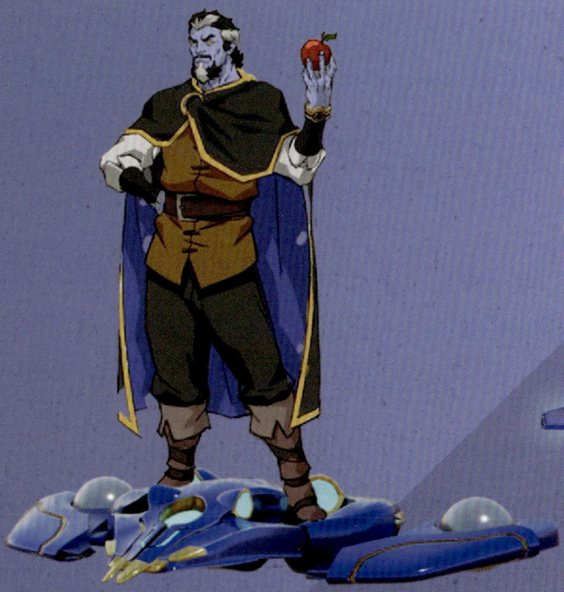

KELDOR'S SLED

Keldor uses advanced hard-light technology from his Gar wristband to conjure a floating sled. But considering this is Skeletor in disguise, you can bet that Motherboard's nanobots played a part in the deception. Keen eyes will also notice a striking similarity to the Ha'vok Staff.

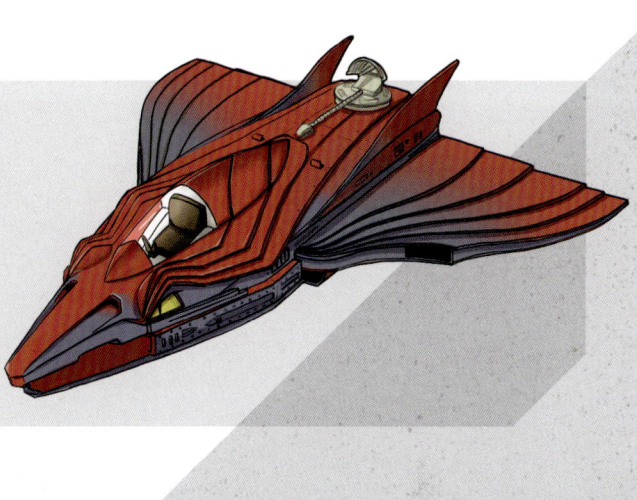

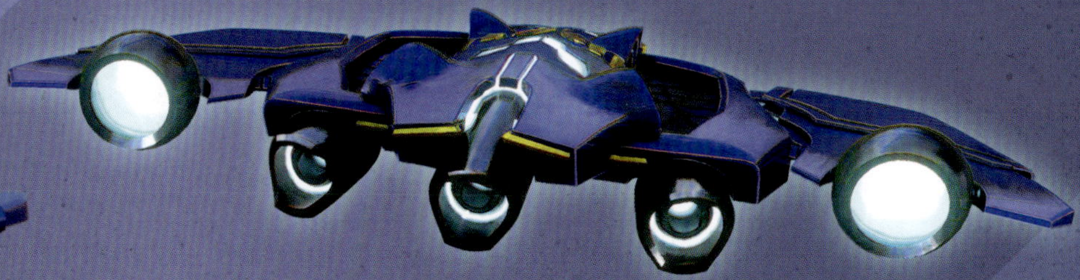

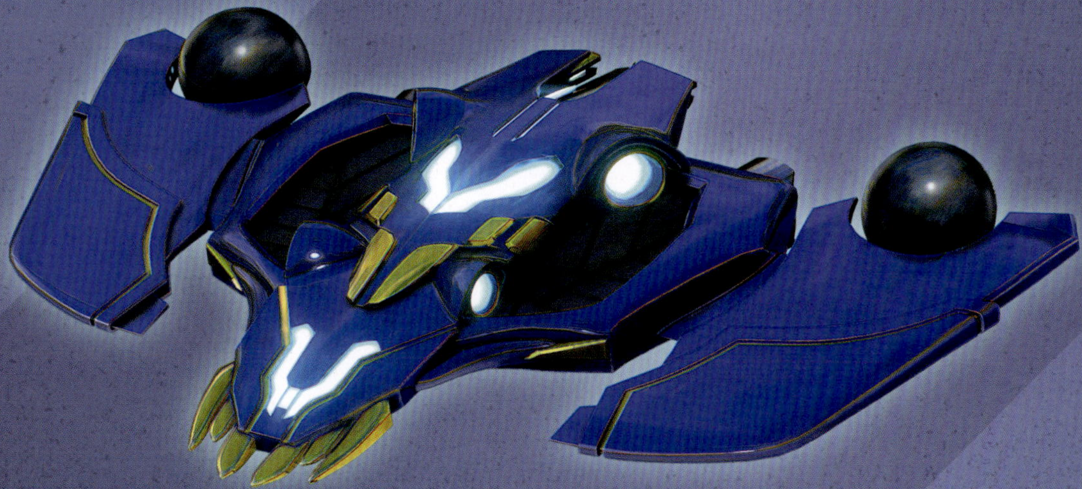

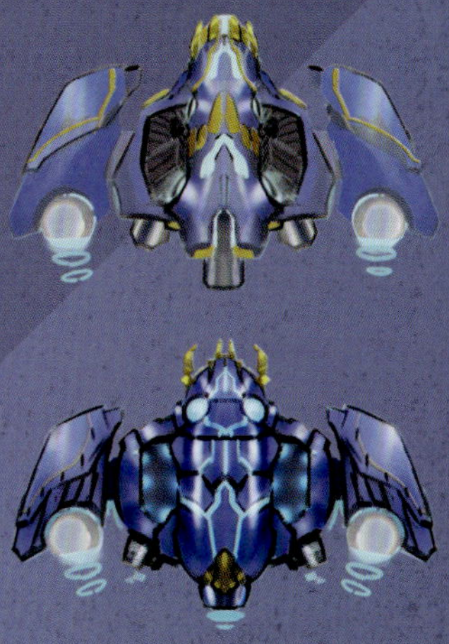

VEHICLES AND ARTIFACTS \\ 95

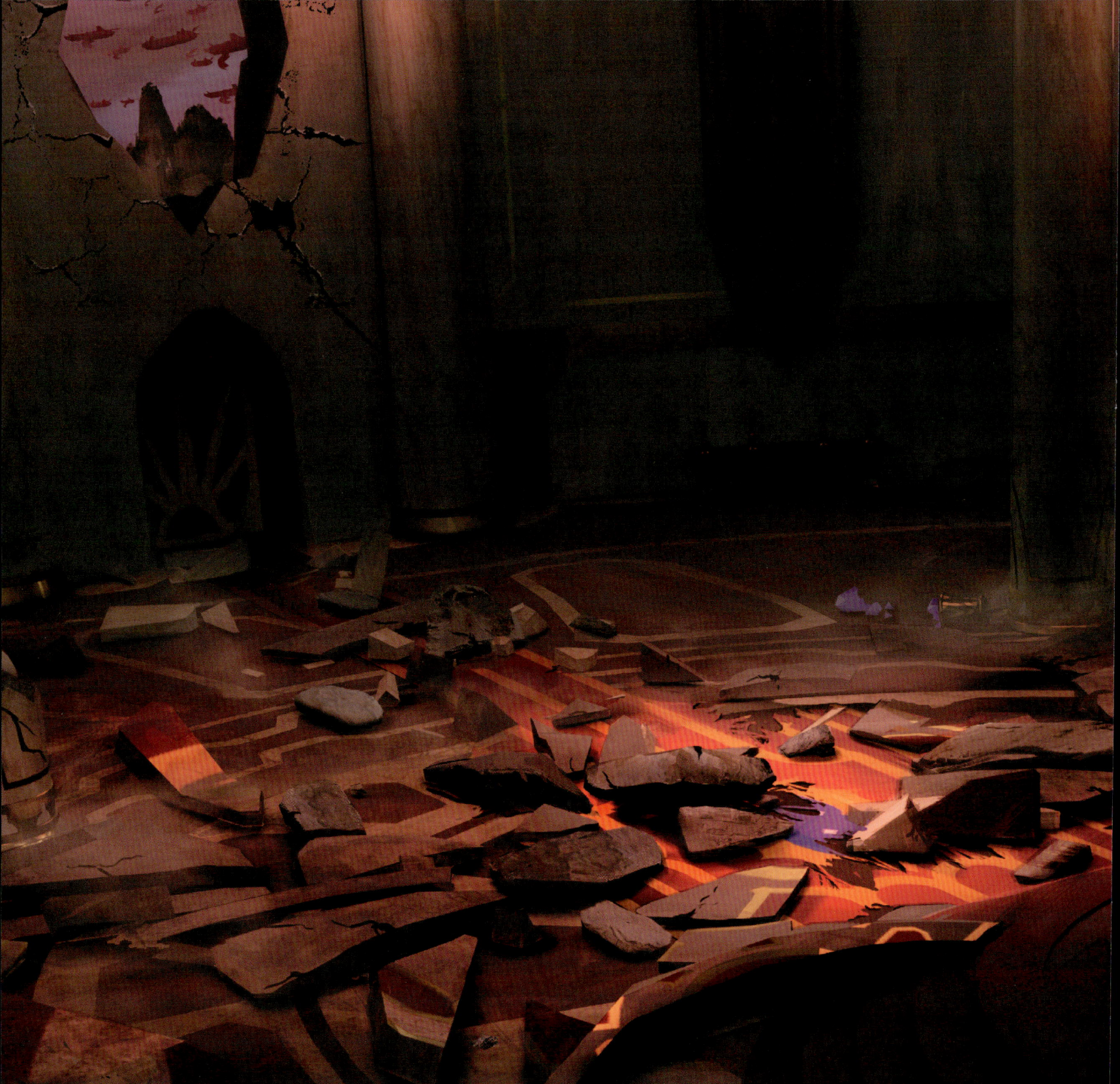

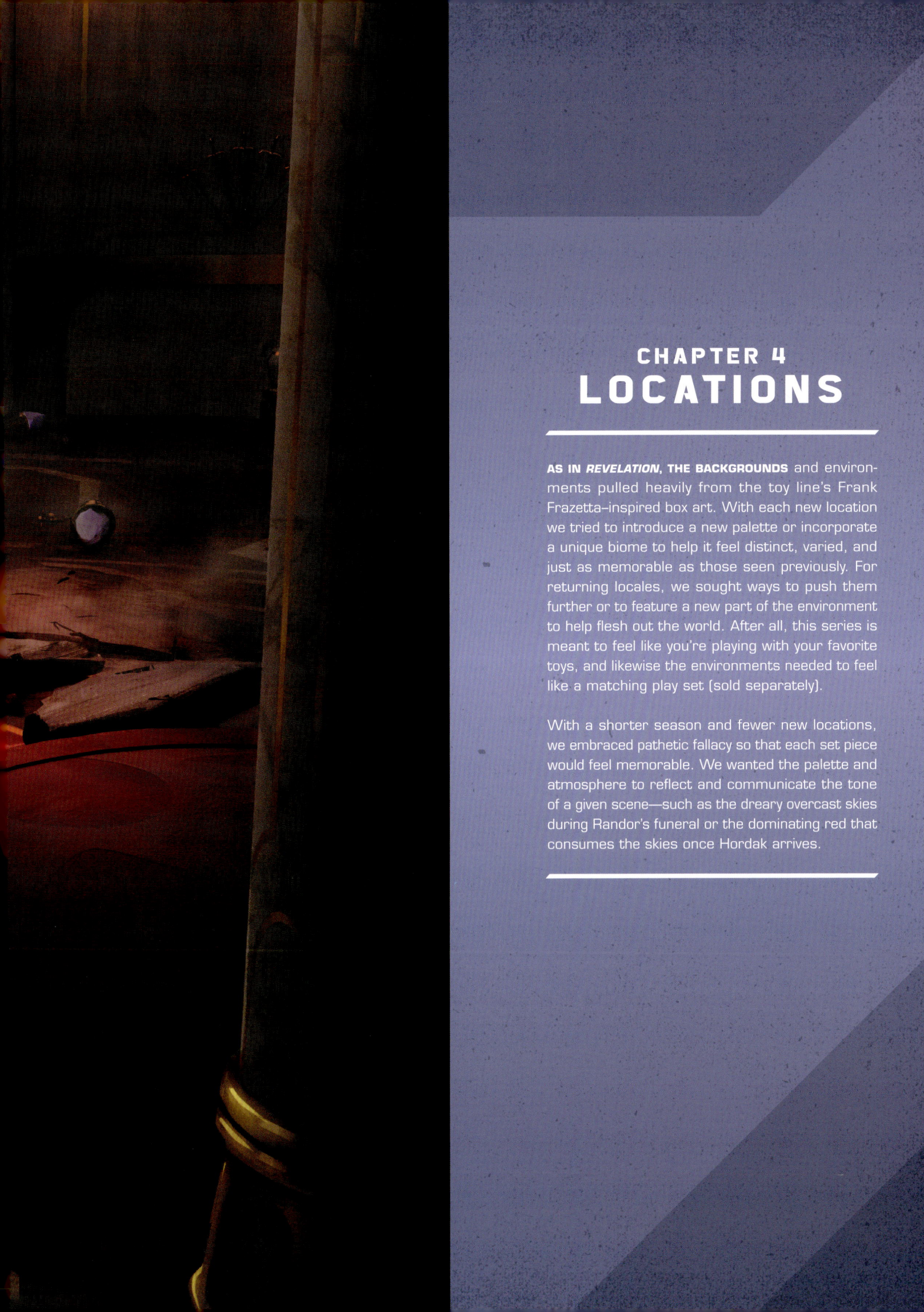

CHAPTER 4
LOCATIONS

AS IN *REVELATION*, THE BACKGROUNDS and environments pulled heavily from the toy line's Frank Frazetta–inspired box art. With each new location we tried to introduce a new palette or incorporate a unique biome to help it feel distinct, varied, and just as memorable as those seen previously. For returning locales, we sought ways to push them further or to feature a new part of the environment to help flesh out the world. After all, this series is meant to feel like you're playing with your favorite toys, and likewise the environments needed to feel like a matching play set (sold separately).

With a shorter season and fewer new locations, we embraced pathetic fallacy so that each set piece would feel memorable. We wanted the palette and atmosphere to reflect and communicate the tone of a given scene—such as the dreary overcast skies during Randor's funeral or the dominating red that consumes the skies once Hordak arrives.

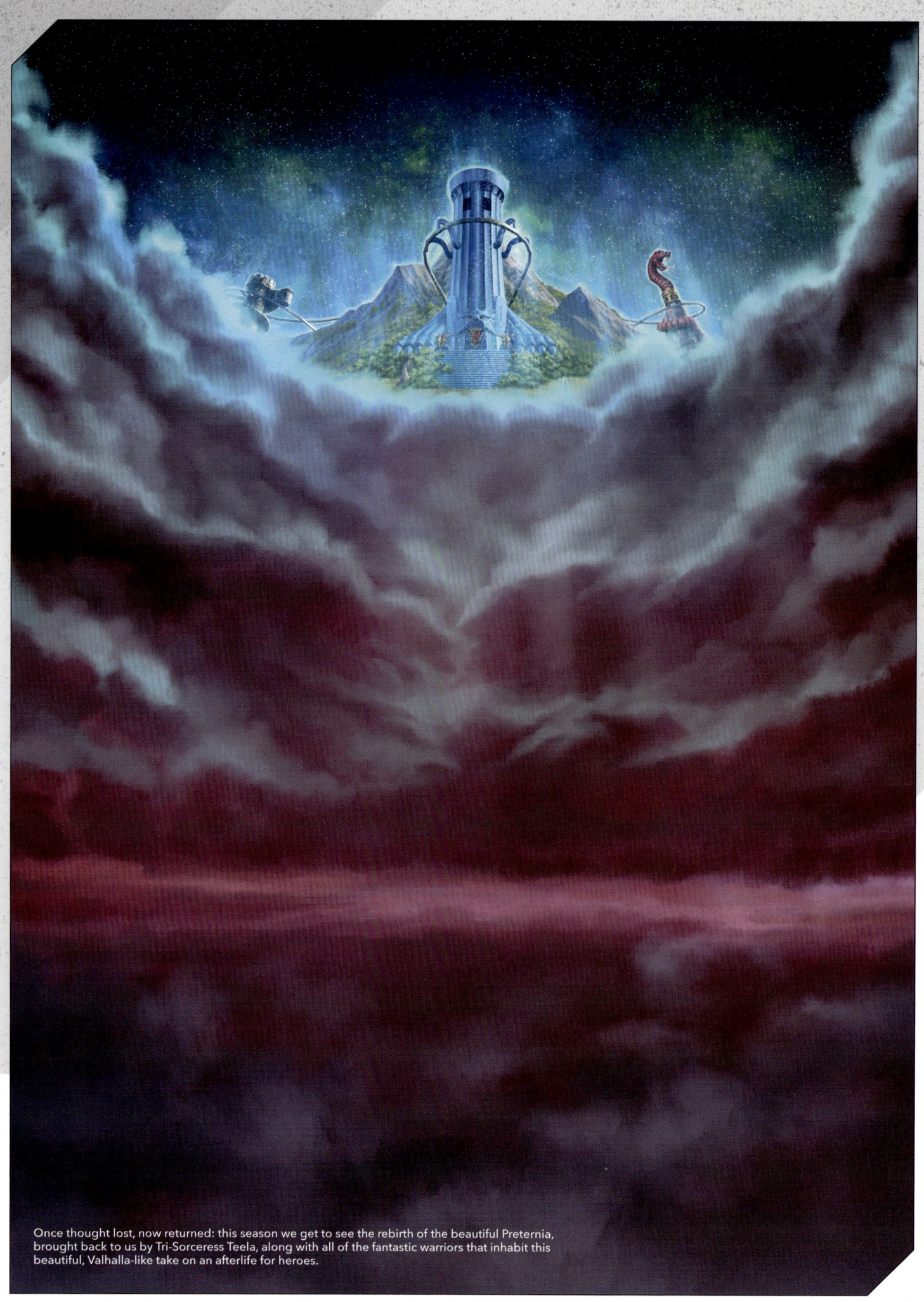

Once thought lost, now returned: this season we get to see the rebirth of the beautiful Preternia, brought back to us by Tri-Sorceress Teela, along with all of the fantastic warriors that inhabit this beautiful, Valhalla-like take on an afterlife for heroes.

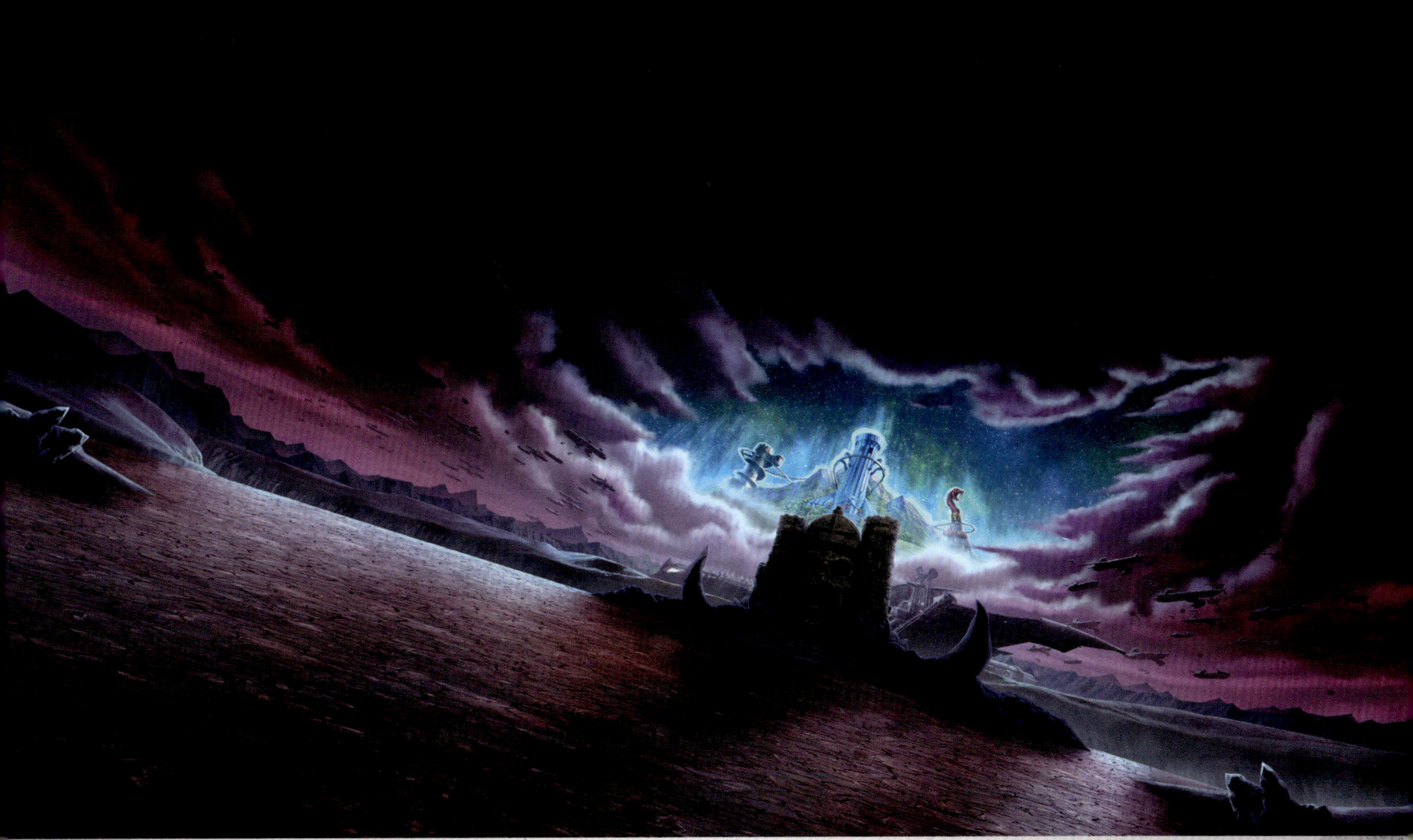

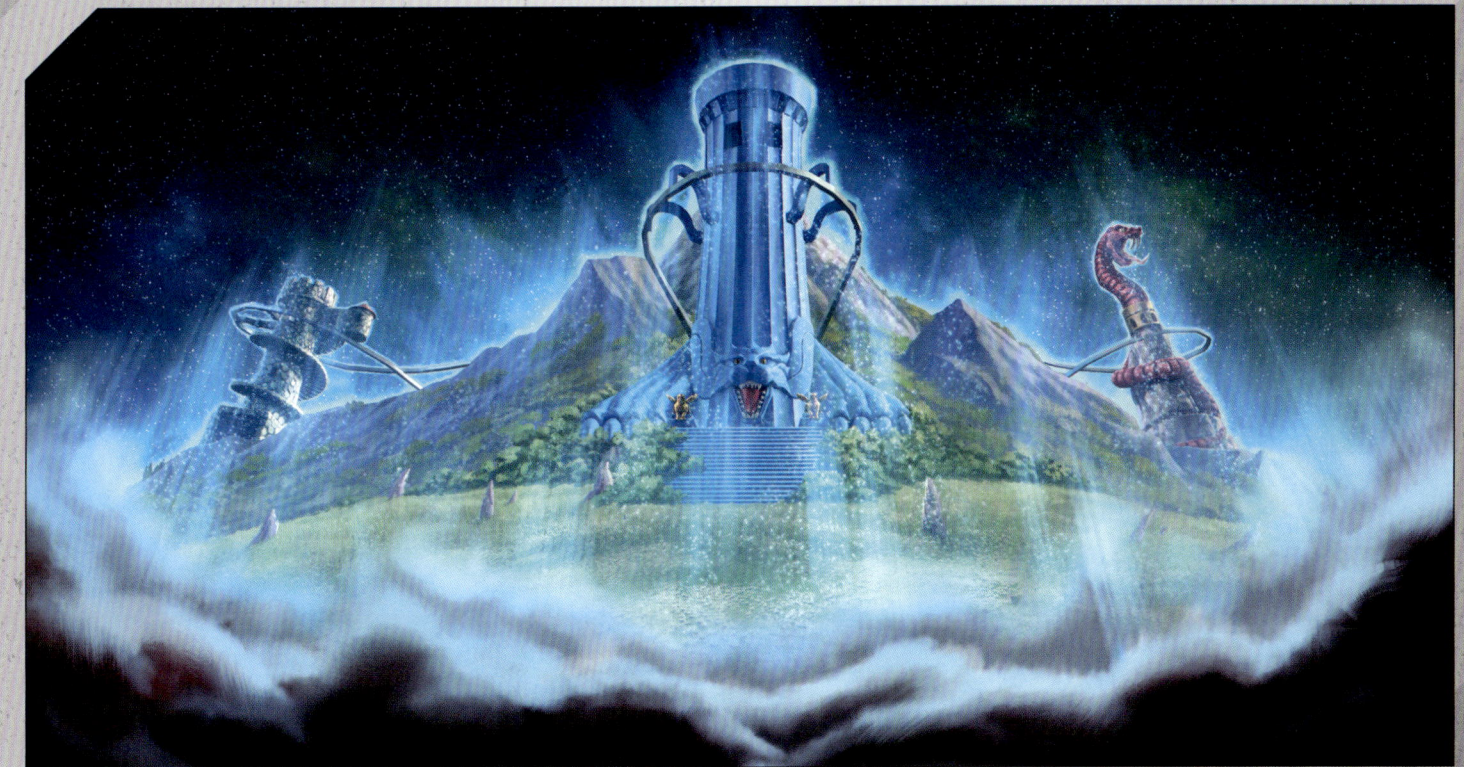
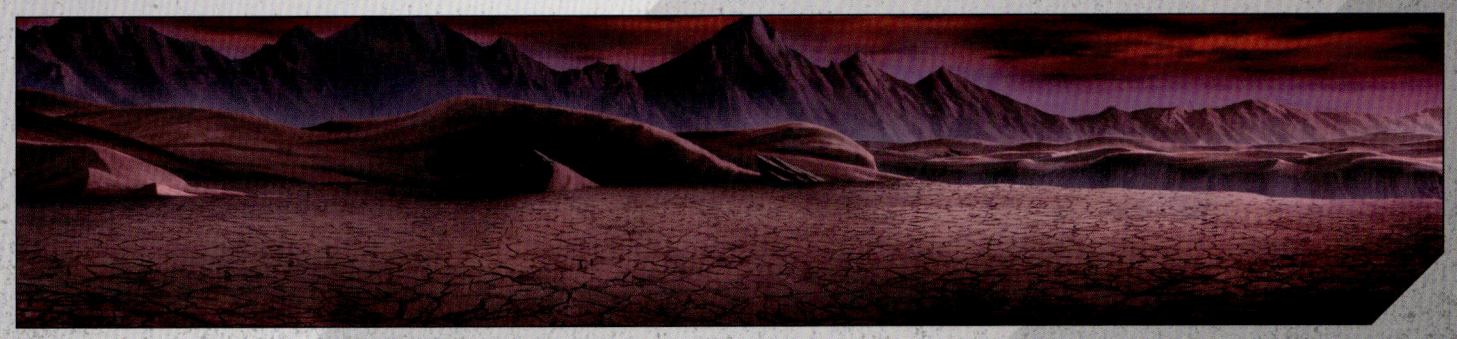

LOCATIONS \\ 99

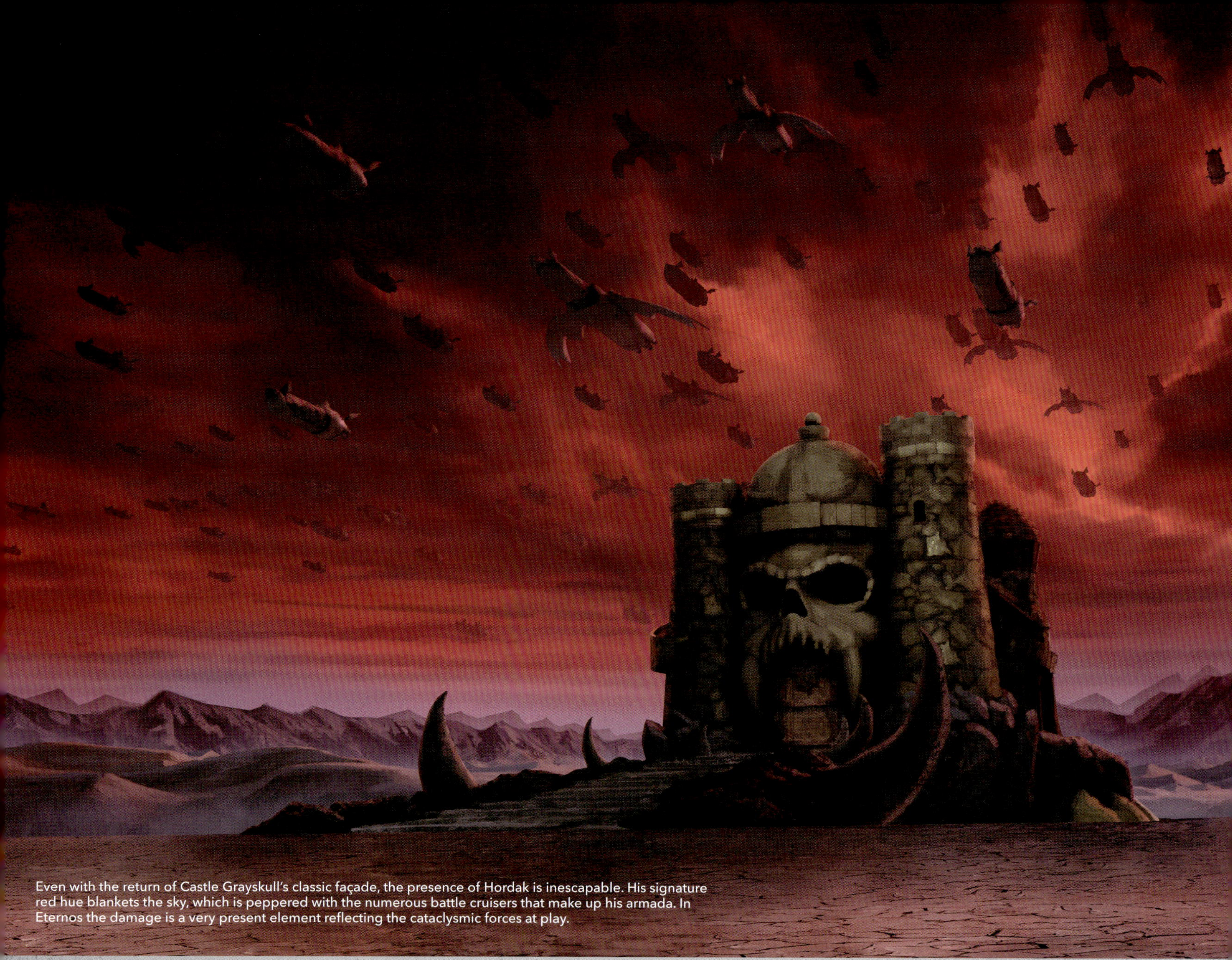

Even with the return of Castle Grayskull's classic façade, the presence of Hordak is inescapable. His signature red hue blankets the sky, which is peppered with the numerous battle cruisers that make up his armada. In Eternos the damage is a very present element reflecting the cataclysmic forces at play.

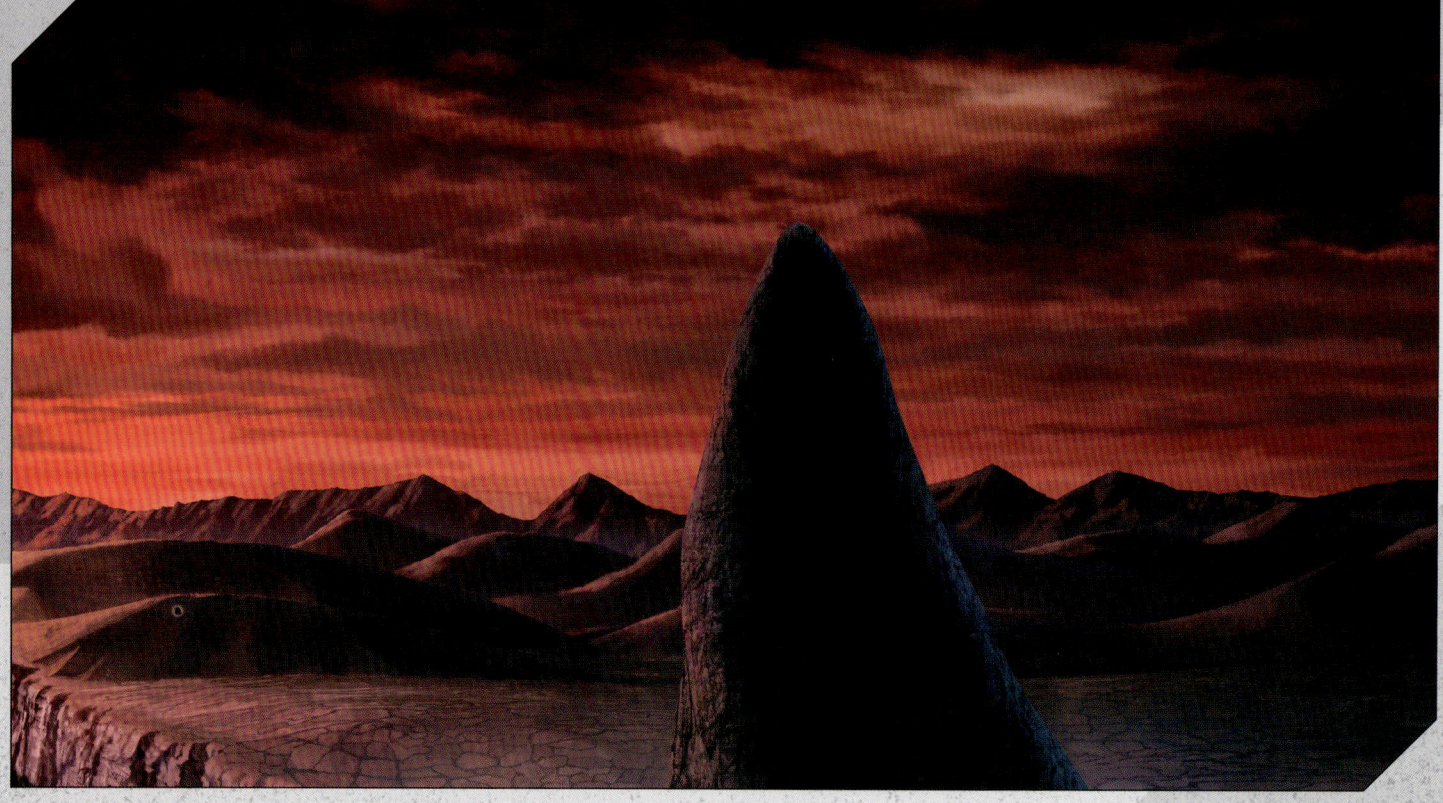

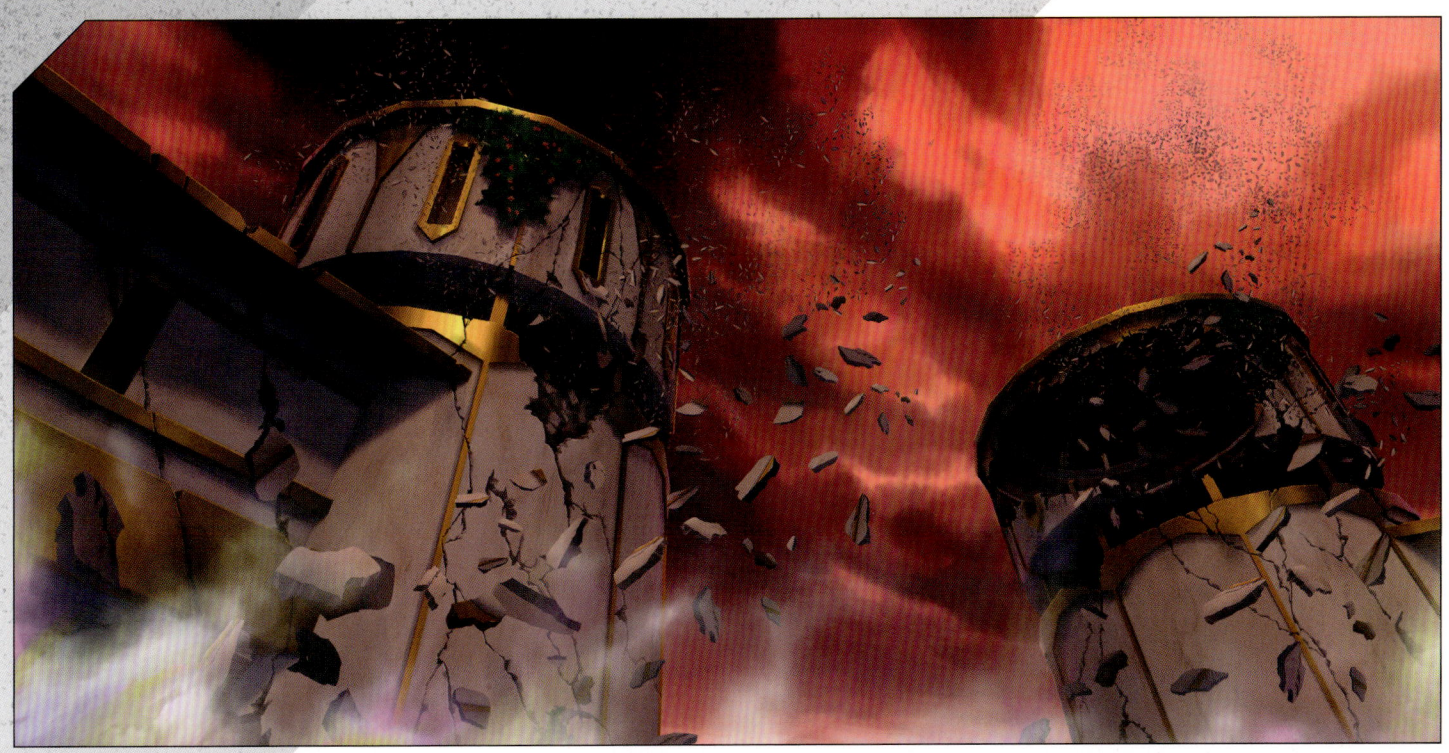
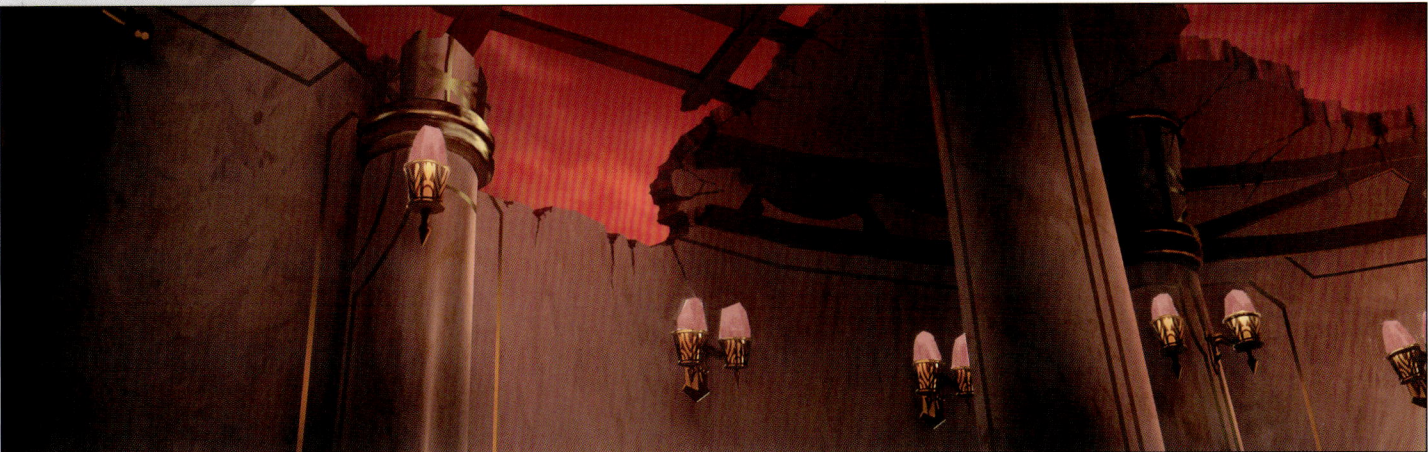
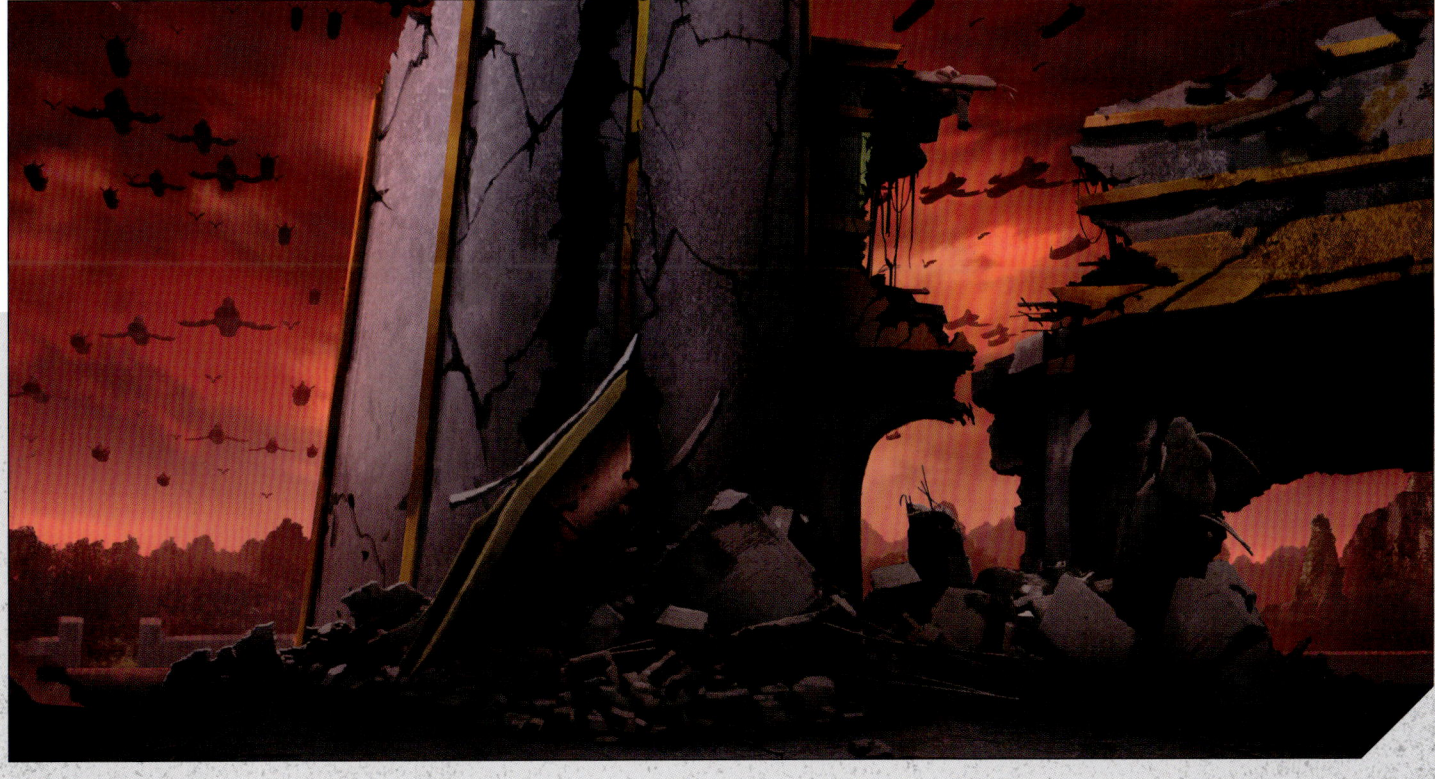

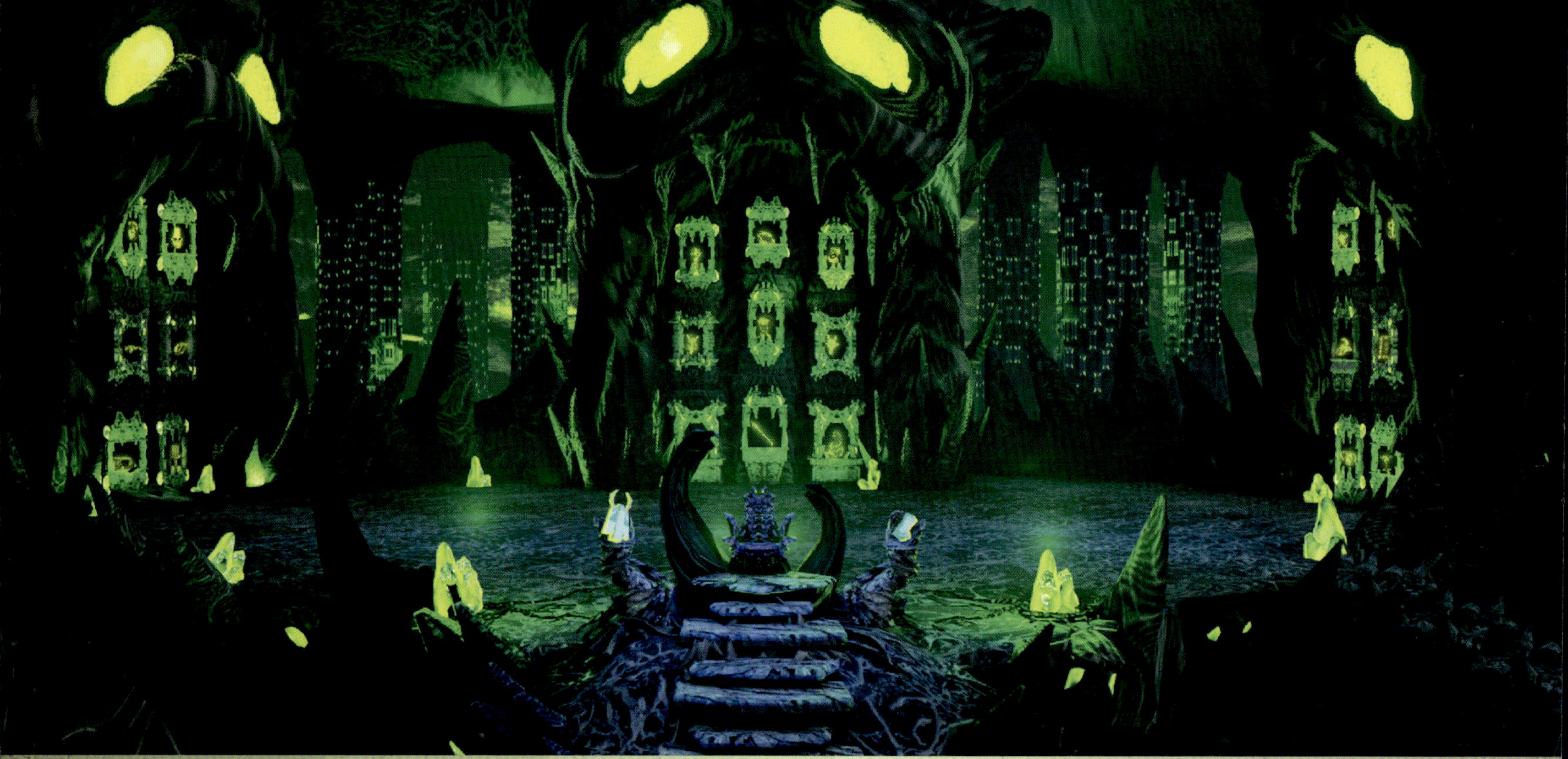

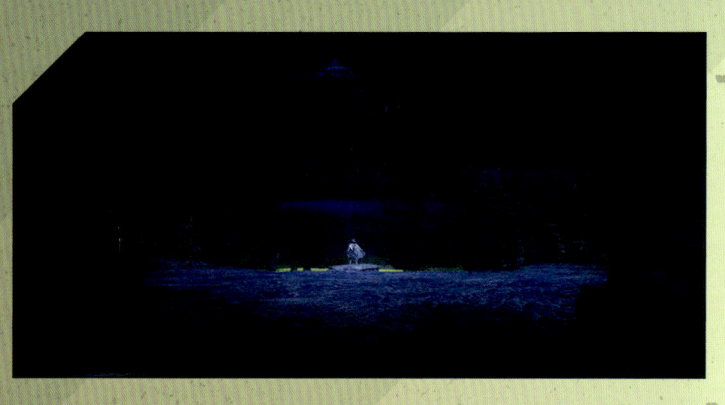
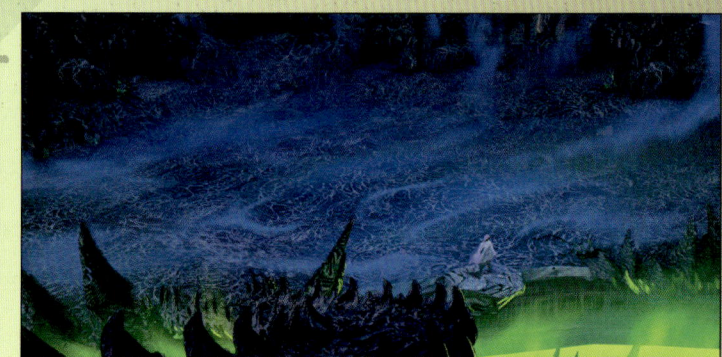
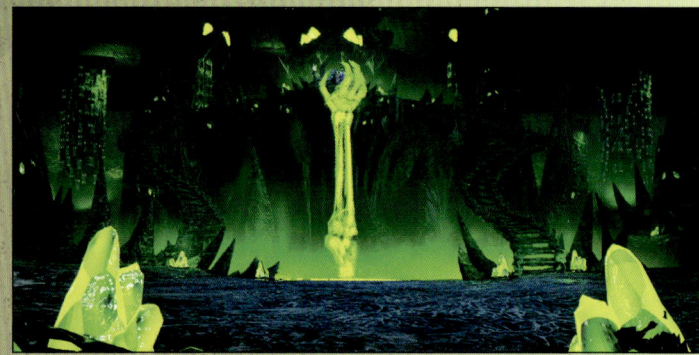
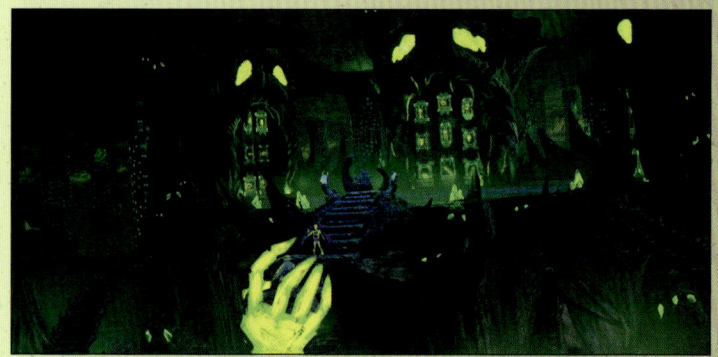
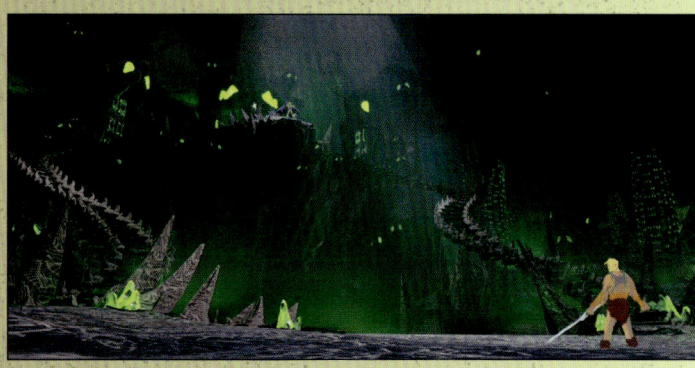
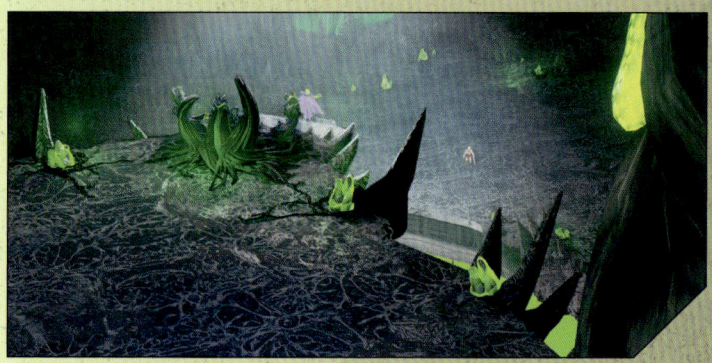

SCARE GLOW'S RELIQUARY
A massive collection of trinkets with columns reaching far back into the mists of Subternia. It was a great opportunity to pack the screen with Easter eggs for eagle-eyed fans who may notice the monstrous cauldron, a dazzling ray of diamond, and a cosmic clock, among many more.

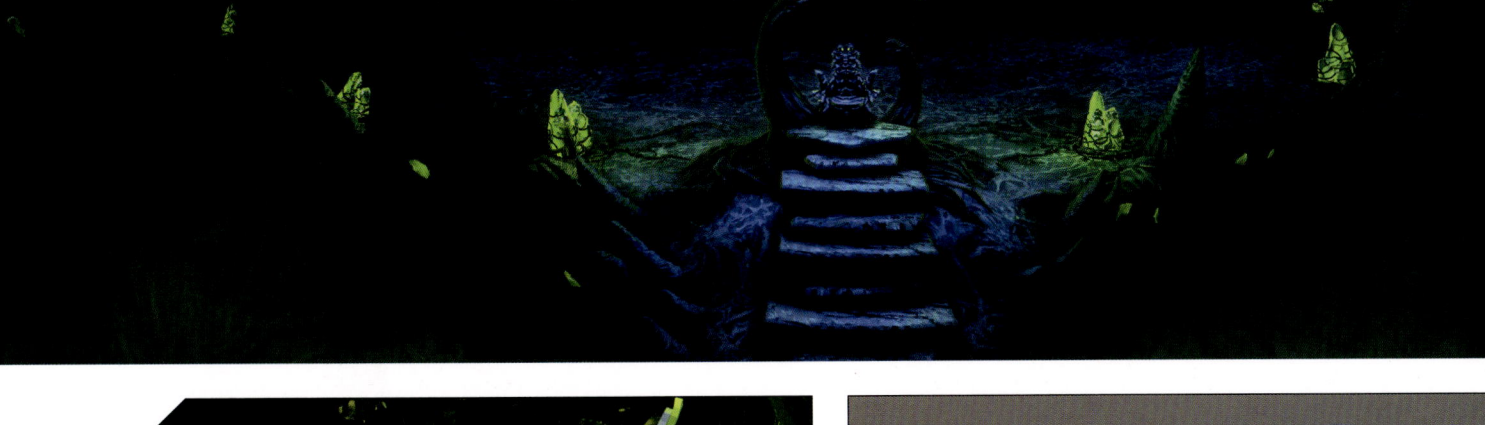
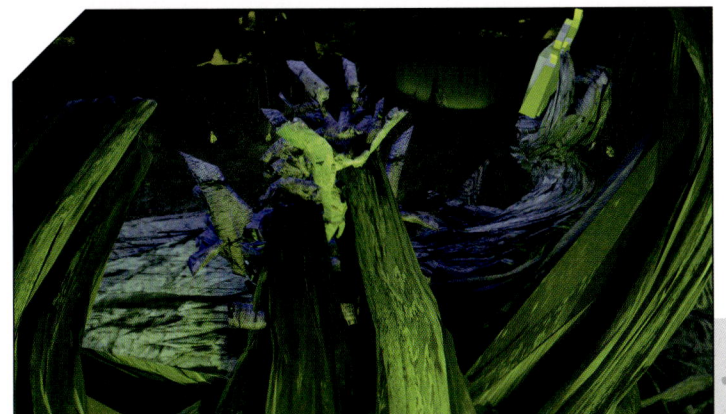
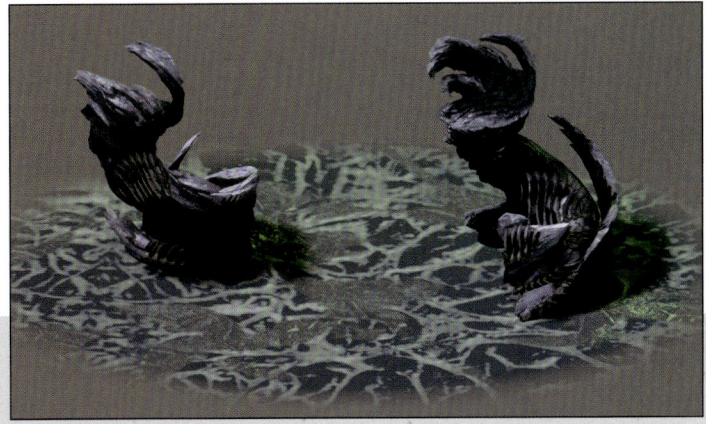

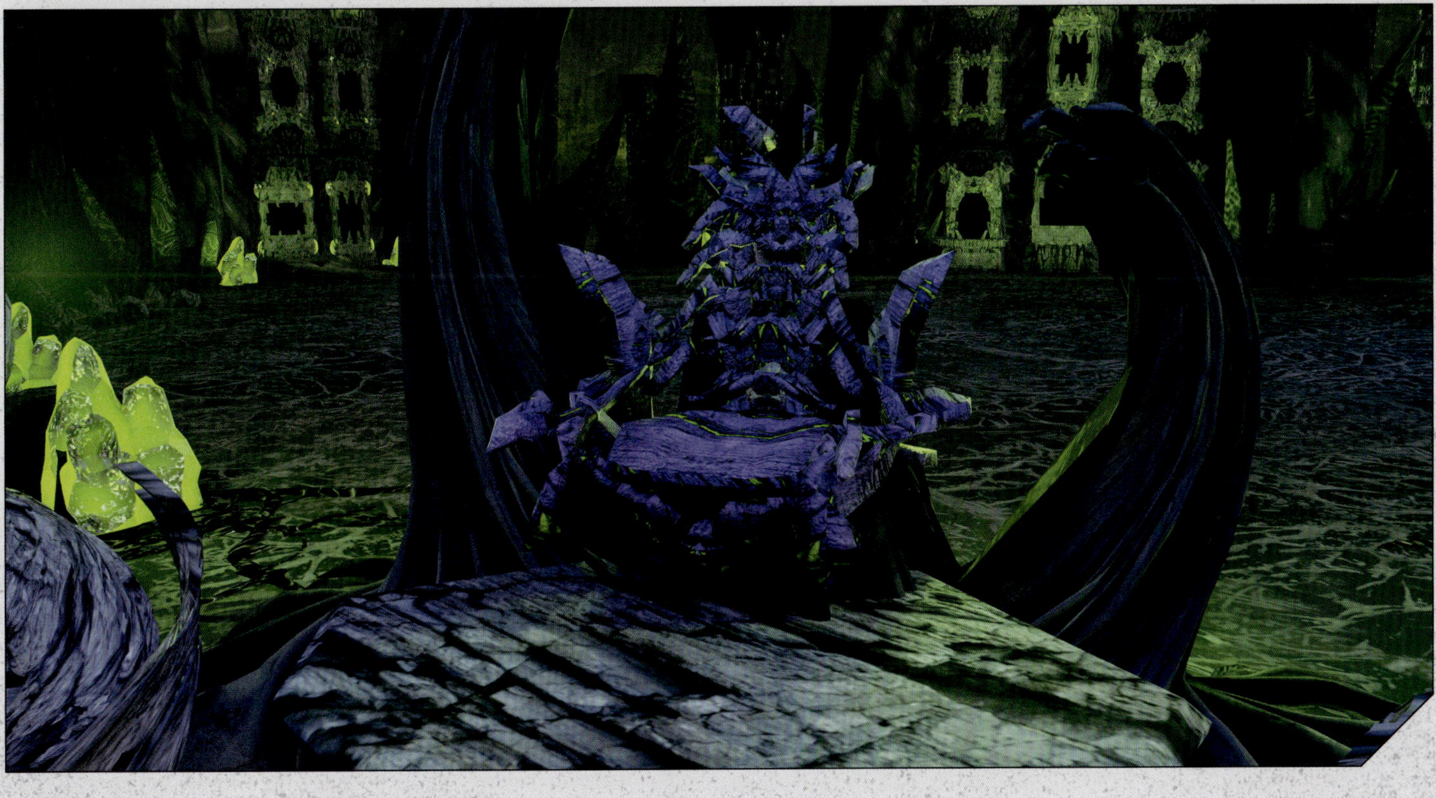

LOCATIONS \\ 103

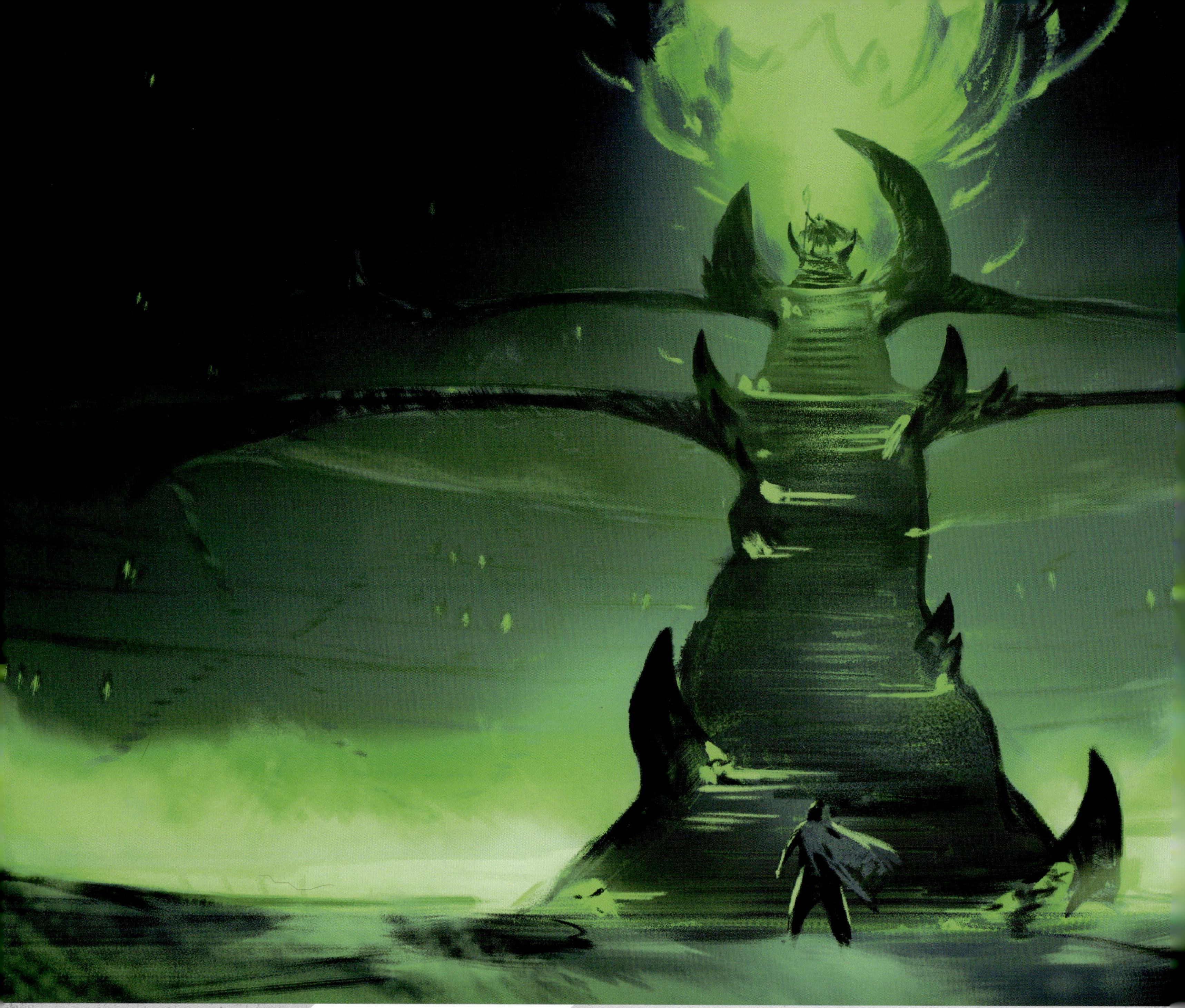

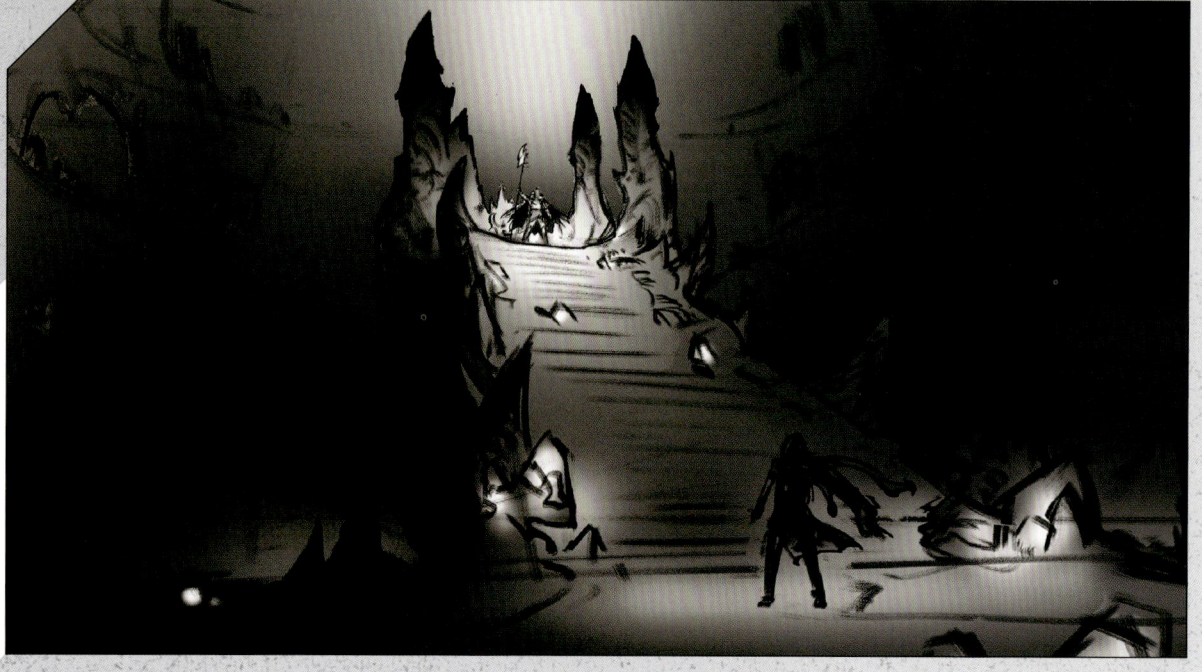
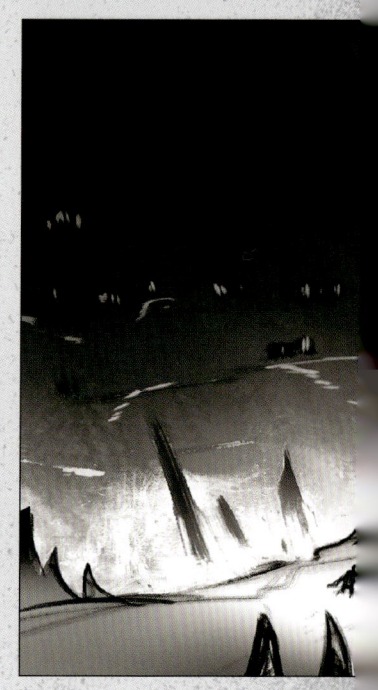

RETURN TO SUBTERNIA

During our last visit to the underworld, the heroes tried to pass through unnoticed. This time, however, Adam heads straight toward the heart of Subternia: Scare Glow's throne room. As it's the first action set piece of the season, we needed a space large enough for all the choreography with plenty of features that showcase Scare Glow's power.

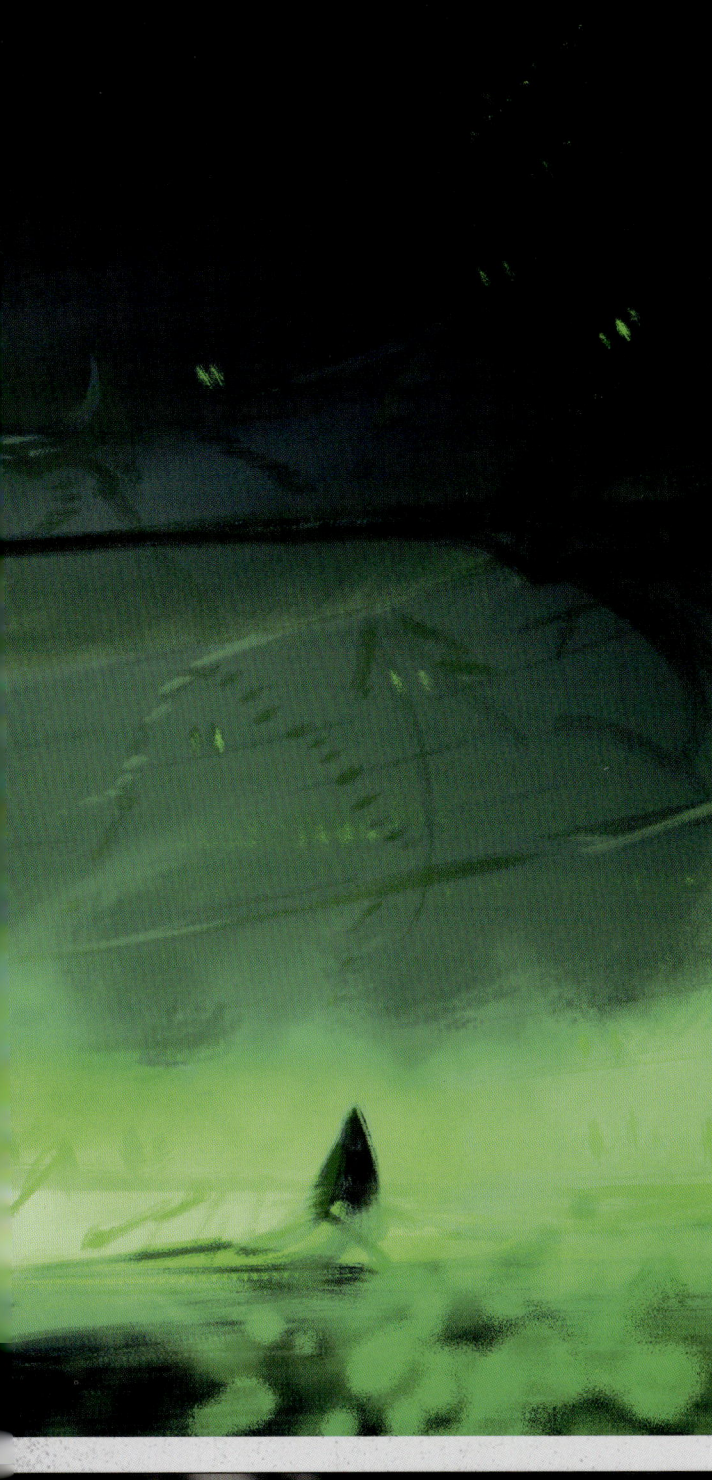

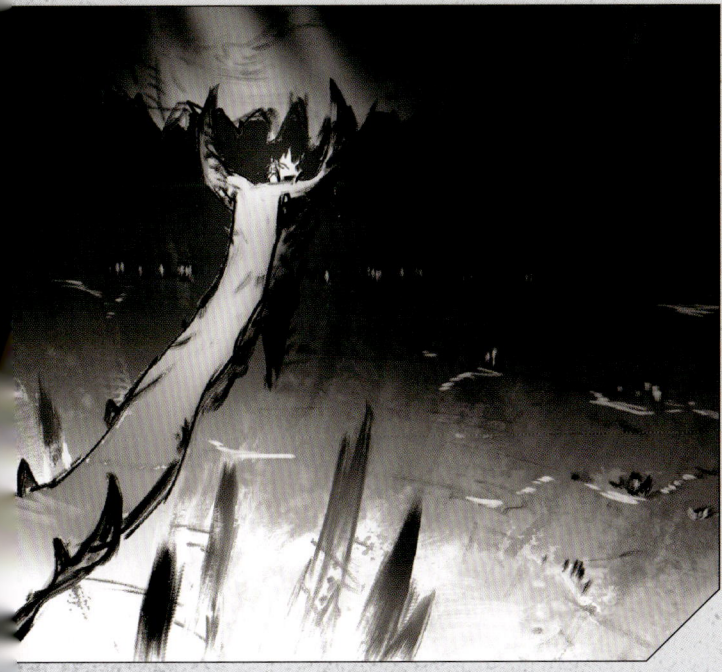

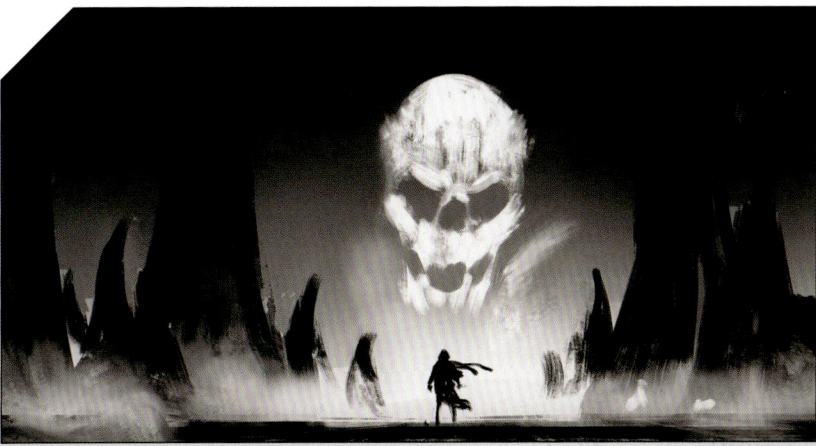

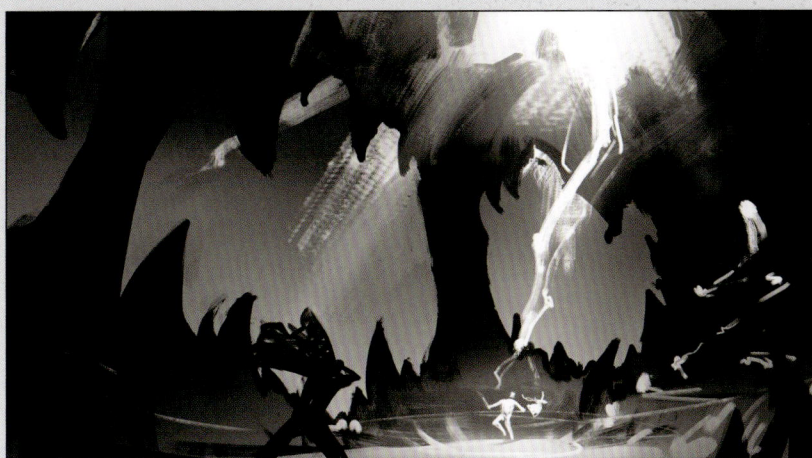

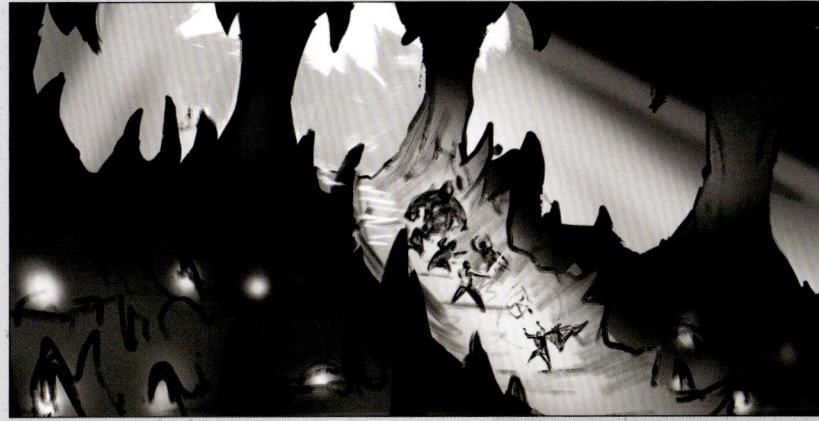

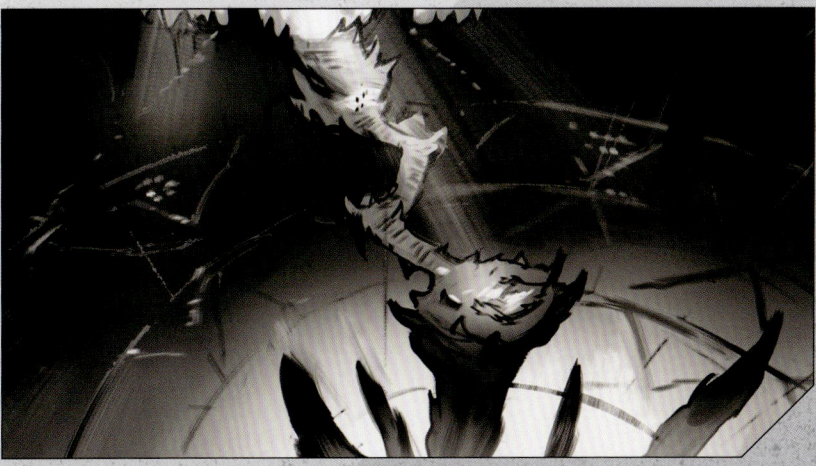

LOCATIONS \\ 105

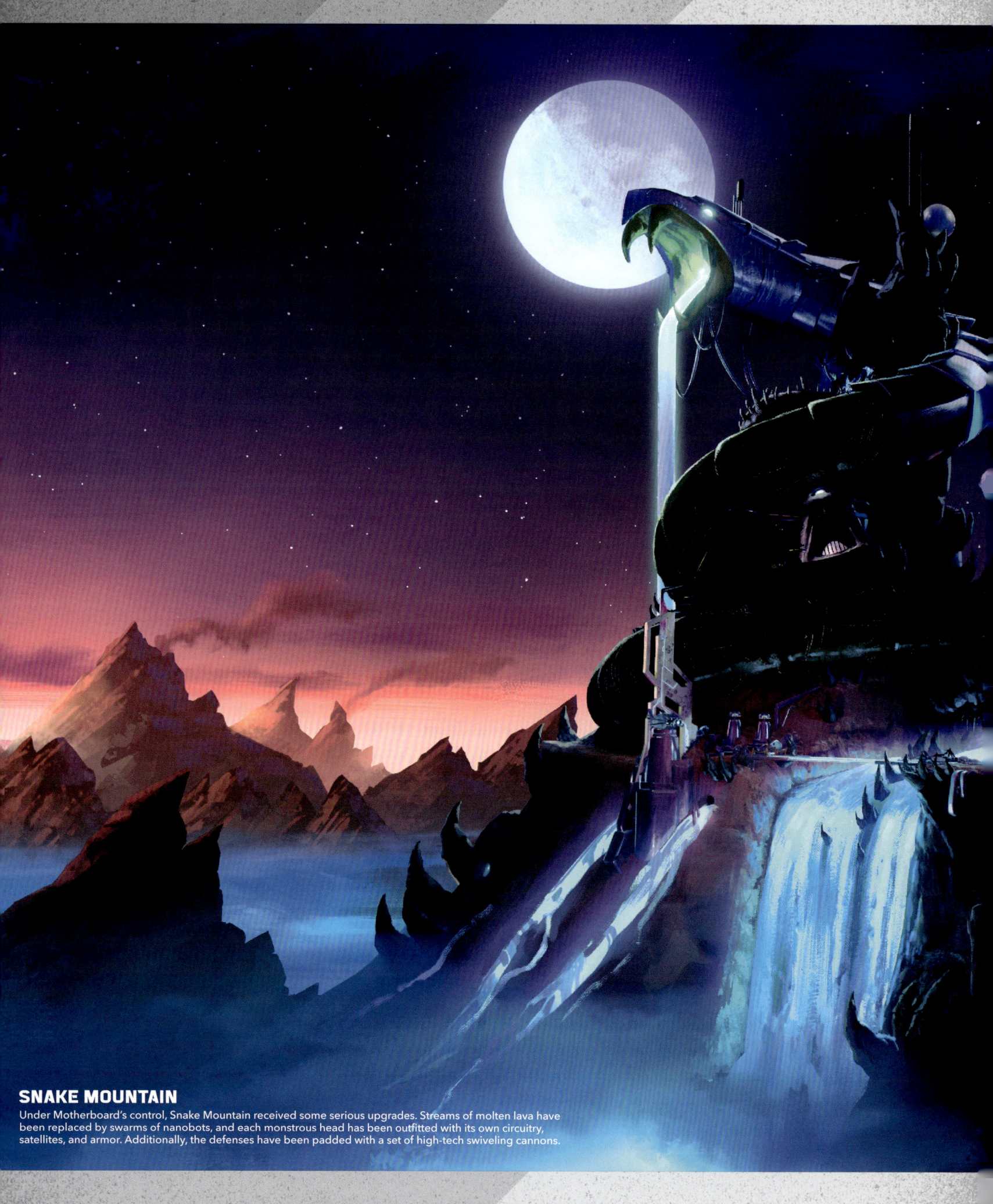

SNAKE MOUNTAIN
Under Motherboard's control, Snake Mountain received some serious upgrades. Streams of molten lava have been replaced by swarms of nanobots, and each monstrous head has been outfitted with its own circuitry, satellites, and armor. Additionally, the defenses have been padded with a set of high-tech swiveling cannons.

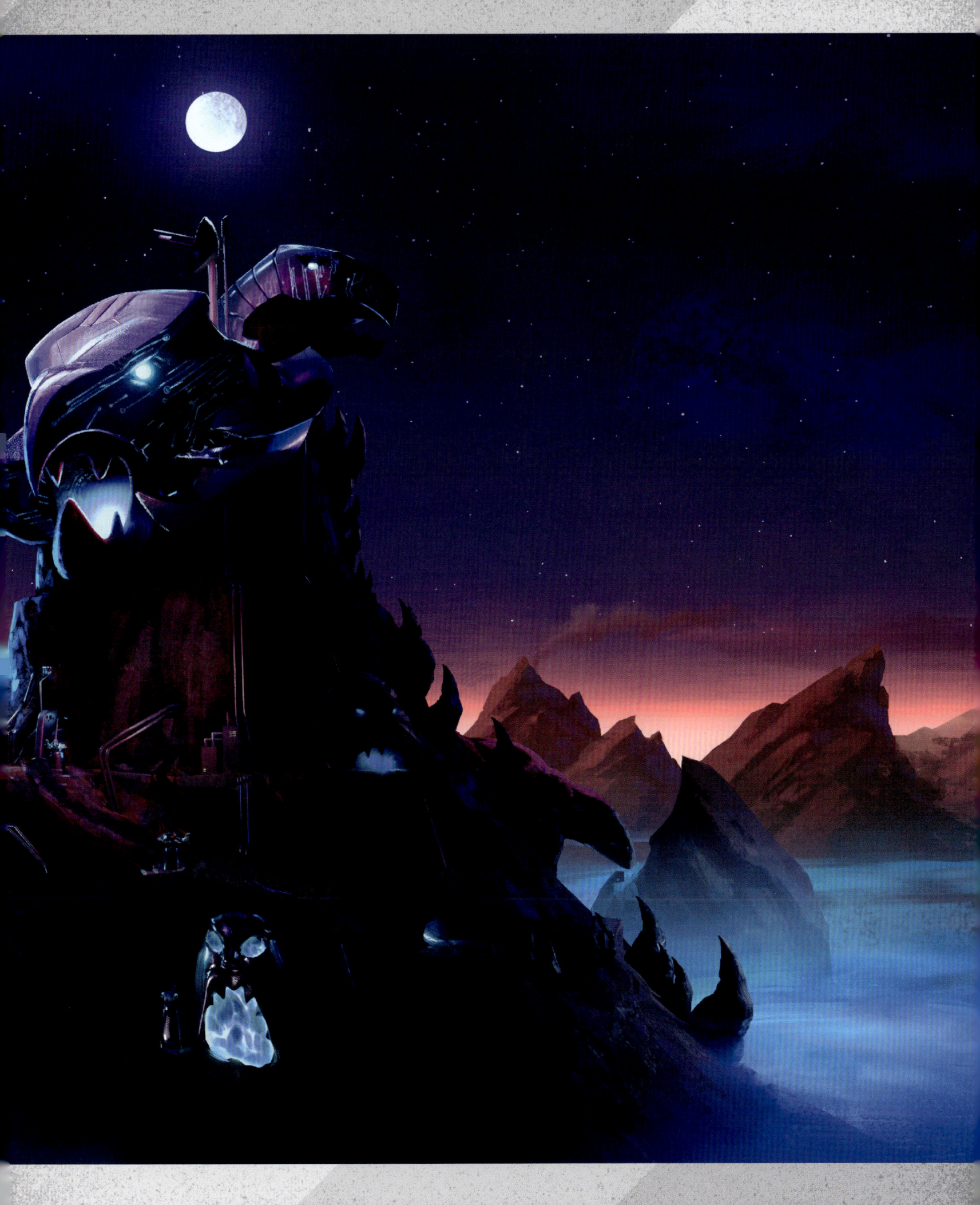

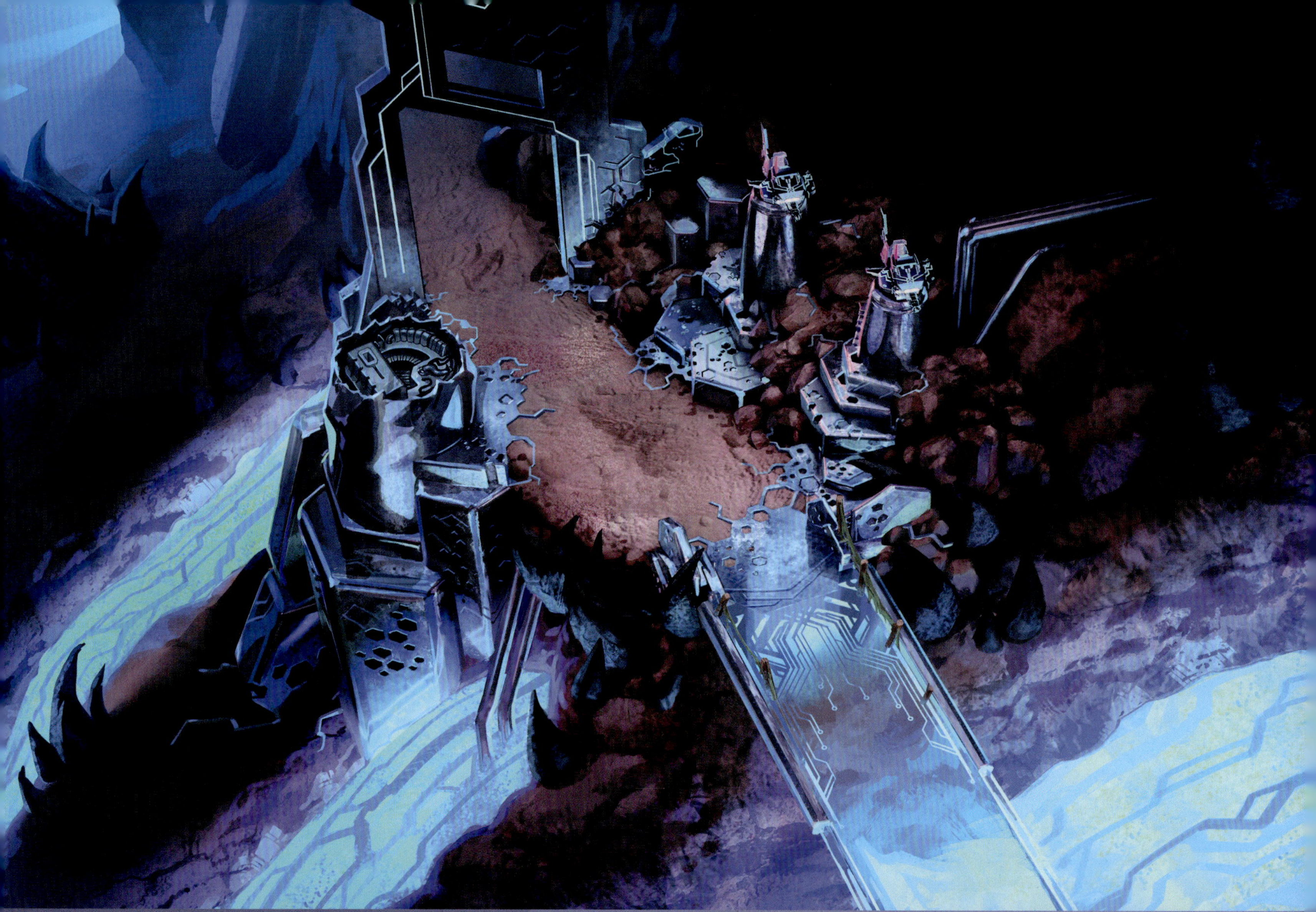

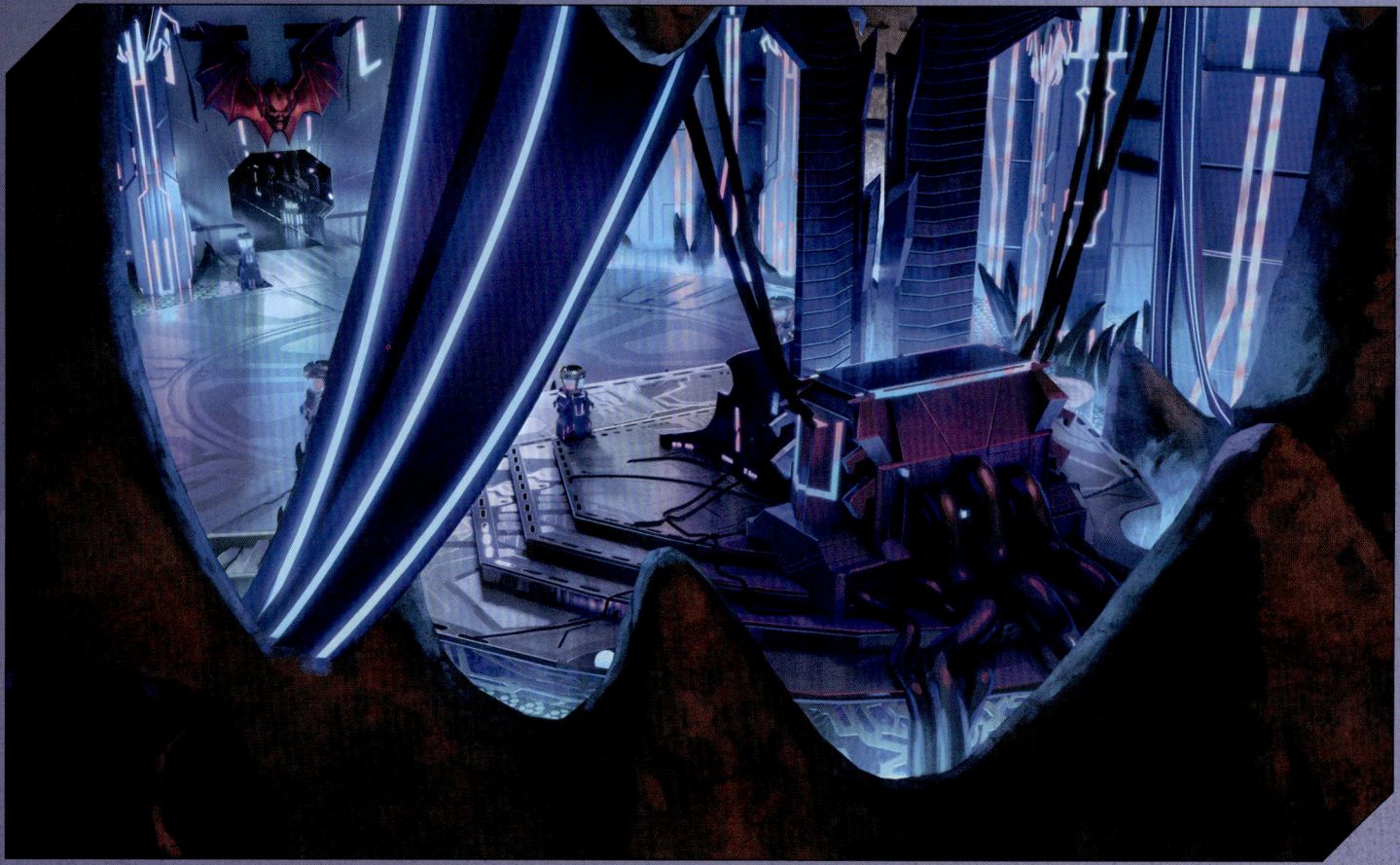

With Motherboard awakened and her allegiance known, Demon's Head has been covered in Horde paraphernalia. Where her Screeech form once rested now sits a grand throne.

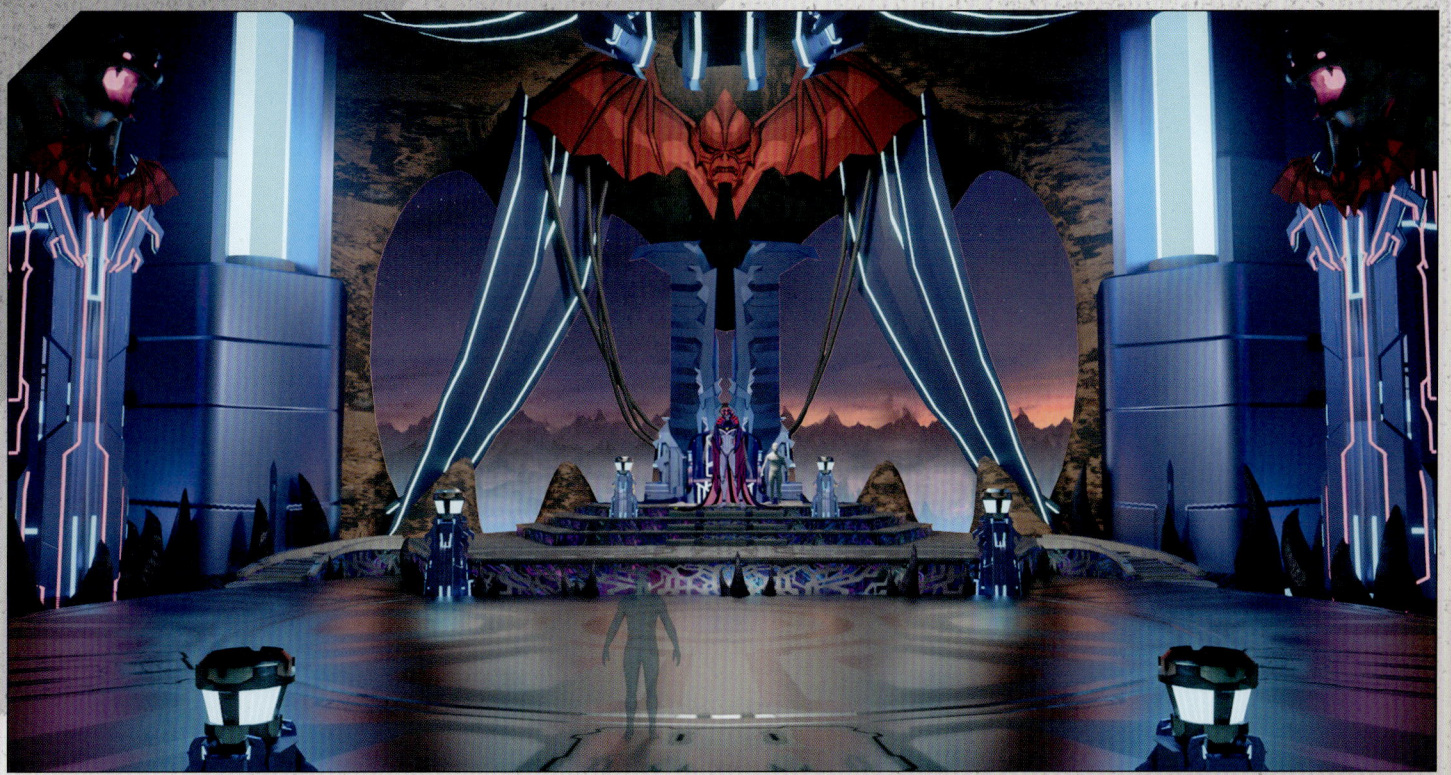

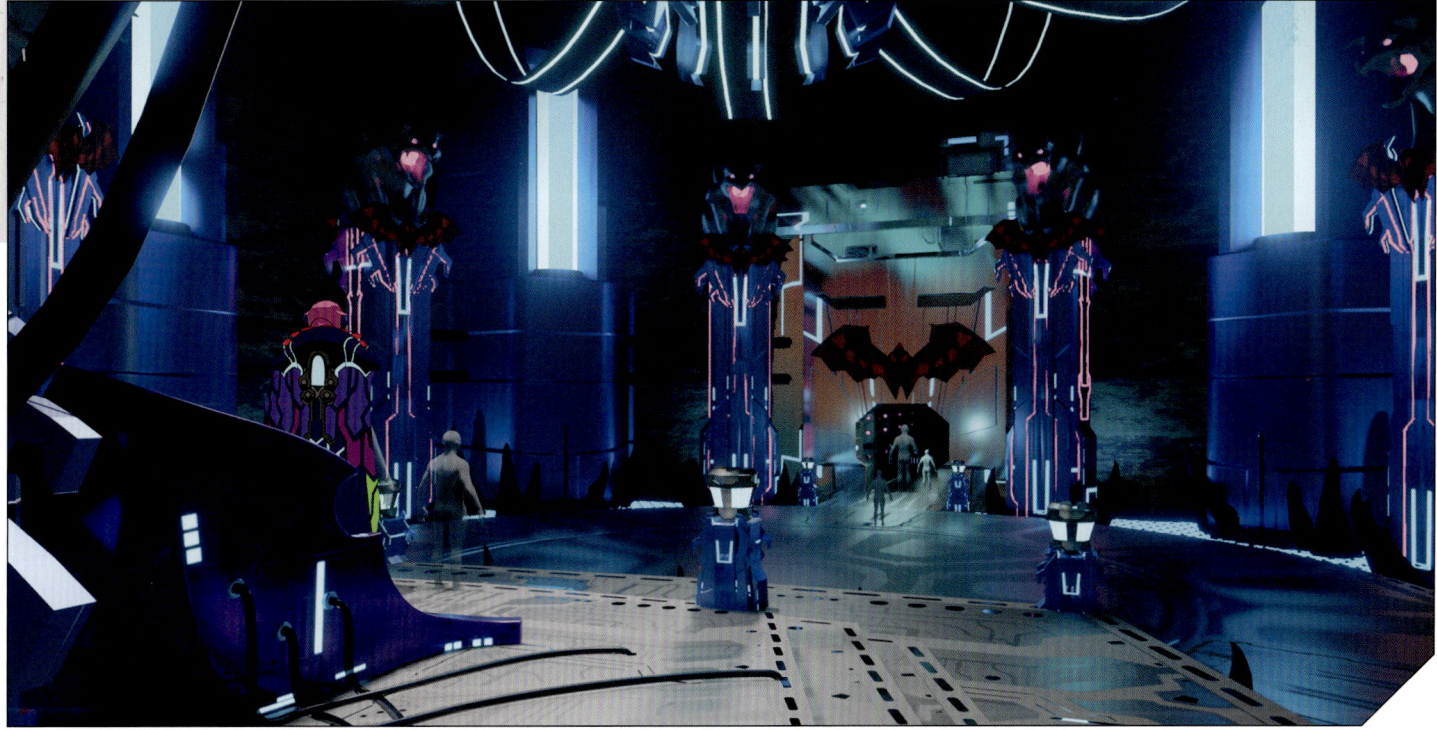

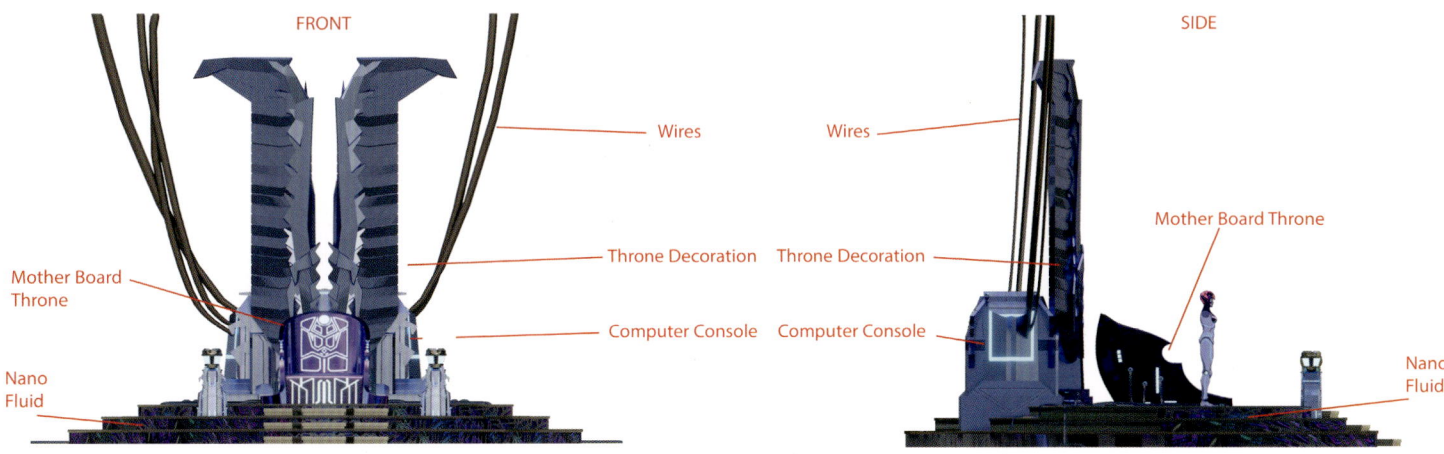

FRONT — Wires, Throne Decoration, Mother Board Throne, Nano Fluid

SIDE — Wires, Mother Board Throne, Throne Decoration, Computer Console, Nano Fluid

LOCATIONS \\ 109

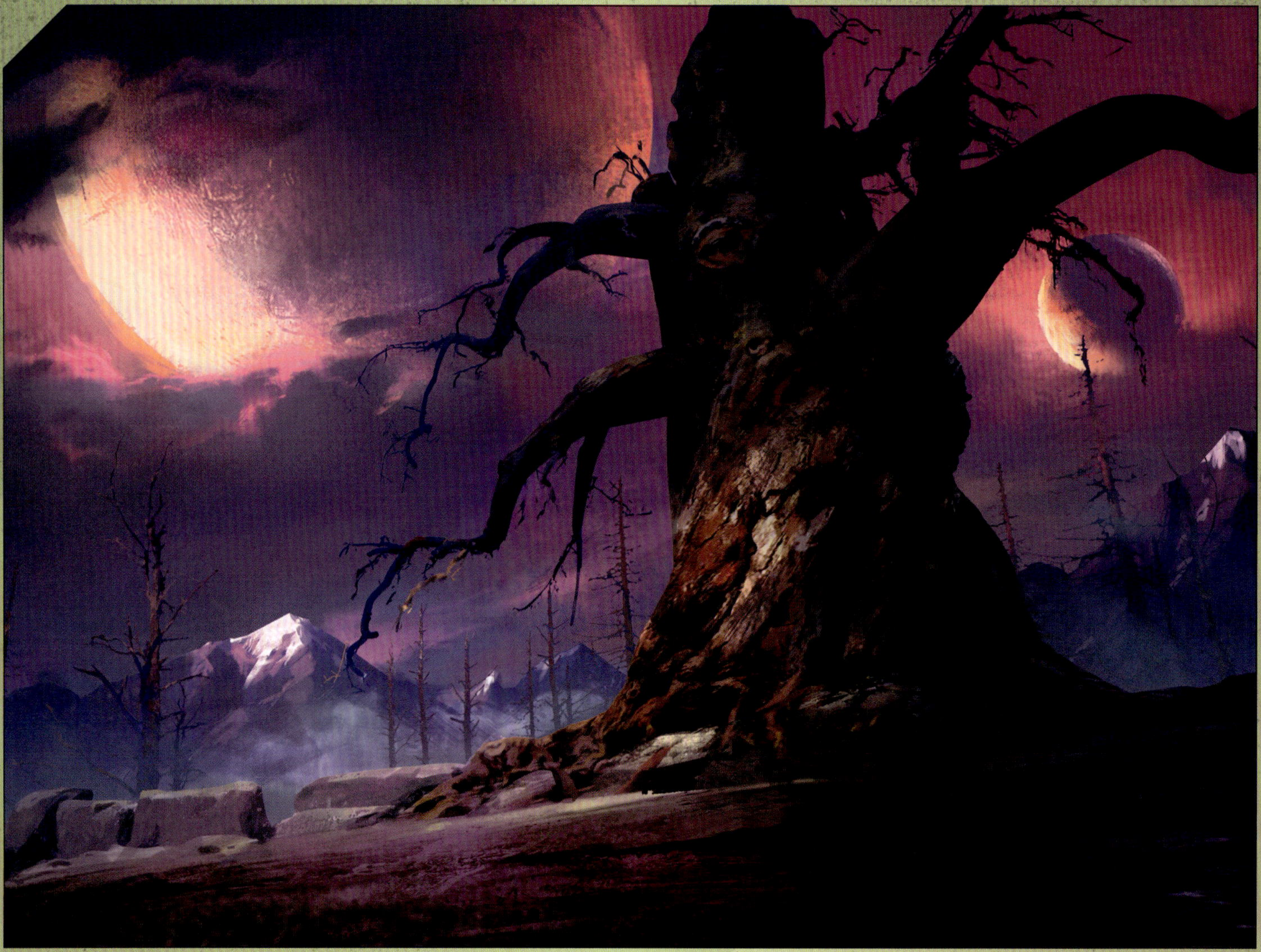

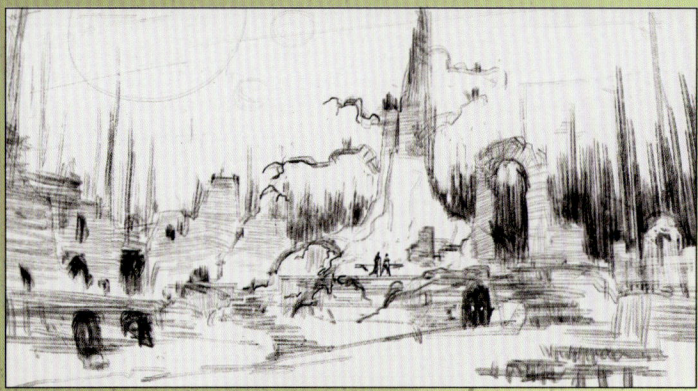
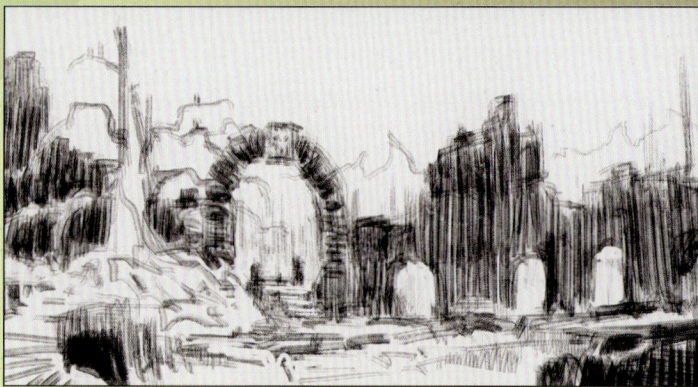
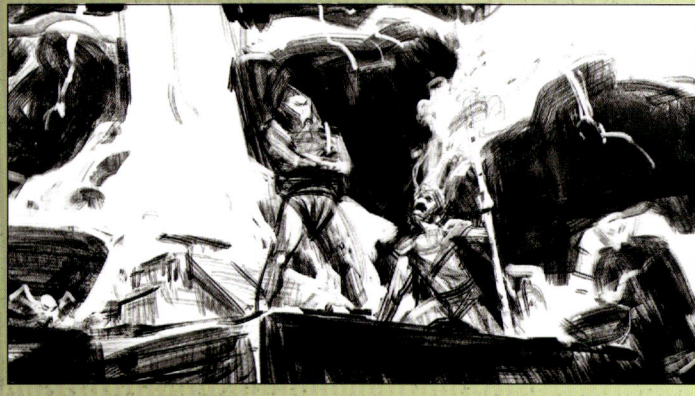
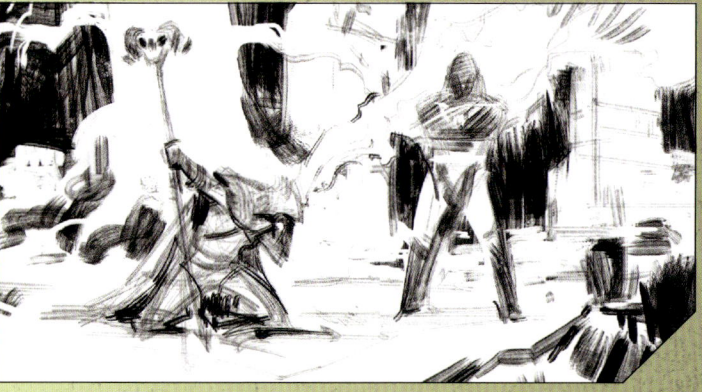

THE FRIGHT ZONE

What better place for Hordak to train young Keldor and bequeath him the Ha'vok Staff than the Fright Zone? Though we experimented with different color palettes, ultimately we decided that this particular Easter egg should be as close as possible to the original box art.

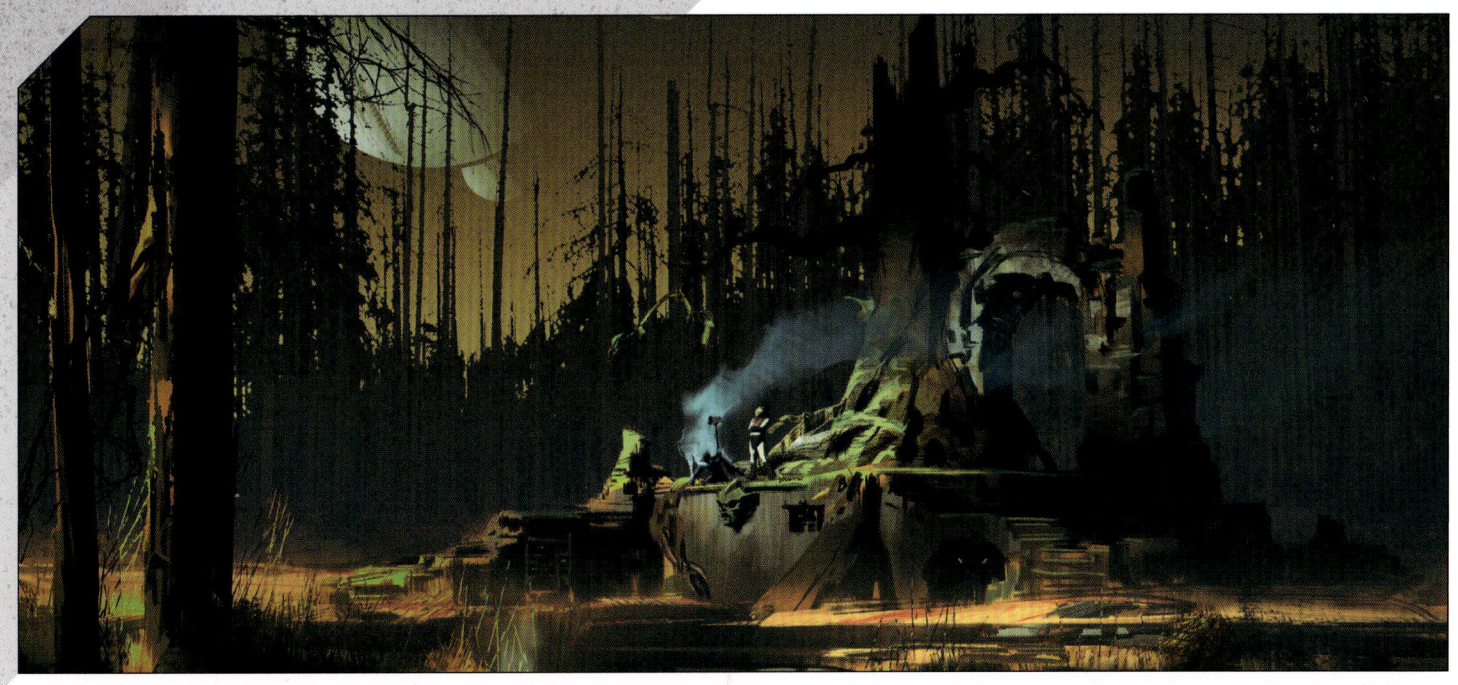
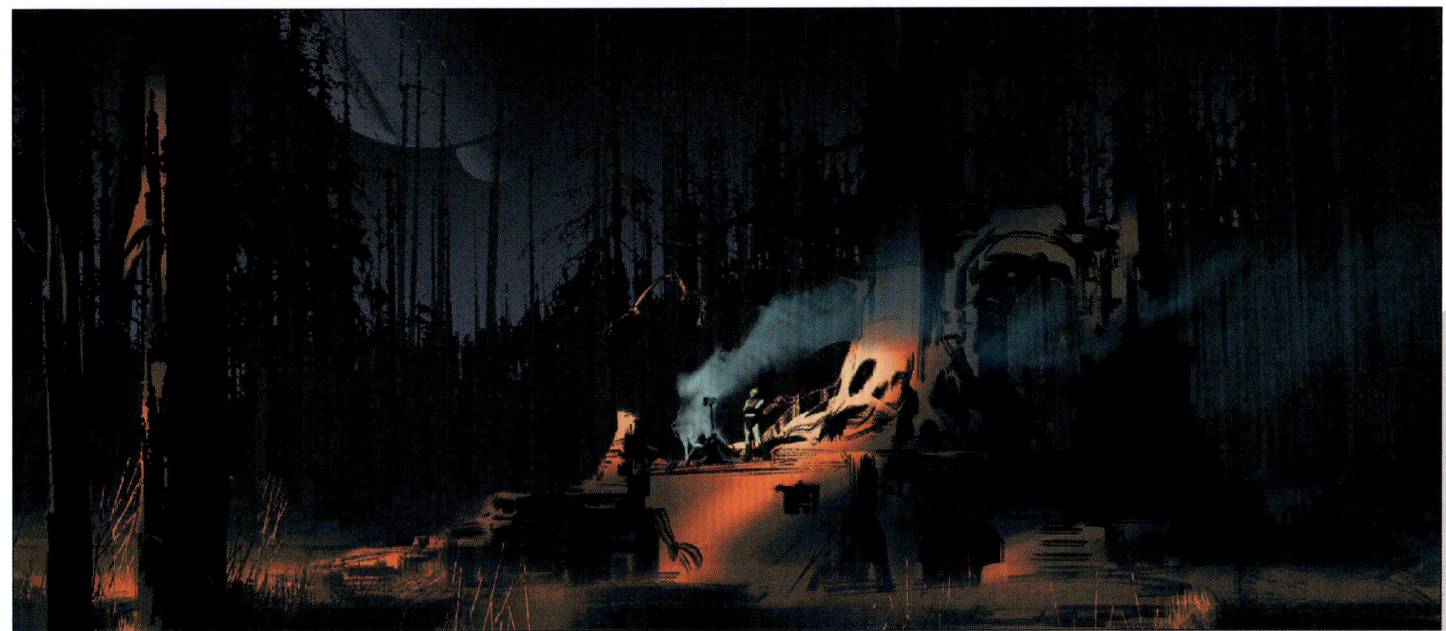
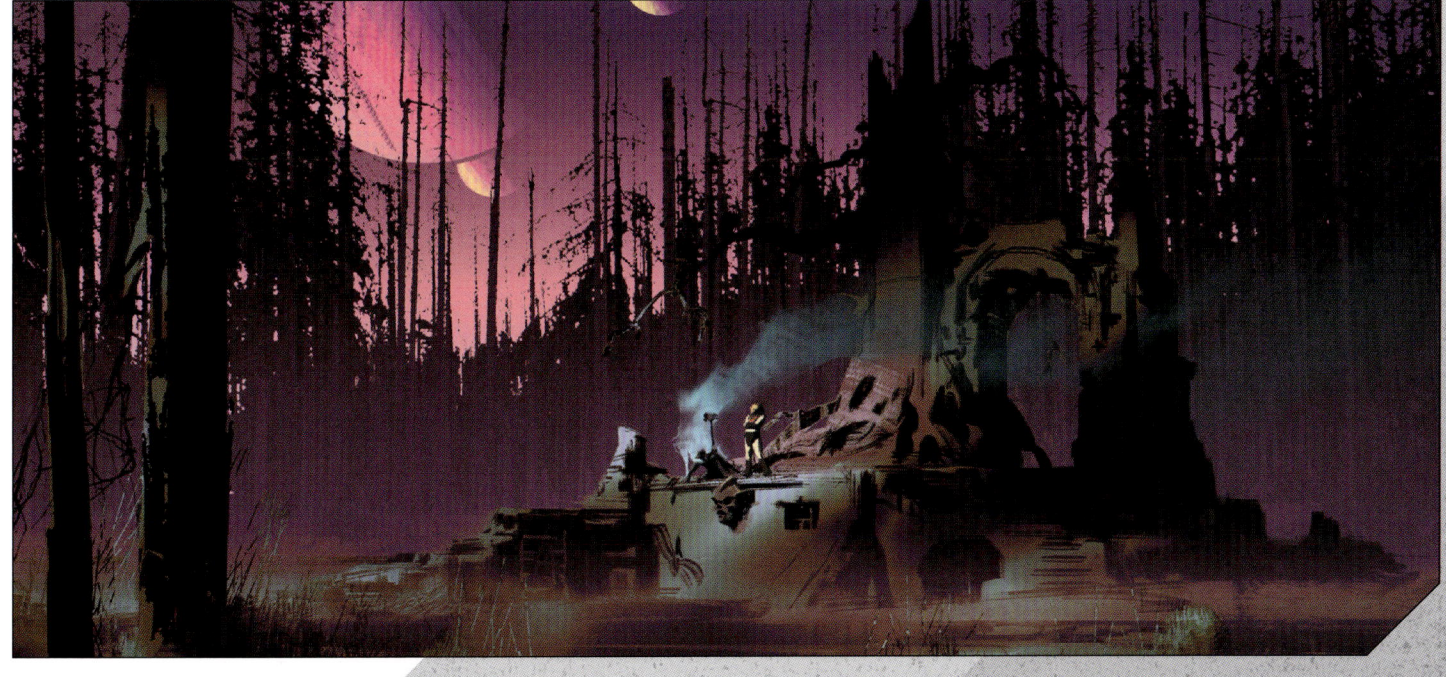

LOCATIONS \\ 111

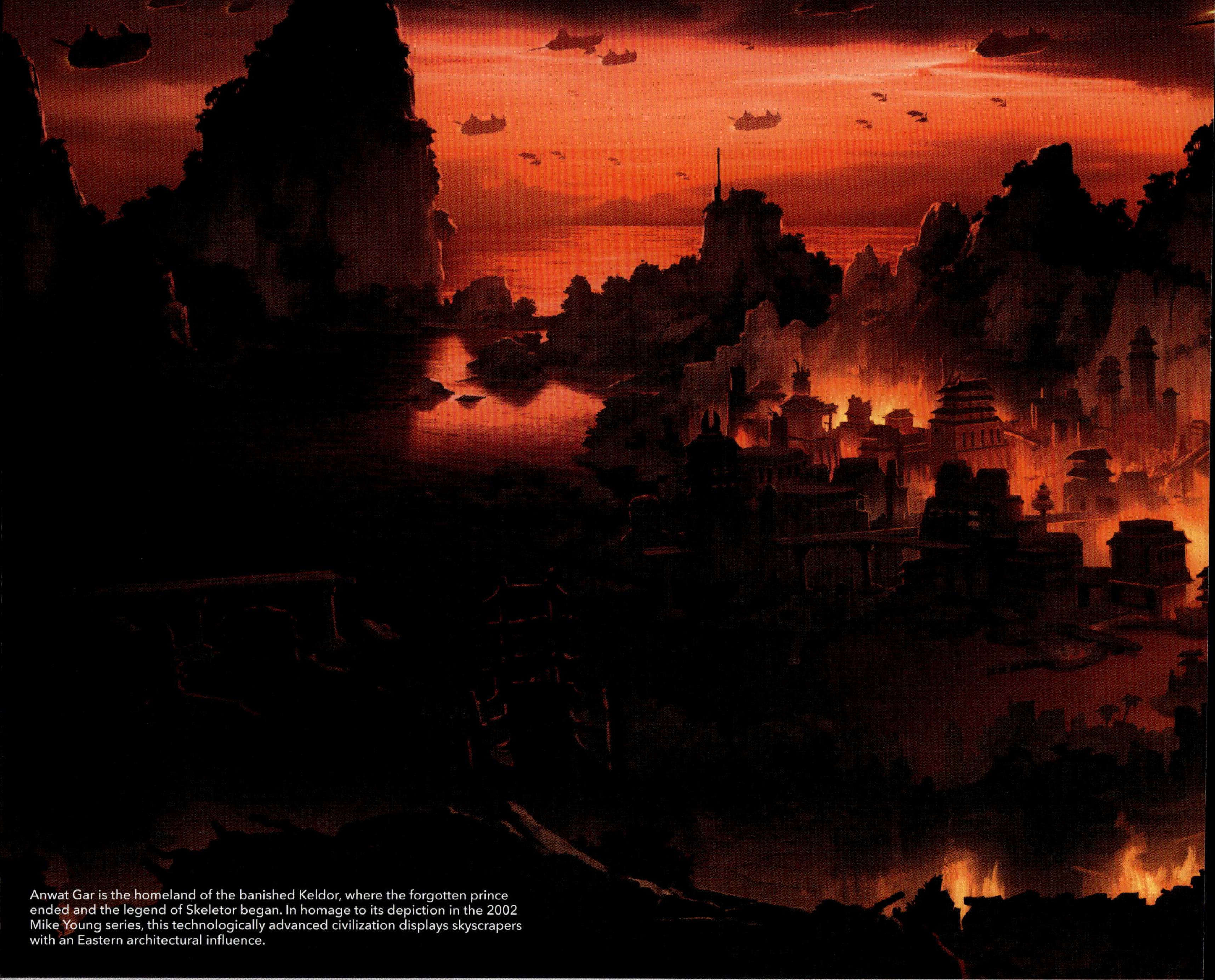

Anwat Gar is the homeland of the banished Keldor, where the forgotten prince ended and the legend of Skeletor began. In homage to its depiction in the 2002 Mike Young series, this technologically advanced civilization displays skyscrapers with an Eastern architectural influence.

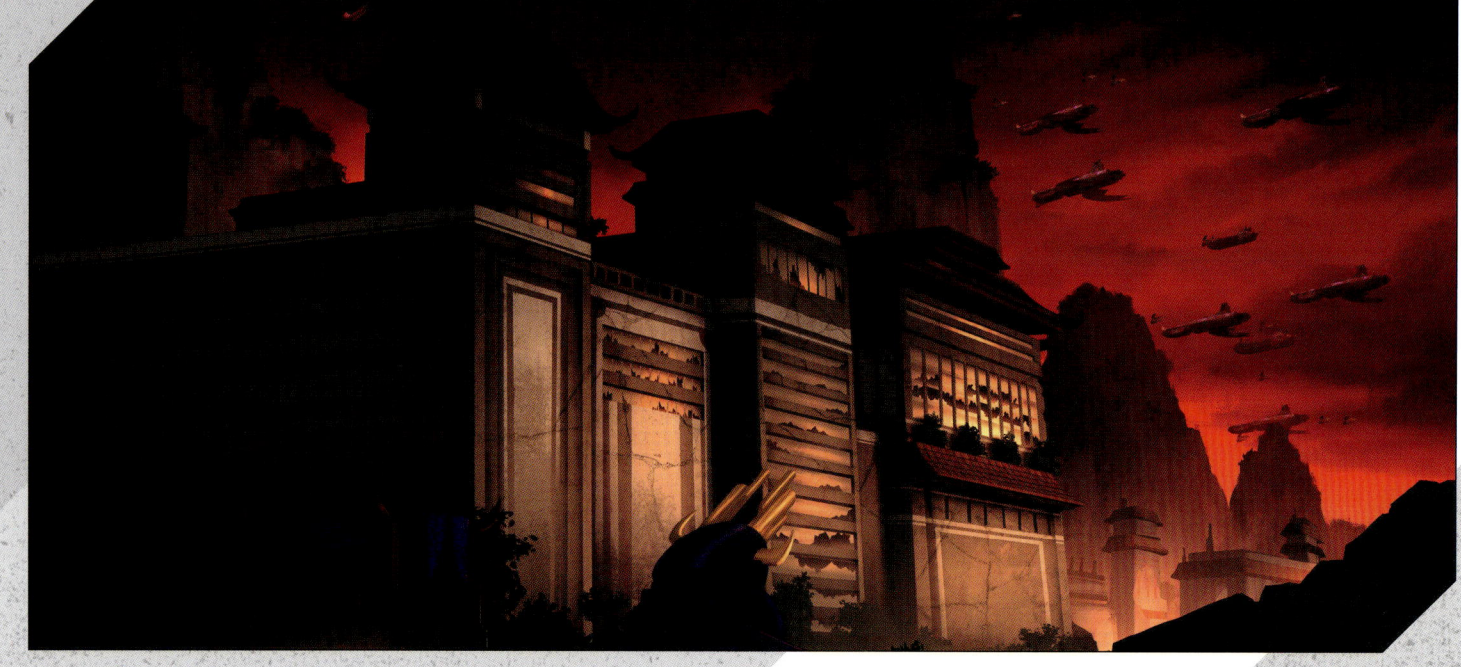

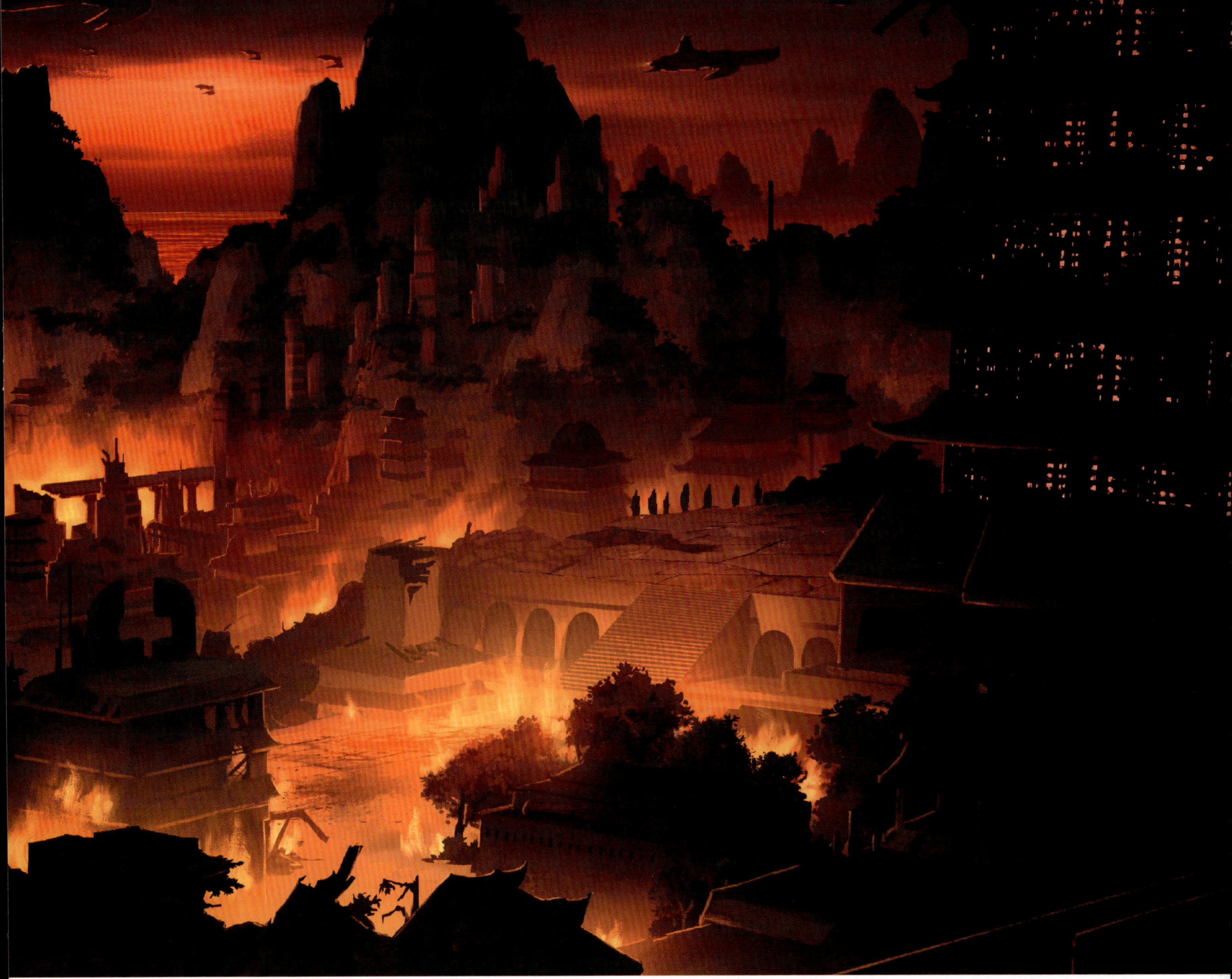

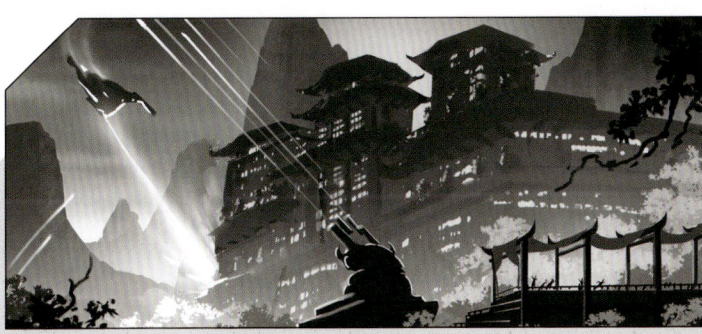
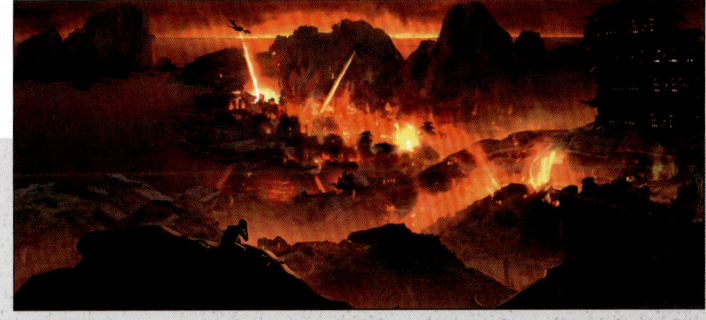
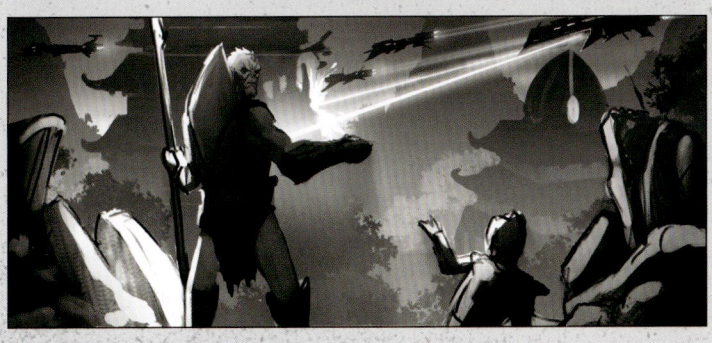
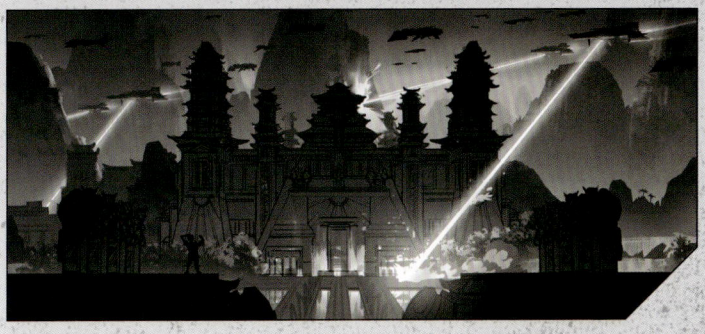

LOCATIONS \\ 113

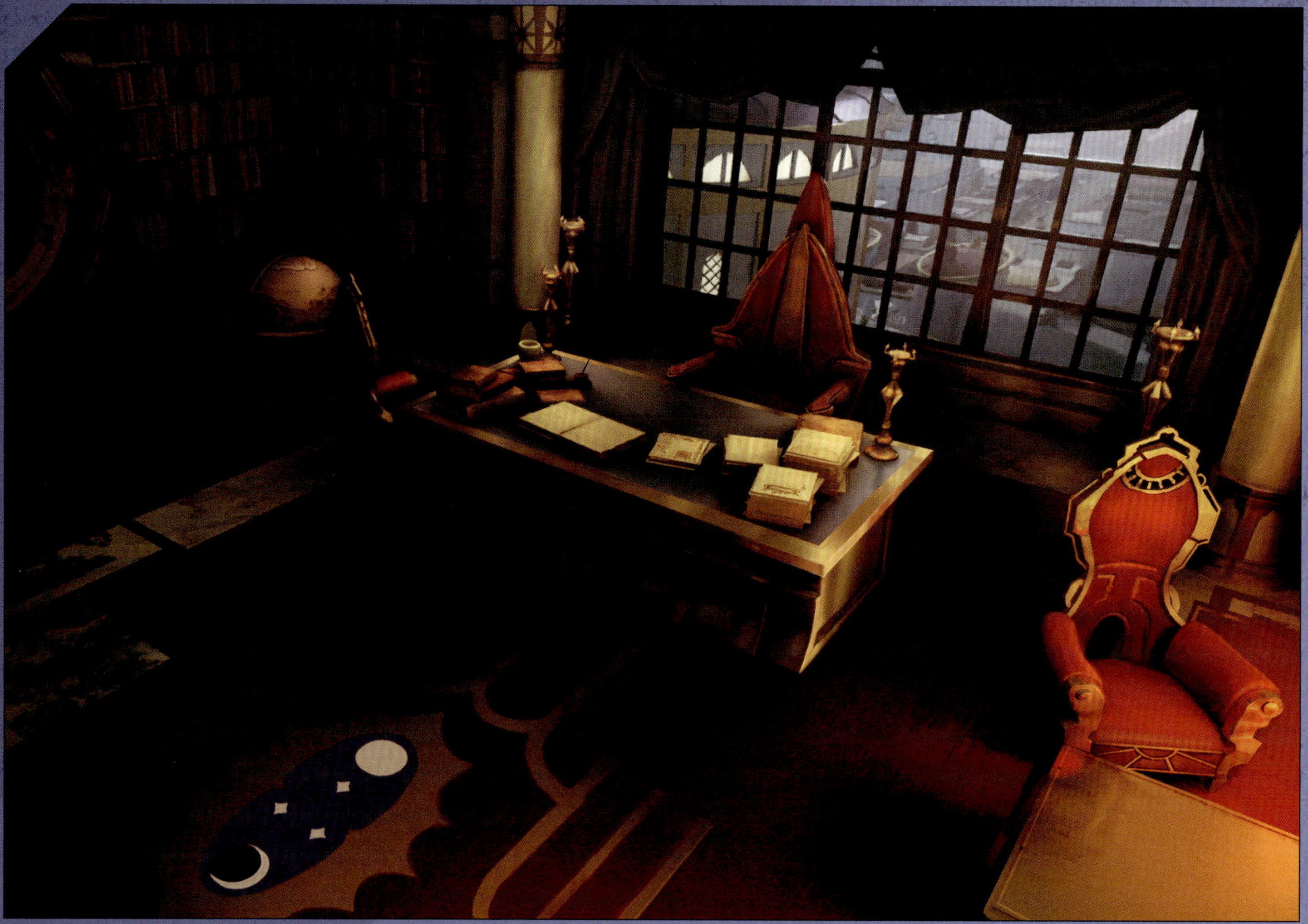

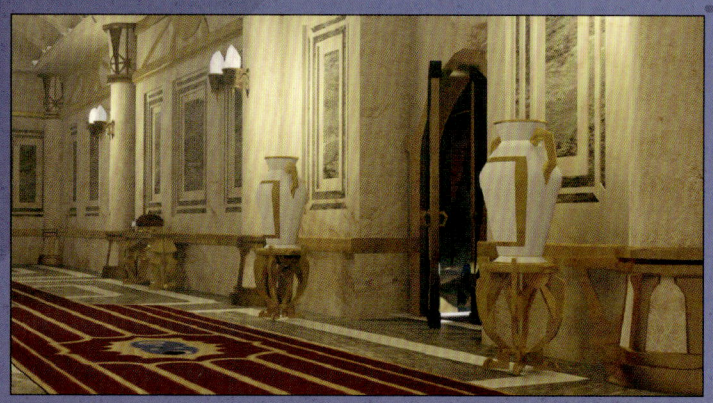

THE KING'S STUDY
A king's work is never done, and not even the unexpected passing of Randor can put a pause on bureaucracy—as evidenced by the mountain of papers piling up on his desk. Though this room has served many a king, it has changed very little over the years.

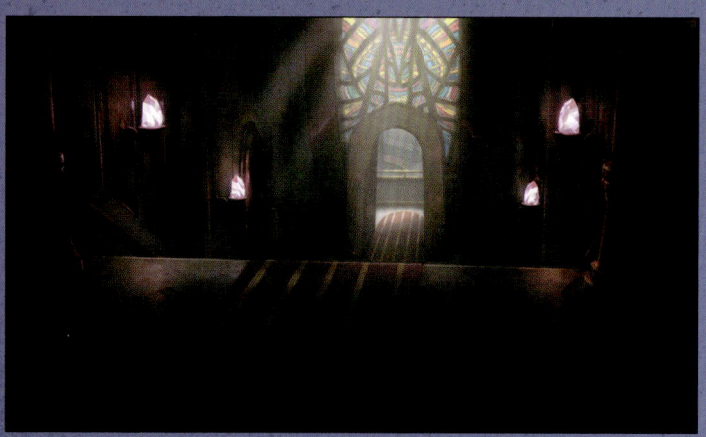

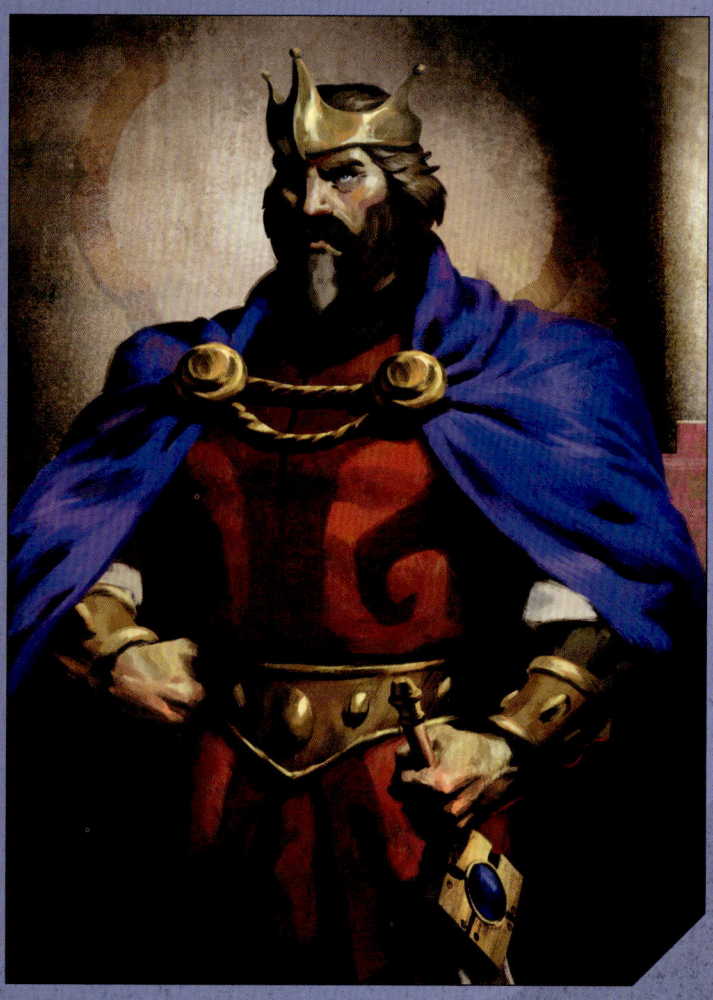

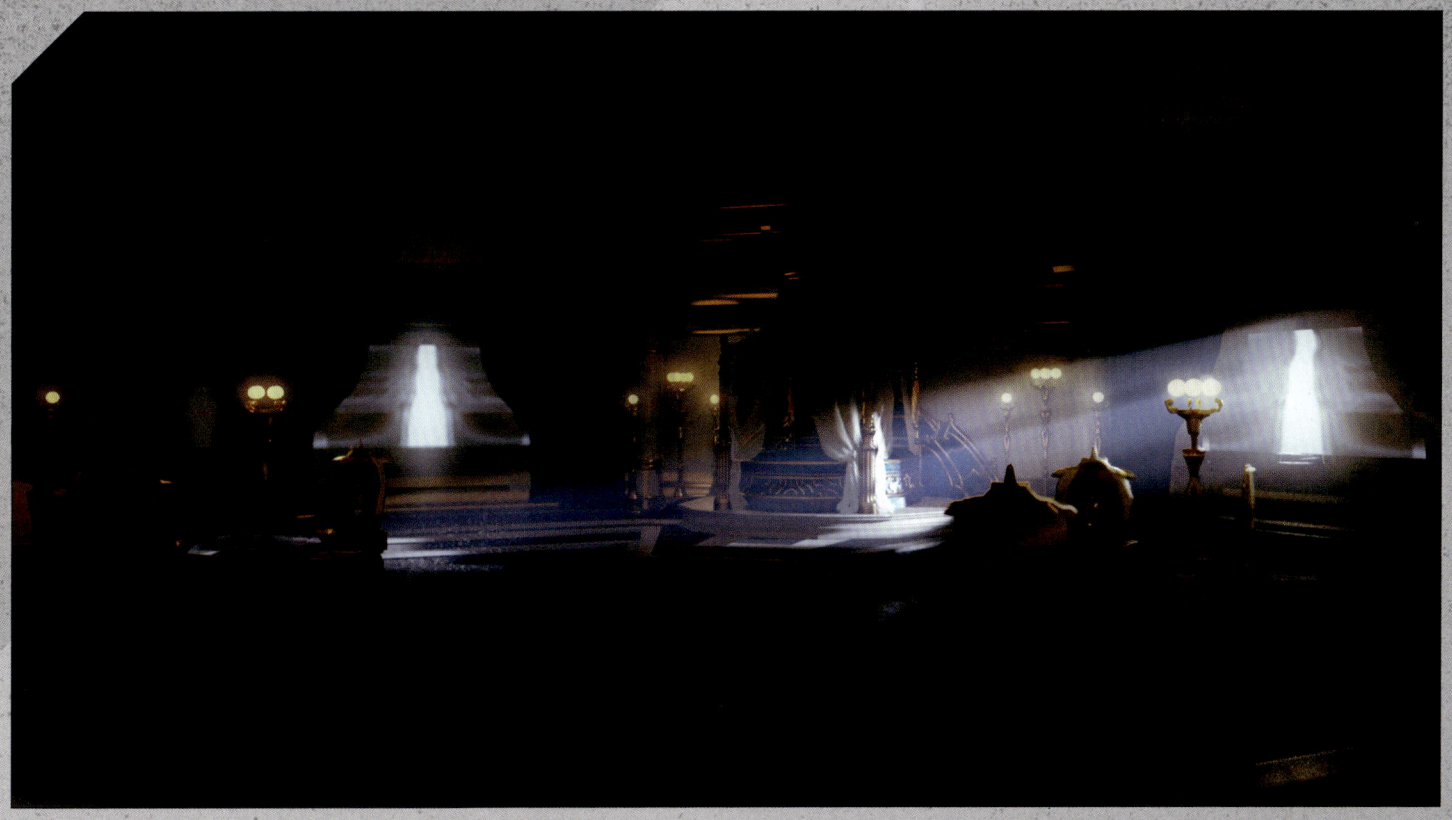

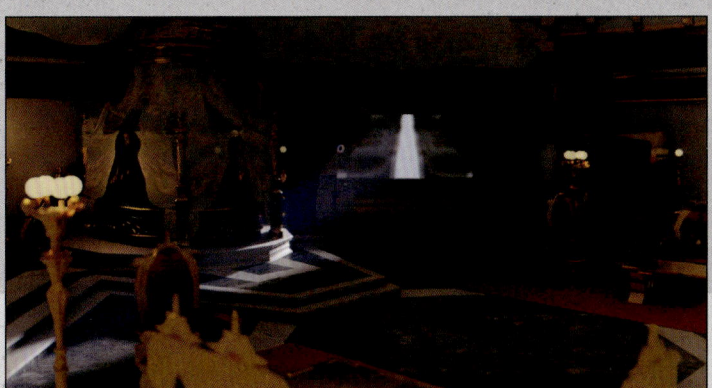
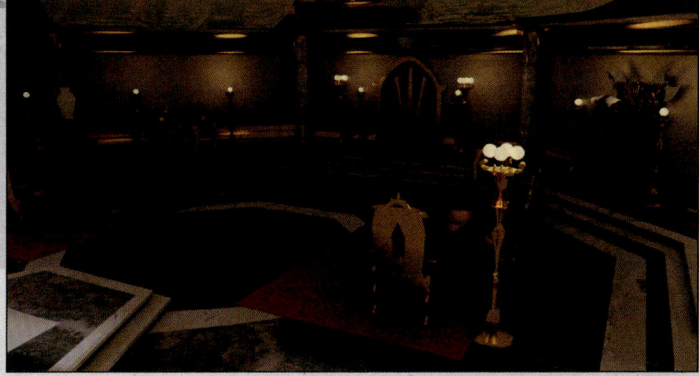

RANDOR'S BEDROOM

The moments surrounding Randor's death demanded a room that was somber and intimate. We utilized the light from the window not just for dramatic effect but also to help suggest the passing of time. As we move from midday to dusk, we are simultaneously watching Randor's reign meet its sunset.

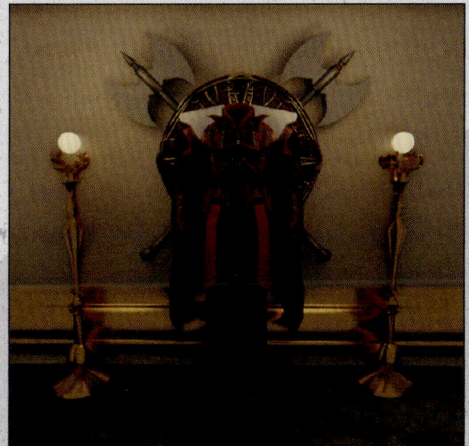
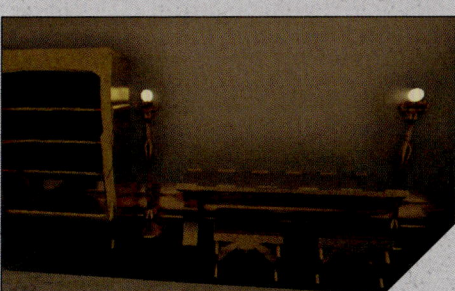
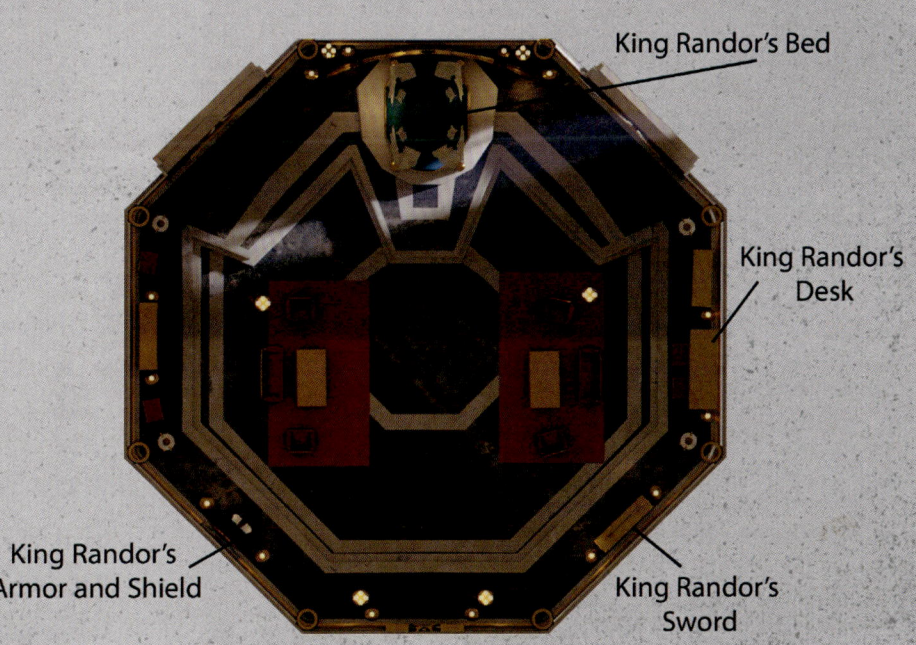

King Randor's Bed

King Randor's Desk

King Randor's Armor and Shield

King Randor's Sword

LOCATIONS \\ 115

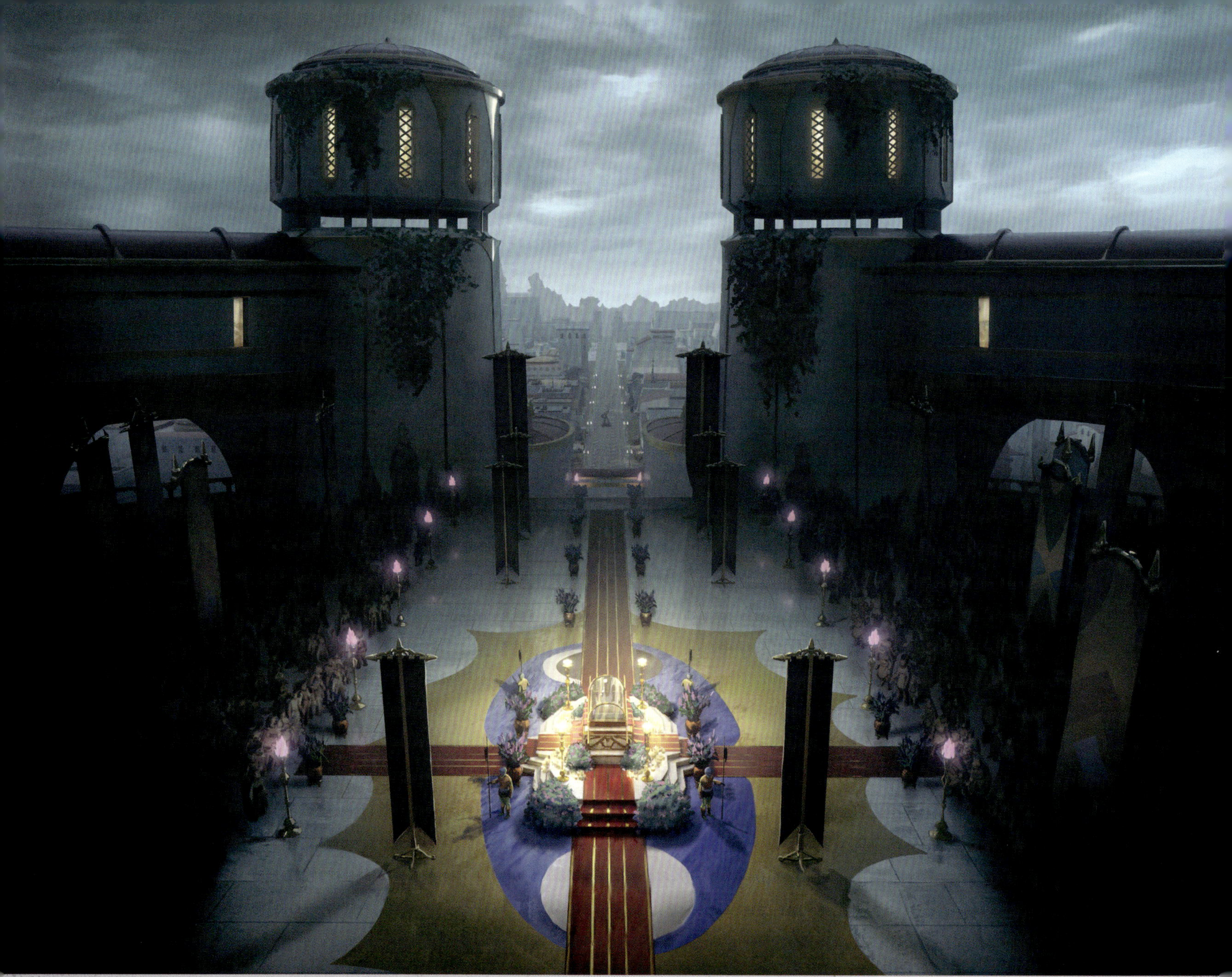

ADAM'S CORONATION
Set to take place immediately upon Randor's passing, Adam's coronation feels more like a funeral as visitors pay their respects to Randor's remains. This is one of the few sequences deliberately bereft of color, and the skies weep for both Randor and the end of Adam's time as He-Man.

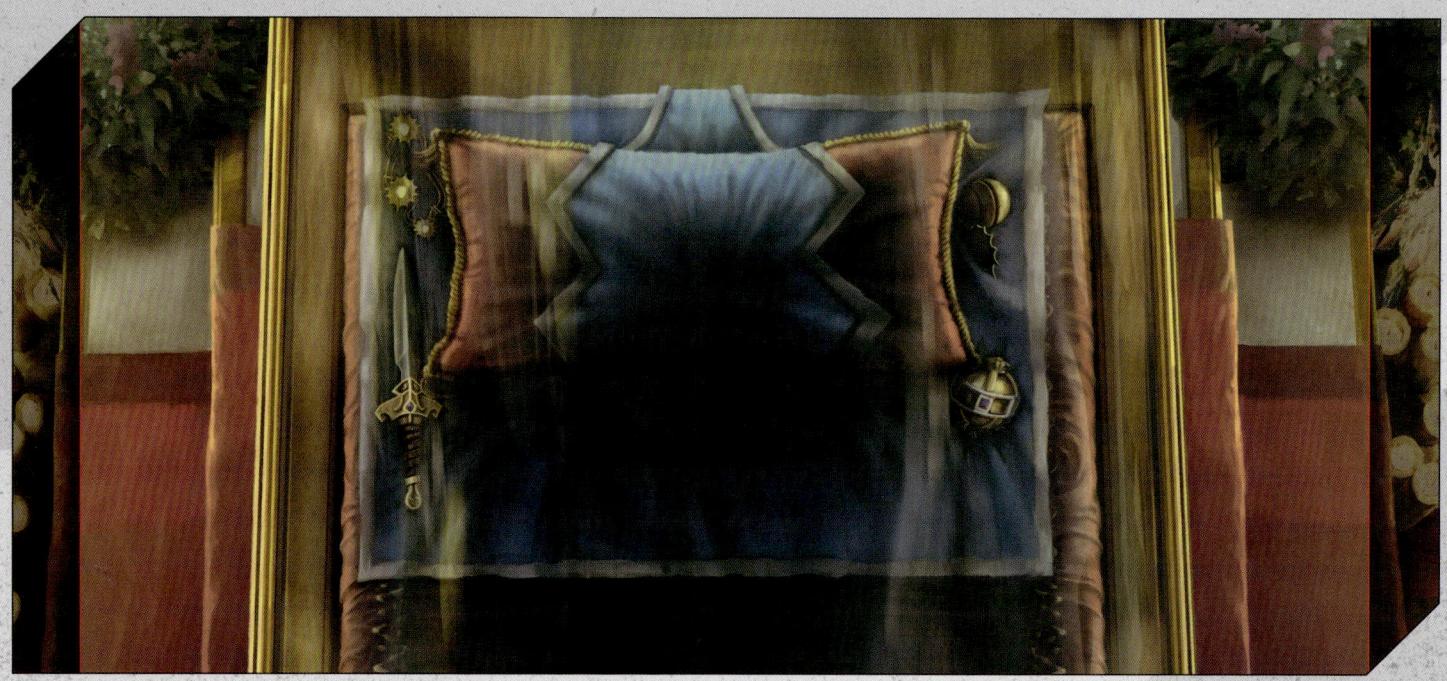

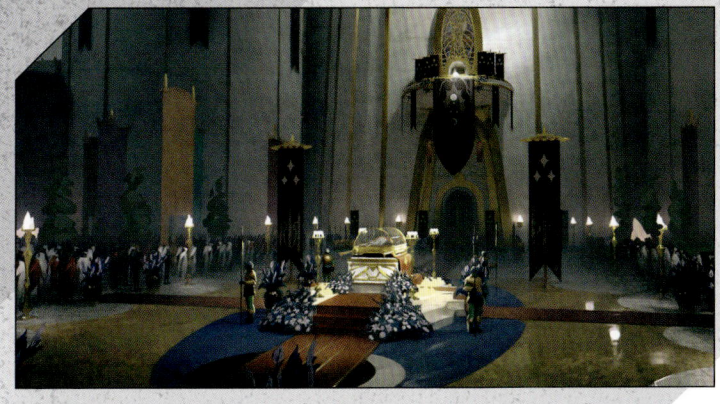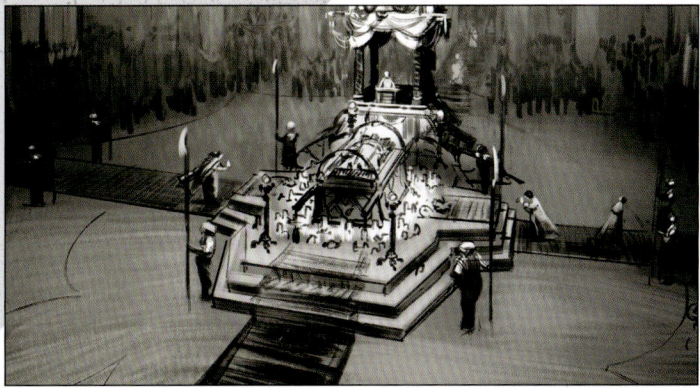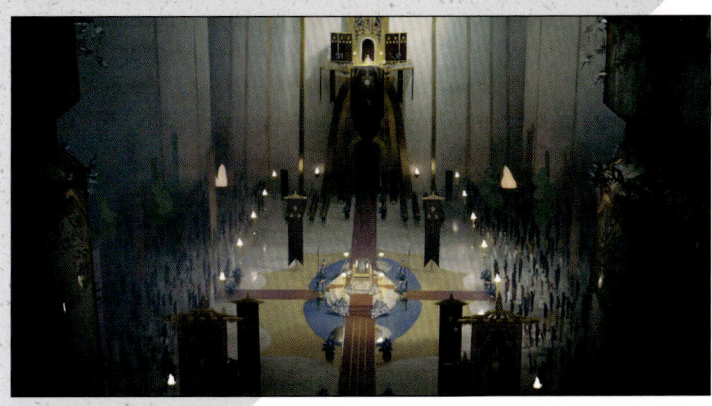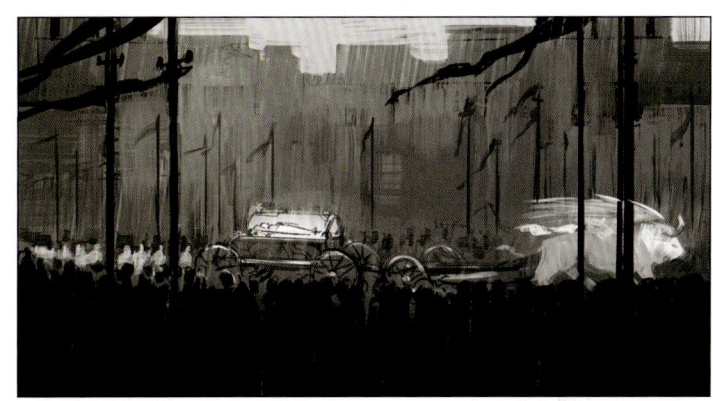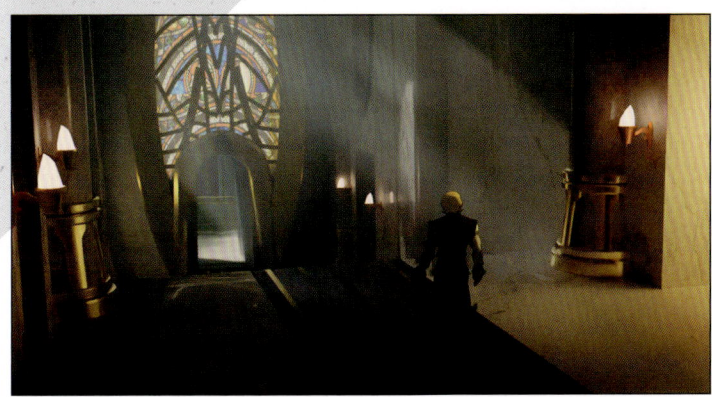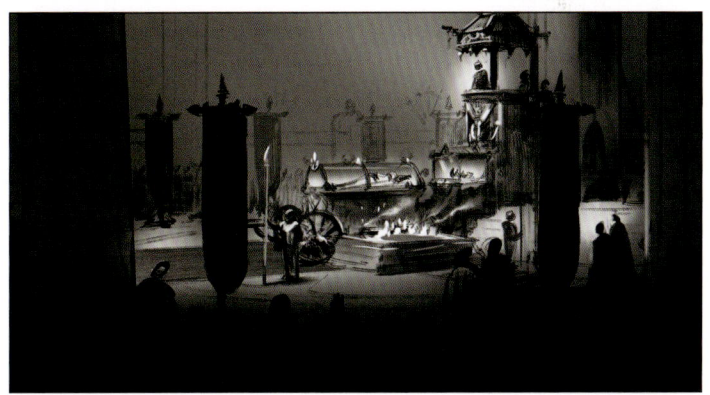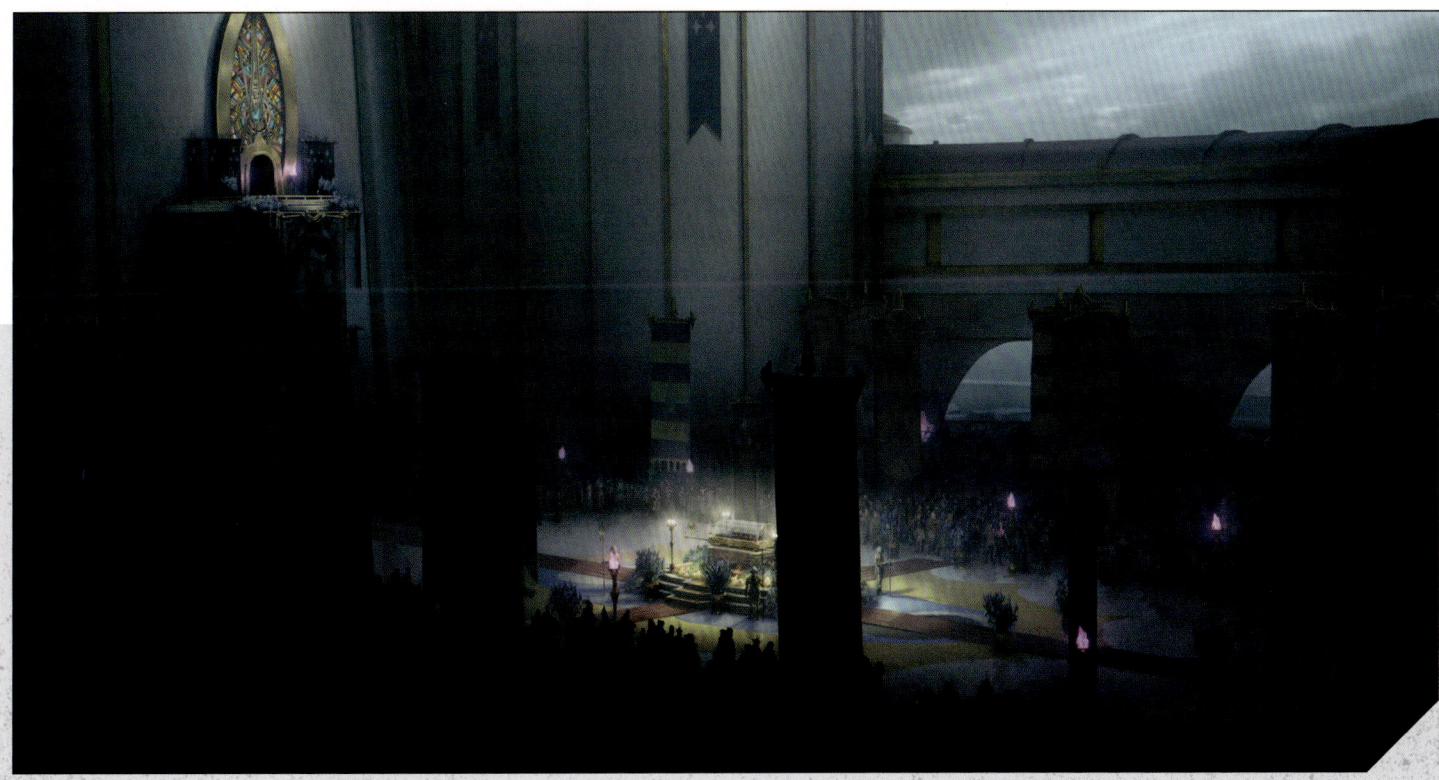

LOCATIONS \\ 117

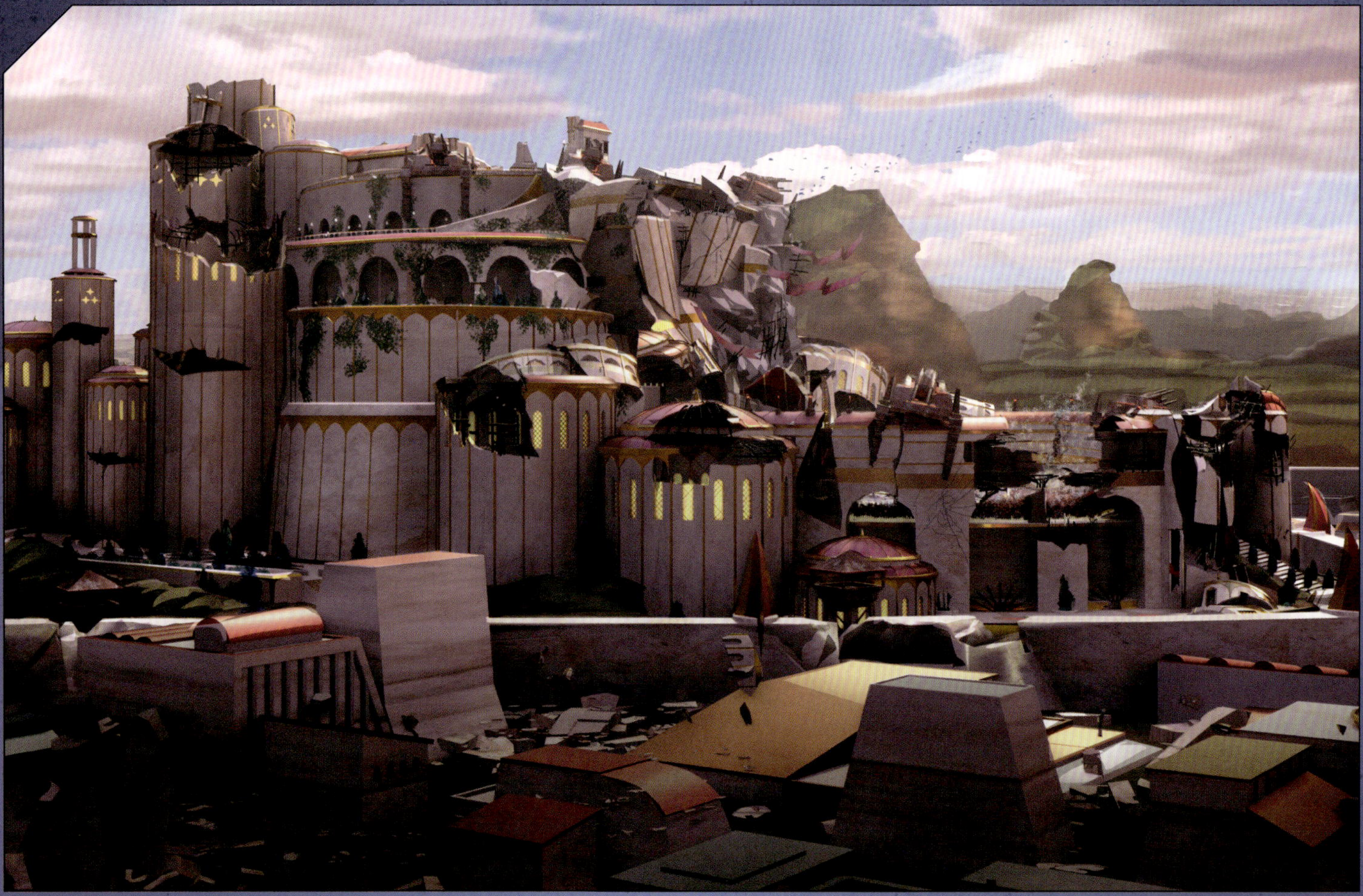

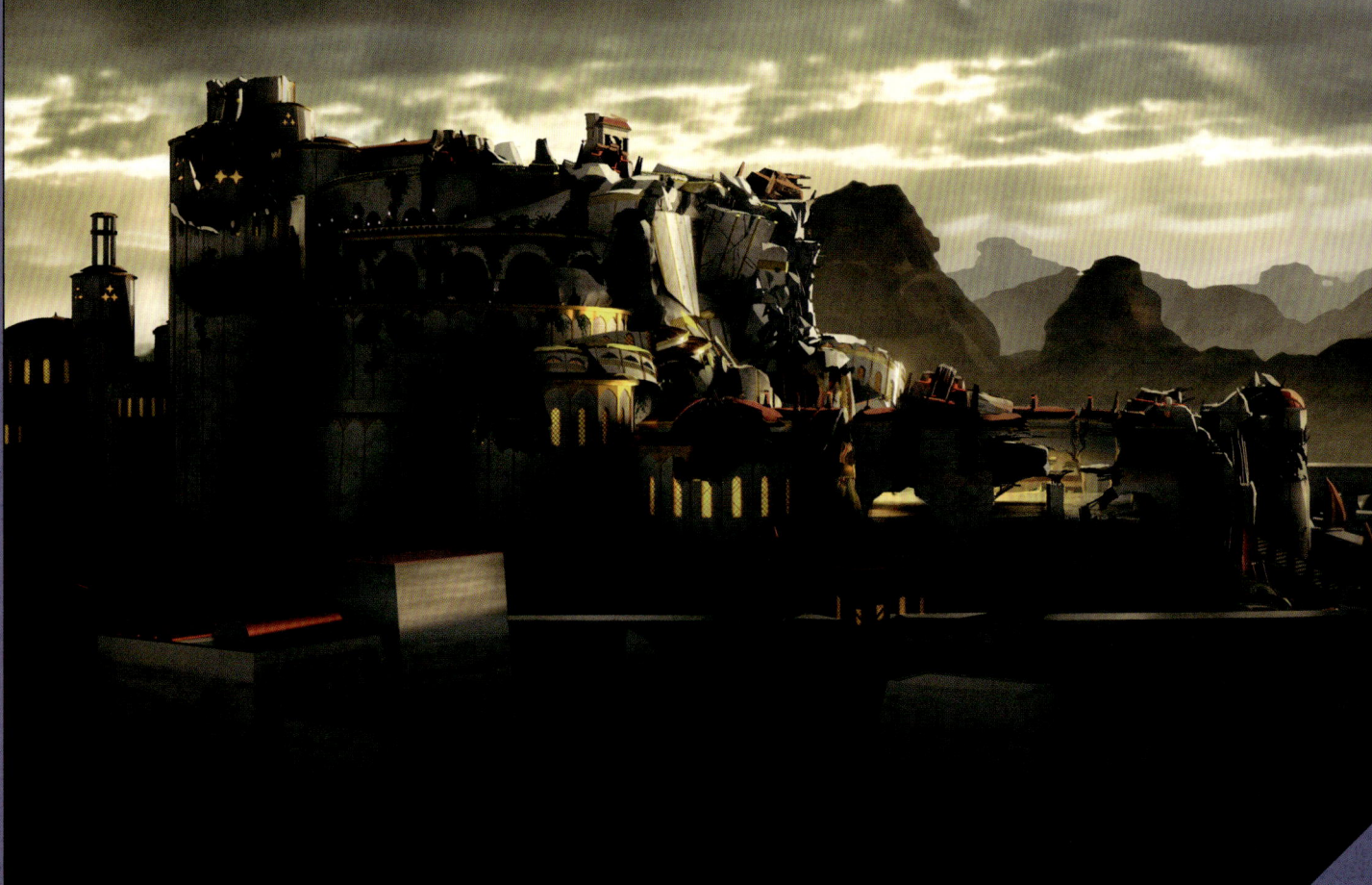

THE ROYAL PALACE RUINS
The aftermath of Hordak and Skeletor's fight leaves the Royal Palace in shambles. However, from its rubble rises Eternos's promise of a democratic future, thanks to He-Man's final royal decree. Despite the palace's dull and damaged state, the crowd of Eternians brighten up the courtyard in their celebration.

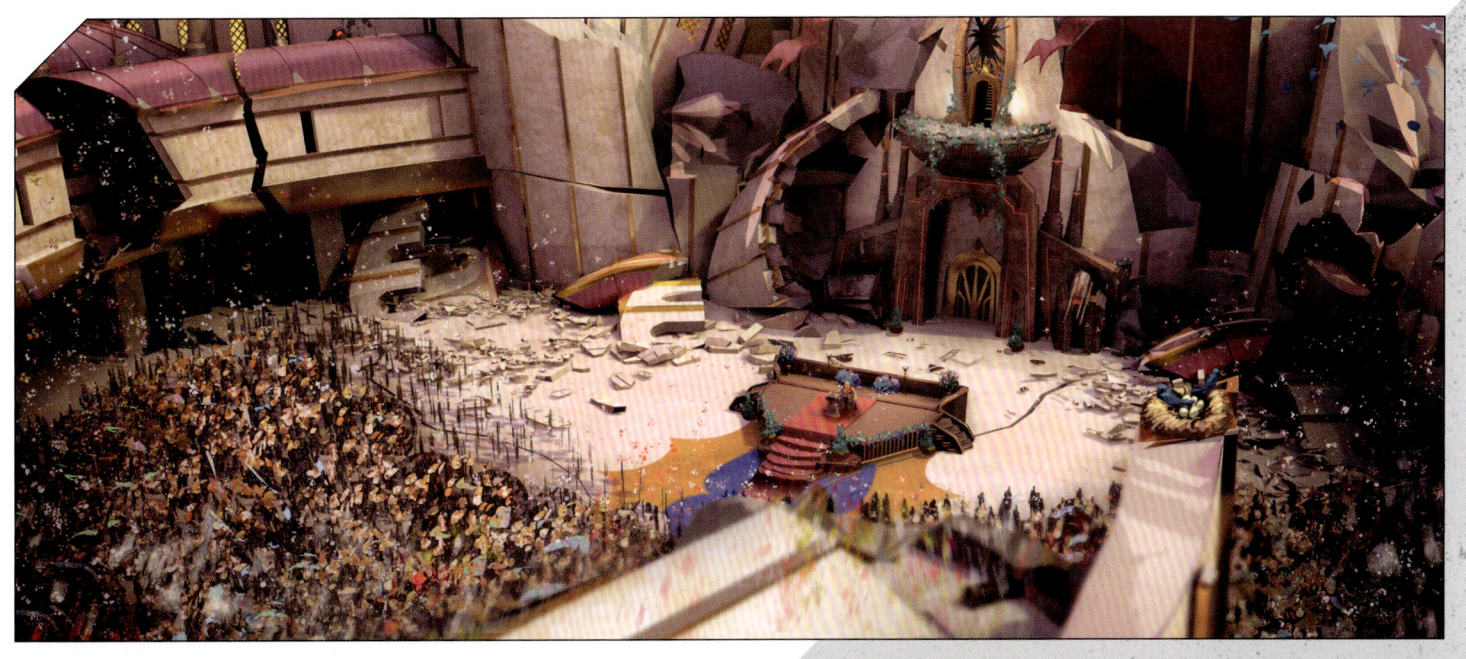
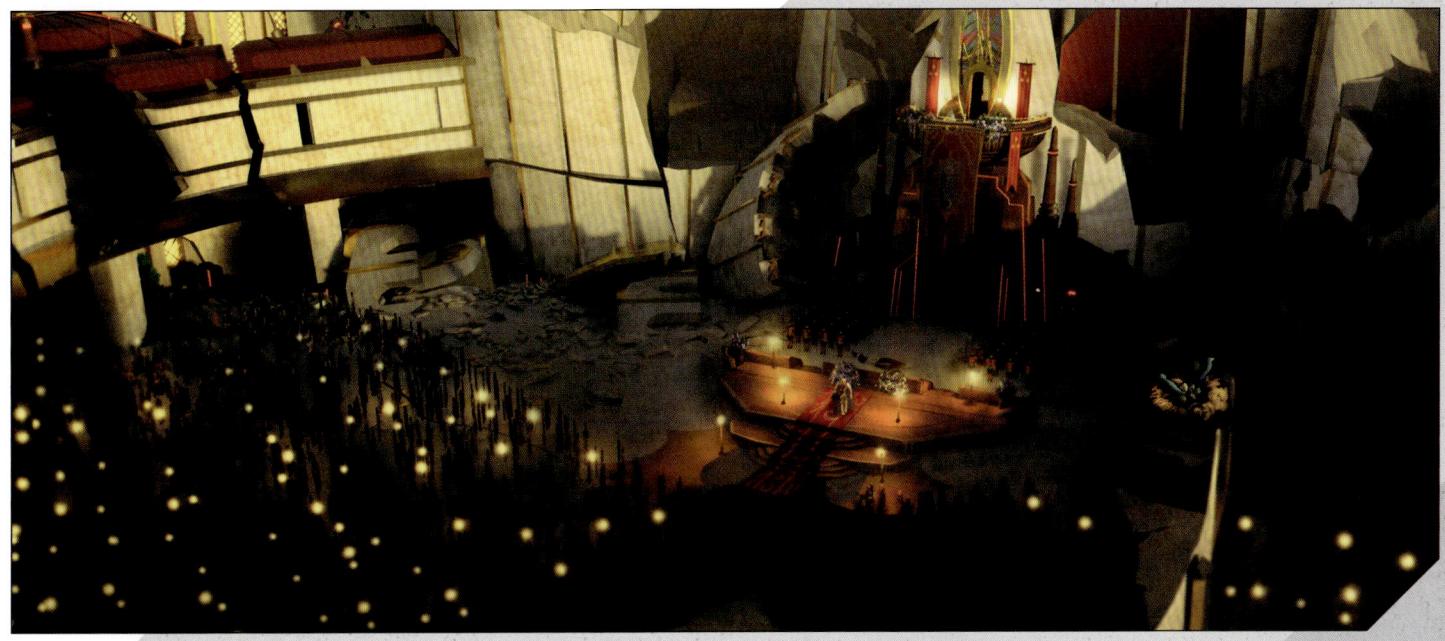
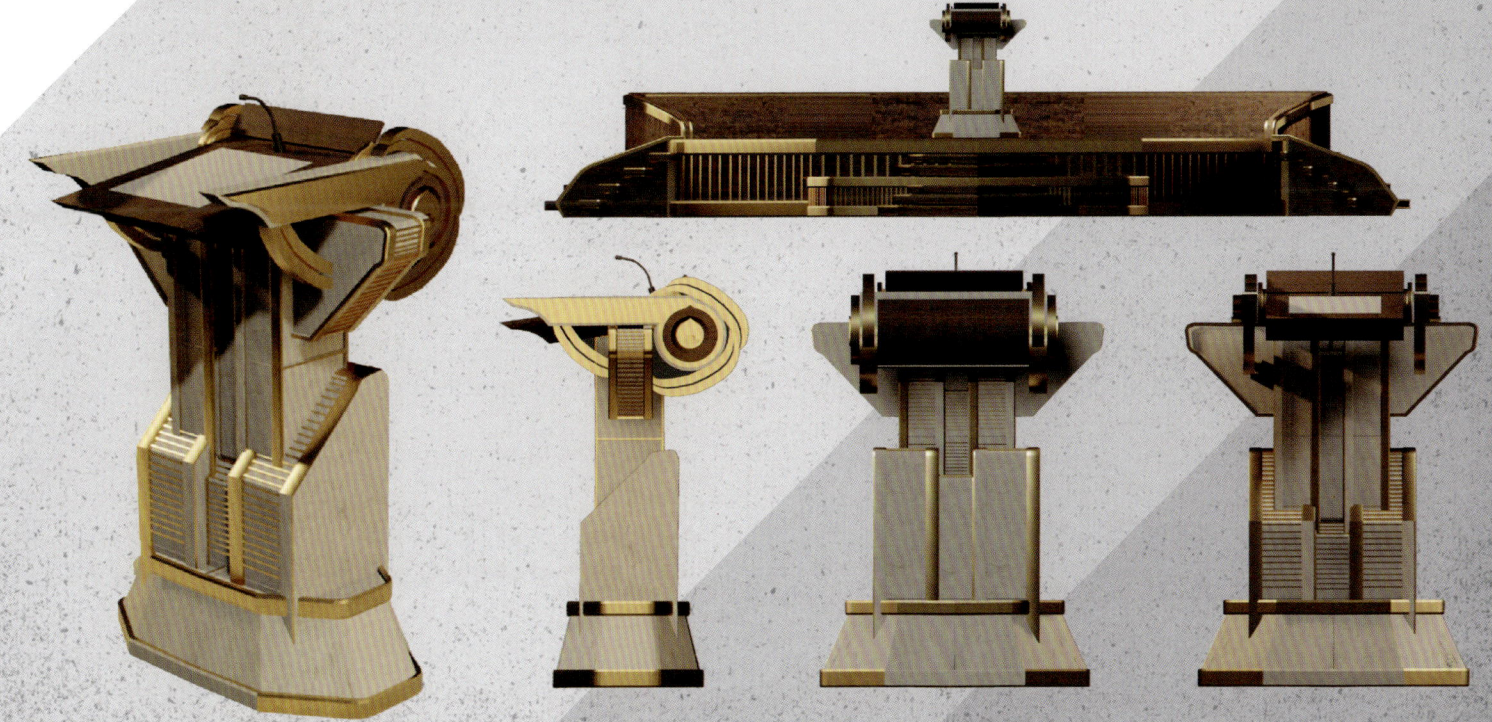

LOCATIONS \\ 119

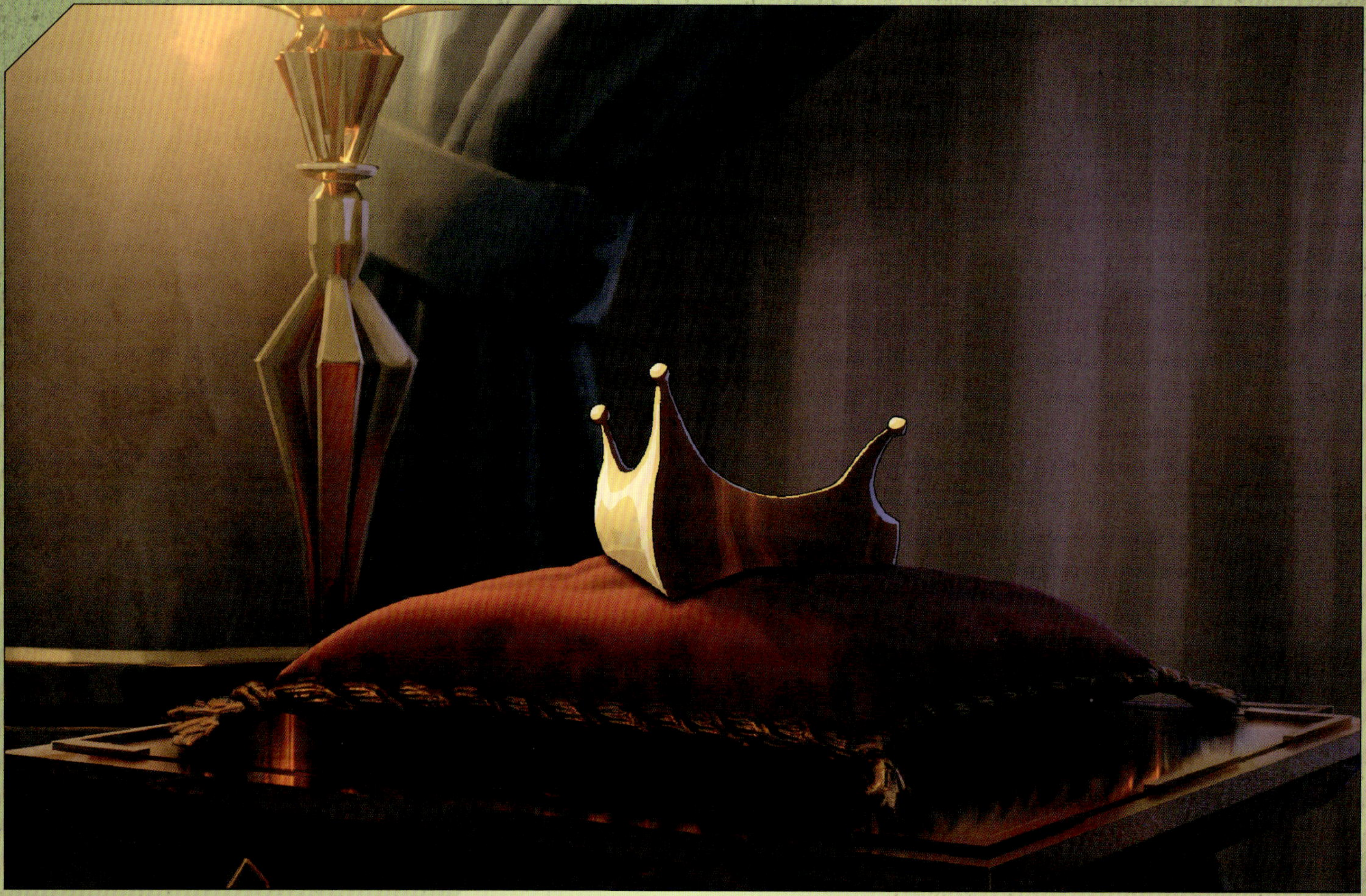

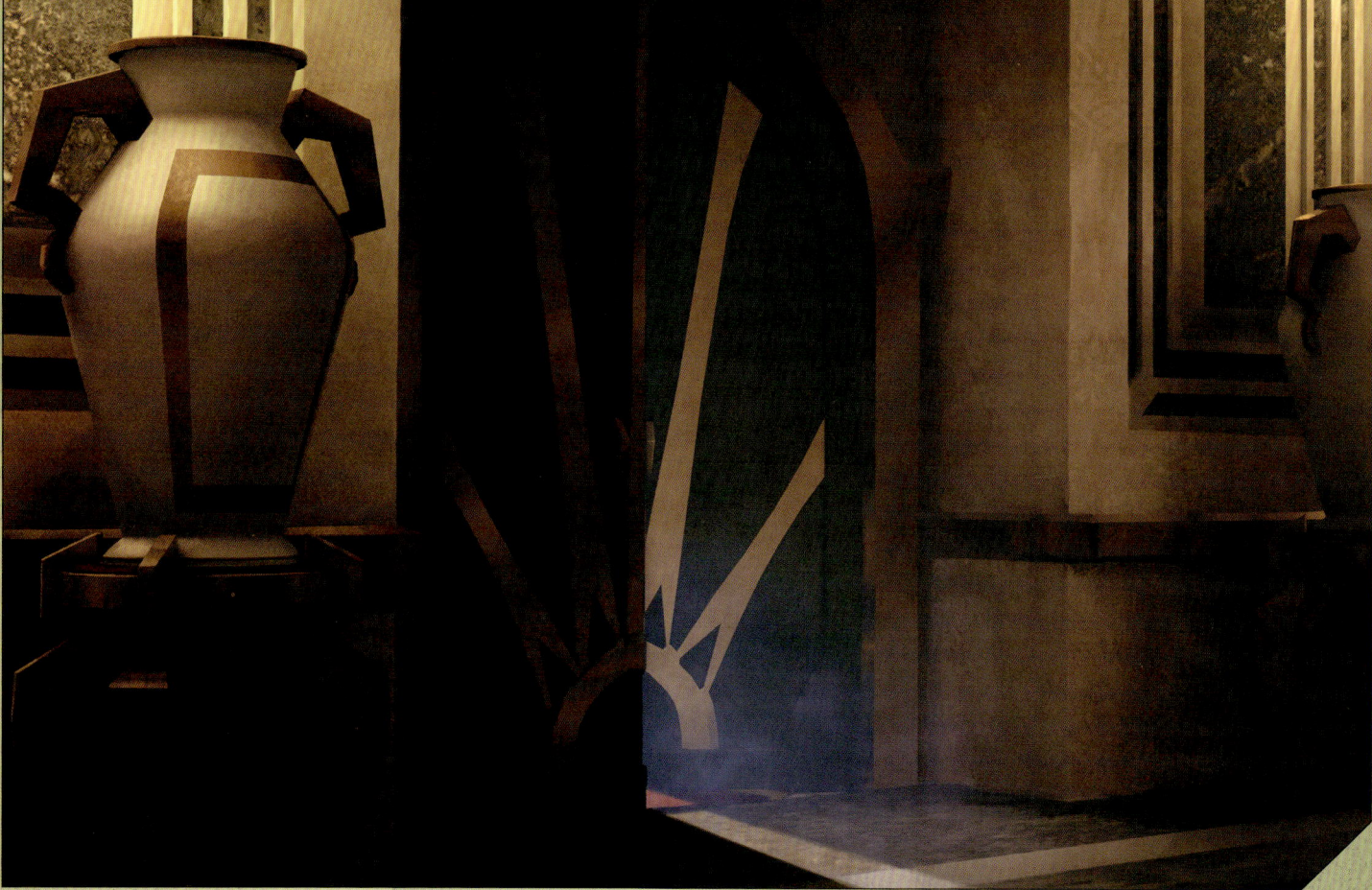

RANDOR'S QUARTERS
As the backdrop for Randor's final words and death, the king's chambers needed to do a lot of heavy lifting. The room has multiple warm and cool light sources, which allowed us to play with shadows and stage the characters in ways that emphasize emotional beats.

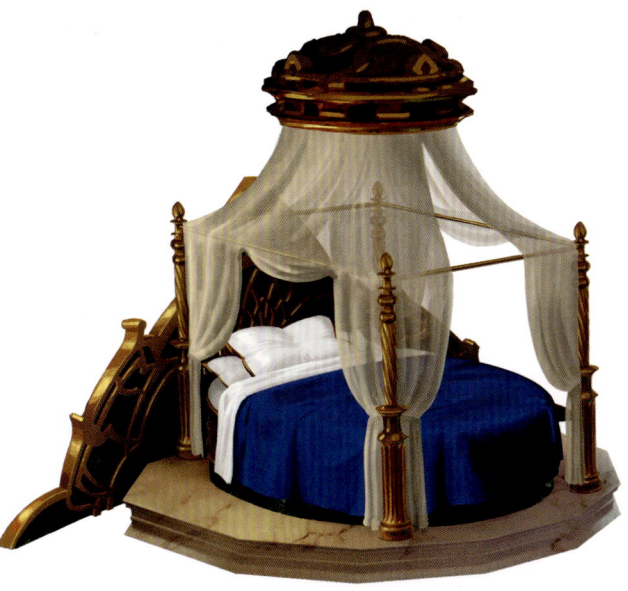
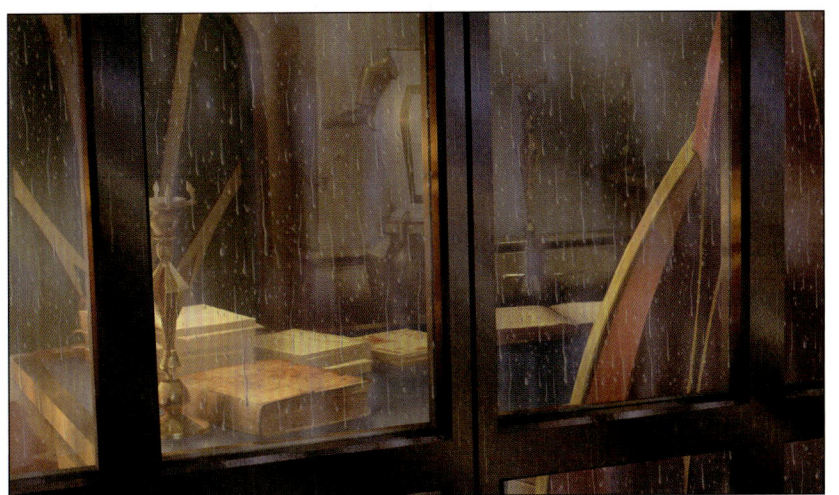
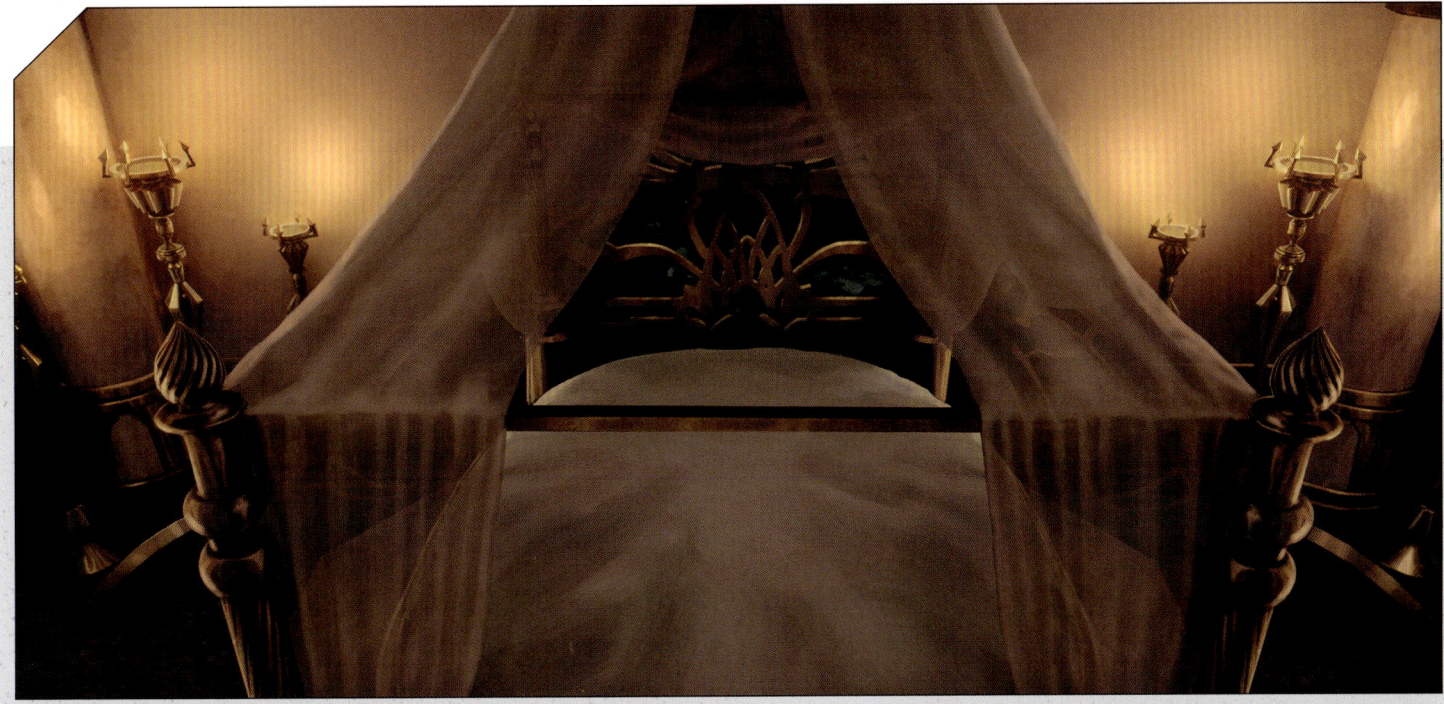
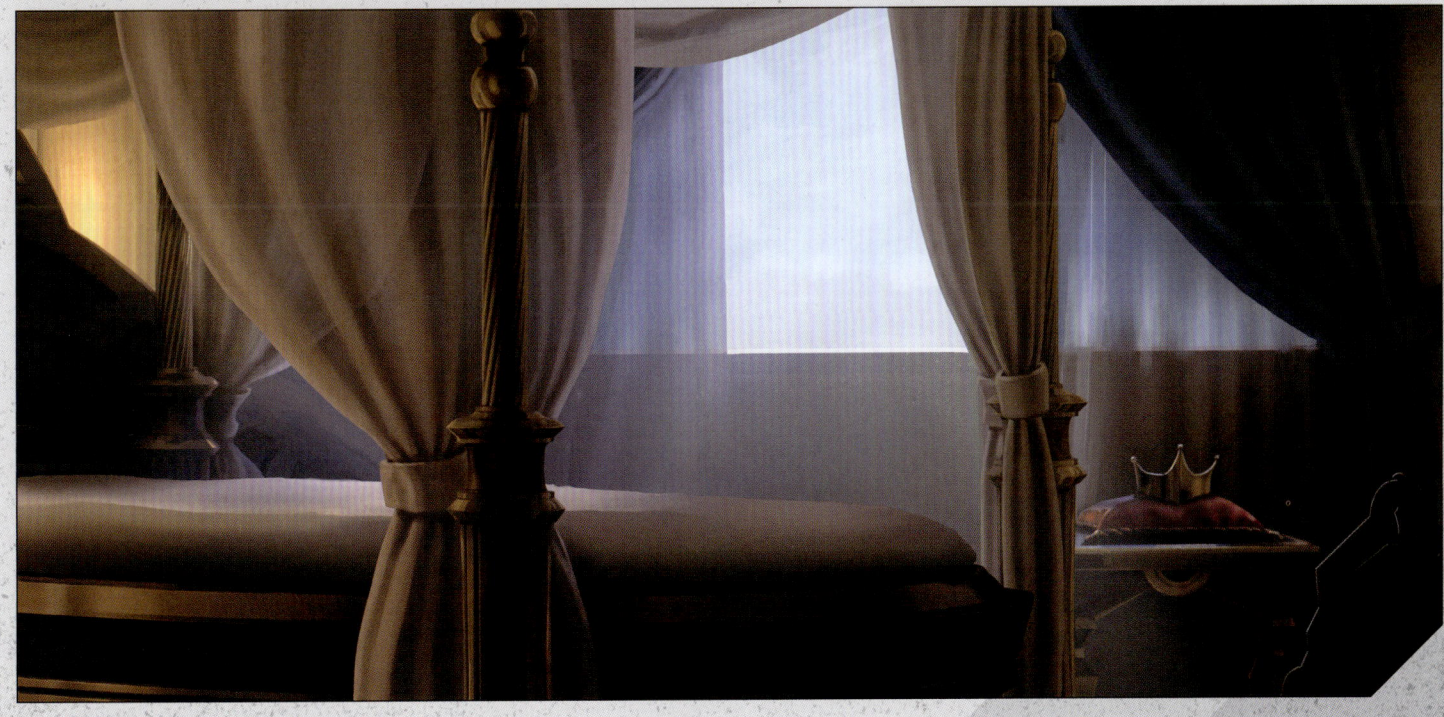

LOCATIONS \\ 121

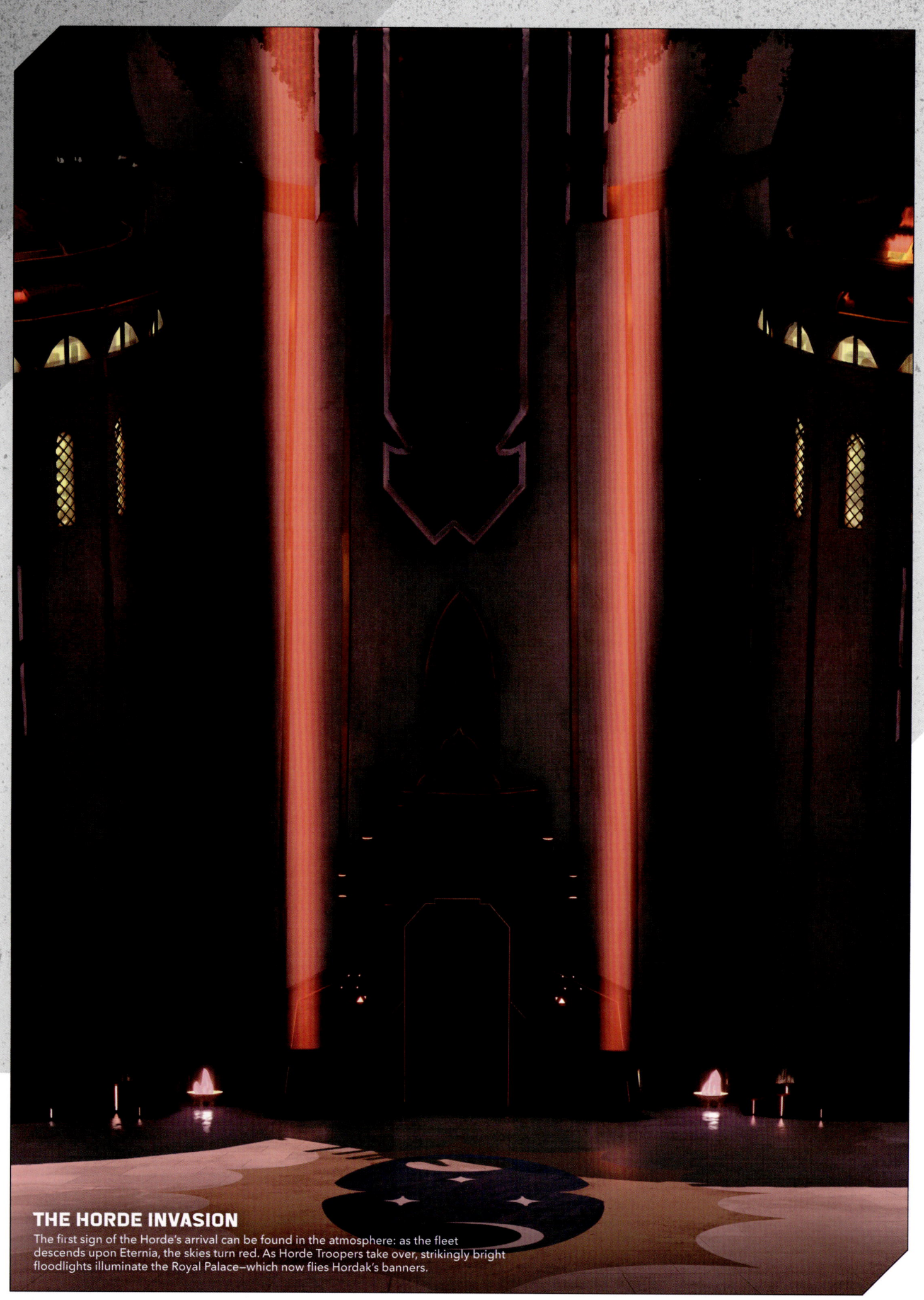

THE HORDE INVASION
The first sign of the Horde's arrival can be found in the atmosphere: as the fleet descends upon Eternia, the skies turn red. As Horde Troopers take over, strikingly bright floodlights illuminate the Royal Palace—which now flies Hordak's banners.

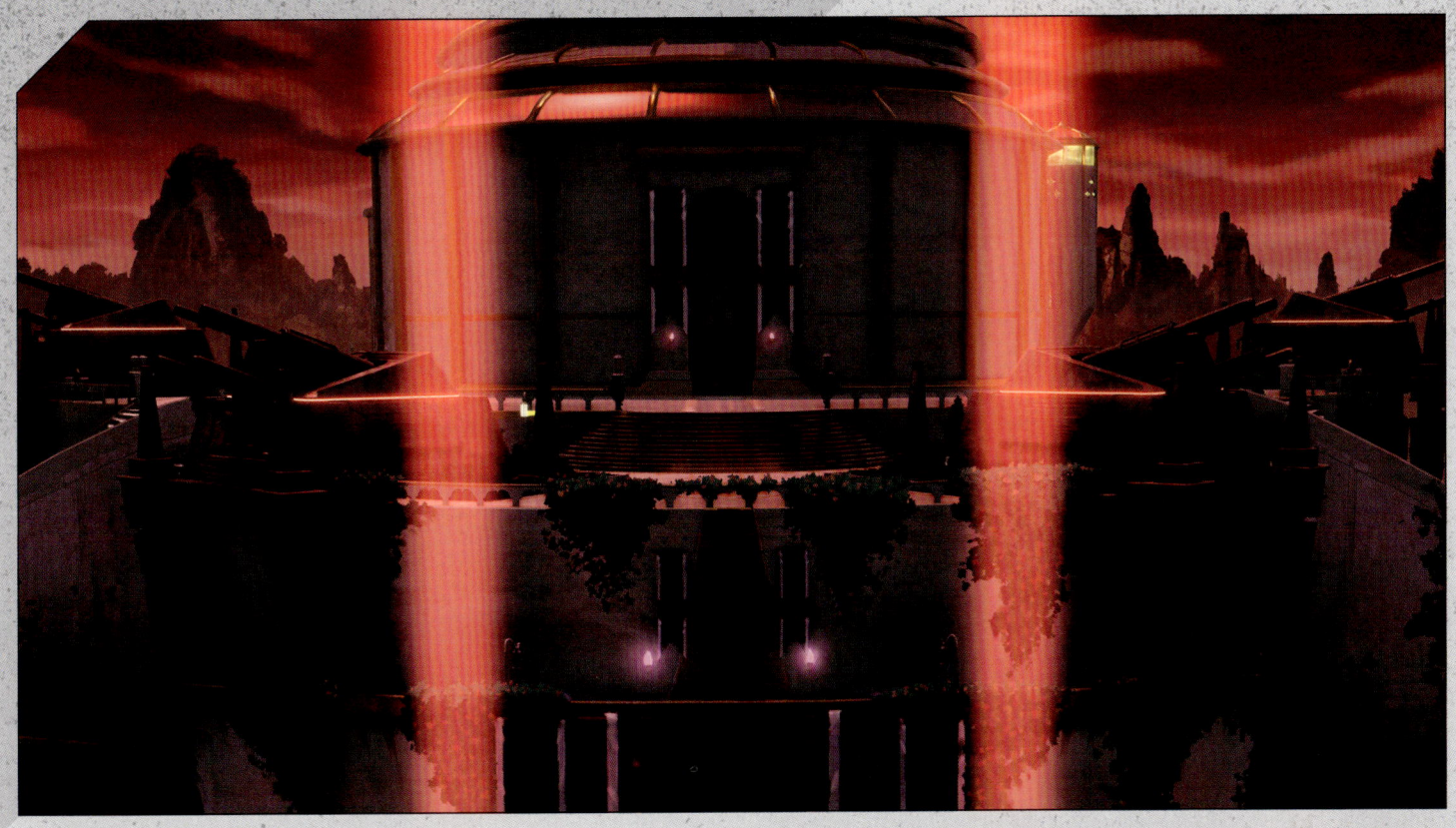
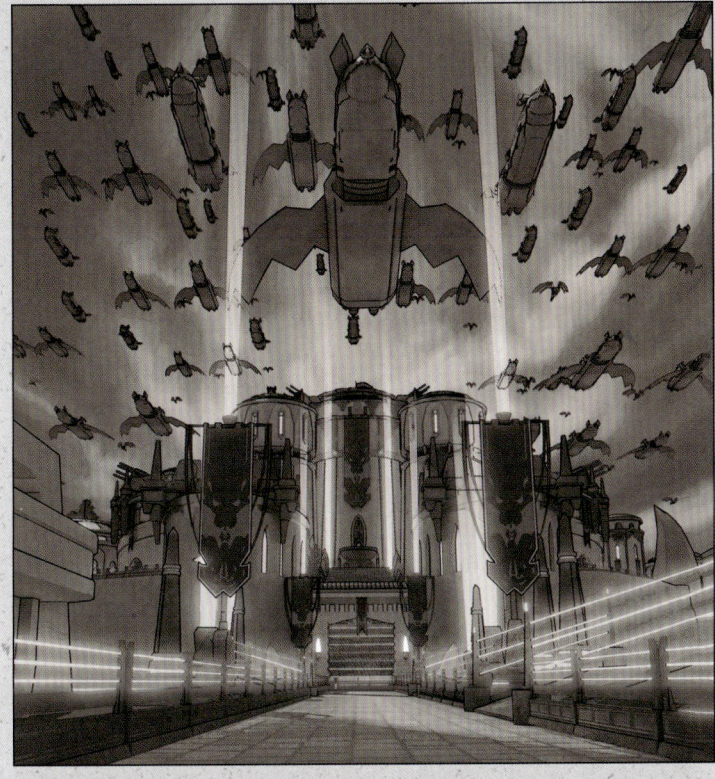
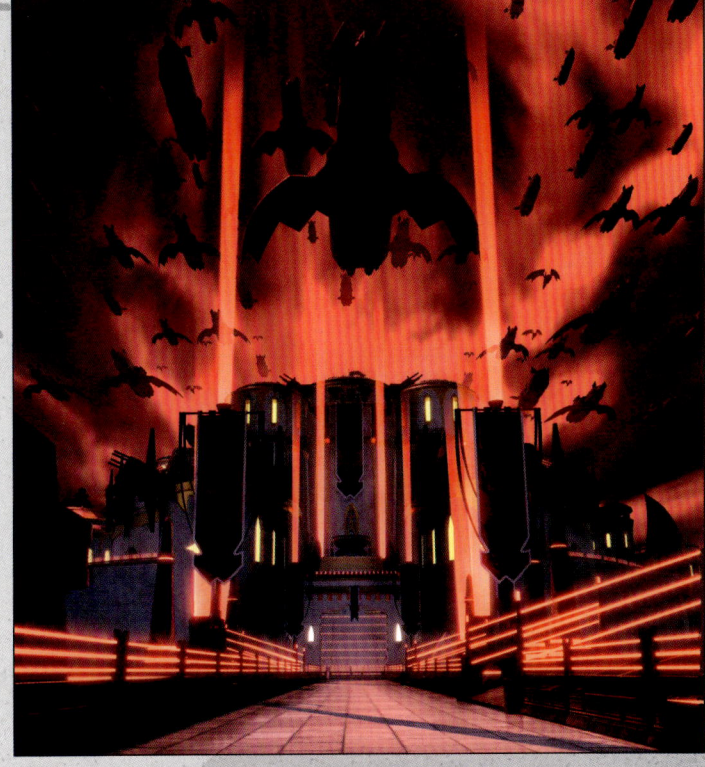
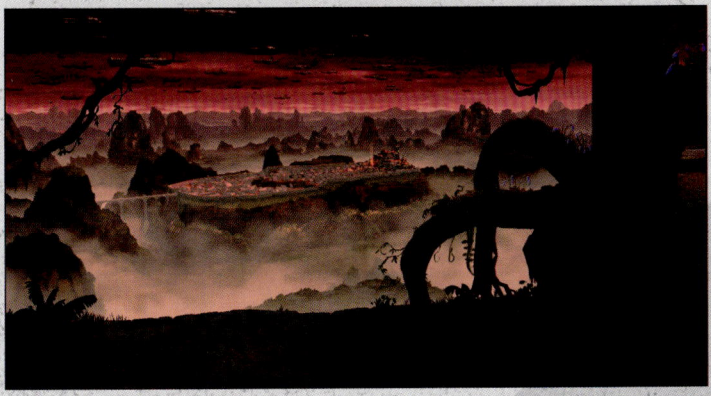
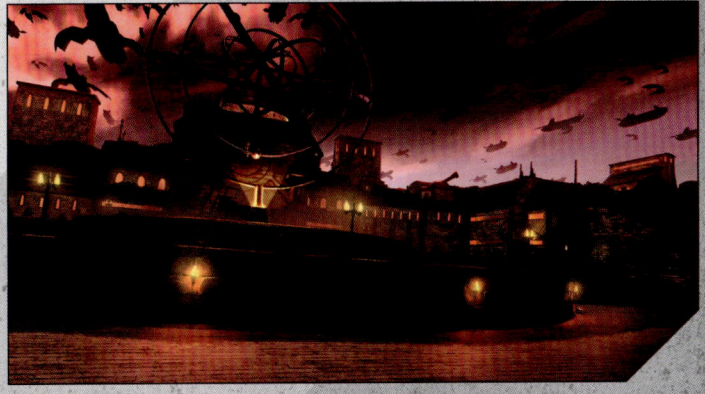

LOCATIONS

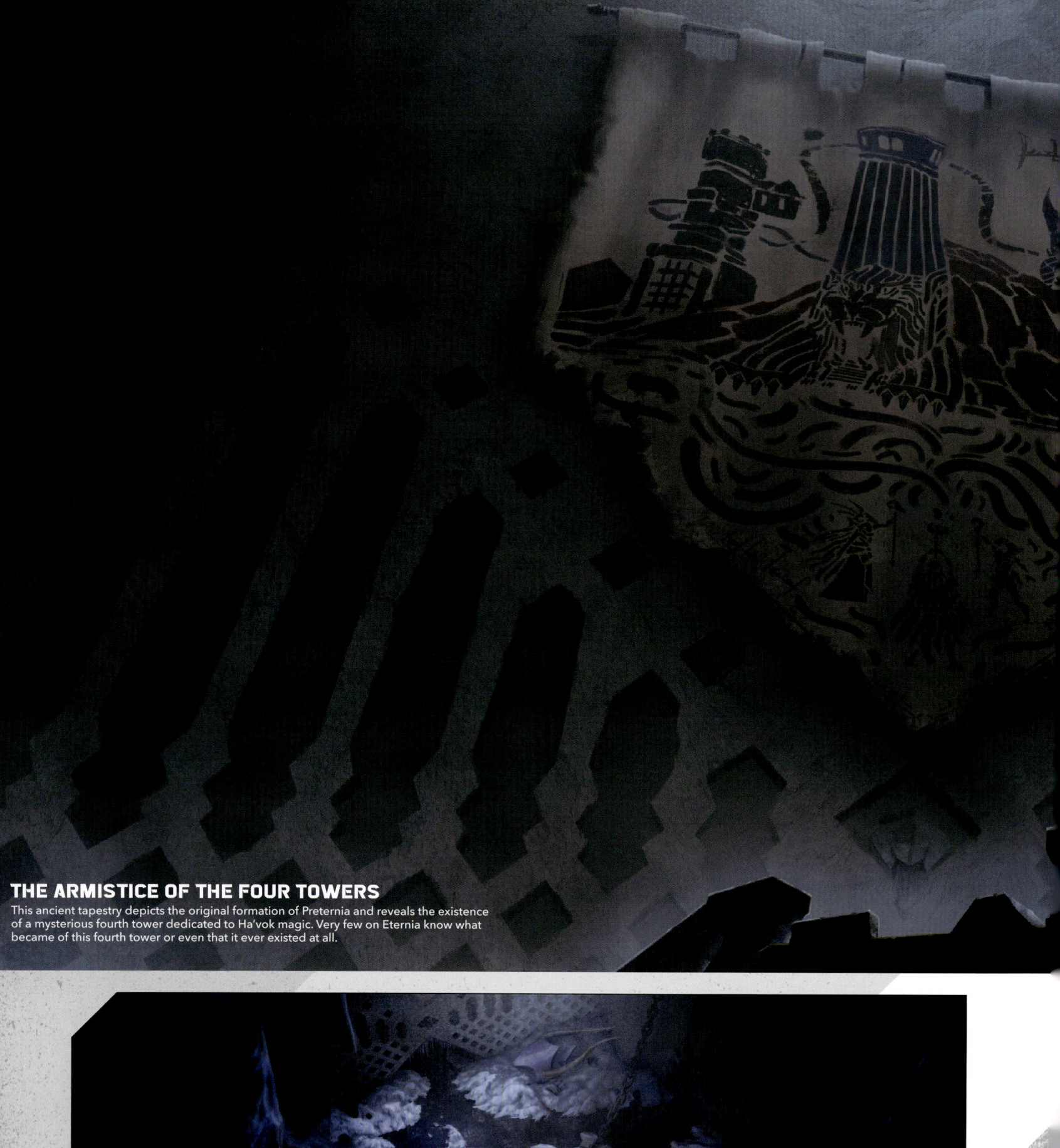

THE ARMISTICE OF THE FOUR TOWERS

This ancient tapestry depicts the original formation of Preternia and reveals the existence of a mysterious fourth tower dedicated to Ha'vok magic. Very few on Eternia know what became of this fourth tower or even that it ever existed at all.

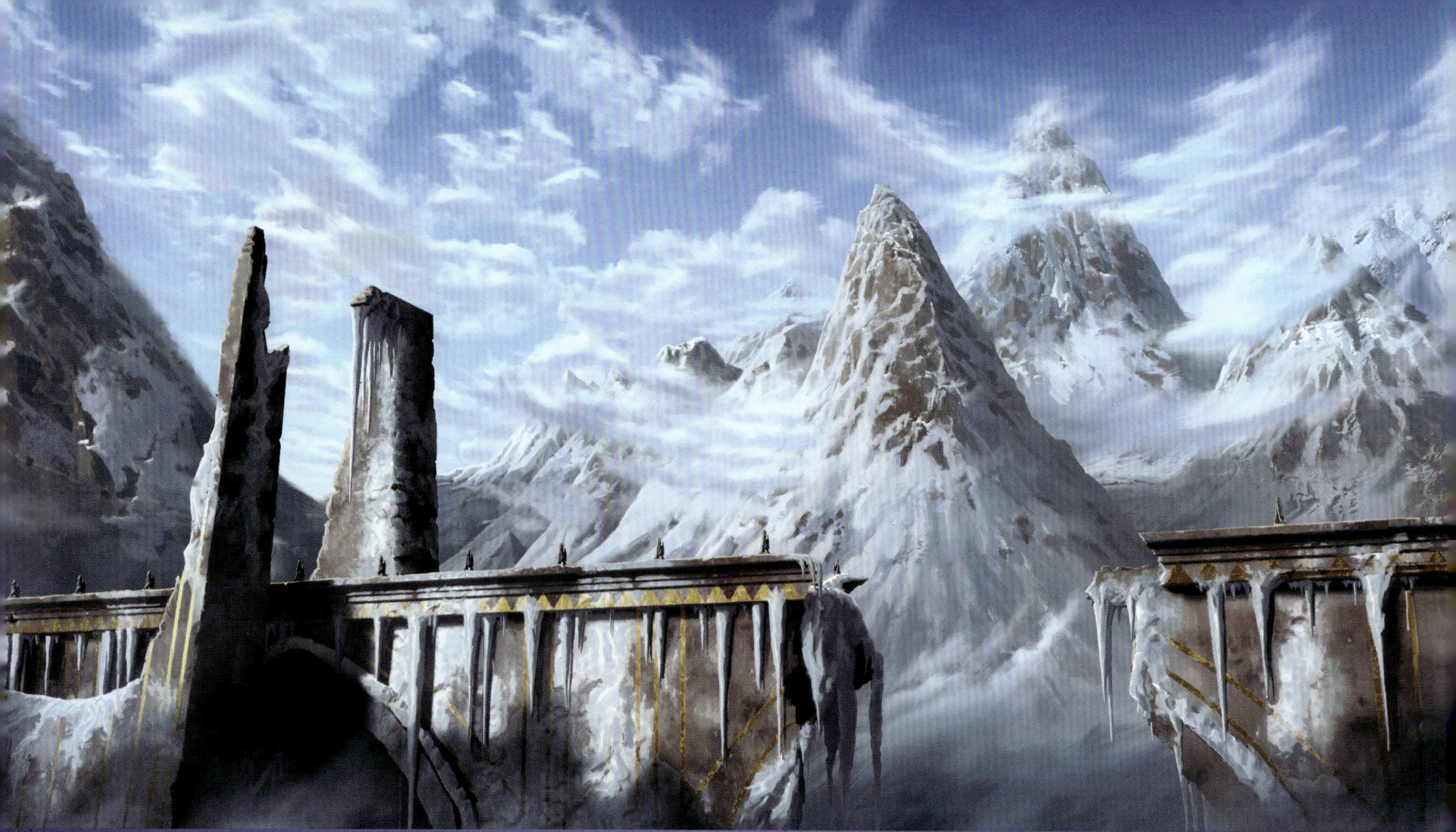

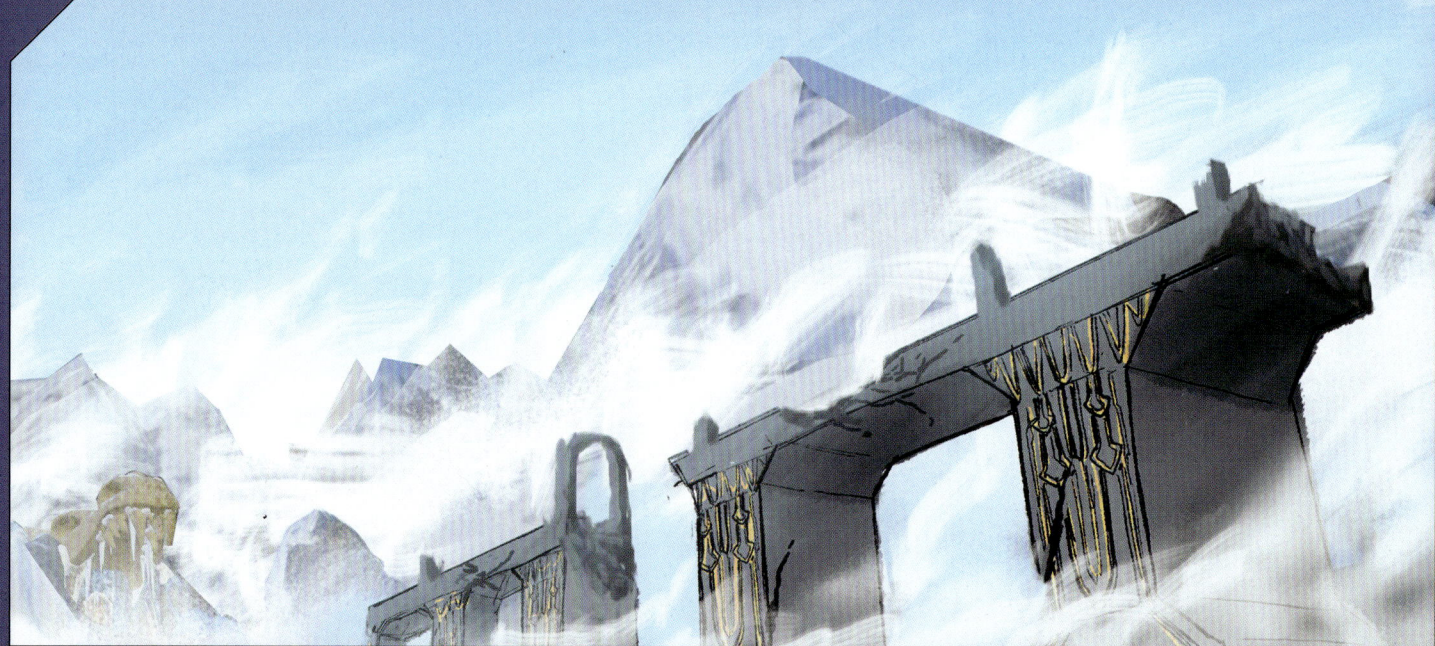

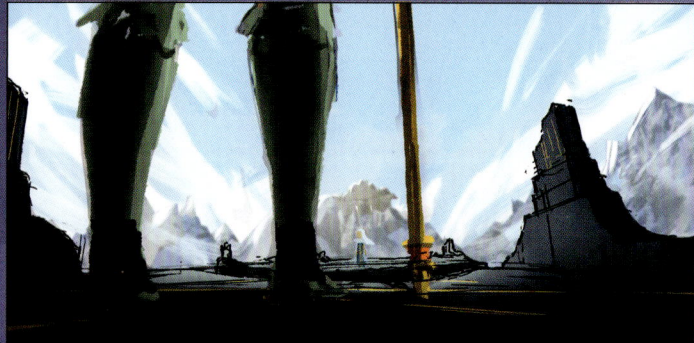
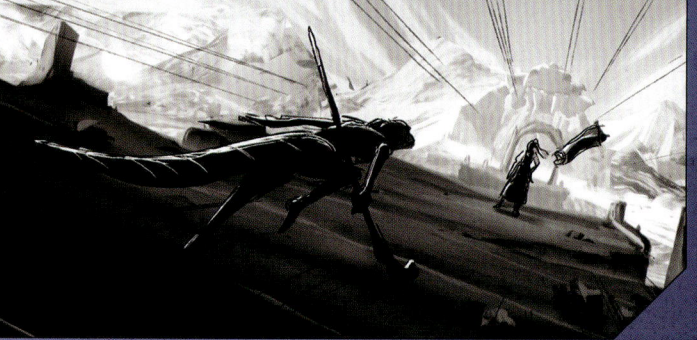

THE MAW OF DARKSMOKE
Everything from the bridge to the massive door beneath a carven skull was scaled up to be dragon sized. They would have been great achievements of masonry were they not left to ruin and erosion by the harsh wintry winds of the mountaintops.

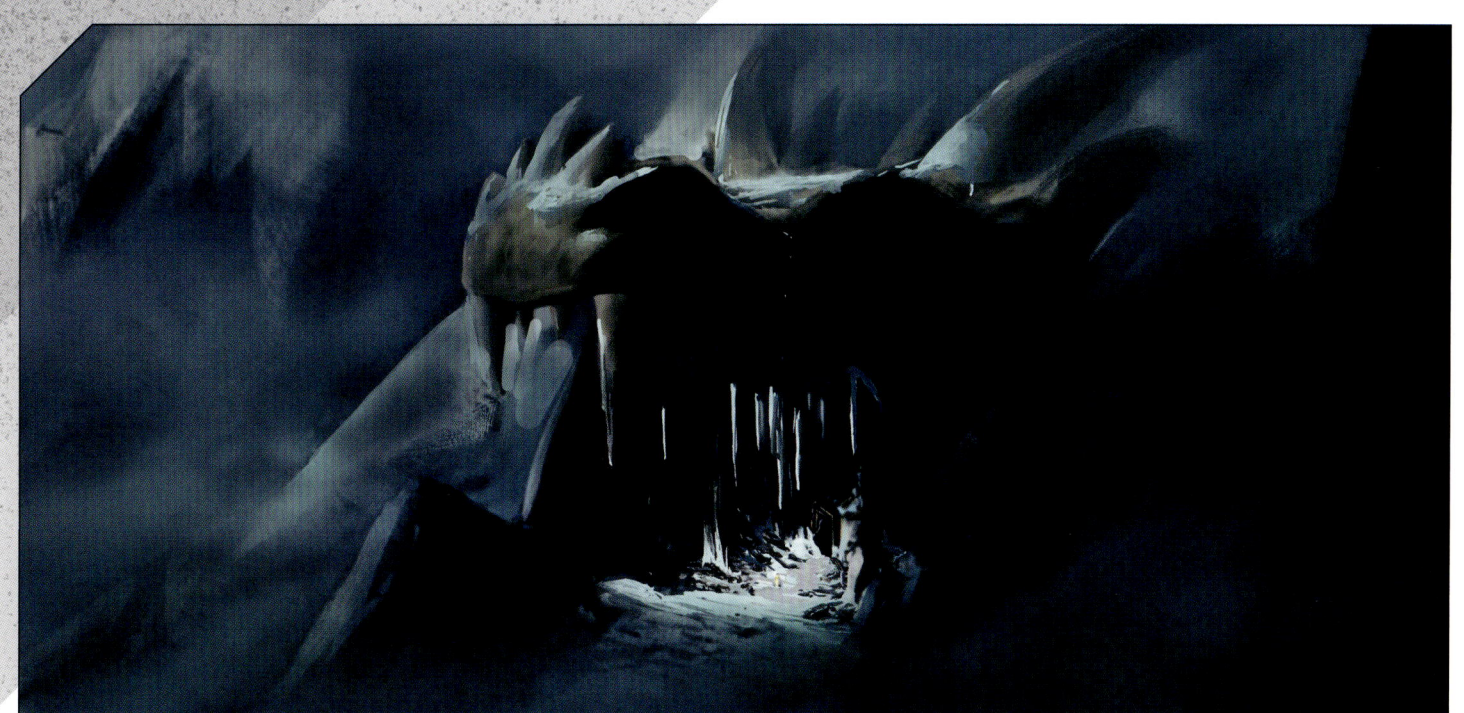
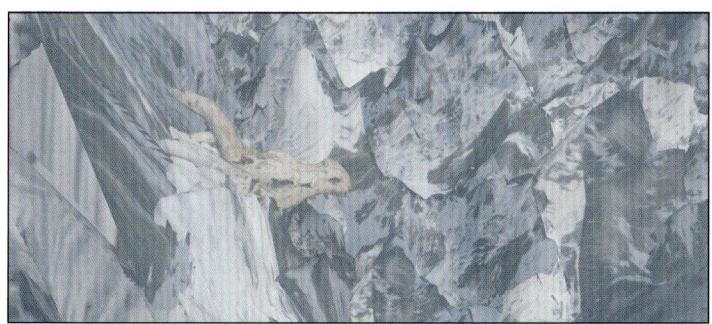
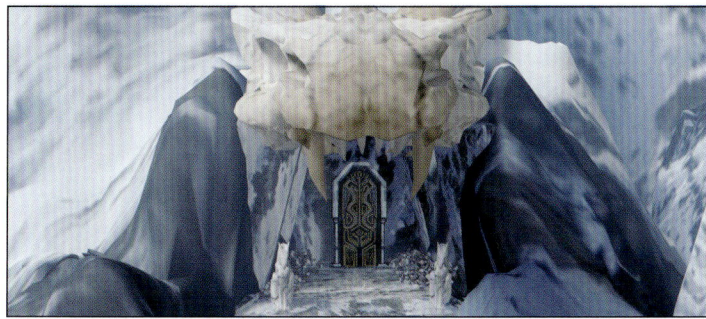
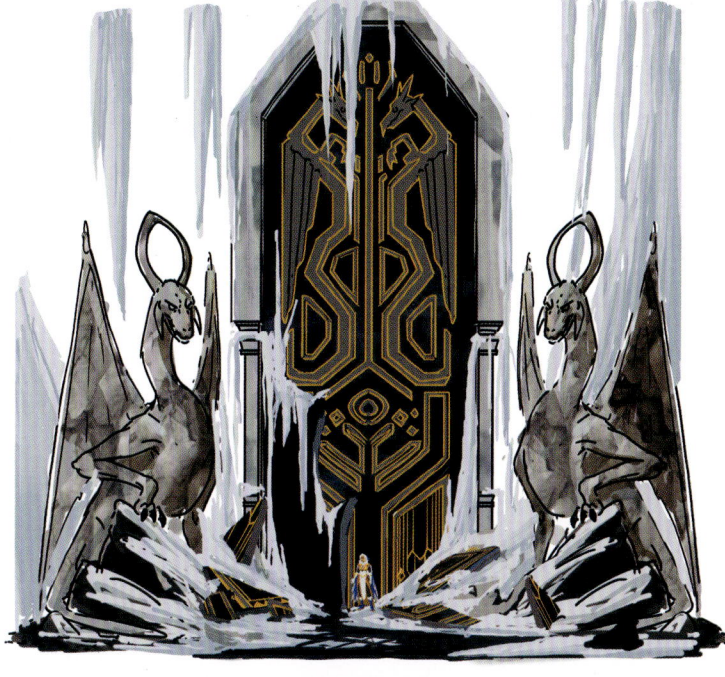
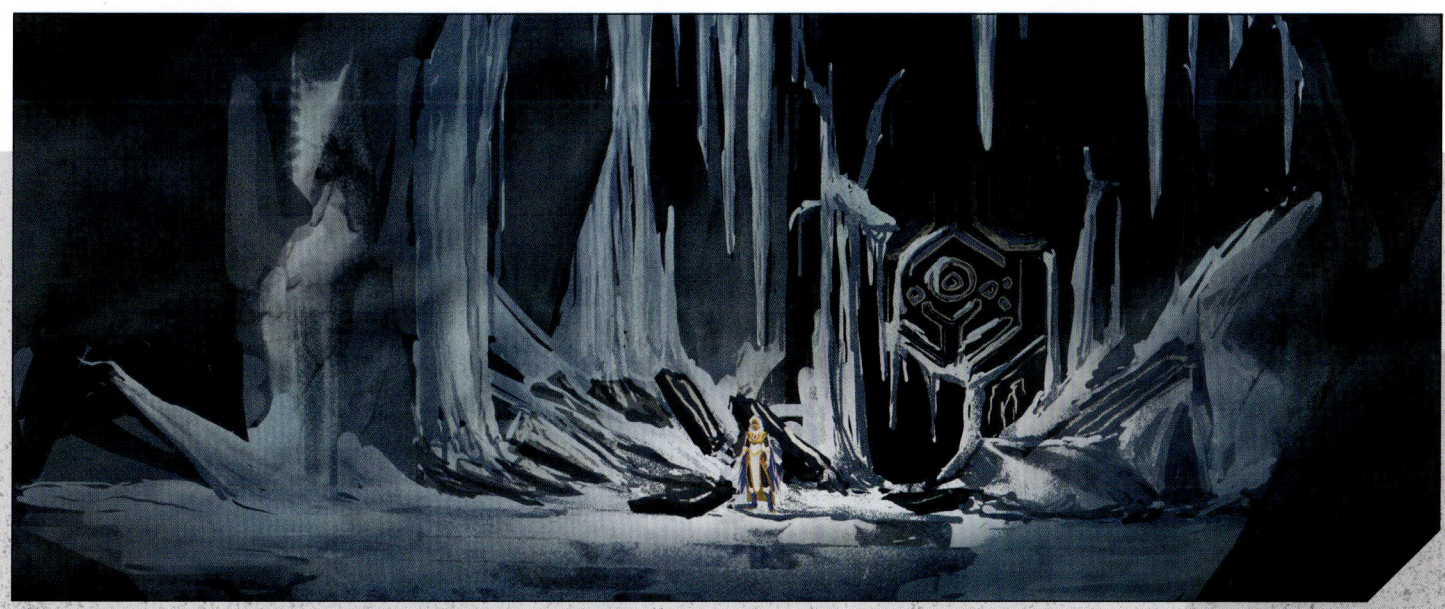

LOCATIONS \\ 127

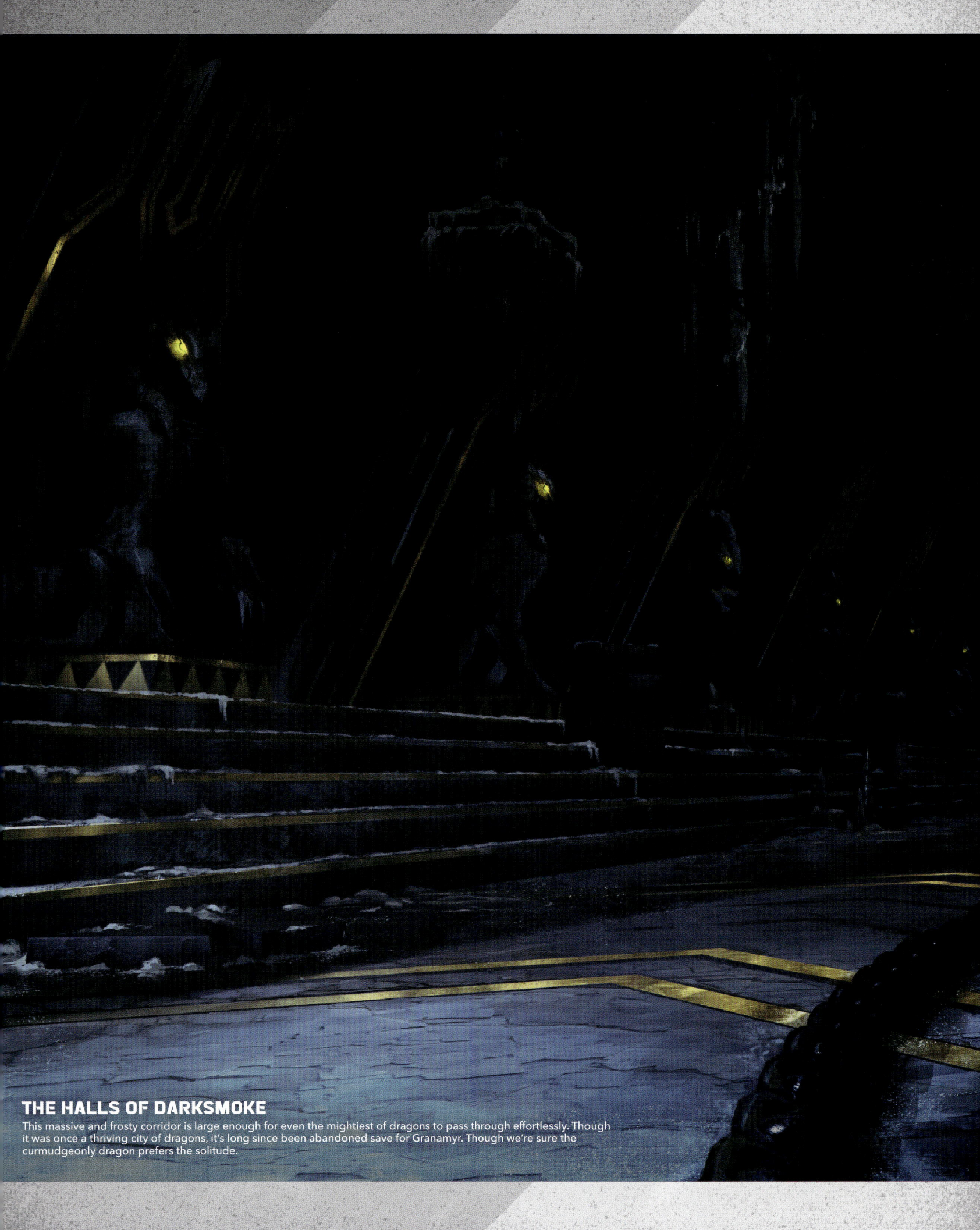

THE HALLS OF DARKSMOKE
This massive and frosty corridor is large enough for even the mightiest of dragons to pass through effortlessly. Though it was once a thriving city of dragons, it's long since been abandoned save for Granamyr. Though we're sure the curmudgeonly dragon prefers the solitude.

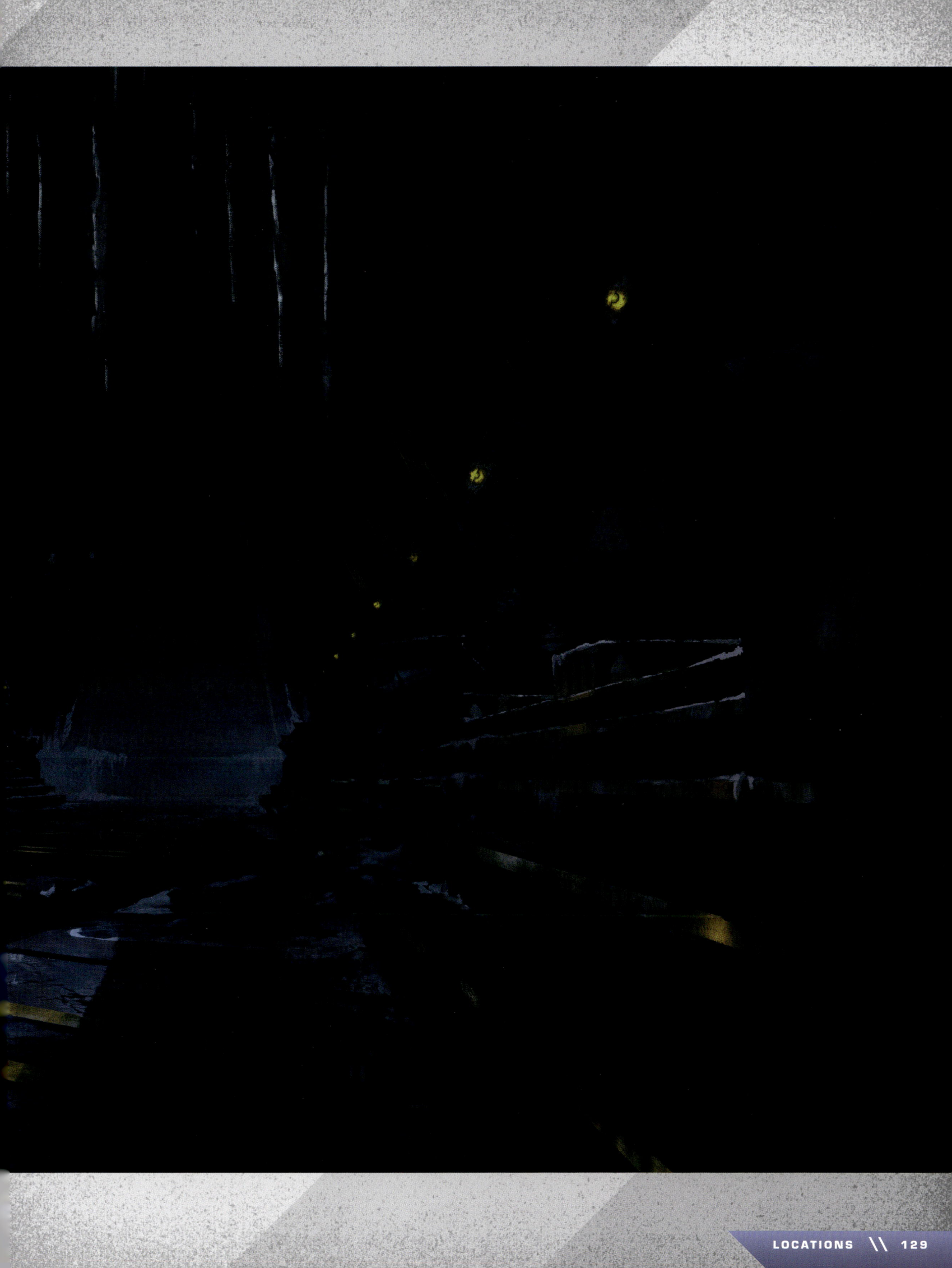

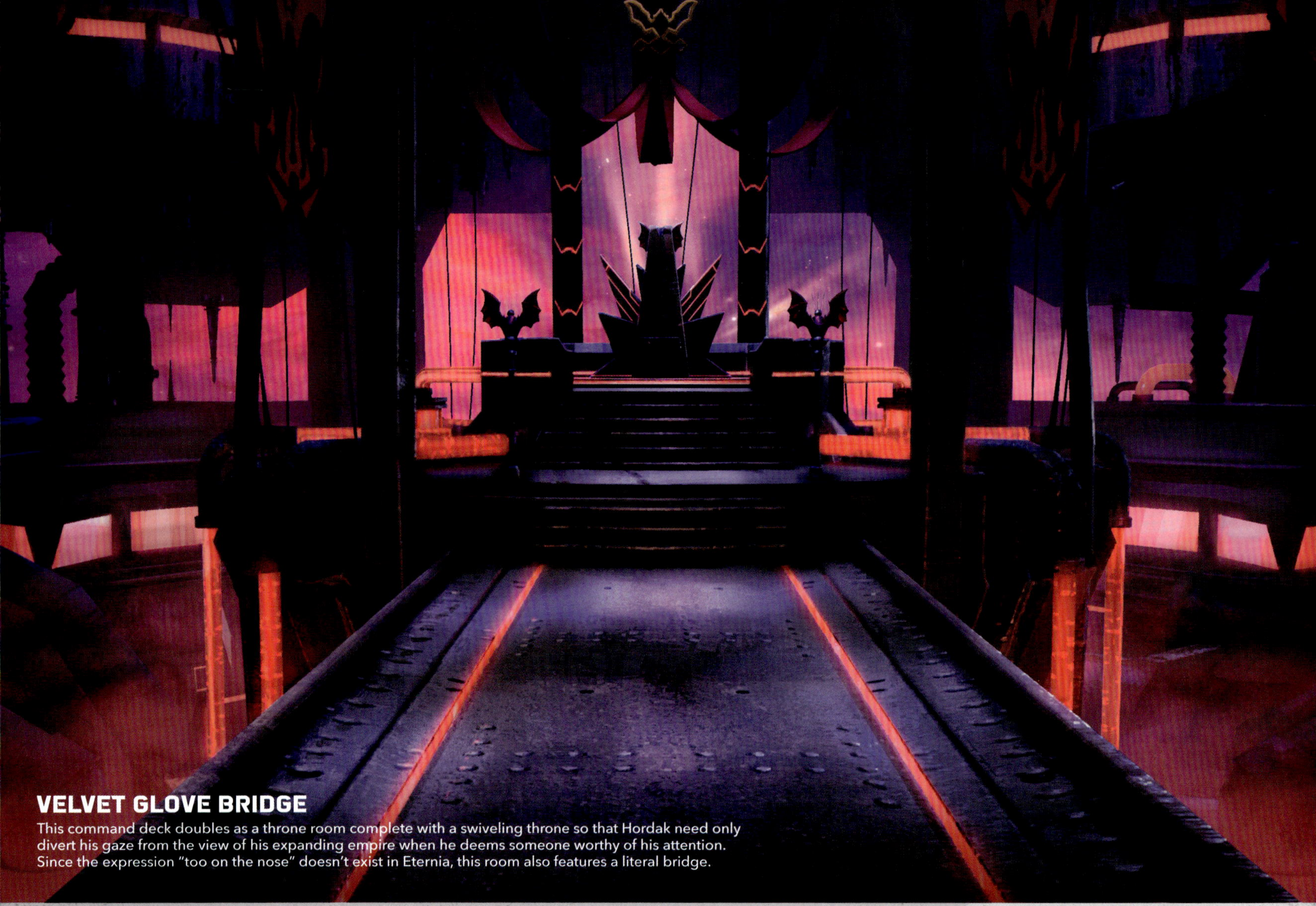

VELVET GLOVE BRIDGE

This command deck doubles as a throne room complete with a swiveling throne so that Hordak need only divert his gaze from the view of his expanding empire when he deems someone worthy of his attention. Since the expression "too on the nose" doesn't exist in Eternia, this room also features a literal bridge.

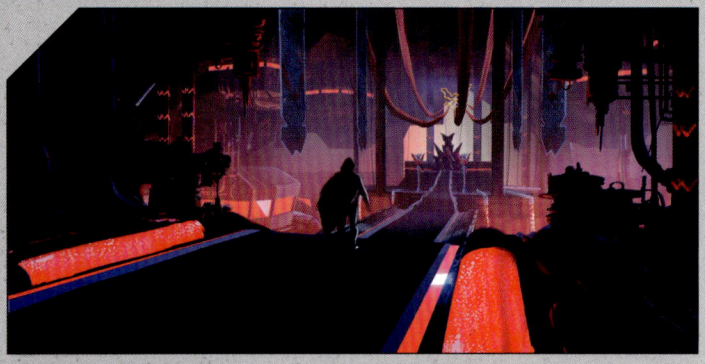
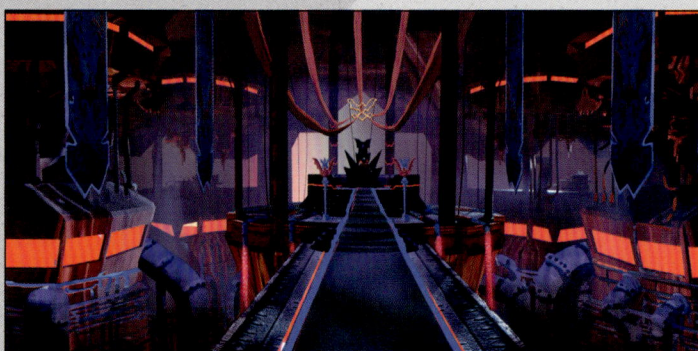
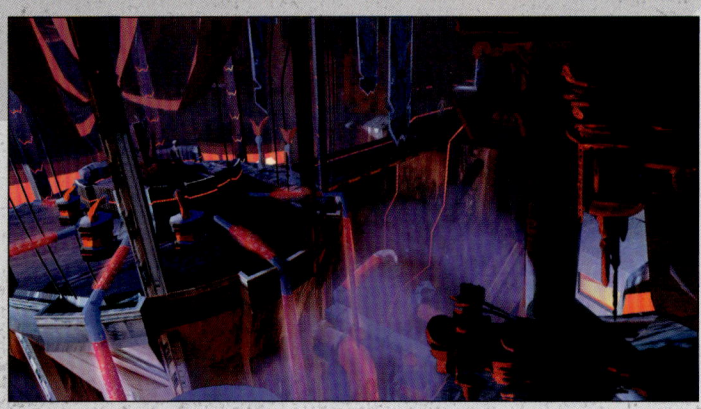
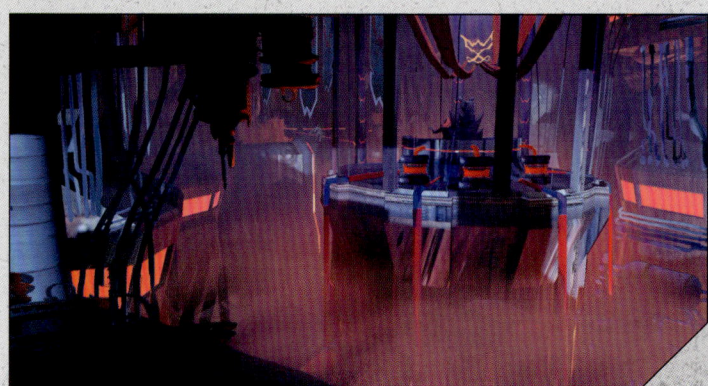

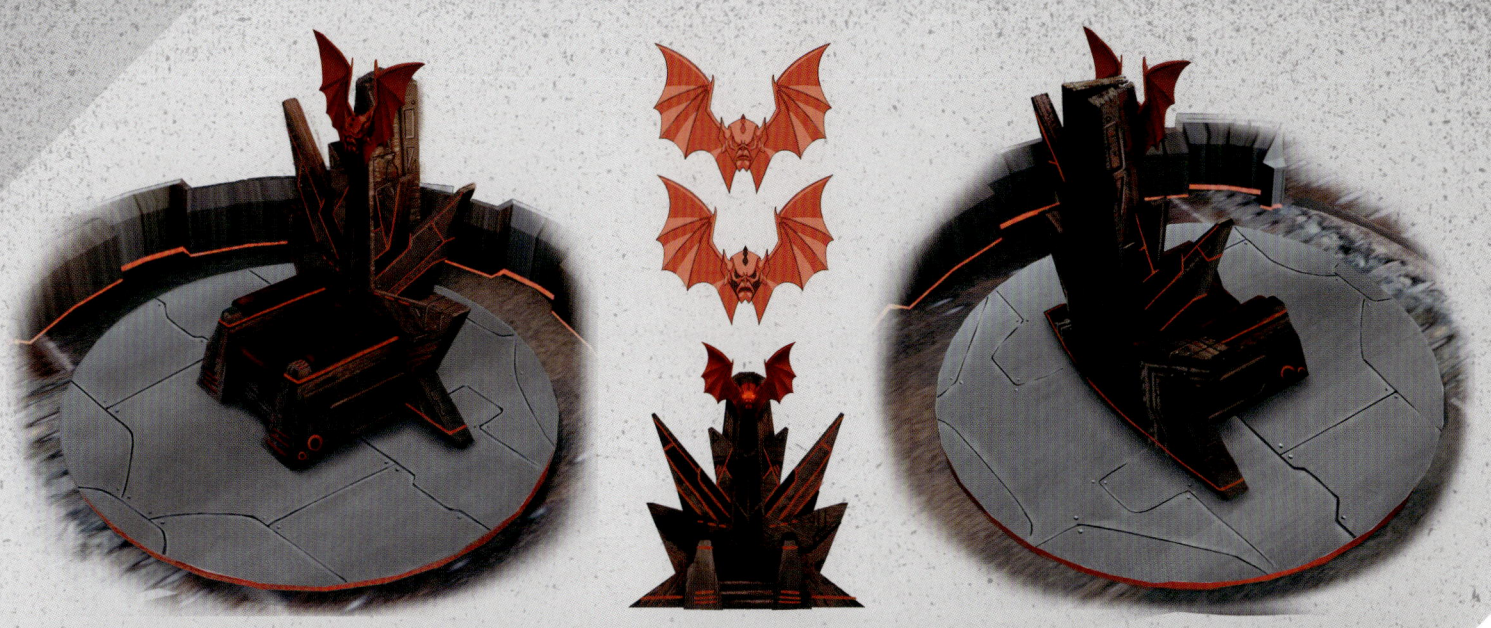
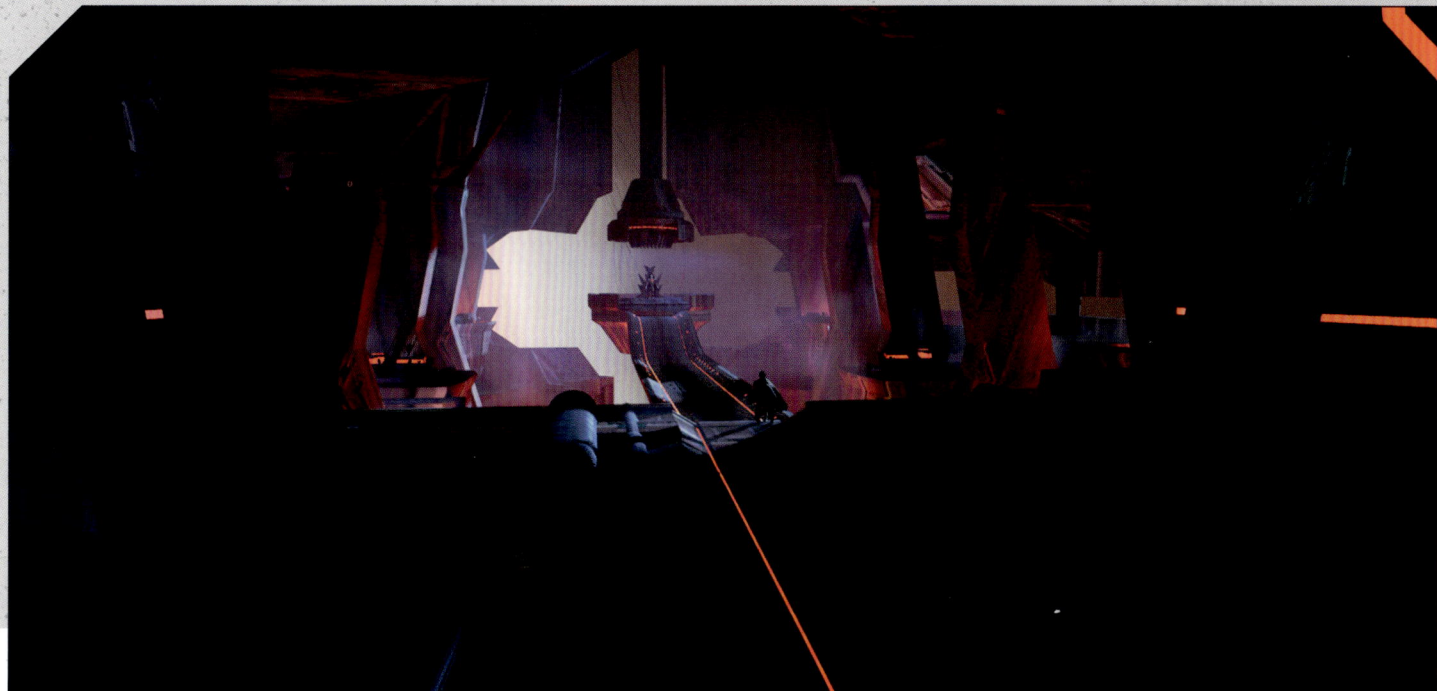
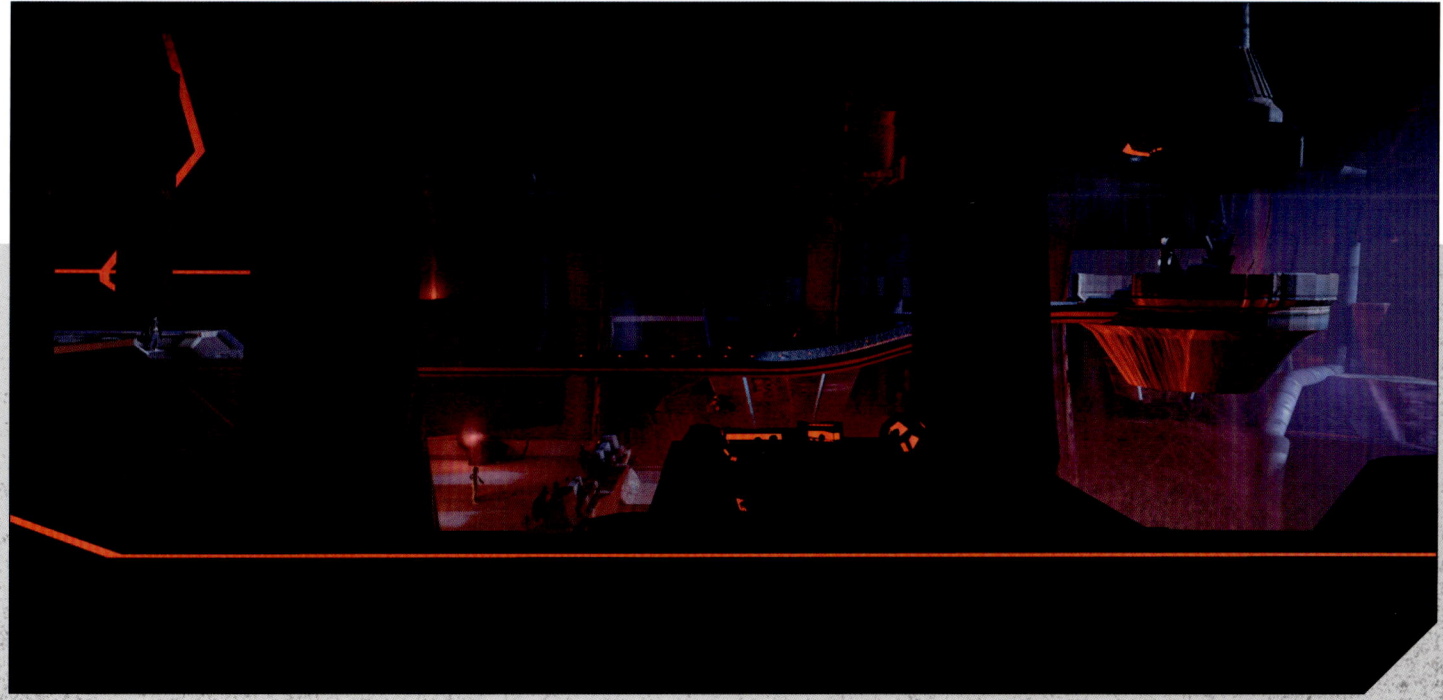

LOCATIONS \\ 131

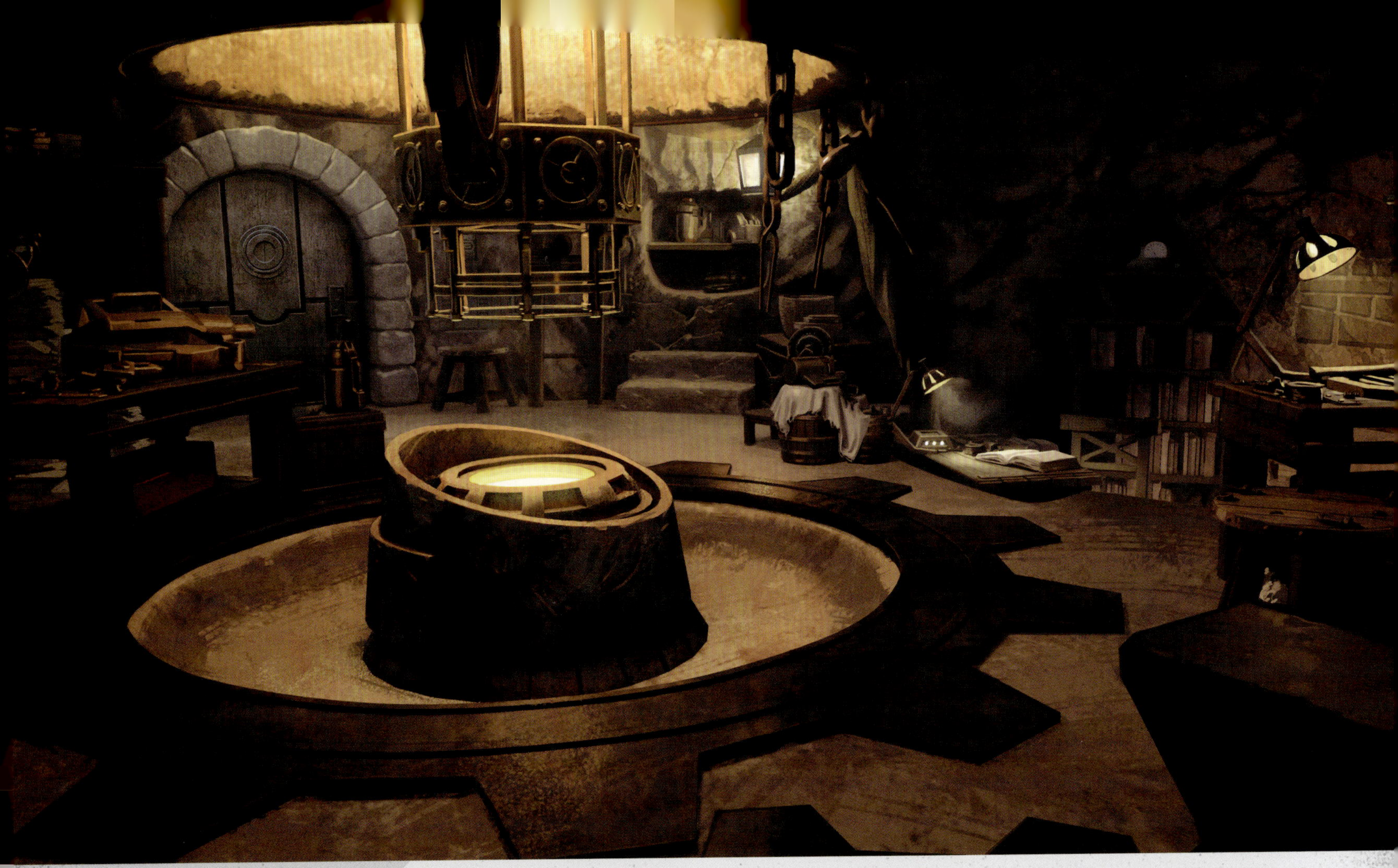

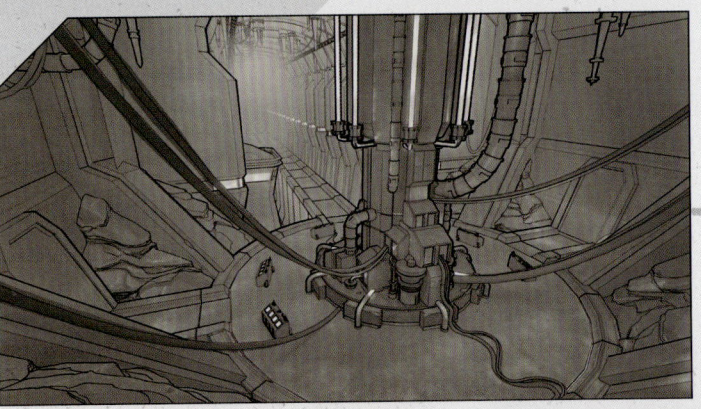
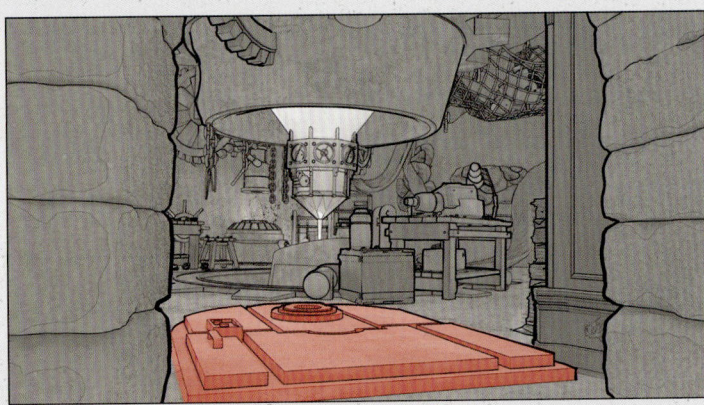
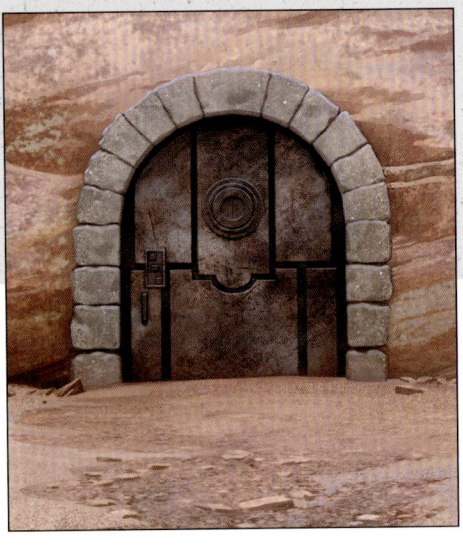
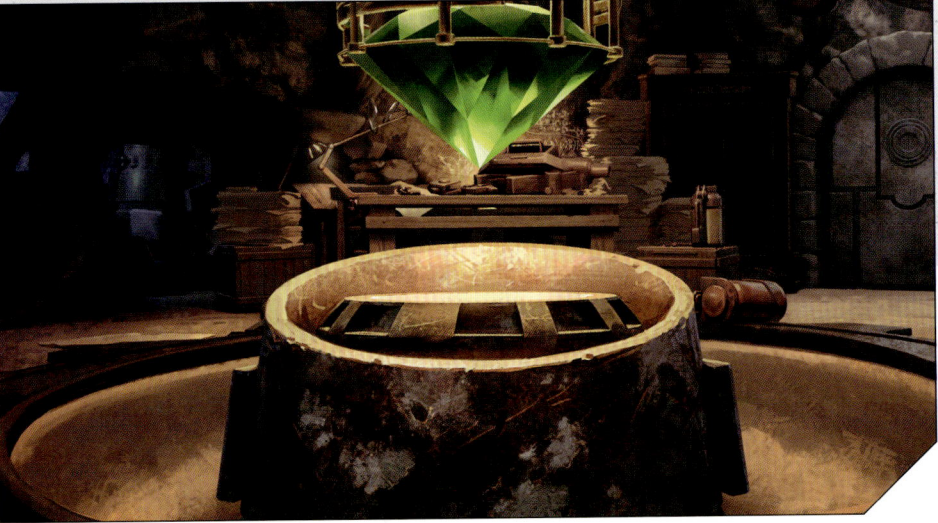

GWILDOR'S HUT

We did our best to re-create the 1987 movie set in the universe of *Revolution*. Some new additions included a large focusing emerald over Gwildor's workbench and Eternian-style foliage around the junkyard, but fans might spot a certain pink Cadillac that looks awfully familiar.

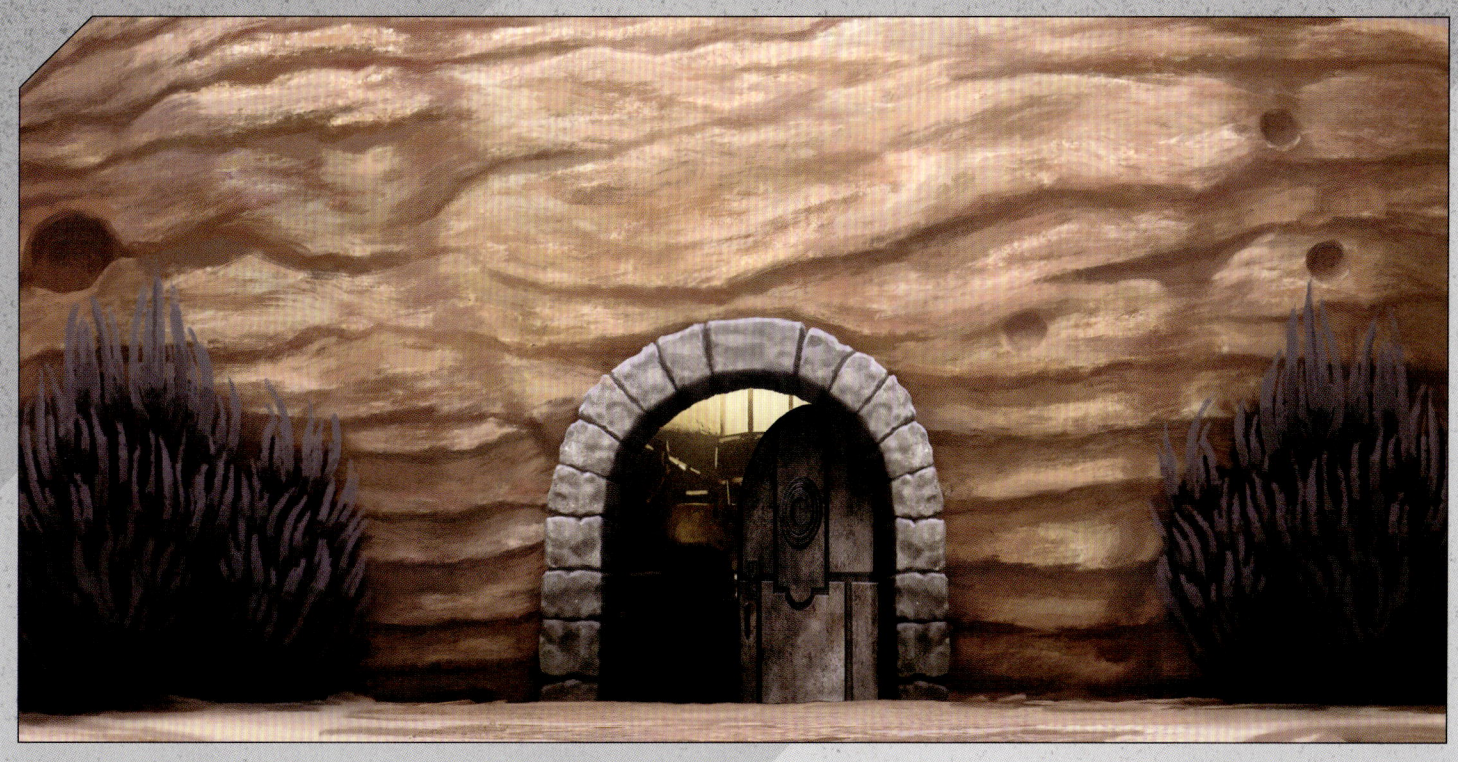
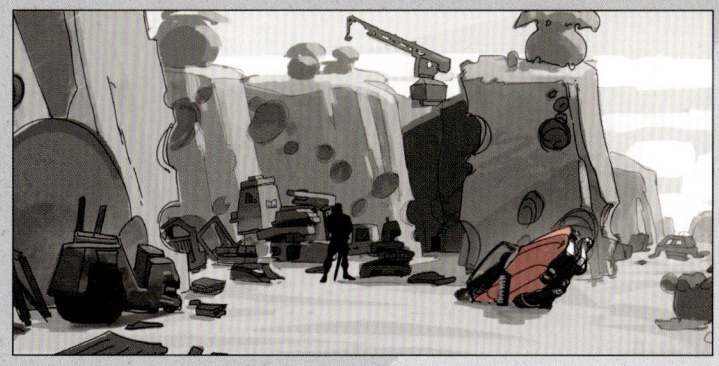
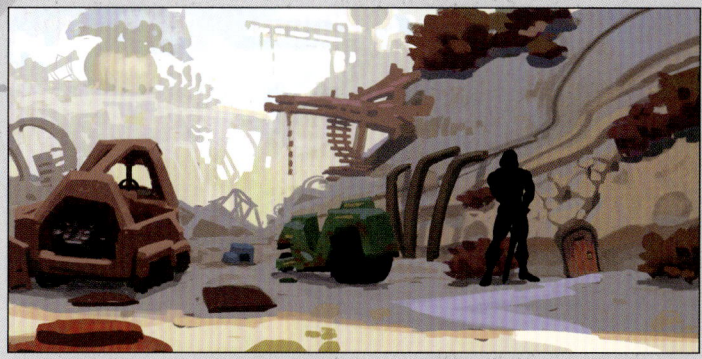
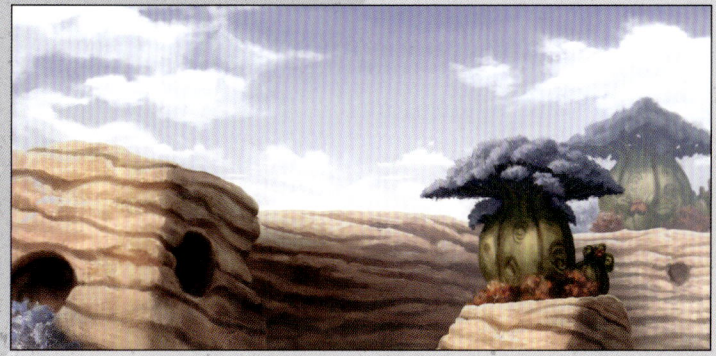
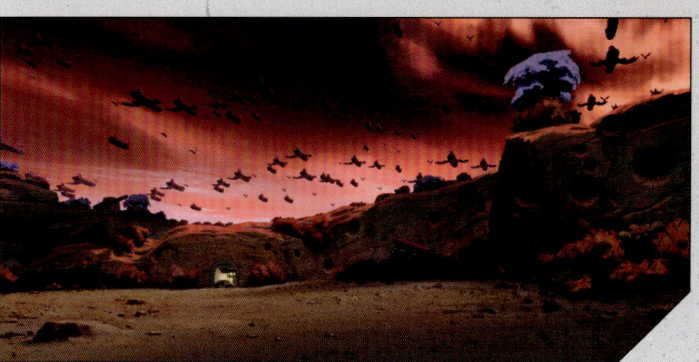
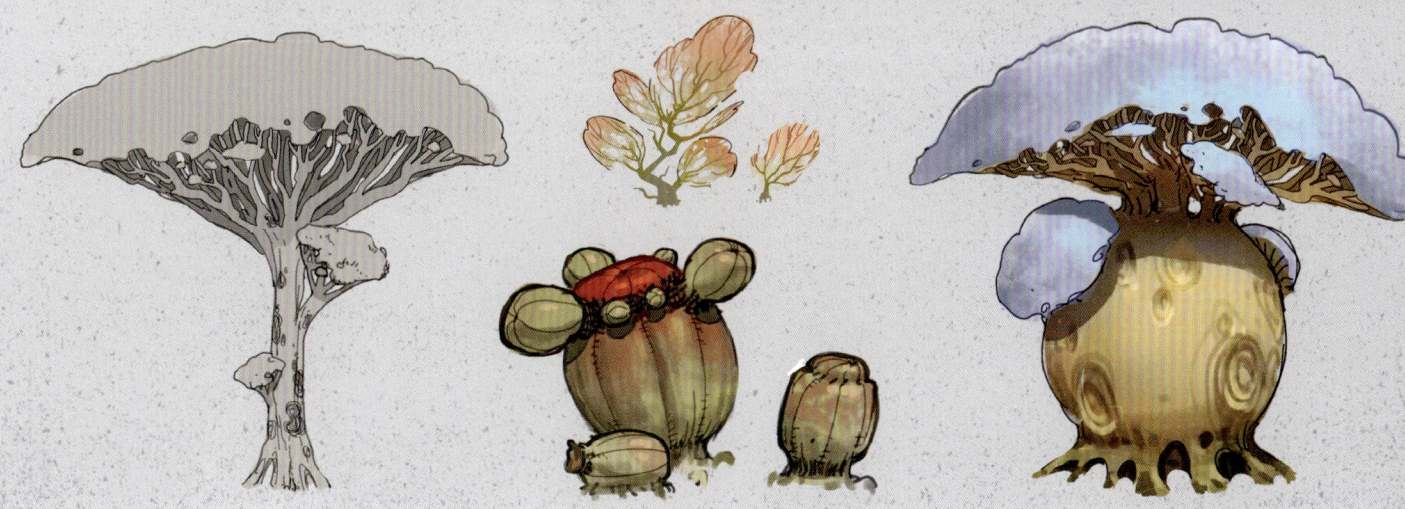

LOCATIONS \\ 133

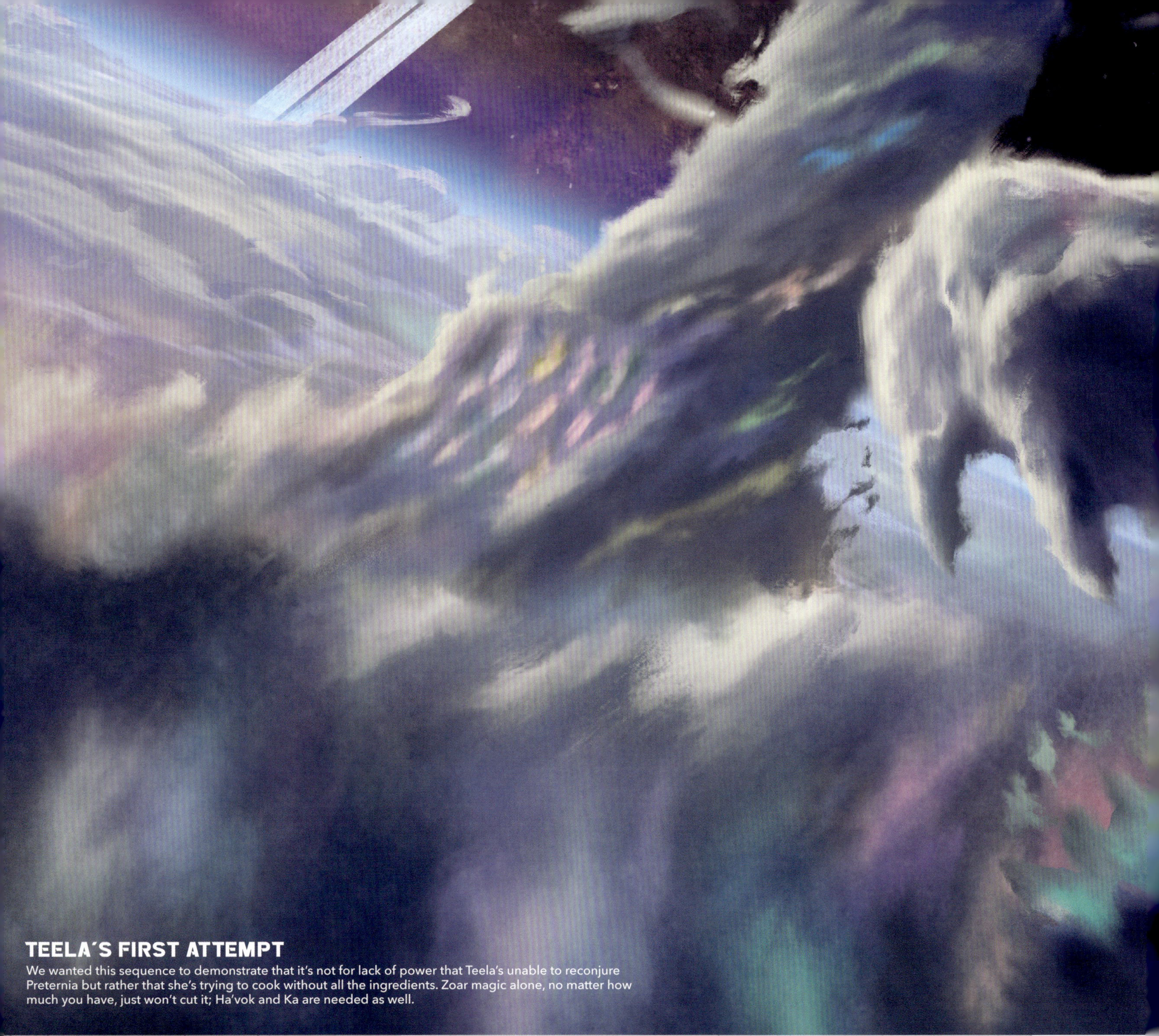

TEELA'S FIRST ATTEMPT
We wanted this sequence to demonstrate that it's not for lack of power that Teela's unable to reconjure Preternia but rather that she's trying to cook without all the ingredients. Zoar magic alone, no matter how much you have, just won't cut it; Ha'vok and Ka are needed as well.

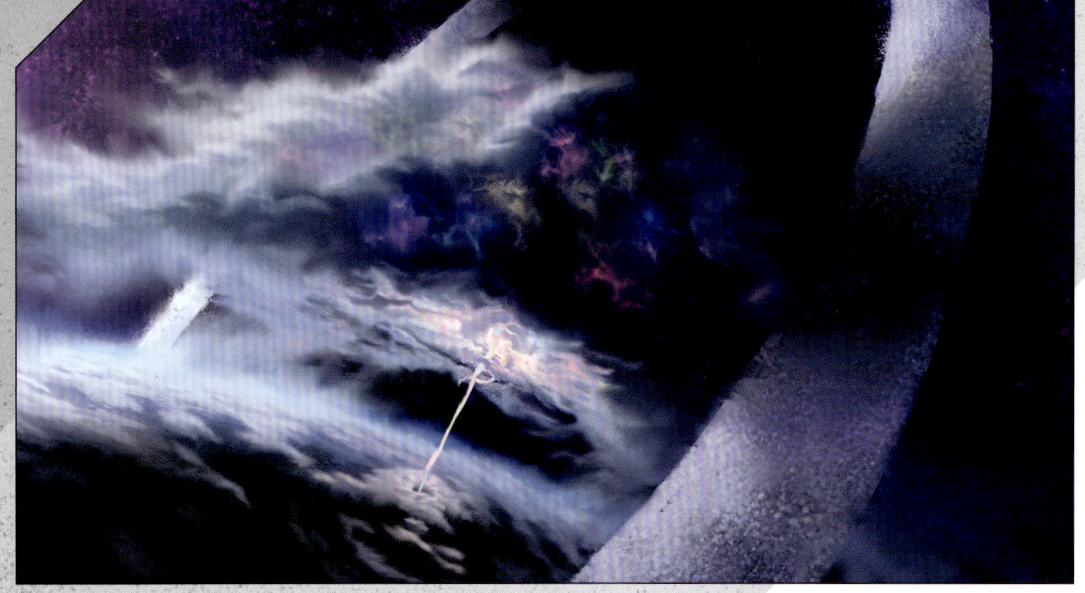
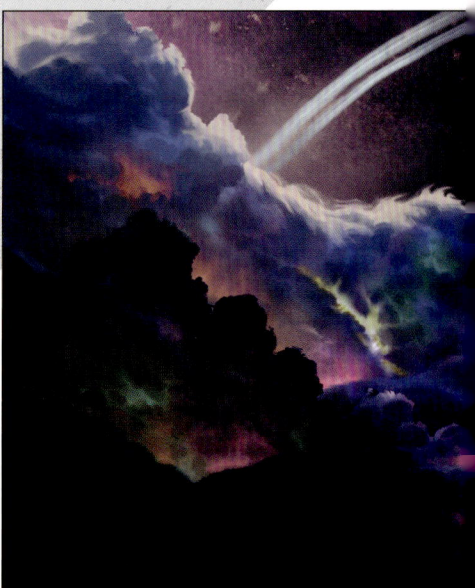

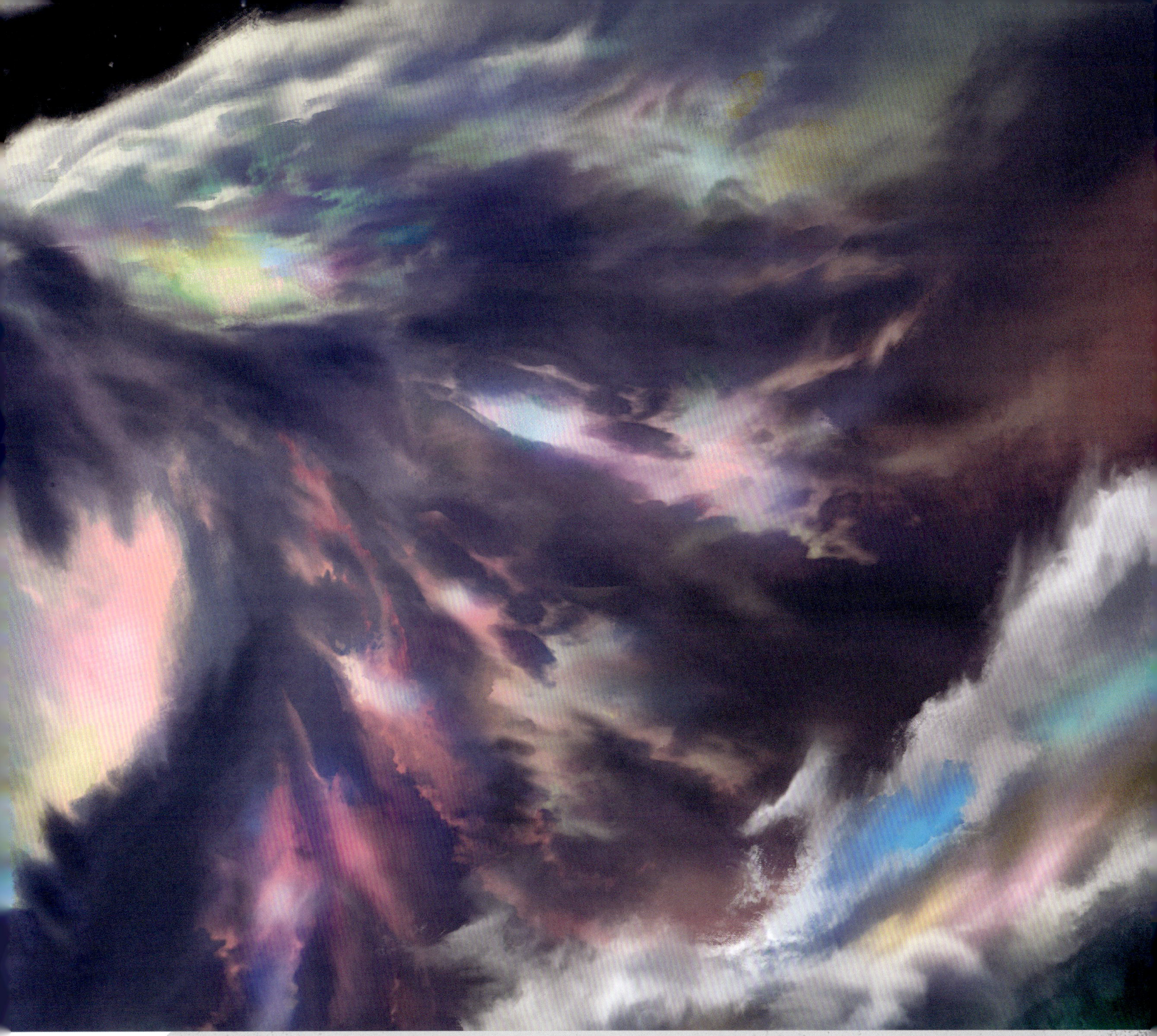

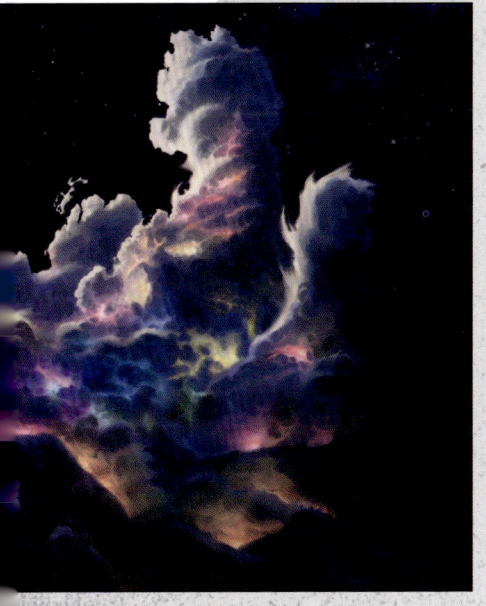
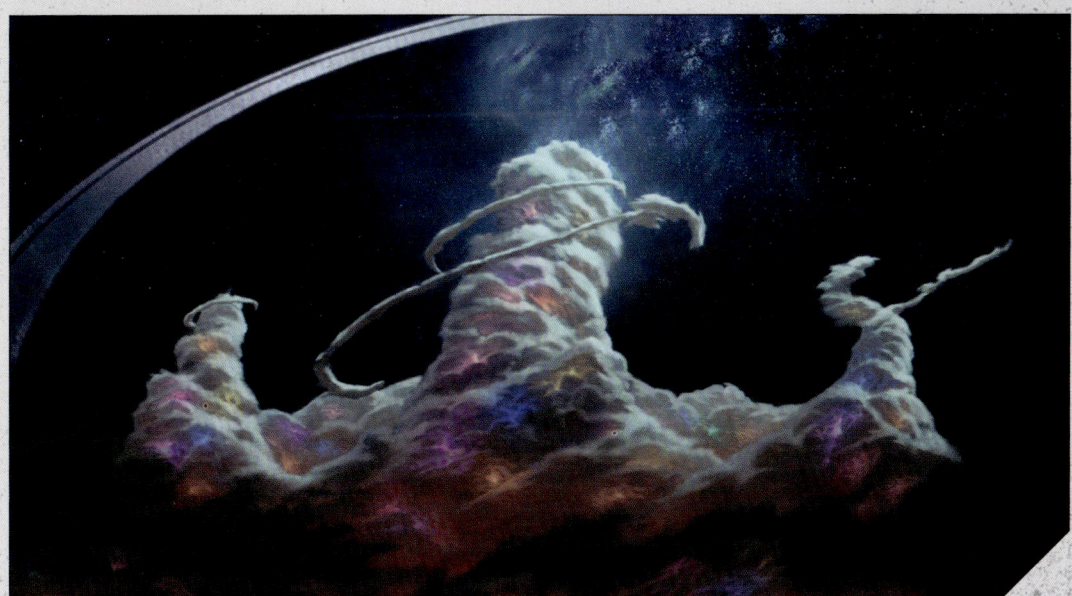

LOCATIONS \\ 135

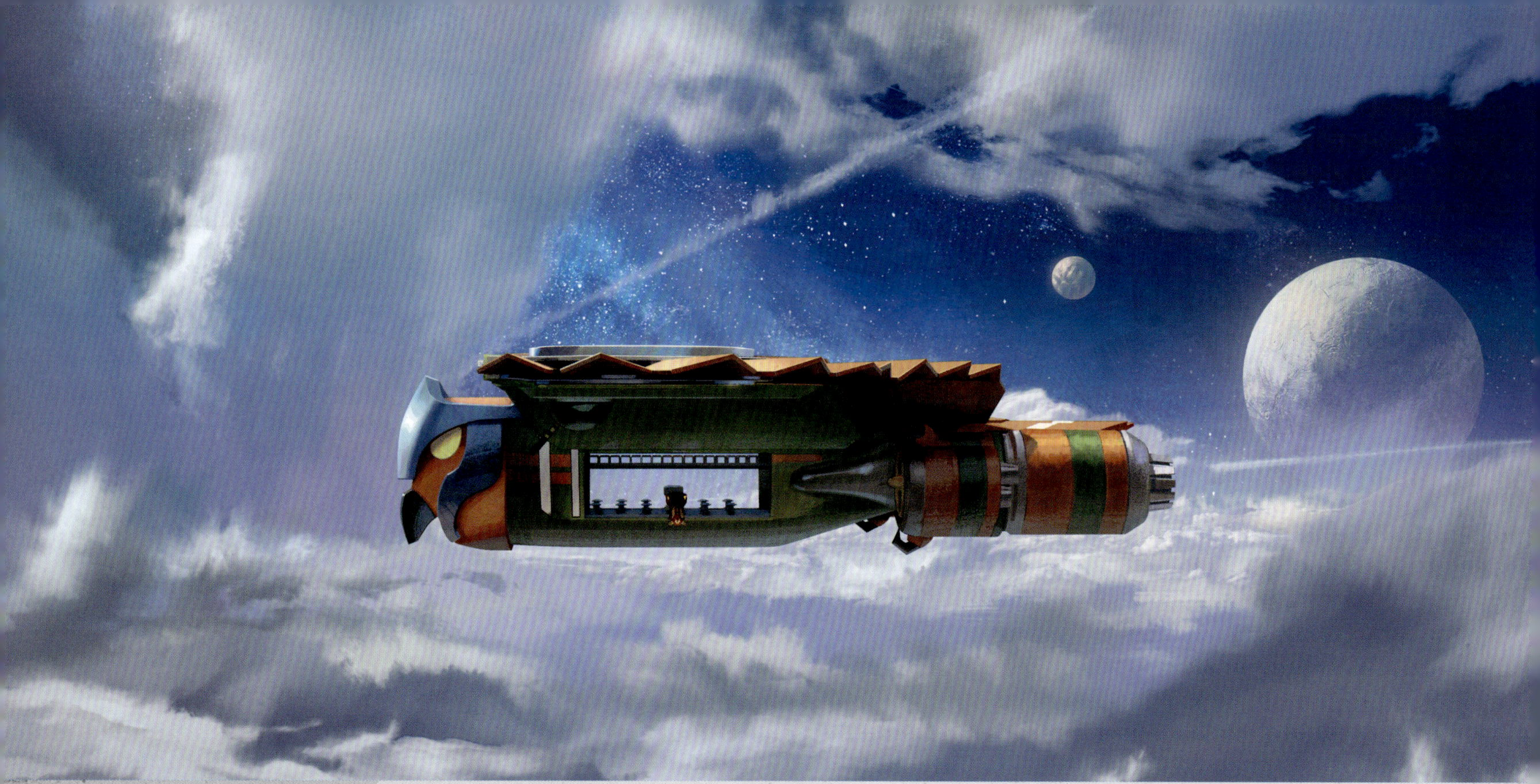

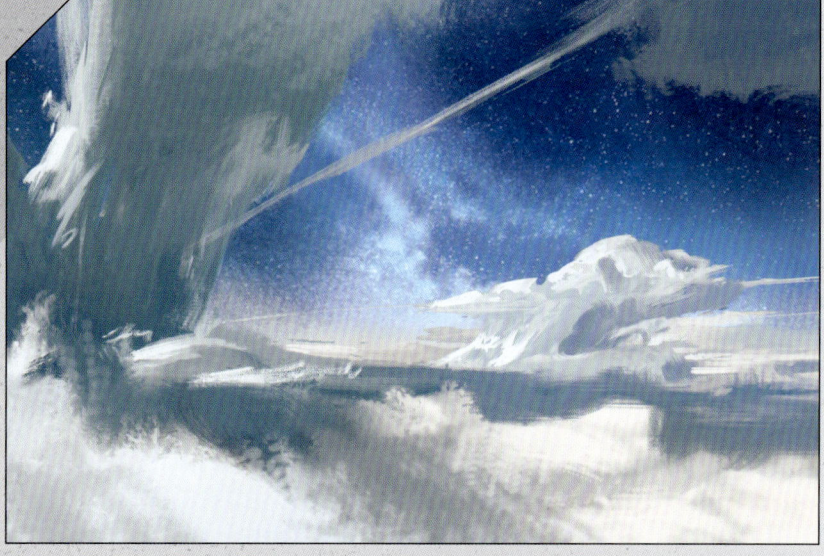

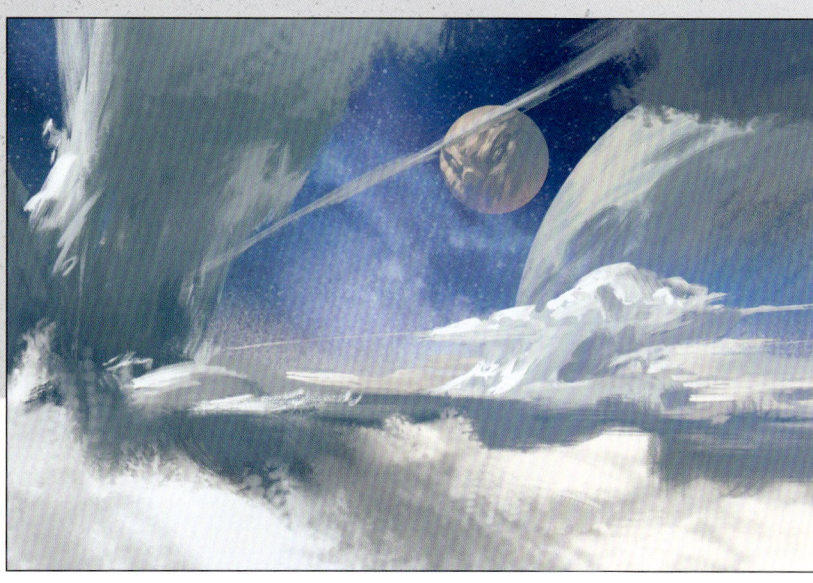

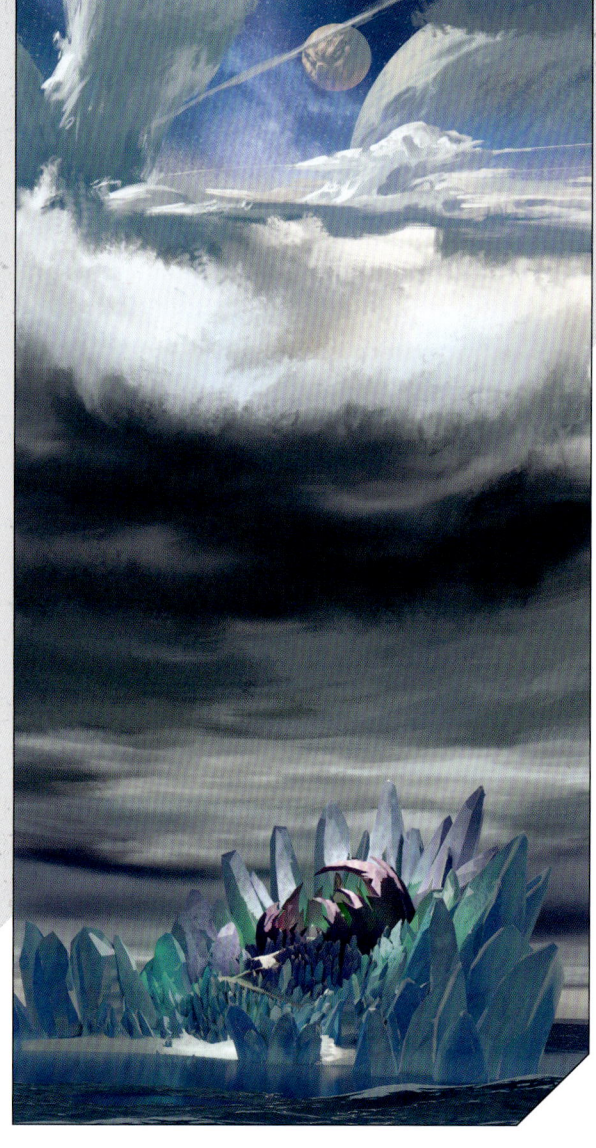

SKIES ABOVE THE CRYSTAL SEA
It was important to us that we conveyed a sense of relief after the intense battle in Subternia. Rising through the overcast storms to the calm cloud tops gives us a moment to rest and celebrate our heroes' victory, though danger may be closer than you think . . .

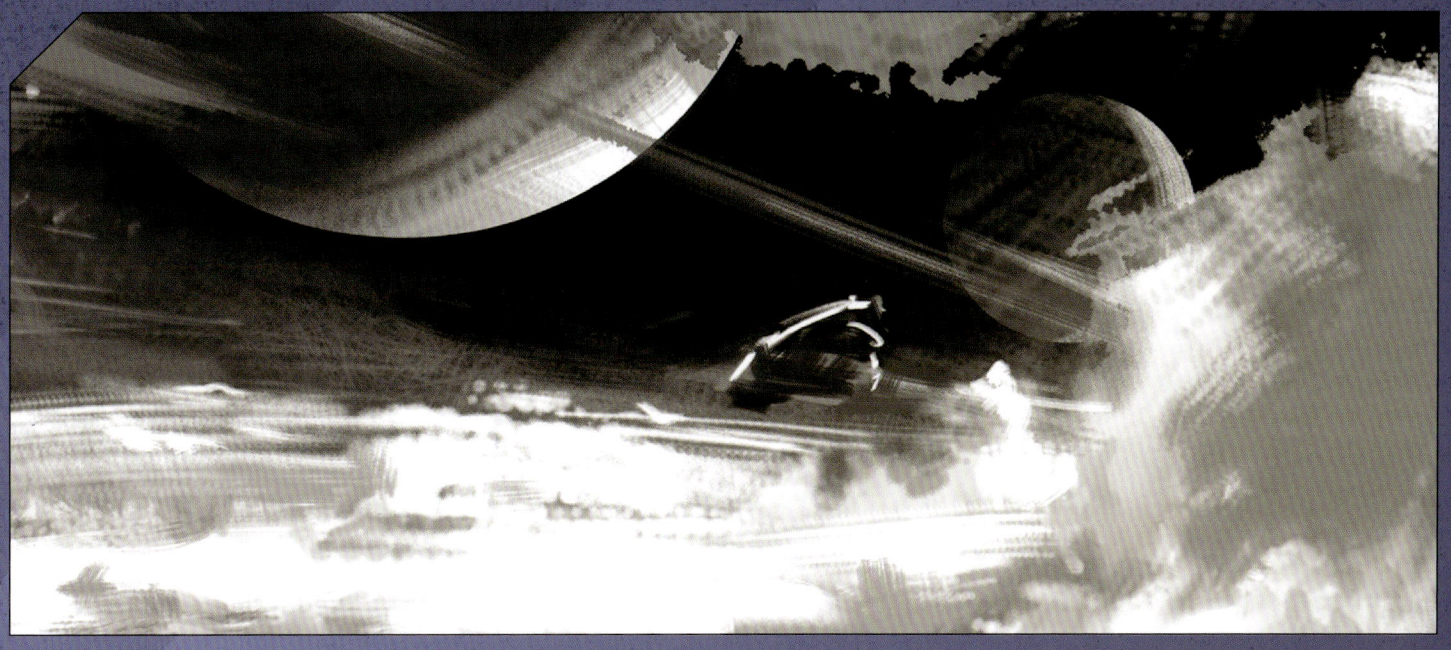
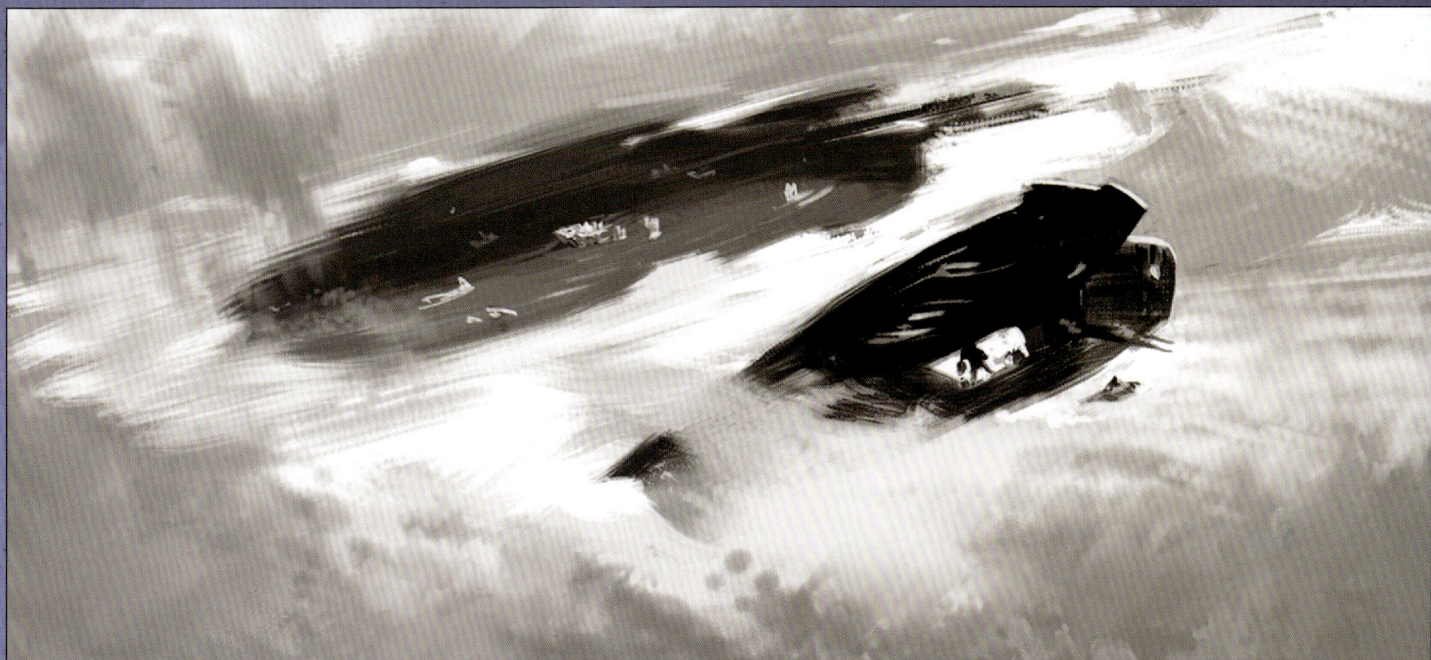
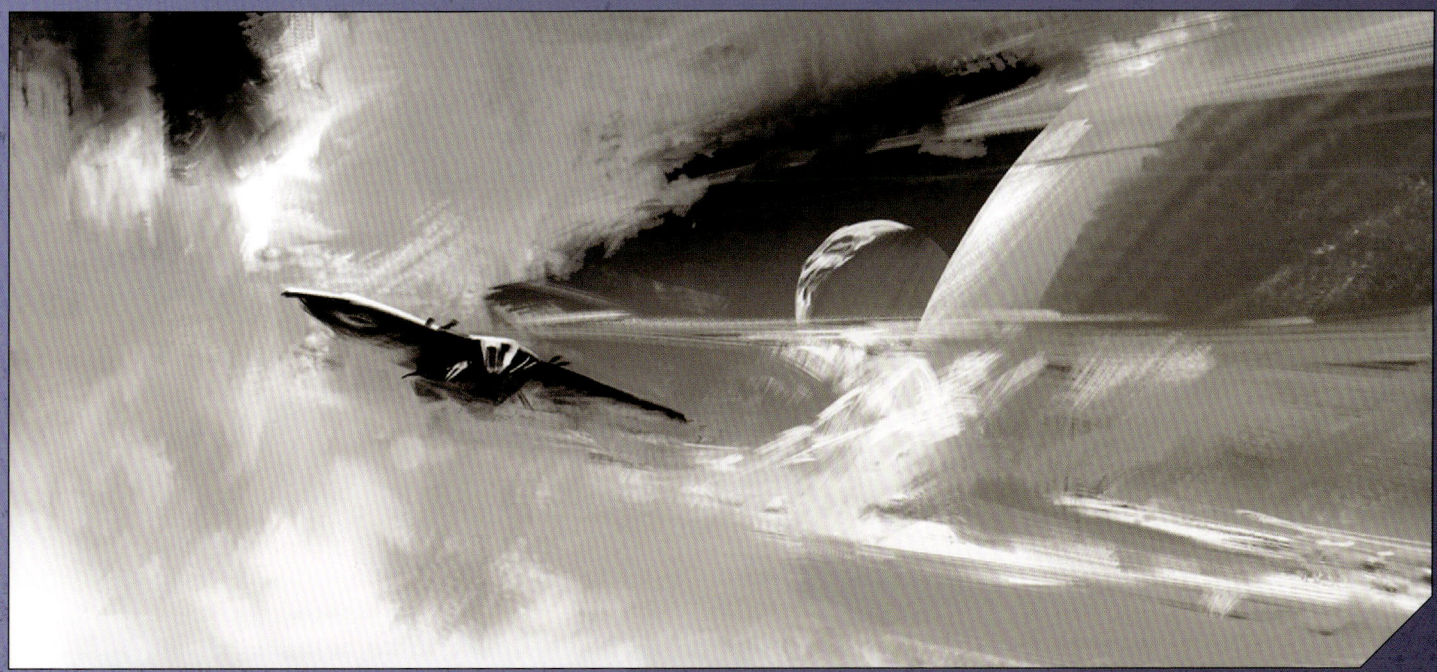

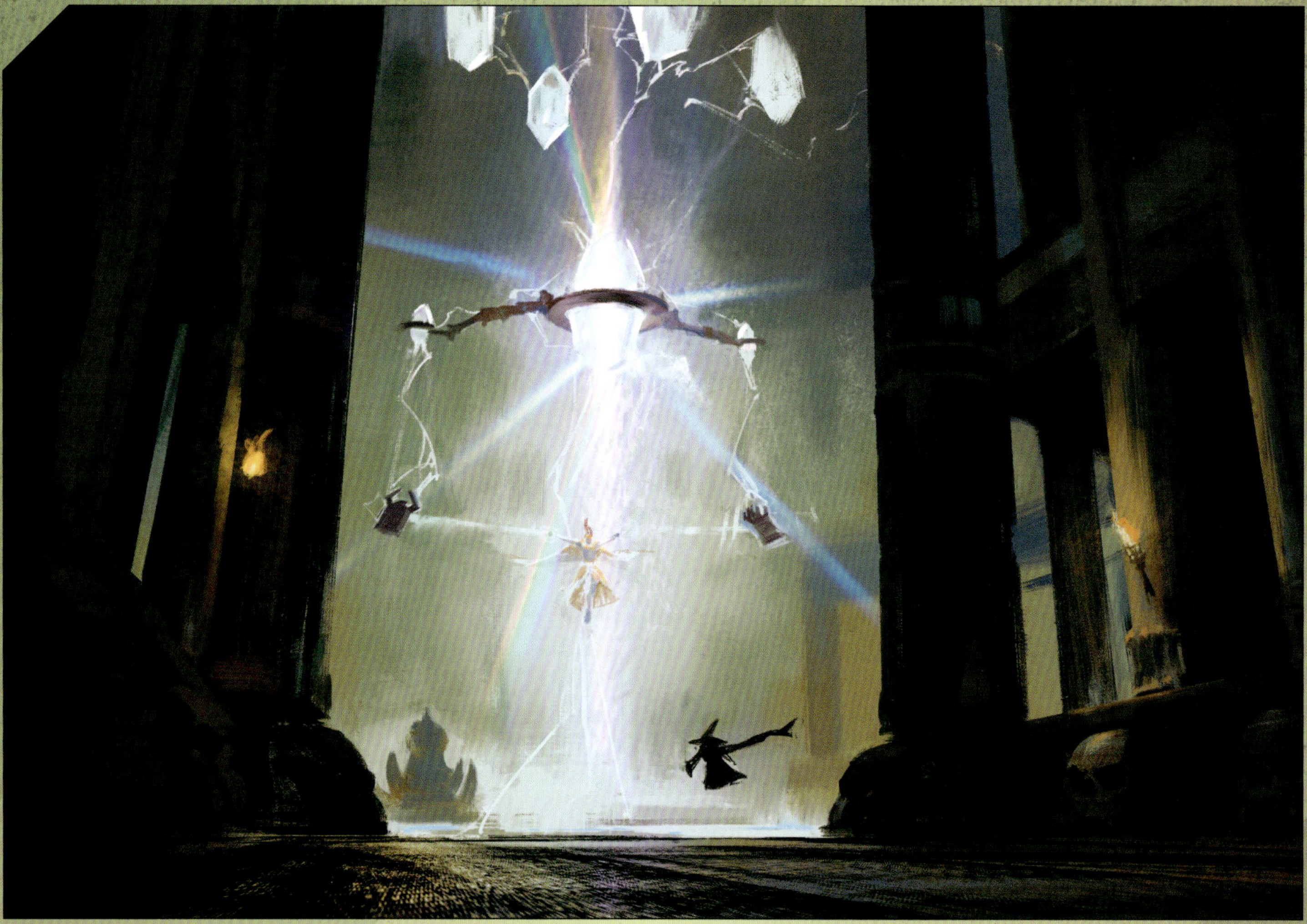

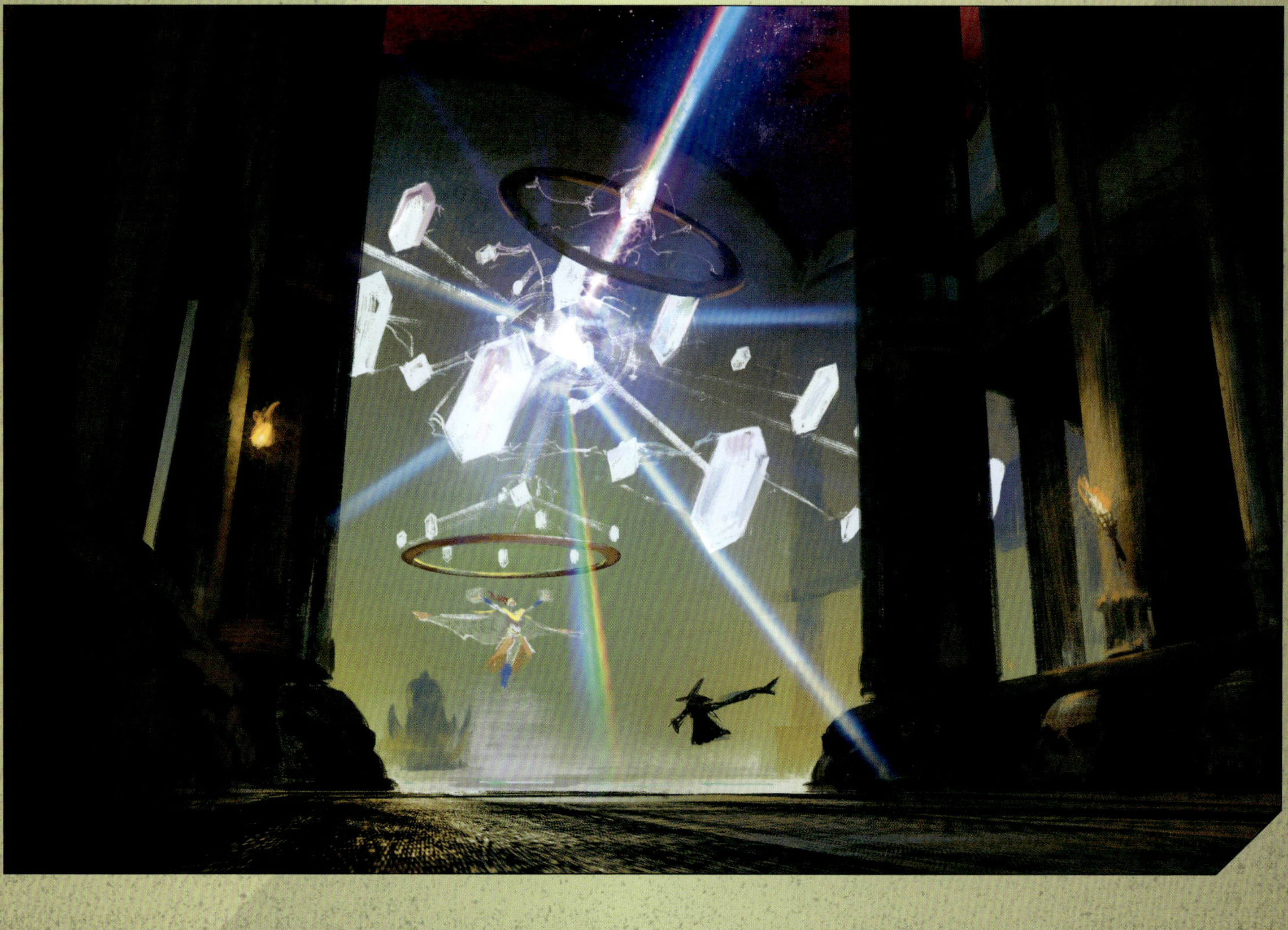

138 // THE ART OF MASTERS OF THE UNIVERSE: REVOLUTION

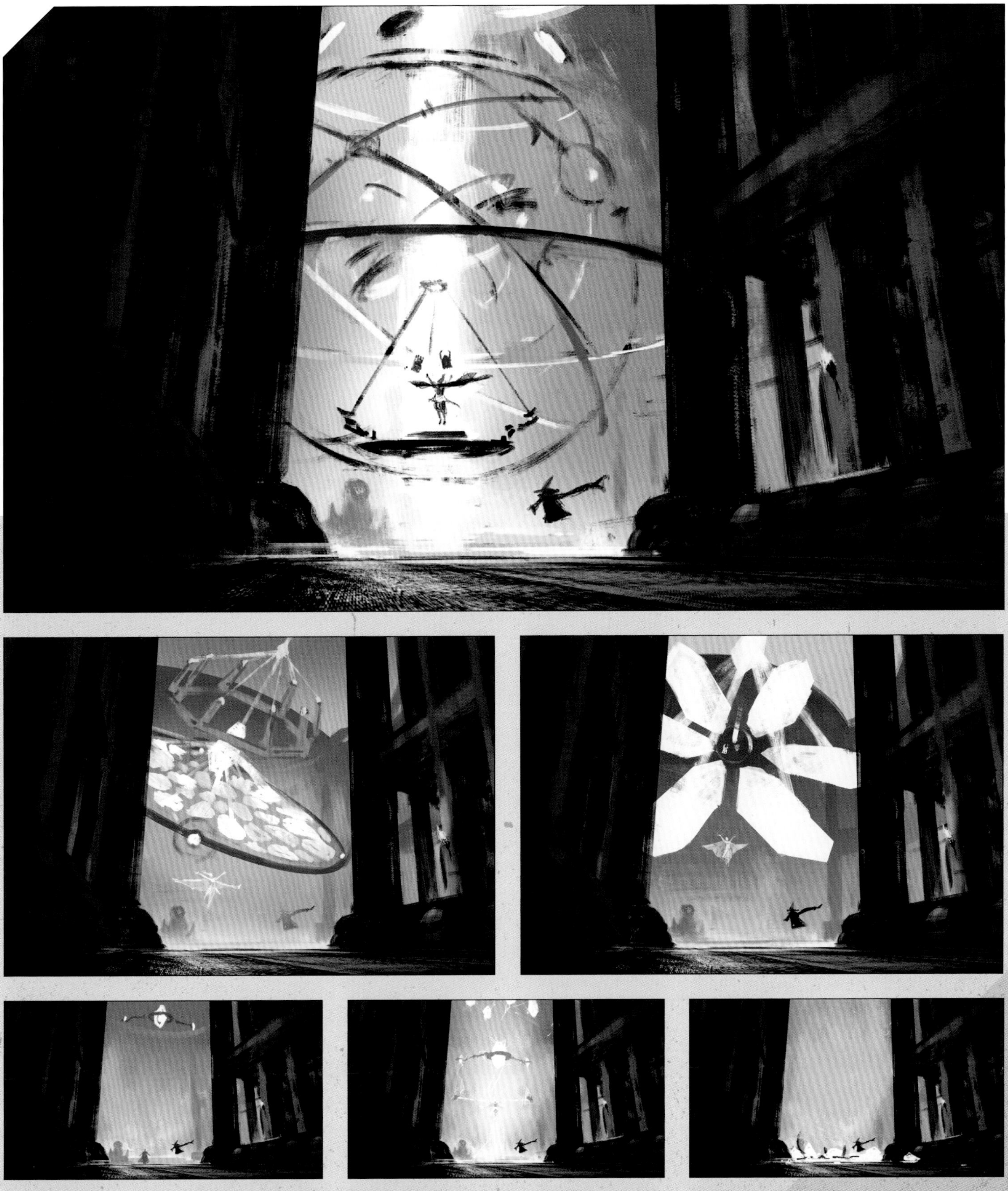

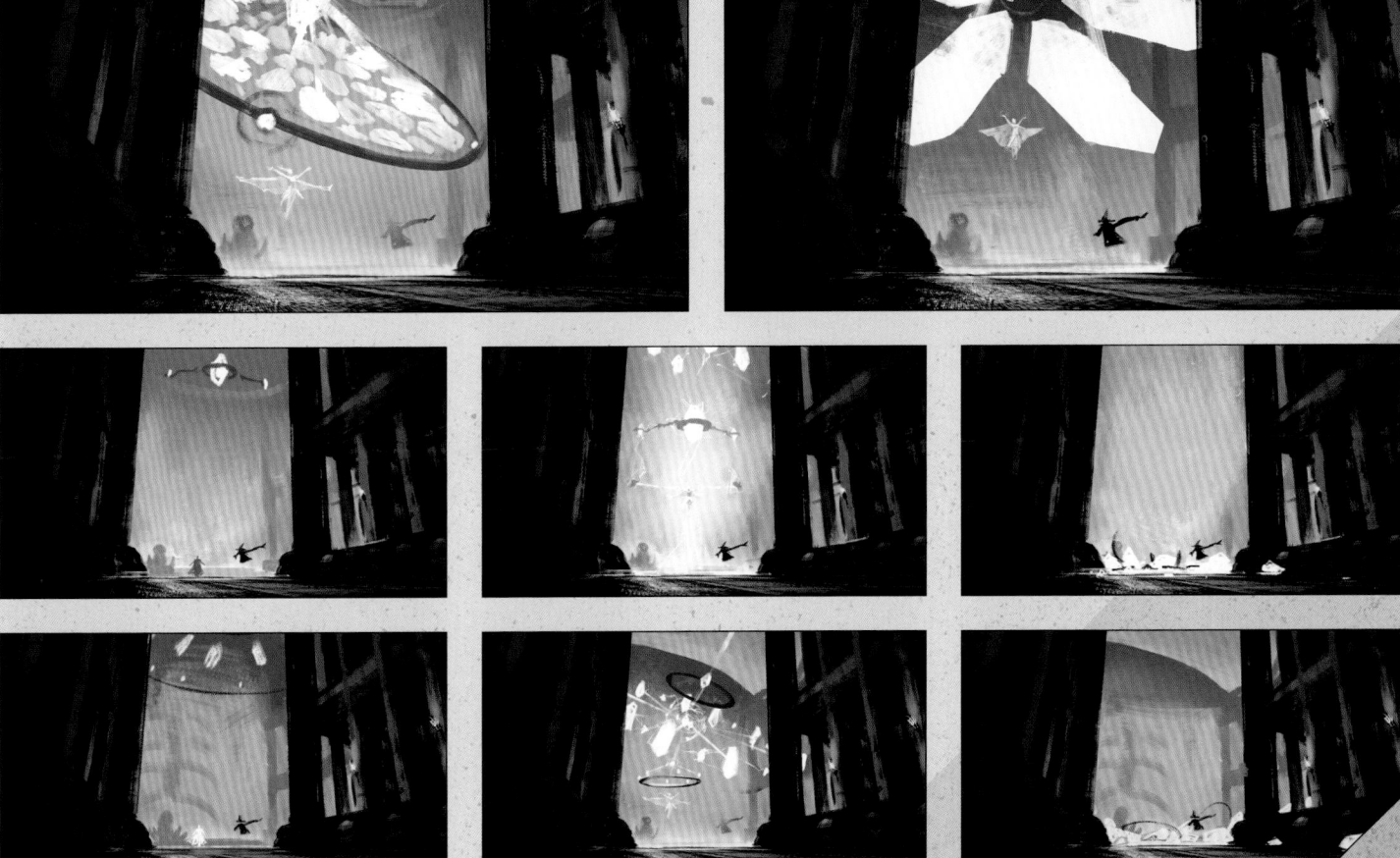

In concepts we incorporated the astrolabe seen in *Revelation* but ultimately decided that this story point would be more clear if the magic came straight from Teela. It also set us up to have an even more torrential display when Teela tries again later with all three magics.

LOCATIONS \\ 139

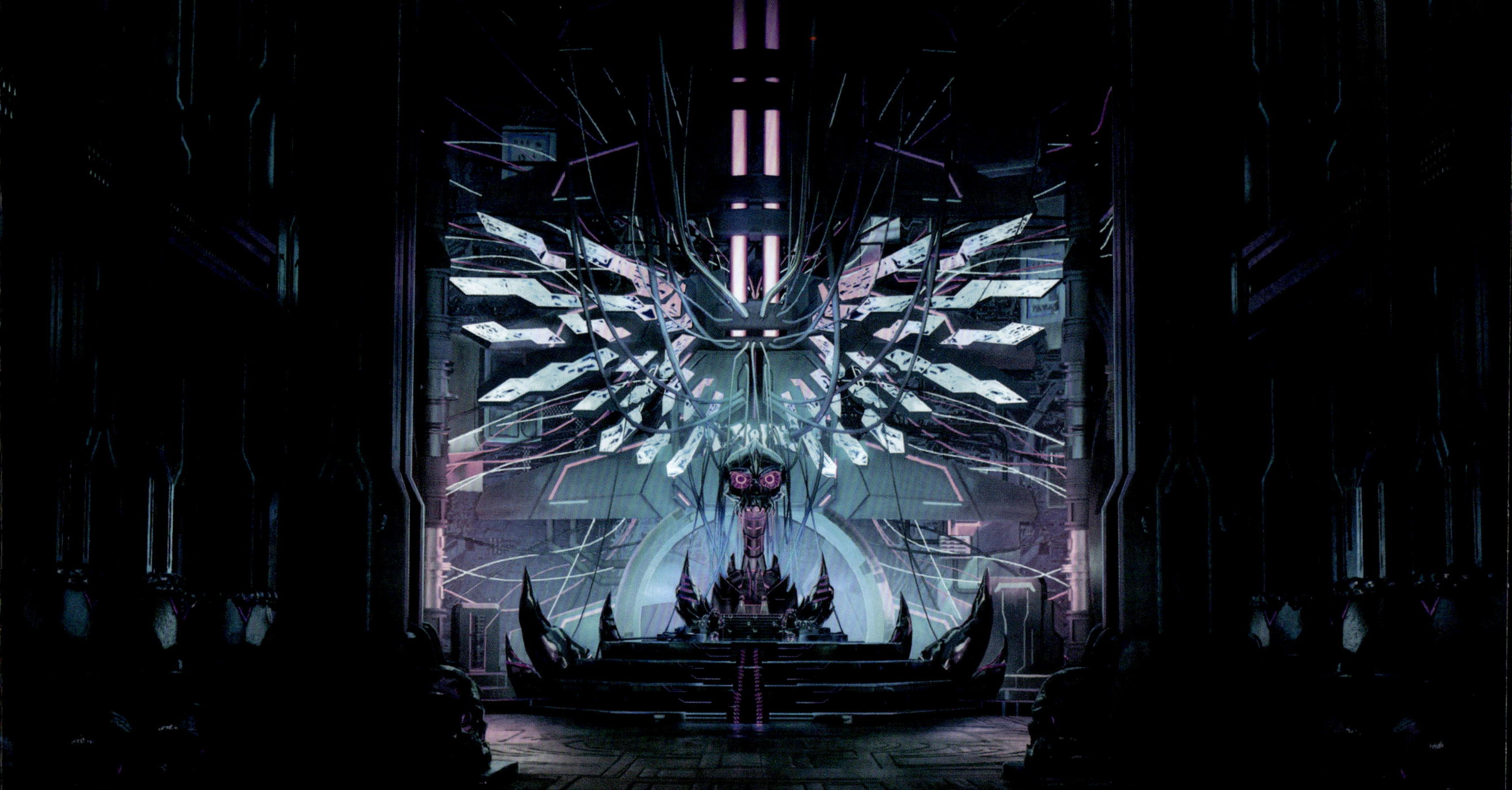

A NEW KIND OF SORCERESS

Motherboard releases nanobots into the environment that transform the magical stronghold into the technological seat of her power while installing herself as a pseudo Sorceress. Keen eyes will also note the large CPU fans mounted to either side of the throne room to keep things running at peak efficiency.

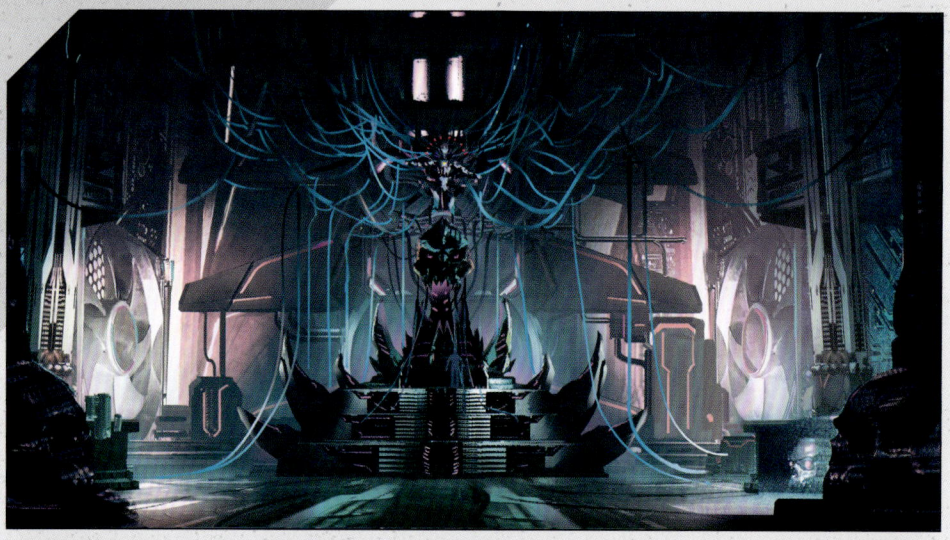

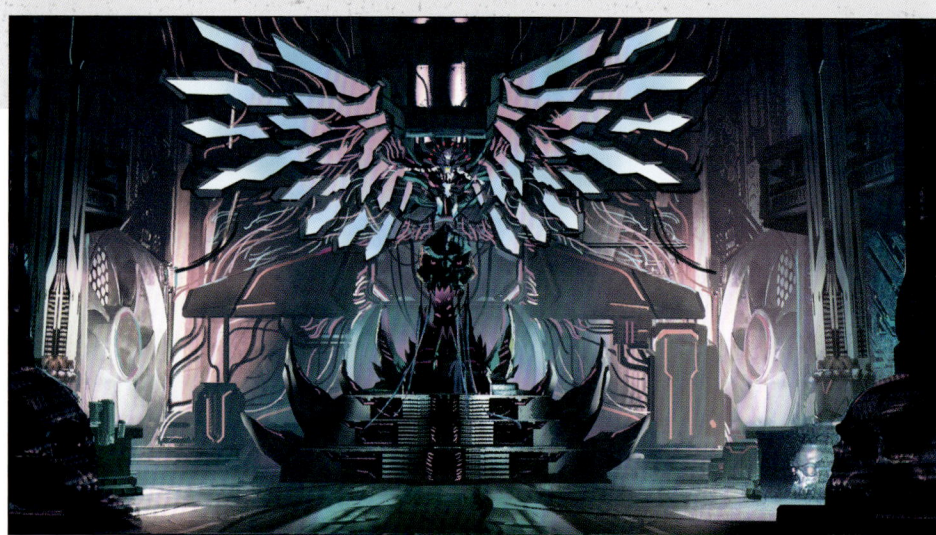

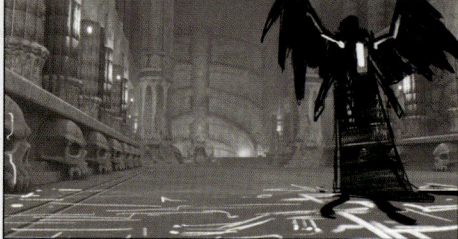

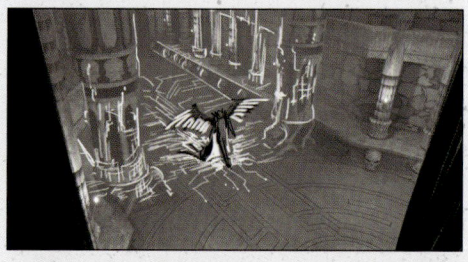

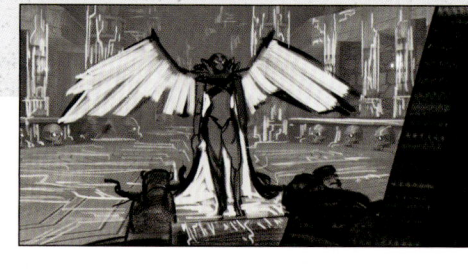

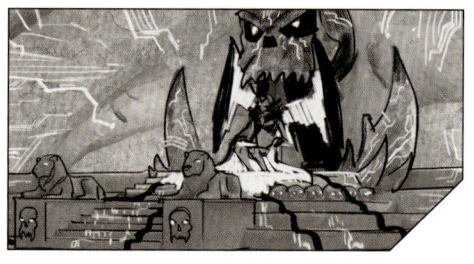

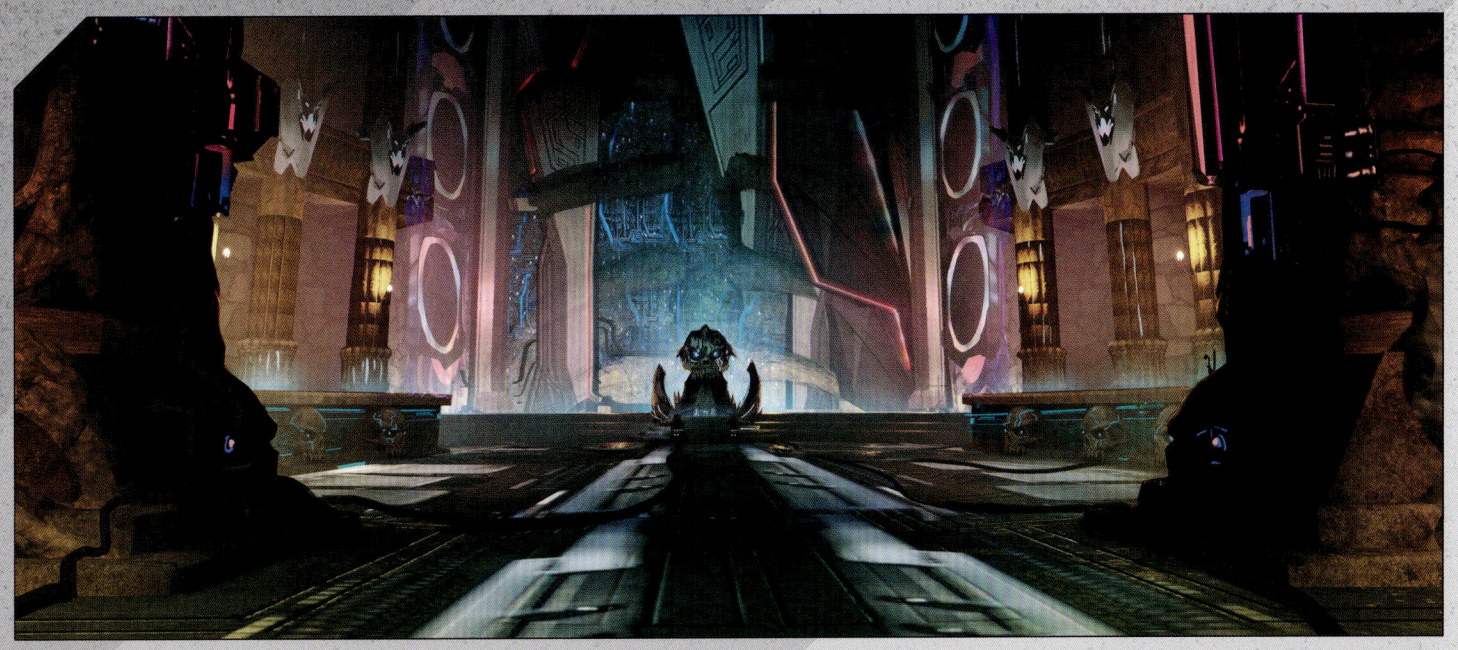
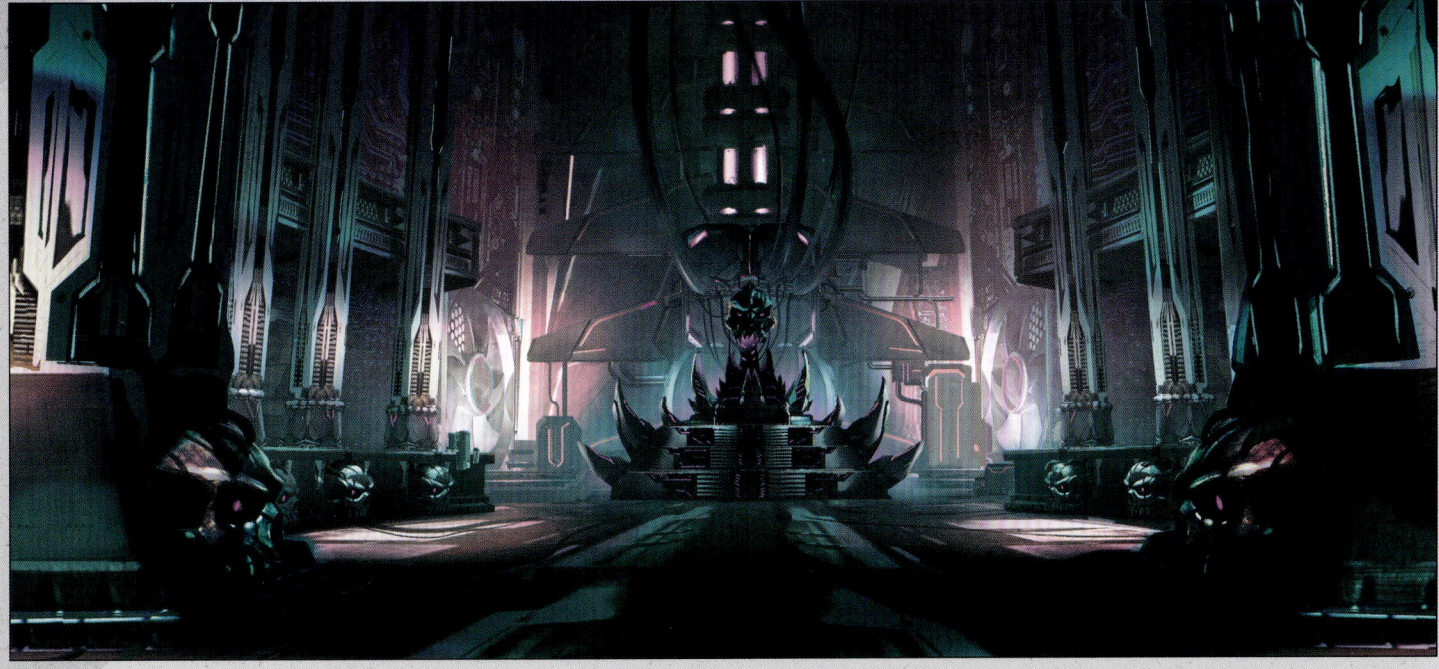
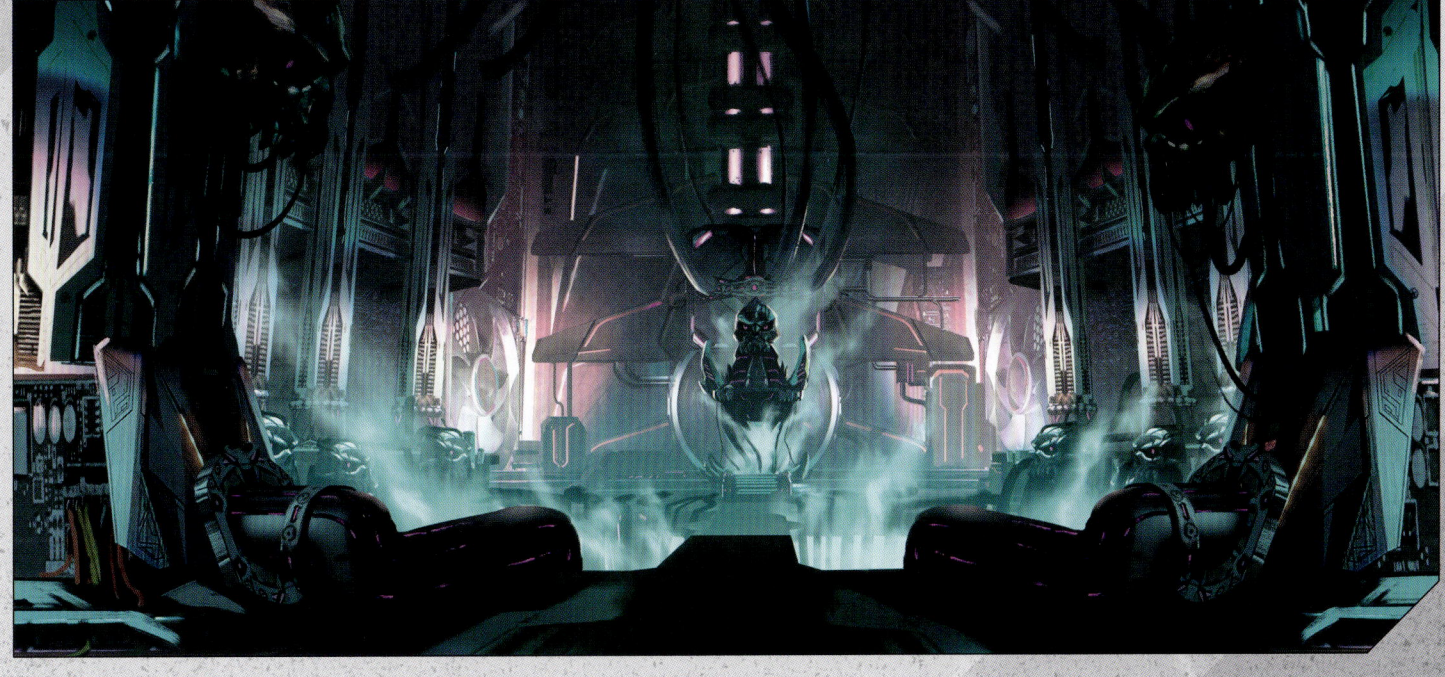

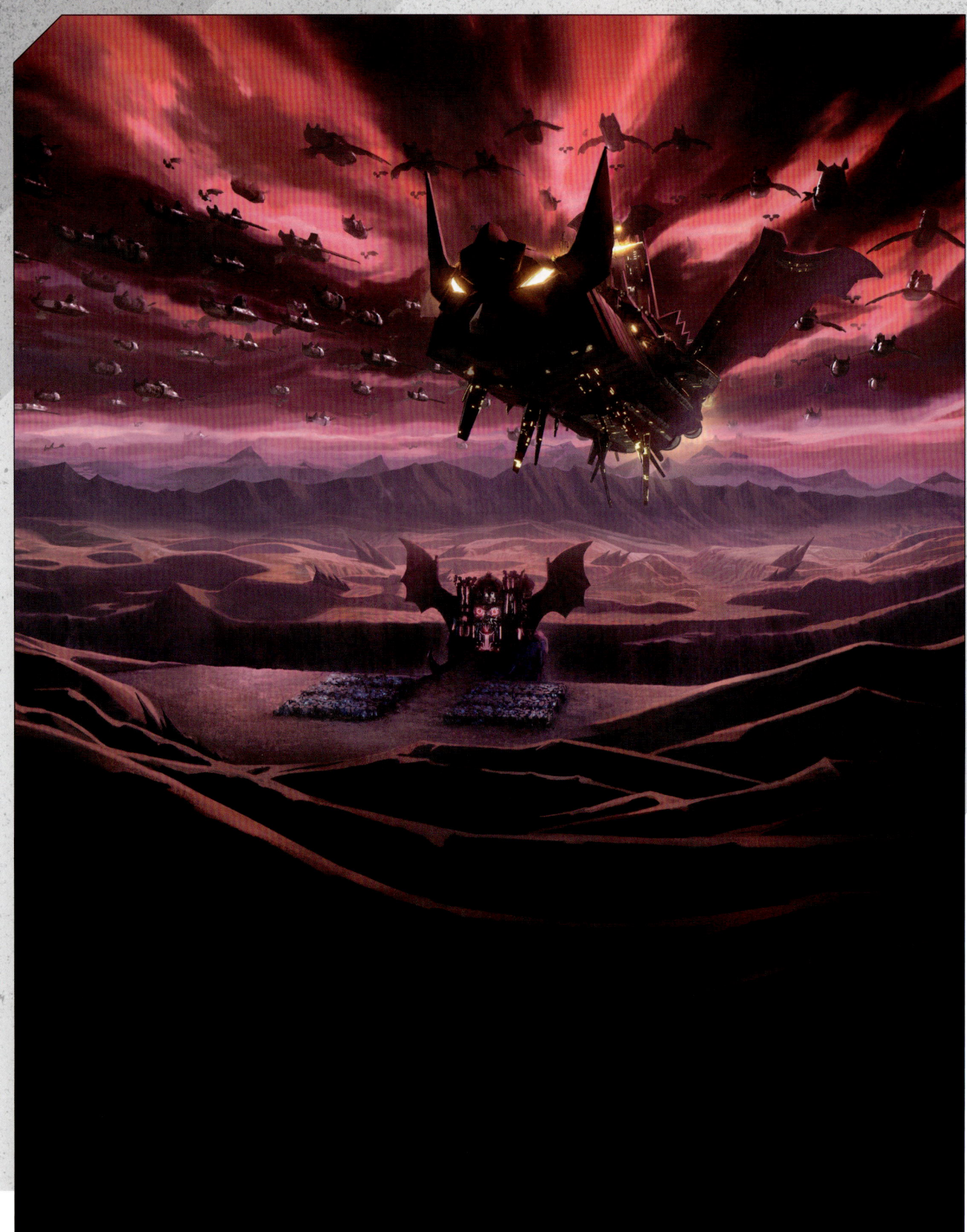

THE TECHIFICATION OF GRAYSKULL
When Motherboard gives Grayskull a technological makeover and brings it under control of the Horde, we wanted it to feel like the desecration of something sacred and familiar. Naturally we decided to parallel the series' title sequence, as if to say that this is Hordak's show now.

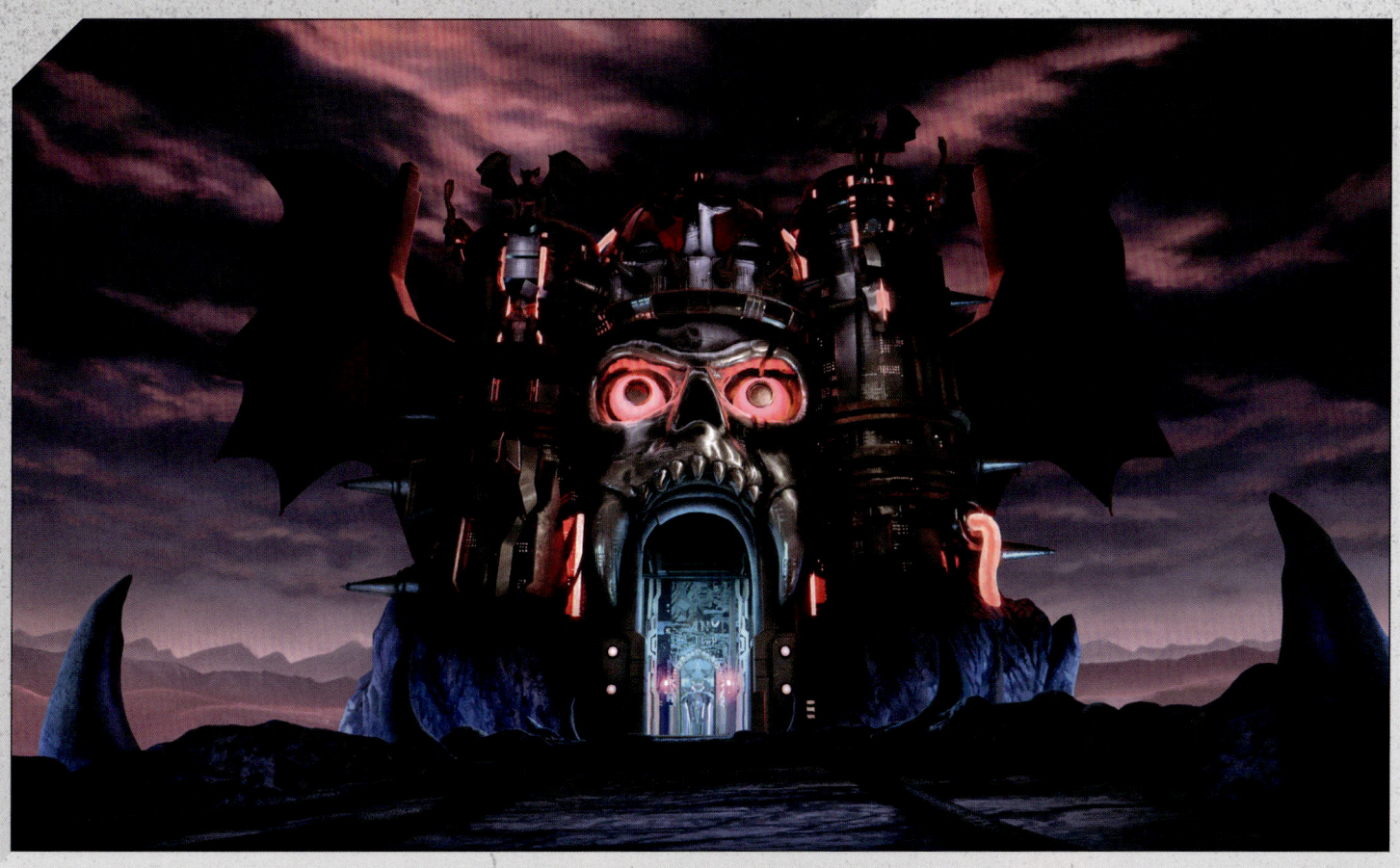

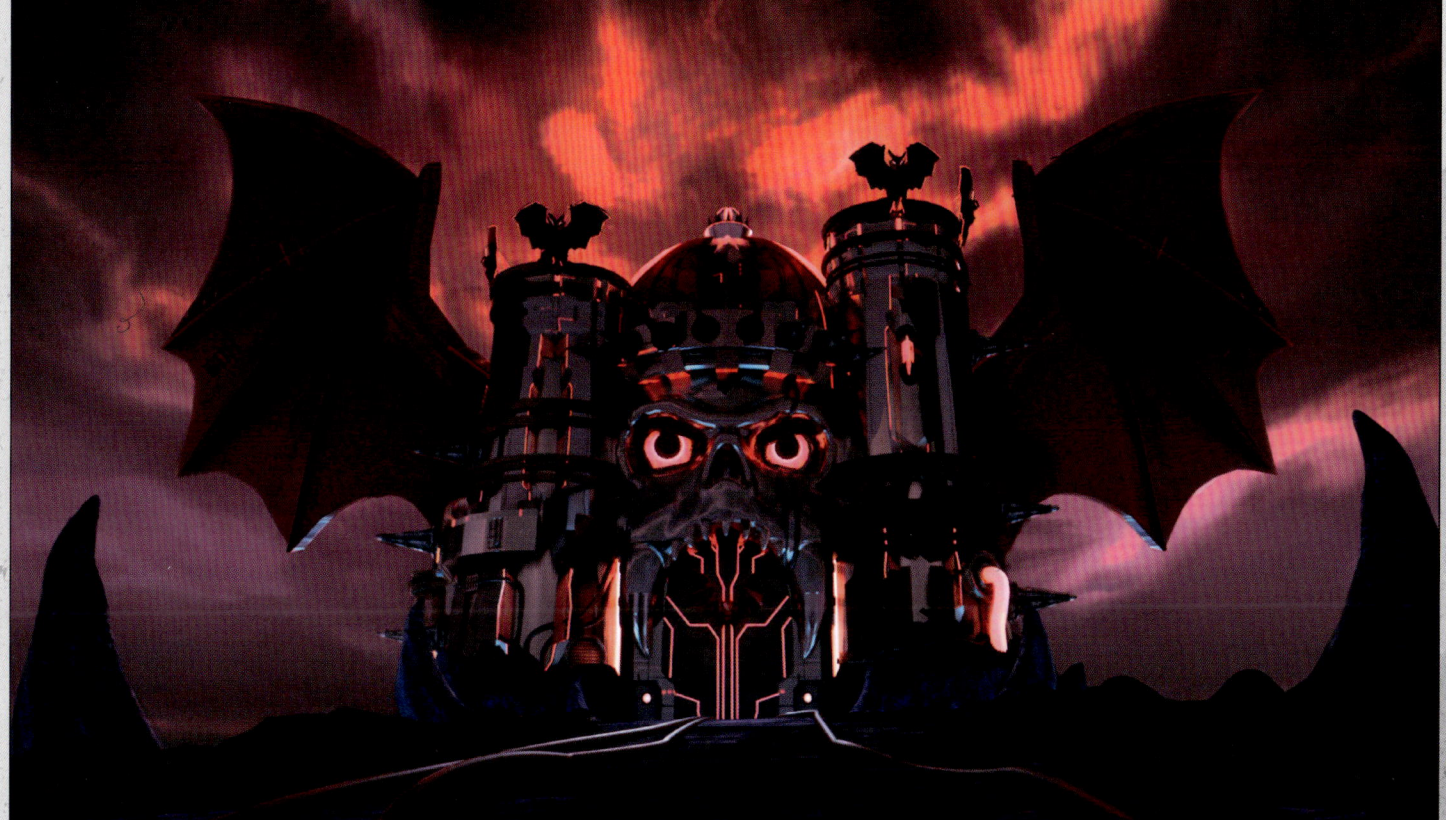

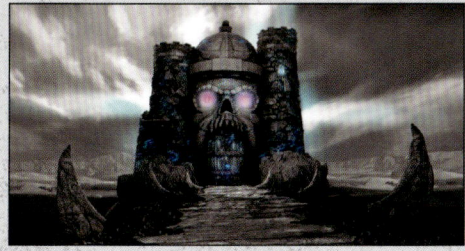
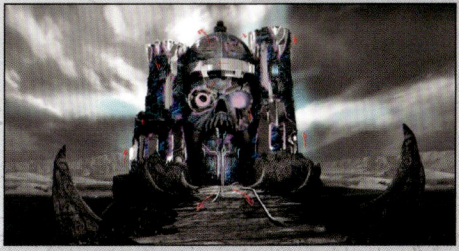
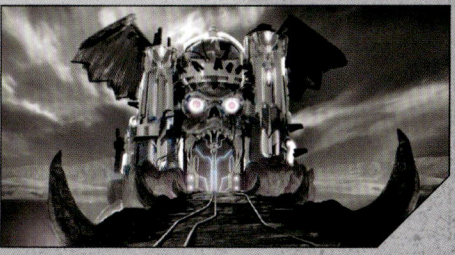

LOCATIONS \\ 143

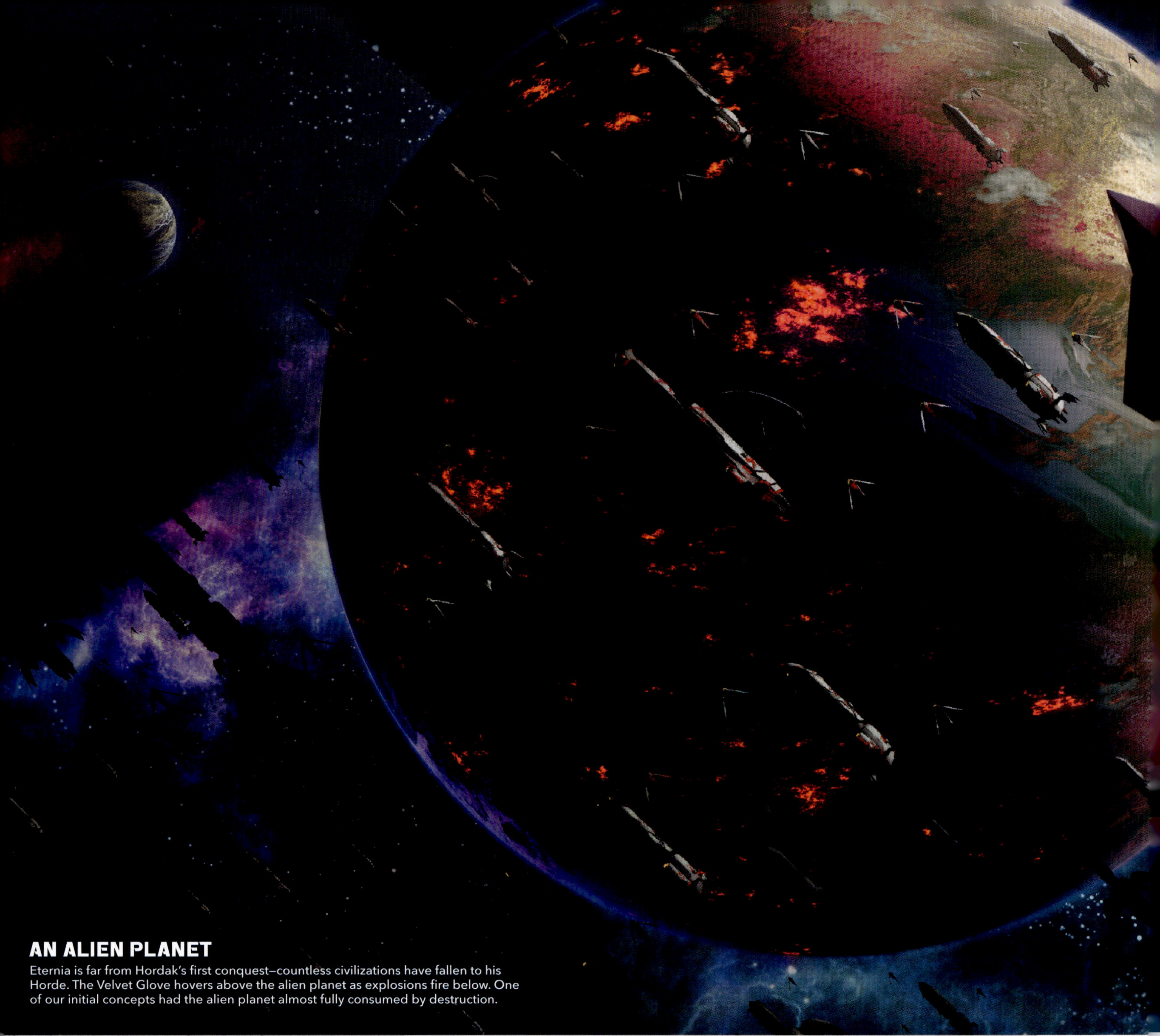

AN ALIEN PLANET

Eternia is far from Hordak's first conquest—countless civilizations have fallen to his Horde. The Velvet Glove hovers above the alien planet as explosions fire below. One of our initial concepts had the alien planet almost fully consumed by destruction.

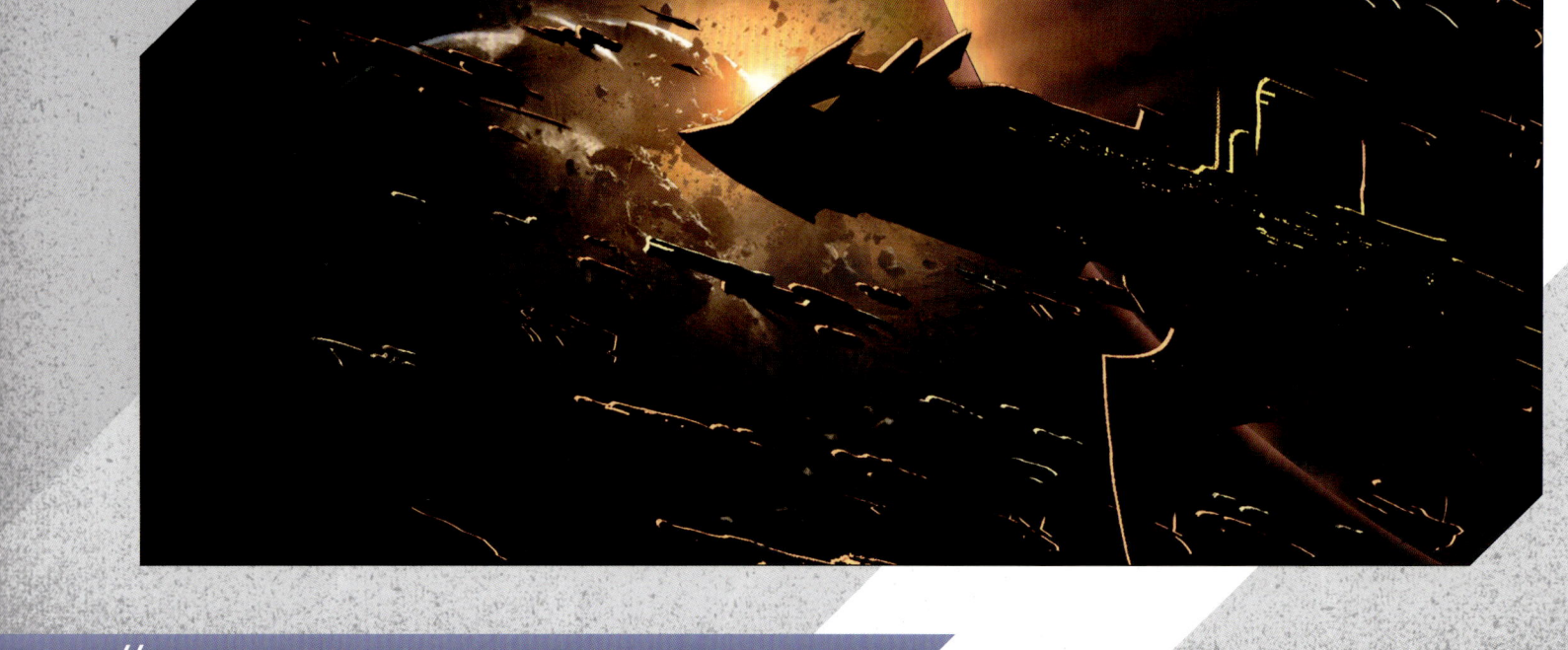

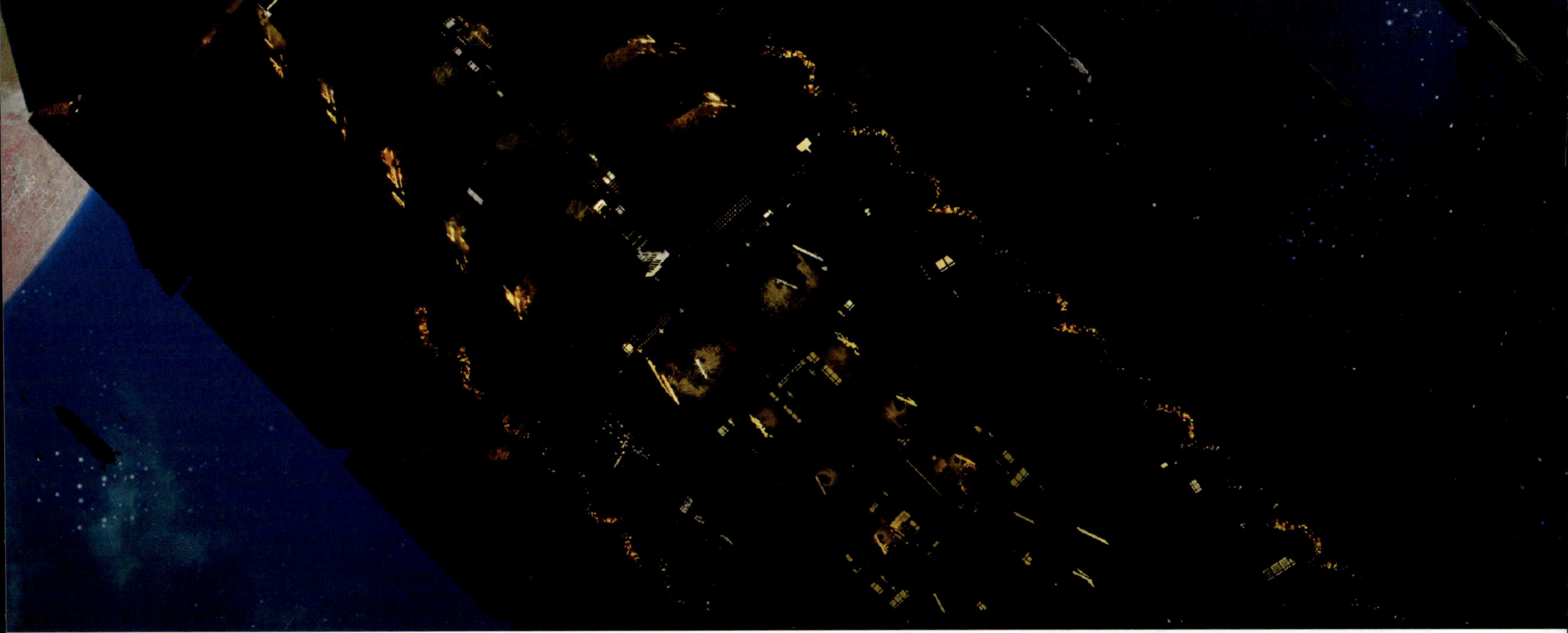

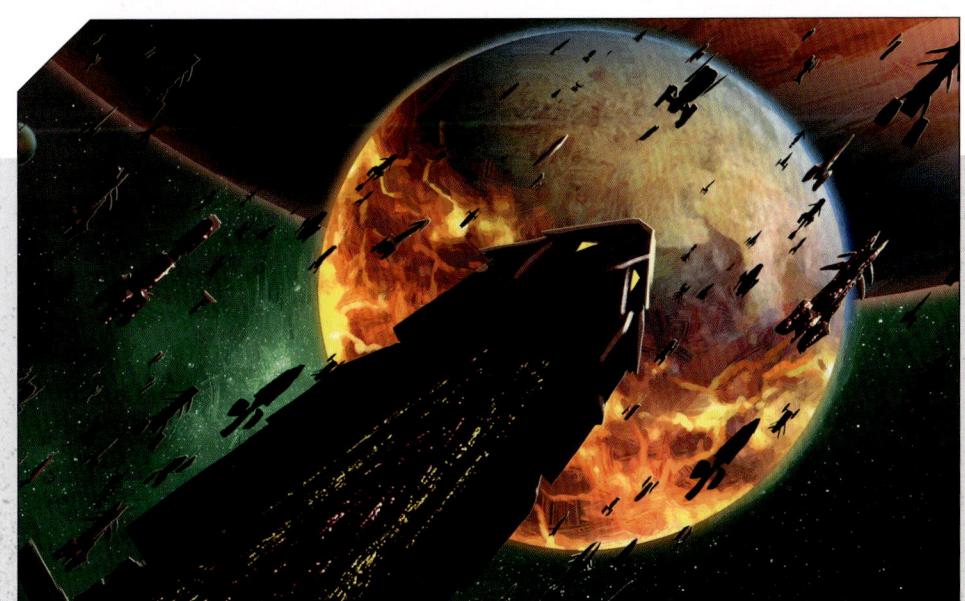
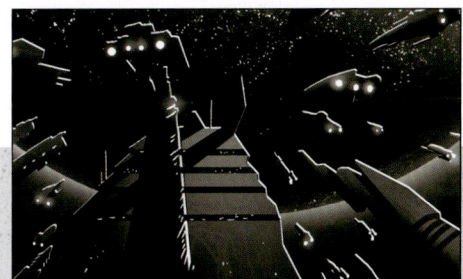
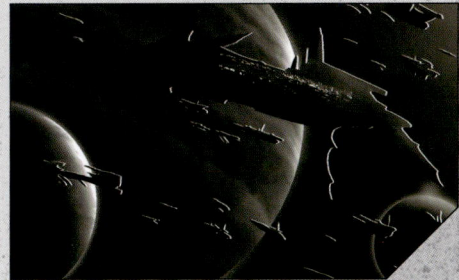

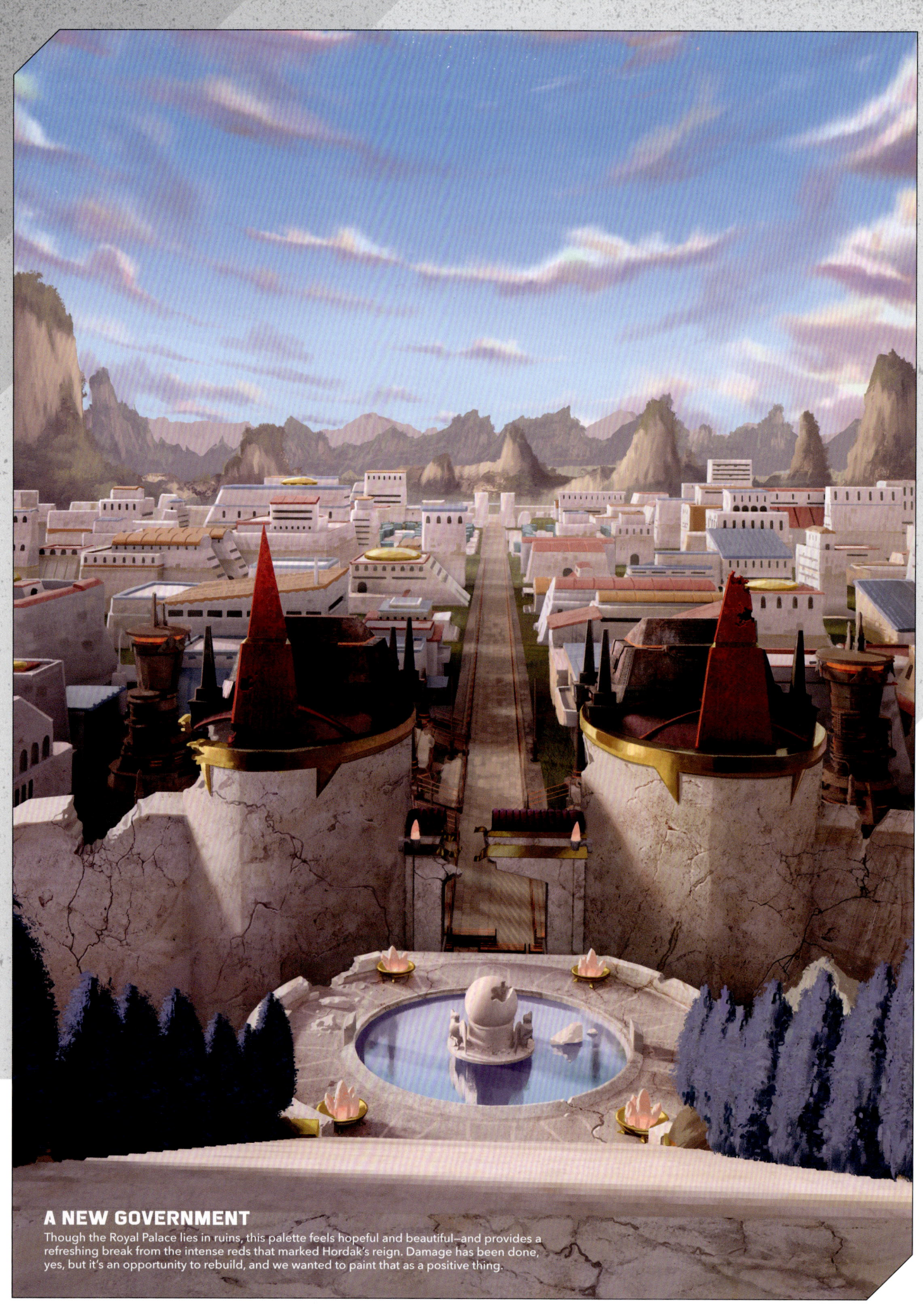

A NEW GOVERNMENT
Though the Royal Palace lies in ruins, this palette feels hopeful and beautiful—and provides a refreshing break from the intense reds that marked Hordak's reign. Damage has been done, yes, but it's an opportunity to rebuild, and we wanted to paint that as a positive thing.

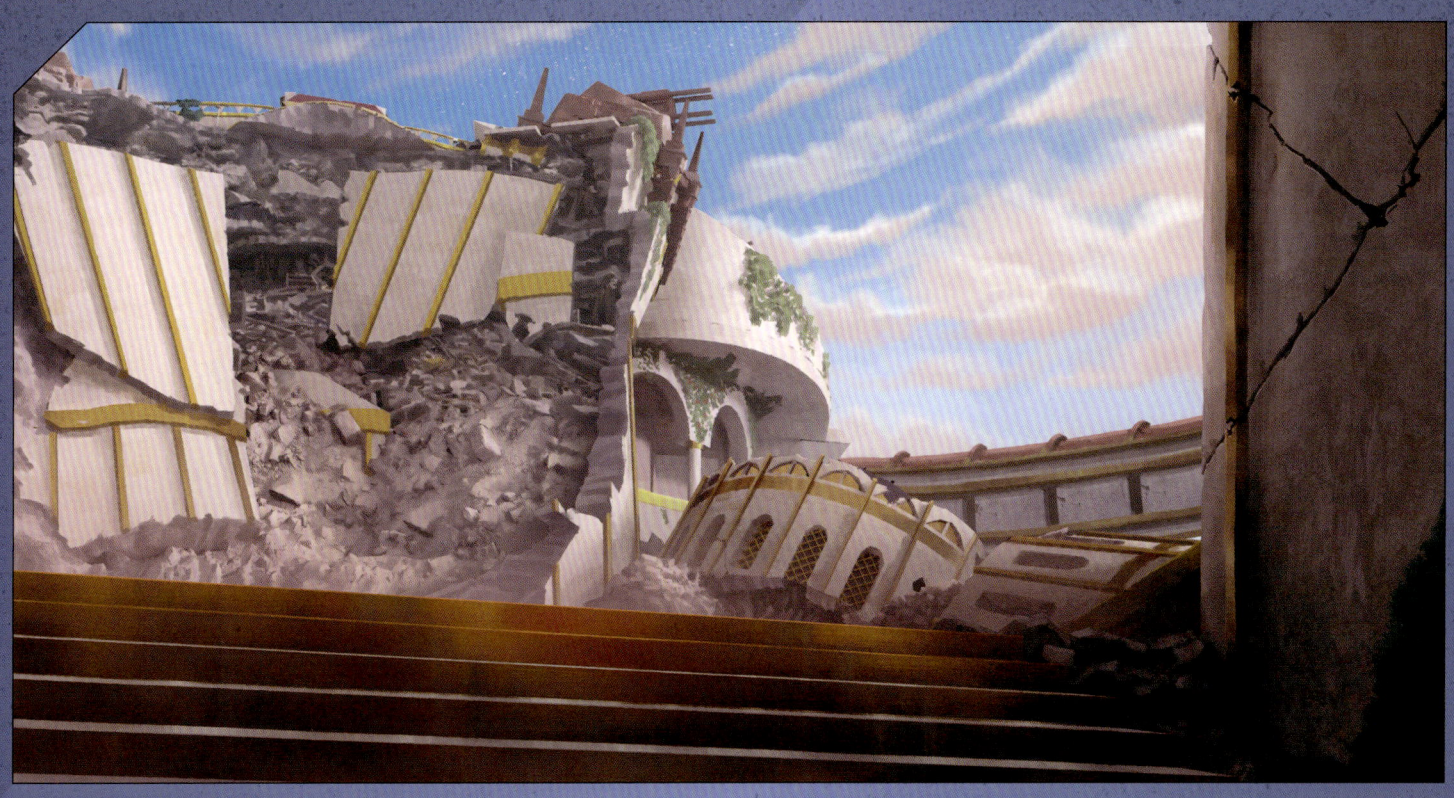
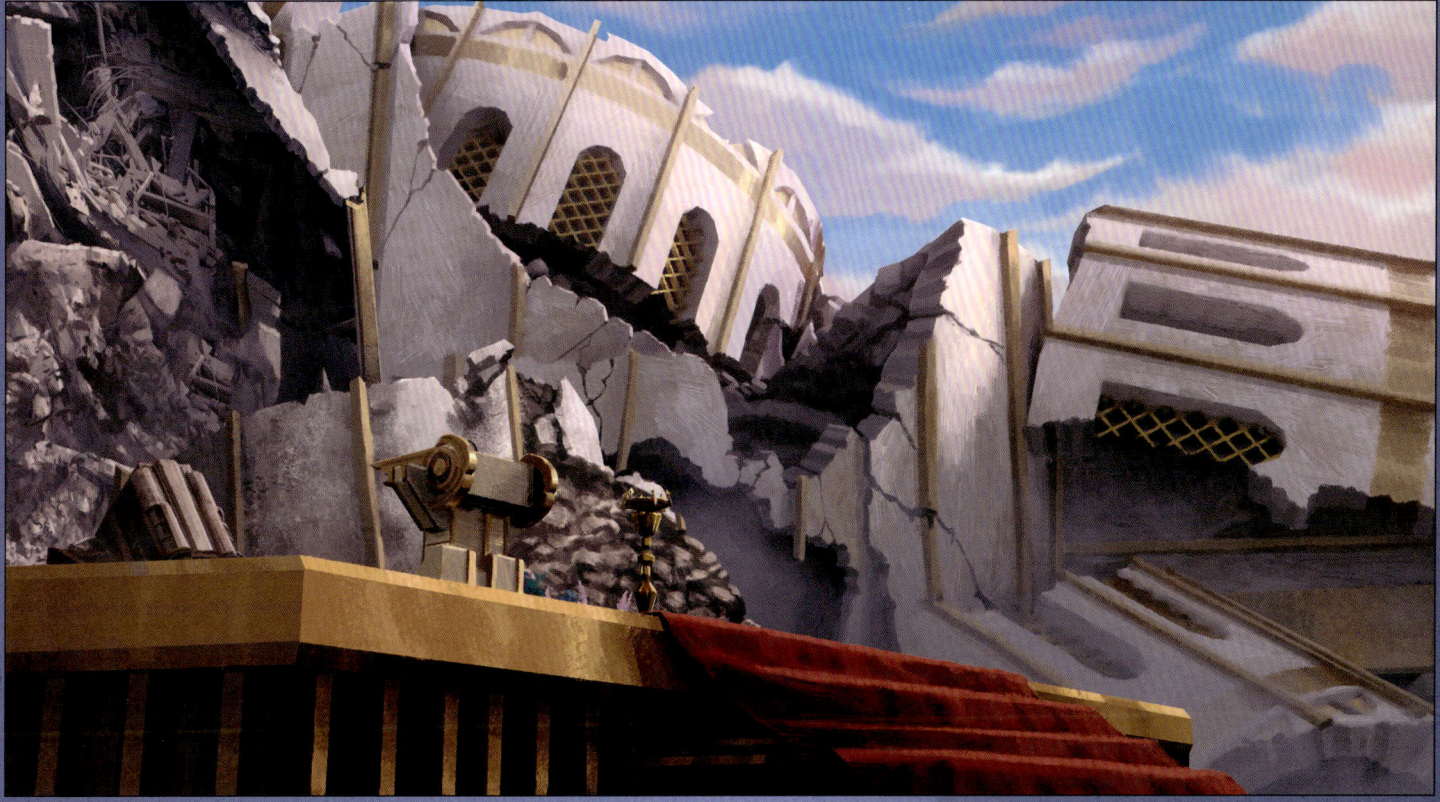
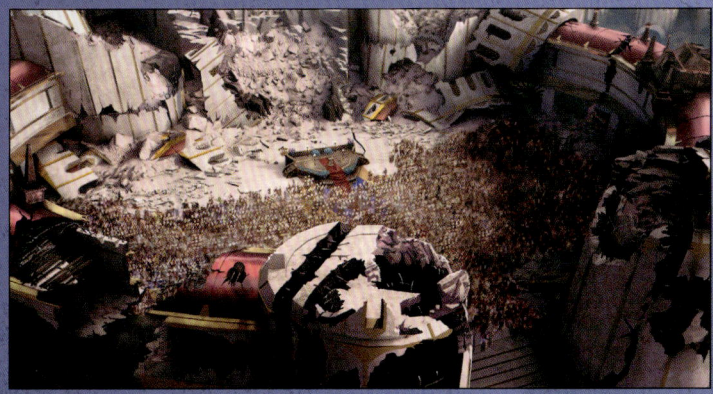
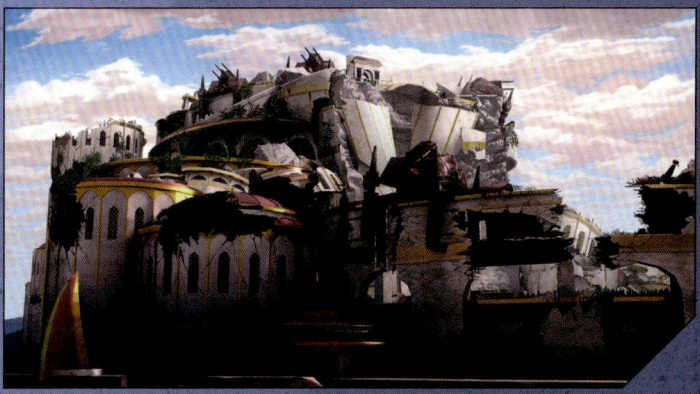

LOCATIONS \\ 147

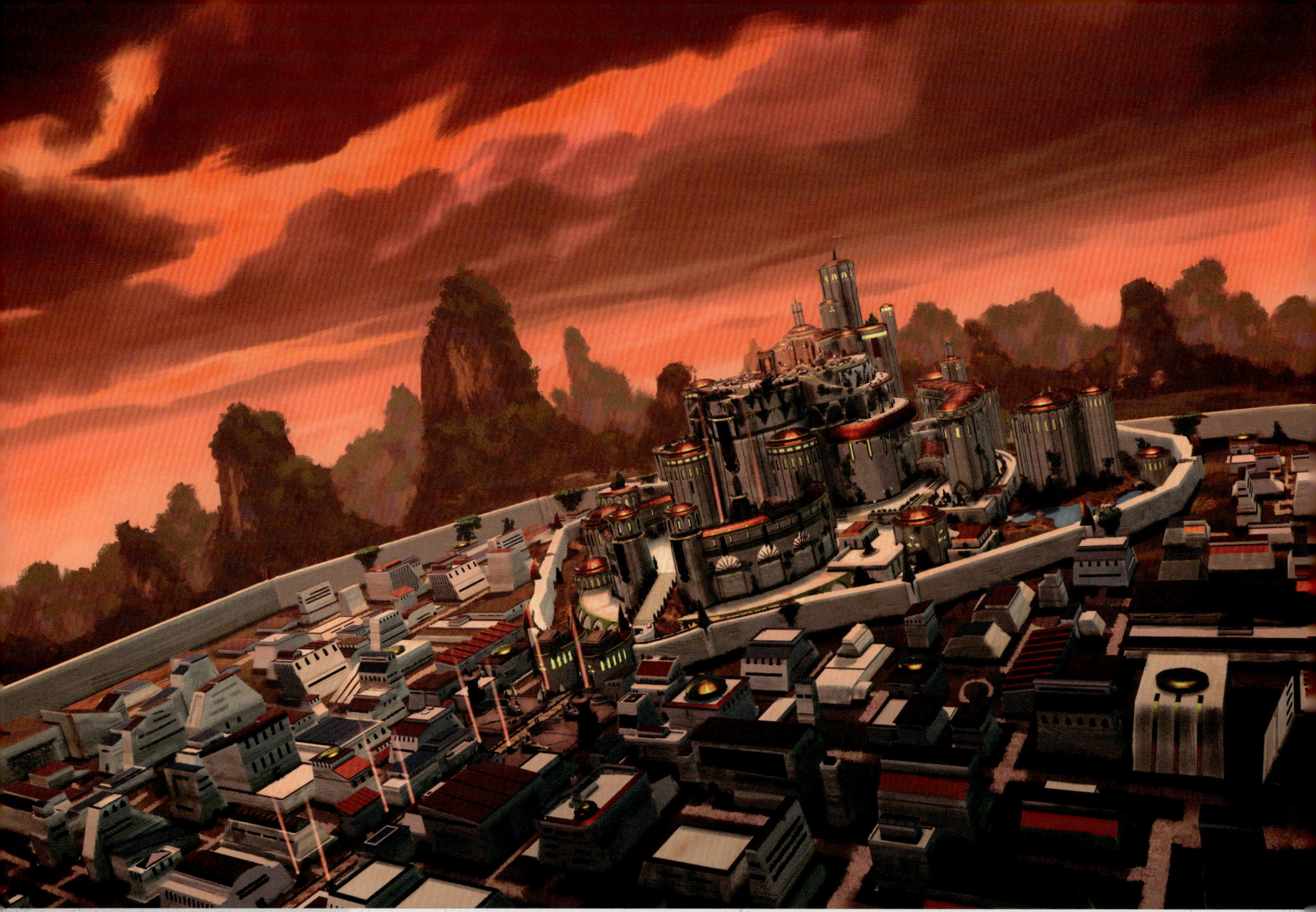

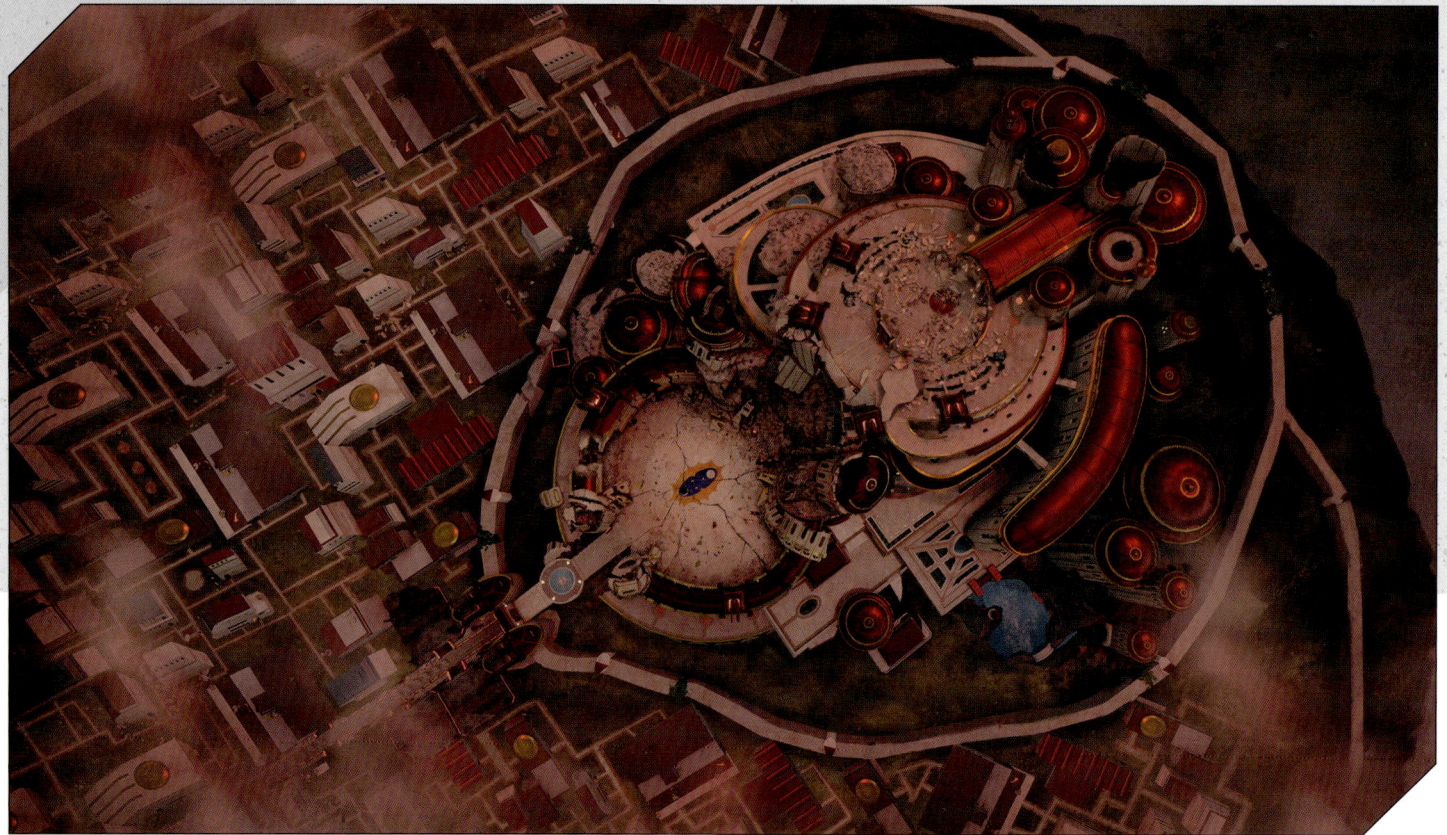

ETERNIA UNDER SIEGE
With dominatingly red skies, the Horde's presence is immediately apparent no matter where you may be on the planet. This grim reminder would naturally help to keep their newly assimilated civilians in line—if they weren't already being mind controlled, that is.

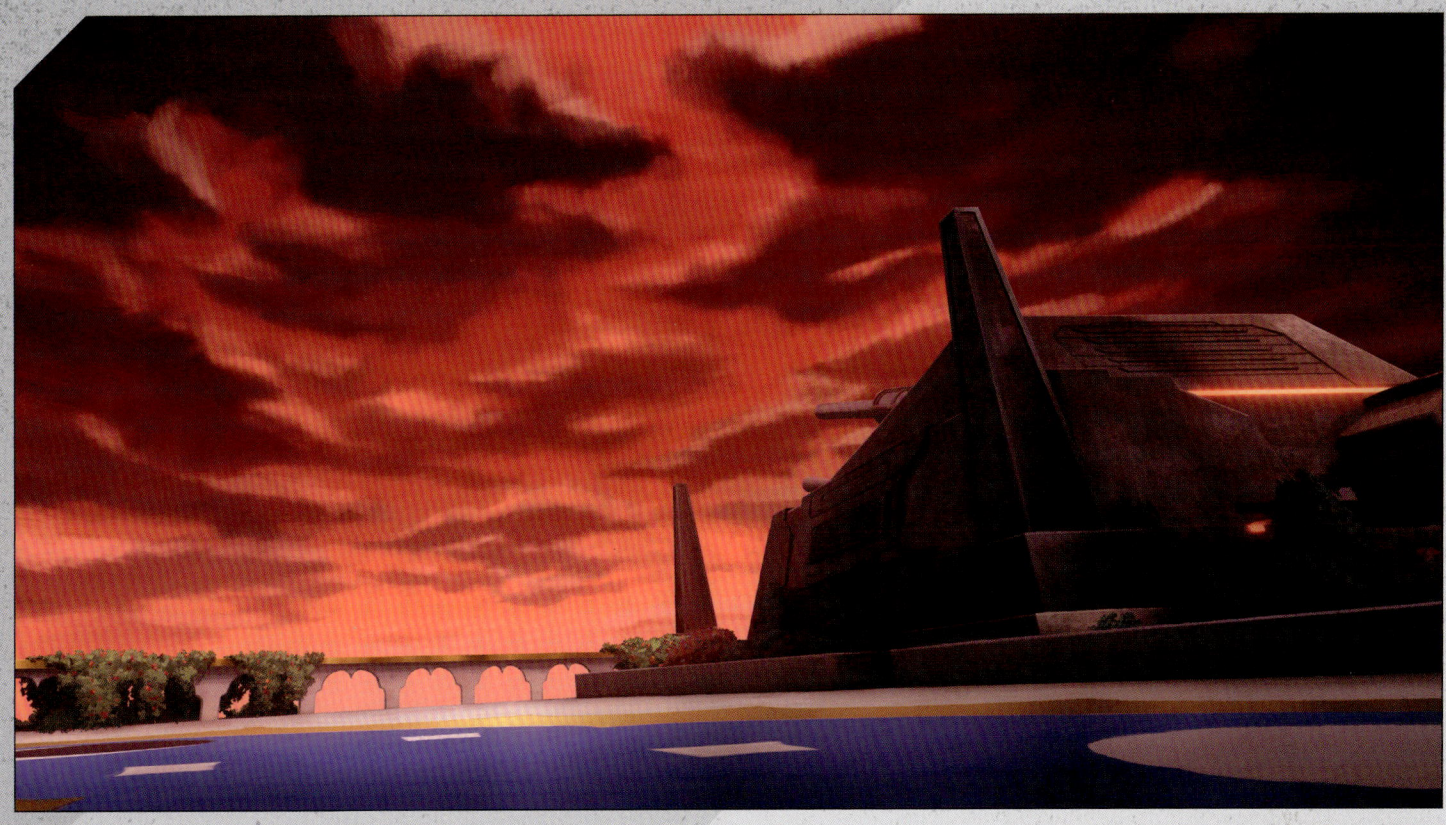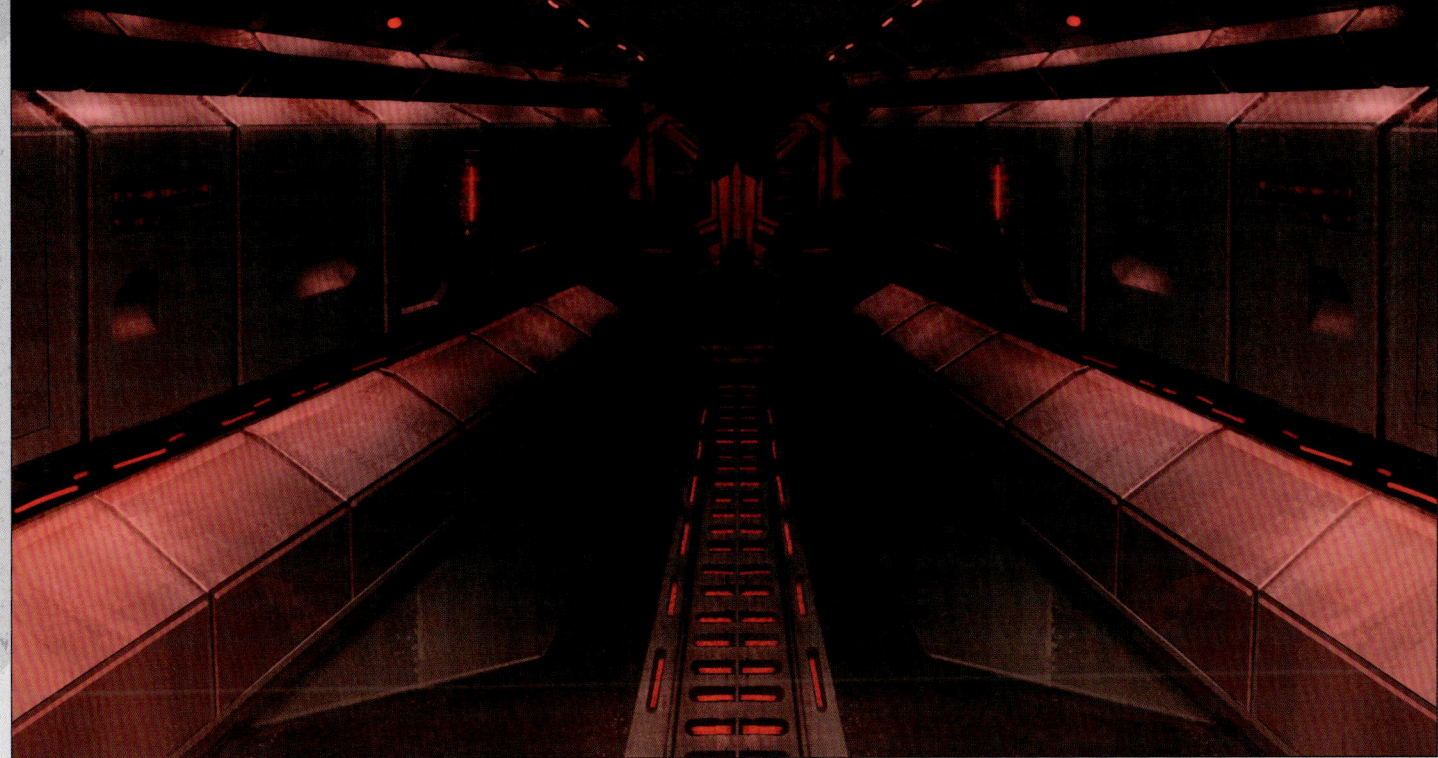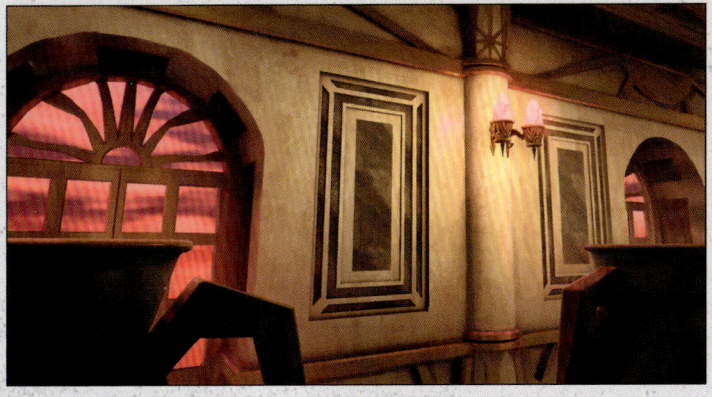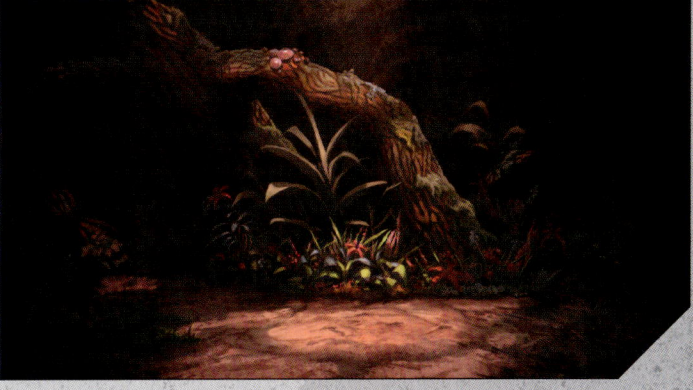

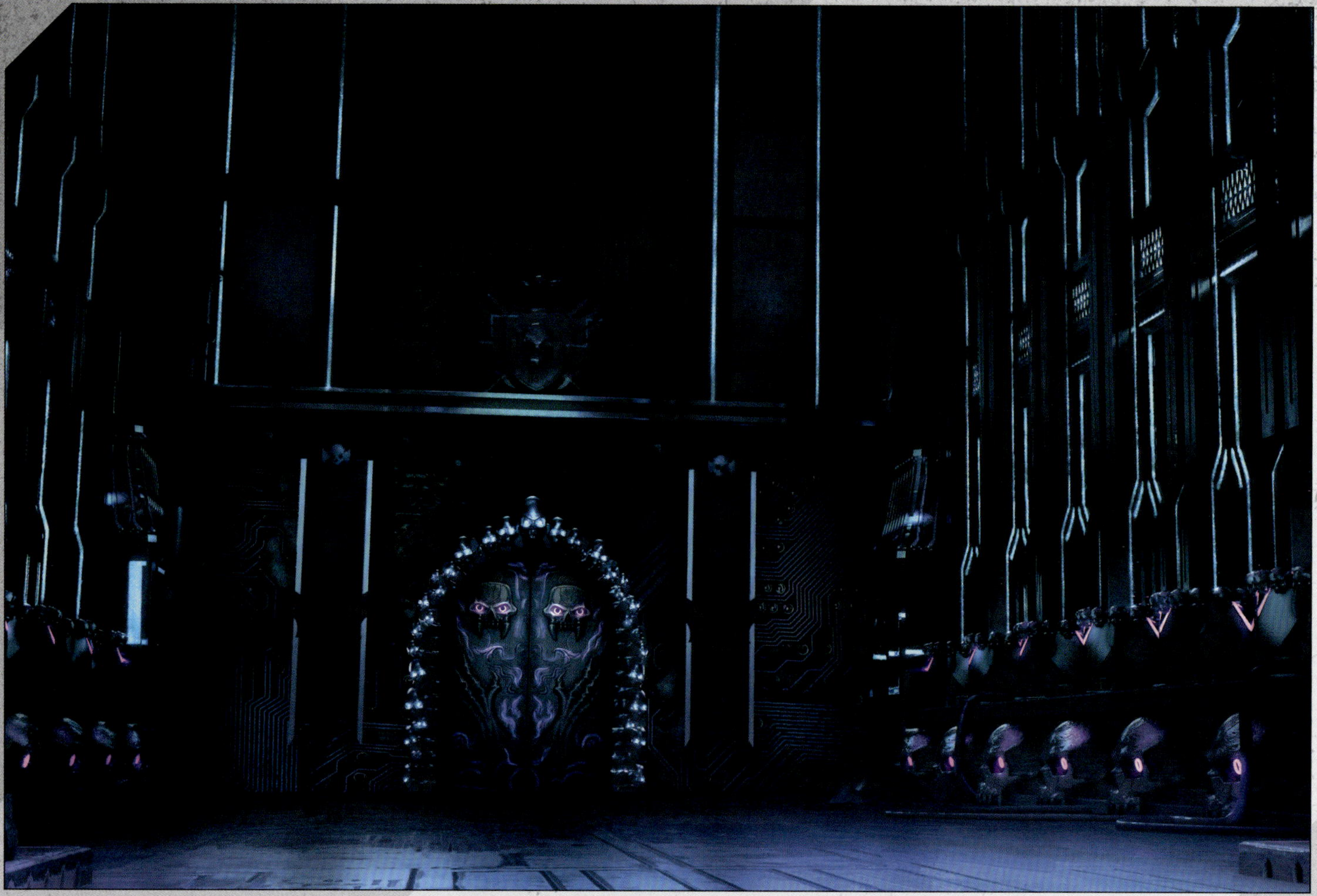

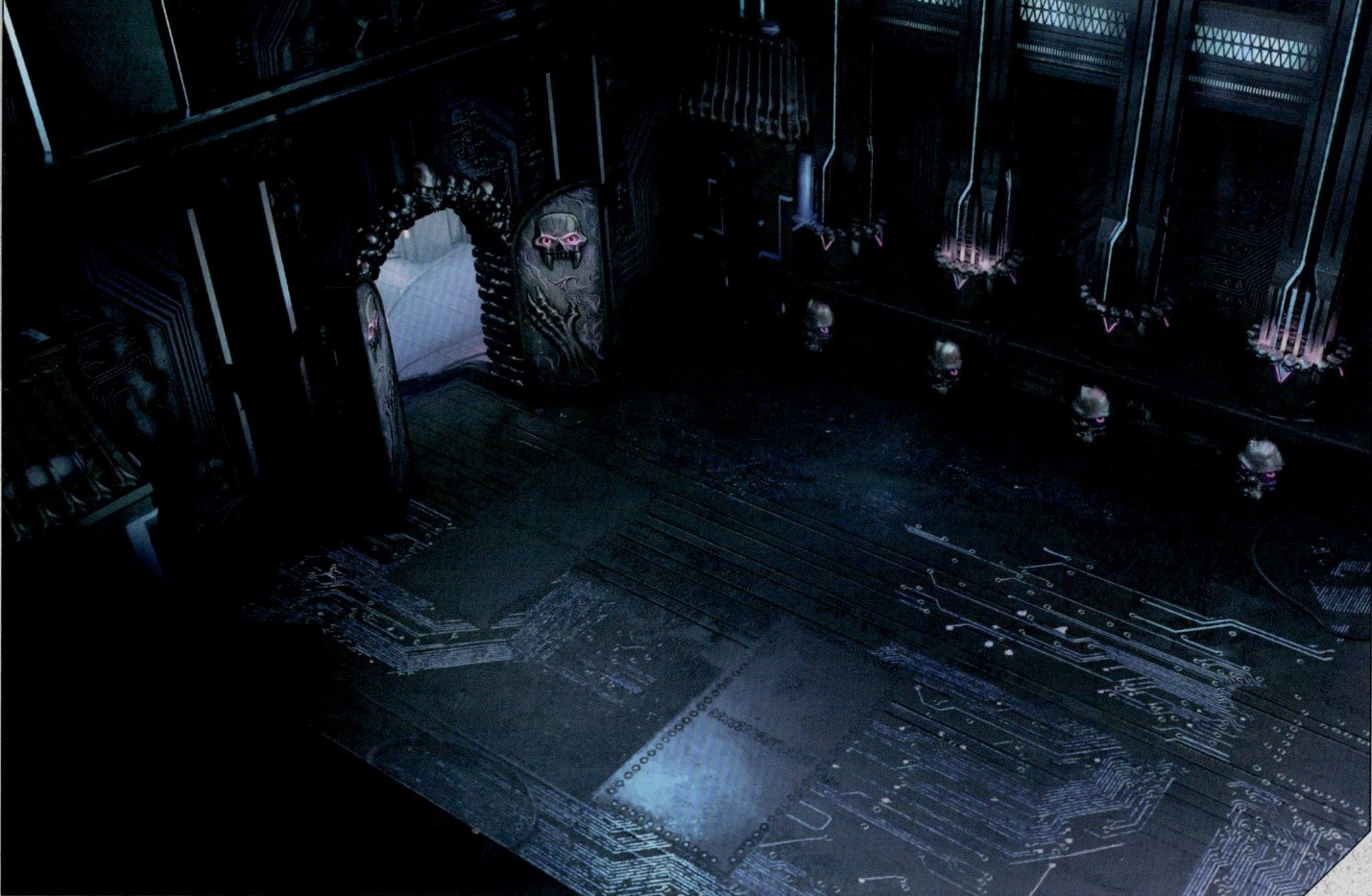

Overrun by Motherboard's infectious nanobots, the whole of Grayskull was taken by the Horde's fearsome technological power. Much like what happened to Snake Mountain, the veneer of the castle changed from one of mythical fantasy to neon sci-fi, displaying the colors and iconography of its new masters.

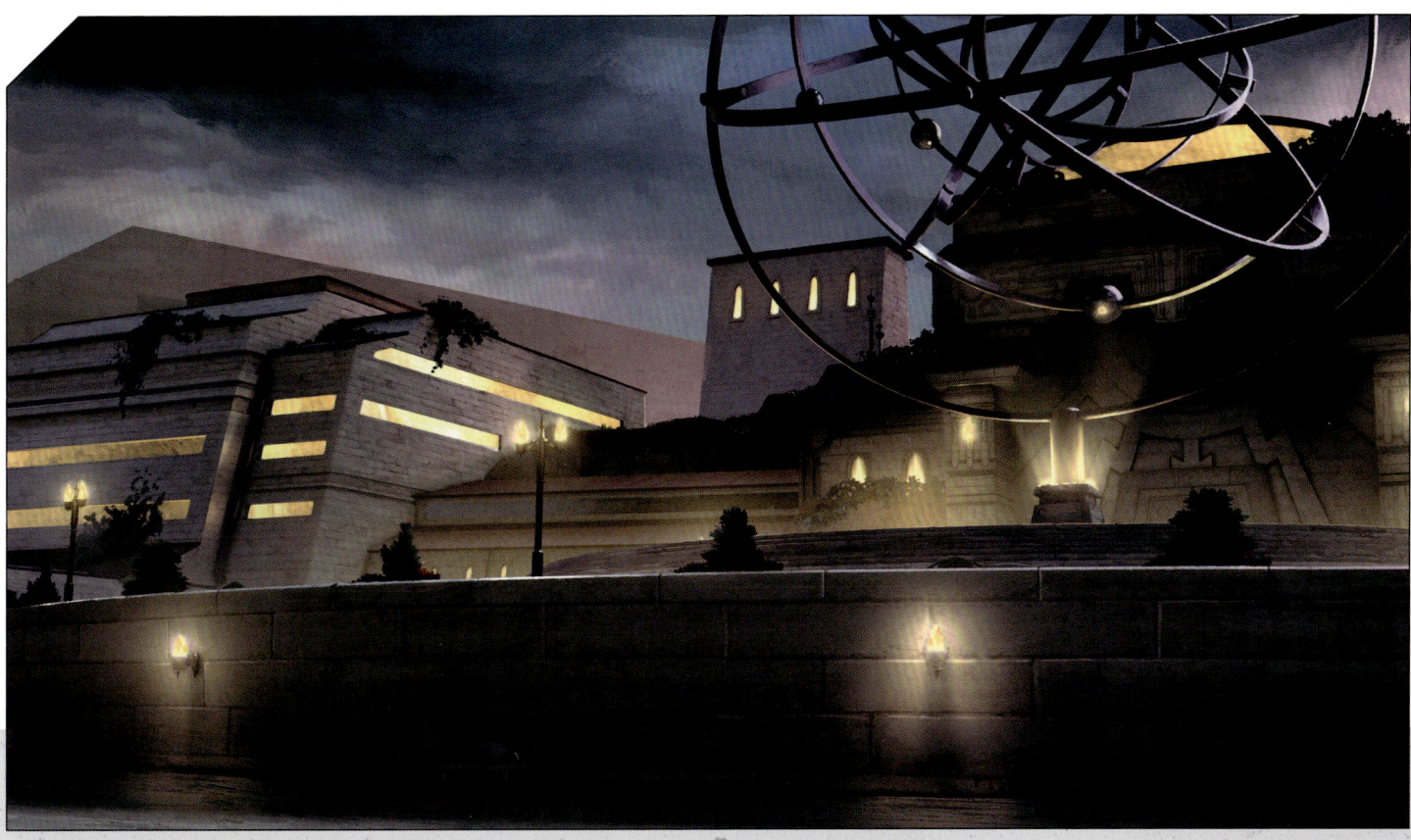

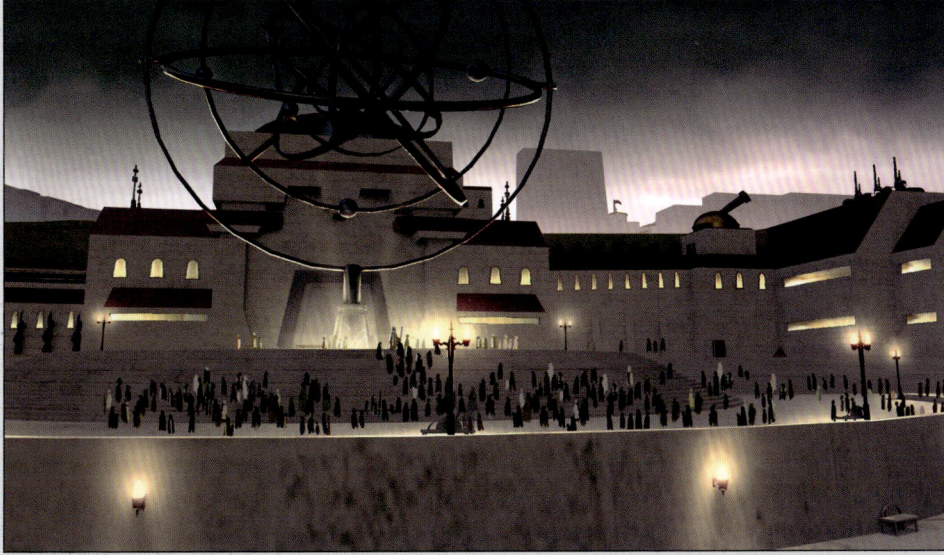

The town square in Eternos was designed to look like the center of research and technology in the capital, the atom sculpture a reference to the Eternos Palace play set. The perfect venue for Keldor to distribute his technological communion.

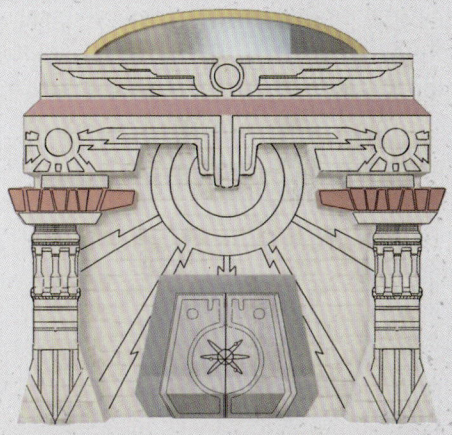

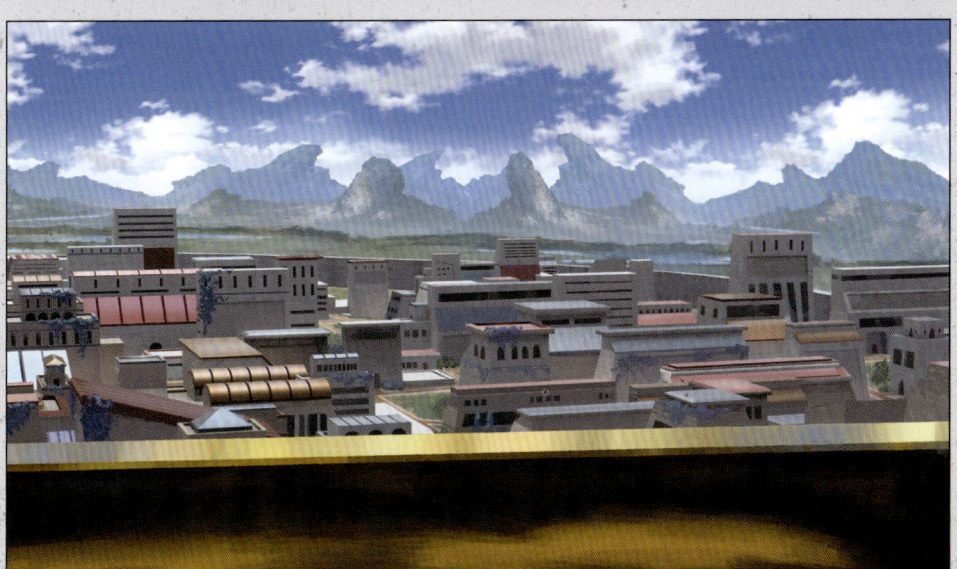

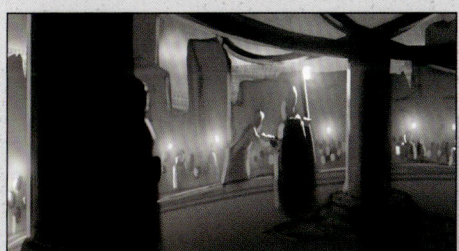

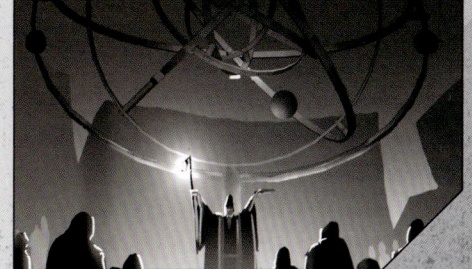

LOCATIONS \\ 151

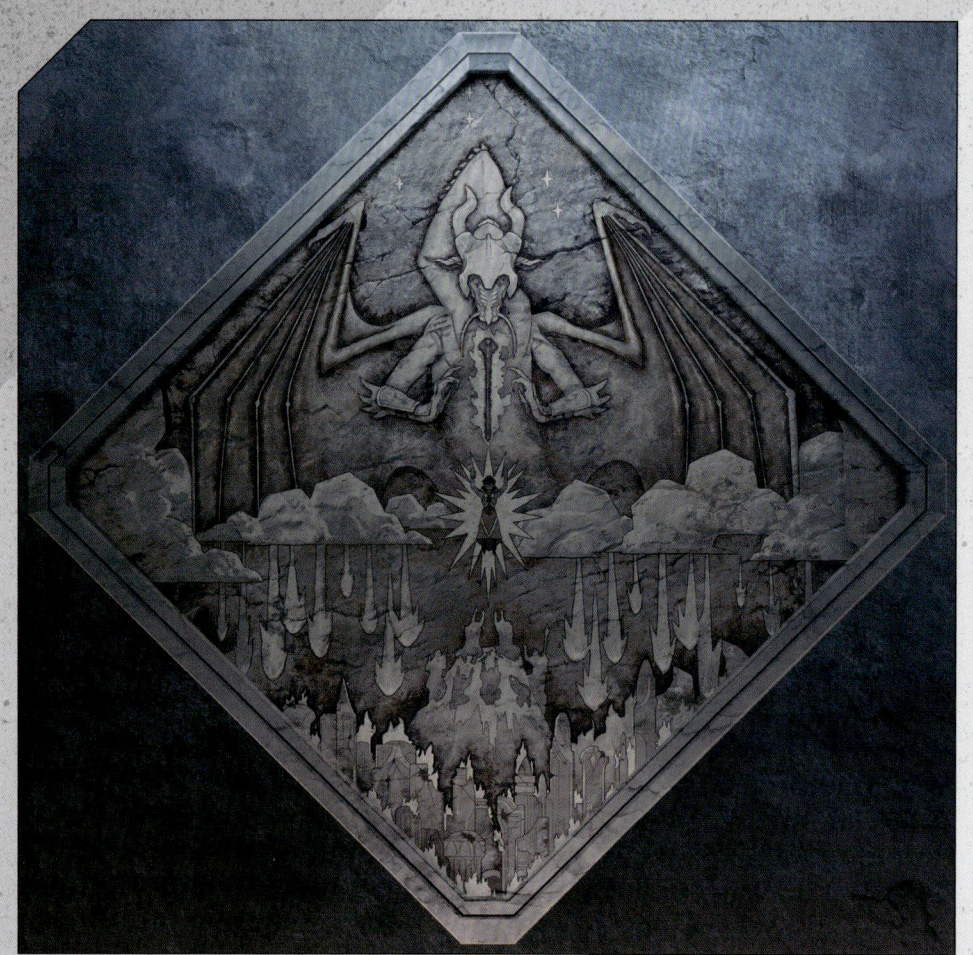
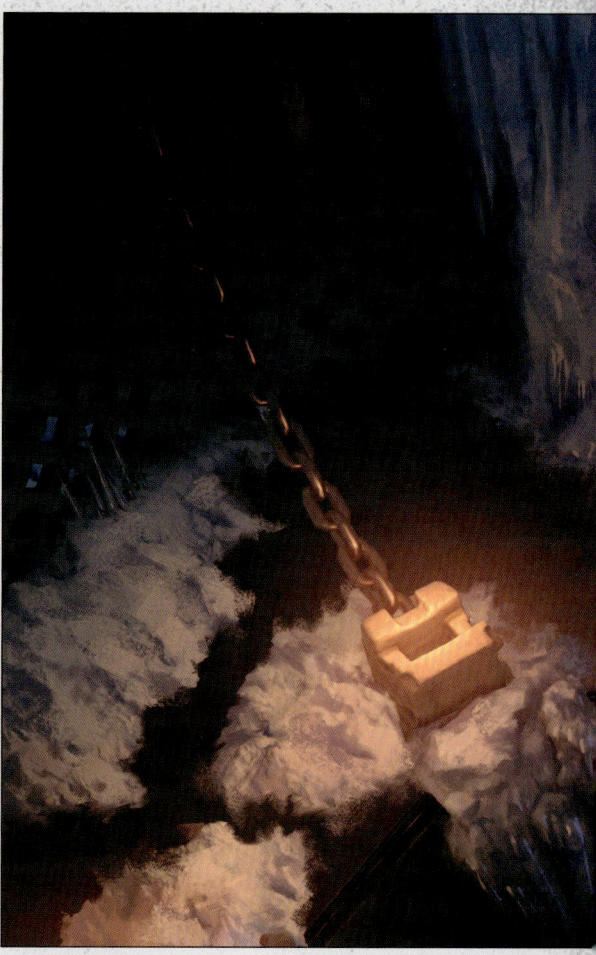

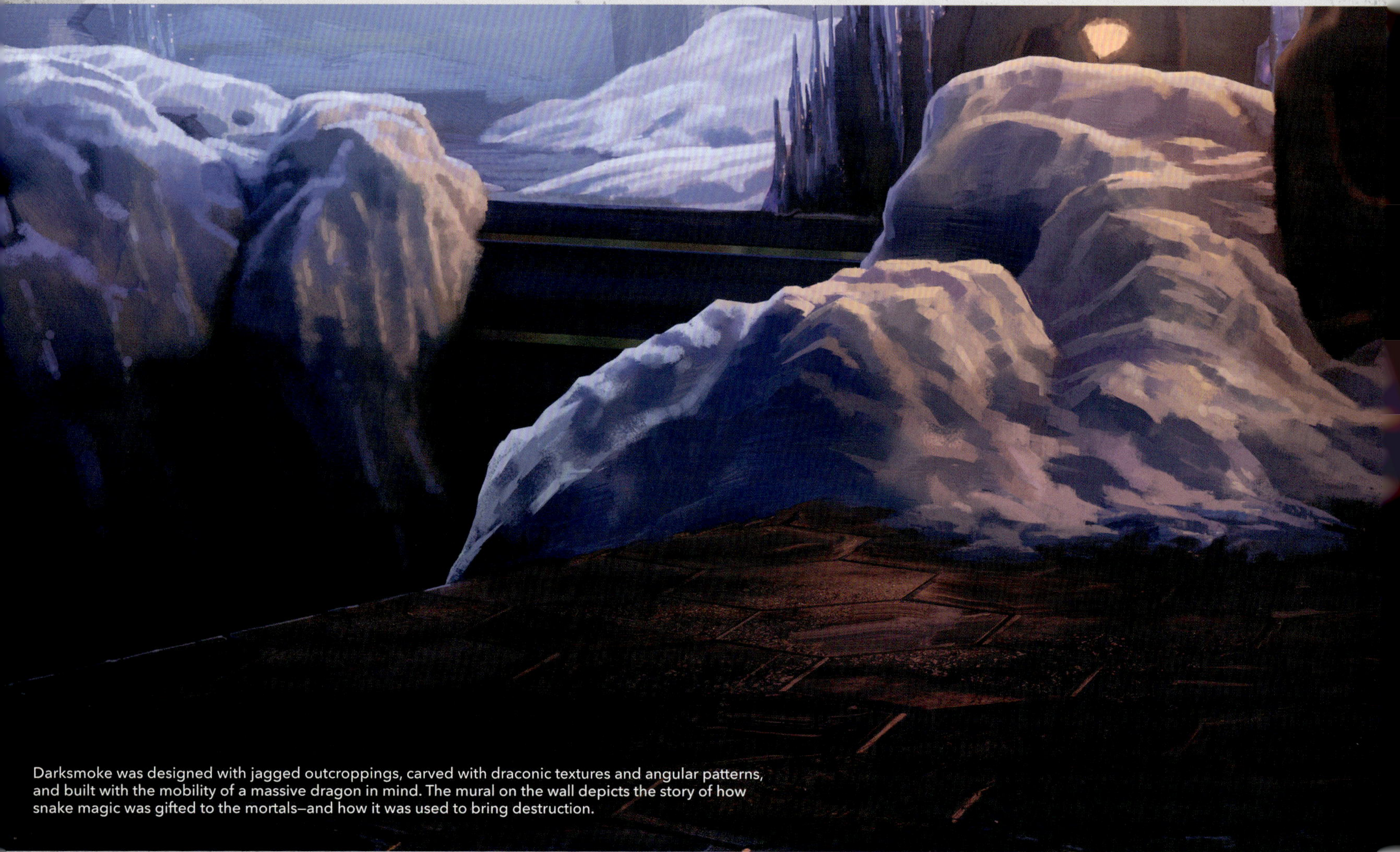

Darksmoke was designed with jagged outcroppings, carved with draconic textures and angular patterns, and built with the mobility of a massive dragon in mind. The mural on the wall depicts the story of how snake magic was gifted to the mortals—and how it was used to bring destruction.

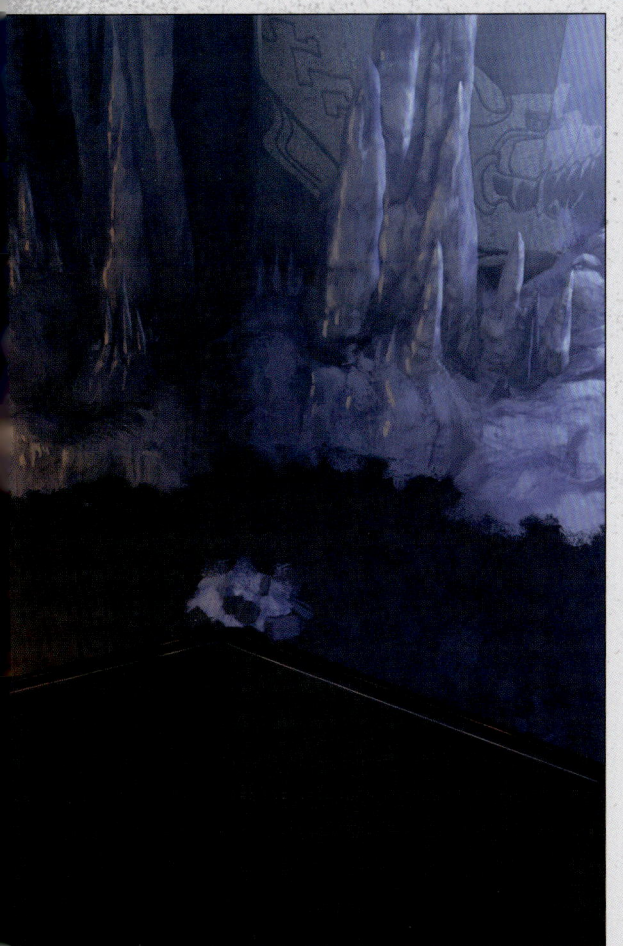
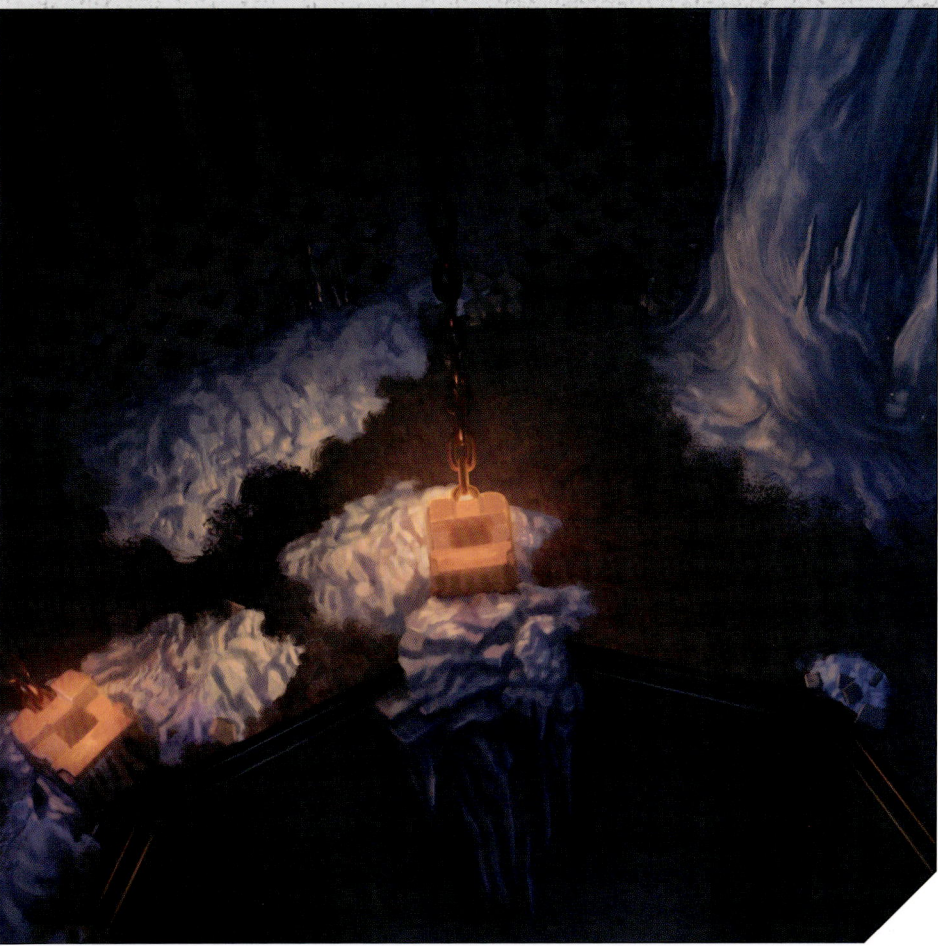

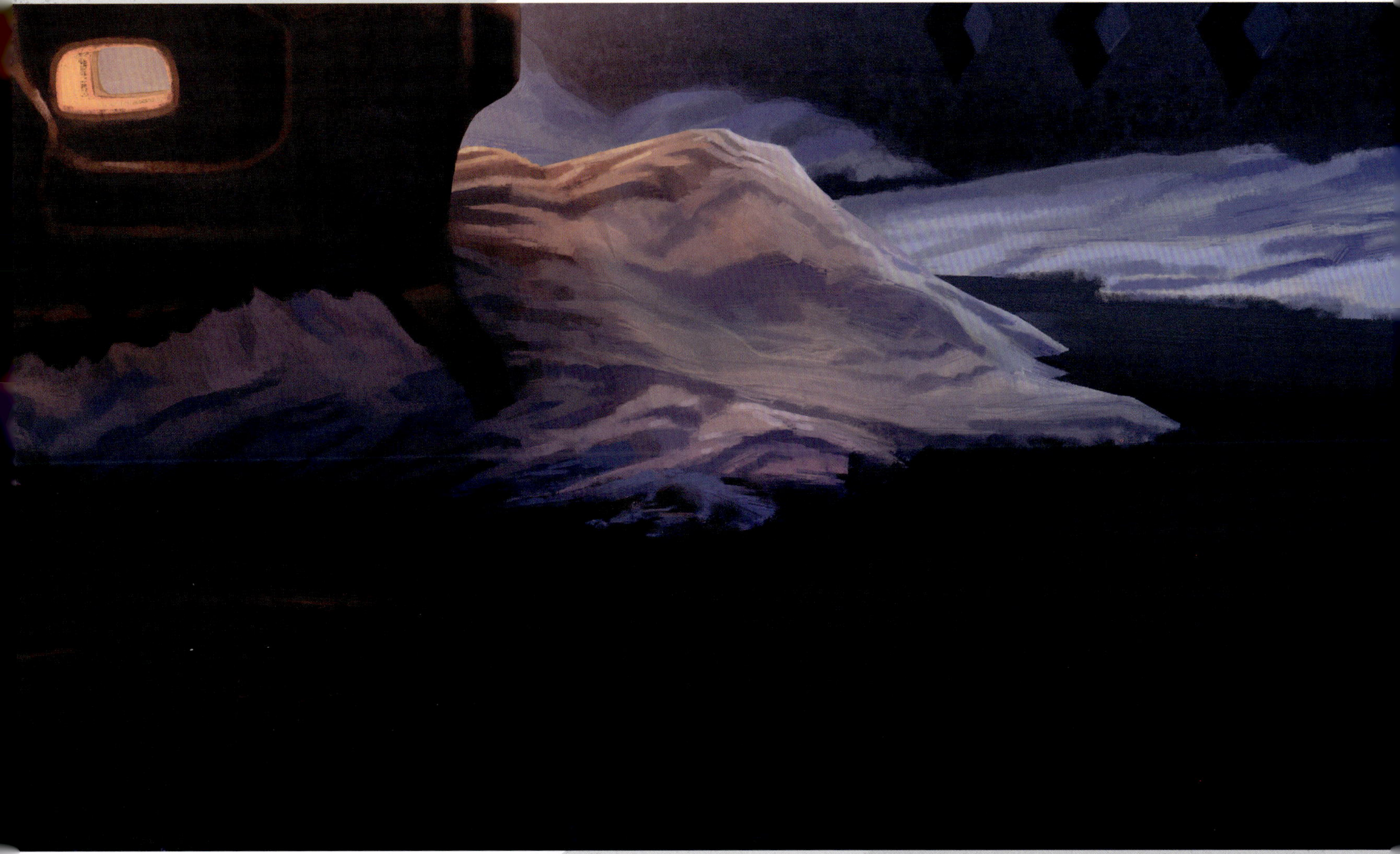

LOCATIONS \\ 153

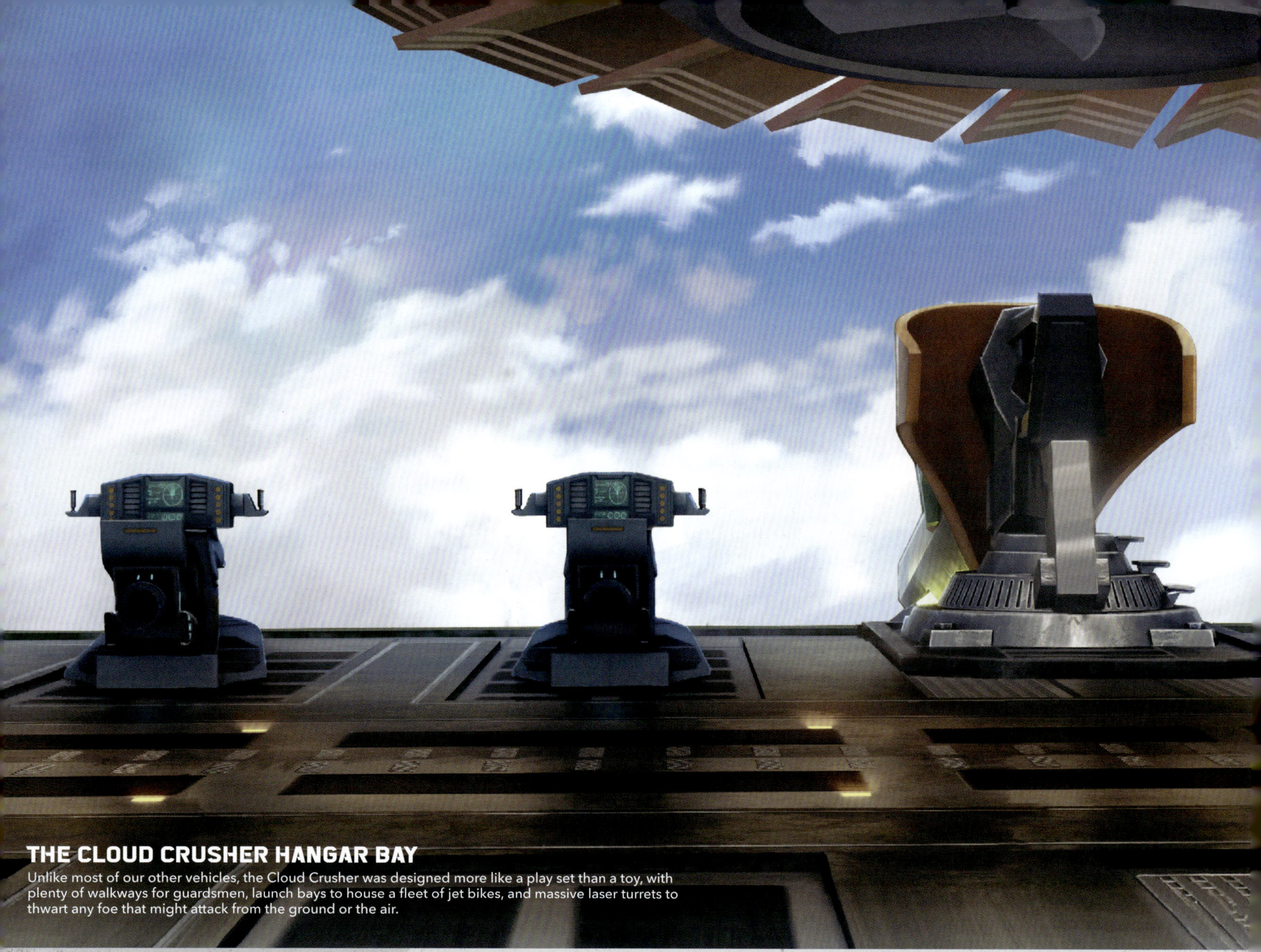

THE CLOUD CRUSHER HANGAR BAY

Unlike most of our other vehicles, the Cloud Crusher was designed more like a play set than a toy, with plenty of walkways for guardsmen, launch bays to house a fleet of jet bikes, and massive laser turrets to thwart any foe that might attack from the ground or the air.

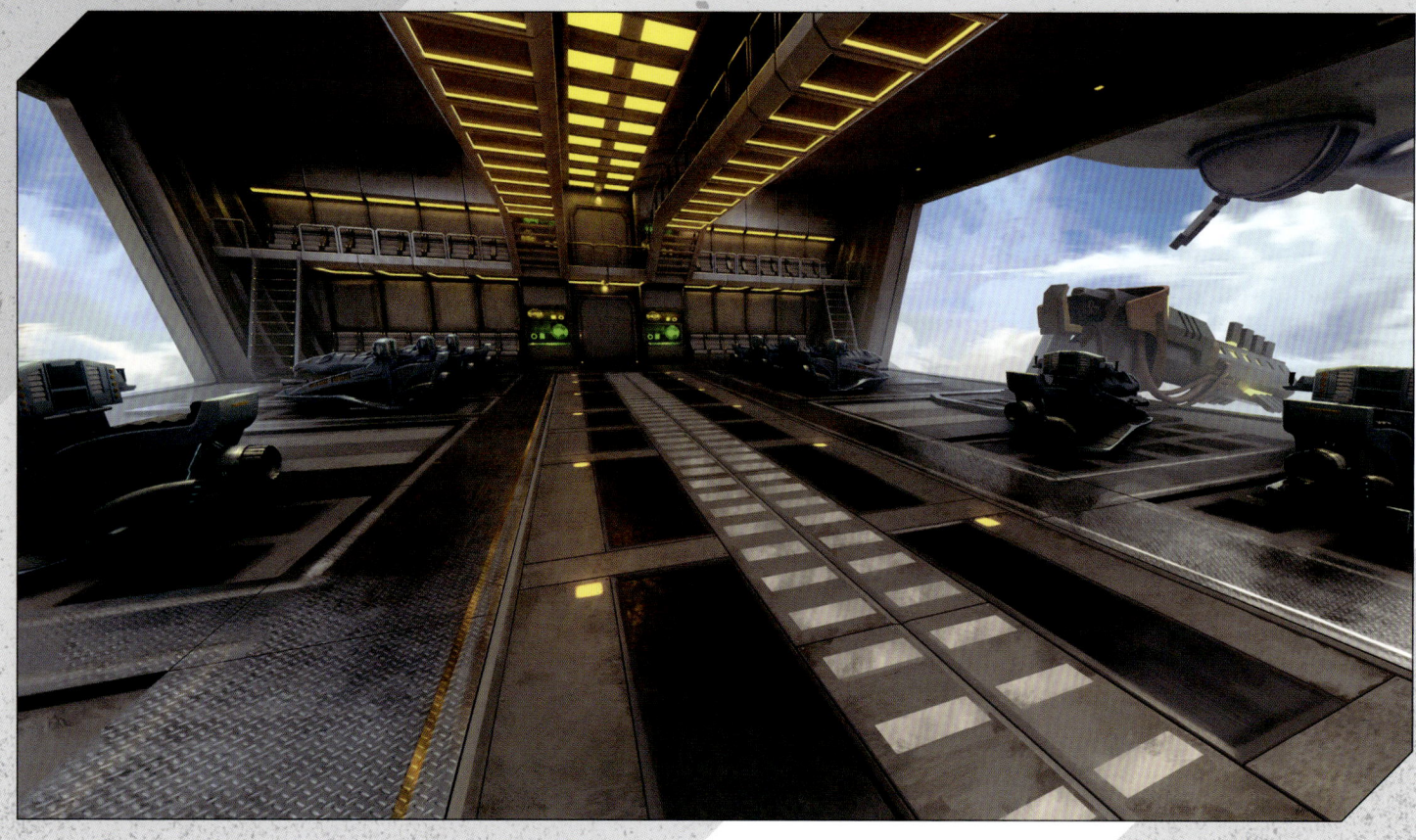

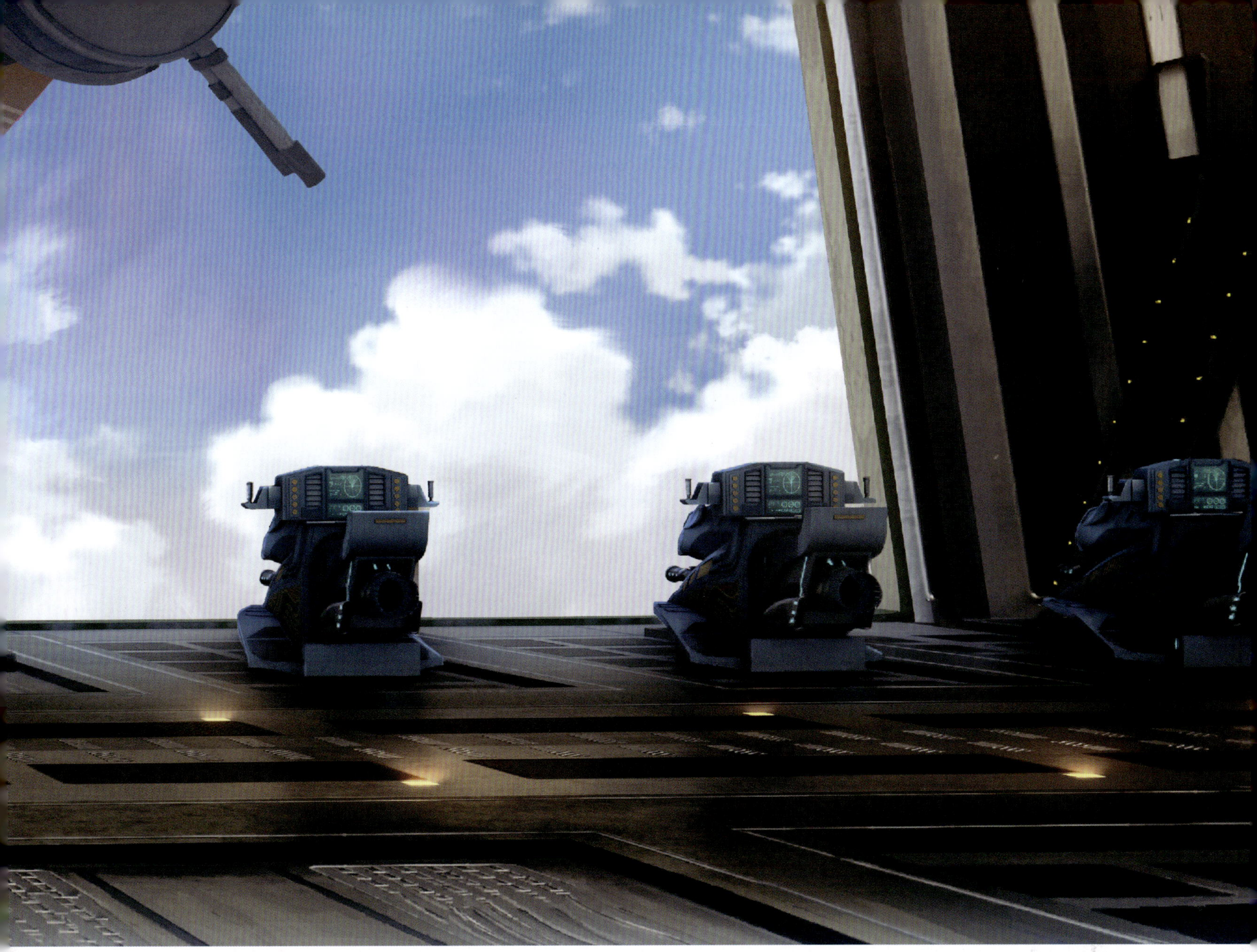

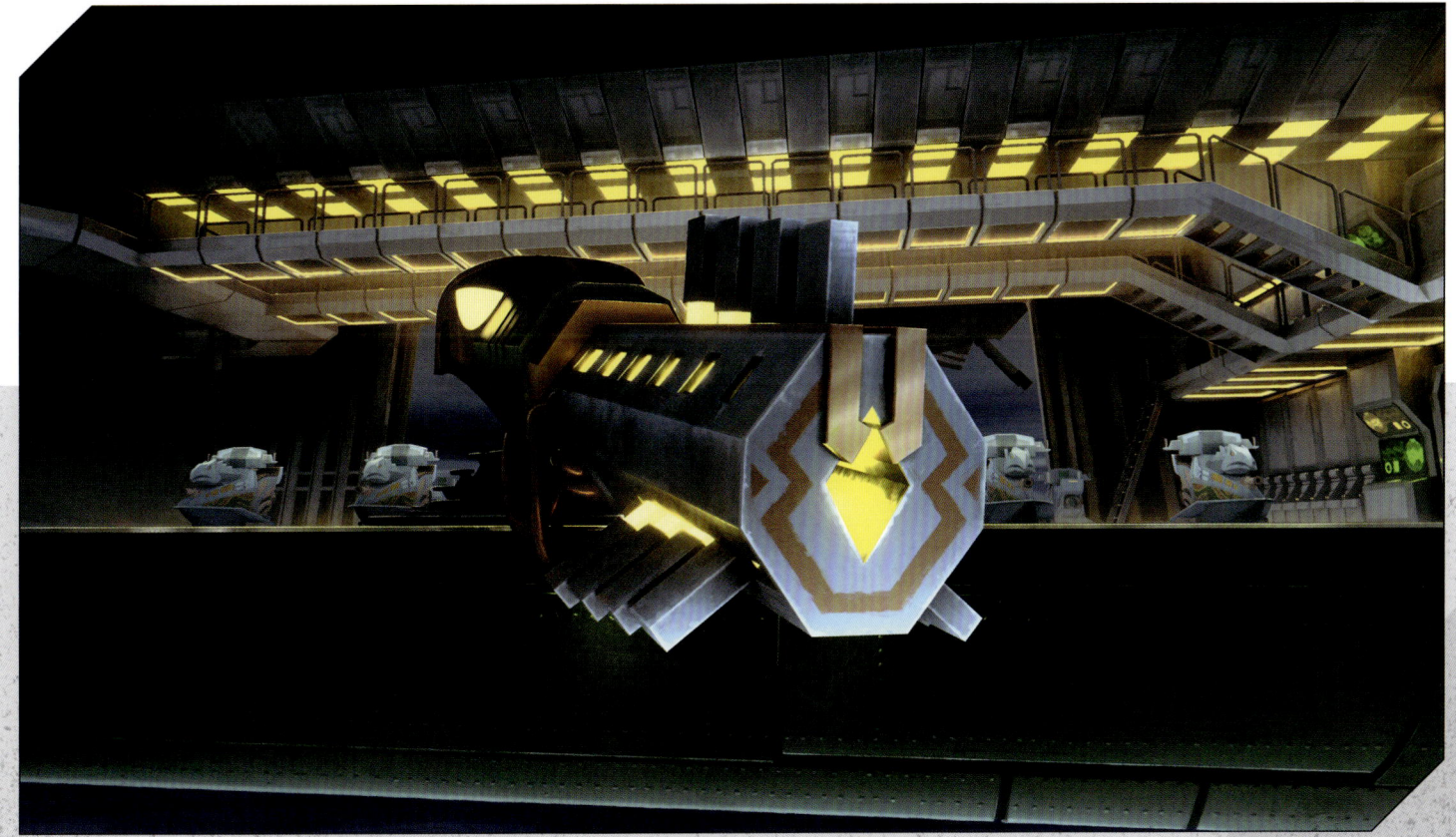

LOCATIONS \\ 155

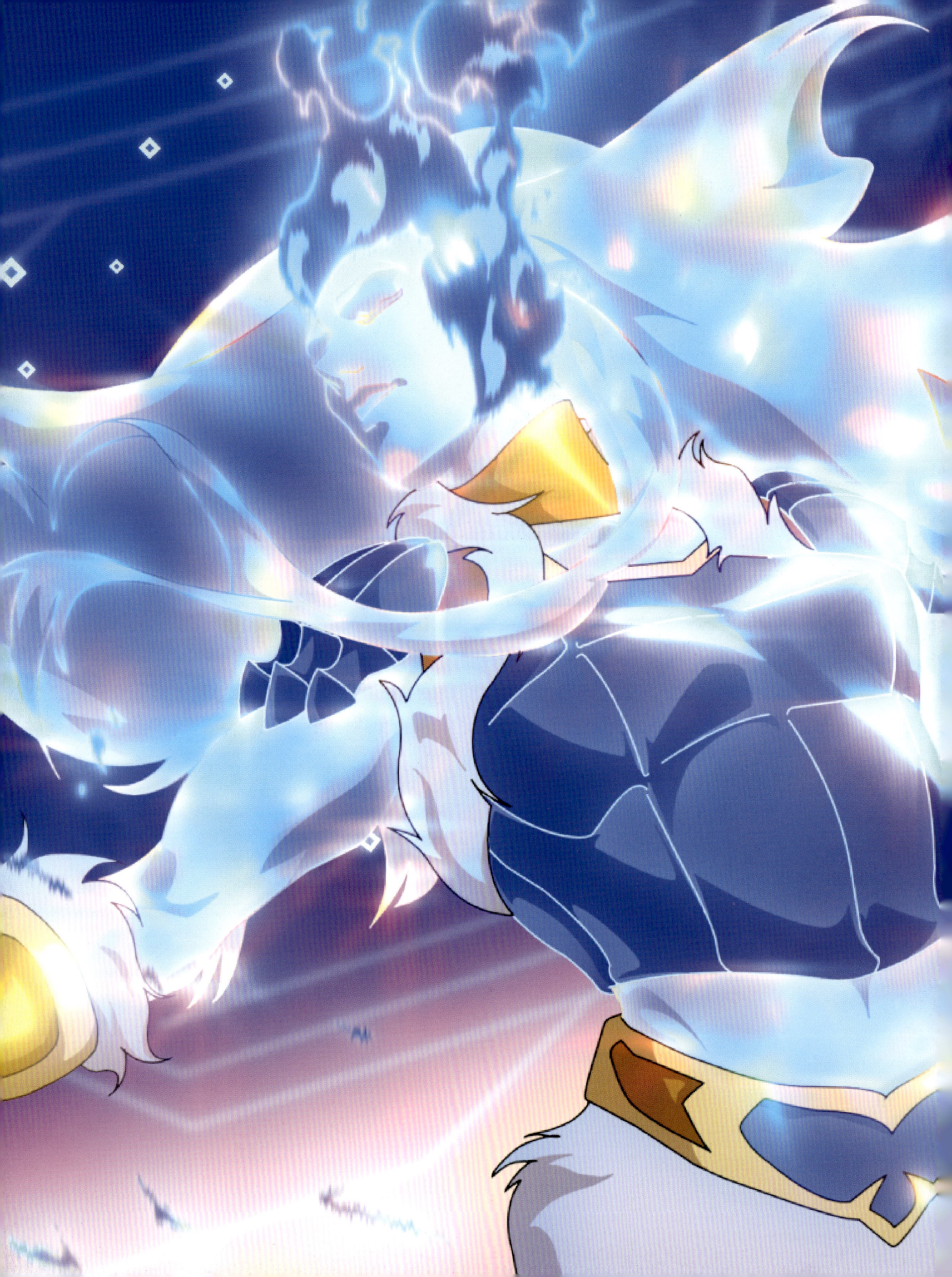

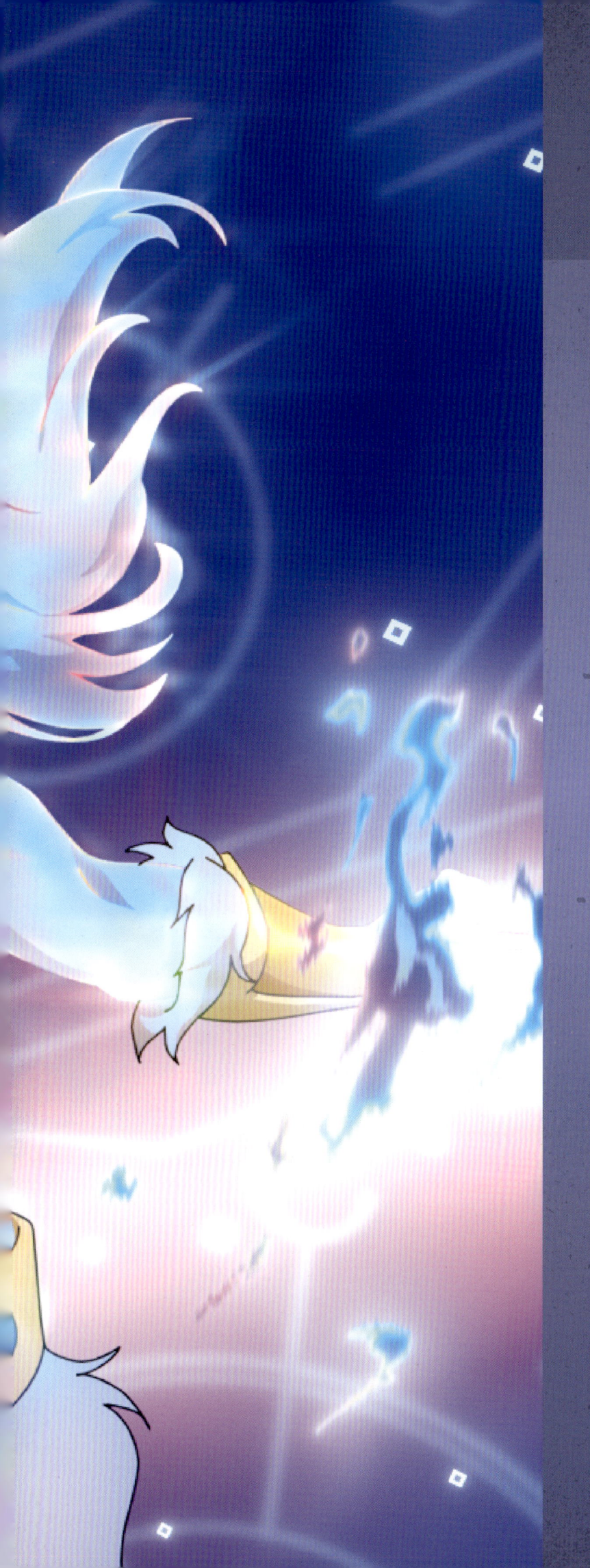

CHAPTER 5
STORYBOARDS AND ANIMATION

THIS SEASON HAS MAJOR "Saturday morning energy" and is best enjoyed wearing a set of comfy jammies while making yourself a big bowl of your favorite breakfast cereal. We took the already-vivid world and colorful cast of characters and sugar blasted them into a smorgasbord for the senses. The colors are more vibrant, the action more spectacular, and best of all, a second season means spending less time on exposition and more time having fun!

With so much for our heroes to do in only five episodes, we had to keep the pacing tight! In fact, the entire season is just barely longer than the 1987 live-action movie from which we drew so much inspiration. Creatively, the faster pacing helped cultivate a sense of urgency as events unravel and allowed us to present an ending as climactic as any movie's. More than just a Saturday morning cartoon, we wanted to make a Saturday morning spectacle!

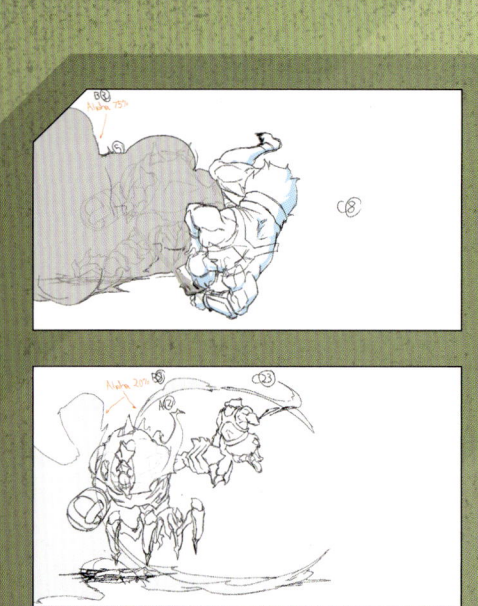
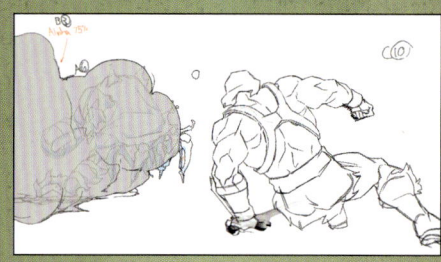
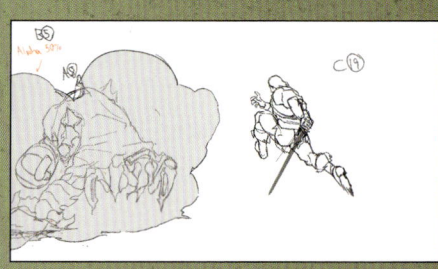
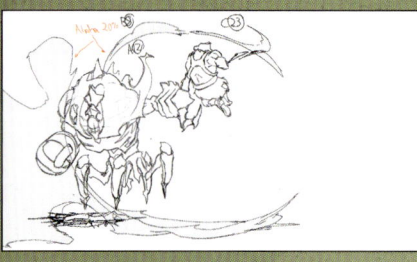
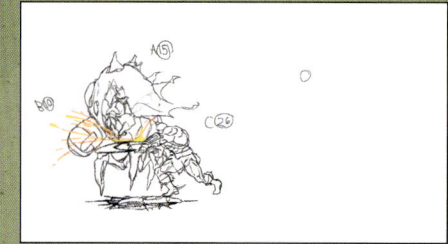
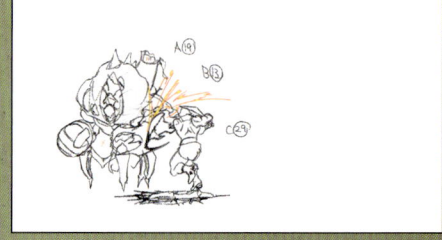
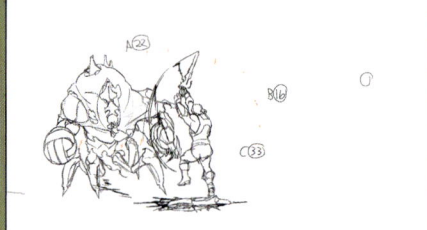
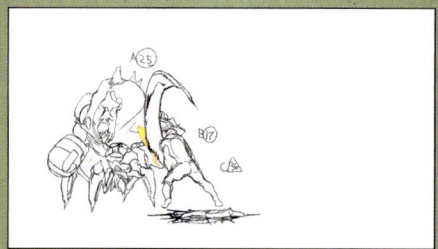
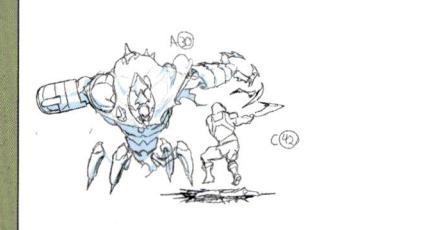
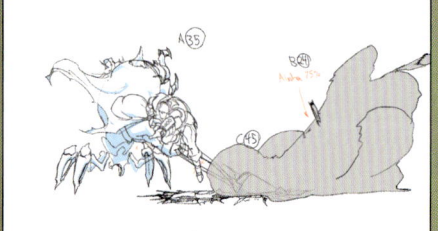
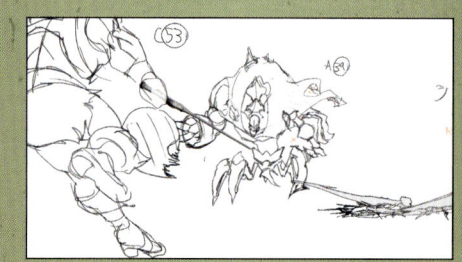

EPISODE 1, SEQUENCE 5
Dominic Ferro animated this amazing action shot between He-Man and the transformed Scare Glow! Even though Scare Glow is an undead wraith, He-Man still pulls his punches when wielding the sword, mainly targeting Scare Glow's arms in an effort to free his friends' souls!

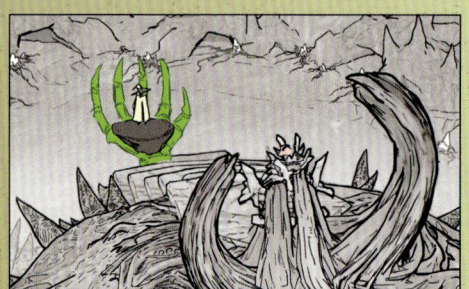
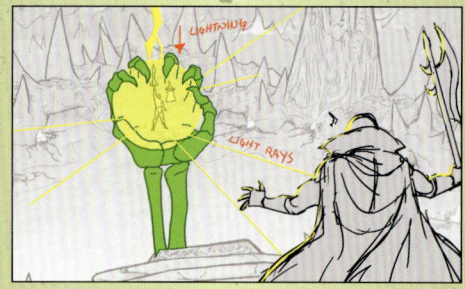
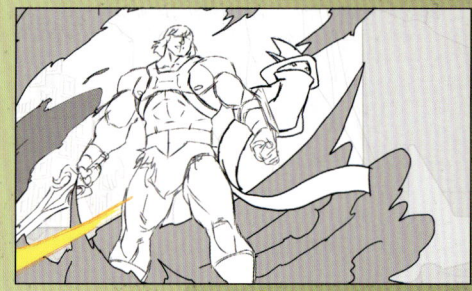
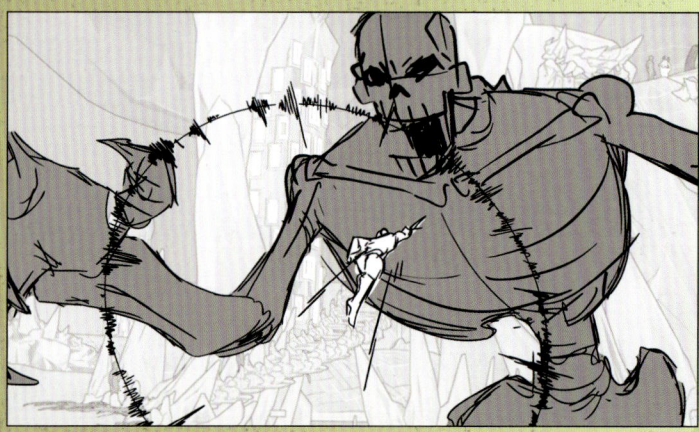
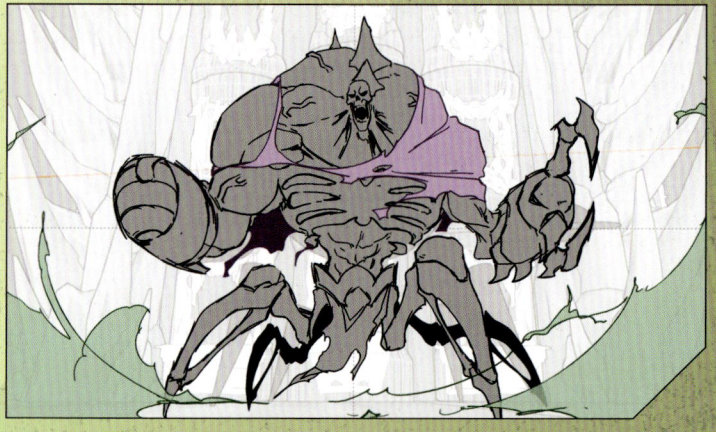

EPISODE 1, SEQUENCE 3
Scare Glow's magic manifests itself in many ways. He first attempts to squash Adam with a giant skeleton hand, then an entire skeletal Titan, and finally he fuses with the souls of both Clamp Champ and Fisto to transform himself into a hideous Goliath!

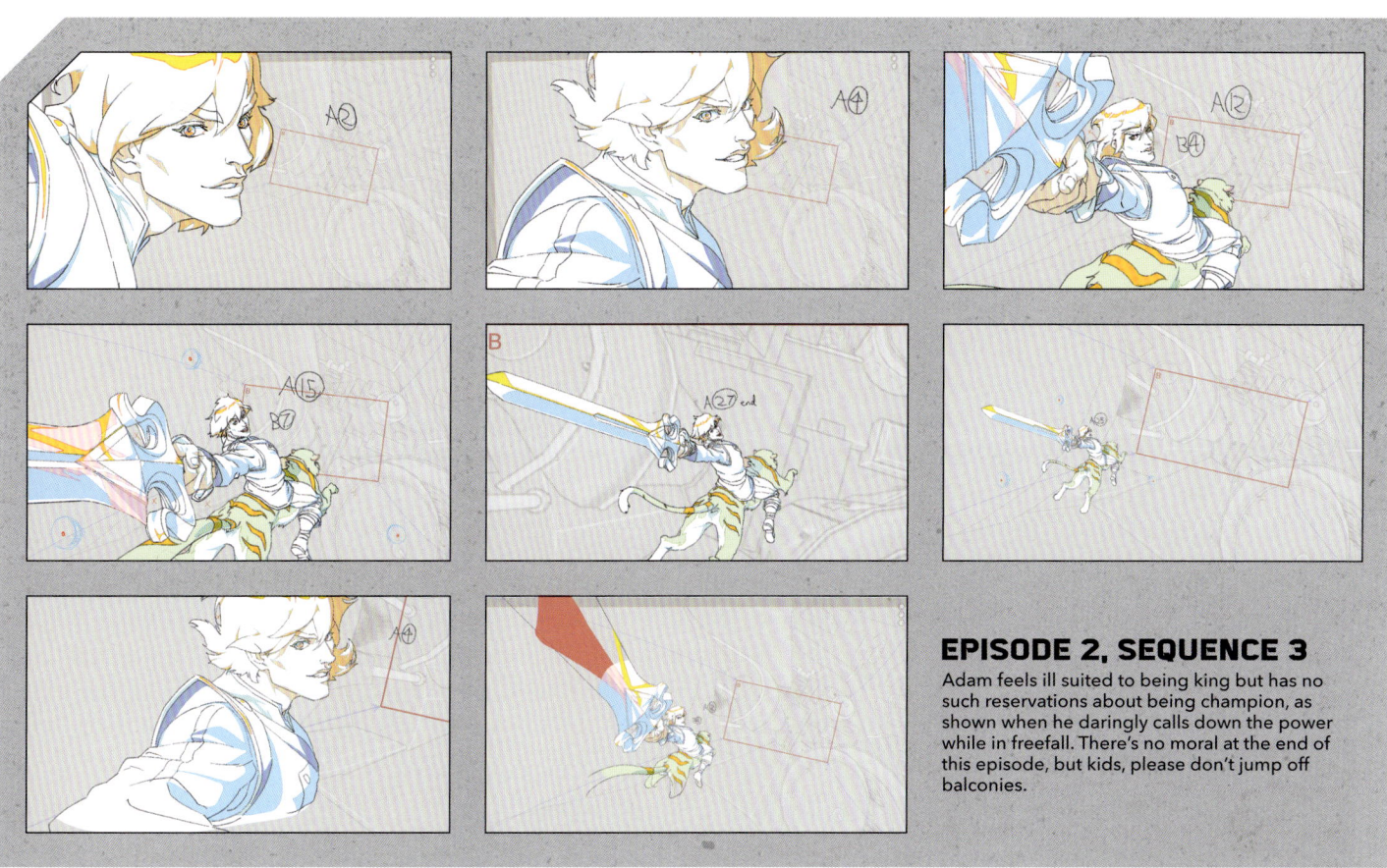

EPISODE 2, SEQUENCE 3
Adam feels ill suited to being king but has no such reservations about being champion, as shown when he daringly calls down the power while in freefall. There's no moral at the end of this episode, but kids, please don't jump off balconies.

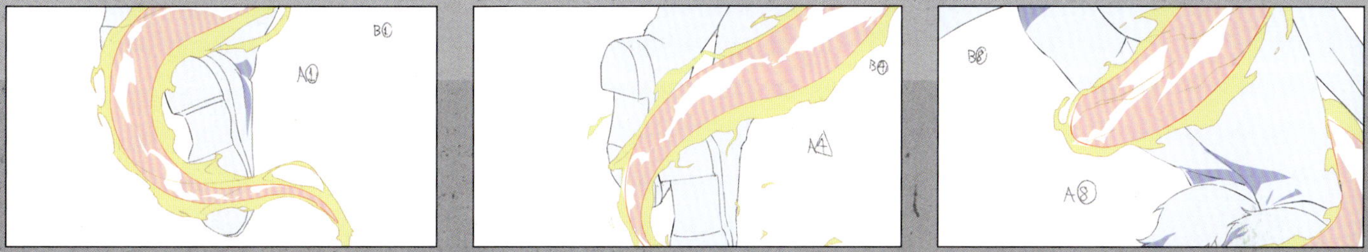

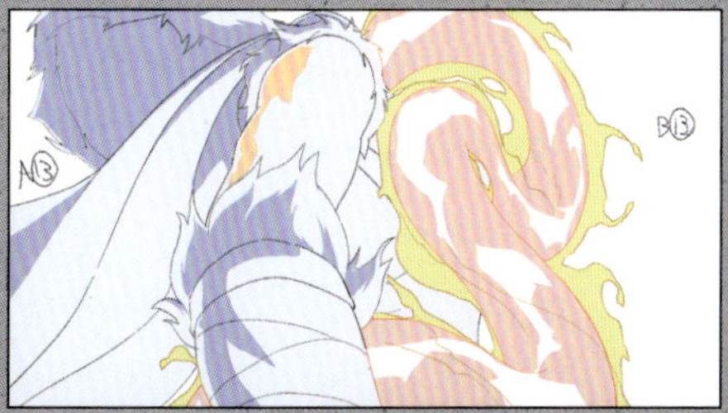

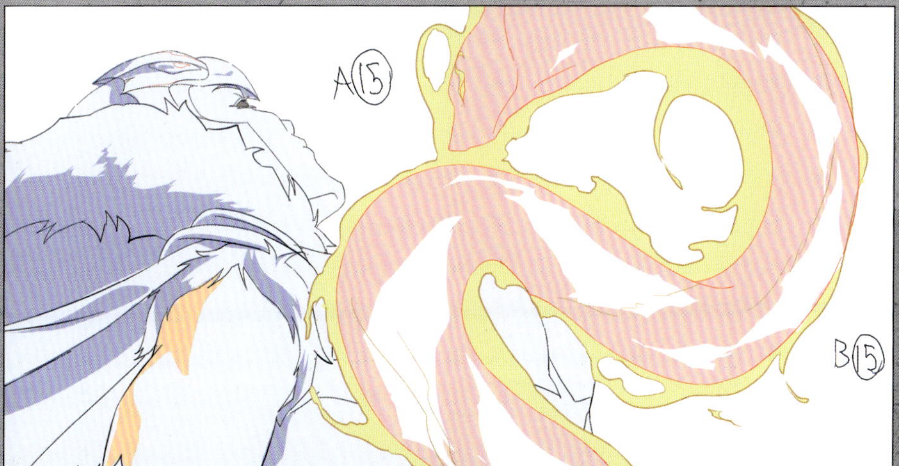

EPISODE 2, SEQUENCE 13
In order for this sequence to have a bit of spectacle, Granamyr performs an ancient ritual that bestows Teela with the Staff of Ka. The powerful artifact first appears as a fiery serpent that evokes the passions from which snake magic is derived.

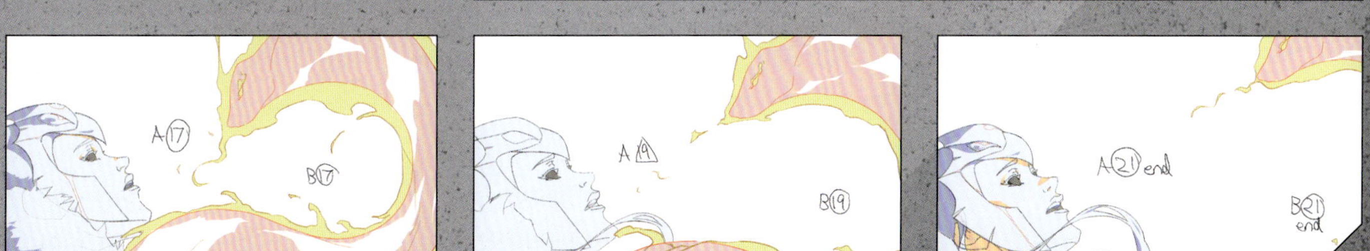

STORYBOARDS AND ANIMATION \\ 159

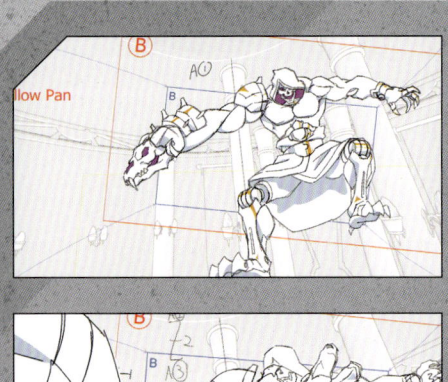
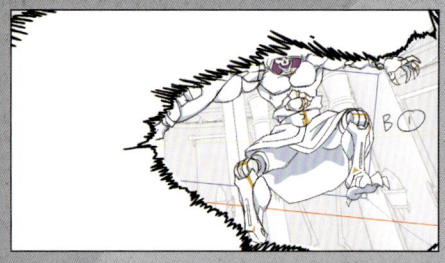
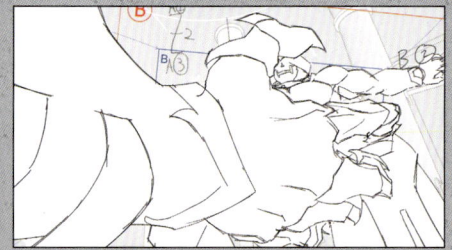
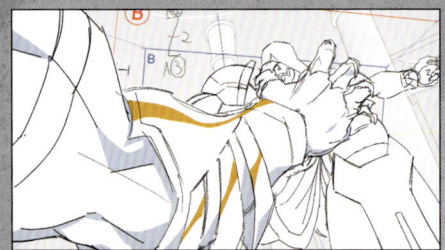
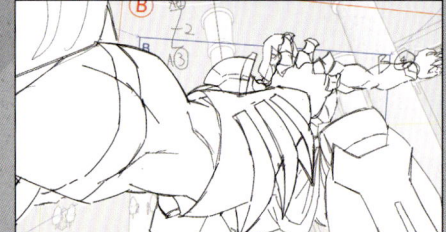
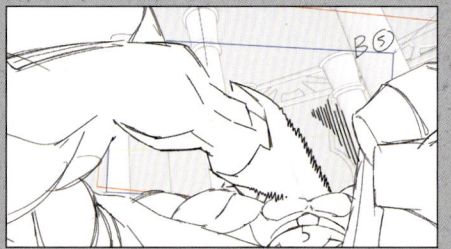
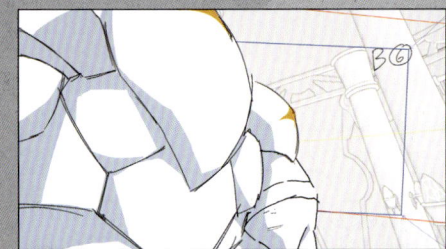
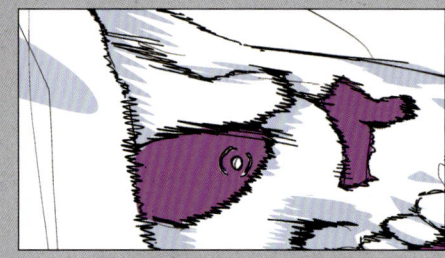

EPISODE 4, SEQUENCE 10
Though of comparable muscle mass to He-Man, Hordak uses combat tactics that are far more cruel. He seizes Skeletor by the face before hurling him into the stone throne. Skeletor's battle with Hordak reduces the throne room to a pile of rubble!

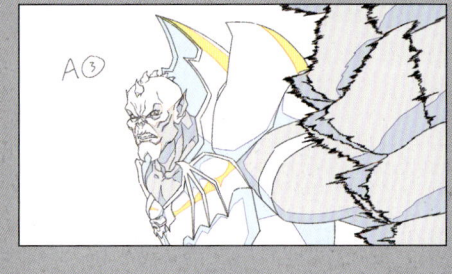
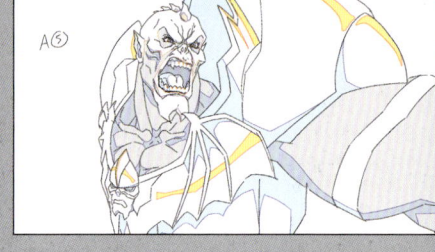
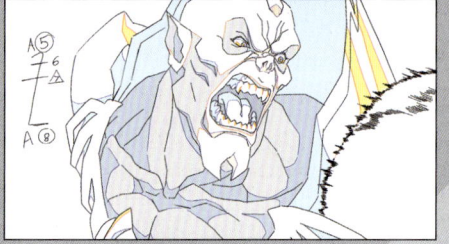
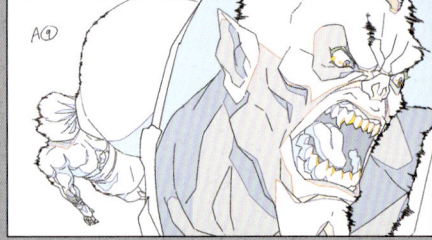
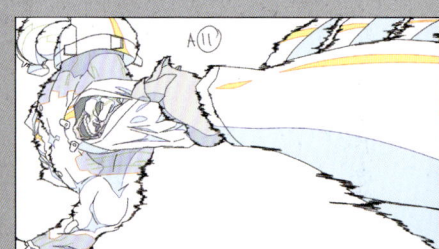
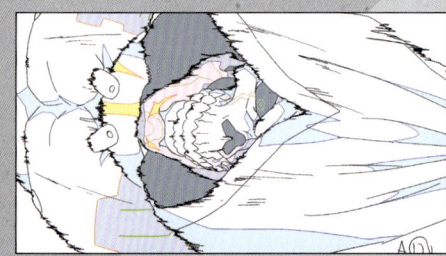

EPISODE 4, SEQUENCE 10
These types of extreme action shots require expert knowledge of anatomy, volume, perspective, and motion from the animator. Sometimes more than one artist is needed to animate something this complex. This scene was handled by Erik Labuguen with assistance from Dominic Ferro.

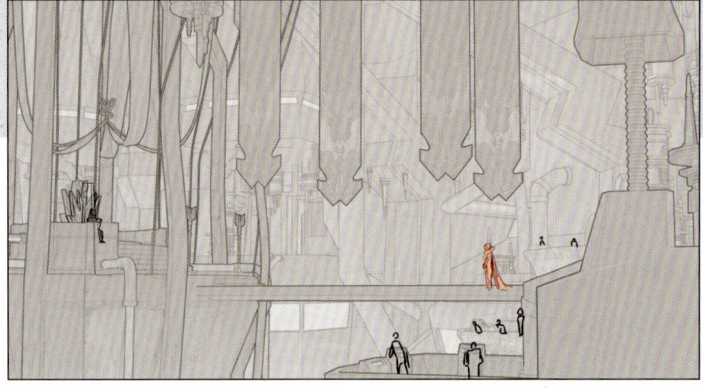
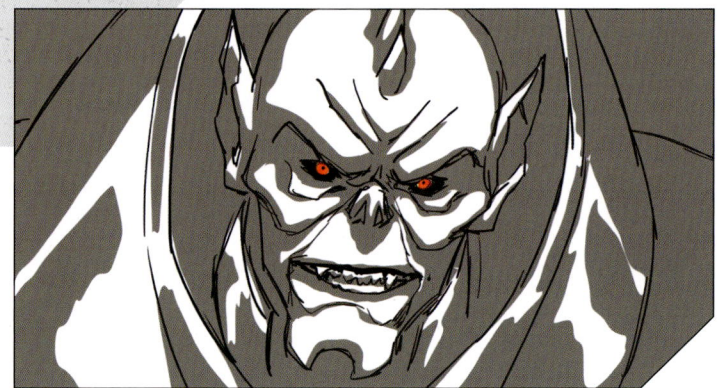

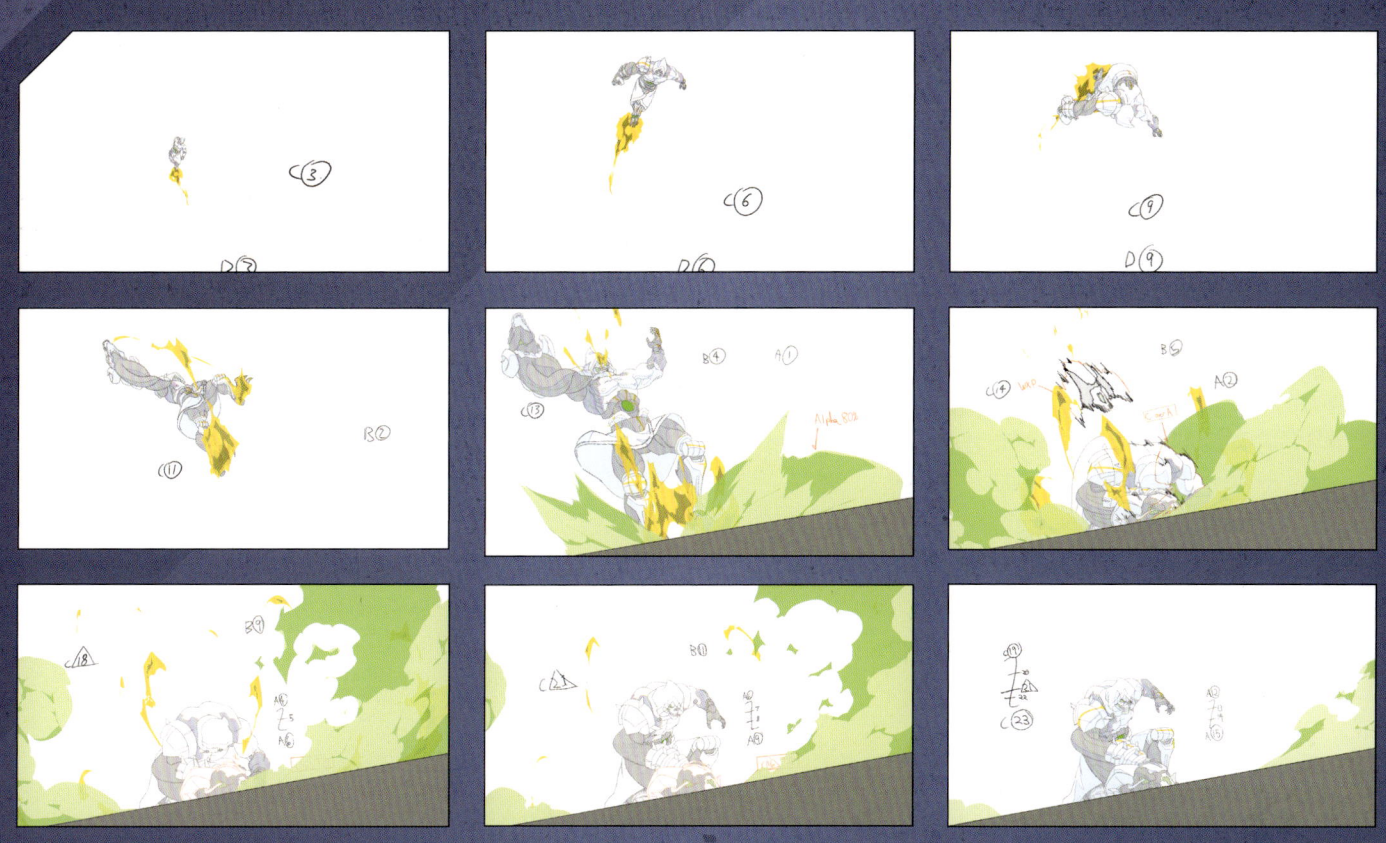

EPISODE 4, SEQUENCE 13
Matting is a useful tool industry artists implement to help define silhouettes and separate elements in the rough draft of a scene. In both animation and storyboarding, these bright colors lay a clear blueprint for the later stages of production.

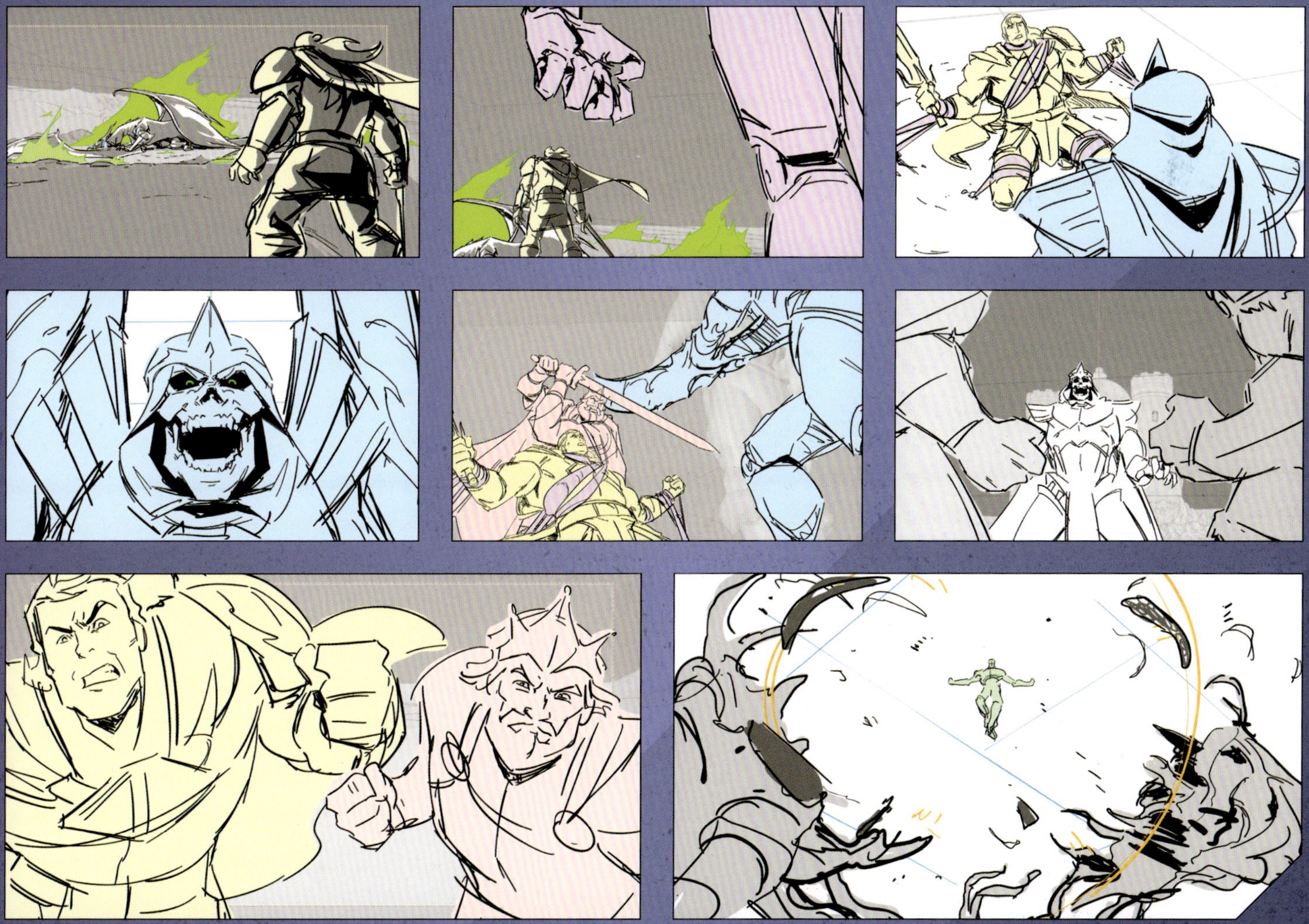

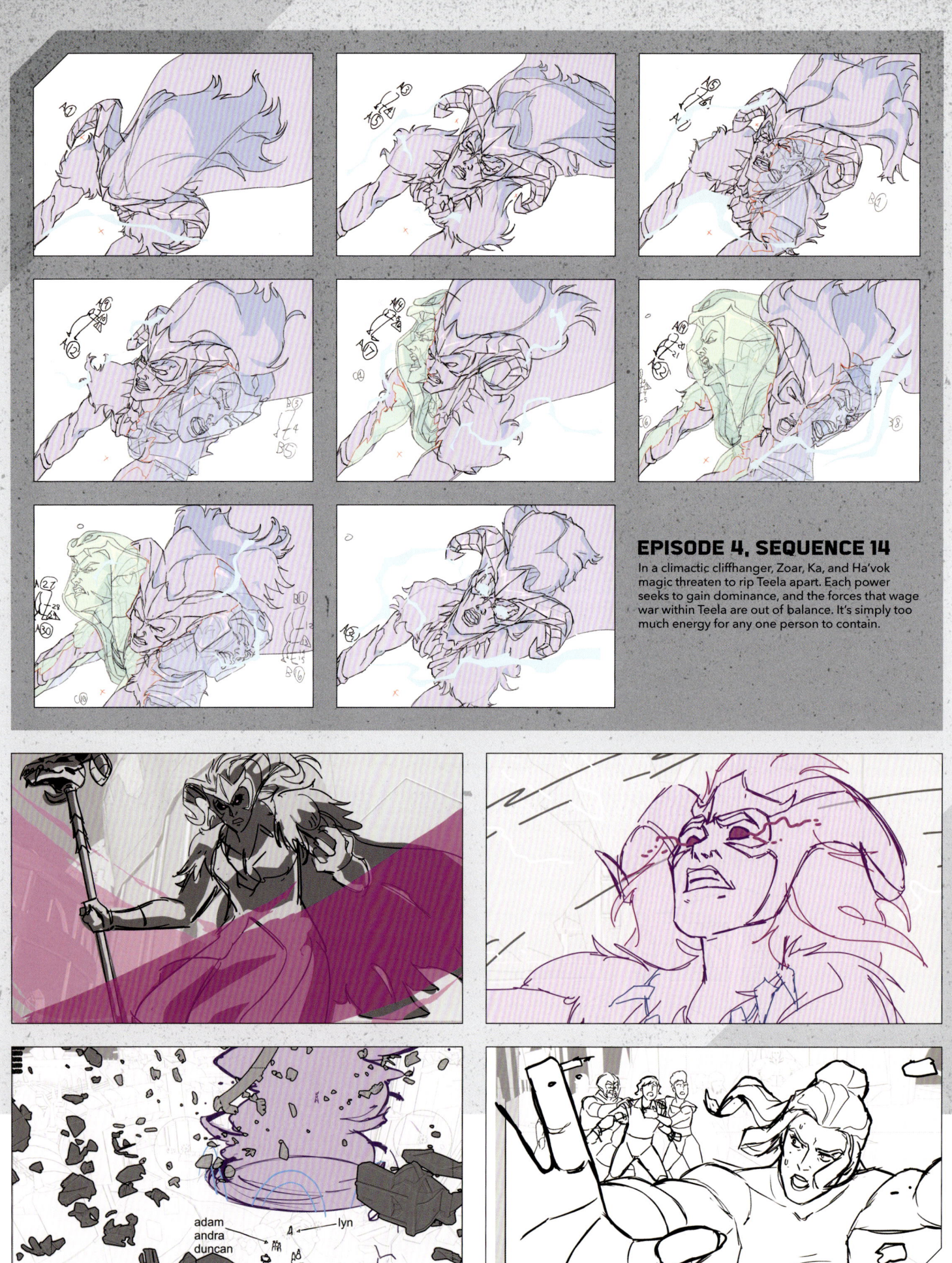

EPISODE 4, SEQUENCE 14
In a climactic cliffhanger, Zoar, Ka, and Ha'vok magic threaten to rip Teela apart. Each power seeks to gain dominance, and the forces that wage war within Teela are out of balance. It's simply too much energy for any one person to contain.

The magics raging within Teela result in a massively magic maelstrom that turns the Royal Palace into rubble. Fortunately, the formerly evil Evil-Lyn is there to erect a magical barrier protecting the heroes, yet even her formidable magic can do little to contain the forces escaping Teela.

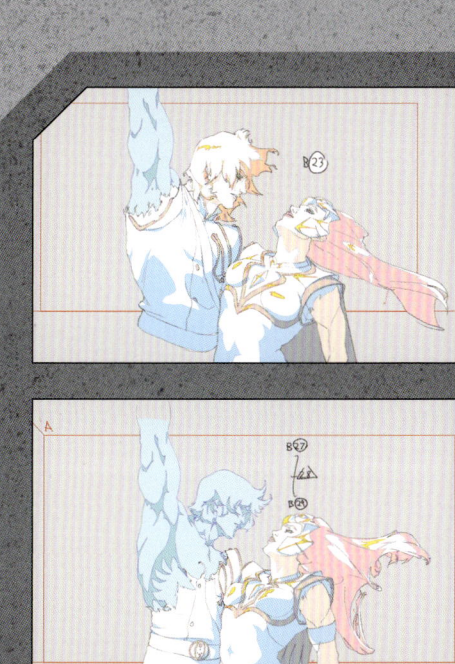
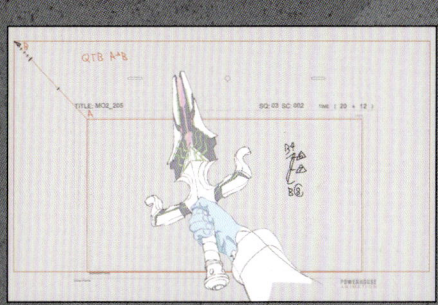
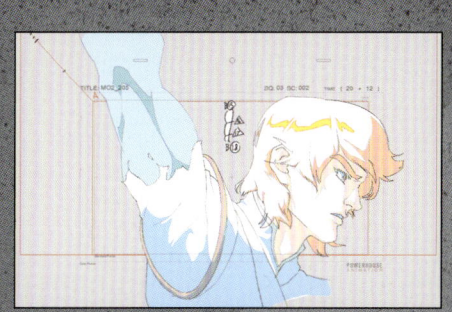
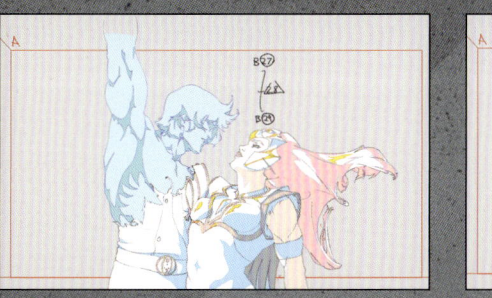
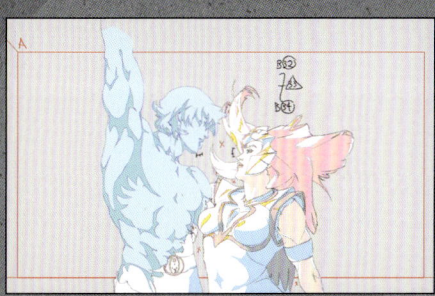
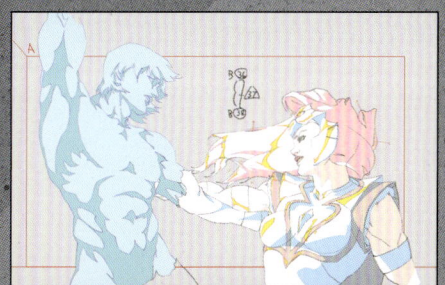
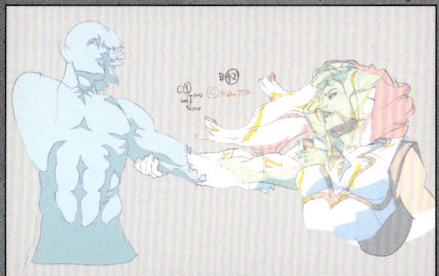
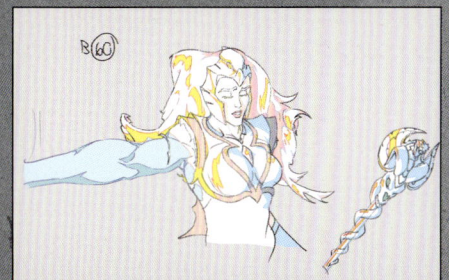
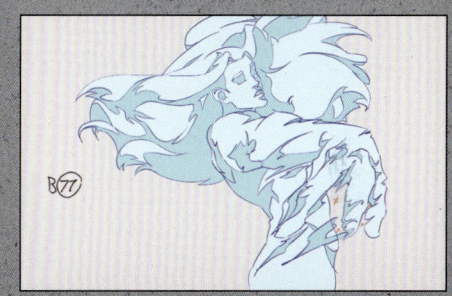
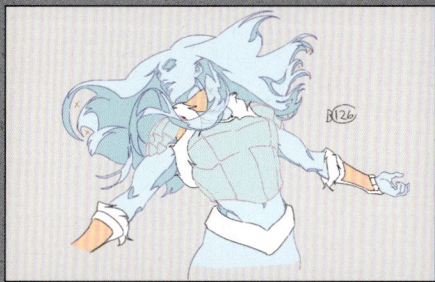
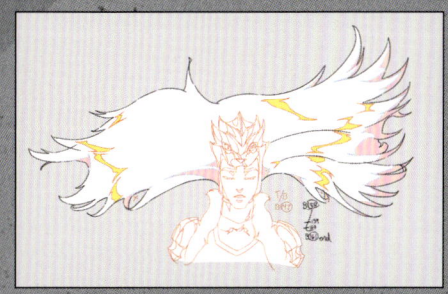

EPISODE 5, SEQUENCE 3

This is the sequence that we were most excited to animate! When Adam calls down the power with the tech-enhanced Power Sword (Thanks, Gwildor!), Adam synergizes magic and technology, and when that energy flows into Teela, it restores balance to the powers warring within her.

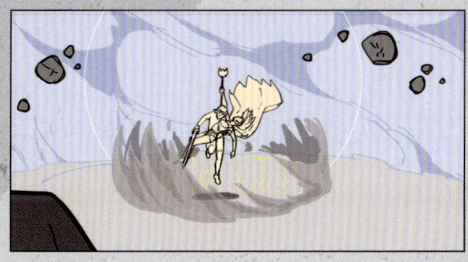
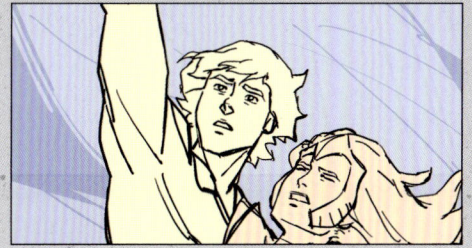
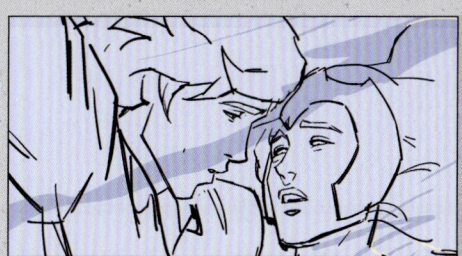
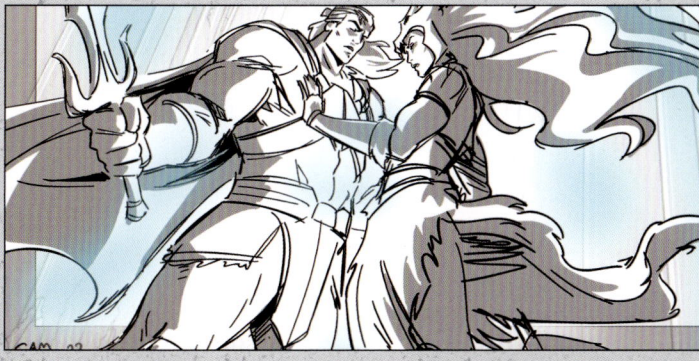
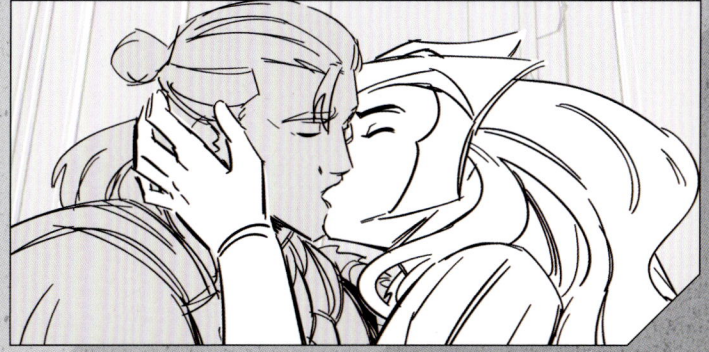

Inside the magical maelstrom, held in Adam's arm, Teela is closer to death than she's ever been before. But from that brink both characters are transformed, and after forty years of setup, we finally get to see these two kiss.

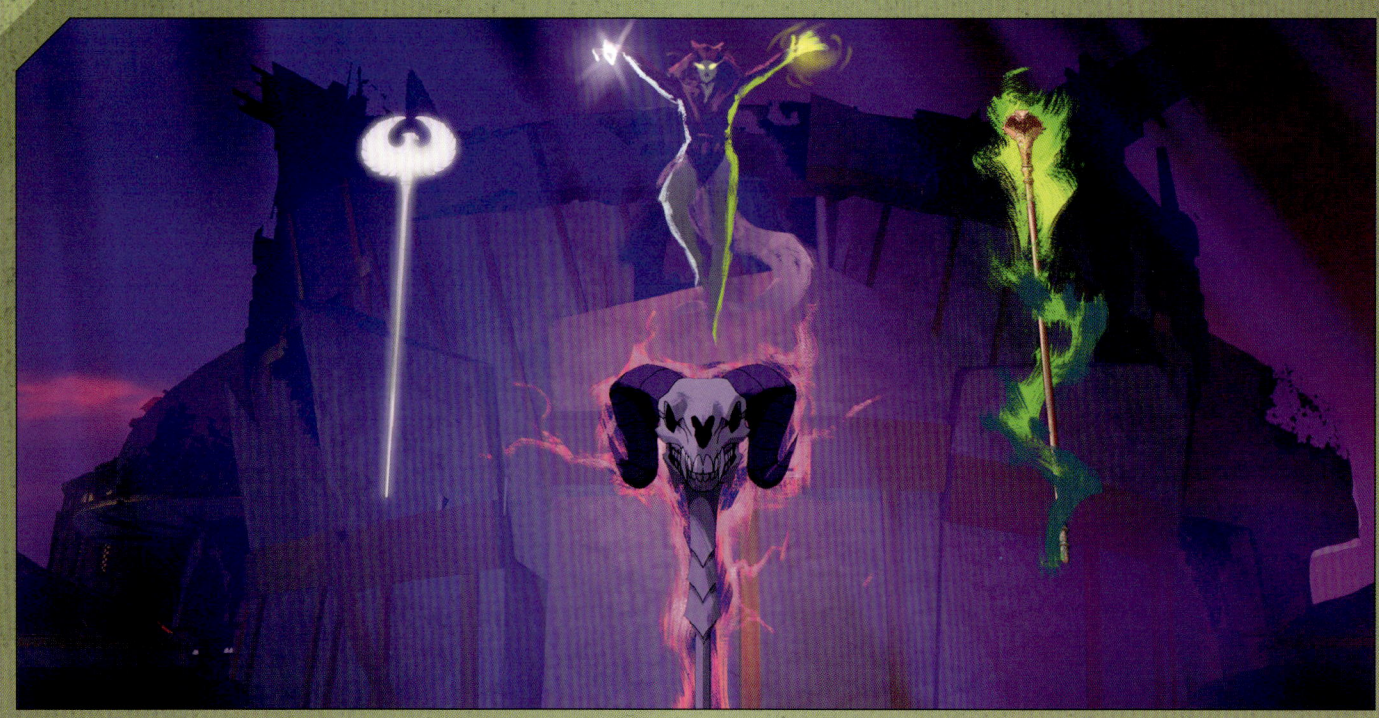

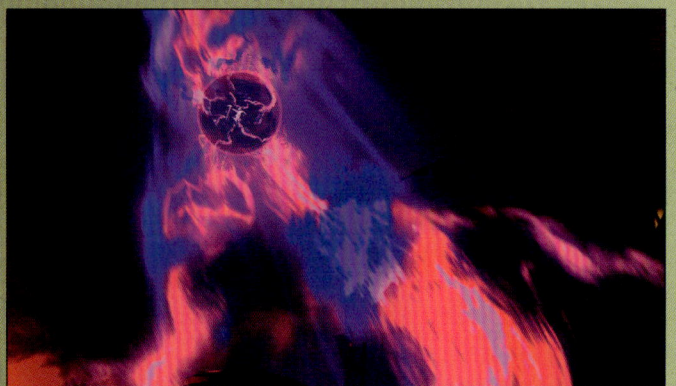
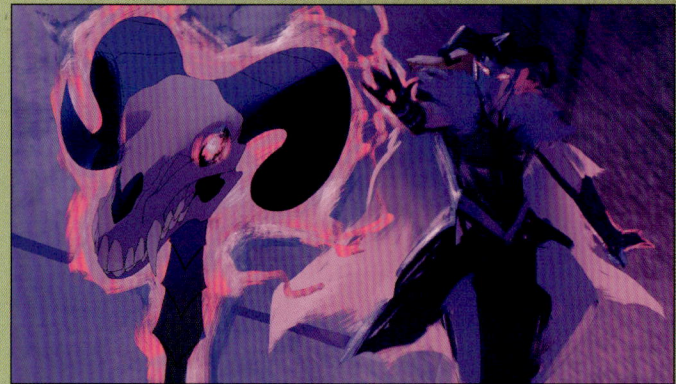

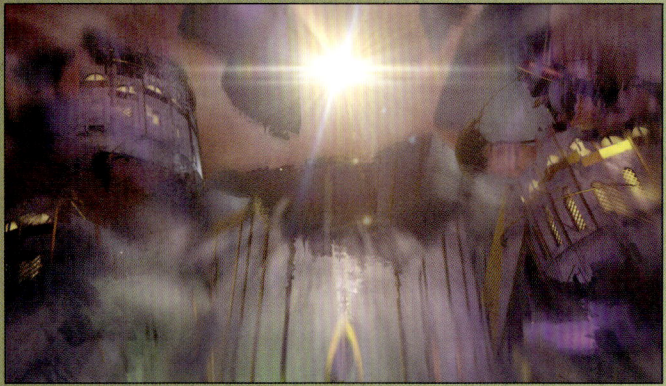
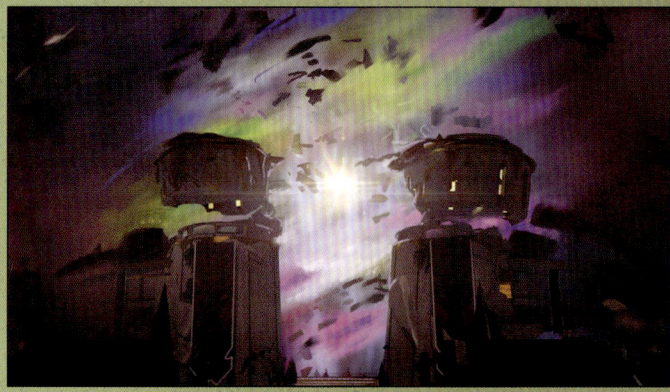

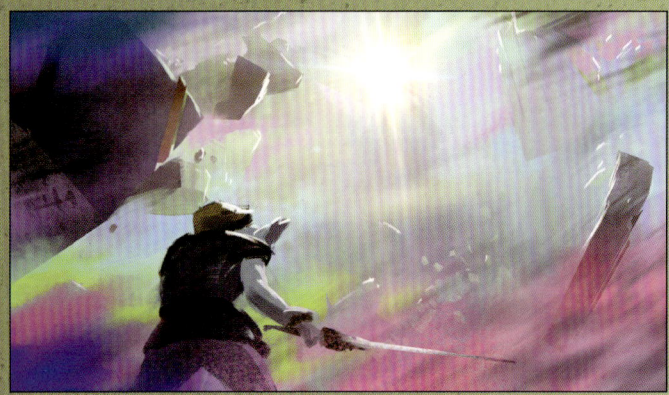

EPISODE 4, SEQUENCE 14

Teela's quest to acquire all three of the ancient magics required to restore Preternia comes to a calamitous conclusion in this episode. These thumbnails helped us plan out the sequence and ensure that this climactic beat would be memorable and full of spectacle!

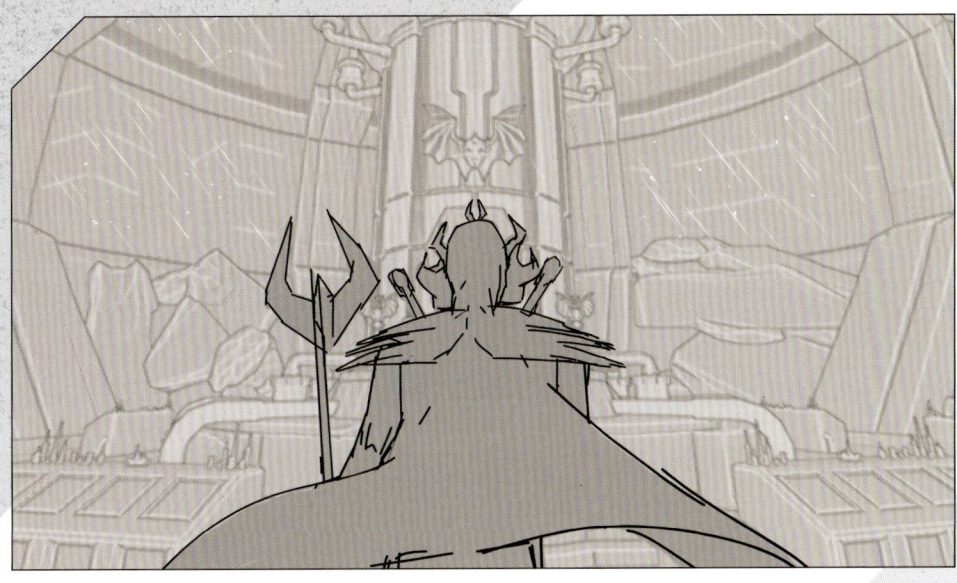
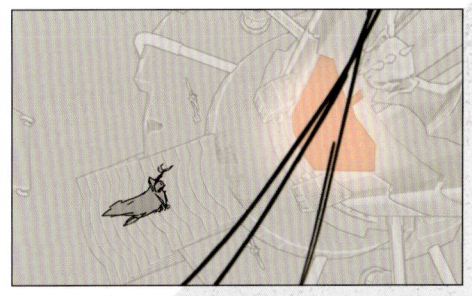
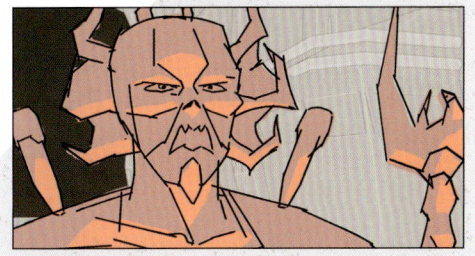
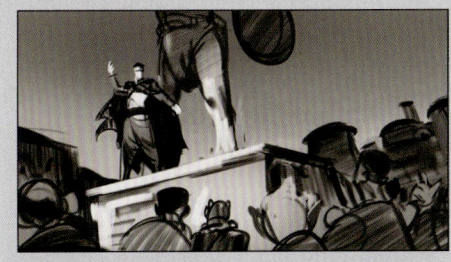
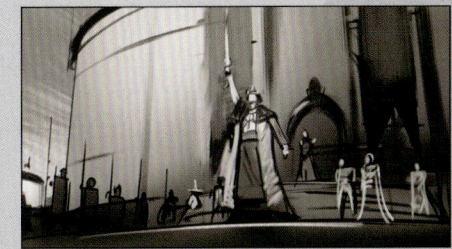
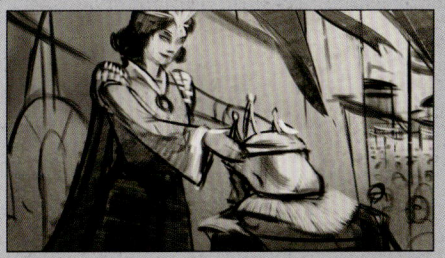
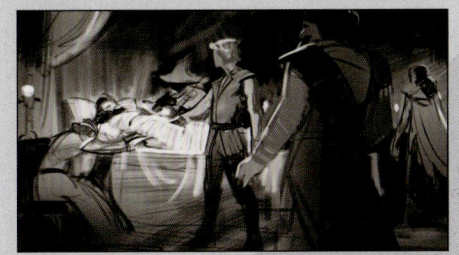
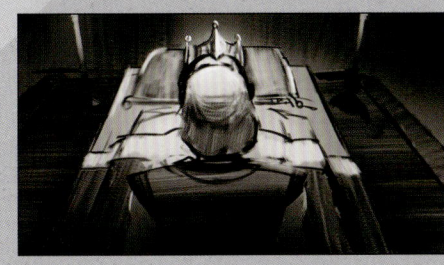
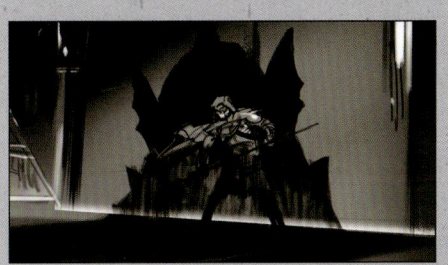
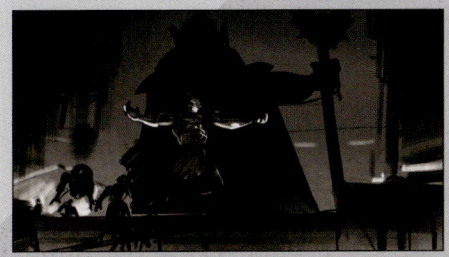
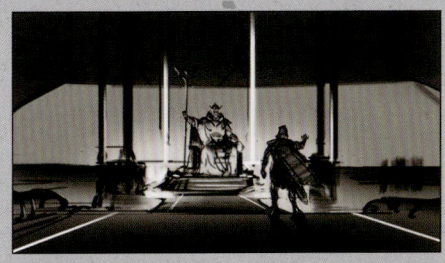
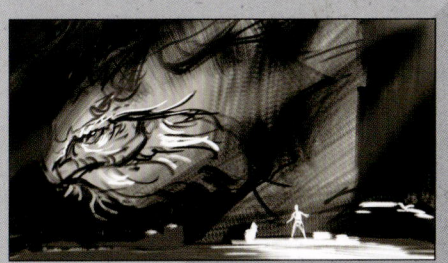
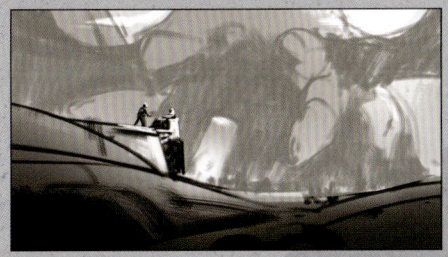
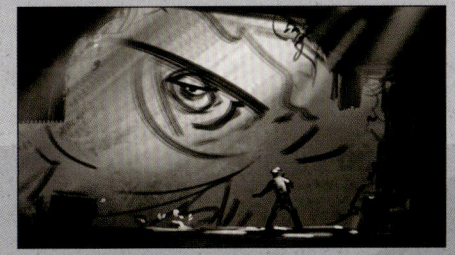
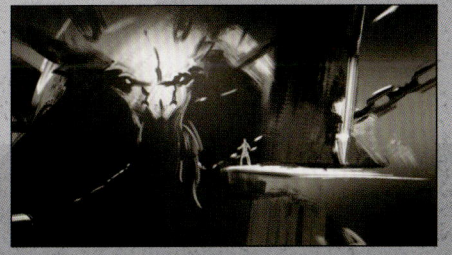
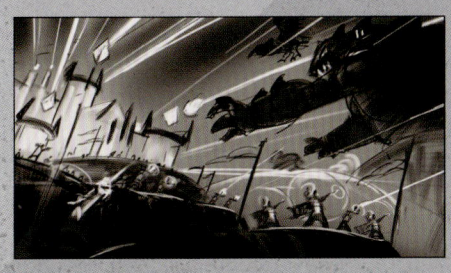
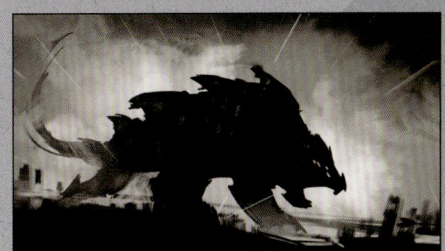

STORY ART
These thumbnails are typically done before character designs and environments are finalized, but they help capture the spirit of a given scene and keep us on track. Even though each of these beats evolved throughout production, you can still trace their origin to these early sketches.

STORYBOARDS AND ANIMATION \\ 165

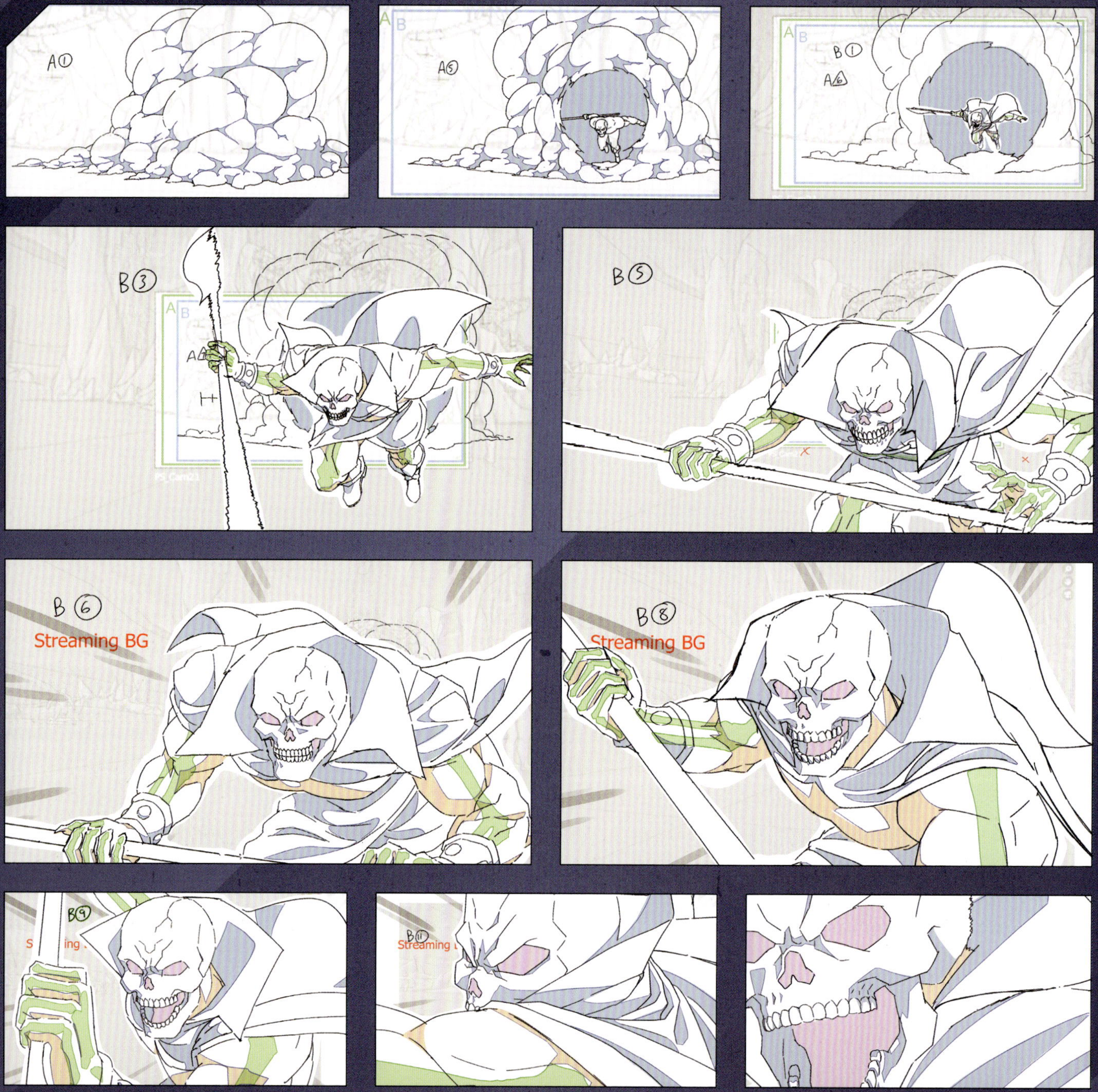

EPISODE 1, SEQUENCE 3

Scare Glow erupts from the smoking crater to cleave a stunned Ram Man with his Scythe of Doom! Scenes such as this have a ton of moving parts, including a camera move, roiling smoke clouds, and a flowing cape!

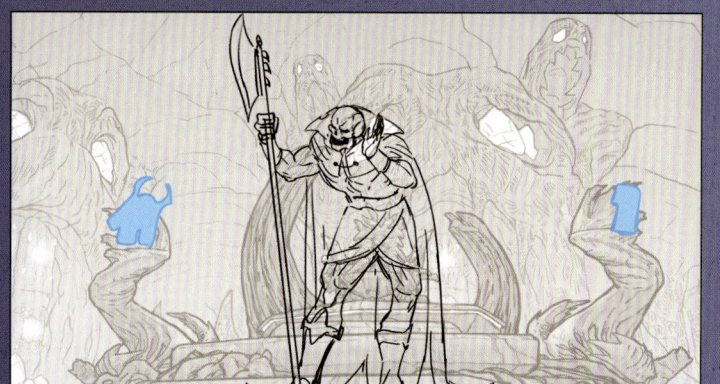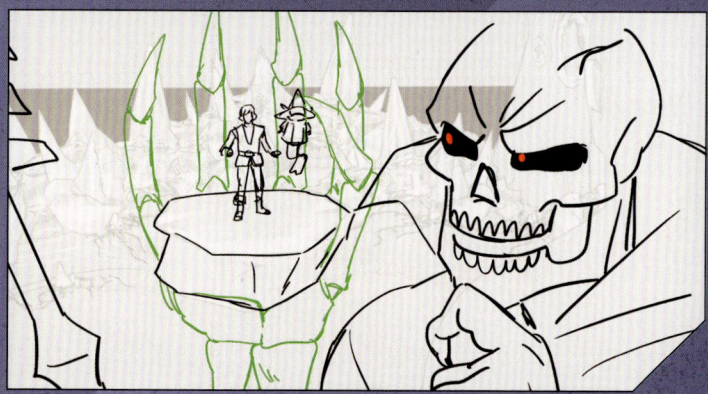

In the storyboarding process, characters are often drawn in what is commonly referred to as "shorthand." Their details, features, and line work may be sparse or roughed in for the sake of expediency, but the performances and proportions are clear and instantly legible.

166 // THE ART OF MASTERS OF THE UNIVERSE: REVOLUTION

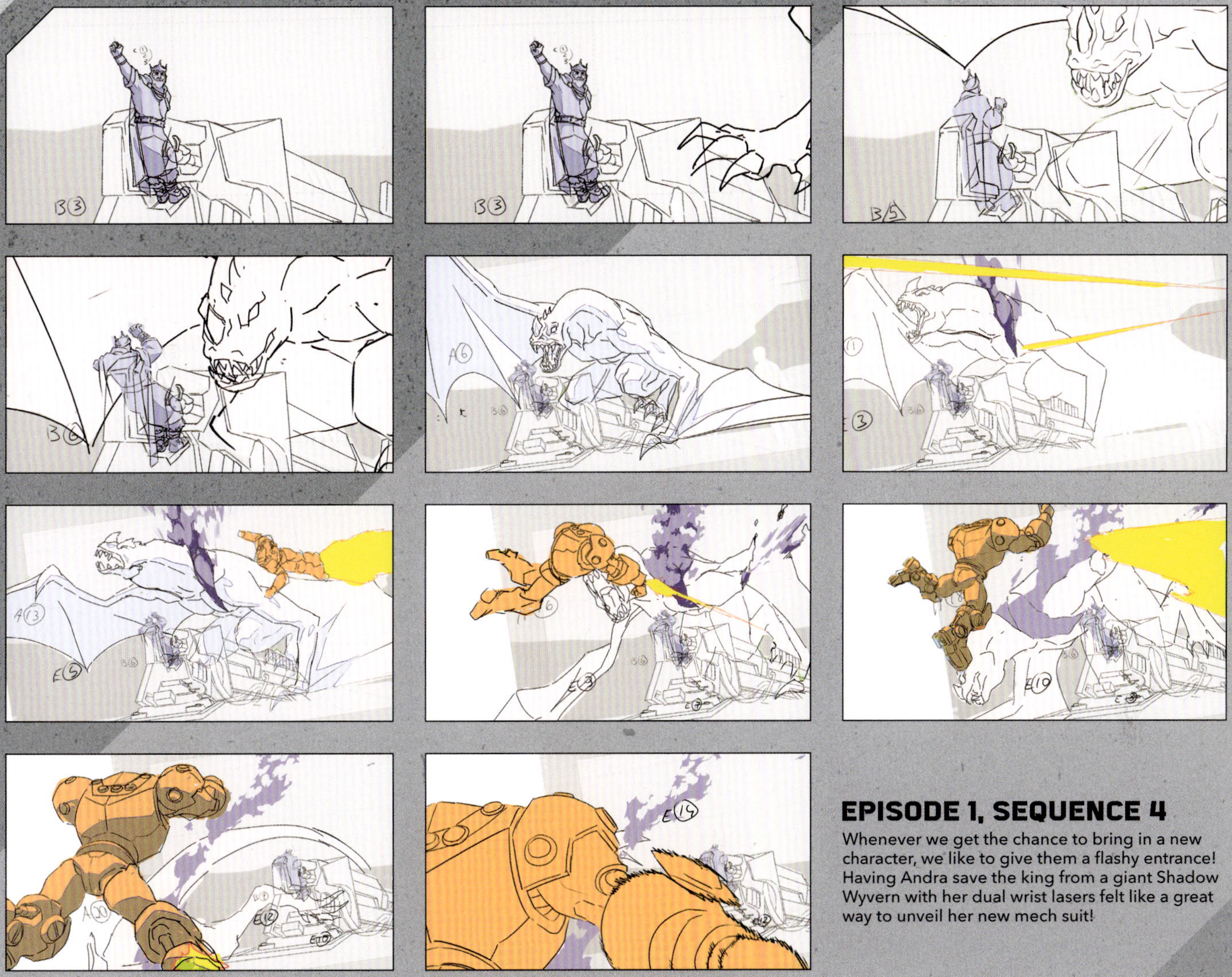

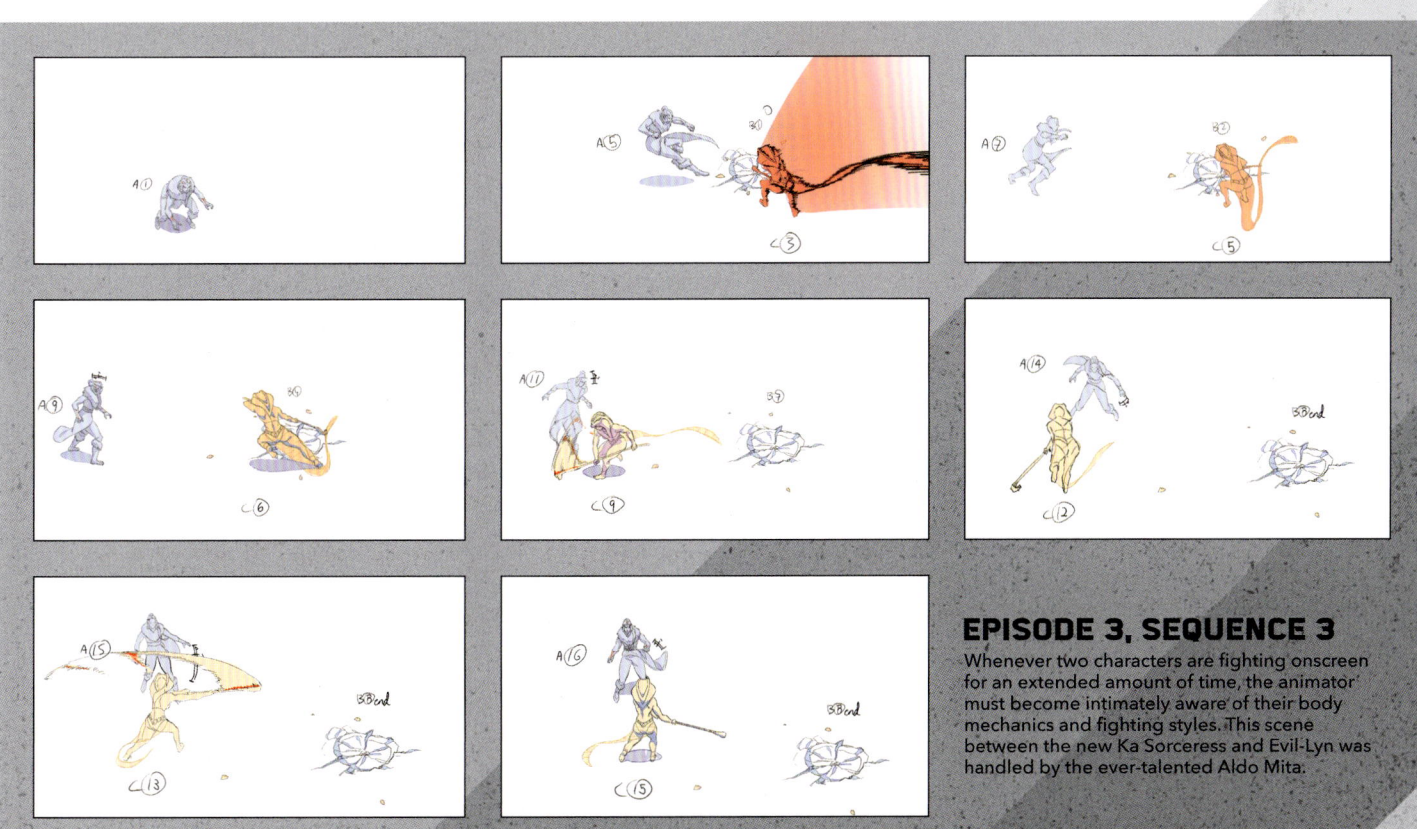

EPISODE 1, SEQUENCE 4
Whenever we get the chance to bring in a new character, we like to give them a flashy entrance! Having Andra save the king from a giant Shadow Wyvern with her dual wrist lasers felt like a great way to unveil her new mech suit!

EPISODE 3, SEQUENCE 3
Whenever two characters are fighting onscreen for an extended amount of time, the animator must become intimately aware of their body mechanics and fighting styles. This scene between the new Ka Sorceress and Evil-Lyn was handled by the ever-talented Aldo Mita.

STORYBOARDS AND ANIMATION \\ 167

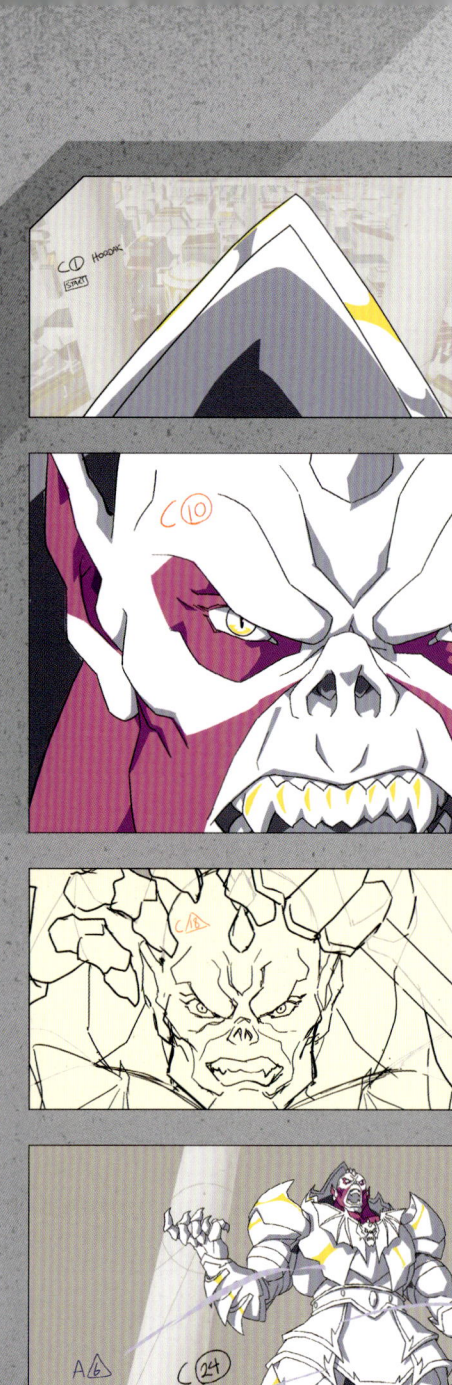
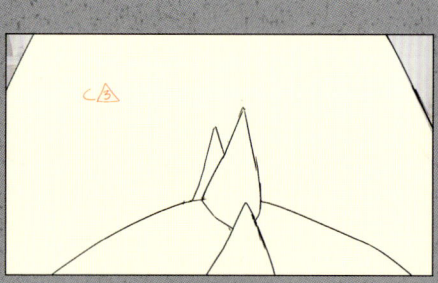
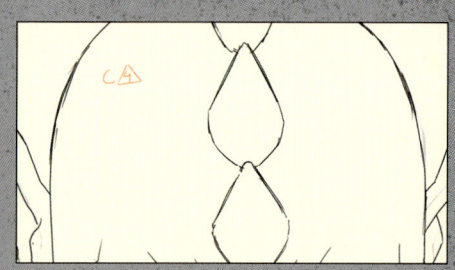
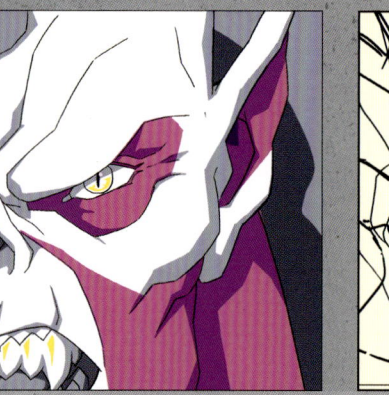
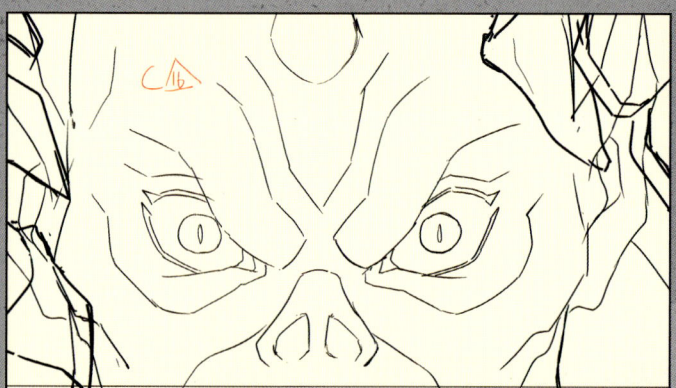
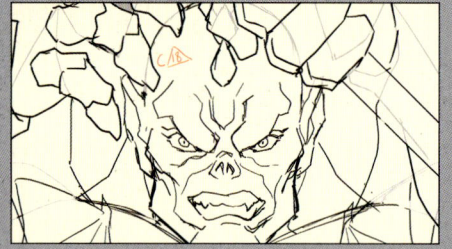
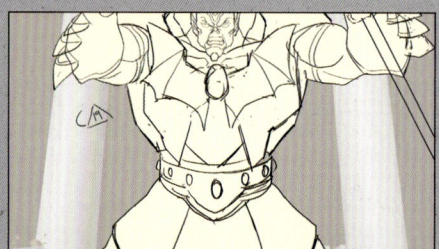
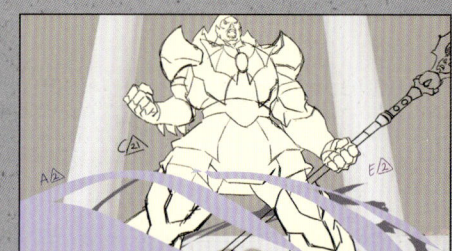
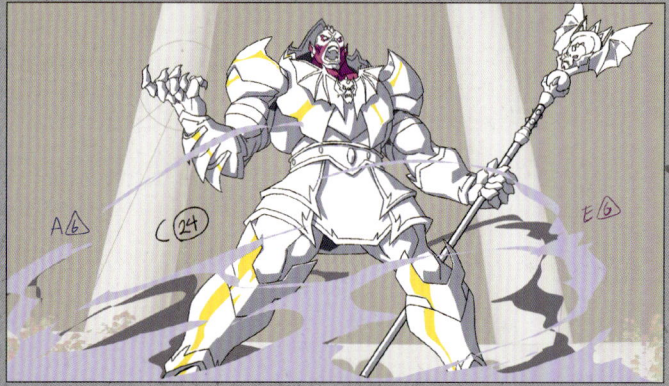
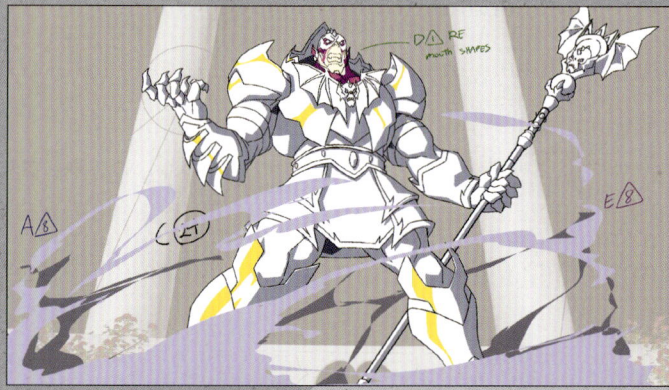
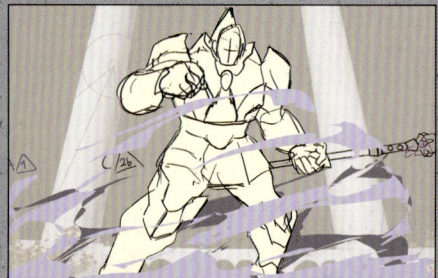
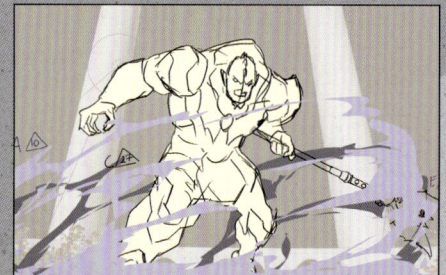
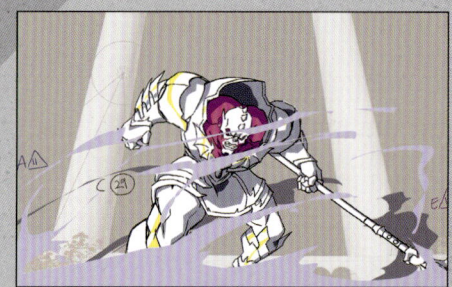
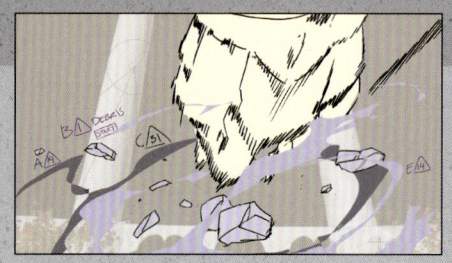
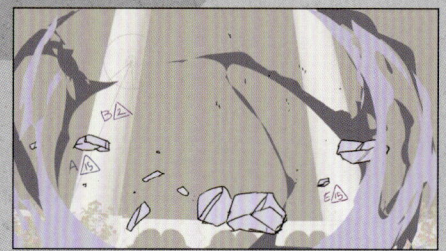

EPISODE 4, SEQUENCE 6

Hordak is conquest incarnate, and in this moment we get to see the full extent of his power! With the power of technology, he is able to transform his body into an armored hulk of doom and destruction!

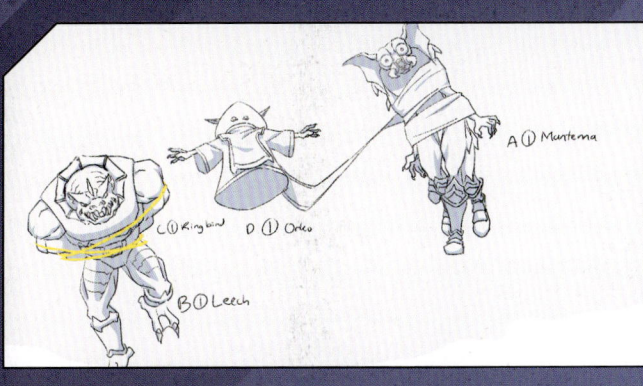
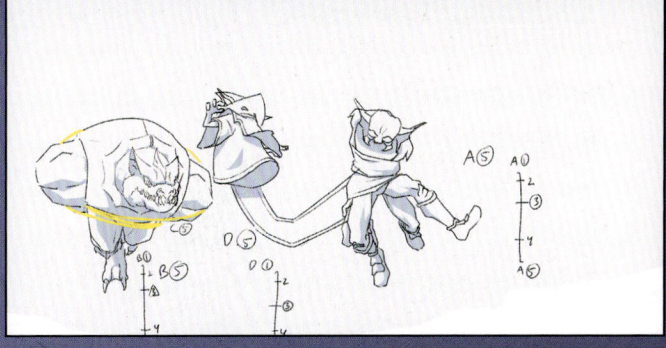
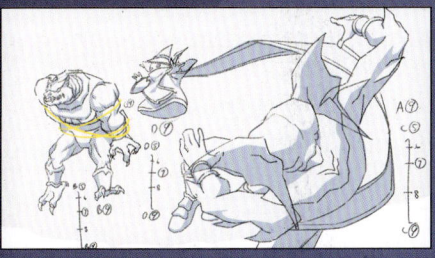
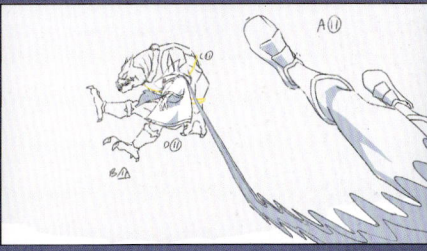
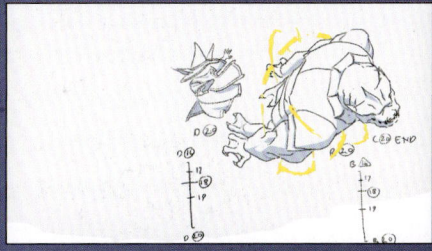
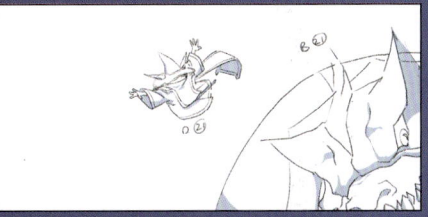
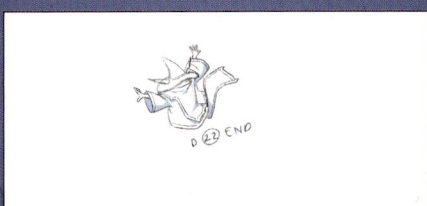

EPISODE 4, SEQUENCE 9

The Horde would do well to remember that Orko is no longer the bumbling buffoon of a magician that he once was. He's now a formidable fighter and single-handedly makes quick work of Hordak's henchmen while Gwildor finishes tinkering with the Power Sword.

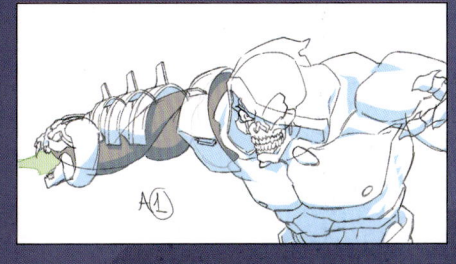
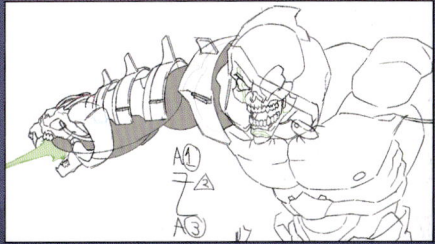
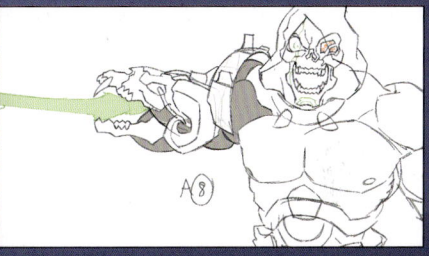
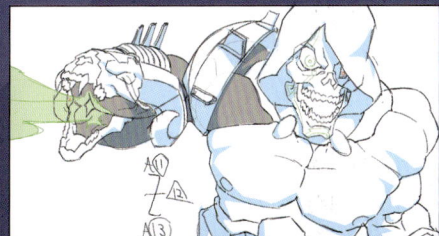
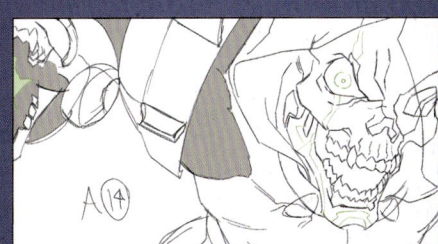

EPISODE 4, SEQUENCE 13

From the moment that Motherboard cracks his cranium, Skeletor is haunted by visions of Keldor. The memories war within his mind and lead him to betray his former mentor and surrogate father. When he deals the deathblow with Hordak's own attack, the visions stop, and his identities are reconciled as Skeletor 2.0.

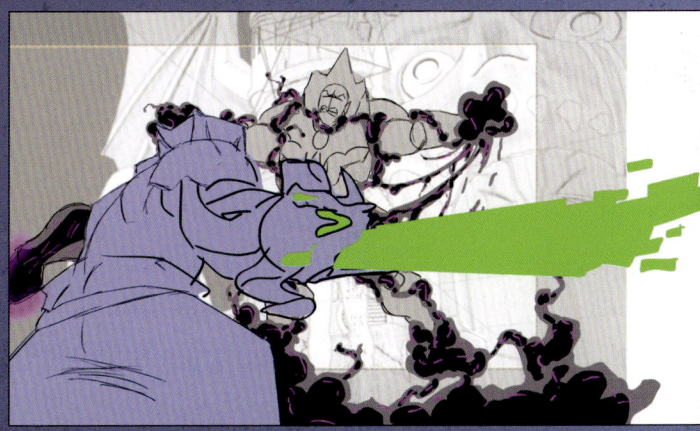
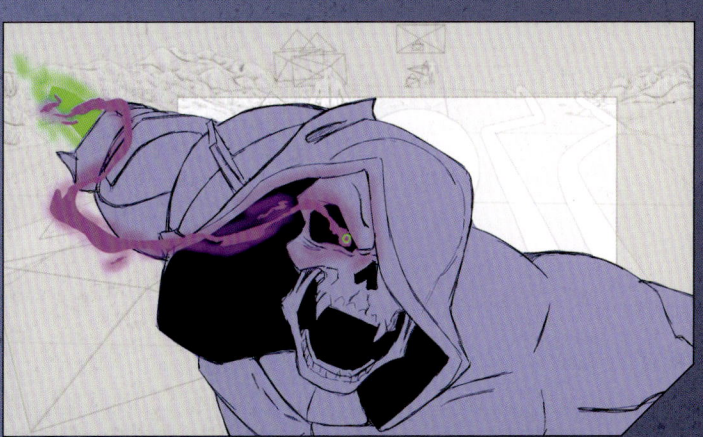

STORYBOARDS AND ANIMATION \\ 169

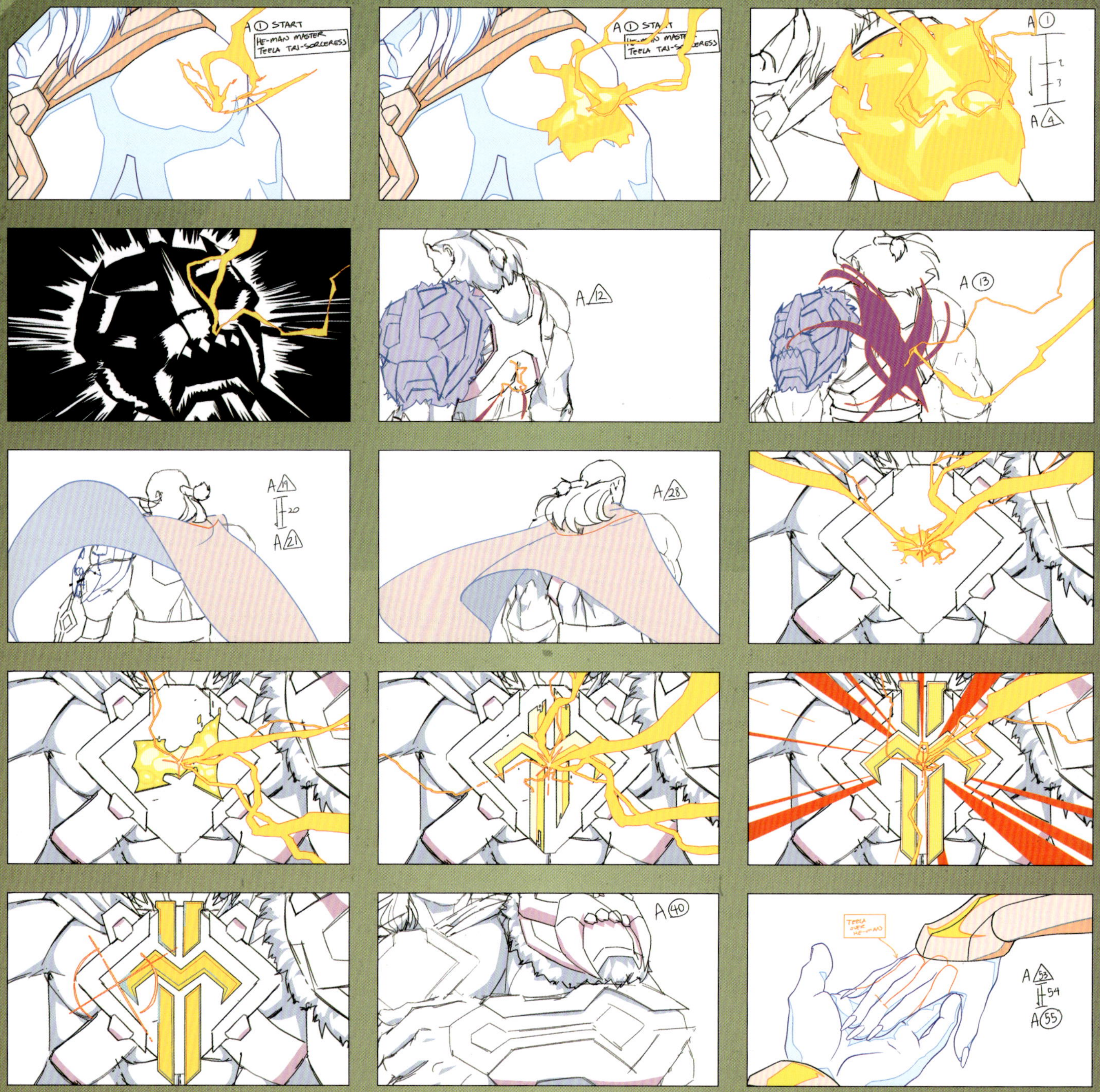

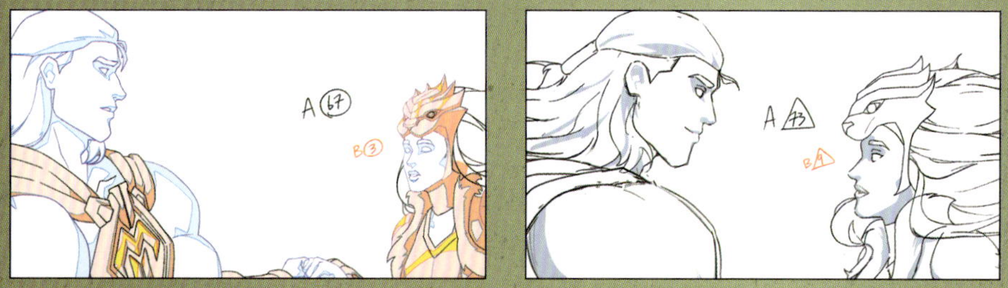

EPISODE 5, SEQUENCE 3

Even though He-Man's armor is now infused with technology, the source of its power still comes from Grayskull. In contrast with Andra's Battle Armor that builds from expanding armor plates, He-Man's tech-infused armor forms from the classic lightning bolts we all know and love.

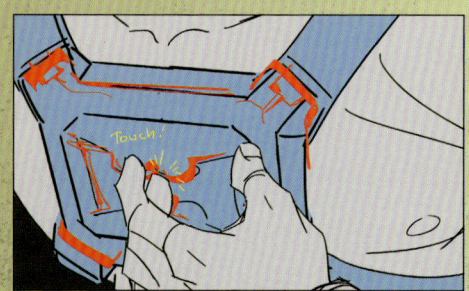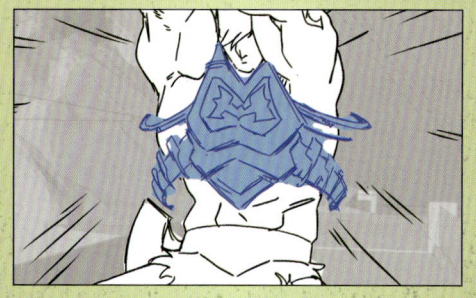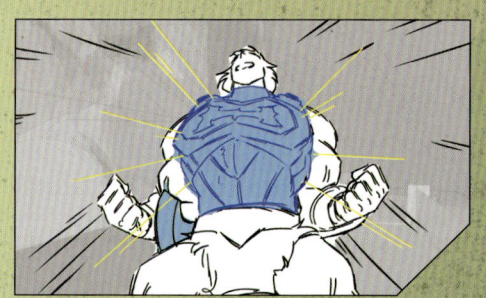

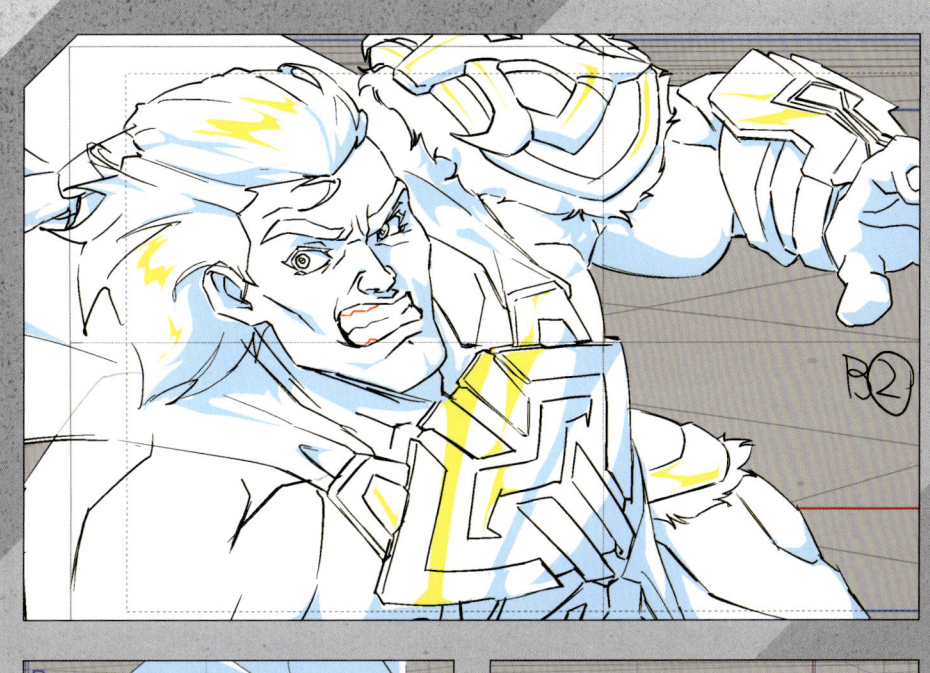
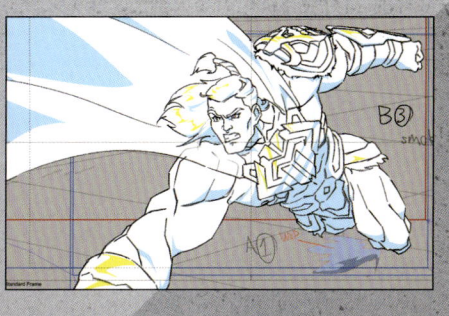
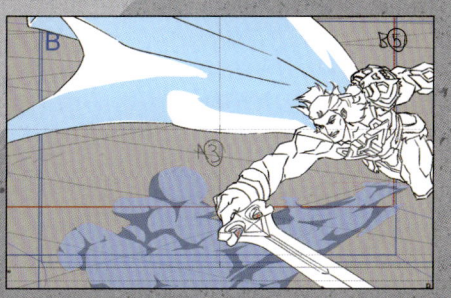
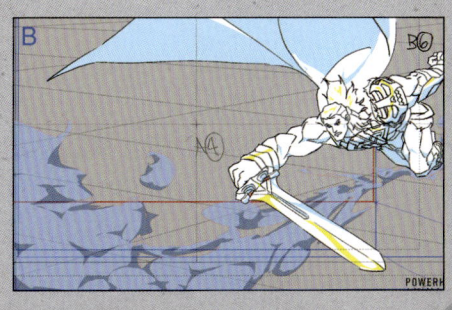
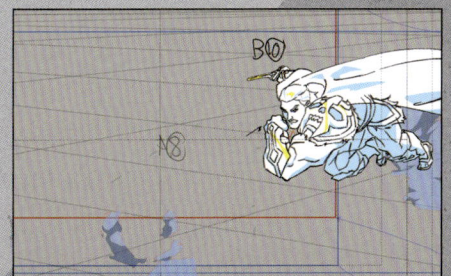
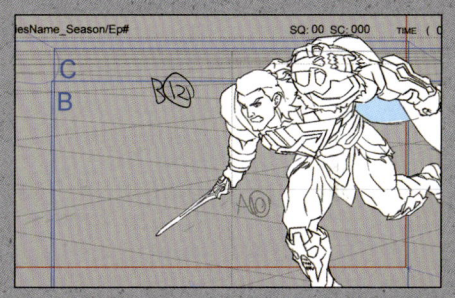
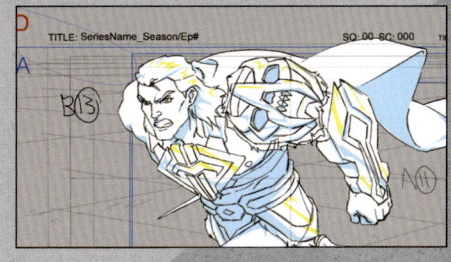
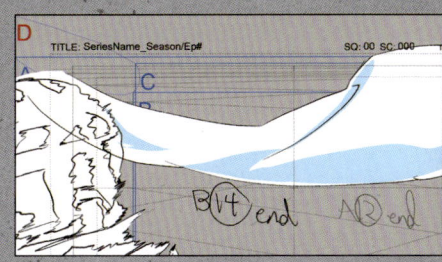

EPISODE 5, SEQUENCE 6

With the power within the sword drained and the panels collapsed, He-Man must engage Skeletor in close combat until an opportunity arises to absorb additional power to charge the tech within! Skeletor, however, will not make this easy for He-Man.

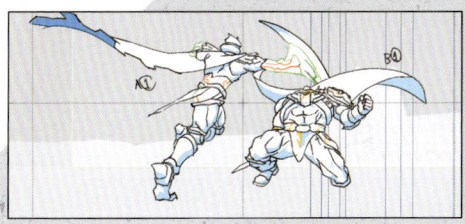
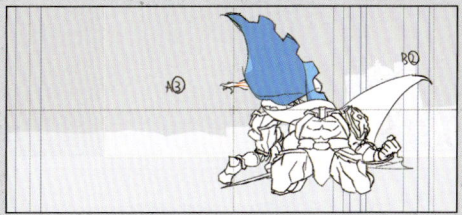
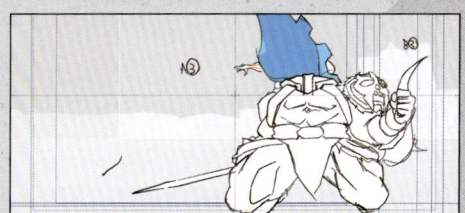
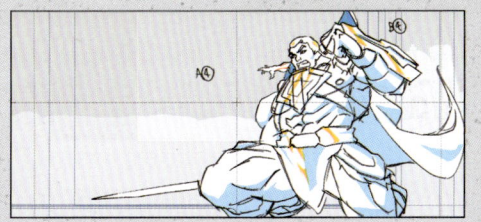
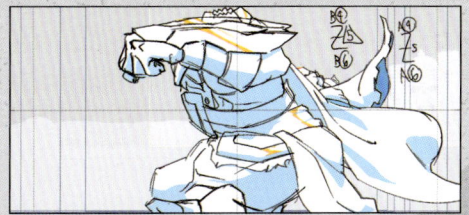
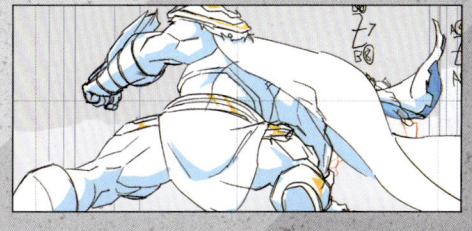
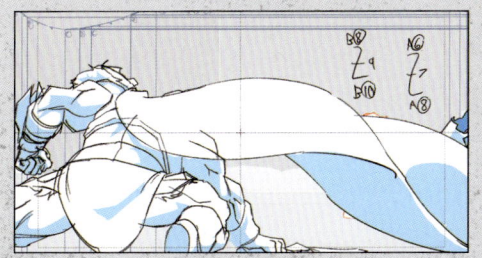
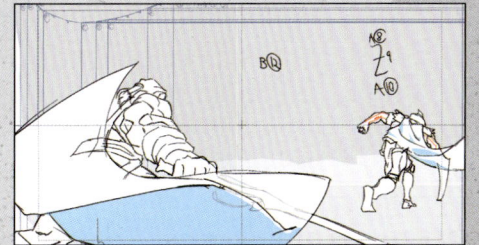
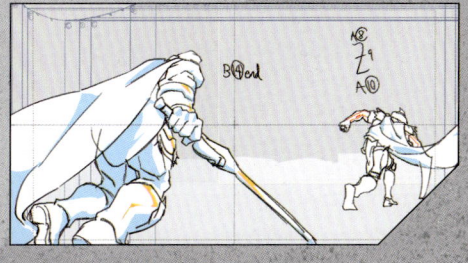

STORYBOARDS AND ANIMATION \\ 171

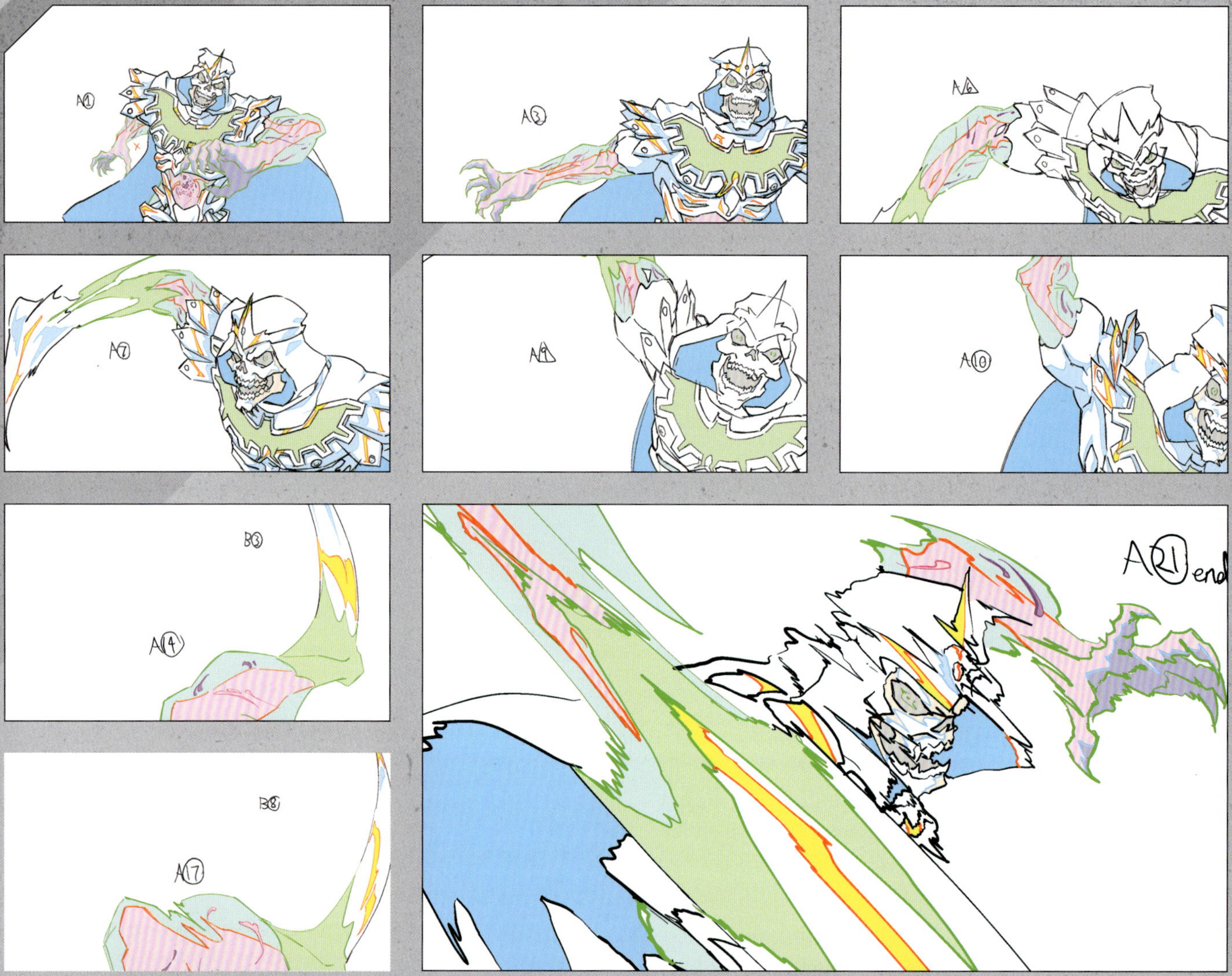

EPISODE 5, SEQUENCE 6
Skeletor's newfound fusion of magic and technology allows him to transform his arms into any weapon he needs at will! He can also duplicate, extend, or throw copies of his limbs to immobilize He-Man while he charges ever-deadlier lasers and spells!

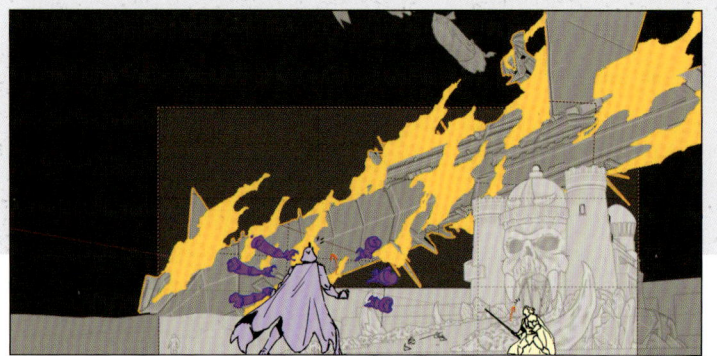
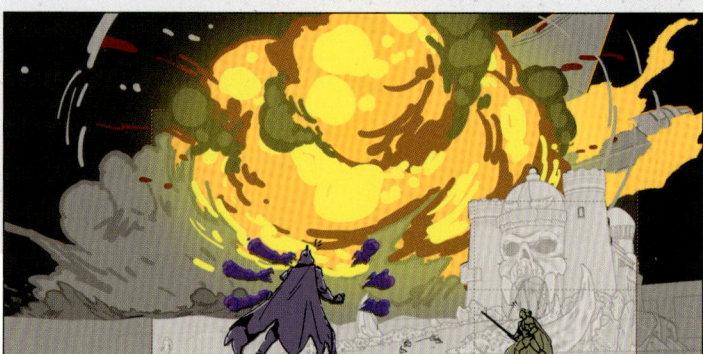
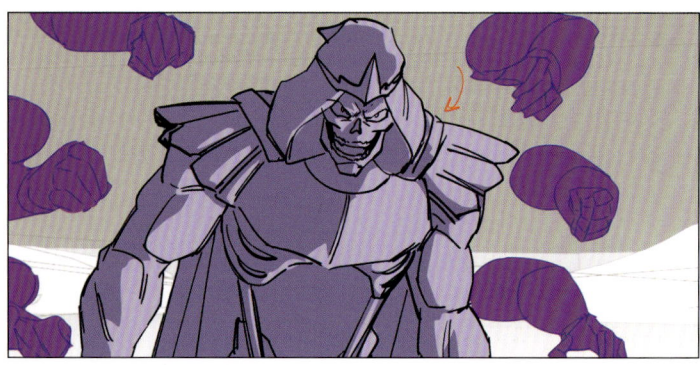
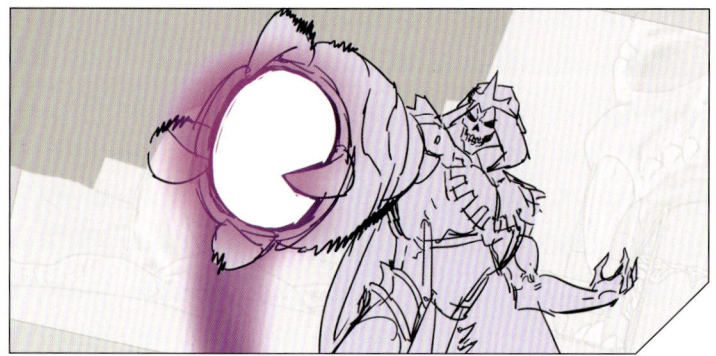

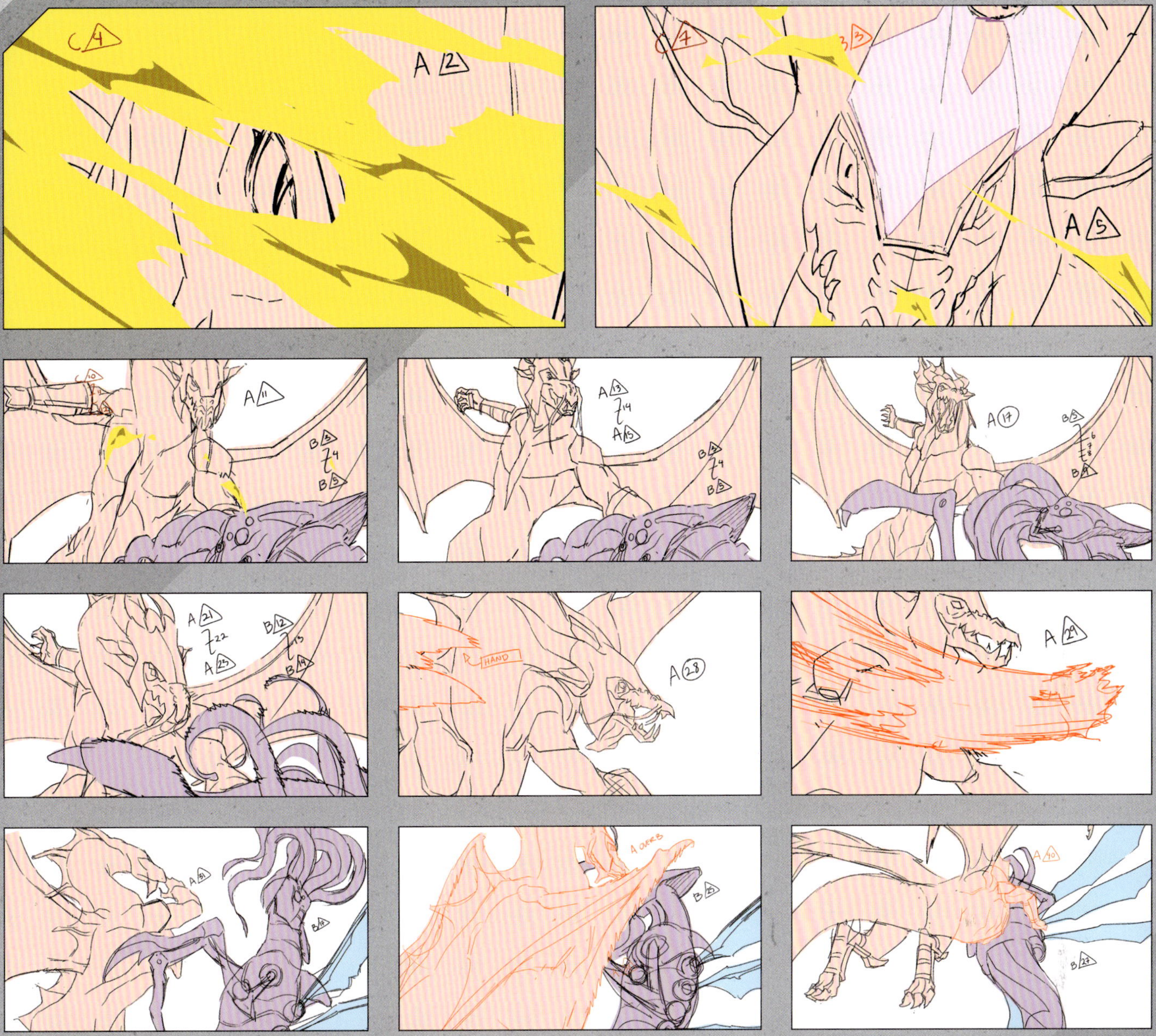

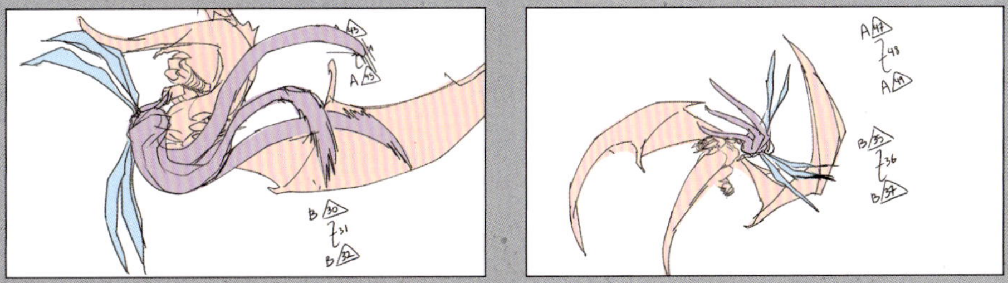

In episode 5 of *Revolution*, we get to see Granamyr in all his power and glory as he appears in the battle to take on the massive Techno-Titan, protecting Orko, Evil-Lyn, and Teela from this beast summoned to stop them from bringing back Preternia.

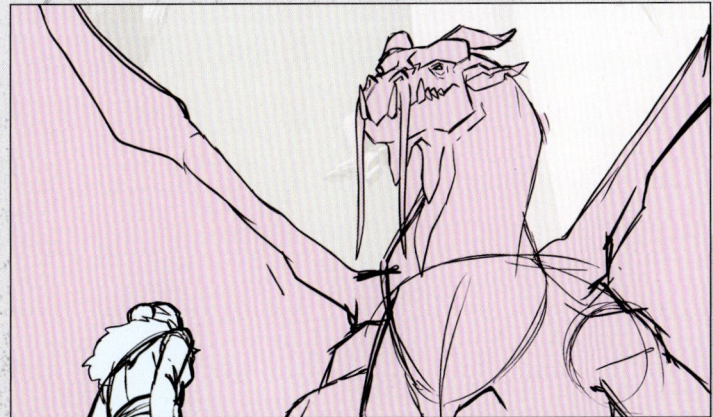
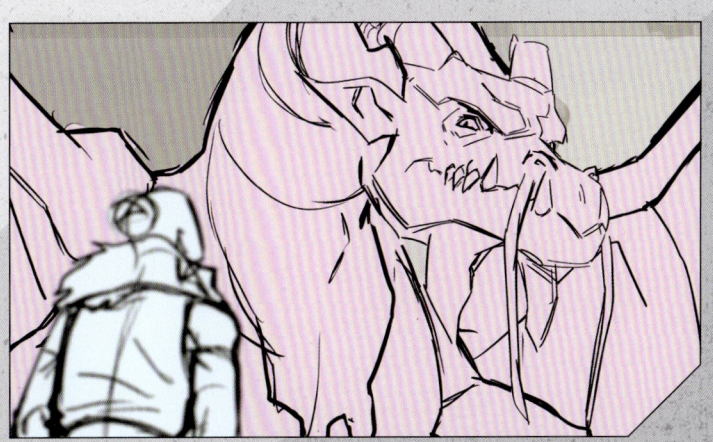

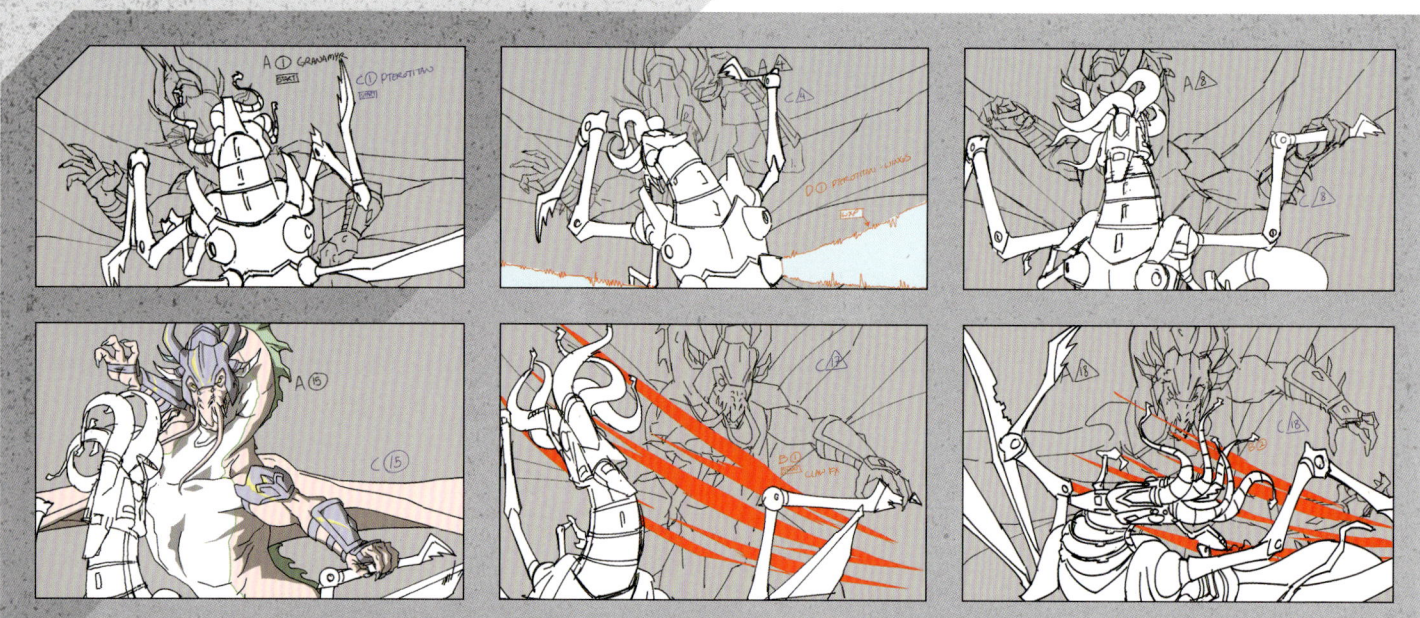

Granamyr's battle with the Techno-Titan continues. He brings all his might of muscle and fire to bear against the technotentacled monster, hoping to earn his redemption. The animators did a fantastic job in handling these two impressive creatures, even with such complicated designs.

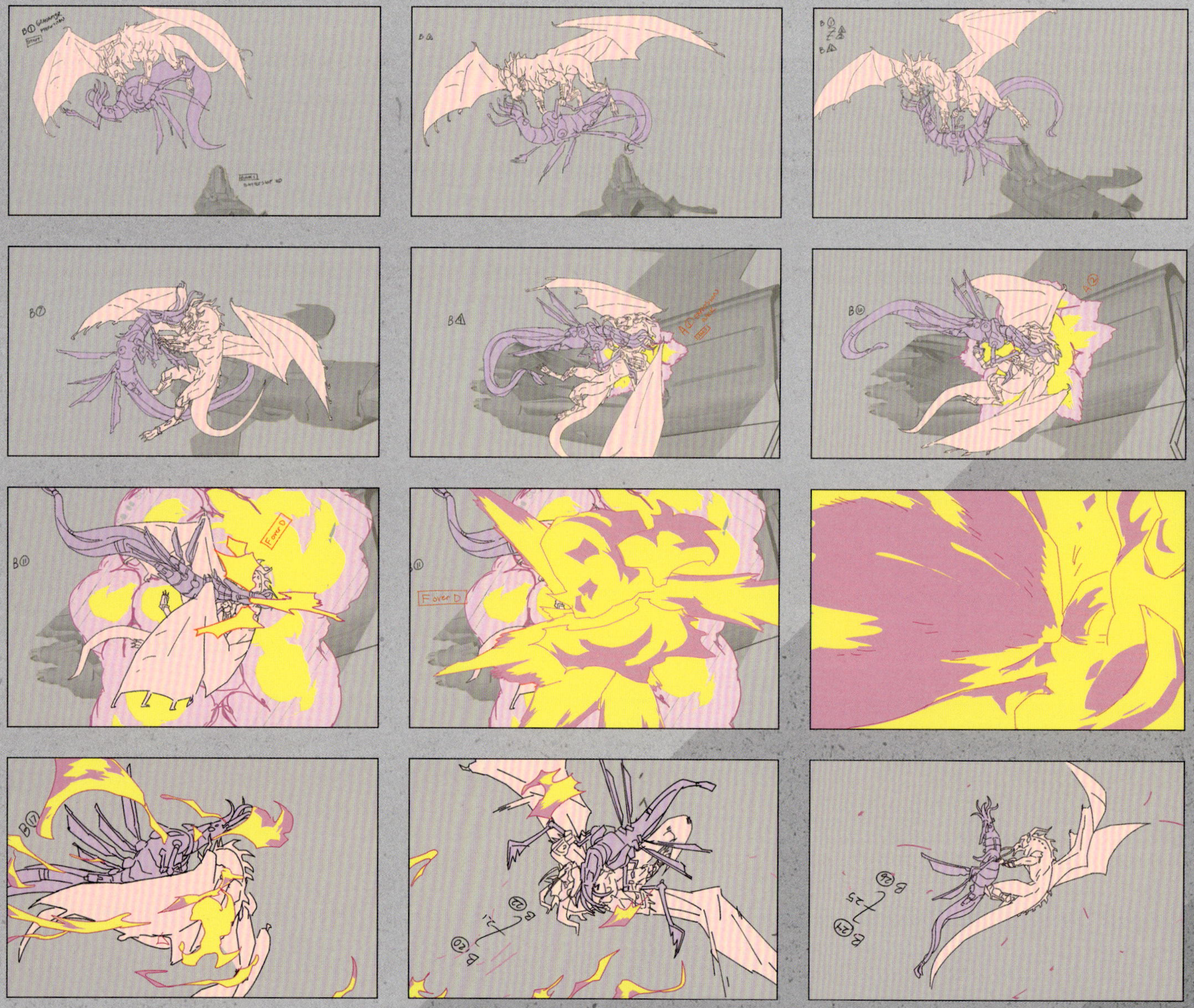

The two creatures are not only battling each other fang and claw but also struggling against the environment around them. Even in the sky, Granamyr not only has to deal with the Techno-Titan but also the onslaught of Horde ships filling the sky of Eternia.

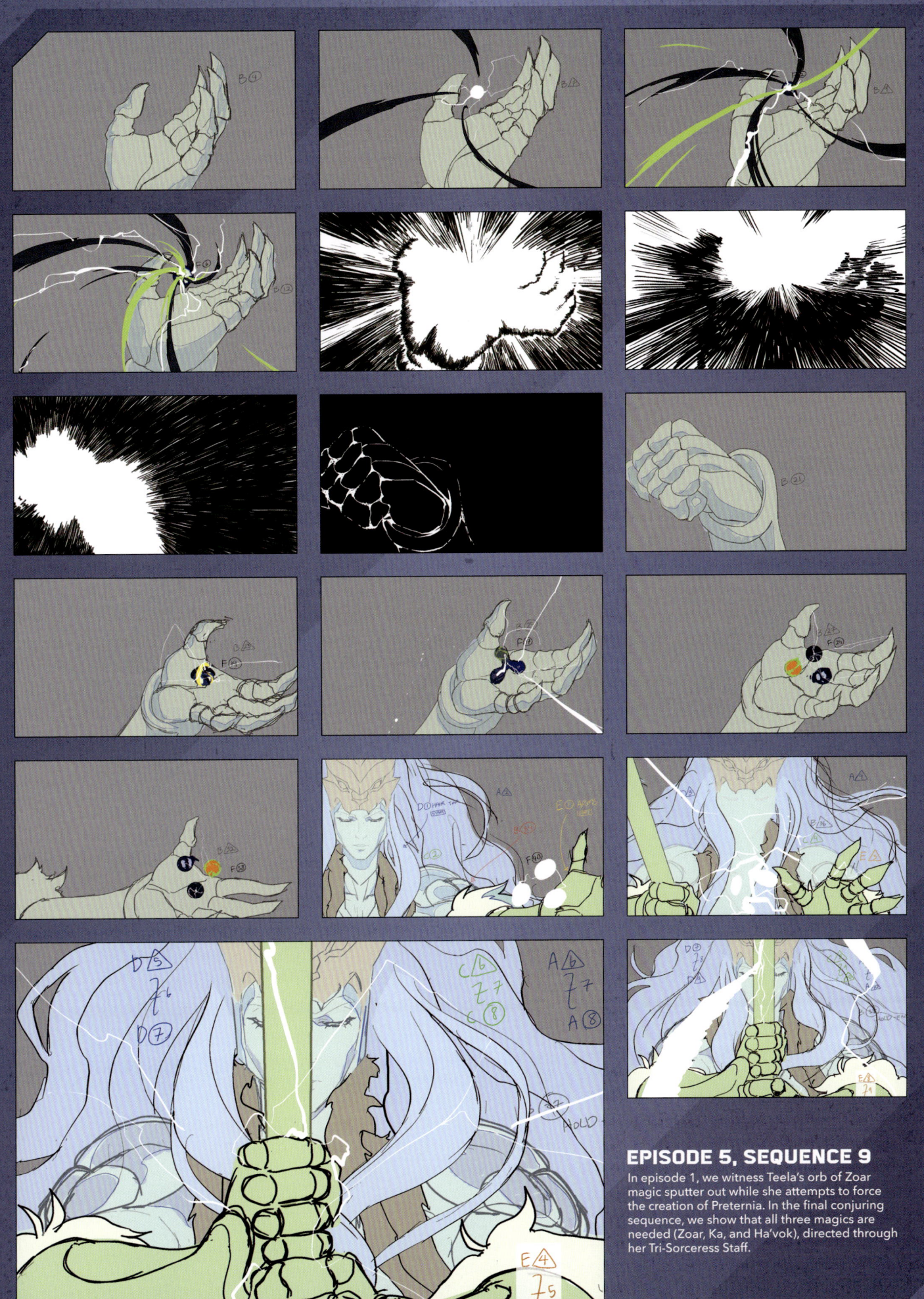

EPISODE 5, SEQUENCE 9

In episode 1, we witness Teela's orb of Zoar magic sputter out while she attempts to force the creation of Preternia. In the final conjuring sequence, we show that all three magics are needed (Zoar, Ka, and Ha'vok), directed through her Tri-Sorceress Staff.

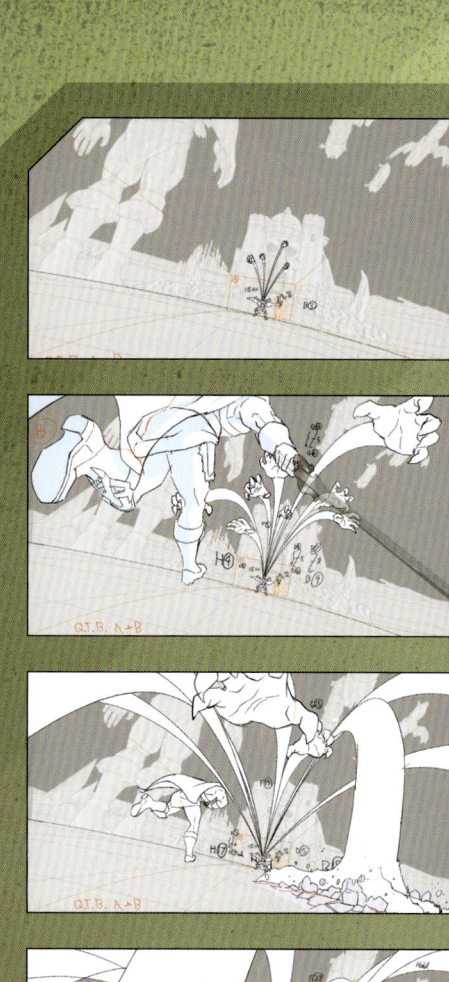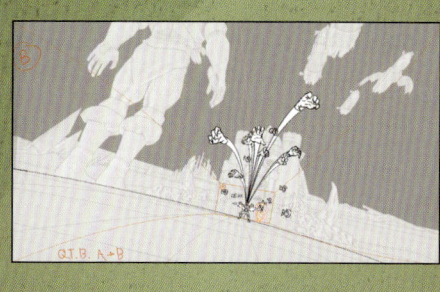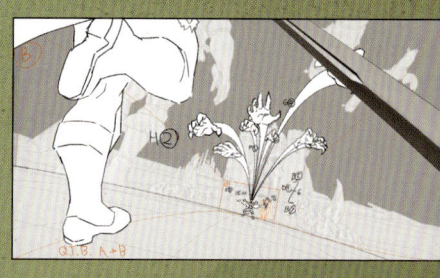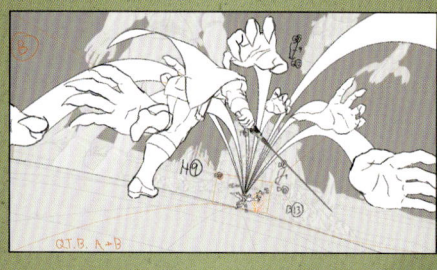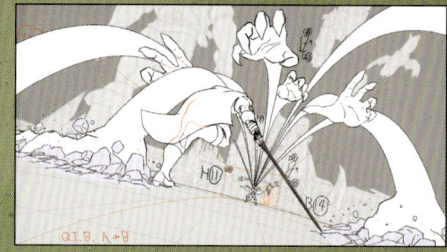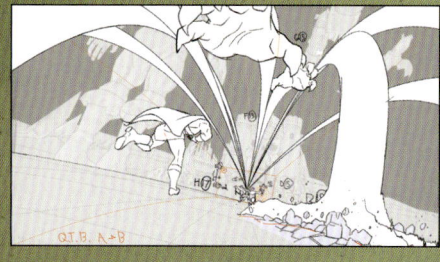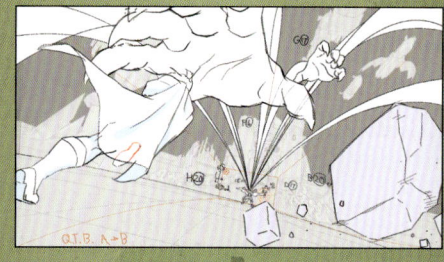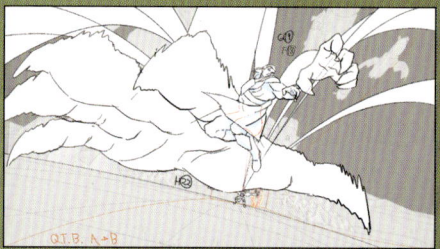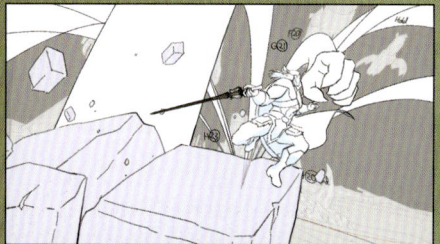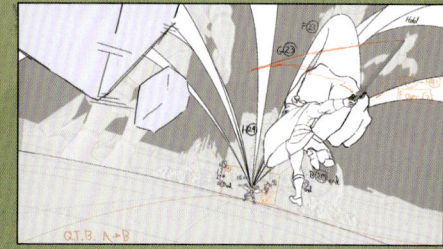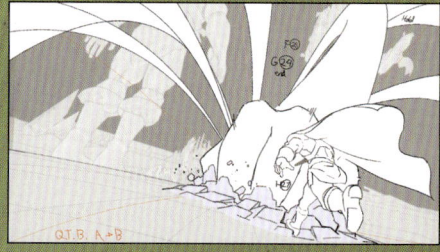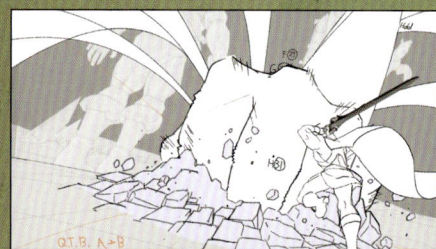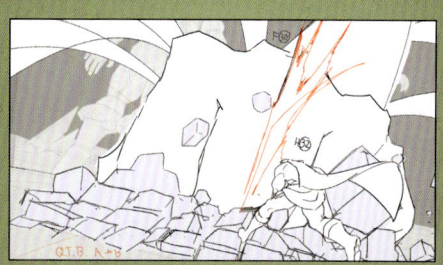

EPISODE 5, SEQUENCE 12

In the end, Skeletor throws everything he has at He-Man but in so doing provides He-Man with the final surge of energy needed to reactivate the Sword of Power, allowing our champion to drain Skeletor of all his tech and his magic!

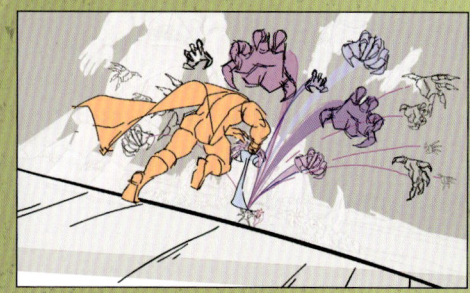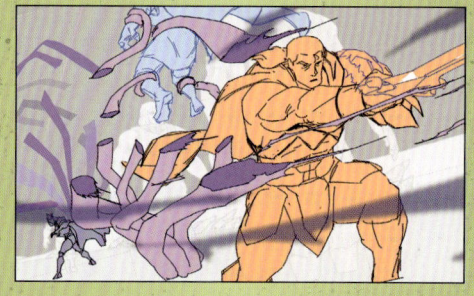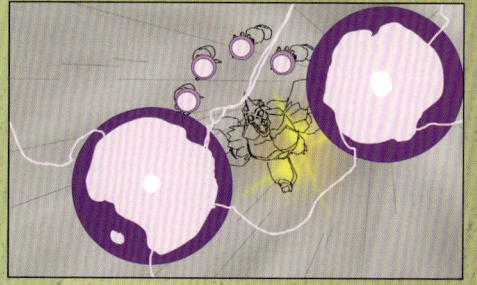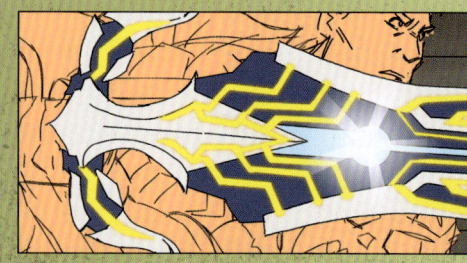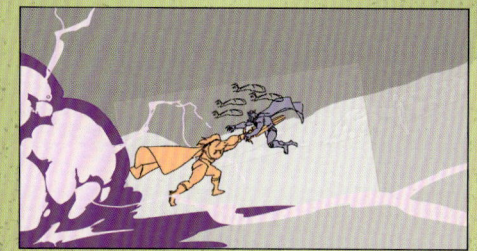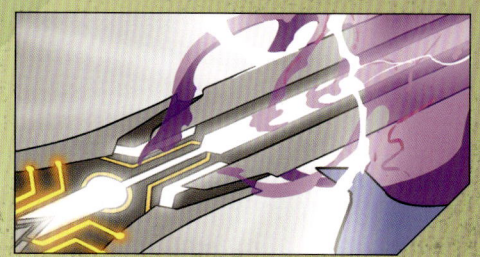

176 // THE ART OF MASTERS OF THE UNIVERSE: REVOLUTION

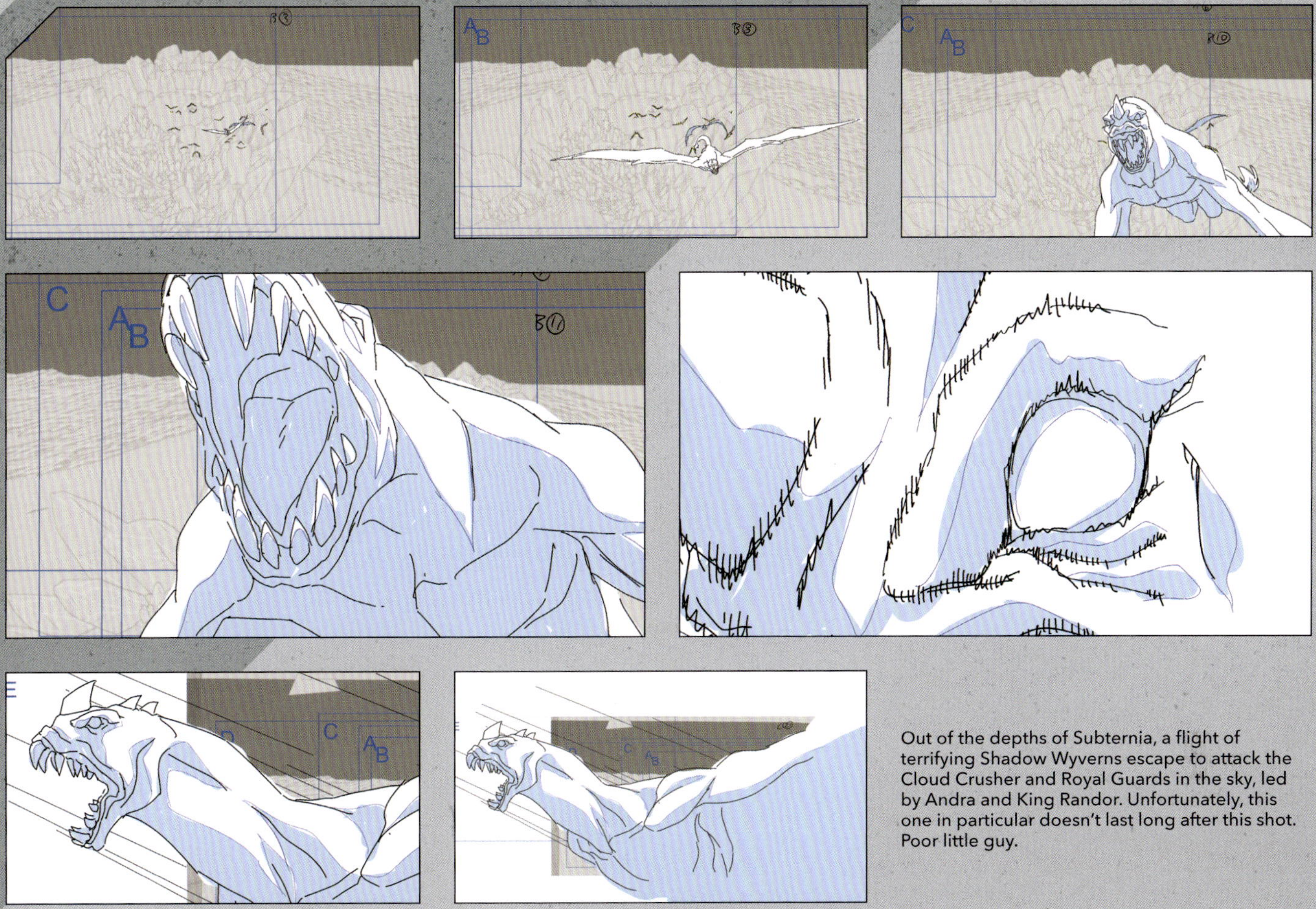

Out of the depths of Subternia, a flight of terrifying Shadow Wyverns escape to attack the Cloud Crusher and Royal Guards in the sky, led by Andra and King Randor. Unfortunately, this one in particular doesn't last long after this shot. Poor little guy.

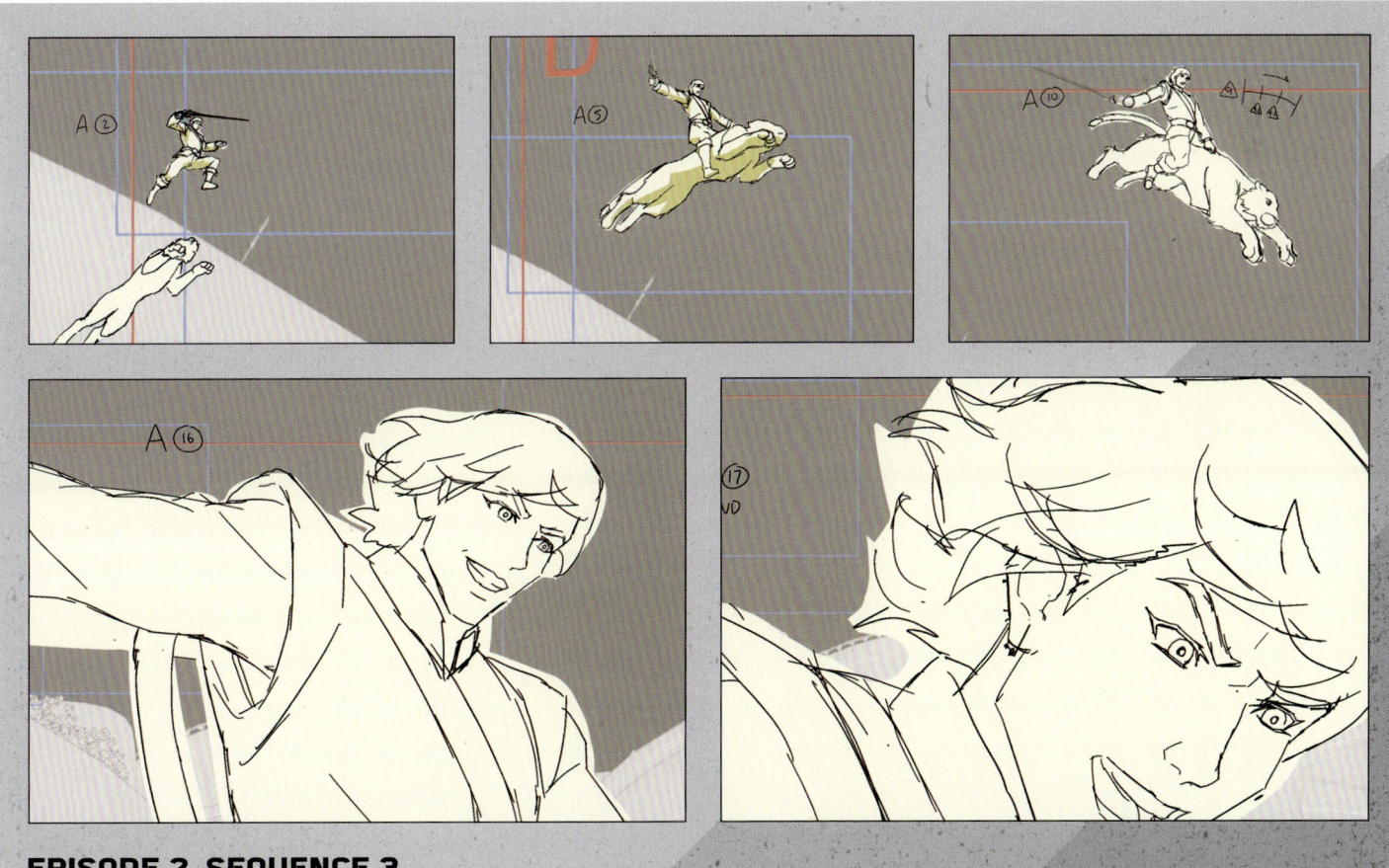

EPISODE 2, SEQUENCE 3
Flashing an impish grin to Keldor as if to say "Check this out," Adam recklessly leaps from the balcony to join the fray. Though Cringer seems reluctant, the fact that he doesn't hesitate is a true testament to their friendship.

STORYBOARDS AND ANIMATION \\ 177

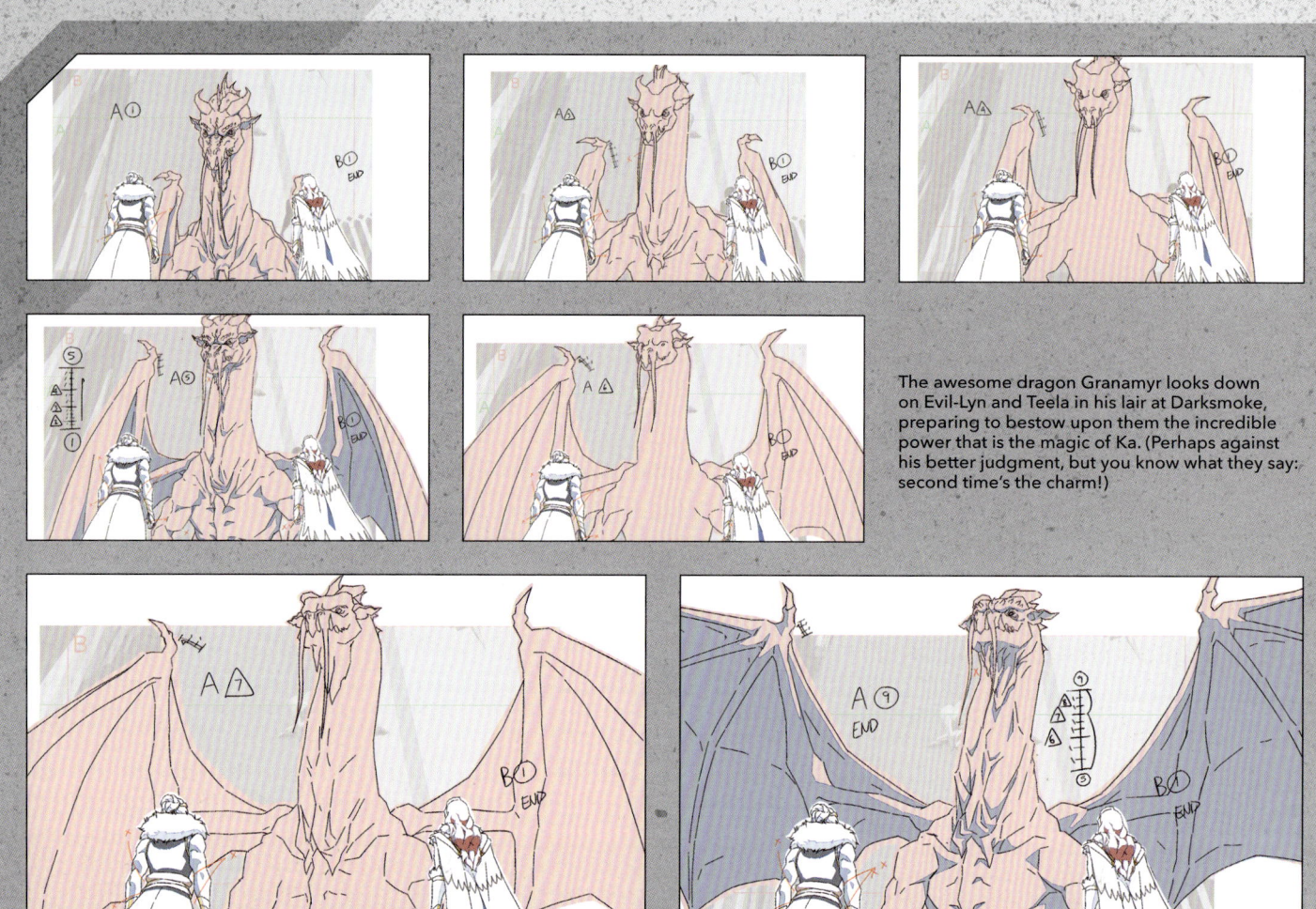

The awesome dragon Granamyr looks down on Evil-Lyn and Teela in his lair at Darksmoke, preparing to bestow upon them the incredible power that is the magic of Ka. (Perhaps against his better judgment, but you know what they say: second time's the charm!)

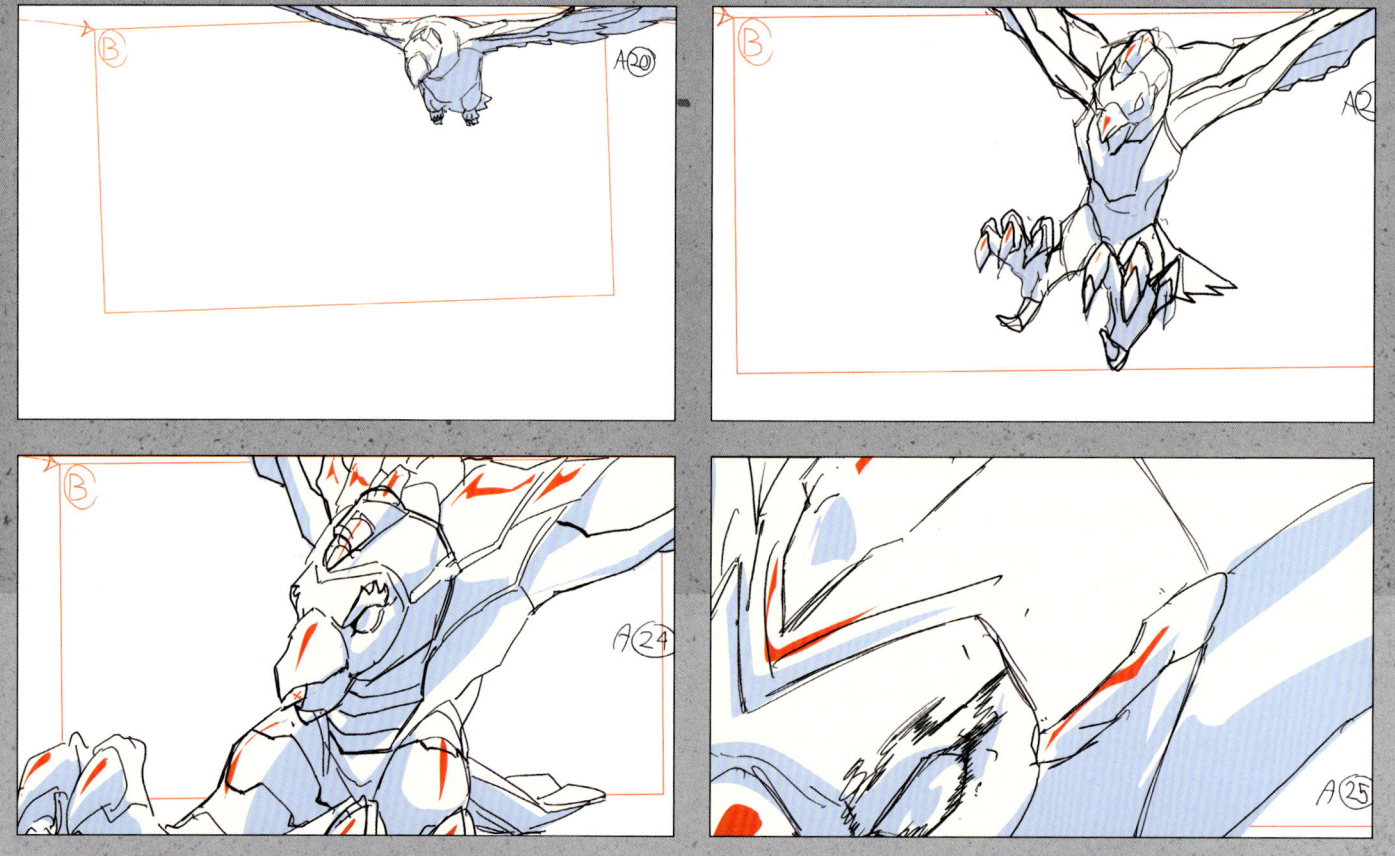

Motherboard returns to her Screeech form, initially seen in *Revelation*, to fly to Castle Grayskull and break through its defenses. Despite Teela's best efforts to safeguard the castle while she was away, her warding spell was no match for Screeech's powerful sonic blast.

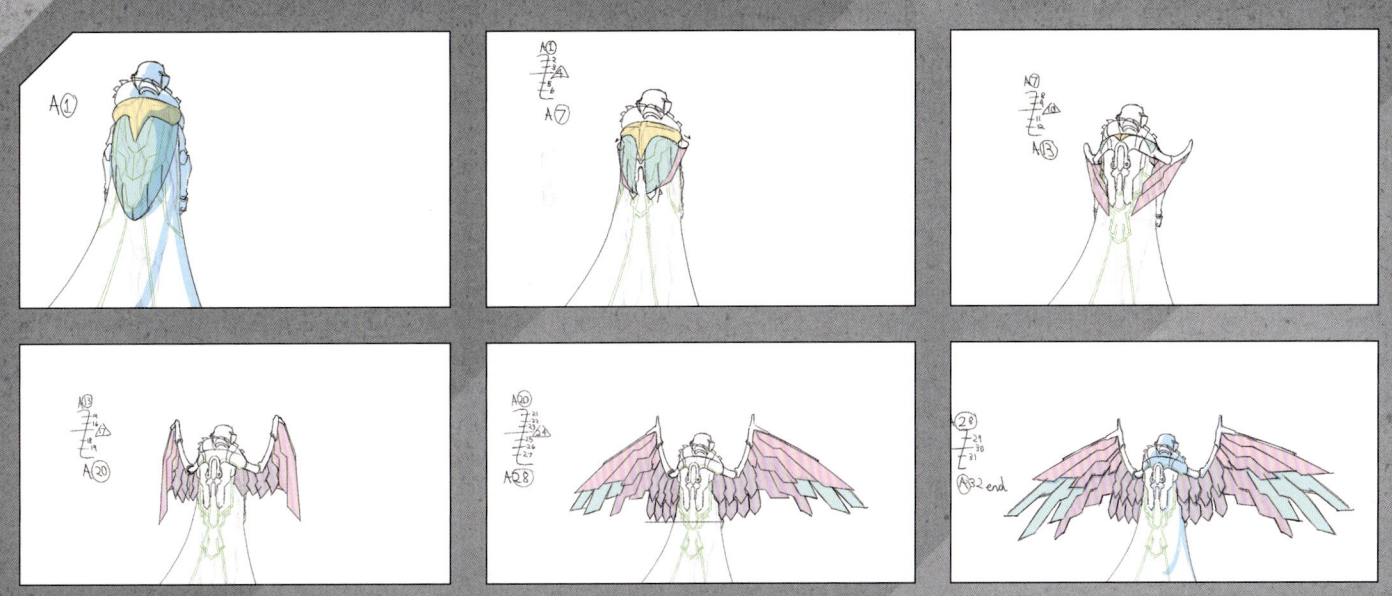

This shot provided a wonderful opportunity to show off the hard work of our design team—and to figure out exactly how Motherboard's wings fold and expand in animation. Large sections of her feathers are color coded to help animators track their positioning.

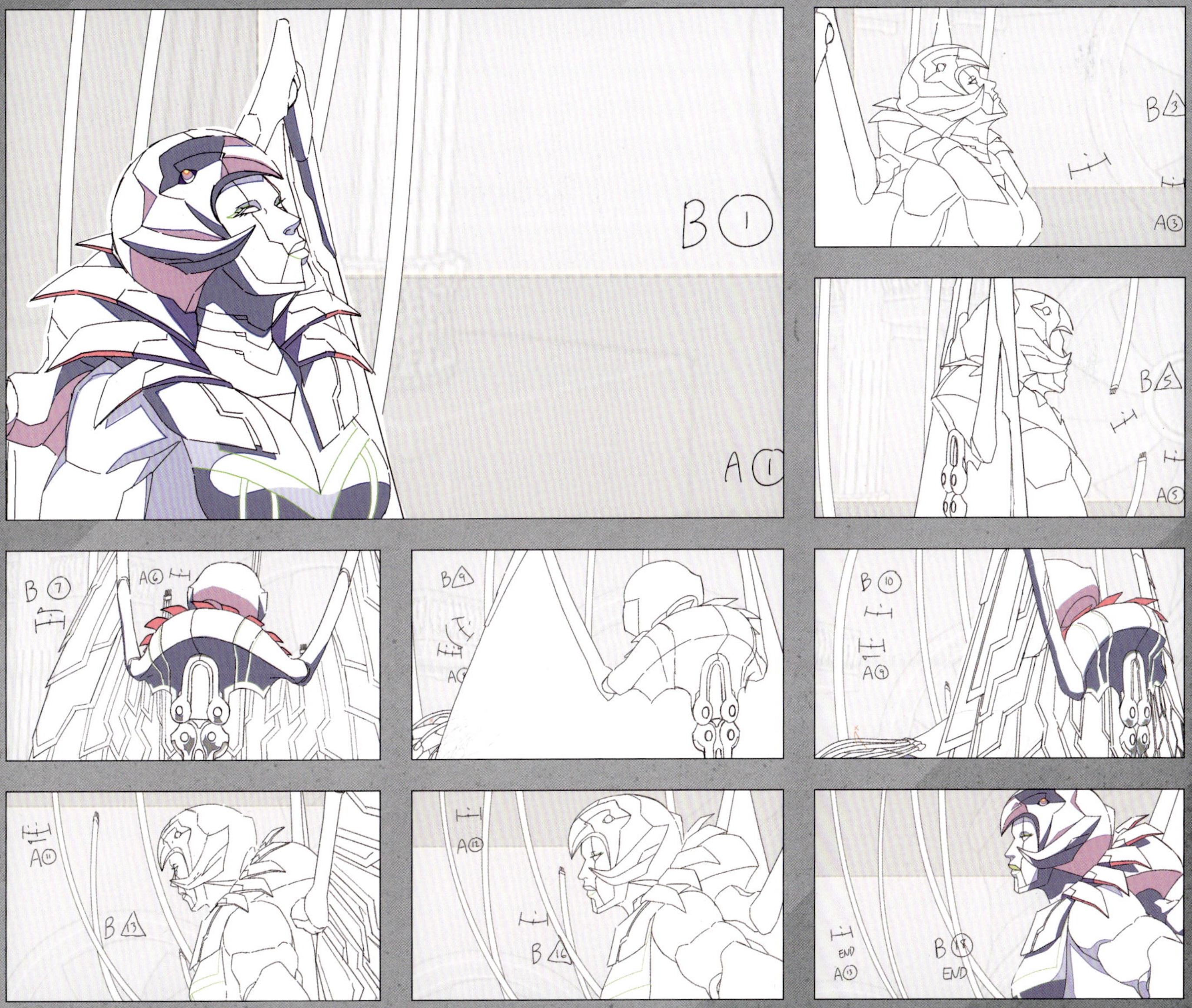

Motherboard triumphantly ascends to the throne of Castle Grayskull, turning as she rises up to survey her new domain. She wastes no time making herself feel completely at home, sending her wires through the castle's every nook and cranny to learn its closely guarded secrets.

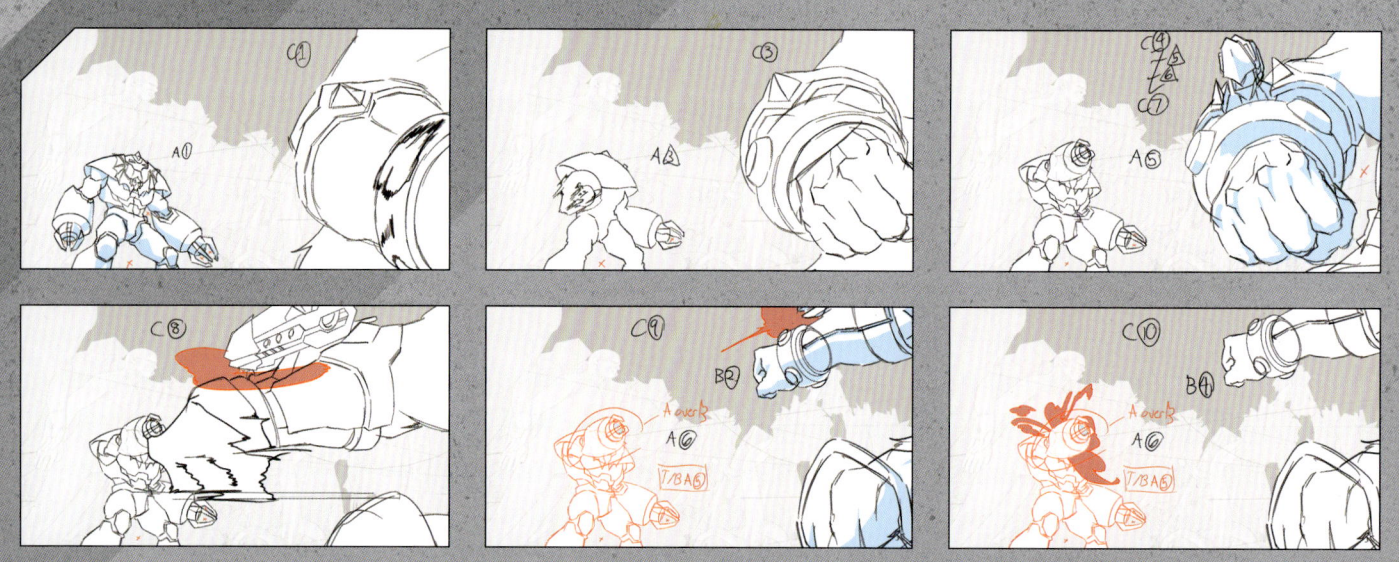

EPISODE 4, SEQUENCE 2

It's always a good idea to introduce a new character design with an action sequence, especially if that person is Man-Of-War! The unsuspecting Horde Troopers proved to be the perfect fodder for testing Duncan's expansive armory of new weapons and gadgets!

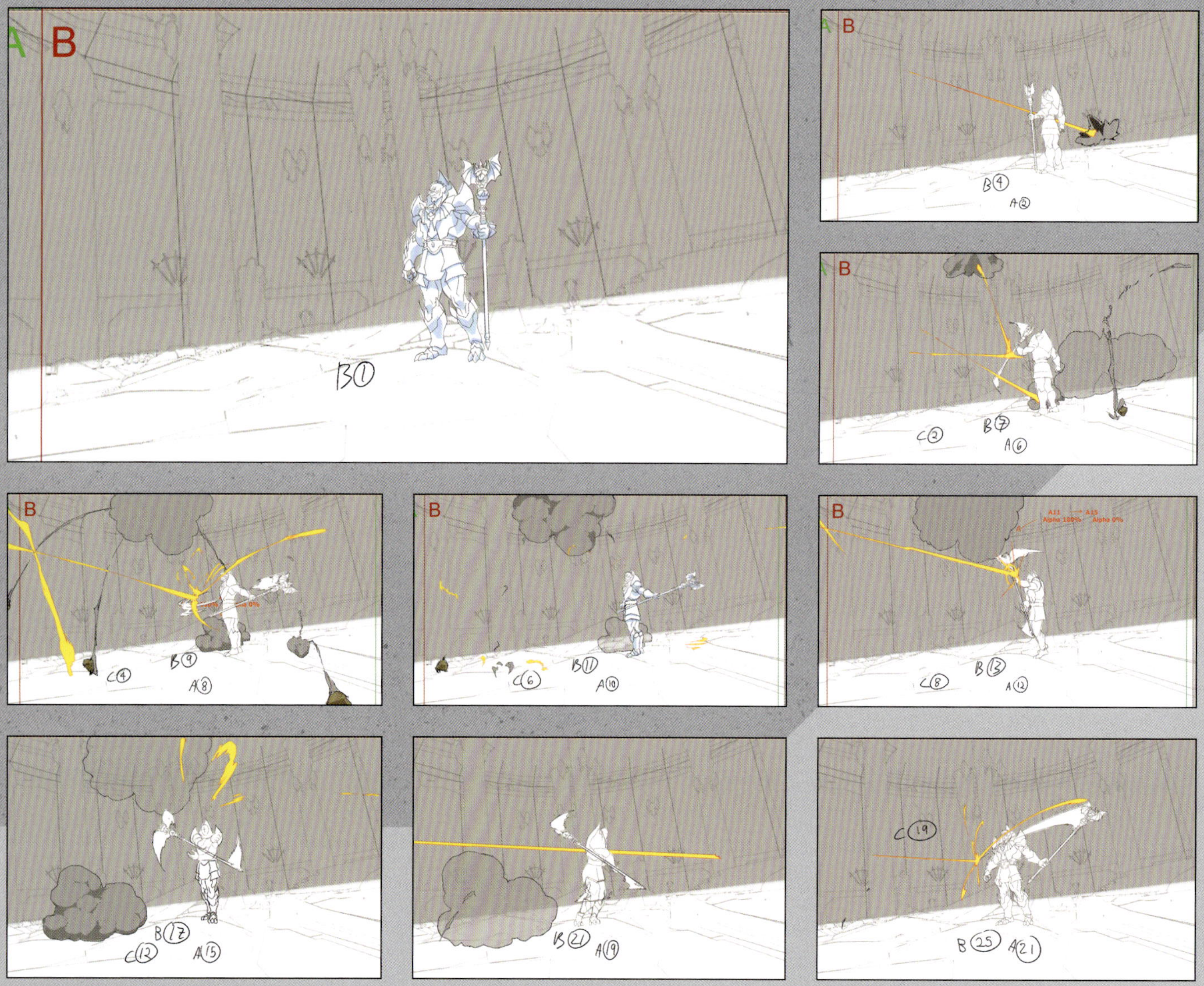

EPISODE 4, SEQUENCE 10

Even someone as powerful as Skeletor has an uphill battle to fight when challenging the mighty Hordak! Skeletor's barrage of homing missiles are deflected with minimal effort by Hordak's staff. Luckily for Skeletor, he always has something else up his sleeve!

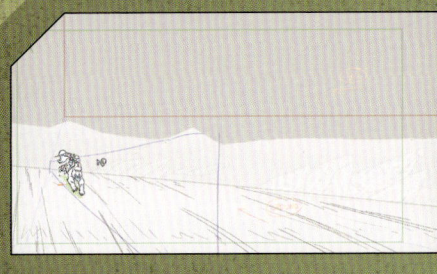 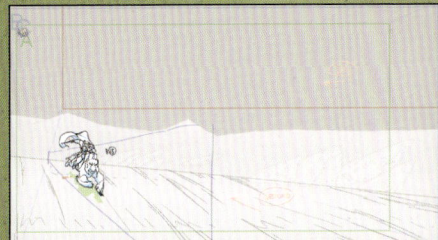 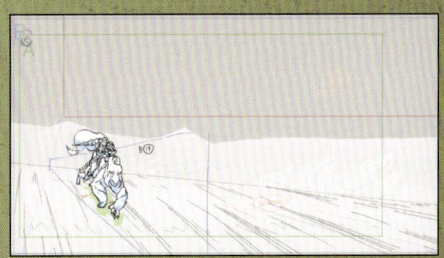
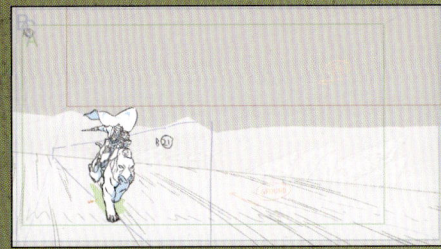 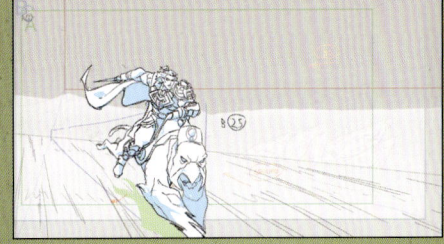 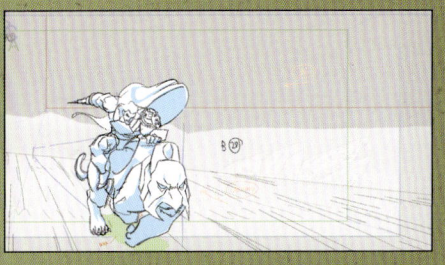
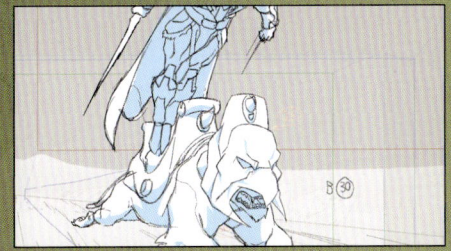 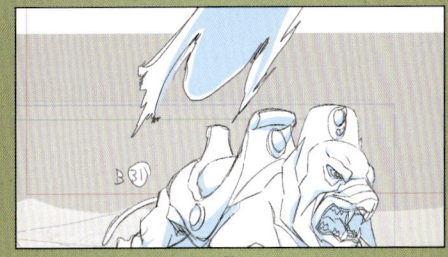

EPISODE 5, SEQUENCE 5
Even in short bursts, scenes that involve a moving background are exceptionally complex to animate and compose. Such applications are reserved for climactic or important events, and any opportunity to showcase Battle Cat and He-Man teaming up qualifies!

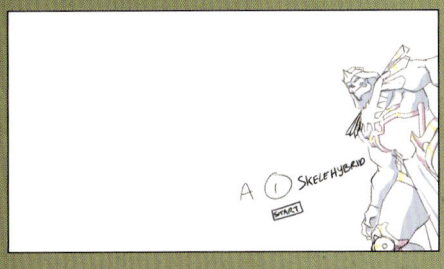 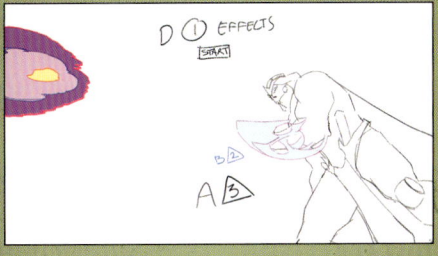 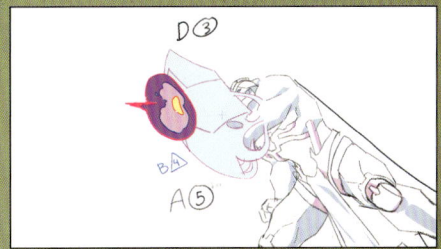
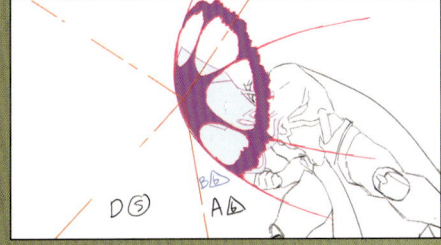 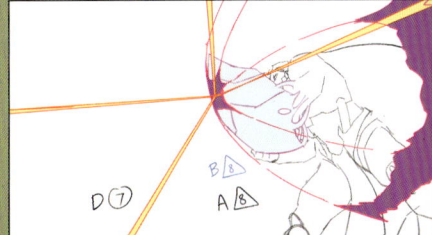 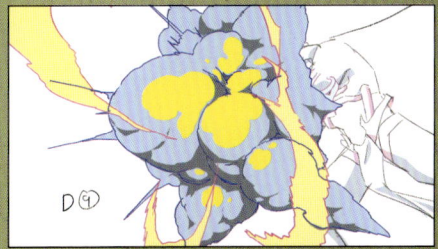
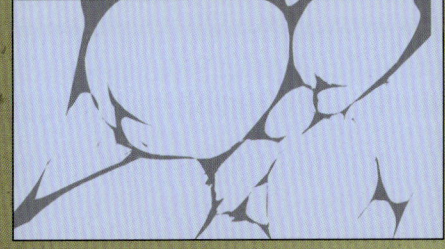 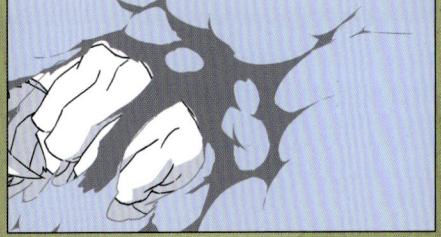 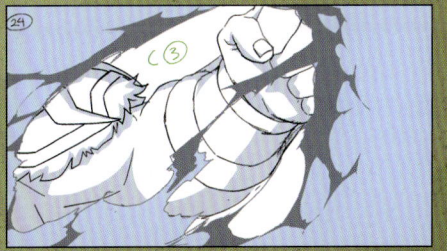
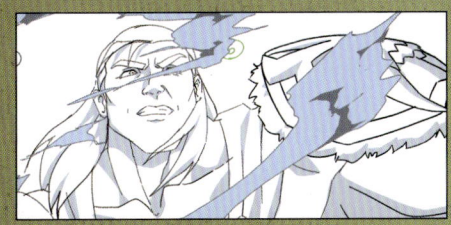 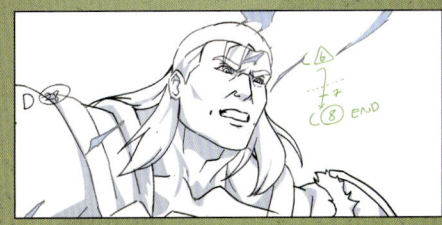

EPISODE 5, SEQUENCE 6
During these high-octane action sequences, we employ a variety of clever transitions to keep the pace elevated and intense. The smoke from the explosion over Skeletor's shield wipes the screen, hiding the cut to the next shot until He-Man pushes through!

STORYBOARDS AND ANIMATION \\ 181

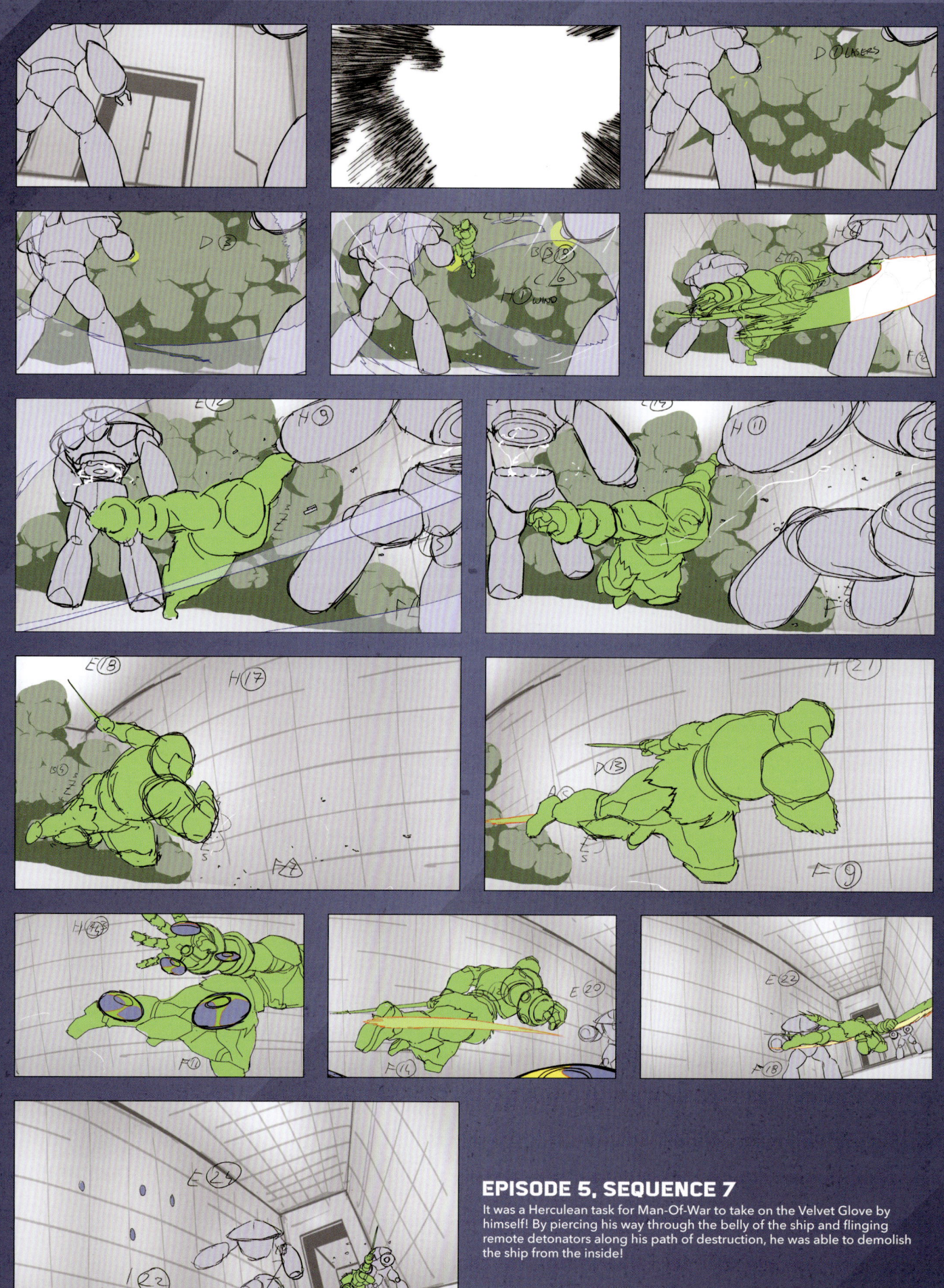

EPISODE 5, SEQUENCE 7
It was a Herculean task for Man-Of-War to take on the Velvet Glove by himself! By piercing his way through the belly of the ship and flinging remote detonators along his path of destruction, he was able to demolish the ship from the inside!

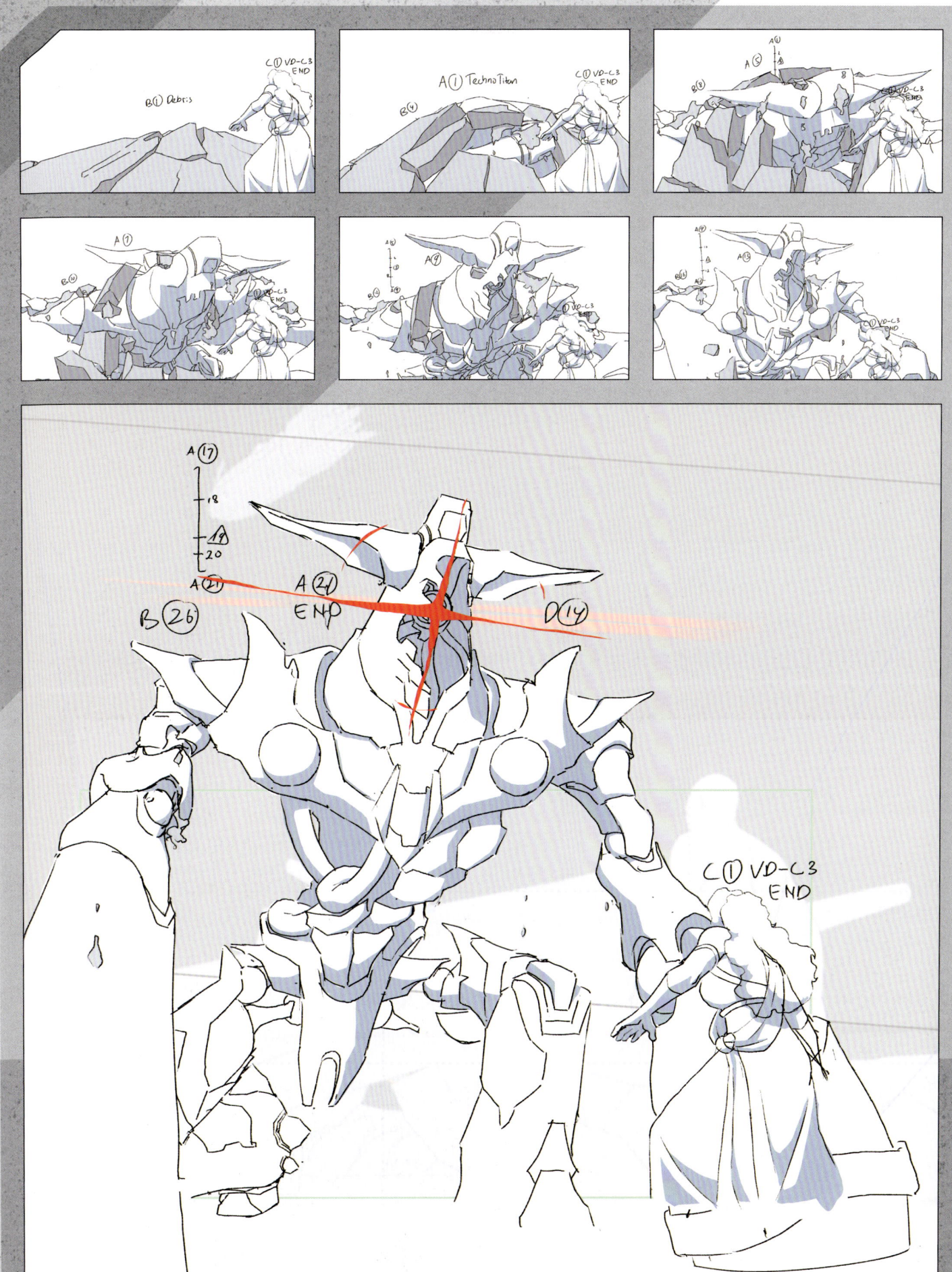

Skeletor taps into the ancient Gar technology left buried in the earth by his ancestors to summon more Techno-Titans. The towering robotic creature breaks through the surface of the wastelands around Grayskull, readying a deadly laser blast to aim at the fleeing Eternian citizens.

STORYBOARDS AND ANIMATION \\ 183

POWERHOUSE ANIMATION STUDIOS

ARTISTS

Abigail Bullock
Adam Connaroe
Aldo Mita
Archer, Aubrey
Arturo Moreno Ruiz
Ashley Lange
Aubrey Archer
Barbara Espinosa Gutierrez
Billy Garretsen
Bingxuan Tan
Edward Booth
Brett Carville
Britt "Dooz" Leslie
Bryan No
Bryant Grizzle
Cesar Arturo Fernandez Zepeda
Chelsea Li
Chris Wilson
Cody Shaw
Craig Nowicki
Dominic Ferro
Eddie Nunez
Eduardo Adsuara
Erica Machida
Erick Choy
Erik Labuguen
Guillem Rodriguez
Hailey Fennelly
Ifesinachi Orjiekwe
Jennifer Fields
Jessica Diaz
Jevon Etheridge
Jin Fang
Jiri Kulhanek
Johnny Villarreal
Jude Murro
Jun Chiew
Jun Wei Chiew (Ian)
Jung-Ha Kim
Kathryn Hall
Lina Ngo
Lina Ngo
Luka Bromley
Madeleine Capen
Mady Neal-Hertz
Marius Millar
Matheus Vincent Hermawan
Michael Leavenworth
Mike Bernhardt
Mikk Dado
Nic Bass
Patrick Stannard
Pedro Ferreira
Pedro Henrique Sardinha Cardoso
Sanchai Somsena
Savannah Ruddy
Shaan Khan
Steven Crowe
Victoria Patterson
William Garretsen
Yohann Abdelnour